Romancing the Past

A CENTENNIAL BOOK

One hundred books
published between 1990 and 1995
bear this special imprint of
the University of California Press.
We have chosen each Centennial Book
as an example of the Press's finest
publishing and bookmaking traditions
as we celebrate the beginning of
our second century.

UNIVERSITY OF CALIFORNIA PRESS

Founded in 1893

Alexander the Great does battle with King Porrus. From *Histoire ancienne jusqu'à César*, Bibliothèque Nationale, fr. 20125, fol. 235.

Romancing the Past

The Rise of Vernacular Prose
Historiography in
Thirteenth-Century France

GABRIELLE M. SPIEGEL

University of California Press

BERKELEY   LOS ANGELES   LONDON

The publisher gratefully acknowledges the contribution provided by the
General Endowment Fund of the Associates of the University of California Press.

University of California Press
Berkeley and Los Angeles, California

University of California Press, Ltd.
London, England

©1993 by
The Regents of the University of California

First Paperback Printing 1995

Library of Congress Cataloging-in-Publication Data

Spiegel, Gabrielle M.
  Romancing the past : the rise of vernacular prose historiography in
thirteenth-century France / Gabrielle M. Spiegel.
      p.   cm. — (The New historicism ; 23)
  "A Centennial book."
  Includes bibliographical references and index.
  ISBN 0-520-08935-9
  1. French prose literature—To 1500—History and criticism.
2. France—History—Medieval period, 987–1515—Historiography.
3. French prose literature—Roman influences.   4. France—History—
To 987—Historiography.   5. Romances—History and criticism.
6. Literature and history.   7. Historiography—France.   8. Rome—
Historiography.   I. Title.   II. Series.
PQ221.S66   1993
848'.10809—dc20   91-42979
                                                                          CIP

Printed in the United States of America
9   8   7   6   5   4   3   2   1

For Marcus and Alix

Because history is consummated only by being narrated, a critique of history may be practiced only as a narrative about how history, in narrating itself, is accomplished.

Jean-Pierre Faye, *Théorie du récit*

Contents

Acknowledgments

Any book as long in the making as this one incurs a list of debts that can barely be acknowledged. Work on the book has been framed by two grants from the National Endowment for the Humanities: the first stage of the research in the manuscripts was facilitated by a National Endowment for the Humanities Summer Stipend in 1979, while a final grant for Travel to Collections enabled me to return to Paris in the summer of 1991 to check my transcriptions. During the years since 1979 a variety of institutions and foundations have generously contributed to sustaining my work. Summer, semester, and year-long grants from the University of Maryland in 1981, 1985, and 1987 furnished me with the opportunity for research in France and leave time for writing. The first two chapters were written in 1988 while I was the recipient of a John Simon Guggenheim Fellowship. I am grateful to the Guggenheim Foundation for its support, as well as to the Rockefeller Residency Fellowship program in Atlantic History and Culture at the Johns Hopkins University, which gave me a study and a home during the tenure of my Guggenheim Fellowship. A year amid the beautiful hills and incomparable facilities of the Center for Advanced Study in the Behavioral Sciences at Stanford University in 1989–1990 afforded me the leisure in which to complete the manuscript. Funding for my stay at the Center came half from the University of Maryland and half from the combined resources made available to the Center by the National Endowment for the Humanities #RA-20037–88 and the Andrew Mellon Foundation. It would be hard to imagine a more congenial setting in which to write than that offered by the Center, whose unfailingly helpful staff, exquisite surroundings, and lively intellectual fellowship will always remain my ideal of scholarly sociability. I am deeply grateful to have been a fellow there and for the financial support that made the opportunity possible.

The staffs of the Bibliothèque Nationale, the Bibliothèque de l'Arsenal, the Bibliothèque de Sainte-Geneviève, and the Institut de Recherche d'Histoire et des Textes in Paris, of the Albertine in Brussels, and of the British Library in London were extremely helpful and enabled me to complete my research with an ease that would otherwise not have been possible. I am especially grateful to the Musée Condé at Chantilly for allowing me to work on its Ms. 869, which contains the recently discovered *Chronique des rois de France* that forms the subject of chapter 6.

During the long course of my research and writing, many friends and colleagues came to my aid, and it is with the greatest pleasure that I take this opportunity to thank them formally. John Baldwin, Brigitte Bedos Rezak, Brigitte Cazelles, J. S. Cockburn, David Cohen, Arthur Eckstein, David Hult, Phyllis Rackin, and the late Ronald Walpole read parts or all of the manuscript in its various stages, sometimes more than once. Charles Segal read the chapter on the translations of Lucan and offered valuable advice and helpful bibliographic references. Gillette Labory of the Institut de Recherche d'Histoire et des Textes in Paris made available to me the Institut's *fichier* on vernacular historiography, as well as various unpublished articles and theses housed there. In particular, her own work on the Latin sources employed by the anonymous chronicler of Chantilly/Vatican has been invaluable in tracing the complex procedures that went into the composition of his *Chronique des rois de France*. Large sections of chapter 6 could not have been written had she not generously shared with me the results of her research. Dr. Léon Wurmser took time out from a busy analytic schedule to verify sections of chapters 2 and 3 for me and helped to refine the psychological arguments therein. Brigitte Cazelles and David Hult consented to check my clumsy translations from the Old French and saved me from many errors. Annabel Patterson, with characteristic generosity and vigor, rescued an overlong text with her incomparable editorial skills. The hours that she spent criticizing the manuscript were exceeded only by the intelligence with which she worked in sharpening the focus and argumentation of the book. I owe her a debt of thanks that can scarcely be redeemed. A similar debt is owed to Kathleen Much, editor in residence at the Center for Advanced Study in the Behavioral Sciences, Stanford, who lent her abundant editorial gifts to reading all the chapters and whose editorial touch is evident on every page. Finally, I take this opportunity to acknowledge the many years of help given me by Carroll Smith-Rosenberg, who similarly read every chapter and discussed the work as a whole with me more times than either of us can enumerate. In the twenty years that we have been friends and colleagues, we have worked so closely together that it is no longer possible to tell where her ideas leave off and mine begin.

Like all families of academicians, mine suffered through the arduous years of work that this book entailed. Begun when my children were still young, the book matured along with them. As a token of my gratitude for the fortitude they have demonstrated under a regime that bordered on (I hope) benign neglect, I dedicate this book to them. The unfailing support of my husband must also be acknowledged, as must the grace with which he accepted the demands that a heavy schedule of teaching, research, and writing imposed. Thanks are due as well to friends and family members too numerous to list, whose emotional support has seen me through some difficult times. They know who they are, and should know how grateful I am to them. Needless to say, whatever errors of fact and failures of understanding that remain are of my own stubborn doing and should not be laid at the door of those acknowledged above.

Parts of several chapters appeared in earlier versions in a series of articles published in the course of my work: "Genealogy: Form and Function in Medieval Historical Narrative," *History and Theory* 22 (1983): 267–288; "Pseudo-Turpin, the Crisis of the Aristocracy and the Beginnings of Vernacular Historiography in Thirteenth-Century France," *Journal of Medieval History* 12 (1986): 207–223; "Social Change and Literary Language: The Textualization of the Past in Thirteenth-Century French Historiography," *Journal of Medieval and Renaissance Studies* 17 (1987): 129–148; "Moral Imagination and the Rise of the Bureaucratic State: Images of Government in the *Chronique des rois de France*, Chantilly, Ms. 869," *Journal of Medieval and Renaissance Studies* 18 (1988): 157–173; "History, Historicism, and the Social Logic of the Text in the Middle Ages," *Speculum* 65 (1990): 59–86; and "De l'oral à l'écrit: la sémantique sociale de la prose française au XIIIème siècle," forthcoming in a *Mélange* being prepared by the Université de Provence in honor of Georges Duby. I thank the various presses for permission to reprint from this earlier work.

Introduction

"Lost causes," C. Vann Woodward once remarked, "especially those that foster lingering loyalties and nostalgic memories, are among the most prolific breeders of historiography . . . particularly so if the survivors deem the cause in some measure retrievable."[1] The search for a usable past, capable of redeeming a cause that has been lost, in ideological if not actual political terms, becomes a compelling task for those who feel the need to mask the failure of their enterprise, to dissimulate the malaise that accompanies a fall from social grace, a decline in political authority, and a sense of the irrelevance of values that had guided comportment and identified the once-prestigious possessors of power and authority as central players in the social game. To fail, and to fail in a contest that discloses the possible historical obsolescence of the principles, beliefs, and prerogatives that had served to define the social and political status of those deeply committed to the lost cause, makes recourse to the past an essential element in the drive to recuperate a sense of social worth. It is here that ideological assertion comes into play, arguing for the continuing relevance of the values that the past enshrines; for the inherent rightness of the social order that had governed political life; for the importance of restoring to their former authority the rules of the social game that had acknowledged the perduring justice of the declining class's hegemony.

Ideology seeks to revive lost dreams of glory, to vindicate motives, and to mantle the discomfort that the contemplation of unwanted and adverse historical change germinates. Because failure is rooted in historical transformations, it is the past that becomes the repository of those dreams and desires, both because it can offer up a consoling image of what once was and is no longer, and because it contains within

1

it the elements by which to reopen the contest and offer an alternative vision to a now unpalatable present. Historical writing is a powerful vehicle for the expression of ideological assertion, for it is able to address the historical issues so crucially at stake and to lend to ideology the authority and prestige of the past, all the while dissimulating its status *as* ideology under the guise of a mere accounting of "what was."

This book examines the use of the past by the French aristocracy in the thirteenth century, as it developed in the patronage of a novel form of historical writing, the Old French prose chronicle. The underlying argument of the book is that both history *and* prose performed critical social functions in the life of the French aristocracy, which sought to embed its ideology in history and thereby endow that ideology with the prestige and imprescriptible character that the past was able to confer in medieval society. At the same time, by adopting prose as the language of history, chroniclers created a novel vernacular historiographic discourse, one that attempted to ground historical truth in a new system of authentication based on prose as a language of "truth," hence uniquely appropriate for the articulation and dissemination of historical knowledge.

One of my concerns in this book is with what might be called the social function of prose. I argue that the rise of literary prose represents far more than a simple fact of literary history, whereby prose composition gradually took its place alongside composition in verse. Old French prose historiography was, rather, the product of a specific historical moment and situation that endowed prose with a particular value for those who patronized, produced, and consumed works written in that discursive register. Global assertions about the literary trajectory and significance of prose tend to assume that its appearance is a natural, if not inevitable, part of any culture's literary history, an assumption that remains undemonstrated and probably unwarranted. To be sure, most literary languages eventually develop prose narratives, but the exact timing, location, and generic embodiment that give rise to prose composition are not necessarily the result of "natural" linguistic progress. It is my belief that the conditions under which prose narratives originate are as various as the cultures that produce them. In some cultures and at some times prose may represent a natural evolution of literary language, while in other places and periods it is socially generated by precise cultural needs and possesses ideological functions and meanings. For this reason, I do not attempt to consider the development of Old French vernacular prose in a comparative perspective, since my methodological goal is to demonstrate the advantages of situating historico-literary texts and developments in a local environment of social and political networks that, I believe, account for their specific form and function. References to other areas could never attain the particularity and density of this treatment and would, at best, constitute passing allusions to complex phenomena.

In France, the turn to prose as the preferred medium of historical writing occurred in service to an ideological initiative on the part of a threatened elite to authenticate its claim to historical legitimacy. At the same time, it worked to distinguish the vernacular chronicle, in both style and oral and fictional sources, from earlier Old French literary forms, namely epic and romance, against which vernacular historiography constructed its generic identity.

The "romancing of the past" represented by the rise of vernacular prose historiography, thus, has meaning on several levels. In its most ordinary and straightforward sense, the project entailed the translation of Latin histories into the rapidly developing language of Old French prose, a *mise en roman* that made available for the first time the historical legacy of both French and classical civilizations to laymen hitherto barred from access to it by their ignorance of Latin. On a more profound level, the "romancing of the past" in vernacular historiography also addressed sentiments of loss and decline that plagued the French aristocracy in the opening decades of the thirteenth century, as the rise of a newly powerful monarchy threatened its traditional autonomy and sought to limit its exercise of traditional political and military roles. From this perspective, the rise of vernacular prose historiography entailed the quest for a lost world of aristocratic potency, one that could be discovered in the past and made, it was possible to hope, a patent for a revised present in which the adverse historical changes suffered by the French aristocracy might be reversed and overcome.

Some historians might argue that the situation of the French nobility in the opening decades of the thirteenth century was not—or not yet—sufficiently serious to suppose that French nobles felt themselves in need of ideological solace and support. Or that, in any case, whatever degree of decline in power the French nobility experienced during these decades, it proved both resourceful and resurgent in reestablishing its prestige in later ages. While it is certainly true that French nobles weathered worse challenges than those facing them in this period, the question is perhaps not exclusively one of "fact" (did French aristocrats really decline?) but includes their perceptions of their situation as well (did they feel themselves to be suffering a loss of power and autonomy? did they know they would be resurgent?). All the evidence, not least the vernacular histories themselves, points to a sense of rupture with the past, a perception of loss of status and function that scholars such as R. Howard Bloch, Georges Duby, Jean Flori, Erich Köhler, Jacques Le Goff, Eugene Vance, and others have long seen as the matrix out of which chivalric ideology and courtly literature in general emerge. The question is, at base, more psychological than social, and our understanding of the social psychology of the aristocracy depends to a high degree on our reading of its characteristic literature.

When I began the research for this book, I expected that I would be tracing the spread of royal ideology as it slowly but progressively diffused downward to the aristocracy via translations and original compositions in Old French. I hoped to be able to chart the geographical and chronological pathways through which royal ideology extended its influence. However, upon close reading, the texts themselves did not seem to me to confirm the generally held view that they were royalist in orientation. Furthermore, when I investigated the social background and political activities of the patrons of vernacular historical texts, I discovered that these patrons belonged for the most part to the anti-royalist party in Flanders. Given this fact, the notion that the texts they patronized were pro-royalist rapidly became untenable. This point is critical. Every *identifiable* patron except one belongs to the English (i.e., anti-Capetian) party in Flanders in the turbulent years of war initiated in the 1180s by the Flemish count Philippe of Alsace and culminating with the battle of Bouvines in 1214.

The highly restricted geographical scope of the patronage phenomenon provides the key to what is fundamentally at issue in this body of texts. In other words, I am not making an argument about the French aristocracy as a whole—for whom, indeed, assertions of decline, impoverishment, and loss of political and/or military autonomy would not be credible—but only about a small group of patrons, whose disastrous social and political histories during the periods when they patronized vernacular prose histories is traced in full in chapter 1. It seems to me incontrovertible that *they*, if not all French aristocrats, suffered from the anxieties and sentiments of decline as described. For *these* nobles, I contend, the patronage and consumption of vernacular historiography represented a search for ethical and ideological legitimacy that was displaced to the realm of culture, taking the form of a re-created past that could correct the deficiencies of a problematic present.

In tracing the rise of vernacular prose historiography, then, it is useful to bear in mind Raymond Williams's dictum that ideology has always to be *produced:* "Social orders and cultural orders must be seen as being actively made: actively and continuously, or they may quite quickly break down."[2] Moreover, as Le Goff reminds us, "times of marked social change are ideal for observing the relationship between material and imaginary realities."[3] The early thirteenth century, in Le Goff's opinion, was precisely such a time, when the attempt to reconfigure the world of imagination in order to comprehend and come to terms with social transformations can be seen in a variety of literatures, both didactic and fictional.

It hardly needs saying that such literary figurations of social realities are scarcely straightforward or "innocent." As Vance compellingly argues, even the most putatively "objective" literary work, one that aims at reproducing the "world as it exists," is inevitably embroiled in the ideologies that "must prevail in the minds of both artist and audience if the system of communication is to remain intact."[4] Indeed, he insists, we should be most on guard in the presence of medieval literature when it pretends to denote the world "literally."[5] Historiography, as the medieval genre par excellence devoted to a "realistic" representation of the social and political world, is at the same time a genre thoroughly saturated with ideological goals. Especially in the Middle Ages, historical writing, precisely to the degree that it claimed to be free of imaginative elaboration, served as a vehicle of ideological elaboration. The prescriptive authority of the past made it a privileged locus for working through the ideological implications of social changes in the present and the repository of contemporary concerns and desires. As a locus of value, a revised past held out for contemporaries the promise of a perfectible present.

Yet, in the end, the Franco-Flemish aristocracy's effort to redeem the present by means of a revitalized past was doomed to failure, for neither past nor present could really address, much less turn back, the long-term historical transformations that were coming to culmination in medieval French society during the reign of Philip Augustus (1179–1223). Ultimately, vernacular chroniclers, in recreating the aristocracy's lost worlds, merely provided a verbal substitute for a social past irretrievably lost; their histories both mask and mark the historical rupture effected by the rise of monarchical authority at the expense of aristocratic autonomy and prestige, which forms the critical historical context in which Old French prose historiography developed.

This study of the rise of vernacular prose historiography assumes that the texts to be considered, although the product of clerical writers, nonetheless represent the aspirations and anxieties of the French aristocracy responsible, by its patronage, for their creation. Although the majority of authors who wrote histories in Old French in the period under consideration remain anonymous, what little we know of them indicates that they were mainly secular clerics attached to noble households. In the small world in which vernacular prose historiography first arises, it is the patron, rather than an eventual public, who can be credited with determining the aims and forms of the chronicle. To the extent that this is so, the Old French prose chronicle does not express a collective image of the community's social past, but instead forms a partisan record intended to serve the interests of a particular social group, inscribing a partisan and ideologically motivated assertion of the aristocracy's place and prestige in medieval society.

A word needs to be said about the relation of these vernacular texts to the Latin sources, whether ancient or medieval, that they translated. That some of the characteristics and transformations occurring within vernacular prose historiography were also true of contemporary Latin historical writing does not detract from the story I am trying to tell. My concern here is primarily with the patrons and audiences for whom prose histories were composed, and with the ways in which such histories addressed underlying issues of aristocratic experience in thirteenth-century France. Since the audiences for Old French histories were effectively denied access to Latin sources by virtue of their linguistic incompetence, they remained ignorant of the developments in Latin historical writing that may have paralleled those in the vernacular. In a more positive sense, the significant change from the point of view of those for whom vernacular history was destined lies in the internal development of vernacular literature as such, which began to offer its audiences novel material couched in new literary modes. This book will deal with the inner progression of vernacular prose history in its earliest stages, as it first emerged by distinguishing itself, sharply and self-consciously, from earlier genres of vernacular literature such as epic and romance (to which, nonetheless, its debt remains clear); and then as it gradually created subject matters and forms of expression proper to it alone, thereby achieving generic autonomy.

But, as I hope will become clear, it is my firm conviction that the rise of vernacular historiography must be seen within the context of

Old French literature and not solely—as has been customary—in relation to the Latin sources that served as the bases of the first works. When relevant and telling, the vernacular texts discussed here are juxtaposed to the Latin texts they either translate or employ. My principal concern, however, is not with that sort of *Quellengeschichte*. Instead, I wish to present these writings as they would have been apprehended by a French audience in the thirteenth century, an audience untutored in Latin and unaware of the sometimes crude, sometimes subtle, reworking of the Latin works from which the narratives they were hearing derived. Only when the changes effected by vernacular translators are particularly revelatory of authorial intentions are they noted in my discussion. If, as was sometimes the case, the vernacular version represents a fairly straightforward or literal translation and adaptation of a Latin text, I remain interested primarily in the image of the past that the vernacular history presented, whatever its ultimate point of origin. It is, moreover, my governing assumption that even literal translations are the product of conscious intentions and that if the Old French texts replicate the substance of Latin texts, it is because the translators believed those Latin works to offer adequate expressions of their own historiographical goals. The instances of revisions to Latin sources, not to mention the wholesale deformation of existing material and the insertion of supplementary sources, are in any case so numerous and pervasive that to assume anything less would do an injustice to the intelligence and purpose with which the creators of Old French prose historiography worked.

Anyone familiar with the development of Old French historiography will notice one notable omission in my selection of texts: the Crusading chronicles by Villehardouin, Robert de Clari, and Henri de Valenciennes. Like the works I have chosen to discuss, these chronicles are among the earliest works of prose history, emanate from the same northern French region that gives us so many of the first vernacular prose histories, and discuss the crusading activities of the same group of northern and Flemish lords among whom the patronage of vernacular historiography was so marked. Hence, they would seem likely candidates for inclusion in a study of this sort. My reasons for omitting them are twofold. First, the chronicles of the Crusade are well known and much written about, in contrast to the works analyzed here, which, with the exception of the *Faits des Romains* and Jean de Thuin's *Hystore de Jules César*, have never been the object of interpretive study—this despite the existence of a large body of secondary literature on the manuscript traditions of various works, and in the case of the *Pseudo-Turpin Chronicle*, the publication of almost all variant versions. Second and more important, my concern in this work is to investigate the place and function of vernacular prose historiography in the life of the French aristocracy, as it attempted to deal with the consequences of rapid and far-reaching social changes taking place in France. Although equally works of prose, the chronicles of the Crusade direct their narratives to an account of deeds performed in distant lands and of an almost exclusively military character. They therefore seemed to me less promising material for my principal interests than texts more closely focused on France, its past history, and contemporary conflicts.

Because my overarching purpose is to demonstrate the ways in which vernacular historiography encodes the historical experiences of contemporaries, albeit via a displacement to the past, my study of the chronicles is preceded by a detailed discussion of the social and political situation of France at the beginning of the thirteenth century. I have not been content merely to invoke secular changes, such as the decline of the aristocracy, the nobility's growing economic impoverishment, and so forth, but have tried to describe with relative exactness the historical experiences of a small group of known patrons for the texts in question. Chapter 1, therefore, sets forth in a traditional historical mode an account of the economic, political, military, and dynastic events that shaped the experiences of those for whom vernacular chronicles were composed. Succeeding chapters are devoted to close readings of the texts that form the object of this study. Thus, in chapter 1 and periodically thereafter, I speak in the historian's voice. For the remainder of the book, I adopt the language of literary criticism. The result is notable shifts in tone, style, and methods as the book moves between historical and literary sections, that is, from context to text and text to context.

To a large extent, the contrast in voice and analytical approach between the historical discussion of chapter 1 and the literary discussions of the following chapters was unavoidable, given my commitment to examining both texts and their contexts in ways appropriate to each. The difficulty in treating both historical context and literary text in a single works stems, I believe, from a series of unrecognized incommensurabilities between the objects, tasks, and goals facing historians and literary scholars. Literary text and historical context are not the same thing. Whereas the text is an objective given, an existing artifact (in its material existence, if not in its constitution as a specifically "literary" work), the object of historical study must be constructed by the historian before its meaning can begin to be disengaged. As a consequence, the historian of texts is a "writer" in his or her function of composing the historical narrative, but a "reader" of the already materially extant text. The task facing the one is broadly constructive, the other broadly deconstructive, and it is not hard to understand why few literary critics or historians of texts have given equal attention to both undertakings.

My book does attempt to do both history and literature. Like any work located on the margins of two fields, it straddles the gap between them and, inevitably, treats each with less thoroughness and complexity than a book more narrowly trained on one or the other. But historiography itself has always fallen between these two stools. The defects of the genre offer at the same time its opportunities. I hope this book will demonstrate in a small way the benefits of a more interdisciplinary and complex analysis of textual production in the Middle Ages than has hitherto been undertaken.

My focus in this book is on what might be called the social logic of the texts, in the dual sense of their relation to their site of articulation—the social space they occupy, both as products of a particular social world and as agents at work in that world—and to their discursive character as articulated "logos," that is, as literary artifacts composed of language and thus requiring literary (formal) analysis. The critical stance I employ begins with the premise, already well stated by Mikhail Bakhtin, that "form and content in discourse are one, once we understand that verbal discourse is a social phenomenon—social throughout its entire range and in each and every of its factors, from the sound image to the furthest reaches of abstract meaning."[6] I therefore assume that particular instances of language use or textuality incorporate social as well as linguistic structures and that the aesthetic character of a work is intimately related—either positively or negatively—to the social character of the environment from which it emerges. Inextricably associated within these histories is a wide range of social and discursive practices, of material and linguistic realities that are interwoven into the fabric of the text, whose analysis as a determinate historical artifact in turn grants us access to the past.

My emphasis on the text's social site stems from my belief that the power and meaning of any given set of representations derive in large part from the social context in which they are elaborated. In that sense, the meaning of a particular text is essentially relational, not stable or inherent in the text itself; it emerges only when the text is situated within a local environment of social and political networks that it seeks to shape and that are being organized around it. Even if we accept the poststructuralist argument that language constitutes the social world of meaning, it remains equally true that "language itself acquires meaning and authority only within specific social and historical settings. While linguistic differences structure society, social differences structure language."[7] Texts, as material embodiments of situated language use, reflect in their very materiality the inseparability of material and discursive practices and the need to preserve a sense of their mutual implication and interdependence in the production of meaning.

At work in molding a literary text is a host of unstated desires, beliefs, understandings, and interests that arise from pressures that are social as well as literary and that impress themselves upon the work, sometimes consciously, sometimes not. All texts occupy determinate social spaces, both as products of the social world of authors and as textual agents at work in that world, with which they entertain often complex and contestatory relations. Texts both mirror *and* generate social realities, are constituted by *and* constitute social and discursive formations, which they may sustain, resist, contest, or seek to transform depending on the individual case. It is this kind of relational reading of text and context, of overt and suppressed meaning, of implied and articulated purposes, together with the variety of literary and discursive modes in which they are given voice, that I have attempted to offer here and which I believe we need to pursue if we are to achieve a genuinely historical understanding of textual production.

It is important to stress the possibly "negative" relation of a text to its context, for it reminds us that, however powerfully the social experiences of the French aristocracy shaped the goals and methods of vernacular historiography, the resulting texts in no way transparently reflect those experiences. On the contrary, like all literary works, these histories are the site of multiple, often contradictory historical realities that may be either present or absent in the works and in both capacities are constitutive of their form and inscribed meaning. Indeed, rather than incorporating and reflecting current social and political realities, I would argue that the rise of prose historiography in thirteenth-century France sought to deny and mask the consequences of recent transformations in the political power and social status of the aristocracy that patronized it. It is precisely this attempt to mantle adverse historical change beneath the calm and deproblematized surface of prose narrative that alerts us to the social function of prose historiography in thirteenth-century France, even as it seeks to disavow the very changes from which it is born.

1 The Historical Setting

The opening decades of the thirteenth century were a crucial moment in the social and political history of medieval France. Long-term transformations in the economic character of medieval society, originating as early as a century and a half before, culminated in these years to produce profound changes in the social and political structures that for centuries had ordered French society. On the one hand, new wealth generated by the rising commercial sectors of medieval society created novel economic cleavages at the heart of France's traditional social hierarchy that undermined the dominance, based on the possession of vast amounts of land, enjoyed for so long by the aristocracy. By the early part of the thirteenth century, French nobles were experiencing a period of progressive impoverishment that made them particularly vulnerable to the shifting gravity of political power—itself a product, at least in part, of the revived prosperity of the twelfth and thirteenth centuries.[1]

Joining with, and reciprocally acting upon, the threat to aristocratic status from below was a new and powerful challenge to the political autonomy of the French nobility, posed by the centralizing policies of the king, Philip Augustus. During his reign (1179–1223) the French monarch relentlessly prosecuted his claims to overlordship of the French realm, repeatedly demanding, in numerous acts both large and small, the service and obedience that the French aristocracy had successfully evaded for centuries. By the beginning of the thirteenth century, the revival of a monied economy and the growth of royal centralization had collaborated to undermine the sources of aristocratic strength and to delimit spheres of noble activity, creating a highly destabilized environment that worked to the advantage of the king.

11

With the triumph of monarchy over the forces of feudal resistance at the battle of Bouvines in 1214, an era of aristocratic domination in French medieval society drew to a close.

It is neither insignificant nor accidental that these same decades witnessed a striking transformation in the historiographical practices of the French aristocracy. For it was during the reign of Philip Augustus that the oldest chronicles in French prose made their appearance, marking a decisive evolution in the historical tastes and concerns of the French laity, whose interest in the past had hitherto been satisfied by rhymed chronicles or epic *chansons de geste*, chanted history with a large component of legend and fiction. By the end of the twelfth century, an expanding body of literate laymen nurtured a growing suspicion of poetized history.[2] Finding the poet's search for rhyme and measure to be incompatible with the historian's pursuit of truth and need for exactitude of narration, laymen increasingly sought to satisfy their curiosity about the past in new ways. Soon after 1200, a popular demand for historical works accessible to those untutored in Latin began to make itself felt.

The earliest products of the movement toward vernacular historiography were the translations of the *Pseudo-Turpin Chronicle*, the largely legendary account of Charlemagne's expedition to Spain, better known through the verses of the *Song of Roland*. Between 1200 and 1230 no fewer than six independent translations of the *Pseudo-Turpin Chronicle* were produced within France, excluding an Anglo-Norman version that dates from the same period.[3] All the translations resulted from the patronage of the French-speaking Flemish aristocracy of northern France, a patronage phenomenon that, in its geographical and chronological concentration, is virtually unmatched in medieval textual production. The first translation was made around 1202 at the request of Yolande, countess of Saint-Pol, and her husband, Hugh IV.[4] Around the same time, certainly before 1206, a "Master Johannes" made a separate translation,[5] a transcription of which was commissioned by Renaud of Boulogne in 1206 and, in the following year, 1207, by Michel III, lord of Harnes and "justiciar" of Flanders.[6] Subsequent translations appear in a version commissioned by William of Cayeux, a lord of Ponthieu, of which only a fragment remains today,[7] and in a version stemming from Artois and dating from about 1218.[8] This version was later used by an anonymous Artesian minstrel in the employ of Robert VII of Béthune.[9] A sixth and final translation stems from Hainaut, composed in the decade between 1220 and 1230 and similarly the work of an anonymous translator who lived and worked in that same region encompassing the counties of Flanders, Hainaut, and Artois that functioned as the center for the diffusion of the vernacular *Pseudo-Turpin*.[10]

Indicative of a deepening interest in the past are the contemporary French histories of antiquity, principally of Rome. Between 1208 and 1213, Roger IV, castellan of Lille, commissioned an *Histoire ancienne jusqu'à César*.[11] Almost simultaneously, between 1215 and 1235, Jean de Thuin composed his *Hystore de Jules César*.[12] In the Île-de-France, the most successful of these ancient histories, the *Faits des Romains*, was composed by an anonymous author in 1213–1214.[13] Trojan history also attracted attention; it was treated in the *Histoire ancienne* as well as in an independent prose version of Benoît de Sainte-Maure's *Roman de Troie*.

By the end of the reign of Philip Augustus vernacular history was adapted to contemporary chronicles. Beginning with a recently discovered *Chronique des rois de France*—which survives in two rather different versions, one at the Vatican (Reg. Lat. 624) and a more complete recension found at Chantilly (MS. 869)—the focus of vernacular historiography shifted to royal history.[14] A contemporary work by the Anonymous of Béthune, also entitled *Chronique des rois de France* and for its early history of France based largely on the *Historia Regum Francorum usque ad annum 1214*, recounted the deeds of French kings for an audience of purely French-speaking laity, professing to answer a widening demand for authenticity of content and clarity of style in vernacular historiography.[15] Shortly before writing the *Chronique des rois de France*, the Anonymous produced a complementary work, the *Histoire des ducs de Normandie et des rois d'Angleterre*, devoted to the history of Normandy and England from the arrival of the Normans to the time of King John.[16] Another instance of royal historiography is a work, now lost, commissioned by Giles of Flagi, a Burgundian lord who charged an anonymous author with composing in French a history of Philip Augustus, doubtless based on the Latin chronicles of Rigord of Saint-Denis and Guillaume le Breton. Fragments for the years 1214–1216 of an additional lost prose chronicle of this monarch, sometimes attributed to Michel of Harnes or a member of his household, have survived as well.[17]

These early-thirteenth-century translations and chronicles marked a critical stage in the development of vernacular historiography and served as important intermediaries between the Latin historiography of the twelfth century and the full-scale vernacular historiography of France signaled by the appearance of the multivolume *Grandes chroniques de France,* the first installment of which was completed by Primat in 1274.[18] Although written at the Abbey of Saint-Denis, the *Grandes chroniques* soon came to be recognized as a quasi-official history of the Capetian kings of France, who were its patrons. With the inauguration of the *Grandes chroniques de France,* it is fair to say that historical writing in Old French was successfully established in France.

What is most notable about the patronage of early vernacular historiography is the extreme chronological and geographical concentration of the texts and their known patrons. Virtually every identifiable patron of an early prose history belonged to a small group of Franco-Flemish lords circulating in the orbit of the count of Flanders in the opening decades of the thirteenth century. Hugh and Yolande of Saint-Pol, Renaud of Boulogne, Robert VII of Béthune, Michel of Harnes, William of Cayeux, and Roger IV, castellan of Lille, shared far more than their common practice of commissioning historical works in Old French prose. They were members of a tightly knit circle of Franco-Flemish aristocrats who lived in close proximity to one another, often intermarried, and, in the crucial years of the early thirteenth century, were caught up in an era of political turmoil unmatched in Flemish medieval history. Only toward midcentury, when the monarchy had imposed its authority and was firmly in control of the realm, did the patronage of vernacular historiography shift to the royal court.

The geographical concentration of the patrons of the first generation of vernacular historical texts implies that vernacular histories addressed themselves with particular relevance to the needs of the Franco-Flemish aristocracy at a moment of crisis and that historiographical innovation was, at least in part, a response to changes in the social and political conditions of noble life. To understand why this should be so, it is necessary to examine the background of the tumultuous events of the reign of Philip Augustus, which had significant consequences for the French aristocracy, both in general and more especially for the Franco-Flemish lords responsible for the rise of vernacular prose historiography.

Philip Augustus and the French Realm

It has long been recognized that the reign of Philip Augustus was a critical turning point in the fortunes of the medieval French monarchy. Under his rule, the royal domain increased dramatically, royal revenue was augmented to an unprecedented degree, and the balance of power between the king and the barons of the realm tipped decisively, and irreversibly, in favor of the monarchy. Philip Augustus's success is all the more notable in light of the condition of Capetian kingship at the beginning of his rule. When in 1179, at the age of fourteen, Philip assumed the governance of the realm from his ailing father, Louis VII, Capetian power scarcely matched that of the great barons, whose counties ringed the royal domain. Weak, with few administrative organs and even fewer servants, the king controlled only a small area of scattered lands, for the most part located within the Seine basin in the territory known as the Île-de-France.

To the west of the royal domain lay the powerful duchy of Normandy, whose ruler, since 1066 also the king of England, disposed of resources far greater than any the king of France could muster. Philip Augustus's grandfather, Louis VI, had engaged in continuous but futile warfare against this threatening neighbor and in 1119, after the battle of Brémule, had been forced to endure the humiliation of receiving back his charger, saddle, and bridle, lost in war, as a gift from Henry I, who kept for himself the French battle-standard as a souvenir of victory.[19] To the east and south of the royal domain—indeed, virtually encircling it—lay the extensive lands of the house of Champagne-Blois; and to the north loomed the rich and powerful county of Flanders, next to Normandy the wealthiest and best organized principality in western Europe at the end of the twelfth century. The counts of Champagne and Flanders, vassals of the French king with respect to their comital tenures, also held lands on their eastern frontiers from the German emperor, a fact that only complicated already difficult relations with their French overlord.[20] Although Louis VI and Louis VII had pacified the royal domain, making it possible for a French king finally to travel between Paris and Orléans without fear of violent attack,[21] the resources that the domain returned to the king, whether in revenue or military service, constituted but a fraction of those routinely available to the king's rivals.[22]

Despite the legacy of a weak and poorly administered domain, however, Philip Augustus was determined from the beginning to assert royal authority and impose his will upon his highly independent and often recalcitrant vassals. The tenacity of purpose and political skill with which he pursued this goal led contemporary chroniclers, looking back at the striking accomplishments of his reign, to attribute to Philip an early and unwavering commitment to defeat his enemies and extend his power. Thus Gerald of Wales reports that in 1174, when not quite ten years old, Philip was taken by his father Louis VII to visit

Henry II at his newly constructed castle of Gisors. As the assembled company of lords extolled the strength and richness of the Plantagenet fortress, the child became angry and burst forth, saying that he wished that the castle were even stronger and made of gold, silver, and diamonds. Asked why, Philip retorted: "The more precious the materials of the castle, the more pleasure I will have in possessing it when it shall fall into my hands."[23]

Perhaps the most striking image of Philip's refusal to be constrained by vassals whom he considered his legal subordinates, however inadequate his own resources, derives from the account of a dream interpolated into Rigord's *Gesta Philippi Augusti*. Before Philip was even born, his father, who had waited many years for the birth of a son, saw in a vision an image of the young prince holding out a golden chalice filled with human blood, which he offered to his vassals, who drank from it (*et omnes in eo bibebant*).[24] The fields of France would indeed be drenched in the blood of Philip's vassals before the king had succeeded in making himself master of the realm.

Few Capetian kings pursued power as ruthlessly or unscrupulously as Philip.[25] Although careful to provide a legal basis for the major acquisitions of his reign, Philip often did not hesitate to break treaties and conventions when it suited him; to compel vassals against their will, sometimes even without their knowledge, to stand surety for their compatriots (both techniques used with notable success in Philip's struggles with the counts of Flanders); and, in general, to employ the full arsenal of available feudal rights to insinuate the monarchy's presence wherever possible throughout the kingdom. Lacking men and money, Philip used guile, patience, and persistence in asserting royal authority over the great barons. Payon Gastinel, a canon of Saint-Martin of Tours, who knew the king well, calls him "expert in the art of intrigue" (*in machinis peritissimus*) and "stingy to his enemies" (*inimicis avarus*), among whom he sowed discord that he might all the more easily "repress the malignity of the great men of the kingdom" (*malignos regni primates opprimens eorumque discordias volens*).[26]

Philip sought to exercise the royal prerogatives that had always adhered to the crown, but which earlier Capetian kings had enforced only with great difficulty, if at all. To that end, he began the slow, painstaking process of creating a machinery of government that would be responsive to the king's will and would enable him to govern the realm effectively. Beginning with the creation of the *baillis*, salaried royal officers owing everything to the king, Philip Augustus inaugurated a field administration that would eventually assume responsibility for the financial and judicial functions of the king on the local level. Although the full impact of the *baillis* on local administration was not felt until after Philip's reign, the growth in royal administration had made sufficient progress that the power of the French king in the thirteenth century became preponderant, transforming irreversibly the traditional balance of authority and autonomy between monarchy and aristocracy.

Of the extensive bureaucratic and judicial innovations of Philip Augustus's reign, a number are particularly relevant here because of their broad implications for baronial independence. Most immediately obvious to contemporary chroniclers was a change in the composition of the royal court. It was the king's practice, the canon of Saint-Martin of Tours reported, to seek advice from "lesser men" (*minorum consilio utens*).[27] The Anonymous of Béthune, in his *Chronique des rois de France*, similarly scoffed at the low-born men and administrative *arrivistes* from whom the king routinely took counsel, men whom, without naming, he characterizes as "un gras chevalier," "un petit chevalier," and another "de basse gens,"[28] who were supplanting the barons and prelates in the royal council.

What these chroniclers noticed was a striking change in the composition of the central curia taking place under Philip Augustus. The Capetian curia, like the household government of the Carolingians from whom it was inherited, had originally consisted of the four standard household officers plus a large and diffuse body of royal *familiares*, who lived at the palace and who formed the royal entourage. These *palatini* traveled with the king, served his needs, filled his embassies, and acted as his counselors.[29] Under Louis VII, the practice of taking counsel from royal advisors became more formal with the emergence of a royal *conseil*, which increasingly functioned as an institutional forum in which the king could consult such *consiliari* as he deemed fit.[30] After the Second Crusade, the men whom Louis VII called to his *conseil* included not only the knights and clerks of his household, but also the great men of the realm, the *proceres* and *optimates* who, as royal vassals, were bound by the conditions of their feudal tenure to offer their lord *consilium* as well as military aid.

This socially complex composition of the royal *conseil*, including both *palatini* and *optimates*, remained Capetian practice until Philip Augustus's return from the Third Crusade in 1191. After that date, however, the number and eminence of Philip's *consiliari* declined consistently. The last great barons to appear in the *conseil* by virtue of their feudal tenure had been men like counts Philippe of Flanders and Thibaut of Blois, both of whom died while accompanying Philip on the Third Crusade.[31] In place of the barons, Philip increasingly relied on a restricted number of trusted counselors who formed part of the incipient "service aristocracy" so distasteful to the chroniclers. These men were creatures of the king, recruited by Philip while still young, generally from among the lesser nobility, who owed their rise to influence and whatever wealth they accumulated along the way to royal favor.

According to the anonymous author of the *Chronique des rois de France*, writing around 1213, Philip confided principally in three men—Walter the Chamberlain, Bartélemy of Roye, and Guerin of Senlis—who, he claimed, were with the king "more continually than any other and aided him with counsel and *chevalerie* and in any way that they could. . . . [Because] in these three in whom he trusted the most, the king was accustomed to take his counsel and open his heart concerning what he wished to do."[32] Although it is unlikely that Philip restricted his search for advice to only three counselors, the exclusion of the magnates from the royal *conseil* and Philip's tendency to rely on lesser knights and clerks of the king—the *milites et clerici regis*—to fill the council and to execute royal orders was symptomatic of a new orientation in Capetian government. No longer was royal government the product of a collaborative effort between the king and *proceres* of the realm, as the Carolingians and early Capetians had envisaged it. Rather, beginning with Philip Augustus, the king based his strength and administrative efficiency on the maintenance of a corps of paid royal servitors responsive to the royal will and personally beholden to the king for advancement. Royal government now possessed the instruments with which to subdue the magnates rather than cooperate with them.

At the same time as Philip Augustus was restricting baronial participation in the royal *conseil*, he sought to extend royal jurisdiction over his vassals and rear-vassals. In 1209, for example, he issued an ordinance respecting the inheritance of fiefs throughout the kingdom, which decreed that whenever a fief was divided, in whatever fashion, all new heirs were to hold their tenures as direct vassals of the original lord, rather than through an intermediary.[33] Effective primarily within the domain itself, the ordinance of 1209 nonetheless signaled Philip's desire to affirm his feudal suzerainty and to insist on the performance of marks of subordination such as homage, owed him in his capacity as feudal overlord. Indeed, Bournazel and Poly have argued that not until the reign of Philip Augustus did the French monarchy become feudal in the strict sense of the term, that is, take the form of a fixed, hierarchical ranking of fiefs, each category of which lay within the *mouvance*, or jurisdiction, of the category immediately above it.[34] Over this structure the king presided, alone free of feudal encumbrances, for, as Philip declared in 1213: "Our predecessors the kings of France were wont to do homage to no one."[35] "Le roi ne tient de nului"—the king receives but cannot himself perform homage;[36] he surmounts but is not part of the feudal order constituted by the totality of fiefs, each dependent one upon the other, which gives the realm its political coherence. This image of the kingdom as an ordered, hierarchical structure of fiefs was precisely that inscribed in the royal registers by the chancery clerks who drew up the feudal inventories (known now as the *Scripta de feodis*), which for the first time projected a mental map of the territories subject to royal authority both within and beyond the domain.[37]

Philip did not confine himself, moreover, to providing a theoretical basis for feudal suzerainty. He exploited the full panoply of rights with which his feudal overlordship endowed him—whether of wardship, marriage, or relief—to augment royal revenues and to expand royal jurisdiction. The citation of King John to the French court in response to the appeal of Hugh of Lusignan in 1202, which laid the legal basis for the conquest of Angevin territories after John failed to answer the royal summons and was adjudged to have defaulted, is the most famous case of Philip's exercise of an expanded feudal jurisdiction over the great barons of the realm.[38] It is not, however, the only one.

Moreover, Philip's ability to enforce the judgment of his court was strikingly new. In 1154, when Eleanor of Aquitaine married Henry Plantagenet, Louis VII had cited him to court for violating a vassal's obligation to consult his lord upon contracting a marriage, and when Henry failed to appear, Louis VII declared his lands confiscate. The war that ensued led to Louis's defeat at the hands of his vassal and ultimately to the humiliating Treaty of Gisors of 1158. By contrast, with the acquisition of the Angevin lands of Normandy, Anjou, Maine, Touraine, and Poitou, realized in execution of the penalty of confiscation for default of law against John, Philip successfully imposed the sentence of his court on a rebellious vassal. That Philip's judgment against John in 1202 led ultimately to the permanent dispossession of his fiefs vindicated the king's claim to feudal jurisdiction beyond the royal domain and served notice that he would no longer tolerate disobedience.

Excluded from central government and made to submit to royal jurisdiction, the French aristocracy was threatened in even such customarily privileged realms as participation in warfare. The use of mercenary armies increased markedly in France during the reign of Philip Augustus, who initially employed the Brabançons, and then military adventurers like Cadoc.[39] After 1181 the chroniclers no longer mention Brabançons as part of French armies, but the general term *cottereaux* (*cotarelli*) appears to indicate the king's use of paid, nonknightly forces.[40] Such bands of professional combatants, of low birth and fighting with weapons considered unworthy of a knight, had been used with increasing frequency since the middle of the twelfth century by English kings,[41] but they had not been resorted to by the Capetians, whose financial reserves before Philip Augustus were inadequate to support large paid armies.[42] Even during Philip's rule, the Capetians relied less on mercenary forces than did the Angevins, whose propensity to expend large sums on military ventures continued to outstrip that of their feudal overlords.

If not strictly mercenary, Philip's army nonetheless contained relatively few knights who served by virtue of their obligation to provide feudal service. According to the accounts of 1202–1203, some 259 knights figured among Philip's troops, which numbered between 2,300 and 2,600 fighters.[43] To a large extent, the royal army was composed of bannerets and lesser knights, whose service was paid from the royal treasury, and of *sergents*, either on foot or mounted. These *sergents à cheval*, although fighting on horseback in the style of knights, formed a non-knightly contingent recruited in all probability both from the lowest ranks of the nobility—those too poor to possess a fief owing military service (according to Audouin)—or from among commoners (according to Duby), including bourgeois from the cities now armed as knights (*armati ut milites*).[44] Guillaume le Breton, describing in the *Philippide* the *sergents à cheval* from Soissons who fought at Bouvines, calls them "sons of the people" (*alumni plebis*).[45] Their appearance among the feudal host during the reign of Philip Augustus signaled the end of the aristocracy's monopoly over war and its right to fight in a distinctively noble manner.

To make matters worse, competition on the battlefield was accompanied by economic competition at home. The late twelfth and early thirteenth centuries witnessed rapid economic change, which worked,

in both the short and the long term, to the detriment of Europe's seigneurial classes.[46] Evidence of a growing pattern of economic impoverishment on the part of the French aristocracy in this period is widespread. Although it is likely that the new monetary economy coming
into full flower at the beginning of the thirteenth century brought
greater revenues to the nobility than their ancestors had enjoyed in
the form of profits from tithes, mills, ovens, *tailles*, and *péages*, it is
also true that the expenses both of seigneurial exploitation and of war
had risen dramatically.[47] To take but one example: the price of a *des-
trier* or medieval warhorse, which in peacetime cost between eight and
ten livres tournois, during periods of war—which is to say, for most
of the first two decades of the thirteenth century—rose to four times
that amount, ranging as high as forty livres tournois.[48] Moreover, in
the regions most deeply penetrated by the new economy, lords no
longer enjoyed absolute monopolies over mills (which, thanks to improved techniques, were a significant source of augmented income),
some of which now belonged to the bourgeois of the towns or to peas-
ant communities, as did other sources of seigneurial income.[49] Profits
from mounting grain prices, which benefited lords who continued to
cultivate their domains directly, were often offset by increases in the
costs of seigneurial exploitation, as the prices for tools, salaries, rec-
ordkeeping materials, and the business of "doing justice" rose precip-
itously in the thirteenth century.[50] In addition, improvements in military technology heightened the expense of serving as a knight, and
feudal "aids" for ransom, voyages to the East and related Crusade expenses, reliefs, and other financial burdens imposed by feudal rulers
similarly expanded.[51]

Doubtless, however, the principal cause of aristocratic economic
embarrassment in this period lay neither in the rising costs associated
with cultivation nor in a decline in landed income. The problem,
rather, was an increase in the expenses entailed by the social requirements of living "nobly."[52] Enormous outlays for food, lodgings, and
especially a growing habit of luxury in dress put unaccustomed strains
on noble purses. Noblewomen developed a taste for green *surcots*, tu-
nics of vermilion silk, dresses of camlet or tiretaine. Their spouses and
suitors began to adorn themselves in cloaks lined with rabbit skins,
capes, and high boots.[53] The greater the social challenge to the old nobility from the rising wealth of the urban bourgeoisie, the more necessary it became for the nobility visually to distinguish itself through
the adoption of a distinctive mode of dress, comportment, and manners. It is hardly accidental that contemporary French romances lavish

such exquisite concern on the details of aristocratic accoutrements and appearance or that the royal virtue most often extolled in aristocratic literature is that of largesse to a warrior class for whom extravagance was rapidly becoming a form of social definition.

To meet the growing costs of a decorated life, the nobility resorted to borrowing. Toward the end of the twelfth century, there is accumulating evidence of aristocratic indebtedness, achieving levels of debt that, after 1200, could be made good only by the sale of homages and property. Sales of lands and manors, rights to tolls and mills, and other sources of economic remuneration generated immediate cash for indebted nobles, but also sapped the economic basis of the noble family's wealth, authority, and social prestige by diminishing the size of its landed patrimony and the rights of governance attached to it. Since land prices remained relatively stable throughout the thirteenth century—a phenomenon attributable to the abundance of available land on the market[54]—such measures in any case provided only limited and temporary relief and risked restricting the family's ability to function in the future. Around 1210, numerous sales of aristocratic properties in northern France are noticeable; among powerful lords like the counts of Ponthieu, the counts of Saint-Pol, and the castellans of Bapaume and Saint-Omer, it is possible to trace sales of important landed possessions to churches through successive contracts representing several generations of the family.[55]

Although the original beneficiaries of such sales may have been churches, considerable territories also went to non-nobles who, in assuming the nobility's titles to land, threatened to acquire the social entitlements that for centuries had marked the barriers dividing noble from non-noble in medieval society. It was to protect themselves against this threat of social decline and to draw indelibly a line between those who, however impoverished, were entitled to access to the nobility by virtue of birth and those who were not that the French aristocracy began to bestow the title of esquire ("armiger," or "ecuyer" in northern France) upon male members of a family whose profligacy or economic ill fortune had deprived them of the means necessary to achieve knighthood and who, therefore, had abandoned all hopes of being dubbed. Without functional significance, the title of *esquire* expressed the social quality of the man whose blood gave him the right to noble status but whose financial resources were inadequate for its maintenance. As Duby has remarked, "Its adoption and diffusion on the eve of the thirteenth century marks more clearly than anything that from then on the aristocracy saw itself as a nobility, a caste closed to all who could not claim good breeding."[56] Threatened from below by the villein upstart who profited from the increased prosperity of the age to raise himself to a position of economic equality with the knight; threatened from within by growing indebtedness, which forced nobles to sell lands and homages; and threatened most of all from above by the rising power of the monarchy with its demand for support and obedience, the French aristocracy responded by closing its ranks, by constituting itself as an *ordo* governed by common juridical rules, accepted manners, and a shared knightly culture.

This shared culture was forged essentially by the diffusion among all members of the aristocracy of the high ideals of chivalry and *courtoisie*. For both high and lesser aristocrats, chivalric ideology functioned as a class code, drawing ever more firmly the lines separating those with claims to nobility from all other manner of men. In the face of the twin threat posed by a rapidly developing monetary economy and a strong centralized state, each of which favored the rise to prominence of non-noble segments of medieval society, the French aristocracy fell back on an essentially cultural model of social superiority through which it sought to assert its continued prestige and centrality.

Flanders

If the aristocracy throughout France underwent an ideological transformation in response to the mounting economic and political difficulties it experienced during the reign of Philip Augustus, in Flanders these difficulties attained crisis proportions. There an abundant agriculture and flourishing textile industry had enhanced the economic prosperity of cities such as Ghent, Bruges, Lille, and Ypres, making Flanders one of the richest and most densely populated regions of western Europe.

The new prominence of the towns in Flanders from the twelfth century onward was the result of the county's rapid economic development. Until the end of the eleventh century, economic activity in Flanders, as everywhere in western Europe, had been essentially local and agrarian. But Flanders was especially well situated to benefit from the commercial renewal that by the middle of the century was quickening the pace of European economic life. The county lay at the juncture of the great commercial routes of western Europe that led from England and the North Sea through France and the Rhineland to Italy. In addition to possessing a long coastline that offered natural sites for harbors, Flanders was traversed by numerous rivers and estuaries, facilitating the transport of bulky goods like grain and wool. To the east, the Rhine offered a natural water route into Germany, and the Meuse drove toward France. In the northwest, the Escaut formed a main trunk for the commercial circulation of goods, with trade fed by subsidiary tributaries like the Scarpe, the Lys, and the Deule on its left bank, and the Haine, Dender, Rupel, Senne, and Dyle on the right.[57] Land routes paralleled the waterways and extended the paths of commercial activity to the fairs of Champagne and the Île-de-France, enabling Flanders to play the same role as a center of international trade in the north that Italy was simultaneously assuming in the Mediterranean.

The counts of Flanders worked to create an environment favorable to trade. Merchants were taken under the count's protection and towns systematically awarded privileges and exemptions from taxes, and harbors and canals, the infrastructure necessary for rapid and sustained economic growth, were constructed under the aegis of comital authority. New ports were built at Gravelines and Nieuwpoort in 1163, Damme in 1180, and Dunkerque and Berliet in 1183.[58] The 1187 *Gros Brief* of Flanders already signals the existence of grain markets in a great number of towns and villages whose revenues to the count, formerly payable in kind, were now calculated and paid in money.[59] Flemish wool-cloth manufacture first developed around 1050 in the region of Ypres-Lille, and as early as 1100 Italian merchants were attending the fairs of those cities.[60] Dependent largely on the high-quality wool imported from the great sheep farms of England (although Flemish wool also circulated from the twelfth century on), the growth of wool manufacture and the wool-cloth trade generated strong economic ties with England, which increasingly exerted a gravitational pull on Flemish political relations with her northern neighbor. In supporting the economic health of the towns and mercantile populations, the counts of Flanders were also thinking of their own purse. They reaped huge profits from the revenues of *tonlieux* imposed on the circulation of men and merchandise at river crossings, bridges, roads, and markets as well as from *péages* and a variety of other rights over production and commerce.[61]

The primary beneficiaries of this burgeoning economic activity were, however, the merchants themselves. By examining the *enquêtes* of 1247, Sivéry has established that at the time of the battle of Bouvines, in 1214, the ransoms demanded from the rich bourgeois of the southern basin of the Escaut, especially those of Arras, corresponded to an annual income of some twelve thousand pounds, a sum that places them at a level of economic parity with the most elevated of the barons and compares favorably with that of the count of Flanders, who disposed of a gross annual income of approximately thirty thousand livres. By the end of the century, while the resources of the counts of Flanders remained relatively stable, a wealthy bourgeois family like the Crespins, moneylenders from Arras, had overtaken the count and attained the literally princely level of forty thousand livres a year.[62]

But the progress of the new economy was not uniformly favorable. Economic growth was, in fact, repeatedly subject to crises caused by the need to readjust market mechanisms to changing conditions of supply and demand, imbalances in the production and distribution of food and manufactured goods, and the problems of provisioning developed urban areas no longer fed solely by their own hinterlands. In the course of the thirteenth century, three such crises struck northern France and Flanders in zones where the new economy was most vigorous, all of them crises of adaptation to the new forces governing economic life, as opposed to subsistence crises generated by war or weather. The common features of these failures were a long inflationary curve in which prices reached extremely elevated levels, followed by a sharp decline first in prices, then in production. As in earlier centuries, such deflationary phases were often accompanied by famines caused by inadequacies in the systems used to provision densely populated urban areas engaged in long-distance trade, areas that, in contrast to smaller centers, tended to import grain rather than rely on local or regional production.[63] The first of these crises occurred on the eve of the thirteenth century in 1197, involving primarily the grain trade. It was followed by symptoms of a crisis in the wool-cloth industry, beginning circa 1214, and in turn by another critical phase in the cereal economy around 1222–1224. These downswings were overshadowed in midcentury by much greater and more prolonged difficulties in both cereal and wool commerce. For these sectors of the economy, economic depression was not wholly reversed until the 1280s.[64]

The dates of these periodic downswings are notable, for they fall in the same years when the Flemish aristocracy found itself in open political conflict with the king of France, thus compounding economic difficulties with the expense and potential tragedies of protracted warfare. The cyclical crises of the thirteenth century naturally were felt most strongly in regions affected by commercialization, of which Flanders was the most advanced in northern Europe. Moreover, to the extent that the cyclical crises represented phases of adjustment to novel economic conditions, participants in the new economy were best able to recover from its oscillations, whereas those who, like the Flemish aristocracy, stood apart from its operation suffered the consequences without being able to take advantage of the benefits it brought.

The most serious economic problem facing the Flemish aristocracy during the first half of the thirteenth century was the long-term effect of steadily rising prices set against the nobility's chronic need for cash and its inability to generate new sources of revenue. It has been calculated that the nominal price of grain rose as much as 51 percent in the first half of the century, which, when adjusted for an inflation rate of 15 to 20 percent over the same period, yields a gain in real prices of between 31 percent and 36 percent.[65] Nor was inflation restricted to grain; it equally affected charges for services, such as salaries for those employed on seigneurial estates, as well as the prices of a broad range of manufactured goods and tools.[66]

Although the rise in grain prices might at first seem to benefit lords with large landed estates, in fact peasants were much better able to take advantage of the new economy than their masters. On older estates, lords generally were confined to collecting a perpetual *cens*, whose rate had long ago been fixed in money and which was, therefore, subject to long-term depreciation caused by inflation. Peasants, in contrast, could easily exploit fluctuating market prices to maximize profits on their cultivated plots.

The depreciation of traditional revenues could, in fact, be considerable. Around 1275 in the Escaut basin, for example, the lord of Pamele Audenarde received only forty-five sous for six *bonniers* of an ancient tenure, but was able to extract seventy-three sous for the same extent of land newly accensed. Genicot has found that in Namur lords were compelled to content themselves with two deniers for the *cens* of *bonnier* held by ancient tenure, a sum as much as thirty times *less* than could be obtained for land recently ceded.[67] Similarly, in Flanders and Picardy, after 1210 there was a slow but steady decline in the monetary value of the *cens*. Both Sivéry and Fossier attribute this slide to the nobility's pervasive indebtedness, which forced them to sell off their *cens* in order to attract peasants little pressed for land to accept new tenures.[68] And as the monetary value of their estates declined, so, of course, did the purchasing power of aristocratic revenues realized from the land, thus occasioning a further round of noble indebtedness.[69]

Chronically short of money in the face of mounting expenditures, Flemish nobles resorted to parceling tenures or to outright liquidation of their property. And when this did not suffice, they borrowed. Among the Flemish sponsors of vernacular historiography, only the house of Béthune was a lender, not a borrower, in this period.[70] Daniel of Béthune, advocate of Arras and brother to Robert VII, patron of the two histories by the anonymous minstrel employed in his household, stood surety for a large number of loans by counts and nobles, apparently convincing the moneylenders that the solvency of his house was beyond question.[71]

Yet even the Béthunes, at first glance free of the financial exigencies of their Flemish compatriots, experienced difficulties at the beginning of the second quarter of the thirteenth century. In 1228, Robert VII complained to Pope Gregory IX that the abbot of Saint-Bertin and others from the dioceses of Arras, Cambrai, and Tournai had extorted money from him by practicing usury (*magnam pecuniae quantitatem per usurariam pravitatem extorserant*) and that they were seeking to deprive him of his landed property.[72] A similar complaint was made three years later by Robert's brother, Jean of Béthune, against Hugh, lord of Châtillon, William his nephew, and others, who had wrongfully retained lands, *villae*, and revenues *en gage*, and again against Hugh of Saint-Pol and others who, Jean claimed, "did not cease to extort by usurious means considerable sums" from him and his wife, Elizabeth.[73] Thus even the lords of Béthune, sought out by their contemporaries as guarantors for loans, seem to have been involved in their own right in the cycle of loans, pledges, and sale of property that was severely undermining the financial health of the Flemish aristocracy.[74]

By 1230, the practice of selling fiefs and landed estates to pay off debts had become a general phenomenon among the Flemish nobility. In 1231, Hugh of Antoing and his wife, Philippa of Harnes (daughter of the patron of a *Pseudo-Turpin* translation, Michel III of Harnes), sold fiefs that they held from the house of Béthune and others in order to repay debts contracted by Michel III during his lifetime.[75] Such sales of patrimony meant a correspondingly diminished legacy to the next generation, which made it difficult for the family to fulfill its obligations to all its members. Younger sons complained that their portions were insufficient to live on, and daughters feared for their dowries. In 1228, for example, Robert VII of Béthune, unable to deliver the thousand livres he had promised as a dowry for his sister, Matilda, instead granted the use of the greater part of his properties at Kalken to Matilda's husband, Gilpert of Zottegern, by way of meeting his responsibilities.[76]

By midcentury aristocratic debt had become so widespread that the countess Margaret, in a charter of 1255 announcing the sale of a fief by Walter of Gistel for 3,750 livres of Flanders to the Abbey of Vaucelles, decried the condition of debt that led Flemish nobles to alienate lands as a voracious plague upon the land, explaining that Walter had been compelled to sell because "gravi debitorum onere premeretur et videret summam debitorum cotidie augmentari, timens ne vorax et semper vigil pestis suam totaliter substantiam devoraret nisi eis occurrendum celeri provideret" and because the unfortunate Walter could find no other remedy for his plight (*non inveniens alibi exitum quo sine graviori dispendio posset a debitorum onere liberari*).[77] The situation was sufficiently alarming to the countess to cause her to issue a charter forbidding the sale of comital fiefs to churches and non-nobles, decreeing that "nule abbeye, eglyze, maisons de religion, priestre, clerc, gens non nobles u autres deffensables a le loy n'acquisiscent en nostre tierre de Flandres fief, rentes, tierres, hyretages u autres samblans acques mouvans de nous et encontre le commandement et le deffence desus dis" (no abbey, church, religious house, priest, cleric, non-noble, or any others forbidden by the law may acquire in our land of Flanders fief, rents, lands, inheritances or anything of the like within our *mouvance* and against the commandments of the above-mentioned prohibition).[78] With this ordinance, Margaret sought to prevent a comital fief from passing to churches or others unlikely to perform the feudal services owed from it or to render the feudal exactions normally levied upon it. In addition, it is clear that she aimed at ensuring the continued solvency of the count's vassals by inhibiting the nobility's tendency to deplete its resources through the sale of property. A similar prohibition was enacted against the sale of allodial property, the nobility's most ancient reserve, clearly intended to address the same issue.

As Countess Margaret's ordinance indicates, when noble land was sold it generally passed into the hands of churches or non-noble burghers from the towns, who, in purchasing noble land, acquired not only the territories included in the sale but also all the appurtenances—the rights of *ban* and other seigneurial prerogatives—attached to it. Rich townsmen thus came to assume more and more of the property and rights of former nobles, a fact that strengthened their political as well as economic standing. Already in 1127, the burghers' intervention in the succession crisis following the assassination of Charles the Good had proven decisive, enabling them to impose their own candidate, Thierry of Alsace, on the comital throne. With the reign of Thierry's son, Philippe of Alsace, the economic dominance of the towns increasingly determined the political strategies of the count of Flanders. His reign marks the beginning of the decline of the Flemish nobility and an important turning point in the history of the county.

Philippe of Alsace

As Philip Augustus was to do in France, Philippe of Alsace (1157/ 1163–1191) laid the basis for an efficient and prosperous administration of the county of Flanders. The brilliance of his rule, which brought medieval Flanders to the apogee of its power,[79] elicited the awe of contemporaries and the flattery of poets. Chrétien de Troyes, who dedicated the *Roman de Perceval (ou le Conte du Graal)* to Philippe, pronounced him the flower of contemporary chivalry and compared him favorably to Alexander the Great:

> qu'il le fet por le plus prodome
> Qui soit an l'Empire de Rome
> C'est li cuens Phelippes de Flandres
> Qui mialz valt ne fist Alixandres[80]

which he composed for the most honorable man who exists in the Empire of Rome, that is the count Philippe of Flanders, who is even more worthy than Alexander,

and the author of *Flandria generosa* asserted that he was "precipuus inter omnes et potentissimus omnium videbatur."[81]

Philippe continued his father's policy of supporting the economic growth of towns, extending to Bruges, Ghent, and Ypres the same privileges of freedom from tolls and duties enjoyed by Arras, Douai, and Lille. He ordered the construction of new ports, as we have seen, at Gravelines, Nieuwpoort, Damme, Dunkerque, and Berliet. At the same time, he reformed the criminal and fiscal laws and replaced the ancient castellans with a new administrative corps composed, for the first time, of salaried and removable functionaries—the *baillis*— who appeared earlier in Flanders than in France. These developments, graced by a favorable marriage to Elizabeth, the daughter of Raoul of Vermandois, which brought Philippe potential claims to the rich territories of Vermandois, Valois, and Amiens, placed the count of Flanders among the political leaders of western Europe, capable of rivaling the power and prestige of his royal neighbors, the kings of England and France.

Yet the spectacular promise of Philippe of Alsace's reign was never to be realized. While the power of the French king grew steadily throughout the last decades of the twelfth century, that of the Flemish count, on the contrary, diminished. From its position as a virtually independent state at the beginning of the century, Flanders was reduced to a fief of the crown, forced to witness the alienation of a significant portion of its southern tier and, finally, threatened with total absorption into the royal domain by the end of the reign of Philip Augustus.

The reasons for this sudden reversal in fortune are intimately bound up with the political conflicts engendered by the Vermandois succession, which brought the count of Flanders into direct confrontation with the king of France, divided the Flemish nobility into a "French" and an "English" party, and, not least, ultimately furnished Philip Augustus with the financial means necessary to defeat his enemies and subjugate a rebellious barony on the field of Bouvines. Although the long-range consequences of economic impoverishment and loss of social status suffered by the Flemish nobility in this period were possibly the more significant, the political reversals and dramatic shift in the balance of power between monarchy and aristocracy struck contemporaries more forcefully. From this perspective, the Vermandois succession and the unresolved tensions left in its wake were the driving forces of change in the world of the Flemish aristocracy, producing both open political strife and a less visible, but equally profound, sense of malaise.

Given that every single patron of the first works of vernacular historiography was involved, either directly or peripherally, in the disputes and wars spawned by the Vermandois succession and its aftermath, it supplies the essential political context for understanding why historical writing in Old French prose should have occurred first in this northeastern corner of France, among a threatened elite whose social and political conservatism would scarcely seem to offer fertile soil for literary innovation. For half a century—from 1164, when the succession first became a point of political contention, until Bouvines in 1214, when the last flashes of resistance to royal authority were quelled by the intrusion of the king's agents into formerly Flemish territory—the complicated sets of negotiations, broken treaties, skirmishes, and full-scale wars occasioned by the Vermandois succession and its attendant events created a highly unstable political environment that increasingly undermined the political autonomy first of the count of Flanders and then of the nobility itself, which had initially sought to profit from the weakening of comital authority by asserting its independence. And if, as I hope to demonstrate, social and political crisis was the ground of historiographical innovation in the opening decades of the thirteenth century, the Vermandois succession bears closer examination than might otherwise seem warranted in a study devoted to medieval historiography, for its vagaries and ultimately disastrous outcome for Flanders led the Flemish aristocracy to defend against its sense of social unease through ideological elaboration and to register its perception of social dislocation through a revision of its customary discursive behavior.

The Vermandois Succession

No one looking at the relative strength of the king of France and the count of Flanders in 1164 could have surmised the changes to come. In that year, Philippe of Flanders, associated with his father as count since 1157, took possession of Vermandois, Valois, and Amiens in the name of his wife, Elizabeth of Vermandois, whom he had married in 1159. Elizabeth was the eldest daughter of the Capetian kinsman Raoul III, count of Vermandois, and his second wife, Petronilla, whose three children—Elizabeth, Raoul the Lepreux, and Eleanor—had been designated his heirs in place of the children of his first marriage to Eleanor of Champagne. When Raoul III died in 1152, Raoul the Lepreux became count of Vermandois. He strengthened his ties to the count of Flanders by marrying Philippe of Alsace's sister, Marguerite. An additional alliance between the two families was contracted in 1172 with the marriage of Eleanor of Vermandois and Philippe of Alsace's brother, Mathieu of Alsace, who had become count of Boulogne through his first marriage to Marie, the daughter of King Stephen of England. The marriage to Eleanor lasted only one year, however, as Mathieu was killed at Neufchâtel in 1173.[82]

When Raoul the Lepreux died prematurely in 1164, Philippe of Alsace took over the administration of Vermandois and its dependencies in the name of his wife, Elizabeth. These included the Amiénois, a relatively small territory centered on Amiens but which included suzerainty over the neighboring fiefs of Pierrepont, Hangest, Boves, Picquigny, Moreuil, and Breteuil; Valois, owing homage to the bishop of Senlis, with its principal territory constituted by the ancient county of Crépy; and Vermandois itself, whose major centers were Saint-Quentin, Ribemont, Péronne, and Montdidier. These lands passed by hereditary right directly to Elizabeth, but in 1175 she consigned them to her husband, the count of Flanders, perhaps as a penalty for her infidelity.[83] Elizabeth's transfer of her lands to Philippe was confirmed by Louis VII in 1179, who thereby lent royal sanction to the grant.[84]

At this moment, the count of Flanders was without doubt the pre-eminent baron at the French court. Philippe accompanied Louis VII on his pilgrimage to the shrine at Canterbury to seek the miraculous aid of St. Thomas Becket in curing the young prince, Philip Augustus, who had suffered a serious hunting accident shortly before the date set for his royal coronation. And in 1179, as the ailing Louis felt the end approaching, he beseeched the Flemish count to protect Philip Augustus after his death and to superintend the activities of the royal court and young ruler.

That the new king seemed destined to be a pawn in the hands of the Flemish count is suggested by chronicle accounts of Philip Augustus's coronation. The count of Flanders bore the king's sword in procession, an honor awarded, as the *Flandria generosa* was quick to point out, to the noblest prince of the realm (*qui ferri debet a nobiliori principe regni*)[85] and whose splendor overshadowed that of his young ward.[86] The addition of Elizabeth's territories to the county of Flanders meant that Philippe of Alsace dominated the Escaut basin and had succeeded in extending his frontiers to the Île-de-France, directly facing the royal domain. He was, at last, in a position to compete with the Capetian monarch for hegemony over northern France. According to Roger of Wendover, Philip Augustus was aware of the count's dreams of glory, having remarked one day that "France will absorb Flanders or she will be destroyed by her."[87]

Philippe of Alsace's first bid to gain control over royal destinies came in the spring of 1180. He negotiated a marriage between the king and his niece, Isabelle of Hainaut, the daughter of his sister Marguerite, who, after the death of Raoul the Lepreux, had married Baldwin of Hainaut. Philippe clearly believed that his niece's presence as queen at the royal court would secure his influence, and as encouragement for the marriage he assigned the territories that later became known as the county of Artois to Isabelle as her dowry. It comprised the towns of Arras, Bapaume, Saint-Omer, Aire, and Hesdin and the *avouérie* of Béthune, ceded to Isabelle on condition that the count of Flanders be allowed to enjoy them during his lifetime. The alienation of these important cities, effectively constituting the southern tier of the county of Flanders, opened the way for the king of France to establish his influence in Flemish territory for the first time in centuries, since title to Artois included suzerainty over the counties of

Boulogne, Lens, Guines, Saint-Pol, Lilliers, Ardres, and Richebourg, all of which would pass into the royal domain if Isabelle succeeded in giving birth to a male heir; otherwise it would revert to her heirs if she died without posterity.[88]

Indeed, it is difficult to understand why Philippe of Alsace should have been willing to make such large concessions to Philip Augustus, even given that the lands were to remain in his possession until his death. Perhaps it was a mark of his confidence in his ability to control events and to manipulate the young king. More likely, Philippe of Alsace sought to use his grant of Artois as Isabelle's dowry as an inducement to the king to confirm Elizabeth of Vermandois's concession of her lands to him, lands that Philip Augustus might himself have sought to claim as a Capetian heir should both Elizabeth and Eleanor die childless. For soon after the marriage, Philip Augustus confirmed Elizabeth's concession to Philippe of Alsace, thus reinforcing his father's confirmation of 1179.

Behind the alienation of Artois, then, stands Philippe of Alsace's desire for legal confirmation of his right to the extensive territories that came to him via his wife's inheritance of Vermandois and its dependencies. The grant of Artois as Isabelle's dowry, in other words, contained a series of gambles. The first, and least likely to come to pass, was the chance that Isabelle of Hainaut might die without an heir and that Artois would automatically revert to Flanders. In light of the youth of both the king and his bride, it is unlikely that Philippe counted too heavily on this possibility. A much more serious gamble involved his own childlessness, which, if it continued (as it in fact would), meant that the county of Flanders would pass upon his death to his sister Marguerite and, if she died while Isabelle remained queen, might eventually pass to France and future royal heirs. Although this outcome was avoided, Philippe's grants opened the way for such an eventuality and demonstrate the high risks the count was willing to take in order to strengthen his claims to Vermandois.

Artois, and especially the cities of Aire and Saint-Omer, were to be the focal point of successive disputes and wars between the king of France and the count of Flanders, always an irritant in relations between the two rulers, roiling up conflicts seemingly without resolution. But the stakes were far bigger than the fate of those two cities, or even of the county as a whole. Artois represented that borderland of uncertainty about whether the king of France would succeed in subduing a powerful and independent barony and make it obedient to his will. Philippe of Alsace, for his part, was apparently willing to tolerate such uncertainty in the hope of furthering his dream of dominating northern France, itself greatly stimulated by the acquisition of Vermandois. In doing so, he made the last of a series of fateful gambles for Flanders.

By 1182, Philippe of Alsace's grand design had begun to unravel. In that year, his wife, Elizabeth of Vermandois, died childless, thus weakening, though not entirely undermining, the count's original claims to the Vermandois succession. In principle, the two royal confirmations of 1179 and 1180 still recognized the legitimacy of those claims and the legality of Elizabeth's bequest of her territories to her husband. But Philip Augustus almost immediately repudiated his confirmation of 1180, on the dubious grounds that it had been extracted from him under duress at a time when he was too young to enter into legal engagements.[89] The king then intervened on behalf of Elizabeth's younger sister, Eleanor of Vermandois, lending to her cause royal favor backed by military force.

Philip Augustus's repudiation of his 1180 confirmation and subsequent endorsement of Eleanor of Vermandois's claims to her sister's inheritance look suspiciously like a pretext to move against the count of Flanders, although it is likely that the king also hoped to benefit materially from his intervention. The precise legal basis for any possible future additions to the royal domain from the Vermandois succession, however, is not entirely clear. The royal chronicler Rigord of Saint-Denis later claimed that the king, in acquiring Vermandois, simply exercised his hereditary right to the succession (*titulo successorio ad reges Francorum jure hereditario*) since the house of Vermandois devolved from a Capetian cadet, and the king, as royal cousin, was the closest living *male* relative to the deceased Elizabeth and thus, next to Eleanor herself, possessed the strongest claim to inherit.[90] But the fact that Rigord, when he came to describe the battle of Boves, which concluded this phase of the struggle over the Vermandois succession in favor of the king, invented a miracle to demonstrate God's support of royal claims (according to Rigord, the fields on which the French forces had been encamped revived and flourished after the troops departed, whereas those trampled by Flemish forces remained barren)[91] suggests the weakness of the king's putative rights to the inheritance and the primacy of political motives for his intervention.

With good reason, the king sought to prevent the formation to the northeast of a powerful, hostile state possessing greater territories and resources than the throne. Support for Eleanor of Vermandois could frustrate the ambitions of Philippe of Alsace and at the same time hold out the possibility that Eleanor, still childless after three marriages, might designate Philip Augustus as her heir. However, the preliminary Treaty of La Grange–Saint-Arnoul, concluded in April 1182, made no mention of the king as Eleanor's future heir. In it, Eleanor received Valois, and Philippe of Alsace renounced any future rights over both Vermandois and Valois, on condition that he be allowed the enjoyment of the former for the duration of his lifetime. Upon his death Vermandois would pass to Eleanor, as her sister's rightful heir. In addition, the count of Flanders confirmed his grant of Artois to Queen Isabelle, and both parties agreed to return territories seized during the hostilities.[92]

Although in the main favorable to Philippe of Alsace, the Treaty of La Grange–Saint-Arnoul scarcely mollified this intemperate prince. In August 1184, still hoping to produce an heir to Flanders, he married Matilda of Portugal and, in a gesture that can only be interpreted as a deliberate insult to the king, assigned part of Artois—the towns of Aire and Saint-Omer—as the marriage dower to his new wife.[93] In retaliation, Philip Augustus called an assembly of barons at Senlis and threatened to divorce Isabelle of Hainaut, an attack clearly aimed not only at the queen and her father, Baldwin of Hainaut, but through them at the whole Flemish coalition as well.[94] It is possible that Philip Augustus had decided he was sufficiently strong to get control of Philippe of Alsace's entire heritage by force and no longer needed the count's support or that of his father-in-law, Baldwin of Hainaut.[95] The divorce itself was averted only because the queen took to the streets of Senlis in beggar's robes, publicly imploring the king's mercy.

By the end of 1184, open hostilities between the king and the count of Flanders had broken out. This time, however, Baldwin of Hainaut, who had invariably supported Philippe of Alsace, was separated from the Flemish party. In a characteristically unscrupulous move, Philip Augustus had named Baldwin, without his knowledge, as a pledge of the earlier agreements on the royal side, thus suggesting to Philippe of Alsace that his former ally had passed over to the king's party.[96] Despite Baldwin's repeated denials, Philippe remained suspicious, and relations between the brothers-in-law continually worsened. Philip Augustus had succeeded in driving a wedge between the two mainstays of the Flemish coalition. In the ensuing war, Philippe of Alsace attacked Hainaut, together with the duke of Brabant and the archbishop of Cologne, driving Baldwin closer to the king in search of military aid.

After five years of war, the count of Flanders was compelled to accept humiliating terms, concluded at Boves in July 1185 and ratified the following year by the Peace of Amiens. Of his wife's inheritance, he retained only the use of Saint-Quentin and Péronne during his life-time. Eleanor of Vermandois, while preserving Valois, gained the re-mainder of Vermandois, Ribemont, Ressons, and Chauny, along with confirmation of the *rente* that Philippe of Alsace had previously as-signed her from Roye. Since these lands came to her by virtue of feu-dal inheritance, she owed the king a large relief for entering into their possession, and it was probably as compensation for the relief due him that Philip Augustus received Montdidier, Roye, Thourette, Choisy, and the county of Amiens, along with the homages of more than sixty-five castles. The addition of Amiens and the southwestern part of Vermandois to the royal domain thus dates from 1185, for Philip Augustus almost immediately began to issue charters in his own name from these regions, even before the definitive conclusion of the treaty in November and its ratification the following March.[97]

Royal possession of Artois was secured in 1187 by the birth of a son, the future Louis VIII, to Philip and Isabelle of Hainaut. The un-happy queen died three years later, in 1190, while giving birth to twins, who also did not survive.[98] Philippe of Alsace, though continu-ing to employ the title of count of Vermandois in all his acts (*Philippo in Flandria et Viromandia comite existente*),[99] had lost all practical authority over the county except in Saint-Quentin and Péronne. The Peace of Amiens put an end to his dream of an independent Flemish state with mastery over northeastern France. Not only had he failed to augment his realm and preserve Flemish independence, but his death in 1191 at the siege of Acre, whither he had accompanied Philip Augustus on the Third Crusade, left to his successors the difficult task of struggling with the consequences of his unsuccessful policies.

Upon Philippe of Alsace's death in June 1191, Baldwin V of Hai-naut, who had the strongest claim to Flanders as the husband of Mar-guerite, Philippe of Alsace's sister, immediately took possession of the county in the name of his wife, assuming the title of Baldwin VIII of Flanders, and thus foiling any plans the king may have had to annex Flanders to the royal domain.[100] Philip had no choice but to acquiesce in Baldwin's succession. In return for the payment of a relief amount-ing to five thousand marks of silver, the king recognized Baldwin as the rightful heir to the county of Flanders.[101]

By 1192, then, the lands of Philippe of Alsace had been subjected to a fivefold division: (1) the county of Flanders itself was secured to Baldwin VIII, count of Hainaut; (2) Matilda of Portugal, Philippe's widow, received as dower Lille, Douai, Guines, and Calais; (3) the king had seized the county of Artois, carved out of former Flemish territories, on behalf of his minor son and (4) was himself confirmed in his possession of Amiens, Montdidier, Roye, Thourette, and Choissy, to which he had joined Péronne and title to the counties of Valois and Vermandois as Eleanor of Vermandois's designated heir; and (5) Eleanor had received her father's lands of Valois and those parts of Vermandois not in royal hands, and had been granted Saint-Quentin as well. She and her husband, Matthew of Beaumont, did liege homage to the king for their lands.

Although the settlements of 1192 did not put an end to the troubled relations between the count of Flanders and the king of France, whose control of the acquired territories was continually contested by the nobility as well as by successive counts, the importance of the Vermandois succession to royal fortunes should not be underestimated. As John Baldwin has strikingly demonstrated, the acquisition of Vermandois and related territories was critical to the growth of royal resources in the decade preceding the conquest of Normandy in 1204. Indeed, Baldwin has shown that the acquisition of Artois and Vermandois provided the financial means required for Philip Augustus to undertake the successful campaign against his Angevin and Flemish rivals in 1204 and 1214.[102] The settlement of the Artois and Vermandois succession thus represented not only an important phase in the ongoing contest for wealth and territory between the king and his great vassals, but also a key moment when royal revenues, hence power, began to outstrip those of the king's rivals.

Although Baldwin VIII, the new count of Flanders and Hainaut, in 1192 had signed the Treaty of Arras recognizing the king's title to Artois, he remained nonetheless unreconciled to its loss. In the following year, taking advantage of the open warfare between Philip Augustus and Richard of England, Baldwin temporarily occupied Aire, Saint-Omer, Péronne, and Roye in an attempt to nullify the alienation of Artois and the terms of the Treaty of Amiens. This effort was undone by the death of his wife, Marguerite, in November 1194, which caused the county of Flanders and all other rights and possessions the count held in her name to pass to their son, Baldwin IX of Flanders.[103] Thus deprived of any legal basis to contest the king's title to the northern territories, from this point until his death in 1195 the count acquiesced in the agreements concluded in 1192 and proved to be a faithful adherent of the king, even seconding Philip Augustus's hostile policy toward the English king.

But the long-term interests of Flanders ran contrary to a politics of anglophobia, however well it suited the needs of the French monarchy. Economic and family ties, as well as traditional habits of mutual cooperation, historically conditioned Flanders to be receptive to English influence. Nor were the Angevin kings loath to use any means at their disposal to ensure the continuance of that influence. Since the beginning of the twelfth century, English kings had been accustomed to lavish gifts and fief-rents on prospective Flemish vassals, and large numbers of Flemish knights can be found among those listed in the *Recognitio Servitii* of 1163 as owing service to the king of England, for which they were remunerated with considerable sums. Throughout the years of conflict between England and France, Richard and John continued to solicit the support of the Flemish nobility with offers of fief-rents and lands far in excess of those offered by Philip Augustus, who competed only halfheartedly in this contest for purchased loyalties. The nucleus of a pro-English party, made up of knights and nobles with strong economic and feudal ties across the Channel, thus already existed in Flanders by the first years of the thirteenth century.

The most significant factors in effecting the reversal of Baldwin VIII's anti-English stance, however, were economic considerations. By the beginning of the thirteenth century, Anglo-Flemish commerce in wool was flourishing. The economic prosperity of towns like Ghent, Saint-Omer, Douai, Bruges, Damme, Arras, Lille, and Ypres depended on the unrestricted flow of wool imports into Flanders, thus placing a powerful weapon of economic sanctions in the hands of English kings. Already in the mid–twelfth century, the king of England had forbidden the goods of any merchants whose princes were hostile to him to circulate in England, in this way creating strong motives for political collaboration with England in regions, like Flanders, where English wool had become commercially indispensable. By the close of the century, as the north experienced the first of those cyclical depressions that would periodically grip the new economy, the need for smooth economic relations had become even more compelling. In the end, the influence of the towns probably determined the political strategies of the count, leading Baldwin IX to repudiate his father's pro-Capetian policies and to ally, instead, with the interests of the English party in Flanders.

Also critical to this decision was Baldwin IX's resentment over the loss of Artois. The new count was no more content to see Artois in royal hands than his father had been, despite the fact that on the death of Baldwin VIII and his own accession in 1195 the count had done homage to Philip Augustus and recognized the concession of Artois, together with the overlordship of the counties of Guines and Boulogne and the fief of Oisy.[104]

Perhaps sensing the growing mood of resistance, Philip Augustus attempted to attach the Flemish more closely to the crown. He insisted that Baldwin IX perform liege homage, excepting only his obligations to the emperor and the bishop of Liège for Hainaut. He then proceeded to arrange a marriage between Baldwin's brother, Philippe of Namur, and the family of the Courtenay-Nevers, who were related to the Capetians.[105] Simultaneously, he married his sister Alix, the rejected fiancée of Richard I of England, to William, count of Ponthieu, thus gaining a familial ally in territory bordering the counties of Boulogne and Saint-Pol. Both marriages were clearly designed to strengthen the French party in Flanders and neighboring lands by creating ties to important political figures in the region.[106] But to little avail. By September 1196, Baldwin IX had signed a treaty of alliance, both offensive and defensive, with John Lackland, who acted in his brother Richard's stead.

Even before the treaty was sealed, practically the entire Flemish aristocracy, led by Baldwin IX, was in open rebellion against Philip Augustus over the Artois succession.[107] According to the Anonymous of Béthune, whose *Chronique des rois de France* narrates the events of these years, only Guillaume, the advocate of Béthune, and Guillaume, the castellan of Saint-Omer, remained faithful to Philip:

> N'en ot gaires baron en cele marche de Flandres, fors Willaumes, l'avoé de Bétune et Guillaume le chastelain de Saint Homer, qui malvais samblant ne li feissent.[108]

> There was scarcely any baron in this march of Flanders, except William the advocate of Béthune and William the castellan of Saint-Omer, who was not against him.

The Anonymous's own patron, Robert of Béthune, in contrast, had joined the Flemish coalition. The alliance of 1197 was, as Malo remarked, "in truth a coalition of the northern feudality against the growth of royal power and the first serious attempt to reverse it."[109]

While Philip Augustus was preoccupied with fighting in Normandy, Baldwin IX and Renaud of Boulogne took Douai, Péronne, Roye, and Bapaume, burned Hesdin, and laid siege to Arras. The king, coming to the defense of Arras, succeeded in forcing Baldwin to lift the siege but, pursuing the count deep into Flanders, found himself cut off near Ypres and was compelled to sue for peace, which was concluded in September 1197. As had happened before in the king's dealings with the counts of Flanders, Philip Augustus was to repudiate this settlement on the pretext that a rebellious vassal could not legitimately impose conditions on his lord.[110] Refusing to abide by the terms of the peace, Philip instead set out to punish the counts of Boulogne and Saint-Pol for their defection. According to the Anonymous of Béthune, the king led his host "up to Hesdin in order to destroy the land of the count of Boulogne and the land of the count of Saint-Pol."[111] They were spared his wrath only because they pleaded for mercy. In April 1198, Renaud and Hugh submitted and temporarily made peace with the king.[112]

By spring the fickle Renaud had already returned to the English alliance, and hostilities between the allies and the Capetian monarch reopened. As Philip journeyed north up the Epte to defend the castle of Gisors against Richard's invading English force, Baldwin IX and Renaud of Boulogne captured Aire and Saint-Omer, which lay in the northern sector of the county of Artois.[113] Richard, meanwhile, had surprised the French forces on the march and sent them scurrying for cover in the castle of Gisors. Shaken, Philip sued for peace, which lasted until 14 January 1199. In April of that year, Richard I died from an arrow wound he had received while besieging the castle of Châlus-Chabrol in Limoges. The day after John's coronation as king on 17 May 1199, Baldwin IX, Renaud of Boulogne, and other members of the Flemish coalition came to render homage to the new English ruler and to claim recognition of their tenures in England. John, desirous of maintaining the loyalty of these important lords, renewed the league which Richard had formed, confirming his brother's previous royal grants of land or money-fiefs to his northern allies.

But John was not to be favored by the fortunes of war as his brother had been. Whereas Philip Augustus had proven consistently unsuccessful on the battlefield against the redoubtable Richard, he now managed to take prisoner Philippe of Namur, the brother of Baldwin IX of Flanders. Fearing for his brother's safety, Baldwin agreed to a truce and in January 1200 a treaty between the king of France and the count of Flanders was concluded at Péronne. Although brought to the bargaining table by the capture of his brother, Baldwin was able to secure at least some of the territories he had won through war, including Aire and Saint-Omer, as well as lordship over Guines, Ardres, Lilliers, and Richebourg and a portion of the land depending on the *avouérie* of Béthune.[114] Flanders thus recovered the northern region of the lands lost at the death of Philippe of Alsace.

Philip Augustus, for his part, was reconfirmed in his possession of Artois, less Aire and Saint-Omer, along with the rest of the contested succession, that is, Amiens and the territories in Vermandois awarded him by the Treaty of Amiens. The king did concede that if Prince Louis—to whom Artois legally passed from his mother, Isabelle of Hainaut—died without heir, the county would return to Flanders. In addition, Philip preserved the homage of the count of Boulogne.[115] At Le Goulet, John recognized the terms of the Treaty of Péronne and conceded the liege homage of the count of Flanders to Philip Augustus. Renaud in 1201 was reconciled with the king. The revival of his allegiance to the king was celebrated by a marriage contracted between Renaud's young daughter and Philip Augustus's newly born son, Philip Hurepel.[116]

Although King John already began to violate the Peace of Le Goulet in 1201 by attacking French territory near Tours, Baldwin IX and Hugh of Saint-Pol were sufficiently satisfied with the outcome of the war of 1197–1200 to take the cross in 1200, departing on Crusade in the course of 1202.[117] Baldwin left behind a two-year-old daughter, Jeanne, and a pregnant wife, who several months later delivered a second daughter, Marguerite. Philippe of Namur, the count's brother, was appointed regent for Flanders and Hainaut, governing with the aid of a college of guardians that included Gerard of Alsace and Guillaume, lord of Béthune.[118] The death of the Countess Marguerite in 1204 and the capture (and, ultimately, demise) of Baldwin IX at the hands of the Bulgars in 1205 placed Flanders under the nominal control of the weak Philippe of Namur, who acted on behalf of the orphaned Jeanne. This unfortunate concurrence of events spelled the undoing of the gains Baldwin IX had realized in the Treaty of Péronne. Whereas the war of 1197–1200 had strengthened Flemish ties to England and seen the emergence of a strong English, anti-Capetian party in Flanders, the death of Baldwin IX left Flanders newly vulnerable to the penetration of royal influence.

The victory of Baldwin IX and Richard I over the French king had demonstrated the strength of the Anglo-Flemish alliance, in the face of which Philip Augustus had proved powerless to impose his authority. The Flemish nobility, like the count resentful over the alienation of Artois, had allied solidly against the French king and exploited the opportunity presented by war to enrich themselves at the expense of English largesse. But this state of affairs was to change very rapidly after 1205, opening the way for the creation of a French party in

Flanders through which the king sought to stem the habits of economic self-interest and loyalty that had prompted the formation of the Anglo-Flemish coalition.

As soon as Philip Augustus learned in 1206 of Baldwin's capture by the Bulgars, he arranged a meeting with Philippe of Namur, which took place at Pont de l'Arche in June 1206. There the regent swore fealty to the king against all others and promised not to marry off his young wards, Jeanne and Marguerite, without the king's consent. As a further inducement to obedience, the king offered to give Philippe his ten-year-old daughter, Marie, in marriage, the terms of which were later negotiated in a convention signed in August. By 1208 Philippe of Namur had relinquished his wardship over the young Flemish heiresses, whom Philip Augustus took into his personal custody, acquiring thereby full rights of wardship over the county of Flanders, although Philippe of Namur's regency technically continued until his death on 8 October 1212.

Throughout the decade of Philippe of Namur's regency (1202–1212), the king employed every means at his disposal to wean the Flemish nobility from their bonds to England. Convinced that John's effectiveness on the Continent in large measure depended upon his influence over Flemish towns and nobles,[119] Philip struggled to parry the English presence in Flanders with the creation of a French party, whose partisans he hoped would neutralize English influence and persuade the county that the destiny of Flanders lay with the Capetian monarchy.

There were inherent difficulties in this strategy that under normal circumstances would have made its success unlikely. Flemish ties to England were of long standing and immensely diverse, and English influence had never threatened to diminish the count's or nobility's freedom of action. A rich source of revenue and military aid, the English alliance offered support with few strings attached, none of which ran counter to the long-term interests of the county as a whole. Even at the height of English prestige in Flanders after the Treaty of Péronne, Count Baldwin IX remained wholly master of his territories and his subjects, pursuing the same goal of securing Flemish independence that had guided the actions of Philippe of Alsace. Had Baldwin IX lived, or had he been followed on the comital throne by an equally strong and resolute ruler, it is unlikely that a French party could have taken root in Flanders, as the king's own earlier failure to garner support among the nobility suggests.[120] Moreover, the growth of French influence in Flanders exerted novel pressures on the county and created serious internal antagonisms hitherto largely absent within the aristrocracy. The very formation of a French party in Flanders, then, was an initial symptom of the broader and more profound political crisis that would shortly overtake the county.

Several factors aided Philip Augustus's efforts to extend royal influence in Flanders. The most important, certainly, was the conquest of Normandy, set into motion by the judgment of John in 1202 and brought to fruition in 1204–1205. John's inability to preserve his most important continental holding raised serious doubts about his military capabilities and dampened Flemish enthusiasm for the English alliance. Aware that his prestige had suffered a severe blow, between 1203 and 1205 the English king sent numerous envoys to Flanders in an effort to prevent further loss of confidence among his followers. Although the Flemish towns remained faithful to John, rising by default to leadership of the English party, support for England among Flemish knights and nobles rapidly eroded.

The conquest of Normandy also provided Philip Augustus with new reserves of land and money with which to woo French partisans among the Flemish nobility. The king's victory over John, joined to the prior acquisitions of Vermandois and Artois, had added extensive territories to the royal domain, which filled Capetian coffers with surplus revenue available for political expenditures. As the English king had done since the eleventh century, Philip Augustus now entered the bidding for Flemish loyalties. Beginning as early as 1203, and with increasing frequency after 1204, Philip Augustus began meting out fief-rents to potential Flemish supporters.

The formation of the French party in Flanders, then, had its beginning with the judgment of John in 1202 and received its most powerful impetus for expansion in the years between 1206 and 1208, when it became virtually impossible for the leaderless Flemish nobles to resist the king's continual pressure to transfer their allegiance from England to their Capetian overlord. It is striking, moreover, that these dates coincide precisely with the appearance of the first works of vernacular prose history under the patronage of Flemish lords caught up in the contest for hegemony over Flanders between the kings of England and France and forced, for the first time, to submit to royal authority.

Interestingly, Philip's policy of economic competition with John for Flemish support in the end proved unsuccessful. Despite his new-found ability to pay, the French king seemed hesitant to match his rival's offers, which so exceeded his own in both number and quantity that Roger of Wendover was moved to marvel at the *pecuniam magnam nimis* that John poured into Flanders.[121] Of the seventeen names that formed the core of Flemish lords on whom Philip Augustus bestowed fief-rents, by 1213, on the eve of Bouvines, all but Michel of Harnes had defected once again to the English party.[122] These men, moreover, represented all the sponsors of vernacular historiography but two: Michel of Harnes, who remained firmly within the royal camp, and Roger IV, castellan of Lille, who, having bound himself as a pledge for the count of Flanders, was barred from joining his Flemish compatriots in the fight against the invading French army. He was, in fact, forced to stand by and watch helplessly as Philip Augustus put the torch to Lille before his eyes. Although lacking these two adherents, the English coalition, at first disheartened and dispersed by the French monarch's successes in 1202 and 1205 and by the evident inability of John to master French forces on the battlefield, revived, sparked by the changed political circumstances created by the marriage of Countess Jeanne of Flanders to Ferrand of Portugal.

The Final Phase

As guardian of the Flemish heiress, Philip Augustus controlled all decisions that pertained to Jeanne's future marriage, in accordance with feudal principles regulating the rights of wardship. In 1211 an initial suitor for Jeanne's hand presented himself in the person of Enguerrand de Coucy, who offered the king a relief of thirty thousand livres for the county of Flanders, later raised to fifty thousand livres.[123] But opposition from the Flemish nobility defeated Enguerrand's candidacy. When the Dowager Countess Matilda, widow of Philippe of Alsace, proposed to match Enguerrand's bid of fifty thousand livres on behalf of her nephew Ferrand, son of King Sancho of Portugal, Philip Augustus accepted with alacrity, assuming no doubt that a ruler foreign to the county and free of prior political entanglements would prove most malleable in furthering the king's plan to strengthen Flemish ties to the crown. The marriage was celebrated in Paris on 22 January 1212, following which Ferrand was knighted by the king and performed homage, secured by pledges, for Flanders.

As eleven-year-old Jeanne and her twenty-four-year-old husband Ferrand prepared to make their return to Flanders, Prince Louis, probably with his father's connivance,[124] hastened on before them and attacked Aire and Saint-Omer, seeking to recapture the northern region of Artois that Baldwin IX had secured for the count of Flanders by the Treaty of Péronne in 1200. After taking the towns into his own hands, Louis summoned the new count and countess to yield, and on 25 February he compelled them to sign the Treaty of Pont-à-Vendin. By this treaty, Ferrand resigned the two cities to the prince and renounced all future rights to them. Among those who witnessed the various acts relative to the affair of Aire and Saint-Omer were Michel of Harnes, Guillaume of Béthune, Guillaume, castellan of Saint-Omer, and Roger IV, castellan of Lille, who at this time was designated one of the pledges named by Jeanne and Ferrand as warrant for the treaty. Roger was required to swear an oath to abandon his lord, the count of Flanders, should Ferrand violate the terms of the treaty or engage in warfare against the king of France.[125]

Although a territorial victory for the royal house, Louis's brazen grab of Aire and Saint-Omer was a serious political blunder, for it revealed all too clearly to the new count the ruthless opportunism governing Capetian policy toward Flanders and served to alienate the count unnecessarily from the king and from Philip's partisans within the French party in Flanders. Moreover, it sowed seeds of discontent among the Flemish nobility, which John was quick to exploit, supported by vigorous maneuvering on the part of Renaud of Boulogne.

Within three months of the Treaty of Pont-à-Vendin, Renaud traveled to England (accompanied by his chaplain, the "Master Johannes" responsible for a *Pseudo-Turpin* translation), where, on 4 May 1212, he formally declared John to be his liege lord once again. Together with Hugh of Boves and Eustache le Moine, he signed an agreement of mutual assistance against Philip Augustus.[126]

In June, John requested Renaud to return with Hugh of Boves to Flanders to mobilize the English party, commissioning the count to negotiate with Flemish lords in his name and to distribute favors as he deemed appropriate, whether in gifts of horses, money, or the more usual fief-rents. So successful was Renaud at this task that Dept calls him the "cheville ouvrière de la coalition," into which he brought his cousin Thibaud of Bar, as well as the Countess Matilda and a large number of the principal nobles of Flanders and Hainaut.[127] Of the twenty-four Flemish nobles mentioned by name in English letters patent, eight were currently in Philip's pay—a good measure of the waning fortunes of the French party at the time.[128]

Although Philip Augustus made some efforts to retain the loyalty of his Flemish vassals—while at Compiègne in June 1212, for example, he renewed the fief-rent of sixty livres, ten sous, on the *péage* of Péronne and Bapaume granted to Michel of Harnes[129]—they pale in significance compared to John's openhanded extravagance. The English party in Flanders was completely rehabilitated, attaining its point of maximum strength at this time. The new count sought to remain neutral, despite his initial anger over the seizure of Aire and Saint-Omer, but neutrality became increasingly difficult in the face of Philip Augustus's repeated interference in the affairs of Flanders, and unfolding events were to render it impossible.

The prospect of war emerged first in June 1212, when John summoned a feudal levy, clearly hoping to launch an attack on France to recover his lost territories. Philip Augustus responded to this act of provocation by seizing all English ships harbored in French ports, a move that John reciprocated in England. The French king, not content to defend his new acquisitions at home, on 8 April 1213 convoked an assembly of great barons at Soissons and called upon his son, Louis, to lead an expedition to conquer England. To this proposal the king received the unanimous assent of his barons, with the sole exception of Ferrand, who refused to perform his feudal service unless Louis returned Aire and Saint-Omer, which by right belonged in the tenure of the count of Flanders. When Philip offered instead to compensate the count for the two cities, Ferrand remained steadfast in his refusal and departed the court.[130]

As Philip assembled his invasion fleet along the coast of Flanders, Ferrand maintained his distance, hoping to avoid a direct confrontation with the king by alleging that his liege homage did not require him to fight for his lord outside the kingdom of France. But Philip was adamant and in May demanded that Ferrand declare his intention to participate in the expedition against England. When Ferrand once again refused on the grounds that his obligations to the king had been nullified by the illegal seizure of Aire and Saint-Omer, the king dismissed him from the court, leaving Ferrand little choice but openly to seek aid from the king of England.[131] John responded immediately to the count's overtures by sending a delegation of Flemish lords already gathered at the English court, led by Renaud of Boulogne, Robert VII of Béthune, Hugh of Boves, and William of Salisbury, to meet with the count and to proceed with ships, troops, and money to the Flemish coast.[132]

Meanwhile the English king, then embroiled in a controversy with the pope over the election of Stephen Langton as archbishop of Canterbury, suddenly capitulated to papal demands that Stephen be allowed to enter his episcopal see and, with the same cunning that John frequently demonstrated in diplomatic matters, proposed to render England and Ireland in fief to the pope and to pay an annual tribute of one thousand pounds sterling to the papal curia. Within a week the papal legate, Pandulf, arrived at Gravelines, where he met with Philip Augustus and demanded that the king abandon the attack on the pope's English vassal, threatening him with excommunication.[133]

With his carefully laid plans thus thwarted, Philip Augustus threw himself at Flanders, ostensibly to punish the obdurate Ferrand for refusing to accompany him to England. In quick succession the king took Cassel, Ypres, and Bruges and laid siege to Ghent, meeting with little resistance except in the latter city. The beleaguered Ferrand was forced to flee to the island of Walcheren while Philip occupied large areas of Flanders. But the English fleet dispatched by John soon landed at Muidon, not far from Damme, where the king had moved the French invasion forces. On 30 May 1213 the Anglo-Flemish allies set fire to the French fleet as it lay at anchor at Damme, destroying any remnant of hope that Philip Augustus may have entertained of continuing with an invasion of England. His navy burned and Flanders reinforced by English troops, the king withdrew, evacuating his army from the county.

Ferrand followed behind Philip's retreating armies and retook possession of his county. Even the garrison that the French monarch had left behind at Lille, thinking to preserve a base of operations in Walloon Flanders, fell as the people opened the gates of the city to the count immediately after the king's departure.[134] The count of Flanders now formally allied himself with the English coalition, in which he was joined by large numbers of Flemish barons appalled at the king's harsh treatment of their territory. The aging Dowager Countess Matilda ordered her vassals to support the count while the bishop of Cambrai, Jean of Béthune, uncle to Robert VII, fomented revolt against Philip Augustus in the southern regions of Flanders. Almost in its entirety, the Flemish nobility united behind Ferrand in opposition to the French king.

Between the destruction of the French fleet at Damme in May 1213 and the battle of Bouvines on 27 July 1214, Flanders was the principal theater of war. Although the English king, as usual, was liberal in his financial support of Flemish knights, the county of Flanders was subjected to extensive devastation. To make matters worse, the Flemish nobility seized the opportunity to prosecute ancient rivalries and avenge old injuries,[135] thus adding local conflict to the wider war between the king and the count.

In July 1214, Philip celebrated his final victory over the Anglo-Flemish coalition. When the dust had settled after the battle of Bouvines, almost two-thirds of the nobility of Flanders and Hainaut had been captured.[136] Among those taken were 5 counts and 25 knights banneret, as well as more than 300 knights.[137] Approximately 130 barons were imprisoned or placed under French custody, among them the most prominent leaders of the coalition: Count Ferrand and Renaud of Boulogne. Of the Flemish patrons of early vernacular histories, Renaud and William of Cayeux were imprisoned, while Robert of Béthune departed for England, where he served as constable in John's army during the French invasion under Louis VIII. Hugh of Saint-Pol had died earlier, and Roger IV of Lille was legally prohibited from participating in the struggle against the French, though, as mentioned above, he was forced to witness the burning of Lille. Only Michel of Harnes, a devoted French partisan, escaped the ruin visited upon his countrymen.

Flanders had suffered a crushing defeat and was forced to submit to royal authority. Countess Jeanne remained the titular ruler of the county, but her sphere of authority was severely restricted by the king, who imposed his partisans Jean de Nesles and Siger de Gand as her counselors. Jean de Nesles was also named *bailli* of Flanders and Hainaut, a position that enabled him to intervene at will in the affairs of the two counties in the king's interests.[138] Towns and communes were required to guarantee their obedience by delivering hostages, and the nobility who had escaped imprisonment were obliged to promise, in writing, no longer to serve the count and to furnish pledges as warrant for their continued good behavior.[139] Similar conditions were imposed on Flemish nobles at the time of their release from captivity.[140]

The king, however, was determined to retain hold of the two chief protagonists of the coalition, Renaud and Ferrand. Renaud eventually took his own life in prison, but Ferrand did manage to secure his release from Louis VIII after Philip's death. According to the Treaty of Melun of 1226, which regulated the conditions of Ferrand's reinstatement as count of Flanders, the count and countess swore to serve the king loyally; to erect no new fortresses below the Escaut; and to compel, under pain of exile or confiscation, the knights and towns of Flanders to swear fidelity to the French monarch and to support him with aid and counsel if either count or countess violated the treaty.[141] After decades of resistance to the French monarchy, the county of Flanders was subdued.

The extent of the damage suffered by Flanders for its resistance to royal authority can be glimpsed, if only in part, through the claims brought during the *enquêtes* of 1247. Although designed by Louis IX primarily to correct the usurpations and illicit actions of royal *baillis* throughout the realm preparatory to his departure on Crusade,[142] the *enquêtes* appear to have functioned at times as a forum for the adjudication of claims for war damages, particularly in the regions affected by the almost uninterrupted strife of the first half of the thirteenth century—that is, Flanders, Artois, Normandy, Poitou, and Languedoc. In the north, the *enquêteurs* made a circuit from Bapaume to Arras, where they entertained complaints from Lille, Douai, Lens, and Hesdin, and finally to Tournai. Those suing for war reparations or compensation for some other grievance were requested to present themselves at these towns with their dossiers, even though the hearings took the form of oral demands.[143] Although past and current illegal exactions by *baillis* and other royal representatives appear alongside a host of complaints referring back to the time of Philip Augustus, in Arras, Lille, and Douai, for example, such claims make up only 18 percent of the total number of petitions.[144] In Flanders and Artois, the vast majority of claims concerned the destruction of property and the seizure of goods, ships, merchandise, and hostages resulting from the war itself or from actions taken by royal agents responsible for provisioning troops and ships.

That both counties suffered disproportionately in comparison to other parts of the kingdom emerges from Sivéry's analysis of the relative level of financial distress indicated in the demands for reparations. In Normandy, where the war was intense but brief, the mean sum claimed by petitioners was only 56 livres tournois, whereas in the Tournaisis it climbed to 664 livres tournois, both figures being in turn far outstripped by the mean of 3,900 livres tournois reached in Artois and Flanders. The same disparity is revealed in the absolute sums requested from both regions, which in Artois and Flanders amounted to 161,941 livres tournois but in Normandy constituted only 62,353 livres tournois, a gap perhaps partially explained by the fact that in Flanders, Artois, and the Tournaisis only 16 percent of the claims were rural in origin, compared to 90 percent in Normandy, the Loire Valley, and western France generally.[145]

Among the largest amounts sought were those resulting from Philip Augustus's habit of taking hostages in Artesian and Flemish cities to enforce their loyalty and then demanding huge ransoms in return for their freedom. At the time of Jeanne's marriage to Ferrand in 1212, for example, Douai, like other Flemish cities, swore fidelity to the king and promised to support him in the event that the count and countess engaged in war against the throne. Unlike Lille, Douai was faithful to its oath and remained loyal to the Capetian king. Yet despite its blameless conduct during the hostilities, when Philip Augustus returned to the city after having burned and destroyed Lille for its "perfidy," he selected twenty hostages from the notables of Douai, imprisoning them for two years at Etampes. After Bouvines, the citizens of Douai were compelled to pay the king sixty thousand livres parisis and to remit twenty additional young men in exchange for the release of the original hostages, the second group in its turn subject to a fee of two thousand livres as the price for their liberty. In 1247, the inhabitants of Douai appeared before the royal *enquêteurs* to claim damages and expenses incurred in the "matter" of the hostages, delicately refraining, however, from stipulating a fixed sum.[146]

Individuals were equally victims of the king's arbitrary actions. In 1198, Philip Augustus arrived in Hesdin and arrested the mayor, Hugh le Roux, whom he imprisoned without cause, freeing him only in return for a ransom of eight thousand livres parisis. Similarly, Henri Troplès, a burgher of Lille, had been seized sometime during the struggles between the king and Philippe of Alsace and secured his release by a payment of a thousand livres parisis. Three decades later, when the hapless Troplès appeared before the royal officials to claim damages, he was still ignorant of the reason for his confinement.[147]

Such sums were trifling in comparison to those demanded, often without any more discernible cause, from the rich burghers of Arras, to whose capacity to pay the king apparently was not insensible. In one extraordinary case, royal agents had extorted as much as 12,500 livres tournois in the form of ransom from a burgher of Arras, a figure greatly exceeding the usual 1,000 livres tournois required of relatively prosperous lords.[148] The scale of this demand comes into high relief when one remembers that the king's ordinary revenue at this time stood somewhere around 195,000 livres parisis, of which the ransom claimed from this single bourgeois of Arras represents approximately 6.5 percent. Indeed, overall in ransoms, seizures of goods, and fines, Philip Augustus had amassed from the citizens of Arras, Lille, Douai, Tournai, Hesdin, and Bapaume 113,000 livres tournois, or 40 percent of his ordinary annual income.[149]

Inhabitants of port cities likewise suffered at the hands of the king and his representatives, especially *armateurs* and merchants who dealt in provisions needed by the French fleets—not only those anchored at Damme in 1213, but those at Gravelines in 1216 as well, as Prince Louis prepared to invade England in response to the appeal of the English barons in revolt against King John. Claims for compensation for ships, arms, wheat, wine, cloth, leather, and other commodities confiscated on royal orders are sprinkled throughout the records of the *enquêtes,* especially those held at Tournai, a major port city of the Scaldian basin. These claims are particularly noteworthy in light of Louis's proclamation in Artois that merchants who were willing to furnish provisions for his army would receive twice the amount of their investment if their ships were lost as a result of English violence—a promise that apparently did not cover losses experienced as a result of French expropriations.[150]

Also appearing in relatively high numbers at the *enquêtes* of Tournai were demands for compensation on the part of knights and lords whose lands had been wasted and castles burned by Philip Augustus as he rampaged through the countryside. Another class of petitioners included men who, having served in the king's army in 1214 and in that of Prince Louis during the English expedition in 1216, came forward to request the *frais de service militaire* still in arrears. So abundant were the complaints at Tournai that the royal *enquêteurs* noted with some surprise the large number of claimants and extensive sums involved.[151] Equally impressive were complaints concerning the destruction of seigneurial lands, both lay and ecclesiastical. Demands for recompense from the king for destroyed property were often made by heirs, whose legacies had been damaged by the actions of royal officials and who now came forward to request the king's liquidation of past injustices.[152]

That baronial discontent over past and present injuries at the hands of royal officials continued to smolder in Flanders for decades after the battle of Bouvines is revealed not only in the complaints presented at the *enquêtes* of 1247 but also by the curious episode of the "False Baldwin," which inflamed the county and unleashed social revolt and civil war in 1225. In that year a man (later identified as one Bertrand de Rains) emerged from a forest not far from Valenciennes where he had been living for some time as a hermit. He claimed to be Baldwin IX, count of Flanders and Hainaut, who had been captured and presumed killed by the Bulgars at the beginning of the century. The pseudo-count instantly became a rallying point for Flemish malcontents. Although ultimately the revolt that broke out over the pretender engulfed all levels of Flemish society, the nobility evidently provided its initial impulse, no doubt hoping to use the lone, ragged figure as a vehicle of political opposition to Countess Jeanne and the royal *baillis* who effectively controlled the affairs of Flanders. It was they who "discovered" the hermit and introduced him to the urban population, for whom he proved to have a strangely powerful appeal.[153]

Flanders had just survived a severe winter that had created terrible conditions of famine, and the urban population, hardest hit by the scarcity of foodstuffs, received the hermit-count as a savior, symbol of the years of deprivation and despoliation that they, too, had suffered.[154] Valenciennes and Lille opened the gates of their cities to him, and within weeks the county was astir as urban workers, animated by the hope of a new leader who would redeem the injustices of the past, agitated the populace. The nobles at first encouraged popular action as a means of weakening comital authority in the belief that they could retain control of events. Even Henry III entered the political fray, recognizing its potential for embarrassing his enemy, Louis VIII, and for undermining the French king's support of Jeanne. On 11 April 1225, the king of England wrote to the False Baldwin, recalling the ancient alliance that had united their ancestors, inviting him to enter into a pact of mutual assistance, and assuring the "count" of his readiness to come to his aid with a strong "helping hand" (*manum auxiliarem*).[155]

Inevitably, the sedition of 1225 provoked intervention by the French king. Louis VIII entered Flanders with troops and systematically set about quelling the rebellion of townspeople and nobility. The misguided Bertrand de Rains was unmasked and put to flight, and later imprisoned and executed at Lille.[156] The result of the revolt was the complete submission of Flanders to the French crown. Since Bouvines, Jeanne had been counseled and supervised by royal *baillis* but had maintained a semblance of comital authority and autonomy. Louis's campaign in Flanders in 1225 forced her to acknowledge her total dependence on the French king, thus destroying even the illusion of an independent Flanders.

Although with greater reluctance, the nobility also recognized the impossibility of opposing the authority of the French sovereign and submitted to royal rule, abandoning its residual ties to the English party and realigning on the side of royal partisans.[157] The failure of the rebellion vindicated the king's triumph at Bouvines. As in 1214, it spelled the end of an autonomous Flemish nobility, who no longer possessed even the possibility of recourse to an English alliance as a protection against Capetian domination. The entire shabby episode of the False Baldwin provides an ironic footnote to the decline in Flemish fortunes from the days of the genuine Baldwin IX, when Flanders had still commanded sufficient resources and prestige to pursue a policy of independence from the Capetian monarchy. It disclosed in equal measure the decisive nature of the king's victory at Bouvines and the impotence of the Flemish nobility in the face of royal authority.

r╱⅄╲┐

Such were the varieties of social and political change experienced by the northern aristocracy within the brief compass of a few decades. Intimately involved in every phase of these transformations—indeed, the most active leaders in the political struggle—was the first generation of patrons of vernacular historiography: Yolande and Hugh of Saint-Pol, Robert of Béthune, Renaud of Boulogne, Michel III of Harnes, and Roger IV of Lille. Except for Renaud of Dammartin, who entered the Flemish sphere by virtue of his marriage to Ida of Boulogne, all belonged to ancient lineages whose origins in Flanders can be traced back at least to the eleventh century.

The original three patrons of vernacular historical texts—Hugh of Saint-Pol, Renaud of Boulogne, and Michel of Harnes—all held lands and tenures in or dependent on the contested region of Artois, as a result of which they were compelled by 1201 to acknowledge royal overlordship. This was also true of the remaining sponsors of vernacular historiography in the years after Bouvines and the collapse of the French expedition to England in 1216, during which Robert of Béthune was enlisted as a constable in the English army. The dates of the earliest translations of the *Pseudo-Turpin Chronicle* cohere remarkably with the troubled political history of Flanders. Nicolas of Senlis produced his version for Yolande and Hugh of Saint-Pol in 1202; the "Johannes" *Turpin* was transcribed for Renaud of Boulogne in 1206 and again for Michel of Harnes in 1206–1207; while at approximately the same date William of Cayeux, an Anglo-Flemish partisan from Ponthieu, solicited his copy. The two remaining early versions stem from the identical region of Artois, Flanders, and Hainaut and appear in the years immediately succeeding Bouvines, 1218 and circa 1220–1230—the same period that witnessed the creation of the two histories by the anonymous Artesian minstrel in the employ of Robert of Béthune. Simultaneously, between 1208 and 1213, Roger IV, castellan of Lille, commissioned the *Histoire ancienne jusqu'à César.*

These years, especially those around 1206–1213, mark the moment when the French party formed in Flanders and the Flemish aristocracy was first made to submit to royal authority during the regency of the weak Philippe de Namur. By 1225, with the crushing of the revolt fomented over the appearance of the False Baldwin, the autonomy of the Flemish aristocracy had been severely curtailed. An era of aristocratic rule in Flemish society had come to a close. Flanders had lost its bid to establish a polity capable of rivaling the French monarchy in power and prestige.

When seen against the events of Philip Augustus's reign, the rise of vernacular historiography at the courts of the Franco-Flemish aristocracy at the beginning of the thirteenth century appears to have resulted from an ideological initiative on the part of Flemish aristocrats whose social dominance and political independence were being contested by the growth of royal power. But the writing of history in Old French prose constituted more than a search for a usable past. It also represented a profound shift in the discursive practices of the French nobility. The distinguishing feature of the early vernacular chronicle lies in its militant insistence on prose as the necessary language of history and its critique of the mendacious tendencies of verse historiography, hitherto the sole language of lay history. If, as this book will attempt to demonstrate, the French aristocracy turned to history as a form of ethical reassurance and political legitimation at a moment of social and political crisis, it seems logical to conclude that the emergence of prose was, as well, functionally related to the transformations occurring within aristocratic society. Political failure and social decline were inscribed in a novel historiographical discourse, which staked its claim to authority on its employment of prose.

The beginning point of this inquiry, therefore, must be the question of the emergence of vernacular prose, for it was in the controversy over the relative truth-value of poetry and prose that vernacular historiography demarcated its own discourse from the aristocratic literary genres and practices that had preceded it, and argued for the truth of the image of the past that it proffered. The emergence of vernacular historiography opens with an intense debate on the truth of history and the authoritative nature of the claims embedded in a past conveyed in the lucid medium of prose. It is, therefore, the problem of prose as presented in the first translations of the *Pseudo-Turpin Chronicle* to which we must now turn.

2 *Pseudo-Turpin* and the Problem of Prose

Voil commencer l'estoire si cum li bons enpereires Karlemaine en ala
en Espagnie par la terre conquere sore les Sarrazins. Maintes genz si
en ont oi conter et chanter mes n'est si menconge non co qu'il en
dient e chantent cil chanteor ne cil iogleor. Nus contes rimes n'est
verais. Tot est mencongie co qu'il en dient car il n'en sievent rienz
fors quant par oir dire.

Li bons Baudoins li cuens de Chainau si ama molt Karlemaine ni
ne veut onques croire chose que l'om en chantast. Ainz fit cercher
totes les bones abeies de France e garder par totz les armaires por
saver si l'om i trouveroit la veraie ystoire . . .

(B.N. fr. 124, fol. 1r)

I wish to begin the history of how the good Emperor Charlemagne
went to Spain in order to conquer the land under the Saracens.
Many people have heard it told and sung, but what these singers and
jongleurs sing and tell is nothing but a lie. No rhymed tale is true.
Everything they say is lies, for they know nothing about it except
through hearsay. The good Baldwin, the count of Hainaut, dearly
loved Charlemagne, but he did not want to believe anything that was
sung about him. Thus he had all the good abbeys of France and all
the libraries searched to see if one might find the true history.

Thus begins the preamble to Nicolas of Senlis's translation of the
Pseudo-Turpin Chronicle, written about 1202, in which the demand
for a novel form of discourse appropriate for the communication of
historical "truth" first appears. Nicolas stakes his claim to authenticity as a historian primarily in opposition to prevailing modes of historical narration. Where those before him who have sung and recited
the history of the glorious emperor were dependent on the uncertainties of oral "hearsay," his work is grounded in the authority of a prior

Latin text; where they employed the deforming medium of verse, producing only "lies" and fictions, he will eschew verse and speak the truth; and where they produced mendacious song, he will produce "true" history. Nicolas's prologue generates a series of dichotomies revolving around the opposing poles of the oral and the written, vernacular and Latin, verse and non-verse, fiction and truth. His insistent representation of difference suggests that the rise of Old French prose historiography was marked by novel tensions in the discursive practices of the lay aristocracy, tensions arising from a broad movement involving the social reevaluation of orality and textuality, fictionality and factuality, poetry and non-verse narrative.

Strikingly absent from Nicolas's polemic, yet central in its very absence, is prose, the missing term toward which the historiographic enterprise of which Nicolas of Senlis is the founding figure is directed. His work stands at the origin of a fundamental change in the literary praxis of the Middle Ages, entailing nothing less than the creation of Old French prose as a literary language. Between Nicolas of Senlis's translation of the *Pseudo-Turpin Chronicle* and the end of the thirteenth century, the use of prose spread well beyond history to include virtually every genre of medieval literary production, requiring the recasting of many earlier romance works into the newly prestigious medium. By the accession of Philip III (1270), Old French prose had become a privileged instrument for the communication of morally and socially valuable knowledge, and it had conquered the domain of imaginative literature as thoroughly as that of history.

Before the thirteenth century, the use of vernacular prose had been confined to juridical texts, charters, translations of the Bible, and homiletic works.[1] Some fifty examples of Old French prose are extant from the twelfth century, almost all concerned with religious subjects. About 1100, prose was employed for the first time for the translation of the Psalms in the *Psalter of Montebourg*, preserved at Oxford,[2] while in the middle of the century the earliest original compositions in French prose made their appearance with the sermons of Maurice de Sully, bishop of Paris from 1160 to 1196. Sully's sermons, of which sixty-four written between 1168 and 1175 remain, were in all likelihood doubly redacted in Latin and French, the latter to serve as instruments for public preaching.[3] Other surviving instances are a lapidary from circa 1150 and a *Description of Jerusalem* written before the city's conquest by Saladin in 1187, as well as biblical commentaries, most notably the *Quatre livres des rois*, dated about 1170, consisting of a glossed translation of the books of Samuel and Kings, translated from the Vulgate with commentaries drawn from the *Glossa ordinaria* and *Glossa interlinearia*.[4] For literature and history, how- ever, there is no Old French prose before the opening decade of the thirteenth century. In those genres, vernacular writing takes the form of verse, even where translations from Latin prose models are con- cerned, and this is as true for overtly imaginative works such as *chan- sons de geste* and *romans* as for historical or pseudo-historical writ- ings such as Jordan of Fantosme's *Chronique de la guerre entre les Anglois et les Ecossois* or Wace's *Roman de Brut*.

The very term "prose" in its nominative form, designating non- verse, non-rhymed literary composition, is lacking in Old French be- fore the thirteenth century. It enters the language only in 1265 with Brunetto Latini's *Trésor*.[5] But even though the word did not yet exist, it is clear that by the end of the twelfth century a debate was emerging over the relative merits of poetry and non-poetry for the expression of historical truth. In this debate, poetry became increasingly suspect, and prose was acknowledged as the proper (or at least preferred) me- dium of historical truth. The argument in favor of historical prose ac- companied the creation of vernacular prose historiography and formed part of the rise to generic autonomy of the vernacular chron- icle. It is important, therefore, to understand the semantic values that medieval writers invested in the idea of prose, for they are crucial el- ements in the ideologically charged conditions under which vernacular prose historiography was first elaborated.

The word "prose" derives from the name of the Roman goddess *Prorsa* (*Prosa*), who presided over births in which the head of the in- fant presents itself first.[6] A *prosator/prosatrix* is, thus, an ancestor, one who begets a natural and straightforward birth, and the Latin ad- jective *prorsus* (*prosus*) describes all things similarly straightforward and direct. Hence, that which is linguistically straight is also denoted *prosa*, the equivalent in literary composition of the straightforward and unproblematic birth of a child with head foremost. Medieval rhet- oricians were not slow to draw the inference that what is straightfor- ward and natural is also true. By contrast, verse (from the Latin *verto*, to turn), to the extent that it deviates from the straightforward path of prose, is a deviant linguistic practice, necessarily implicated in the convoluted ways of lying. This intimate link between verse and falsehood as transgressions against the pristine propriety of prose ap- pears clearly in the declaration by Buoncompagno da Siena in 1200 that "tota scriptura trahit originem a prosa. Nam rithmi et metra sunt mendicata suffragia, que a prosa originem trahunt.'"[7] To be sure,

Buoncompagno's confident assertion of the priority of prose as an originary literary language is patently incorrect, but his facile equation of rhymed verse with mendacity is significant testimony to the clerical belief in the inherently deviant nature of poetic language, which lacked the straightforward properties of truthful discourse. This suspicion of verse, moreover, was implicated in the much broader and more powerful distrust of all literary language from late antiquity on, a consequence of the dominance of Christianity in the world of letters.

As is well known, the early church fathers propounded a complex series of arguments concerning the posture Christians should assume toward the vast legacy of profane letters that the early church had inherited from the Greco-Roman world. At issue was not just the question of which works Christians might profitably employ for their own purposes and which must be jettisoned as inimical to Christian morality, but a more profound inquiry into the nature of human language and its usages in relation to the unitary and revealed Word of God. Not merely were pagan authors seen as potentially subversive of Christian morality, but human language itself, insofar as it imitated the creative power of God, appeared to rival the unique authority that reposed in Scripture. A stark contrast between the stable, univocal *Verbum* (the Word of God) and the multiform, mutable *verba* (the words of men)[8] became the starting point for an extended patristic critique of the arbitrary nature of human signs, a critique rooted in a belief in the primary reality of the revealed Word and the secondariness of all human symbolic activity.[9]

Thus Augustine, whose *De doctrina christiana* offered a prolonged meditation on the nature of language, condemned those Christians who allowed themselves "to be satisfied with signs instead of realities and [who were] not able to elevate the eye of the mind above the sensible creation to drink in eternal light" (III, 5:9). For Augustine, to take a text literally amounts to a "carnal" use of the letter, understood as the body of the word. Such carnal apprehension of signs "enslaves the soul" by inhibiting it from progressing to a true understanding of the figurative nature and transcendent spiritual significance of words. The rejection of the figurative and spiritual in favor of the literal constitutes for Augustine, as for many early church fathers, both a "fornication of the soul" (II, 23:35) through its "carnal" fixation on the literal, and a form of idolatry (II, 23:36), the misguided worship of a thing created by man which usurps and transgresses the proper devotion owed to God. "God," Tertullian insisted, "is not pleased by what

He Himself did not produce. . . . Therefore, those things cannot be best by nature which do not come from God, who is the Author of nature."[10] To adhere to the arbitrary *verba* of men in place of the unique truth of the *Verbum* is to engage, Augustine maintains, in a "pernicious union of men and demons" (II, 23:35), in a veritable act of intercourse between the Devil and the "fornicating soul." This patristic distrust of the corrupting potential of human language as the material embodiment of a rivalrous creation to the *Verbum Dei* facilitated the associations between signs, carnality, fornication, and idolatry that were deeply to mark the medieval understanding of literary creation.

In the eyes of the church fathers, the literary text, as an imitation of the divine *Verbum*, both rivals the Word of God and threatens to subvert the hierarchy of meaning and truth that, in Christian theology, necessarily subordinates the human and the temporal to the eternal and the divine. Literature's subversive force derives from its specific tendency to divert the mind from its due reverence to God by offering an alternative object of contemplation. But whereas the contemplation of the Word of God leads to truth, the contemplation of literary texts, of "imagined fables and falsities," as Augustine calls them, is "deceitful and mendacious" (II, 25:39). Literature beguiles with its "frothy nexus of words (IV, 14:31), which causes the reader to "cling to it with affection for its own sake," rather than, as a Christian should, "to use this world and not enjoy it, so that the invisible attributes of God may be clearly seen, 'being understood through the things that are made' (Rom. 1:20)." Imaginary signs were ordained by God to develop the love of God, not to pervert the "hearts of unhappy creatures through their own individual longing for temporal things" (II, 23:36).

To Tertullian, authors who adorn their literary works with rhetorical ornamentation are like women who sin against God by anointing their faces with creams, staining their cheeks with rouge, and lengthening their eyebrows with antimony. Both are artificers who "are not satisfied with the creative skill of God but in their own person seek to perfect and add to His work." The beauty they create is "naturally the exciter of lust" and lies at the root of all concupiscence and its consummation in fornication.[11] All means of adornment, for Tertullian, are attempts to deceive by belying the true nature of the things they cover. Feminine adornment and poetic ornamentation are commensurate forms of lying, hence by nature adulterous. The artful imitation of natural forms constitutes an infraction of the natural order of things,[12] an illicit use of the forms created by God for the satisfaction of merely human desire.

The seductive power of literature lies precisely in its ability to dissemble its true nature. Thus Lactantius speaks of pagan literature as "sweets which contain poison,"[13] and Alain de Lille denounces poetry as an art that mantles falsehood in a pretense of credibility.[14] Indeed, Alain's De planctu Naturae functions as an exhaustive elaboration of the analogous relationship between poetry and perversion. The sodomizer disports himself as a man, but in truth he has had "his sex changed by a ruleless Venus in defiance of due order," transforming what is a "straightforward attribute of his." In this, he resembles the "sophistic pseudographer," who poses as the purveyor of truth but who actually "abandons the true script of Venus" and perverts the truth of logic for personal gain.[15] Sodomy and sophistry—sexual deviance and linguistic deviance—are, like poetic verse, dissembling departures from the straight paths of truth, alike subverting the proper practices of human intercourse, whether sexual or discursive. Unlike grammar and correct logic, which follow the straight way of truthful discourse, poetry moves within the realm of the deviant, the deceitful, and the perverse.

By the twelfth century, this longstanding equation of poetry with seductive error and sexual and linguistic deviance had created an abundant repertoire of theological topoi hostile to literary creation, which the vernacular chronicler could use in his attack on verse as inherently mendacious. Yet the success of that attack and the increasing vogue of prose bespeak a broader crisis in courtly romance literature, one that ultimately gave rise to the demand for a new form of historical discourse more relevant to the historical needs of its public than the versified histories of epic and romance—a demand, in effect, to forge a new version of the past. The rise of the vernacular prose chronicle joined to the censure of verse a censure of the content, style, and oral and fictional sources of epic and romance. Its emergence thus suggests not simply an important shift in the historical tastes and habits of an aristocratic audience, but a more profound crisis in that audience's sense of the past and its relation to history, hitherto adequately served by epic and romance.

An indication of a crisis in courtly romance genres appears as early as the late twelfth century in verse prologues to various works in which, as in the Turpin prologues later, the mendacious tendencies of romance versification are singled out for criticism. The earliest such complaint, found in La mort Aimeri de Narbonne, written circa

1180, already discredits the truth-purveying capacity of the *chanson de geste:*

> Nus hom ne puet chançon de geste dire
> Que il ne mente là où li vers define
> As mos drecier et à tailler la rime.
>   (lines 3055–3057)[16]

No one is able to recite a *chanson de geste* without lying at the place where the verse ends, to order the words and shape the rhymes.

Although the author of *La mort Aimeri* takes his stand on technical grounds, denouncing the poet's search for rhyme and measure as incompatible with the demands of truth and the need for exactitude of narration, it seems clear that far more is at stake than the ways in which the technical requirements of versification subvert the truthfulness of epic narration. For what was most threatening in imaginative literature of the twelfth century, whether epic or romance, we may infer, was its tendency to constitute itself as a self-consciously fictional world, complicating thereby its representation of a past reality and its relation to the authority embedded in it.

This had not, of course, been the case earlier. As Michel Zink has demonstrated,[17] the earliest romance authors of the *romans d'antiquité* tended to legitimize their work by calling attention to their role as cultural transmitters, responsible for the transferral of ancient Latin learning to those whom Benoît de Sainte-Maure describes as "cil qui n'entendent la letre" (those who do not understand writing).[18] The truth of the romance author's version of the past resided in the authority of his Latin model, whereas the activity of the writer was framed in the act of translation—in the dual sense of the transmission of classical learning to a contemporary French audience otherwise barred from access to it and of the linguistic transformation from Latin to Old French. So fundamental was the notion of the inherent authority and veracity of the past contained in Latin *auctoritates* that romance authors often simply invented fictional sources when genuine Latin ones were lacking in order to avoid the suspicion that they were engaged in autonomous literary invention.[19] Abandoning any claim to creation ex nihilo, vernacular literary activity at first presented itself merely as the recasting of earlier tales,[20] and this was true even of such supposedly oral epics as the *Chanson de Roland* in which, on occasion, the *geste* the singer enacts is described as having already been written down: "il est escrit en la geste Francor" (it is written in the French *geste*).[21] The aim of this highly ambiguous reference to a prior written source was to guarantee the documentary nature and historicity of the events recounted, despite the fundamentally presentist ethos created by the oral performance of epic as an unfolding account brought into being by the poet's voice and existing only within the compass of his enunciation.[22]

In the *romans d'antiquité*, the truth of the past transmitted in the act of translation rests, in the final analysis, on the philological competence of the translator, whose *mise en roman* effects the *translatio studii*, the transferral of knowledge from antiquity to the present. Yet paradoxically, it was precisely this critical location of the translator at the juncture between past and present that tended ultimately to transform the *roman d'antiquité* from a literary genre into an intellectual exercise, thereby enhancing the significance of the author's own meticulous work of reconstruction, adaptation, and translation.[23] If, as Benoît de Sainte-Maure pointed out in the prologue to his *Chronique des ducs de Normandie*, literary meaning is not inborn—"sen ne naist pas es cuers humains" (meaning is not born within human hearts)[24]—then it must be the work of a literary artificer, who establishes meaning through the felicitous exercise of his craft.

The effect of this emphasis on the art of translation was to displace the authority of the Latin source to the *roman* and thus to make way for the personal creativity of the author, who imposes his presence in the text and endows his function with an importance otherwise denied it, all the while maintaining his allegiance to the authority of his Latin model. By drawing attention to the centrality of literary expression, the romance author/translator liberated himself and his text from dependence on classical models (whether real or fictional) and created a distance between source and translation in which the creative imagination of the writer found legitimate room for play.[25] Both Benoît de Sainte-Maure's *Roman de Troie* and Wace's *Roman de Brut* locate their tales within a literary space suspended between history and fable, where, Wace proclaimed, the reader will find "ne tut mençunge, ne tut veir" (line 9793).[26] Neither wholly a lie nor wholly true, the image of the past offered in the *romans* of Benoît and Wace is a fiction that purports to tell the truth about past facts, and thus is a fiction implying that its fiction is not simply a fiction.[27] By means of this "fictional factuality" the *roman* formulates its own reality, which exists somewhere in the interstices between fable and history.

As Jean Bodel had already recognized in the prologue to his *Chanson des Saisnes*, it was with the emergence of Arthurian romance, and more particularly with the works of Chrétien de Troyes, that medieval romance came finally to acknowledge its status as a self-created fabrication, whose aim was to present an agreeable fiction—"vain et plaisant"—for the literary entertainment of the reader.[28] In contrast to the epic "matter of France," which purported to be "true" (*vraie*), and the "matter of Rome," which was recommended for its moral utility (*sage*), the Arthurian romance announces itself as an autonomous literary invention whose authority lies in the creative virtuosity of the writer. But for the romance writer openly to acknowledge the fictional nature of his work, it was necessary to relegate the truth of the past to a secondary status and to embrace a frankly doubtful history, a move that occurred with the shift from the *romans d'antiquité* to Chrétien's employment of the *roman breton*. By systematically privileging the Breton "fable" and making the praise of *mençunge* the foundation and justification of a literary method, Chrétien was able to become, in effect, the author of the authority of his text.[29] The truth of Chrétien's tale lay not in its referential fidelity to a past ensconced in a prior recounting, but in the pleasure of its form and in the meaning it engendered—in its *sens* and *conjointure*, in Chrétien's famous terms.[30] No longer at the service of historical or religious truth, Arthurian romance inscribes itself as a literary game in which the playful artifice of the writer produces in the reader that pleasure in the text which is at the same time the sign of its literary autonomy.[31] Thus Chrétien, in the prologue to *Erec et Enide*, no longer professes to preserve the memory of the past, but boasts that the future will, instead, preserve the memory of his work:

> De or commencerai l'estoire
> Qui toz jors mes iert an mimoire
> Tant con durra crestiantez
> De ce s'est Crestïens vantez.
> (lines 23–26)[32]

Here now I will begin the story which evermore will be remembered, for as long as Christianity endures; of this does Chrétien boast.

The *estoire* that Chrétien begins to recount is the product of his own artifice, of his personal literary prowess, neither founded in the superior authority of an antecedent text nor justified as the transmission of prior tales. It is the past of "fable" and accepts itself as such.

It is important to stress the self-consciously "fabulous" character of vernacular romance, both as created "fable" and as a depiction of an imaginative realm of the wondrous and magical. For it was romance's

literary construction of the fictional, together with its avowed intention to please and instruct through the elaboration of *sens* and *conjointure*, that operated to reinforce clerical hostility to vernacular
literature as an attempt to rival the authority of the divine *Verbum*
and to usurp the moral role of the church in the spiritual guidance of
the laity.[33]

By situating itself between the vaguely demarcated boundaries of
history and "fable," courtly romance had problematized, by invert-
ing, the traditional relationship between the historical "truth" of
the past and the imaginative "truth" of fiction, calling into question
the moral utility of the former through its implicit validation of the
latter. In so doing, however, it flew in the face of the fundamental
distinction that medieval authors had inherited from classical rhetoric
between, as Walter Map professed, "historia, que veritate nititur, et
fabula, que ficta contexit."[34] It comes as no surprise, therefore, that
the rejection of verse and adoption of prose was accompanied by a
turn to historical writing, in which for the first time Old French prose
is used as a literary language. The persisting medieval belief that poetry was inherently suspect meant that the attempt to rescue the
"truth" of the past from the corruption worked upon it by the created
fictions of vernacular romance privileged historical writing as the locus of truth.

History was associated not only with the "true" but with the written as well. In that sense, the censure of verse as false entailed a parallel disparagement of the oral sources of romance versification. Thus
Bodel contrasts the authentic written tale—"dont li livre d'estoire
sont tesmoing et garant" (of which books of history are witness
and guarantee)—with the jongleur's capricious practice of oral
recitation.[35] Poetry was fictional and oral; history was truthful and
written. The one relied on a vagrant practice of performance, the
other on the scribal practices of an increasingly textualized literary
world. Involved in this dichotomy, so central to the claims that accompanied the rise of vernacular historiography, were the results of a profound transformation in medieval literary practices effected by the
growth of literacy and a widespread movement of textualization
occurring everywhere in medieval Europe in the twelfth and thirteenth centuries.

Until the spread of literacy, the defining mode of medieval vernacular literary communication had been oral recitation.[36] The performed text represented a periodic ritual reenactment of the basic val-

ues of lay culture by means of a shared, public recitation of traditional stories. Indeed, oral "song" as such did not merely signify spoken language; rather, it stood for "an emblem of harmony, of unison, of consonance and order that makes the world . . . intelligible and beautiful."[37] All texts, to the degree that they formed part of the oral culture of lay society or entered into it by being read aloud, enjoyed a public, collective status as vehicles through which the community re-affirmed its sense of historical identity.

The nature of oral culture is such that human action is normally understood through comparison with traditional patterns of behavior preserved in the legacy of stories about the past.[38] Since the community depends on oral narrative for the knowledge required to perform social tasks, such knowledge, once acquired, has to be constantly re-stated or it risks being lost. This patterning of social experience into fixed, formulaic expression facilitates the memory's retention of the collective wisdom that society has built up about its nature and functioning.[39] But oral culture tends to collapse past and present, allowing little room for alternative versions of the past, apart from those conserved by communal memory, to surface publicly. The spoken word is essentially evanescent, allowing the hearer little time to challenge its referential veracity within the framework of its public enunciation.[40] The power of oral vocality lies in its expressive, emotive qualities—those we still call "evocative"; it encourages empathetic identification with the subject matter being sung about or recited, not analytic distance. The fundamental goal of oral recitation is, precisely, to revivify the past and make it live in the present, to fuse past and present, singer and hearer, author and public, into a single, collective entity. In such an environment, the question of historical truth—or, more precisely, of any truths other than the communally agreed-upon precepts ritually enacted in the course of oral performance—can scarcely surface.

But the spread of literacy ultimately challenged the authority of orally communicated history as the source of lay society's self-knowledge. As late as the 1190s, romance authors still affirmed the superiority of their remembered, recited tales to those contained in writing. Béroul, for example, when referring to himself and his art in *Tristan*, although acknowledging the authority of texts, nevertheless claims that his oral recounting of the story of Tristan surpasses other versions, since he more fully "knows"—that is, has a better memory of—the tale:

> Li conteor dient qu'Yvain
> Firent nier, qui sont vilain
> Ne savent mie bien l'estoire!
> Berox l'a mex en sen memoire.
> (lines 1239–1243)[41]

The storytellers claim that Yvain was drowned; but they are scurrilous. They hardly know the story, which Béroul has much better in his memory.

Béroul's insistence on the superior cognitive capacity of his memory compared to that of his competitors marks his text, written after 1191, as the product of an oral, not written, tradition. It is obvious, however, that Béroul's claim makes sense only in a society beginning to experience the growth of literacy and a widening process of textualization, in which the social prestige of the oral account must compete with the authority of the written text.

Until the twelfth century, medieval language use had observed a strict diglossia—two distinct linguistic codes—associated with the bilingualism created by the clerical employment of Latin and the lay use of the vernacular, themselves in turn associated with a more profound division between writing and orality, literacy and illiteracy. That these linguistic distinctions reflected a genuine cultural diglossia, creating a hierarchy of discourses each of which represented a different set of values, behavior, and attitudes, and was not simply a form of bilingualism is certain.[42] Indeed, the inferior status of the vernacular in relation to learned Latin was etymologically prefigured in its derivation from *verna*, meaning a house-born slave.[43] Latin was a "high," learned, written, and fully textualized language,[44] the vernacular a "low," basically oral language, the bearer of the laity's social experience and collective memory but lacking any connection to formal educational institutions. So socially stratified was medieval linguistic practice that mention of the term *literatus* instantly identified a cleric instructed in Latin letters, whereas *illiteratus* correspondingly designated the lay user of oral vernacular.[45]

By the last half of the twelfth century, however, a rapid increase in the use of writing in the vernacular, for both literary and legal purposes, fundamentally changed this traditional picture.[46] The intrusion of writing into the oral realm of the vernacular helped to raise its prestige by analogy to the authority of Latin as a written language. Indeed, by 1209 Walter Map, responding to Gerald of Wales's complaint that his works had only a narrow diffusion, recommended that Gerald translate them into French, contrasting the declining popularity of

Latin *scripta* with the large audience eager for vernacular *dicta*.[47] Map's essential divide remains that between Latin *scripta* and French *dicta*, but the latter term in this case refers to an orally transmitted *written* text. Most striking, though, is Map's novel appreciation of the communicative possibilities of the vernacular, in whatever fashion disseminated.

The late twelfth and thirteenth centuries witnessed a progressive loosening of the bond between the vernacular and orality as vernacular composition was realigned with writing. Although originally *mettre en roman* meant the process of translating into the vernacular, irrespective of the ultimate medium of communication—oral or written—quite quickly the phrase *mise en roman* acquired the implication that the translated text was preserved in written form and so was distinguished from orally transmitted *contes*.[48] It is interesting, in this connection, that the term *roman* hardly ever appears in the *chansons de geste*, the closest thing to a purely oral genre in the Middle Ages, but is associated rather with the beginnings of courtly romance—the *roman*, par excellence, through a semantic restriction of its meaning.[49] Despite its original definition as a register of spoken language, then, *roman* rapidly assumed a generic connotation as a particular type of vernacular literature, suggesting a written or potentially written performance. Once this had occurred, the cultural competition between orality and textuality as communicative modes was no longer limited to the contrasting discursive registers of Latin and Old French, but was displaced to within the vernacular itself, a struggle that was to have broad significance for the eventual debate over the value of poetry or prose in the communication of "true" historical knowledge.

From the perspective of the communicative situation, oral recitation does not, of course, disappear. Most members of the lay audience for vernacular literature doubtless continued to be personally illiterate and remained dependent on performance for access to texts. Lay audiences for romance literature came to form, in Brian Stock's felicitous phrase, "textual communities," groups of hearers assembled for the reading of a text, as the word "audience" itself suggests.[50] Well into the thirteenth century and even beyond, vernacular literature retains all the marks of works intended for oral delivery and a heavy residue of verbal art forms associated with primary orality.[51] Actual written composition designed for silent reading appears only much later, and until that time all forms of writing are heavily conditioned by oral patterns derived from speech, a phenomenon as true of prose as of verse narration.

Nevertheless, it is undeniable that the spread of literacy and the passage of romance literature from a primarily oral to a primarily written culture significantly changed the character of medieval literary production. Orality was transformed by a gradual process of acculturation with the written, which not only modified the nature of romance narration[52] but, more importantly for our purposes, also revalued the relative authority of oral utterance with respect to writing. The denunciation of verse in *La mort Aimeri de Narbonne*, cited above, as inherently mendacious because it sacrifices truth to the enunciative requirements of oral delivery indicates that by the end of the twelfth century the authority of the oral had been severely undermined by the growth of vernacular textuality. Verse, even when written, is "burdened by its former life in the now devalued oral culture."[53] No longer the communicative center of society's most important cultural and historical legacies, orality is gradually displaced to the realm of fiction, error, and hearsay. The tendency within Arthurian romance to emphasize the fictional status of its discourse no doubt contributed to this process, which at the same time continued to be fed by the traditional medieval distrust of poetic language in general, always closely associated with orality. By the beginning of the thirteenth century, both epic and romance appear to suffer from the opprobrium that in earlier centuries had been visited upon pagan Latin poetry; and the issue that came to the fore in the course of this reconfiguration was the problem of "truth."

Recent research into the implications of literacy has argued that the penetration of romance oral culture by writing provided a new linguistic model of truth, one based on written, not spoken, language. That model implied that written communication directly reflected reality, but that oral exchange, when not supported by a text, did not.[54] "Truth," in other words, was lodged in texts, not speech. Early vernacular histories, although in fact orally transmitted, could reap the ideological benefits of this displacement of authority from speech to writing, a phenomenon that perhaps explains why the question of truth should have emerged so powerfully in the debate that accompanied the introduction of prose historiography.

To be sure, the shift from an oral model of consensual truth as the bearer of society's self-knowledge to a written model proceeded slowly and gradually. Written texts remained heavily permeated with the values and signifying practices of orality. But, progressively, those signifying practices most closely tied to orality—epic, verse, and poetic language generally—were increasingly stigmatized as suspect and liable to error: as, in effect, "lies." Textuality, in contrast, came to serve as a sign of authenticity, establishing prima facie its own authority. Written verse remained closely associated with the circumstances and rituals of oral performance, and thus inevitably suffered from the growing suspicion of verse as necessarily implicated in the uncertainties of orality. Prose, to the extent that it created a textual space of its own, a space clearly differentiated from that of performance,[55] was to gain from this transformation a newly legitimized status as a privileged literary form for the communication of socially valuable knowledge, hence as a preferred medium for historical writing.

The new prominence of prose, which first appears in the prologues to the *Pseudo-Turpin* translations, signals the rise of textuality as an instrument of aristocratic culture. Yet we may still ask why prose appeared when and where it did, within such a highly circumscribed circle of aristocratic patrons—a pattern that was in sharp contrast to earlier forms of aristocratic patronage of epic and romance, in which a much broader segment of the French aristocracy had participated. We may also ask why the argument in favor of prose emerged most powerfully in historical texts, rather than in derhymed or, ultimately, prosed versions of epic and romance tales. And finally, in the broadest sense of the question to which the *Pseudo-Turpin* translations are merely the first response, we may ask what problematic aspects of aristocratic experience or ideology were being defined and expressed with the production of the vernacular prose chronicle.

The Latin *Pseudo-Turpin Chronicle* was easily one of the most popular literary works in the Middle Ages, representing an audacious clerical rewriting of the largely legendary account of Charlemagne's expedition to Spain and the epic matter of Roncevaux, best known through the verses of the *Chanson de Roland*. Assembled in its present state about 1140, it comprises an awkward mix of epic narrative and clerical sermonizing, and purports to be an eyewitness account by the Archbishop Turpin, who figures as a central character in the *Chanson de Roland*.[56] In all likelihood it was the work of ecclesiastical propagandists, who were attempting at one and the same time to control the legacy of the *Chanson de Roland*[57] and to take advantage of the poem's enormous appeal by insinuating within it a series of theological debates, moral exempla, digressions on the Seven Liberal Arts, and miraculous events that function to tame and moralize the heroic force of the vernacular poet's account. Its translation into the vernacular is,

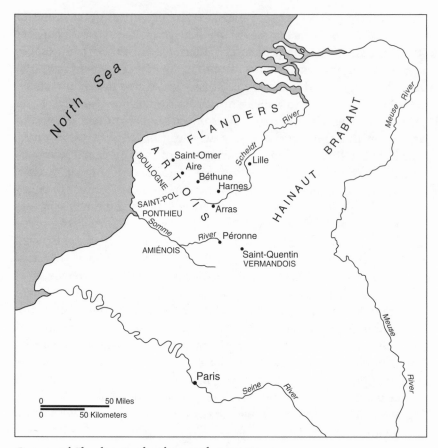

County of Flanders in the thirteenth century.

thus, in some sense a re-translation, a reappropriation of the vernacular epic in its newly sanitized state by writers in Old French.

Between 1200 and 1230 no fewer than six independent translations of the *Pseudo-Turpin Chronicle* were made within the confines of the French realm, exclusive of an Anglo-Norman version that dates from the same period.[58] Strikingly, all these translations resulted from the patronage of the French-speaking Flemish aristocracy of northern France (see map). The first was made by Nicolas of Senlis about the year 1200 at the request of Yolande, countess of Saint-Pol, and her husband, Hugh IV.[59] Yolande was the sister of Count Baldwin VIII of Flanders (Baldwin V of Hainaut), who, sometime between 1180 and 1189, had dispatched his clerks to Cluny, Tours, and Saint-Denis to search out and copy a text of the "true history" of Charlemagne. This he did, according to Nicolas, because "le bons Baudoins . . . si ama molt Karlemaine ni ne veut onques croire chose que l'om en chantast" (the good Baldwin, the count of Hainaut, dearly loved Charlemagne, but he did not want to believe anything that was sung about him), thus he dispatched his clerks throughout Europe in search of "la veraie ystoire." This text—the fictive *Pseudo-Turpin*, doubtless recovered from the Abbey of Saint-Denis—Baldwin bequeathed to Yolande at his death in 1195, requesting that she preserve it as long as she might live ("que par amor de lui gardast le livre tant cum ele vivroit").[60] It was in Yolande's possession when Nicolas translated it. Although his original French version no longer survives, it was later associated with a corpus of local history known as the *Chronique Saintongeaise*, through which it is preserved in three extant manuscripts.[61]

A second branch of the vernacular *Pseudo-Turpin* derives from a translation executed sometime before 1206 by a "Master Johannes," possibly the same "Johannes" whose presence is recorded at the court of King John of England as the chaplain of Renaud of Dammartin, count of Boulogne.[62] This "Johannes" created the most popular version of the vernacular *Pseudo-Turpin*, for his text was copied and adapted several times within a few years of its appearance. Pierre de Beauvais transcribed it, also before 1206, joining to it his own translation of the Latin account of Charlemagne's legendary journey to Jerusalem, the *Descriptio qualiter Karolus Magni clavum et coronam a Constantinopoli transtulit*.[63] Pierre's *Descriptio* was in turn highly abbreviated and utilized as a prefatory chapter to Johannes's *Turpin* by a second anonymous redactor, and it was in this combined form, as a *Descriptio-Turpin*, that Johannes's text was to find favor at the courts of the Flemish aristocracy. In 1206, Count Renaud of Boulogne sponsored a transcription of the Johannes *Turpin*, and in the same or following year another copy was made for Michel III, lord of Harnes and "justiciar" of Flanders. Although both Renaud of Boulogne and Michel of Harnes claimed to have commandeered translations directly from a Latin text (found, naturally, in the library of Saint-Denis), Walpole has conclusively demonstrated that the two patrons can be credited only with having sponsored independent copies of the second French redaction, or composite *Descriptio-Turpin*.[64]

Another offshoot of this redaction appears in a version commissioned by William of Cayeux, a lord of Ponthieu, of which only a fragment remains today, preserved in B.N. fr. 2168. The prologue states that Pierre de Beauvais made a copy of his translation of the

Descriptio "pour l'amour son bon segnour Williaume de Caieu qui volentiers ot verité mis de Latin en romans comment et par quele ochoison Charlemaine ala outremer devant le voie d'Espaigne" (for the love of his good lord, William of Cayeux, who had the truth translated from Latin to French of how and for what reason Charlemagne went to the Holy Land before the voyage to Spain).[65] The Johannes *Turpin* seems to have been part of the original text made for William, as indicated by the mention of the *voie d'Espaigne*.[66] The county of Ponthieu lay generally within the Flemish/Anglo-Norman sphere of activity. William of Cayeux was a companion of Richard Lion-Heart on the Third Crusade and fought with the Flemish on John's side at the battle of Bouvines, where he was taken prisoner.

A fifth translation of the *Pseudo-Turpin* is found in a version stemming from Artois and dating from about 1218.[67] It was subsequently utilized by an anonymous Artesian minstrel in the employ of Robert VII of Béthune, whose fortunes he followed during the period when Robert served among the mercenary forces of King John of England in his wars against Philip Augustus. To the pen of this Anonymous we owe two of the most important early histories in Old French prose: a *Histoire des ducs de Normandie et des rois d'Angleterre* and a companion *Chronique des rois de France*, the latter completed before 1223, in which the account of *Pseudo-Turpin* was for the first time inserted into the body of the text as an integral part of the Carolingian history of the French monarchy.[68] The sixth and final translation of the *Pseudo-Turpin Chronicle* was made in Hainaut in the decade between 1220 and 1230. It is the work of an anonymous translator who in all likelihood lived and worked in the same region bordering the counties of Hainaut, Flanders, and Artois that functioned as the center for the diffusion of the vernacular *Pseudo-Turpin*.[69]

Numerous, with close textual affiliations, these *Pseudo-Turpin* translations constituted the first stage in the adoption of prose for historical writing in Old French. Walpole rightly expressed surprise at the fact that none of the translators seemed to know the work of any others,[70] although Hugh of Saint-Pol, Renaud of Boulogne, and Robert of Béthune were political allies, and Michel of Harnes, who claims to have borrowed the Latin text from Renaud's library (but did not), was constantly involved with all three. Indeed, all the sponsors were intimately connected in the political struggles that beset Flanders in this period. Although far from socially homogeneous, by the twelfth century all (except Renaud of Dammartin, who married Ida, heiress to the county of Boulogne) can be identified as belonging to the upper echelons of the Flemish nobility, whom Galbert of Bruges, a superb guide to and commentator on the social world of Flanders, terms "peers" and "barons" (*pares et barones*).[71]

The peers of Flanders belonged to the class of free, militarized land-owners who were the noble descendants of the ancient *viri illustres*,[72] and Fossier has suggested that the frequent use of the term *pares* in charter attestations between 1180 and 1210 reflects an attempt to revive the old nobility,[73] a process whose full significance can be appreciated in light of the political turmoil affecting Flanders in these decades. Like the more usual term *barones, pares* clearly indicates not only those highly placed in the feudal hierarchy, but also an ancient nobility of blood.

Among those whom Galbert of Bruges specifically associates as peers or barons of Flanders are Robert IV of Béthune and Roger II, castellan of Lille.[74] He probably included in that select group the count of Saint-Pol as well. By the early thirteenth century, in any case, Hugh of Saint-Pol was married to Yolande, who as the sister of Count Baldwin VIII stood at the summit of Flemish noble society. Clearly noble as well were the counts of Boulogne and castellans of Harnes,[75] the latter having been named hereditary constables of Flanders by Thierry of Alsace in 1128 and castellans of Cassel between 1128 and 1139,[76] at which time members of the family bore the title of *baro*.

In a curious passage, Gervase of Canterbury claims that when the marriage between Philip Augustus and Isabelle of Hainaut was celebrated in 1180, the nobles of France were unhappy that the king "per comitis Flandriae consilium uxorem de tam humili progenie sibi associare voluerit in reginam" (on the advice of the count of Flanders, the king wished to associate with himself a wife of such humble descent as queen),[77] which suggests that the status of the Flemish nobles was somehow inferior in the eyes of the court barons. The so-called *Scripta de feodis*, however, drawn up by Philip Augustus's chancery clerks, ranks the counts of Flanders, Saint-Pol, and Boulogne in the highest category of the feudality, while the *avoué* of Béthune appears among the *barones*.

Only Michel of Harnes, noble within the context of Flemish lords, is placed below in the ranks of mere *vavassores* and, when listed under Artois, *milites*.[78] Yet Michel's father, Michel II of Harnes, was mayor of Harnes, castellan of Cassel, lord of Boulaere, *avoué* of Ninove, and hereditary constable of Flanders.[79] The family, in fact, was sufficiently important in the late twelfth century to be courted by both English and French kings. Michel II is found among the castellans who in 1163 witnessed the *Recognitio servitii* acknowledging service owed to Henry II, in return for which he may well have received a money-fief or grant of land. It appears that, additionally, he received a fief-rent from the Capetian king, since in June 1212 Philip Augustus renewed to Michel III a fief-rent of sixty livres, ten sous, on the *péage* of Péronne held by his father: "sicut pater eius Michael predictum redditum tenebat de domino perone."[80] That a Michel de Harnes collected a fief-rent from the French king is proven by an entry in the "budget" of 1202–1203, which accounts for a disbursement to "Michel de Harnes pro suo feodo LX l. et X s.,"[81] although it is difficult to determine whether the recipient of this payment is Michel II or Michel III.[82]

It may be significant that among the Flemish nobility active in the sponsorship of vernacular histories, Michel, who ranked lowest in social status, was the only one to defect outright to the French cause. The clearest evidence that he had joined the French party in Flanders derives from the confirmation charter, cited above, renewing the fief-rent on the *péage* of Péronne. But it is likely that Michel had already passed over to the king's side sometime between 1206 and 1208, when the French party in Flanders was in the process of formation.[83] By 1208–1210 he was already identified as one of the king's followers by Jean Renart, who in his *Roman de Guillaume de Dole* artfully divided contemporary French and imperial partisans into opposing sides at the fictive tournament of Saint-Trond.[84] Few Flemish lords served Philip Augustus as loyally or as well as Michel. He fought bravely with the king at Bouvines and joined Prince Louis's expedition to England in 1216, for which there is preserved a fragment of a chronicle possibly written by Michel himself.[85] Whatever his standing in the eyes of the royal chancery clerks, it is obvious that the French monarch considered him a valuable ally.

Walpole believed that the intense interest in the *Pseudo-Turpin* exhibited by this group of Flemish aristocrats was primarily literary and that the patronage of independent copies was the result of literary competition: "They were probably rivals in the field of letters as they were in other fields, jealous of their reputations as sponsors of the arts."[86] But sponsorship of multiple versions of the same text is not the most obvious way of establishing a reputation as a literary patron. Indeed, the large number of copies of these manuscripts would seem to suggest that the *Pseudo-Turpin Chronicle* possessed a particular appeal for Flemish lords that went beyond mere rivalry in literary patronage.

The distinguishing feature of the initial *Turpin* translations lies in their militant insistence on prose as the necessary language of history and their critique of the mendacious character of verse historiography. As the first translator, Nicolas of Senlis, recognized: "many peoples have heard told and sung [the story of Charlemagne's expedition to Spain], but what these singers and jongleurs sing and tell is nothing but a lie. No rhymed tale is true; everything they say is lies, for they know nothing about it except through hearsay." This is so, as the prologue to Michel's *Turpin* explains, because "in order to fit the rhyme, it borrows words outside of history."[87] Boldly rejecting any history that, as one manuscript proclaimed, when "treated in rhyme seems a lie,"[88] these translations insist on the veracity of their tale, whose truth is guaranteed by its faithful transmission via the lucid medium of prose. Thus Johannes, in the prologue to his translation, asserted the authority of his version against its predecessors on the basis of his faithful reproduction in French of the Latin prose of his exemplar: "Whatever the others have taken away from or added to [this history], here you can hear the truth of Spain [*la verité d'Espaigne*] according to the Latin of the history that Count Renaud of Boulogne had with great effort caused to be sought out in books at the Abbey of Saint-Denis"[89]—the latter invoked, falsely, as an additional guarantee of the text's historical authenticity. Johannes's sentiments are precisely echoed in the prologue to B.N. fr. 1621, which similarly asserted that "because history treated in rhyme lies, this history is translated into French [*mise en roman*] without rhyme, according to the order [*le raison*] of the Latin that Archbishop Turpin himself made and treated [*fist et traita*]."[90]

The vernacular *Turpin*, therefore, makes a privileged claim to authority on the basis of its utilization of an authentic Latin text found at Saint-Denis, which is accurately reconstituted in French by means of a literal prose translation. The proclaimed "truth" of the chronicle separates it from fictional genres such as epic and romance, whose veracity is disparaged by the dismissal of their content as mere "hearsay," in contrast to the *Turpin*'s founding in an authoritative Latin text. This "truth" is further reinforced by the listing of acknowledged guarantors of veracity—author, patron, and manuscript owner. The aim here is to surround the translation with an aura of credibility, lent by the discussion of the circumstances of the work's composition, the historian's awareness of the difficulty of his task, and his avowed commitment to remain faithful to historical truth where others before him had failed.[91]

It is obvious, of course, that the *Turpin* is forged history, taken by patrons and translators from texts either already transcribed in French or, if from the Latin, existing in versions circulating within their own courtly libraries.[92] Virtually every claim articulated in these prologues—the text's foundation in a prior and authoritative Latin manuscript, discovered after much effort at Saint-Denis, which has been laboriously translated with the utmost care from Latin into French—can be shown to be false. Thus, despite the fact that the prologues to Renaud's and Michel's translations insist that they were made directly from the Latin (in Renaud's case based on a text found at Saint-Denis; in Michel's, on a Latin version located in Renaud's library), both versions are in fact independent copies of the second redaction of Johannes's Old French *Turpin*.[93]

Although the irony of this enterprise surely strikes us more forcefully than it did its perpetrators, the assertions of truthfulness and accuracy that abound in the prologues are nevertheless significant, for they bespeak a desire to create or answer a demand for a new form of historical discourse, one free of the content, style, and oral and fictional sources of epic and romance. This demand amounts to an attempt to ground historical truth in a novel system of authentication and authorization, one that relies on (and therefore ultimately competes with) the prior authority of "authentic" Latin histories preserved in written form among the most prestigious guardians of historical truth in medieval France, the monks of Saint-Denis.[94] And the question remains: Why did such a demand come so powerfully to the fore in the first decades of the thirteenth century, among a narrow group of Flemish patrons, whose requests for new modes of historical edification promising greater veracity than the versified histories of romance literature seem so at odds with the very choice of *Turpin* as the originating text of vernacular prose historiography and with the falsity of the claims with which they hedge their enterprise?

In the main, scholars concerned with Old French historical writing have tended to see it as a late, and not altogether welcome, addition to a centuries-old and already sophisticated tradition of Latin historical writing, in relation to which vernacular historiography received rather low marks. This view of vernacular history seemed to be justified by the fact that the earliest texts consisted of translations of Latin works and, thus, naturally invited comparison with their Latin sources. But although it is true that early vernacular chronicles translated Latin texts, they did so in a way that clearly demonstrates their ties to an already existing vernacular literary culture distinct in its origins and modes of operation from Latin literature. Indeed, the evolution of historical genres—from *Pseudo-Turpin* translations, to ancient histories, to political and military chronicles—strikingly recapitulates the evolution of romance genres from epic, to *romans d'antiquité*, to courtly romance, while recasting them in prose.

The curious parallel between the generic evolution of romance literature and vernacular historiography suggests that vernacular culture itself generated Old French historiography and that Old French historical writing is perhaps best viewed as one among a variety of literary genres through which the French aristocracy sought to resolve the tensions created by its changing social status. In addition, this parallel opens up the possibility that the emergence of prose historiography in particular, accompanied by the censure of verse and oral performance, is functionally related to the transformations occurring within aristocratic society, although the specific ways in which that might be true remain to be discovered.

As a starting point for such an inquiry, it is useful to note that modern sociolinguistics has demonstrated that social groups most affected by transformations in status tend to be especially conscious of alternative modes of discursive behavior—that they are, in other words, particularly sensitive to the power of language to register social change.[95] Language games, Lévi-Strauss insists, are essentially power games, and it follows that disputes over language domains and usage are contests of power. The profound shift in language use from poetry to prose among the French aristocracy of the thirteenth century appears, therefore, to point to a perception by that group of dislocations in the social order, a perception registered in a revision of its customary discursive behavior. However, where earlier romance genres sought to explore the newly problematic aspects of aristocratic life— to forge, that is, a literary language by which "to articulate the crisis of [the aristocracy's] own changing status"[96]—the adoption of prose as the language of vernacular history represented, I would argue, an effort to *deproblematize* aristocratic culture in an age of anxiety whose social ground was the radical challenge to aristocratic autonomy and prestige posed by the revival of monarchical authority.

In the *Turpin* prologues, history is demarcated as a discourse distinguished by its commitment to truth, a commitment enabled and guaranteed by its rejection of verse and adoption of prose. Whereas verse "lies," prose, in contrast, is presented as a "natural" language, one existing prior to the imposition of any form[97] and thus able to serve as a lucid medium of communication, untainted by literary ornamentation and its deceits. A profound irony, therefore, accompanies the emergence of prose as the literary language of history, created by the paradox that verse, in its evident artificiality, openly illustrates what it is that language is—a deceit, a system of arbitrary signs harboring opaque meanings—whereas prose, in its claim to lack of artifice, enacts a myth of transparency, promulgating the deceit that it is a language free of form and mimetically truthful, hence uniquely appropriate as a mode of historical discourse. Involved here is not simply the devaluation of history's artistic properties as traditionally defined,[98] but an ideological privileging of prose as a natural language, inherently superior for the acquisition and dissemination of historical truth. In literary terms, the substitution of prose for verse represents the displacement of linguistic mediation toward a "naturalized," "realistic" mode, employing a language of transparent factuality that sets itself off from the overt use of fiction, fable, and hearsay in epic and romance. This suggests that the failure of earlier romance genres to satisfy the aristocracy's need for historical edification occurred on the level of metaphor,[99] in the sense that the specific literary devices employed by courtly romance, and to a lesser extent by epic, were no longer perceived as adequate to articulate the aristocracy's sense of crisis.

To say that romance and epic were no longer adequate, however, does not explain the choice of Pseudo-Turpin as the originating text of prose historiography. Nor does it explain the work's special attraction for the northern lords who commissioned the translations, a patronage phenomenon almost unmatched in medieval literary history in terms of the relatively large number of independent commissions executed within a highly restricted chronological and geographic span. Indeed, to Omer Jodogne, the success of Pseudo-Turpin "paraît étrange,"[100] a sentiment recently echoed by Diana Tyson in her study of the patronage of French vernacular history writers in the twelfth and thirteenth centuries.[101] Paul Meyer, Ronald Walpole, William Sayers, and Ian Short, to be sure, have attributed the work's popularity to an awakening French patriotism, which settled on the Pseudo-Turpin Chronicle because of its exaltation of the French monarchy in the guise of Charlemagne. To these scholars, the vernacular Turpin constitutes a kind of proto-national chronicle, awkwardly anticipating sentiments of devotion to the national ruler that were fully voiced only later.

Yet everything we know about the patrons for these translations should make us suspect the validity of this interpretation. For as we saw in chapter 1, with the exception of Michel of Harnes, all the patrons of *Pseudo-Turpin* chronicles belonged to the English, anti-Capetian party in Flanders, were hostile to the advance of the French monarchy into Flemish territories, and struggled persistently, if unsuccessfully, to prevent the extension of royal authority over their lands. To varying degrees, all suffered the consequences of their opposition to the French king, experiencing financial stress, imprisonment, and loss of autonomy. At the same time, it is clear that the patronage of the Flemish aristocracy—rather than the existence of an indeterminate prospective audience—was the crucial factor in the creation of vernacular prose historiography, and in the determination of its aims, tone, and form.[102]

At first glance, the declining political fortunes of the Flemish aristocracy would appear unrelated to any motives that might have inspired the patronage of *Pseudo-Turpin* chronicles so copiously practiced in the courts of Flanders. What possible connection could there be between the fields of Flanders and the fantasies of Charlemagne's exploits in the Spanish hills of Roncevaux, between the all-too-real sting of political defeat at home and the all-too-fictive glory of temporally and spatially distant chivalric combat in the past? Why should this banal, Latin appropriation of the epic *Chanson de Roland* for the purposes of ecclesiastical propaganda have seemed valuable for the expression of aristocratic crisis, especially since it required retranslation into Old French and the reintroduction of those very epic elements, excised from the clerical Latin version, that accounted for so large a part of its appeal? To answer these questions, we must return to the prologues to the translations, for they contain important clues that allow us to situate the *Pseudo-Turpin* histories within the sociopolitical context outlined in chapter 1 and to begin to understand the possible sociocultural roles of vernacular historiography.

The *Turpin* prologues disclose a surprising unanimity concerning the motives and goals that prompted their authors to undertake the laborious task of translation. In general, their claims can be divided into four programmatic statements present to varying degrees in all the texts: first, a desire to revive chivalric virtue deemed to be in decline; second, a belief in the exemplary value of Charlemagne and the moral profit to be gained from a knowledge of his crusading deeds; third, a less overt but nonetheless clear pride in Charlemagne as the distant progenitor of the patron's own lineage, for whom the *Pseudo-Turpin* chronicle served as ancestral history; and finally, the explicit adoption, as we have seen, of prose as the proper language of history, with a corollary condemnation of epic and romance styles of historical writing. Taken together, these statements frame the revolution in historical writing represented by the rise of the vernacular prose chronicle.

The first of the chronicle's stated aims—to revive chivalric virtues—received its most powerful articulation in the prologue to Renaud of Boulogne's *Turpin*, a work he commissioned, the prologue asserts, because

> les bones vertus sont au siecle auques defaillis et les courages des grans seigneurs afoibliz pour ce que on ne voit mais si voulentiers comme on souloit les fais des preudomes et les anciennes histoires es queles on treuve comment on se doit avoir envers Dieu et contenir au siecle honnorablement.[103]

> the good virtues are in our times in decline and the courage of the great lords enfeebled, for one doesn't see as readily now as one used to in the past the deeds of *prud'hommes* [nor does one come across] the ancient histories, in which one finds how one should comport oneself with respect to God and how to live honorably in the world.

For, the prologue warns, "vivre sans honneur est mort et descroissement" (to live without honor is death and diminution). The secular decline in virtue and progressive enfeeblement of knightly virtue resulting from ignorance of the past recommends the reading of the *Pseudo-Turpin* to "tous haus homes," among whom "si doit estre ciere tenue et volentier oie" (it ought to be cherished and willingly heard).[104]

Pseudo-Turpin is here offered as an antidote to chivalric decay, in the hopes that the perusal of its pages might work a salutary effect on the minds of an aristocratic public fully conscious of a crisis in its code of behavior and in those values of honor and courage to which it lent support. The prologue's implicit assumption of the power of history to provide such ethical stimulus is seen in the author's corollary assumption that it was the neglect of the past, the inattention paid to the "deeds of *prud'hommes* and the ancient histories," that led to the loss of moral virtue and courage to begin with—a criticism leveled not only, one suspects, at the ethical comportment of contemporary society and its presumed noncompliance with chivalric codes of behavior, but also at the relative neglect of history due to the rise of the courtly romance in the second half of the twelfth century. The vogue of romance had diverted aristocratic literary preferences away from the public recitation of precisely those epic *chansons de geste* and versified histories of which the prologues complain.

The *Turpin*'s program for the revival of chivalry, therefore, has as its literary counterpart the revival of epic, which, by the circuitous logic of medieval historical thought, in turn becomes the literary instrument for the revivification of noble virtue. But since oral epic proper was vulnerable to the charge of falsity, of a linguistic *défaillance* parallel to the *défaillance* of military prowess and boldness thematized in the prologue, a simple reprise of the *Chanson de Roland* could no longer perpetuate those heroic values now deemed in decline. *Pseudo-Turpin*, to the extent that it possessed the inherent authority of an ecclesiastical Latin model, avoided the possible stigma attached to epic, oral narrative—aided, of course, by the fact that it employed the linguistically straightforward language of prose, thereby avoiding the suspicion of linguistic impropriety that the *Turpin* itself so powerfully casts on verse.

From this perspective, the choice of *Pseudo-Turpin* as the initial historical text of vernacular historiography indicates a desire to revive the moral and political conditions of an earlier age of aristocratic glory, as a form of ethical reassurance to an intended audience of aristocratic hearers and readers that they still occupy a vital place in the social order. Given the situation of the Flemish aristocracy in the early thirteenth century, facing invasion from above and below of its age-old prerogative to wage war in a distinctive noble style, the appeal of the *Pseudo-Turpin* chronicle becomes more understandable, for it allowed the patrons of these texts to assert their need for an ethically valorized past, without at the same time implicating them in a web of linguistic "deception." The revival of an epic, heroic, valorized, "absolute past," to use Bakhtin's phrase,[105] achieved by the retranslation of the *Pseudo-Turpin* Latin chronicle back into a vernacular language heavily laden with traditional epic themes and linguistic practices, enabled the chronicler to provide a verbal substitute for a social past irretrievably lost, and thus to cover an absence.[106] In this sense, the *mise en roman*—the translation of history into Old French—is a genuine "romancing" of the past, a search for the missing term, a quest to recover a lost, idealized world of chivalric potency and aristocratic valor, the memory of which haunts the pages of the *Pseudo-Turpin* chronicle. Like the *Chanson de Roland*, the *Turpin* recounts an epic of defeat spiritually transcended, a military rupture overcome in moral triumph, memorialized and thus perpetuated for all time as a literary artifact, transforming a socially absent past into a living vocal presence.

In its relation to the *Chanson de Roland*, the *Pseudo-Turpin* achieves a similar economy of transcendence, for it overcomes the loss of time inherent in the evanescence of oral epic by its inscription as text. Thus, both as textual history and as historical text, the

Pseudo-Turpin Chronicle monumentalizes a historiography of lost causes, in which the decline of the Flemish aristocracy is answered in the historically transcended defeat of Roncevaux; the loss of aristocratic military power is morally transfigured into a myth of chivalric virtue; the loss of linguistic propriety entailed in epic verse is rectified by prose; and the evanescence of oral performance is overcome in the permanence of textual inscription.

Yet the *Turpin* prologue's very recognition of chivalric decline indicates that the recovery of the heroic past has been displaced to an ethical realm, in which the military vocation of the knightly classes is defined more as a set of moral predicates than as a practical, political reality. The Carolingian past has been transmuted into a moral vision of the battlefield as an arena of personal honor, furnishing examples of how to live *honnorablement*.[107] The *Pseudo-Turpin* chronicle thus implicitly acknowledges that the heroic age of Charlemagne, although it continues to offer a storehouse of exemplary ideals, is a past definitely gone, and its literary revival as moral epic serves primarily to render visible the process of decline, of *décroissement*, already under way. The laments on the decadence of chivalric prowess disguise a pervading sense of resignation in the face of a history that cannot be recuperated. The evocation of the moral conditions of the heroic past is a gesture that seeks to renew the thread of continuity broken in the near past, whose effect is simultaneously to mark and to mask a rupture.[108] History no longer provides precedent and legitimation for a viable complex of political claims and initiatives; it is directed, rather, at the encouragement of a cultic code of social comportment revolving around the notion of honor. As Johannes put it:

> Molt sont bien a oir les oevres et les bones estoires ou li bien fait et
> li bon essample sont qui ensaignent comment on se doit avoir en
> Deu et maintenir au siecle honorablement. Car vivre sans honeur
> valt pis que morir en terre.[109]

> It is very good to hear works and good histories where there are
> good deeds and good examples, which teach one how to behave to-
> ward God and how to conduct oneself honorably in the world. For to
> live without honor is worse than to die on earth.

"Honor" becomes the watchword of a class whose political efficacy has been undermined and which takes refuge in a sense of moral superiority, by means of which it endeavors to disavow its consciousness of the present futility of former knightly endeavors. The *Pseudo-Turpin* translations are directed at "tous haus homes," to whom they offer a nostalgic vision of a glorious, collective past, whose moral seriousness both contrasts it with the "vain et plaisant" conceits of courtly romance and compensates for its lack of political relevance.

The totalizing vision of the past that the *Turpin* offers is most clearly marked in its suppression of the tensions and antagonisms that were such crucial elements in the plot of the *Chanson de Roland.* There is no trace, either in the Latin *Turpin* or in the vernacular chronicle, of feudal independence; of Ganelon's wounded honor or Roland's fierce pride, which leads to epic *démesure;* of Charlemagne's indecision, which renders him unable to prevent the fatal unfolding of the quarrel between Ganelon and Roland that engulfs the epic world in tragedy. Instead, both king and aristocracy are treated in wholly homologous terms, in an epic celebration of a unitary, deproblematized world, where Charlemagne becomes the ideal knight and Roland is presented in language borrowed from the moral conspectus of royal virtues.

Charlemagne first enters the chronicle as a young man, forced in exile to seek refuge at the palace of Toledo, where the Emir Galaffre knights him: "cestui Charle fist Galafres chevalier en son palés a Tolete quant il fu de France essilliez" (Galaffre made this Charles a knight in his palace at Toledo, at the time when he was exiled from France). From the outset, then, Charlemagne appears on the stage of history not as an imperial persona, but in the chivalric guise of a knight. In return for his "ordination" as a knight, Charlemagne fights against Galaffre's enemy, Braimant, whom he slays, inaugurating with this act of chivalric prowess his glorious campaign of conquest ("aprés conquist mainte terre"), which carries him to the heights of power as emperor of Rome and king of France, England, Denmark and Germany, Bavaria, Lotharingia, Burgundy, Italy, Brittany, "et plusors autres terres de l'une mer desi a l'autre" (and many other lands from one sea to the other).[110] Even after becoming emperor of all these lands, Charlemagne continues to fight as a knight. Thus Johannes, in his portrait of the emperor, emphasizes his status as a "chevaliers tres aigres" (a very ardent knight),[111] of such great strength that with his sword Joyeuse he could slash a knight in half— "et lui et son cheval" (he and his horse)—in a classic epic gesture of chivalric prowess.

In a similar fashion, the anonymous translator of the version found in Vat. Reg. 624 transforms the bland account of his Latin model (narrating how Charles, when his horse was killed beneath him in battle, "oppressus fortitudine paganorum, resumptis viribus cum suis

exercitibus peditus interfecit multos illorum") into an extended paean
to the emperor's chivalric deeds:

> mais il comme chevalierz vaillanz et preuz traist sa bone espee et
> ambraça le fort escu et se feri an la presse tot a pié et prist Sarrazins
> a ocierre et detranchier, ne nus qui i soit nés ne vos porroit dire ne
> retraire la mervoille qu'il fist ce jor de soi, car par sa ruste proece
> furent le jor Sarrazin vancui et desconfit comme cil qui durement
> estoient lassé des crestiens qu'il avoient ocis; et il qui puis ne porent
> sofrir les rustes cops Karlemaigne lor ce ferirent an la cité.[112]

> But he, like a valiant and doughty knight, wielded his good sword
> and grasped his strong shield and threw himself into the ranks all on
> foot, and began killing and slashing Saracens. No one could say or
> describe the marvels that he performed that day himself, for by his
> robust prowess the Saracens were vanquished that day, beaten like
> men who were harshly exhausted by the Christians whom they had
> killed, and those who could no longer withstand the brutal blows of
> Charlemagne then hastened into the city.

So, too, Pierre de Beauvais, in his *Descriptio-Turpin*, introduces a
heavenly vision of Charles, fully armed in the shimmering accoutrements of a knight, who appears to the beleaguered emperor of Constantinople as he ponders how to rescue Jerusalem from the Saracens,
prepared to offer the full panoply of his chivalric weapons for the recovery of the Holy Land. Charles appears

> en semblance d'un chevalier armé, les escus est tous vermauz et li
> ponz de s'espee vermauz et la lance qu'il tenoit estoit toute blanche
> dont la pointe du fer giete flambe sovent. Il tenoit .i. hiaume doré en
> sa main. Il ert auques d'aage et mout biaus de vout et noble d'esta-
> ture. Si oeil resplendissoient com estoiles et ses chiés blanchissoient
> de chagnes. Ce ne fait mie a douter que telle vision ne venist de
> Dieu.[113]

> in the form of a knight in arms: his shield is all red, and the point
> of his sword was red and the lance that he held was completely white
> while its iron point threw forth flames; he held a golden helmet in
> his hand. He was advanced in age and extremely handsome in ap-
> pearance and noble in stature. His eyes sparkled like stars and his
> hair was shining white. It cannot be doubted that such a vision came
> from God.

Gone is the image of the hoary ruler of the *Chanson de Roland*,
who tears his white beard and weeps bitterly at the burdens that history and divine providence have laid upon him. In its place is a *chevalier* among *chevaliers*, who matches their prowess blow for blow and

shares their knightly travails as an equal. The effect of this erasure of Charlemagne as a superannuated figure of authority is to integrate him more closely into the chivalric order of knights, among whom he figures as a *primus inter pares*.

In the *Pseudo-Turpin*, Charlemagne's virtues and behavior conform to aspects of the chivalric ideal that stressed royal largesse, the wise taking of counsel, and justice in the king's relations with his barons. The emperor is praised as "molt larges de granz donz doner et outroiers juigierres et biaus parliers et molt savoit bien doner un haut consoill" (very generous in giving great gifts and just judgments and graceful in speech, and he knew very well how to bestow high counsel).[114] He is, moreover, consistently depicted as aware of the need to attend to the dictates of noble counsel, without which he does not initiate action. Indeed, throughout the translation from the original Latin there occurs a pattern of interpolation regarding the privileged participation of the aristocracy in matters of government and war, a pointed response to the contemporary movement among Capetian kings to exclude the great barons from the royal *conseil*. Emperor and nobility move in concert, embracing a system of mutual respect, support, and adherence in which the tension between royal and baronial imperatives that gives to the *Chanson de Roland* so much of its narrative power is glossed over in the representation of a unified chivalric world, miraculously free of internal stress and division.

Only occasionally is the unspoken anxiety concerning the threat of aristocratic social debasement, against which the *Turpin*'s totalizing vision of chivalric harmony is projected, allowed to break through. When, for example, letters from the emperor of Constantinople arrive in France beseeching Charlemagne's aid in the recovery of the Holy Land, the king determines to undertake the journey to Jerusalem and sets about raising a host. All those capable of bearing arms—in principle, all knights, that is—are commanded to join the royal forces. But

> cil qui porroient armes porter et avec lui n'iroient, devroient .iiii. deniers de lor chief a toz jors mais, et il et lor ligniee, celle qui ert presente et a venir.[115]
>
> those who were able to bear arms and would not go with him owed four pennies a head henceforth, they and their line, both in the present and to come.

Those who refuse to accompany the king are threatened with debasement as serfs, for four pieces of money, usually four *deniers*, ordinarily constituted the *chevage*, the *capita propria* paid by serfs to their seigneurs, and these men were, as a consequence, often called *homines quatuor nummorum*.[116] Johannes's abbreviation of Pierre de Beauvais's account makes explicit this threat, stating, more simply, "qui n'i iroit, il seroit sers, et il et si oir, a toz jorz" (he who will not go shall be a serf, both he and his heirs forever).[117] Conversely, when Charlemagne receives word that Agolant awaits him at Pamplona to join battle, the emperor hastens to France to gather an army:

> Il manda et commenda par tote France que tuit cil qui serf erent de lor chars par les mauveses costumes des seignors, fussent franc permenablement, et il et lor ligniee, cele qui ert presente et a venir. Ensint le fist de toz cels qui en Espaigne avec lui iroient.[118]

> He directed and commanded throughout all France that those who were serfs in their persons on account of the evil customs of lords should be free in perpetuity, they and their line, both in the present and to come. Thus he commanded on behalf of all those who would go with him to Spain.

Not content to rely on traditional sources of military recruitment among barons and knights, Charles emancipates those enserfed "par les mauveses costumes des seignors," promising them and their posterity perpetual freedom if they participate in the expedition to Spain. Reaching further into the social pool, the king releases those languishing in prison, clothes the poor and the naked, and restores the disinherited to their honors.[119]

The *Turpin* thus displaces to a fictive past aristocratic anxiety over a world in social confusion, where nobles await enserfment and serfs can hope for emancipation and where the liberation of felons, the clothing of the poor, and the restoration of dispossessed heirs are represented as acts of equal value. The image of hierarchical disorder, dysfunctional mobility, and loss of intrinsic social value expresses, and in expressing contains, the nobility's underlying fear of social competition from non-aristocratic classes, both on and off the battlefield. Yet the threat of social disorder is characteristically resolved by a final image that betokens the restoration of a unitary chivalric world, in which those skilled in the use of arms, and even squires (noble by blood but, in the thirteenth century, financially incapable of pursuing a knightly vocation), are uniformly elevated to the order of chivalry and all tensions between the king and his followers dissolved:

> Les sages d'armes et les escuiers ordena de l'ordre de chevalerie et cels qu'il avoit deseritez de s'amor de tot en tot a s'amor converti. *Car autrement ne le doit fere rois qui bien velt tenir terre.*[120]

Those skilled in arms [i.e., knights] and squires he ordained into the order of chivalry, and those whom he had removed from his love he completely converted to his favor. For a king who wishes to possess lands should not behave otherwise.

The good king who wishes to rule well, Johannes stresses by interpolating the italic sentence into his Latin text, respects the precedence of the warrior classes and returns (in fictive principle) the financially disabled squires to their rightful place alongside their noble blood brothers.

Significantly, the preoccupation with money intrudes itself into the very heart of the plot of the *Pseudo-Turpin Chronicle,* transforming the contest over honor between Roland and Ganelon that had motivated the tragedy of the *Chanson de Roland* into a base pursuit of gold and silver on Ganelon's part. Ganelon's treason here is activated not out of a sense of rivalrous pride with Roland, but because Marsiles promises him twenty packhorses laden with gold and silver if he will deliver Charlemagne's host for killing:

Iluec fu decuez Ganes par la covoitise de l'or et de l'argent, dont maint home ont esté deceu et sont encore. [121]

Thus was Ganelon deceived by the desire for gold and silver, by which many men have been deceived and are still.

Not only is Ganelon deceived by his greed into betraying his sovereign and compatriots, but he is cast from the outset as a figure of deception: "il sembla bien prudome, mes li cuers se despareilla molt du semblant" (He seemed to be an honorable man, but his heart [i.e., intentions] belied his appearance). [122] He is the dissembler, who, on the face of it, presents the image of a fixed, known value but whose true worth, like money itself, is deceptive, changing, hence treacherous for the standards by which the chivalric world determines social value. [123]

Moreover, just as the emergence of an economy of monetary exchange penetrates and transforms the stable values of an older, agrarian society, so Ganelon's greed spreads and infects Charlemagne's host, exciting avarice, drunkenness, and fornication. In addition to his own gains, Ganelon returns from Marsiles's camp with thirty packhorses of gold and silver and forty horses of wine and a thousand Saracen girls with which to work his corruption upon the French host. [124] Ever sensitive to the formal hierarchies of this stratified social world, the anonymous author of the *Turpin I* reports that "the great barons of the host received the wine" (intoxication, seemingly, an appropriate moral equivalent for the self-deception of the socially superior), while "the *menues genz* took the women"[125]—those lower on the social scale thus indulging in physically lower, and baser, forms of self-degradation. Ganelon's pursuit of pecuniary advantage unleashes deceit, treachery, and sexual deviance. Those whom it entraps are destined to die at Roncevaux ("si pechierent as fames sarrazines et as crestienes qu'il avoit amenees de France; si en furent mort" [they sinned with the Saracen women and with the Christian women he had brought from France; thus they died]);[126] but they are not alone. For once let loose into the world, the desire for money threatens to engulf all other values, which become subject to its transactional modalities, so that nothing remains what it seems, all is negotiable and subject to loss, and the social currency of the aristocracy appears destined to be devalued, redeemable only through the ethical transcendence that defeat is able to effect.

The agent of that redemption in the *Pseudo-Turpin*, as in the *Chanson de Roland*, is Roland himself. Whereas Ganelon is presented as a figure of deception, Roland is the figure of truth: he is faithful where Ganelon is false, self-denying where Ganelon is greedy, honorable where Ganelon is treacherous. Ganelon exploits his semblance of truthfulness to beguile Charlemagne into returning to France, leaving behind the best of his host as the rearguard to be destroyed by the Saracens. Roland, in contrast, never lies. He is, as Charlemagne proclaims in the *planctus* delivered over Roland's dead body, a *langue qui ne sot onques mentir*,[127] a tongue (a clear synecdoche for language) incapable of lying, thus free of the deceptions and seductions of the false linguistic currency by means of which Ganelon transacts his treason. As a "truthful language," Roland recuperates for the chivalric epic the transcendent ethical values threatened by Ganelon's dissembling acts. At the same time, he is emblematic of the truth of the *Pseudo-Turpin* chronicle in relation to its literary antecedents, whose deforming "lies," as the prologues intone, had perverted literary meaning and destroyed historical authenticity. His authority underwrites the authority of the text. In his transparent veracity, Roland restores the transparency of historical discourse itself, and guarantees in his fidelity its faithful recounting of the past.

As guarantor of the truth of history, Roland embodies the whole range of values that the past enshrines, royal as well as aristocratic, clerical as well as lay. In addition to the standard chivalric virtues of prowess, honor, boldness, prudence, and justice, he exhibits specifically royal traits:

Desfendierres de Crestiens! Murs de clers! Baston d'orfelins! Escuz
de vueves dames! Viande et refections de povres et de riches, amours
de chevaliers! Li sires d'armes! Relevierres et essaucierres de Sainte
Eglyse![128]

Defender of Christians! Fortification of clerics! Bastion of orphans!
Shield of widows! Food and nourishment of the poor and rich, love of
knights! The lord of arms! Redeemer and savior of the Holy Church!

He engages the pagan Ferragut not only in single combat but also in
theological disputation, preaching the truth of the Christian faith to
him. Unlike his literary avatar in the *Chanson de Roland*, this Roland
is untouched by false pride or *démesure*, untrammeled by bonds of
family or female affection, prepared to die as a *beneoit martir* (holy
martyr)[129] for the Christian faith and to receive his apotheosis: "vi-
erges et chastes ies montez es cieus" (virginal and chaste he ascended
to the heavens).[130] He is the perfect knight as the new military orders
of the twelfth century imagined him: virginal, chaste, devout, dedicated to the eradication of pagan superstition and the spread of Christianity, who employs his fierce strength and courage in the service
of God.

This representation of Roland as a *somme* of chivalric and Christian
virtues is imbricated in the *Turpin's* larger project of moralizing and
spiritualizing the ethical aspirations and knightly codes of conduct that
had for so long defined the aristocracy's sense of itself and its role in
feudal society, but that now stand revealed as dysfunctional in a new
era of monarchical consolidation and authority. The displacement of
chivalric ideology to an ideal plane works to gloss over the contradictions between the goals of chivalric conduct and the realities of royal
power; at the same time, it dissimulates the aristocracy's powerless-
ness to master in life the realities that are slowly emptying out the
meaning of the very ideals that the *Pseudo-Turpin* chronicle so insistently invokes.

It remains true, however, that in the *Pseudo-Turpin* chronicle the
principal exemplary figure is Charlemagne, and the principal exemplary matter of history derives from his crusading exploits in Spain—
the *verité d'Espaigne*, as the translators call it. Already by the twelfth
century, Charlemagne had become a privileged theme for the laity,[131]
for whom he was both present moral exemplar and nostalgic talisman
of past greatness.

The exemplarist aims of the *Turpin* translations were, of course,
common to all forms of medieval historiography, whose didactic and

mediatory practices were rooted in a belief in the mimetic capacity of history to furnish models worthy of imitation. No less than other historical texts of the Middle Ages, the *Turpin* chronicles are permeated with a moral conception of history whose primary function is the encouragement of virtue and the disparagement of evil through an objective narration of examples drawn from the past. As Johannes put it:

> Si doit estre chiere tenue et volentiers oïe de toz hauz homes. Car por ce sunt les bones vertuz el siegle auques defaillies et li cuer des seignorages affebloié, que l'en n'ot mes si volentiers com en soloit les oevres des enciens, ne les estoires ou li bon fet sunt qui enseignent coment l'en se doit avoir en Deu et contenir el siegle honoreement.[132]

> This should be held dear and willingly listened to by all high men. Because for this [reason] the good virtues in our times have now failed and the hearts of lords become enfeebled, that one no longer listens so willingly as was customary to the works of the ancients nor to the histories in which appear the good deeds which teach how one should comport oneself with respect to God and how to live in the world honorably.

And the stated purpose of his translation was "por refreschir es cuers des genz les oevres et le non del bon roi" (to revive in the hearts of the people the works and the name of the good king).[133] The desire to create sharply drawn positive and negative *exempla* meant that medieval historical works exhibited many of the traits characteristic of orally composed work: characters are "heavy" (hence memorable) and agonistically toned (containing heroes and villains); events are episodic and concrete and close to the human life-world; and the narration is oriented toward action rather than analysis.[134]

It comes as no surprise, therefore, that the most consistent theme of the *Pseudo-Turpin* chronicle is the glorification of Charlemagne in the most exalted language that the translators could muster. In their work, monarchy serves as an emblem both of value and of power. Thus, the anonymous author of the *Chronique des rois de France* opens his version of the chronicle (a variant of *Turpin I*) with a song of praise to the emperor as the greatest prince ever to rule in France:

> De maint roi cretien qui ça an arriers ont esté sont eure a nostre tans prisié et loés et renomés par lor san et par lor valor et par lor proece qu'il eure an aus an lor tans et par lor vertu, bien doit donques estre bien prisiee la grans vertuz et la grans poissance a nostre fort roi Karlemaigne, la cui valors et la cui vertuz fu par desus touz les rois qui a son tans furent an terre ne qui ancor aient esté jusqu'a jor

d'ui, por ce si ne pout estre celee ne reposte sa grans vallance ne sa
redoutee poissance, et c'elle poïst non deüst ele pas estre, quar si
grant fu et si fiere sa force que tuit cil qui a lui marchisoient li
obeisoient, et cil d'estranges terres qui de son non et de sa fierté
oïrent parler le redoutoient a mervoilles. [135]

Many Christian kings who have been before are now in our time
praised and renowned for their blood and their valor and because of
the prowess which they exhibited in their time and for their virtue.
So, too, surely, should the great virtue and power of our strong king
Charlemagne be admired, whose valor and virtue were far greater
than that of all the kings who had been on earth until his time and
all who have existed since, down to our very day. For this reason his
great valiance and fearsome power should not be hidden; it neither
can nor should be, for so great and so fierce was his strength that all
those who marched with him obeyed him and those from foreign
lands who heard tell of his name and ferocity feared him marvelously.

The *Pseudo-Turpin* chronicle takes up the myth of the emperor and
enhances it with epideictic exaggeration and with a specific stress on
the emperor's role as an instrument of God by virtue of his crusading
efforts on behalf of the faith, directed by providence and sustained by
miracles. Charlemagne is not just the most powerful lord in the world,
but has been so created by God in order to promote His causes on
earth, as the apparition of St. Jacques to Charles declares:

"si com Deus t'a fet plus puissant de toz rois terriens, autressi
t'eslist il a delivrer mon sarqueu." [136]

"since God has made you more powerful than all other earthly
kings, so does he enlist you to deliver my tomb."

Whereas other kings of France before Charles conquered parts of
lands and converted many of their peoples, "cil Charles a son tans les
conquist toutes" (this Charles in his time conquered them all). [137] The
importance of crusading themes to the sponsors of the translations
doubtless explains the addition of Pierre de Beauvais's Old French *Descriptio* at the head of the account of Roncevaux in the Latin *Turpin;*
for as Pierre himself asserted, while many peoples knew of Charlemagne's exploits in Spain, few were acquainted with the voyage he
had made *outremer* to deliver the Holy Land, despite the fact, Pierre
emphasized, that "ce fu la voie dont France ot onques plus d'onor et
a encore si con vos orréz" (this was the journey from which France
had the greatest honor and has still, as you will hear). [138] Both Pierre's
Descriptio and the *Pseudo-Turpin* stress the crusading character of

Charlemagne's undertakings, muting the aspect of pilgrimage also present in the Latin texts.

Here again, the personal background of the patrons doubtless was a conditioning factor in the nature and popularity of the vernacular *Turpin*, for Flemish participation in the Crusades ran high,[139] and in a large number of manuscripts *Pseudo-Turpin* is bound together with material pertinent to crusading themes. Translated after the Third and Fourth Crusades, which had given the West its final military successes in the East, the *Turpin* chronicle offered the aristocracy an image of itself in its traditional role as warrior and thus vindicated its claim to possess a unique historical mission at the very moment when that sense of mission was being undermined at home.[140] Adventure and feats of arms in the Orient provided a lone, distant arena of glory for a class threatened with the loss of its functional definition in medieval society. But this attempt to validate the nobility's historic mission as *bellatores* and defenders of the Christian faith by means of historical fictions attributing comparable crusading exploits to Charlemagne only indicates how little there remained of the aristocracy's sense of its military importance to society.

Of far greater significance than the Crusade to the patrons of the translations was the *Pseudo-Turpin*'s utility as ancestral history. As Duby has shown, one indication of the coalescence of the aristocracy in this period is provided by the emergence of genealogical literature, which gave voice to a growing sense of dynasticism centered on the veneration of ancestors, itself a product of the rise of the agnatic family organizing itself into a *lignage*.[141] Genealogy was both cause and consequence of this development, for its appearance as a literary genre in the twelfth century helped to impose dynastic awareness on members of the lineage group. Genealogical literature exalted aristocratic families through the demonstration of their noble origins and the virtually genetic transmission of that nobility by blood and semen to succeeding generations.[142] At the same time, such genealogies carefully elaborated principles of social exclusion and thus served to draw ever more firmly the lines separating those with claims to nobility from all other manner of men. The appearance of genealogy as a literary genre, a phenomenon that in the county of Flanders can be traced to the end of the eleventh and beginning of the twelfth centuries, thus signals the aristocracy's consciousness of itself and its illustrious past. And it was this awareness of the ideological prestige to be garnered from the ancestral past that influenced the choice of *Pseudo-Turpin* as the initial subject matter of vernacular historiography.

Although most scholars who have studied the texts argue that the sponsors of vernacular history turned to *Turpin* because it offered them a vehicle through which they could give form to inchoate sentiments of patriotism, centered on the person of Philip Augustus as an *alter Karolus*, we have already seen how little this interpretation conforms to the social logic of the textual situation. Rather, I would argue that the sponsors saw in the *Turpin* chronicle the history of their own most glorious progenitor. The genealogical claims of the *Turpin* prologues act as "charters" of present social institutions,[143] grounding aristocratic ideology in a particularized memory of an ancestral past that underwrites the aristocracy's claims to greatness and autonomy.

According to Nicolas of Senlis, Count Baldwin had searched far and wide for a copy of *Turpin* because "si ama molt Karlemaine," from whom he claimed descent through Judith, a daughter of Charles the Bald, as did his sister Yolande.[144] Interestingly, the one patron of a *Pseudo-Turpin* translation not of Flemish origin, that is, Renaud of Dammartin, adjoined to his text a false genealogy of the counts of Boulogne and the counts of Flanders in which he pretended descent from Charles of Lorraine through Ermengarde.[145] To those Flemish lords who could not boast direct ties to Charlemagne, *Pseudo-Turpin* appealed, as Walpole has noted, as "the story of their own forebears, whose exploits they sought to emulate in the feudal and crusading life of their own day."[146] Virtually every prologue affirms the importance of knowledge of ancestral deeds to be learned by the recitation and reading of *Pseudo-Turpin*:

> Por che qu'il fust as vivans et as haus homes en mimoire et raconte que à venir estoient et i presissent garde et lor sovenist des anchiseurs.[147]

> So that it might be to the living and high men in memory and report what was to come, that they might be warned and remember their ancestors.

The translations of *Pseudo-Turpin* can, thus, be seen as a continuation of the dynastic impulse that in the preceding century had disseminated genealogical literature.

Here again, the epic toning of the *Pseudo-Turpin* is significant, for as Bakhtin has argued, "the formally constitutive feature of the epic as a genre is the transferral of a represented world into the past."[148] This representation of the present in the past, in the time of "founders" and "ancestors," creates a distant world of beginnings that, by its separation from the present, is distanced and preserved from the ravages of the contemporary world and thus provides a source of authority and privilege that is both "absolute," in Bakhtin's sense of a hierarchically valorized category, and immutable, therefore impervious to relativization. The appeal of such a protected and distanced image of the past for the Franco-Flemish aristocracy is obvious. Far from being proto-nationalist, the vernacular chronicle erects an ideology based on family origins and to that extent is ethnocentric in focus and, I would argue, anti-royalist—or, more precisely, anti-Capetian—in motive.

The ideal character of Charlemagne as presented through the legitimizing lens of the original ecclesiastical author of the Latin *Pseudo-Turpin* made him an apt figure for the aesthetic correction of the present on the basis of the past.[149] Like Arthur in courtly romance, Charlemagne is not so much a sovereign king as the symbol of an ideal ruler.[150] As such, he could be set forth as an antitype of the increasingly assertive French monarchy under Philip Augustus, an exemplar of royal power and value from which the French monarchy had hopelessly, and wrongfully, derogated.

Moreover, Flemish ties to Charlemagne and the Carolingians were much stronger than those of the royal family, which, despite repeated marriages with women who could claim Carolingian blood, had not yet framed its own claims to Carolingian descent. These were to emerge only in the thirteenth century with the appearance of the *reditus* doctrine, the notion that the throne of France had returned to the heirs of Charlemagne in the person of Louis VIII, Carolingian stirps through, significantly, his mother, Isabelle of Hainaut.[151] In this connection an interesting *exemplum* appears in a Franciscan collection of the latter part of the thirteenth century: Philip Augustus one day lamented that there were in his time no knights like Roland and Oliver; to this the well-known *jongleur* Hugh le Noir is reported to have replied: "True, Sire, but there isn't any longer a Charlemagne either."[152] Clearly, the Carolingian legend could cut both ways.

Viewed in this perspective, *Pseudo-Turpin* worked as a mediated criticism of Capetian kingship by a group of Flemish aristocrats acutely aware of the challenge to their own independence posed by the revival of royal power. Clearly intended as a performed text, *Pseudo-Turpin* functioned, in this sociopolitical setting, as a ritualistic confirmation of the shared values of an aristocracy in the throes of social change. At the same time, by making Charlemagne into an ideal-type and ancestor, it became the vehicle for a historiography of resistance, verbalizing hostility to the monarchy in the guise of a widely shared fantasy masquerading as historical fact concerning a glorious, collective past, which, by the genetic logic of historical consciousness then current, was potentially present in each succeeding generation of noble heirs. Such an interpretation of the vernacular *Turpin* connects it to the tradition of the French epic of revolt and, more generally, to Arthurian romance—in other words, to that body of vernacular literature created for and by the French aristocracy to explore and valorize its own ideological premises in opposition to the hegemonic aspirations of monarchy.[153] And it is this ideological context, I would argue, that provides the most plausible explanation for the adoption of prose as the language of history and that connects the formal demand for a new system of historical authority and authentication to the social and political crisis out of which vernacular prose historiography arose.

Scholars concerned with the beginning of prose history have identified the demand for a new form of historical discourse expressed in the *Turpin* prologues as one for greater factual accuracy and realism on the part of an increasingly sophisticated and literate public. According to William Sayers, for example, the chronicler's choice of prose over verse "seems a necessary complement to the passage from romance to reality, from literary ornamentation to factual communication."[154] Typically, such an advance in historical consciousness has been attributed to the expansion of aristocratic literacy, which in turn facilitated the replacement of public recitation—for which poetry was best suited—by individual, private reading. With the spread of aristocratic literacy, Bernard Guenée recently argued, historical prose could be reconciled with truth without losing the chance for public success.[155] Once this happened, verse yielded its natural place in chanted history to prose, whose advantages in terms of accuracy made it the preferred medium for the communication of historical truth set down in books intended to be read, rather than recited.

Although it is certainly possible that the ultimate consequence of the adoption of prose for writing history was greater realism and, perhaps, accuracy, such consequences are not necessarily identical to the motives that impelled chroniclers to utilize prose in the first instance. Apart from the problematic nature of *Turpin* itself as history (surely more apparent to us than to them), the procedures employed by the first translators run counter to the proposition that they were interested primarily in greater accuracy or facticity.

In the first place, all the translators replaced the indirect discourse of the Latin text with direct speech, in an obvious attempt to enliven the narrative in conformity with forms of discourse characteristic of epic and romance. At least one translator, the Anonymous of Béthune, inserted additional episodes taken from epic themes to relieve the plain recounting of historical "fact" found in his model;[156] and all of them reworked their received material to suit the literary tastes and expectations of audiences formed by the experience of vernacular literature. The most striking additions to the Latin *Turpin* are, in fact, those that show the influence of French heroic poetry, especially the *Chanson de Roland*.[157] Identifiable epic techniques such as the doubling of verbs, the use of oral interjections such as "oyez" (hear) and "voyez" (see) to invoke audience participation,[158] and the rendering of historical situations in vividly realized, dramatic form were part of the vernacular chroniclers' technical repertoire and were extensively used to recreate the past in ways similar to fictional narrative. By adapting epic technique and, in particular, epic's capacity for vivid realization, the *Turpin* chronicler invited the audience to visualize and to participate in the history he was recounting. In this respect, the *Pseudo-Turpin* translations have all the marks of works written for oral delivery and were clearly intended to be read aloud in public performance, rather than read silently in private. The very use of the vernacular for history almost necessarily meant that the translators drew upon the linguistic resources provided them initially by the language of epic and romance.

For all these reasons, the use of prose does not appear to me to indicate an attempt to achieve historical accuracy. Rather, I would argue, the substitution of prose for verse was the product of an ideological initiative on the part of the French aristocracy, whose dominance in French society was being contested by the rise of monarchical power during the very period that witnessed the birth of vernacular prose historiography. By appropriating the inherent authority of Latin texts and by adapting prose for the historicization of aristocratic literary language, vernacular prose history emerges as a literature of fact, integrating on a literary level the historical experience and expressive language proper to the aristocracy. No longer the expression of a shared, collective image of the community's social past, vernacular prose history becomes instead a partisan record intended to serve the interest of a particular social group and inscribes, in the very nature of its linguistic code, a partisan and ideologically motivated assertion of the aristocracy's place and prestige in medieval society.

That the backward-looking nature of the aristocracy's response to crisis served as the breeding ground of literary invention should not, perhaps, surprise us. Social loss and political decline are powerful agents of historical desire and fertile generators of the desire for history, all the more so when the sting of defeat is recent and palpable and the possibilities for more direct expressions of discontent and dissidence appear momentarily closed. Disempowered and unable to discuss overtly what was too painful and too political to be confronted directly, the Franco-Flemish aristocracy displaced to a mythic, epic past an idealized image of social order, represented in a novel historiographic discourse through which it sought to recuperate a sense of its own authority. As a language of transparent "truth," prose became both a literary means by which to signify the truth of the values that the past enshrined and a mediated language in which to assert the perduring validity of the aristocracy's once-potent political presence, potentially recoverable precisely because it was alleged to be historically "true." For northern French lords of the early thirteenth century, the Carolingian legend embodied in the *Pseudo-Turpin* chronicle supplied a medium for the propagation of a historiography of resistance to royal centralization and did so with the borrowed authority of an ecclesiastical Latin text set forth in the newly historicized language of vernacular prose. Social conservatism became the unwitting accomplice of literary progress, and from this unnatural alliance was born vernacular prose history.

The vernacular *Pseudo-Turpin*'s representation of a lost world of Carolingian glory achieved its specific meaning and authority within the social space in which it was articulated in the early thirteenth century, a meaning completely different from what it had possessed in the hands of its original clerical authors, and from what it would come to signify when finally incorporated into royal history. At the prompting of its Franco-Flemish patrons, *Pseudo-Turpin* inaugurated a profound transformation in the discursive behavior of the French aristocracy, in which the authoritative nature of prose history was harnessed to the ideological aspirations of a declining social class. This social function of prose continued to operate in subsequent phases of vernacular historical writing, as later texts reiterated and expanded on the *Turpin*'s insistence on the distinctive propriety of prose for the communication of historical truth.

Succeeding stages in the production of vernacular prose historiography, however, greatly enlarged the chronological scope and thematic content of the Old French chronicle, reaching far back beyond the legendary "matter of France" embodied in the Carolingian past. The next identifiable stage in the development of vernacular prose history emerges with the translations of classical histories of antiquity, which sought to attach chivalric ideology to the most ancient and prestigious past known to the Middle Ages. At the same time, complementing this expansion in the subject matter of history was a corresponding expansion in the patronage of vernacular historiography. This sponsorship was no longer confined to Franco-Flemish lords, although they continued to play a critical role in soliciting and supporting the composition and diffusion of prose vernacular texts. Just as the vernacular chronicle augmented its range and sense of historical filiation with the past, so also does it come to speak to the aristocracy as a whole, seeking to ground aristocratic ideology in a past of unquestionable authority, into which it attempted to inscribe the perduring values and codes of conduct that, it tacitly argued, possessed continuing relevance and viability in the thirteenth century. In turning to ancient history, vernacular chroniclers addressed a past acknowledged to possess special power and significance for the lay world of medieval France. In refiguring that past in the image of medieval society, they appropriated classical antiquity as the basis for a revised understanding of the nature of contemporary culture. Whether this effort to furnish aristocratic ideology with a new, antique pedigree that, in turn, could valorize the social roles and prerogatives of the nobility was inherently feasible remains to be seen. Let us now turn to a consideration of ancient historiography as it was elaborated in a series of translations of classical authors that appeared in northern France in the early thirteenth century.

3 Past Politics and the Politics of the Past

Ancient History I

The Historiography of Secular Culture

In the introduction to *Cligès*, written about 1176, Chrétien de Troyes offered to a prospective audience of French-speaking laity an *estoire* that he claimed to have discovered in an ancient book at the library of Monseigneur Saint Pierre de Beauvais, the truth of which was guaranteed by its venerable age and the high seriousness of its content.[1] For, he claimed,

> Par les livres que nos avons
> Les fez des anciiens savons
> Et del siecle qui fu jadis.
> (lines 27–29)

By means of the books that we have, we know the deeds of the ancients, and of the times that came before.

The necessity for such an undertaking, Chrétien lamented, stemmed from the fact that

> . . . des Grezois ne des Romains
> Ne dit an mes ne plus ne mains;
> D'aus est la parole remese
> Et estainte la vive brese.
> (lines 41–44)

No one any longer discusses the Greeks and Romans; talk of them has receded, and its glowing embers extinguished.

No longer discussed, the history of ancient Greece and Rome was wrapped in silence, and the glowing embers (*vive brese*) of glorious deeds and famous exploits that it enshrined extinguished. From

Chrétien's perspective, the cultural situation confronting romance authors and audiences in the last third of the twelfth century was the potential loss of the cultural legacy bequeathed to the medieval world by its classical predecessors, a rupture with the past that his verses at once mark and seek to repair. Chrétien's recuperation of ancient history was to be achieved not merely by breathing new life into the dying embers of medieval society's knowledge of Greek and Roman deeds, but, more important, by translating that knowledge into a language and literary form accessible to those untutored in Latin letters. For as is well known, it is precisely the notion of *translatio* that stands at the heart of Chrétien's cultural project. Embedded in the musty book of Saint Pierre de Beauvais was an *estoire* that Chrétien deemed to be of great pertinence to the social life and cultural horizons of the medieval French nobility:

> Ce nos ont nostre livre apris,
> Que Grece ot de chevalerie
> Le premier los et de clergie.
> Puis vint chevalerie a Rome
> Et de la clergie la some,
> Qui ore est an France venue.
> (lines 30–35)

This is what our book taught us: that Greece has the first renown of chivalry and of learning [*clergie*]. Then chivalry came to Rome, and with it the sum of learning, which now has arrived in France.

His "translation" of *les fez des anciiens*, thus, assumes as an enabling condition the existence of a historical process through which *chevalerie* and *clergie*—chivalry and learning—were themselves translated from Greece to Rome and came finally to rest in France, whence, he prays, the honor that has alighted there shall nevermore depart.[2]

One may be justifiably skeptical about the relative neglect of ancient *matière* against which Chrétien inveighs in the prologue to *Cligès*. He writes, after all, considerably later than the initial flourishing of the *romans d'antiquité*—begun as early as the 1130s with the first redaction of the *Roman d'Alexandre* by Alberic de Pisançon and continued in the 1150s and 1160s with the appearance of the *Roman d'Enéas* and the *Roman de Thèbes*—and he outlines a program whose didactic goals are not very different from those announced by Benoît de Sainte-Maure in the prologue to his nearly contemporary *Roman de Troie* (1172).[3] Indeed, by the end of the twelfth century, Marie de France complained that too many romance authors had devoted themselves to adaptations of Latin works and that, as a consequence, she had lost her appetite for the task:

> Pur ceo començai a penser
> D'aukune bone estoire faire
> E de Latin en romaunze traire
> Mais ne me fust guaires de pris
> Itant s'en sunt altre entremis![4]

> I had begun to think that I might make a good story of them, and translate from the Latin into French. But such a project would scarcely have benefited me, since it had already been done so much by others.

And it hardly needs saying that Chrétien's *Cligès* is not, in any case, an adaptation into French of a classical book discovered at Beauvais, but a wholly original work, which employs this fiction of authority as warrant for its own creative act of authorship.

Yet the terms of Chrétien's complaint are noteworthy. His "translation" into French of the *translatio* of *chevalerie* and *clergie* from Greece to Rome to France suggests that ancient history itself served as a *translatio* in the medieval rhetorician's sense of the word—that is, as a metaphor by which contemporary French society in the twelfth and thirteenth centuries sought to explore and to articulate historical dimensions and cultural components of its existence with which it had scarcely been concerned before. The literary passage from the Old French *chanson de geste*, involving the oral recitation of the Carolingian "matter of France," to courtly romance, inaugurated, significantly, with the *roman d'antiquité*, enormously enlarged the temporal, spatial, and cultural boundaries within which the imagination of French writers and audiences operated, supplying a much broader range of subjects, images, and traditions against which to interpret their own cultural performance.

Yet somewhat paradoxically, this newly enlarged domain of the past, receding back into classical antiquity, was relentlessly rewritten in the image of medieval chivalry. Simultaneously recovered and transfigured, ancient history provided a capacious field of metaphors through which medieval French society could project onto the screen of the past an image of itself in historical perspective, an image that functioned less, perhaps, as a measure of its accomplishments than as the bearer of its political and ethical anxieties and aspirations. When romance authors transferred to the distant shores of Troy, Greece, and Rome the feudal-chivalric world of the twelfth and thirteenth centuries, they effaced the temporal distance that separated their world from the classical past. At work in this rewriting of ancient history in shapes and hues borrowed from contemporary society was neither ignorance of classical antiquity nor bad faith toward the past, but an intellectual attitude that refused to acknowledge the past as either irretrievably lost or ethically irrelevant. By transforming ancient history into a metaphoric equivalent of French chivalric society, romance authors established an implicit, metaphorically effected connection to ancient civilization that enabled them to convert that past from a cultural legacy into a social patrimony. Ancient history was figured as a genuine forebear of the medieval world of *chevalerie* and *clergie*, which could now be seen as the last link in a cultural chain of transmission that stretched in unbroken succession, as Chrétien proclaimed, from Greece to Rome to France.[5]

The same forces within vernacular literature that helped to promote the generic shift from epic to romance, and with it the extension of the temporal boundaries and *matière* informing vernacular culture, also were at work in historiography. The generic evolution of vernacular historiography recapitulated in prose the generic development of romance verse forms. Just as the *roman d'antiquité* succeeded the *chanson de geste*, substituting for epic's treatment of the Carolingian "matter of France" a focus on the "matter of Rome" (to use Jean Bodel's famous formula), so also the translations of the "Carolingian" *Pseudo-Turpin Chronicle* were followed in the domain of Old French historiography by translations of ancient histories. Not surprisingly, these histories were subject to many of the same impulses as the *romans d'antiquité*, to which the histories owed an unacknowledged but primary debt of influence. The recasting into prose of the literary themes and historical concerns of the *romans d'antiquité* was accomplished within the framework of new translations of classical historians, into which the amorous and chivalric exploits originally created in courtly romance were inserted.

This *mise en prose* was impelled by the same distrust of verse and desire for "truth" that had inspired the first translations of the *Pseudo-Turpin Chronicle*. Yet the task facing the translators of ancient history was inherently different from that confronting translators of the Carolingian myth. If the Carolingian past of thirteenth-century France could, almost without question, be considered the "true" and legitimate prehistory of thirteenth-century French society—a past to which members of the French nobility were bound by ties of blood, geography, and a "national" tradition continually reaffirmed within oral performance—the same could not be said of classical history. The ancient past lay buried in Latin texts whose pagan authors described a world divided from the Middle Ages not only by time and space, but also by religion, political practice, social custom, moral outlook, and intellectual heritage. Ancient history lacked exactly that self-evident continuity with the present that endowed the deeds of Roland and Oliver, Charlemagne and Archbishop Turpin, with their power to move, and that gave to their commemoration in song and history an elegiac tone of collective mourning for a social world that had been, though was no longer, present, but which remained accessible through the collective memory that medieval Europe had preserved about its distant past. In contrast, the creation of a sense of continuity between the classical past and medieval present was an act of intellectual will, conscious, even contrived, and inevitably artificial. It required, as a basis for its success, the conversion of the "other" represented by the ancient world into a fictive "sameness," and the thoroughness with which the ancient "other" was converted into a medieval "identity" furnishes one index of the goals that motivated the patrons and authors of these translations.

It is within this context that the question of anachronism, which has so long plagued the study of the *romans d'antiquité* and the histories alike, must be judged. Although most scholars who lament the medieval penchant for anachronism acknowledge that it was accompanied by an awareness of the classical past as a distinct historical era,[6] they do not necessarily focus on that awareness of distance as itself a force in reshaping the past. For some literary historians, like Monfrin, the intrusion of anachronism is an inevitable by-product of the translation procedures employed by medieval authors, who accepted as the basis of their practice a widespread belief that all works destined to instruct were inherently perfectible: "du moment qu'on le transcrit et qu'on le traduit, on ne voit aucune raison pour ne pas le modifier au goût du jour ou l'améliorer en le complétant à l'aide de renseignements puisés à d'autres sources."[7] Since the translation of pagan authors, in particular, justified itself on didactic grounds as making available to lay audiences those kernels of *clergie* and wisdom preserved in the Latin past, the very didacticism of such works laid them open to the "perfectionist" impulses of the translators.

Other scholars believe that the anachronisms that abound in translations and adaptations of classical texts serve a simpler purpose of familiarizing an alien world, enhancing an author's ability to communicate with and be understood by a public ignorant of the realities of antiquity, and thus contributing to the work's overall intelligibility.[8] In this view, as Cormier points out, medieval anachronisms can be considered necessary mediators between past and present, translating foreign institutions and beliefs into terms readily grasped by contemporary readers. From a technical point of view, he insists, the necessity of communication within adaptation explains the widespread existence of anachronisms.[9]

The prevalence of "mimetic anachronisms"—of decor, costumes, customs, usages, institutions, even psychology—Frappier also suggests, helped to typify the ancient hero and to create an idealized world with exemplary value for the moral instruction of the laity.[10] The exaggerated character of these sorts of anachronism contributed to the rhetorical intensity of the romance author's depiction of antiquity and hence to its persuasive force as exemplarist history. Mimetic anachronisms superimposed upon the body of classical works, from this perspective, were the result not of historical "naïveté" but rather of a general, hyperbolic style that affected all didactic and exemplarist literature in the Middle Ages. For Frappier, what shocks the modern reader of medieval *romans d'antiquité* and ancient histories is not the presence of anachronism, but its global character, which engulfs moral and religious beliefs as easily as details of dress and fashions of fighting.[11] Behind it lies a moral and aesthetic conception of antiquity that seeks to garner from the past an aestheticized view of human conduct in which ancient, medieval, and Oriental practices meld together like figures at a masked ball, at once enriching the poetics of the romances and histories and endowing the past with a sense of dramatic renewal.[12]

As Frappier and others have demonstrated, this tendency to "typify" classical heroes within an idealized, almost dreamlike world of exotic adventure, extraordinary luxury, riches, beauty, and exemplary behavior both "actualized" the past and suppressed the historical distance between antiquity and the Middle Ages.[13] Although far more pronounced in the *romans d'antiquité* than in the thirteenth-century translations of ancient history, where temporal markers underlining the historical remove of antiquity are much more in evidence, in both genres the use of anachronism addressed the same underlying problem of how to effect a temporal connection with an absent and discontinuous past whose relationship to medieval society could not easily be assumed to exist. The re-creation of classical civilizations in the image of medieval society worked to relocate the past in the zone, as Gilson once called it, of the "eternal present," while at the same time historicizing the present by furnishing it with ancient ante-cedents.[14] In this bi-directional renovation, both past and present were elevated, as it were, into a kind of atemporal equivalence, which was the temporal corollary of the translators' use of ancient history as a metaphoric field.

It is worth noting briefly the implications of this use of ancient his-tory as a metaphoric field on which the self-projections of the medi-eval world were displayed, for it helps to explain many of the pecu-liarities both of the *romans d'antiquité* and of the prose histories that were their literary heirs in the thirteenth century. To begin with, it meant that there was relatively little interest in remaining faithful to either the letter or the spirit of the Latin texts being translated. To have transmitted classical authors without adaptation, revision, or the addition of invented episodes (a literary phenomenon that begins only in the fifteenth century) paradoxically would have generated the very sense of alienation from the past that the translators sought to overcome through its recovery. Even allowing for the varying linguis-tic properties of Latin and Old French, it can be assumed that a me-dieval author capable of translating a classical text was also capable of doing so *tout court*. No deficiencies of Old French required the level of adaptation and invention characteristic of the medieval approach to ancient history.[15] At issue here is not a question of simple additions made to a text in order to familiarize medieval audiences with alien classical practices, or even of the clothing of ancient actors in medieval garb to encourage identification with the past, but the wholesale re-creation of the past in the image of the medieval world. The refigu-ration of classical antiquity in the forms of contemporary chivalry can only be understood as a deliberate strategy, deliberately executed.

Thirteenth-century French adaptations of classical texts privilege an ideological reading of ancient history in which the past is seen less as a prefiguration of the present than as a material replica of the me-dieval world.[16] And as with all ideological readings, the goal was to naturalize, by historicizing, those aspects of the contemporary world sensed as problematic. In that sense, thirteenth-century ancient his-toriography in France operated very much in the fashion of "high" epic genres, in which, as Bakhtin has explained, "the important point is not that the past constitutes the content of the epic. The formally constitutive feature of the epic as a genre is rather the transferral of a represented world into the past, and the degree to which this world participates in the past." For Bakhtin, this process of representing the present in the past derives from mythological and artistic modes of thinking that consider the past to be the repository of society's valorized categories: "in the high genres, all authority and privilege, all lofty significance and grandeur abandoned the zone of familiar contact for the distanced plane. . . . It is in this orientation to history that the classicism of all high genres is expressed."[17] By locating present ideals in the past, the valorized categories of contemporary society are endowed with the authority and prestige of the past and at the same time protected from the ravages of contemporary reality because separated from the present. They are, in a sense, cut off from history and "saved," their value intact and immutable, no longer subject to historical forces that might reveal them as dysfunctional or problematic. Contemporary reality enters into the high genres in an already valorized state, suggesting that the ideological function of such historical inversion is to preserve and protect the *present*, to cut *it* off from the criticisms and challenges of the familiar, hence vulnerable, world of contemporary experience and, thus, to hedge it with an aura of the unquestionable.

Since this temporal manipulation had as its ideological goal the elimination of distinctions between socially significant aspects of ancient times and medieval society, it did not, needless to say, operate evenly across the whole spectrum of the ancient past, but was directed at facets that paralleled contemporary concerns and anxieties. This explains the extremely uneven application of anachronism to the body of Latin works translated into Old French, a procedure that allowed large segments of past time and behavior to be reproduced authentically according to the letter of the texts under scrutiny even as other parts were systematically deformed. It is, perhaps, this inconsistent play of anachronism in the medieval view of antiquity that has proven so confusing to scholars, since it accommodated the growth of a critical spirit in the translation of ancient works of history, which some scholars have pointed to,[18] yet at the same time recast the form and meaning of certain kinds of events within its own evaluative framework.

It is the deformed aspects of the past, then, that hold the greatest interest for us, since they point most clearly to the issues that medieval authors and audiences sensed as problematic. Far from representing annoying embellishments to otherwise "authentic" texts, the anachronisms that so profoundly mold the character and tone of thirteenth-century translations of classical histories provide our surest points of access to the motives and aims inspiring the translations.

What were, in the broadest sense, those goals? In what ways was ancient history relevant to the nobility's consciousness of itself in historical perspective, and to what extent did ancient historiography expand and redefine the French laity's awareness of its ideal attributes and sociopolitical roles? And why, in the first instance, did Frenchmen seek to extend their sense of historical filiation with the past back beyond their own legendary traditions connected with the "matter of France" and the "matter of Britain" to the pagan past of Troy, Thebes, Greece, and Rome? The answers to these questions are in part already present in the *romans d'antiquité* and in part discoverable only through close readings of the texts, such as will be offered later in this chapter. But a few preliminary points can be made by way of introduction.

The two principal concerns identified by Chrétien de Troyes in the prologue to *Cligès* continued to preoccupy producers and consumers of ancient history in the thirteenth century. The revival of *clergie* and *chevalerie* were, if anything, objectives addressed more directly in these works than in the earlier *romans*, which tended to refract a belief in the historical mission and intellectual attainments of ancient heroes through the lens of amatory exploits.[19] Indeed, the translators self-consciously stigmatize the courtly themes of the romances as "fables," which their own "true" histories eschew, a claim to authenticity of content enormously aided by the fact that the histories are said to be translations of genuine classical texts, free of the "fictions" against which prose historiography in general demarcates its generic identity and makes its bid for credibility.

A striking instance of the concern to liberate the vernacular prose chronicle from its evident dependence on prior romances, which at the same time seeks to promote a movement from authorial presence to textual objectification, can be traced in the manuscript tradition of the *Histoire ancienne jusqu'à César*.[20] This text, the earliest universal chronicle in Old French prose, was written at the behest of Roger IV, castellan of Lille, sometime between 1211 and 1230.[21] According to the verse prologue, the author planned to cover the history of the world from the creation down to the Norman Conquest and the peopling of Flanders. In fact, for reasons that remain unknown, the chronicle abruptly terminates with an account of Caesar's conquest of Gaul, after the defeat of the Belgae in 57 B.C. The work as a whole is divided into seven sections beginning with Genesis (I) and progressing through the history of Assyria and Greece (II), of Thebes (III) via a somewhat confused section that treats the history of the Minotaur, the Amazons, and Hercules (IV), and continues with an account of Troy (V) and Aeneas (VI), closing with the history of Rome (VII), which contains an oddly placed and extremely lengthy interpolation devoted primarily to the career of Alexander the Great.[22] Although the author shares the general aversion to romance characteristic of early vernacular chroniclers, it is striking that the best-realized portions of his history are those that cover the terrain of earlier romances—that is, the accounts of Thebes, Troy, Aeneas, and Alexander—works which he clearly knew and used, all the while fiercely maintaining his textual independence of such "fables" and his strict reliance on Latin sources whose truth was to be believed ("que de verité iert creüe").[23]

Forty-seven manuscripts exist today of the first recension of the *Histoire ancienne*, of which eight date from the thirteenth century.[24] Of these, two (and only two) preserve a series of twenty-one moralizations in which the anonymous clerical author engages in a personal appeal to his listeners to hearken to the moral lessons that his history proffers, lessons ranging from the necessity to do good, fear death, and avoid envy and greed, to the benefits of loyal servitors, humility, virtue, and the political advantages of *largece* as exemplified by Romulus.[25] The verse moralizations are scattered throughout the text in fairly regular intervals, but are notably absent from the sections that deal with Theban and Trojan history and that recount the deeds of Aeneas and Alexander—that is, from precisely those parts of the work most indebted to romance verse narrative. The absence of verse moralizations in these sections suggests a conscious strategy on the author's part to avoid contamination of his own verses by a too close association with the *matière* of the *romans d'antiquité*, whose mendacious treatment of history is routinely criticized.[26]

On four occasions, the moralizations are clearly marked in the text as establishing the author's personal voice, being introduced with well-rubricated titles announcing that "ci parole cil qui le livre fait," or "ci parole le maistres qui traite l'estorie."[27] Elsewhere, the author initiates his moral commentary with a direct address to his audience of *seignors et dames*, a live voice calling to a live and listening public, whose participation in the recitation of the great deeds of the past he hopes will bring them moral profit.

Later manuscripts of the *Histoire ancienne* progressively suppress both the verse moralizations and the interpellations to the audience. First to disappear is the extensive prologue in which the author had located his enterprise in a personal context of patron and purpose, doubtless deemed overly specific by later copyists operating in other milieux and for new patrons. Manuscripts such as the thirteenth-century B.N. fr. 9682 not only suppress the prologue, but also transcribe the verse moralizations in a prose format—without, however, bothering to rewrite the verse, so that they remain embedded in what appears, visually, to be a uniform prose text. The effect of this method of transcription is textually to efface authorial presence without actually silencing the author's voice, for when the passages are read aloud, that voice instantly reemerges in the octosyllabic couplets that still make up the moralizations. This masking of authorial presence is the first step in a steady process by which the verse portions of the *Histoire ancienne* are little by little abridged, prosed, or dropped altogether (as is the direct address to the audience)[28] in favor of a textually coherent prose narration that has lost all traces of the author's original moral preoccupations (see table, pp. 110–111). The burden of the moral lessons that ancient history conveys is, in the end, carried by an "objective" historical narration, unassisted by authorial commentary, which refuses engagement in a direct dialogue with its public.

By offering their public "faithful" translations of authoritative Latin histories free of the fictions and forms of versification that had characterized romances, French histories of antiquity vastly expanded the scope of the laity's knowledge of the past, satisfying a desire for learning that seems to have become increasingly important to the nobility's sense of self-worth in the High Middle Ages. One thinks, for example, of the extraordinary collection of books that, according to Lambert of Ardres, Baldwin II, count of Guines, had translated and read aloud to him (*ante se legere fecit*), works ranging from the scriptural and theological to the musical and scientific and even works *in fabellis ignobilium ioculatores*.[29] Jacques Le Goff, in fact, hypothesizes that one of the primary motives for the creation of the historical *roman* was the intellectual insecurity of the French nobility in the twelfth century, a sentiment of inferiority that recourse to an ancient history furnishing brilliant examples of chivalric heroes pursuing amorous adventure and military glory did much to assuage.[30]

Thirteenth-century vernacular histories of antiquity opened up a vast cultural legacy from which the laity had been barred by ignorance and linguistic incompetence. The translation of classical works hitherto available only in Latin liberated the nobility from its dependence on clerical preceptors while linking it to a pre-Christian past of extraordinary authority and prestige. The appropriation of *clergie* independently of the clergy created a novel potential for cultural competition with the clerical classes who had for so long monopolized learning in medieval society. In a more general sense, thirteenth-century histories of antiquity provided French audiences with a model of secular culture and source of moral wisdom, providing thereby the

Verse Moralizations Omitted, Retained, or Rendered in Prose in Thirteenth-
Bibliothèque Nationale, Paris, using B.N. fr. 20125 as the base MS.

Folio in B.N. fr. 20125	Text	B.N. fr. 9682	B.N. fr. 20126	B.N. fr. 1386
1–2v	Verse Prologue	omitted	omitted	omitted
10r	Beau Sire	omitted	omitted	
20v	Por ce doit	omitted	omitted	
14r–14v	Li parole	omitted	omitted	
21v	Les paroles	omitted	omitted	
24r–24v	les paroles	omitted	retained	
28v	Peches de Sodom	prose	omitted	
30v	He! Segnors	omitted	omitted	
41v	Que envie	omitted	omitted	
43r	Doivent mort	omitted	omitted	
62r	loiaus sergans	prose	omitted	
122v	Serve God	omitted	omitted	
180v	Romulus/Largesce	prose	retained	prose
212r–212v	Doute la mort	retained	omitted	prose
[2132v	humilier]	[retained]	[retained]	[retained]
[233r	meisme]	[retained]	[retained]	
252v	d. of Alixandre	omitted	omitted	
273v–74r	covoitise	retained	omitted	
283v–84r	Mort	omitted	retained	retained
288v–89r	coarts	prose	omitted	
304r–305r	covoitise de deniers	omitted	omitted	
Nos. Retained	21	8	5	4

[ ] = nonverse moralization
↓ = MS. incomplete, hence portion of text not included.

basis for a collective history of chivalry on which to construct a specifically historical identity. The conflation of classical past and contemporary chivalry argued for the historical antiquity of the aristocracy's political roles and codes of behavior and helped to valorize its
claim to an autonomy that was at once political and cultural.

It would be a mistake to underestimate the importance of time itself
to this cultural agenda, for it was precisely the antiquity of ancient
history that made it such a powerful symbol of authority in a society
accustomed to look to the past for legitimation.[31] The recuperation of
the classical past and its transfiguration into an image of medieval

and Fourteenth-Century Manuscripts of the *Histoire ancienne,*

B.N. fr. 3576	B.N. fr. 168	B.N. fr. 251	B.N. fr. 182	B.N. fr. 9685	B.N. fr. 821
omitted	omitted	omitted	↓	omitted	↓
omitted	omitted	↓		omitted	
omitted	omitted		↓	omitted	
omitted	omitted		omitted	omitted	
omitted	omitted		omitted	omitted	
omitted	omitted		omitted	omitted	
omitted	omitted		omitted	omitted	
omitted	omitted		omitted	omitted	
omitted	omitted		omitted	omitted	
omitted	omitted		omitted	omitted	
omitted	omitted		omitted	omitted	
omitted	omitted	↓	omitted	omitted	
omitted	omitted	omitted	omitted	omitted	↓
retained	retained	retained	prose	prose	omitted
omitted	omitted	omitted	omitted	omitted	
[retained]	[retained]	[retained]	[retained]		
[retained]	↓	[retained]	[retained]		
omitted		omitted	omitted		
omitted		retained	retained		
retained		retained	omitted		↓
omitted		omitted	omitted	↓	
omitted	↓	omitted	omitted		
4	2	5	4	1	0

chivalry invested chivalric ideals with universality,[32] transforming them into patterns of behavior continually expressed and re-expressed down through the ages. Ancient history became in the process not merely a source of moral wisdom and exemplary deeds, but a repository of precedents newly available to a class threatened in the exercise of its traditional functions and thus attacked at the very source of its prestige in medieval society. In turning to ancient history, the French aristocracy conformed to what John Pocock has taught us about the processes that stand at the origins of the study of the past in pre-modern societies. According to Pocock, the study of the past within a society, or within a particular segment of society, originates when a traditional relationship to the immediate past has broken down. The elements of society affected by the disturbance to traditional continuities respond by reshaping myth, historicizing or constructing a novel image of the past in terms of some new continuity.[33]

On this model, the thirteenth-century translations of ancient history, in converting antiquity into an image of feudal-chivalric society, represented an effort on the part of the French lay aristocracy to mask social change through the articulation of a newly created continuity between it and the lay society of classical antiquity. The result was a universalization of chivalric ideals and codes of behavior, now endowed, as Maurice Keen has remarked, with a "faultlessly antique and highly evocative pedigree."[34] And it is surely significant that this universalizing impulse increasingly made itself felt at a time when the Capetian monarchy was rapidly establishing itself in a space that could, eventually, be understood as "national."

The growth of royal power in the late twelfth and thirteenth centuries, most striking during the reign of Philip Augustus, necessarily entailed the gradual restriction of the territorial and jurisdictional scope of the nobility's spheres of activity. Would we be wrong to see in the nobility's attempt to connect itself to a universal past of unquestionable power and authority, effected through its attachment to the great deeds of antiquity, a response to the diminution of its political authority, martial roles, and territorial possessions enforced from above by the actions of a newly aggressive king? The temporal extension into the past of the aristocracy's codes of conduct compensated, so to speak, for its present-day constrictions in territory and power. By refiguring a classical "other" into a medieval "identity," vernacular historiography relegated a troubled present to a deproblematized past, a present/past protected from the incursions and vagaries of the contemporary world by its (re)location in a temporal zone of absolute value. To that extent, Le Goff's judgment concerning the *roman historique* of the twelfth century remains true for thirteenth-century ancient historiography in the vernacular as well: "The historical romance is nothing other than a psychodrama played out, under the trappings of history, by a social class struggling against its destiny."[35]

What perhaps differentiates these thirteenth-century works from their romance predecessors is their greater focus on the specifically martial and "chivalric" aspects of the classical past, in place of the highly eroticized adventures of the twelfth-century *romans d'antiquité*. Although the Old French histories include and even interpolate amorous tales, they deliberately downplay such romance elements—the love affairs between Achilles and Polixena and between Caesar and Cleopatra being notable exceptions—and relegate the erotic economy of the *roman* to a secondary place. This shift is in keeping with the worsening military and political environment for the thirteenth-century French aristocracy and its correspondingly greater need for social and political legitimation. To an aristocracy challenged in the exercise of its defining roles and powers, ancient history offered a realm of fantasy and escape, the continuation in daydreams of a glorious past and an expression of historical crisis.

The repetitive patterning of ancient history according to chivalric models takes on new meaning in the light of these social and political preoccupations. If an essential aim of the Old French histories of antiquity was to universalize the dominant features of contemporary aristocratic society that were threatened by the expansion of royal power, the rewriting of the past by the addition of epically styled battles and the attribution of chivalric codes of behavior and values to ancient actors can be seen as a powerful instrument for the realization of this aim.

The significance of these interpolated sequences stems from their function as synecdoches of the implicit intertextual corpus from which they derive and which, as part, they represent as a whole. As interpolated units they represent only a fragment of the world of the absolute past for which they stand. The absolute past, Bakhtin notes, "is closed and completed in the whole as well as in any of its parts. It is, therefore, possible to take any part and offer it as a whole."[36] Since one cannot embrace in a single epic the national past in its entirety, the part must stand for the whole, whose structure and meaning are repeated in each of its parts.

The interpolation of epic segments into the histories of antiquity thus summoned up the entire structure of epic discourse, which in turn implicitly served to reinterpret the whole of the narrative in reference to the inserted part. At the same time, it conjured up in the minds of the audience that vast repertoire of motifs and values embedded in romance literature, enabling translators to rewrite the ancient *auctores* so as to make the past conform to the lineaments of medieval chivalric culture. The widespread presence of this literary procedure in the Old French histories of antiquity, despite their differing concerns and styles, suggests that its prevalence was overdetermined, responding to more than one need. It therefore seems reasonable to inquire what other sorts of purposes the repeated epic patterning of the text might have served and to what extent its utility lay in the very fact of repetition itself.

Literary critics such as Northrop Frye have argued that the appearance of symmetry in any narrative means that historical content is being subordinated to mythical demands, and anthropologists have long noted the centrality of repetition to myth in all its contexts.[37] In archaic societies, human life is given over to the conscious repetition of received paradigmatic gestures—paradigmatic in that such gestures reflect not merely social order, but the supernatural order upon which men should seek to pattern their lives.[38] It is instructive to look at the ways in which narrative repetitions function within the histories as laicized, textualized versions of ritual, endowing secular culture with the same timeless quality usually associated with the divine. Although pretending to be narrative accounts of enacted deeds, the interpolated epic sequences are not so much mimetic as paradigmatic, despite their surface appearance of historicity. Indeed, it is precisely the repetitive nature of the deeds recounted that belies their veracity, betraying the mythic demands at work in the construction of the narrative. The return to the past, together with the seemingly obsessive character of the recurring epic motifs, reveals the insecurity of contemporaries and betokens the wish to recapture a historical experience that has been lost. Repetition on this level, as E. Jane Burns has tellingly argued in her analysis of the Vulgate cycle, can be equated with a desire for the missing term, for a past that can only be recuperated through textual reenactment.[39] And one function of textual reenactment is to stimulate desire for the missing term, to enlarge the demand for a mythic past that is, like all history, by definition absent.

What is inscribed by means of discursive recurrence, therefore, is not plenitude but lack: the loss of legitimate domains of aristocratic experience that discursive repetition attempts in vain to revive in words. The endlessly repeating cycle of chivalric deeds and amatory exploits assigned to historical characters manifestly incapable of having performed them discloses an underlying anxiety about the brokenness of contemporary experience brought about by adverse historical change, which the search for historical continuity and identity endeavors to repair. Ironically, the discontinuous character of aristocratic experience is textually embodied in the narrative ruptures to which the Latin sources are subjected by the interpolation of epic sequences and romance themes. The very procedure employed by the thirteenth-century translator in his desire to impart pattern and continuity to the representation of the past, thus, wreaks upon the Latin source a narrative analogue of the historical process for which the texts were intended to serve as antidotes.

The centrality of the cultural component of this agenda should not be missed. Nor should it be seen in isolation, as somehow unrelated to the political program for which the newly reinterpreted history of antiquity was a vehicle. In a sense, the issue of political autonomy was merely displaced to culture. The acquisition of cultural autonomy at a moment of political loss indicates the extent to which political and cultural aspirations operated, Janus-like, as interrelated phenomena. The translation of ancient texts into vernacular prose for consumption by the lay aristocracy of France served to redefine that class's status with respect to the whole cultural patrimony of antiquity and signaled a revived relationship between history and writing that, as Vance has pointed out, had been essentially Roman and classical.[40] In appropriating the cultural legacy of antiquity as its own, the French aristocracy laid claim to the prestige and durability of a written, historical culture into which a historical mythology of chivalry had been introduced and which, thus, by association, assumed a commensurate degree of authority and permanence.

The fact that, in its now mythologized origins, chivalry could be located in a pre-Christian past raised the prestige of a secular world that had long labored under a sense of cultural inferiority with respect both to the clergy, who acted as the guardians of culture in medieval society, and to kings, who had succeeded in elevating themselves into the representatives of God on earth. Whether cultural in the narrow sense or political, the autonomy that ancient history could confer on the medieval French aristocracy helped to heighten its aura of legitimacy and to strengthen its resolve to compete in cultural arenas formerly closed off. In both aspects, the connection to a distinct and distant past reinforced aristocratic ideology: politically, by liberating chivalric forms and functions from their strict dependence on royal grants, since chivalry could be said to antedate the rise of kingship in France; culturally, by legitimating through the assertion of its antiquity a lay vernacular culture increasingly besieged by clerical critics for its moral transgressions and literary mendacity.

It is hardly surprising, then, that the tie sought with the Greek and Roman past in these adaptations of ancient history went well beyond the imitation and assimilation of the legacy of classical learning. In effect, Old French translations attempted to create a genealogical attachment to Troy, Thebes, Greece, and Rome as proof of the historical basis for its claims to autonomy. Thus Roger IV, castellan of Lille, in commissioning the *Histoire ancienne jusqu'à César,* conceived of the classical past as a vast prologue to the history of Flanders. The work was to offer a historical account running from the creation of the world to the peopling of Flanders ("des quels gens Flandres fu puplée / vos iert l'estoire bien contee")[41] and expressly indicates that the histories of Thebes, Troy, and Rome are to be understood as the prehistory of Flanders. The author is, in general, scrupulously attentive to royal genealogies within the text and to the chronological concordances that, in his eyes, they authorize.[42] Throughout the text, elaborate genealogical interpolations trace the patterns of descent binding the peoples and cities of Flanders to classical founders.

The author of the *Faits des Romains* is similarly concerned to demonstrate the ties that link the various inhabitants and cities of France to ancient forebears, whose Roman names are consistently replaced by thirteenth-century French designations. All the translations, in fact, routinely practice this substitution of medieval French names for Roman equivalents (or nonequivalents, in many cases), the effect of which is nominally to fuse medieval and classical identities. The impression created by this fusion of ancient and medieval *nomina* is to suggest the active presence of French peoples and places in the distant classical past, an impression strengthened by the invention of erroneous etymologies for medieval place-names that purposely create false genealogical ties between medieval and ancient sites and populations.

In this way, ancient history comes to function not merely as a prologue to the history of French chivalry, but as the very ground of a genealogically inherited system of status, prerogatives, values, and functions, the right to which, as a historically transmitted legacy, could not be denied. In contrast to the *romans d'antiquité* that circulated in the Angevin realm,[43] in these texts it is not so much empire as lineage that forms the keystone of a system of values, rights, and codes of behavior. The aristocracy's assertion of historical affiliation with ancient civilization, thus, is corroborated by the creation of a genealogical filiation between past and present, the aim of which was to proclaim the imprescriptible nature of aristocratic claims. Antiquity as the ancestral ground of the medieval French nobility is integrated into a historical vision in which the most important persons and events of the ancient world acquire paradigmatic force for contemporary life. The recuperation of the ancient past becomes, thereby, a process of self-definition. The great *gestes* of the ancient world become the thematic nodes around which a discussion of the most troubling aspects of medieval noble life are organized. As we shall see, these themes—of chivalry, love, desire, liberty, morality, counsel, and money—are present with varying emphases in all the texts that make up the corpus of ancient historiography in the thirteenth century. Both singly and as a group, these texts disclose the political and cultural forces at work in the literary strategies adopted on behalf of an aristocracy in search of a historical mission and the moral wisdom with which to carry it out.

That ancient history was addressed principally to the concerns of the aristocracy is made clear not only by the social status of the patrons who commissioned the translations, but also by the class-specific character of its intended audience, one clearly marked in the texts. The prologues open with exhortations to their audience to attend to the moral lessons that the past proffers, assuming that audience to be made up, as Jean de Thuin specified in the initial lines of his *Hystore de Jules César*, of those "ki tiere ont a garder et a gouvrener" (who have lands to protect and to govern).[44] All the texts stress that they will deal with material useful to the conduct of noble life and will trace the actions and affiliations of the great lineages of the past. *Bonté* (virtue), *loiauté* (loyalty), *droiture* (righteousness), *noblece* (nobility), *hautesce* (loftiness), and *parages* (lineage) are all topics present in the ancient past that, the translator of the *Histoire ancienne* declares, had never before been treated in Old French ("C'onques fust an nos lengue traite"). In his work, they will be set forth for the benefit of those who care to learn—a timely lesson, the anonymous author believes, for "li siecles chascun ior enpire" (the times daily worsen).[45] Like the translators of the *Pseudo-Turpin Chronicle*, these writers begin their works with an evocation of secular decline, which their histories both address and seek to redress by furnishing accounts of past glory.

According to the prologue of the *Faits des Romains*, the special utility of ancient (in this case, Roman) history for men of *haut lignage* derives from the extraordinary power amassed by the Romans, who "par lor sens et par lor force et par lor proesce conquistrent meinte terre" (by their wisdom and by their strength and prowess conquered many lands). The Roman achievement of world domination endows Roman history with its exemplary status, for "en lor fez puet on trover assez connoissance de bien fere et de mal eschiver" (in their deeds one can find much to learn about doing good and avoiding evil).[46] This suggests that the cultivation of classical history among the French aristocracy of the thirteenth century is intimately tied to issues of political power and authority. Whether as a guide to *gestes* or as a compensation for the loss of martial and political potency, "wisdom" cannot be divorced from "chivalry," from the attempt to use cultural competition as a displaced arena for political competition.

The intertwined nature of culture and politics, morality and authority, virtue and power, is powerfully articulated by Jean de Thuin, who fears the effect of evil speakers, calumners and low-born (*vilain*) counselors, whose tongues poison the atmosphere of reason that should guide the exercise of power. Against them, Jean proclaims, present rulers must learn from the classical past "biel parler sans fol gas et sans mesdire d'autrui" (fine speech without foolish prattle and without speaking ill of others).[47] Correct speech becomes the ethical counterpart of a corrected social order.

The medieval belief in the ethical dimensions of language, understood as a discursive order both expressing and fostering social order, helps to explain the attraction that ancient history held for thirteenth-century vernacular chroniclers. Insofar as ancient history presented a model of lay society founded on correct linguistic usage, it held up a corrective mirror to the threat of social decline and hierarchical confusion so insistently invoked in the prologues to vernacular histories. And because, in medieval thought, speech and behavior, virtue and power, culture and politics, are never far removed from one another, the presentation of an appropriate linguistic model of lay society is equally a program of social renovation, a vehicle of political legitimation, and a template of cultural attainment. Vernacular translations of ancient history constantly move among the strands of a broad range of goals that are at once political, moral, and sociocultural. Literary language preempts more violent modes of social reform,[48] a strategy well adapted to the needs of a class that was slowly losing its ability to impose its authority in less mediated forms. Although the prologues to the texts stress the mimetic and hortatory functions of classical historiography in recounting the great deeds of the past, the logic of the procedures employed in the literary reconfiguration of the past in the image of medieval society suggests that the primary aims of Old French histories of antiquity are not mimetic. Rather, they displace to linguistic mediation the conflict between king and nobility that constitutes the underlying problematic of vernacular historiography in this period. Nowhere is this process so clearly at work as in the *Faits des Romains*, which is also the first work produced by vernacular translators of ancient history in the thirteenth century.

The Faits des Romains

The *Faits des Romains* is not merely the earliest but arguably the most influential work of ancient historiography to appear during the first phase of vernacular translations of classical texts. One character-istic to be noted at the outset is the novelty of its treatment of Roman history and of Caesar, which departed sharply from the topics hitherto addressed in the *romans d'antiquité*. In France, the first *romans d'an-tiquité* take their themes from Greek or Trojan history. The *Roman d'Alexandre*, the *Roman de Thèbes*, the *Roman de Troie*, and even less well known works like the *Roman d'Apollonius de Tyr* and the *Ro-man d'Hector et Hercule* are all set in the Greek or Trojan world. Even the *Roman d'Enéas*, the one exception to this rule, might be consid-ered a continuation of the Trojan legend, as Aeneas and his Trojan remnant make their way through the world after the destruction of Troy.

Moreover, Caesar's appearance as a subject of Old French narrative clearly coincides in France with the emergence of prose historical nar-ratives, in contrast to developments in Italy, where the use of Caesar as a literary subject preceded the legends of Alexander, Troy, and Thebes in verse compositions.[49] The vernacular chronicle's novel fo-cus on Caesar suggests that early-thirteenth-century writers turned to this period of ancient history with a specific political purpose, moti-vated by the historical developments outlined in chapter 1. Comple-menting a generalized desire to resuscitate *clergie* and *chevalerie* in the light of a new Roman historiography that stood for the idea of a resurgent and educated French aristocracy was a more specific political desire to recover precisely those phases of Roman history that could serve as analytical models for the confrontation between a centralized and a decentralized view of political authority. At issue in a Roman past centered on Caesar was the confrontation between late Republi-canism and Caesarism, a confrontation that Philip Augustus was seen to have modeled by his very name: Augustus. In medieval France, the opposition between senatorial rule and imperial authority could be understood only in terms of a confrontation between the feudal aris-tocracy and centralized kingship. But precisely for this reason, the sit-uation of France in the thirteenth century, if not an exact match, nonetheless resonated powerfully with this critical juncture of Roman history.

Looked at from this perspective, the choice of Caesar's rise to power and his threat to the Republican ideals of senatorial authority as a pri-mary subject for the vernacular historiography of antiquity was hardly accidental. As would occur in later European historiography for similar reasons, the story of Caesar's destruction of the Roman Re-public and the advent of imperial rule functioned as an analogue for contemporary history. Thus, it is perfectly clear that Caesar functions in the *Faits des Romains* as an analogue for Philip Augustus—but not, as Jeanette M. A. Beer proposes, in order to legitimize Capetian territorial ambitions by presenting Julius Caesar's program of territorial expansion as a historical precedent for a French monarchy claiming to be heir to the Roman *imperium*.[50] Rather, Caesar is a pejorative analogue of the French king, who, like his Roman predecessor, weakened advisement and made the monarchy less a consultative and more an absolutist form of rulership, thereby moving it closer to the imperial model furnished by Caesar.

To be sure, Caesar himself never attained imperial status, having been cut down by Brutus before he could bring to a successful conclusion his seizure of the Roman polity. But by the Middle Ages, Julius as Roman general and military leader and Caesar as emperor are collapsed into a single imperial image. In the thirteenth century, "Caesar" means emperor, a fact that renders intelligible the author's use of Suetonius as an overall frame for the *Faits des Romains*. In Suetonius's *Vitae*, medieval readers found a negative representation of Caesarism, seen as an overall phenomenon (despite Suetonius's relatively benign treatment of Julius) leading inexorably to Nero and Tiberius. The translation of Lucan in the second half of the *Faits des Romains* merely strengthens this interpretive tendency, since in Lucan there appears an absolute fusion between Caesar and Nero. This collapsing of Caesar and the pejorative imperial tradition that was his long-term legacy to the Roman world thus adds another level of anachronism to the *Faits des Romains*, one already embedded in the historical sources selected for presentation.

The *Faits des Romains* survives in some fifty-nine manuscripts, of which eleven date from the thirteenth century, eighteen from the fourteenth, and thirty from the fifteenth—compelling testimony to the popularity that it achieved and sustained throughout the High Middle Ages, for which it served as a basic manual of lay culture. Although the author announced at the beginning of the book that he intended to trace a vast tableau of Roman history from the time of Julius Caesar to the reign of Domitian, with Suetonius's *Lives of the Caesars* as his obvious model, he did not realize this design. Instead of the planned history of the twelve emperors, he offers only that of Julius Caesar, terminating the work with the death of the Republican conspirators against Caesar—that is, in the last chapter of Suetonius's *Vita*. The work was originally called *Li fet des Romains, compilé ensemble de Salluste, et de Suetoine et de Lucan*,[51] but later copyists, finding this title both unduly long and inadequately descriptive of the material treated, changed it in subsequent manuscripts to *Le livre de Julius César, Comment Julius César regna et conquist plusieurs terres, Le granz afaires dou livre de Juille César, La vraie histoire de Julius César,* and the like, *tituli* that better reflected the scope of the work.[52]

The identity of the author of the *Faits des Romains* remains unknown, for none of the extant manuscripts bears his name, nor does internal evidence allow for speculation. As Flutre indicates, he was assuredly a cleric, who knew the rules of rhetoric and who reveals throughout his history the influence of the schools, not least in his utilization of scholastic glosses (*scholies*) on Lucan.[53] But whether this means, as Guenée has suggested, that he was aiming primarily at a clerical audience is, perhaps, a different question. Focusing on the learned character of the sources consulted by the anonymous author, Guenée concluded that the *Faits des Romains* was "l'oeuvre savante d'un clerc nourri de la culture historique qu'offraient les écoles en général et celle d'Orléans en particulier, dont ni le sujet ni la conception n'étaient particulièrement propres à séduire, en 1214, des laïques."[54] The basis for Guenée's opinion is the immediate use made of the *Faits des Romains* by subsequent authors, such as Jean de Thuin in his *Hystore de Jules César,* a work Guenée also characterizes as learned in inspiration and execution, dependent on Jean's access to rare texts and glosses such as those from the school of Orléans, to which he refers several times and which would have been available to him in Paris. The same argument applies to Brunetto Latini, who was living and teaching in Paris after his exile from Florence at the time that he composed his *Trésor,* in which several passages borrowed from the *Faits des Romains* are present. On these grounds, Guenée asserts that for the first fifty years of its existence, the *Faits des Romains* "restent essentiellement ce qu'ils étaient d'abord, une oeuvre universitaire."[55] Only in the second half of the thirteenth century, he claims, did the *Faits des Romains* achieve a wider audience, primarily (although not exclusively) among the nobility of northern France and, in particular, Flanders, where its employment by Baudouin d'Avesnes for the composition of his *Chronique* created a secondary center of diffusion.

The pattern of manuscript diffusion on which Guenée's thesis rests is beyond question. Even so, it is reasonable to ask why a cleric, writing for a university audience, should have laboriously rewritten this material not only in French (which clerics could have enjoyed as easily as the laity), but in the epic and courtly styles to which, in principle, a clerical, university audience would have been hostile. Why systematically deform learned texts for a learned audience in ways inimical to their tastes and interests? Moreover, if copies of the *Faits des Romains* did not proliferate in the north of France until the middle of the century, perhaps the reason lies in the virtually simultaneous appearance of the *Histoire ancienne* (ca. 1220), a work identifying itself as the product of aristocratic patronage, which may in part have satisfied the aristocracy's demand for ancient history. Judging from the literary styles employed by the anonymous author, his obvious familiarity with *chansons de geste* and Old French *romans*, his persistent refiguration of the classical past in the image of medieval chivalric society, and his avowed desire to instruct the laity in the exercise of authority, there seems little reason to reject the notion that at least one important audience that he envisaged was the nobility of northern France, among whom, in fact, the *Faits des Romains* had a substantial success.

If the authorship of the *Faits des Romains* remains elusive, the date of its composition is relatively easy to determine from a scattering of interpolated remarks. The work must have been written after 1211, since it mentions as still standing a Roman amphitheater, *les arènes*, whose construction the author mistakenly attributes to Chilperic. The amphitheater was situated on the Left Bank of Paris between the abbeys of Sainte-Geneviève and Saint-Victor and lay in the path of the city walls with which Philip Augustus was encircling Paris in the early years of the thirteenth century: "de ce theaitre duroit encore une partie en estant au jor que li rois Phelipes conmença Paris a ceindre de mur par devers Petit Pont" (of this amphitheater there still remained a part standing in the days when King Philip began to encircle Paris with walls [in the section] around the Petit Pont).[56] According to Guillaume le Breton, this part of the construction of the left-bank *enceinte* was begun in 1211.[57]

It also seems likely that the *Faits* was completed before July 1214, the date of the battle of Bouvines, at which a coalition of Anglo-Norman, Flemish, and German forces was defeated by Philip Augustus. This conclusion emerges from an allusion that the author makes, in the midst of describing the horrors visited upon Rome by the wars between Marius and Sulla, to a *planned* invasion of France by English and Norman forces, aided by the excommunicated emperor, Otto IV— a plan he derides as misguided:

> Totes eures que il me membre de ceste chose, je tieng por fox et Anglois et Normanz, qui ont fole esperance et quident que Octes li escomeniez, que Diex et seinte Eglise ont degité, doie France envaïr par itel gent.[58]

Whenever I am reminded of this matter, I hold as foolish both the
English and the Normans, who have vain hopes and believe that
Otto, the excommunicated, whom God and Holy Church have set
aside, could invade France with such people.

Otto was excommunicated by Innocent III in June of 1210 and joined
the coalition in mid-1213. Since the reference to the invasion occurs
toward the middle of the work, it seems reasonable to fix the composition of the *Faits des Romains* in the years 1213 and 1214,[59] which
makes the *Faits des Romains* the oldest extant vernacular translation
of ancient authors.

The author not only is well informed about the rumors of war preceding the battle of Bouvines, but also claims to have seen King Philip
Augustus. Reporting from Suetonius that Sulla had once warned the
Senate to beware of the young Caesar, "that boy with the loose
clothes" (literally, "badly belted": *le valet mau ceint*), he draws a
comparison to Philip Augustus as *mau pingnié* when he was young,
and demonstrates his awareness that the king was illiterate as well as
disheveled:

> Quant ge lis de Juilles Cesar que Luces Silla l'apeloit le valet mau
> ceint, si me membre de monseignor Phelipe le roi de France, que l'en
> pooit bien apeler le valet mau pingnié quant il estoit joenes, car il
> estoit torjors hericiez. Ne il n'a pas mains de sens en lui que il ot en
> Juilles Cesar, fors seulement de letres, ne n'a pas meins eü affere que
> Juilles ot; et encontre ce que Juilles fu letrez, est li rois sanz malice,
> car la letreüre aguisa Juilles a meint malice.[60]
>
> When I read that Lucius Sulla called Julius Caesar "the boy badly
> belted," I am reminded of my lord Philip the king of France, whom
> one might well have called "the boy ill combed" when he was
> young, because he was always disheveled. Nor did he possess less
> sense in him than there was in Julius Caesar, with the exception of
> [learning in] letters, nor did he accomplish less than Julius; and in
> contrast to Julius, who was literate, the king was without malice, for
> literacy goaded Julius to a great deal of malice.

Although Beer argues from the presence of this comparison in the
Faits that the anonymous author must have been a royal partisan, the
passage itself indicates only that at one time in his life he had seen
the ill-combed king and that he excused royal illiteracy on the (somewhat strained) grounds that literary attainments had made Caesar vicious. He equally reveals a knowledge of Parisian topography, especially the Left Bank, and displays a rather precise understanding of the
ecclesiastical divisions of France, as well as of the countryside of the

Île-de-France.[61] All these indications firmly locate the author in Paris and its environs, although they tell us little else.

In compiling his history, the anonymous translator employed the main Latin sources of ancient history popular in the West, to which he added a series of medieval works on which he drew for amplifications, explanations, and incidental material. The *Faits des Romains* is made up of successive translations of Suetonius's *Life of Caesar;* Sallust's *Catiline Conspiracy;* Caesar's *Commentaries on the War of the Gauls,* with the continuation by Hirtius; and Lucan's *Bellum civile,* or, as it was more familiarly known, *Pharsalia.*

Rather than simply following Suetonius's *Life,* however, the compiler uses Suetonius as a frame for the insertion of the principal texts to be translated. The prologue is loosely based on the first chapter of Sallust, to which the author adds his own reflections on the nature of Roman history and the lessons to be learned from it. It is followed by a chapter on Roman magistracies taken from Book 9 of Isidore of Seville's *Etymologies.* Clearly, the anonymous author feared that his audience would not be sufficiently acquainted with the Roman political system to follow the maneuverings of Caesar's political career. Only then does he begin a "life" of Caesar, using Suetonius to recount Caesar's birth and early youth, and the beginning of his military and official career through the Roman *cursus honorum* of questor, aedile, pontifex, and praetor.

Since Caesar was praetor during the Catiline conspiracy, the author inserts a complete translation of Sallust's *Catilina* before returning to Suetonius's account of Caesar's election as consul and his subsequent alliance with Pompey. After a series of digressive episodes that treat Pompey's military exploits against the Jews and the formation of the Triumvirate by Caesar, Pompey, and Crassus, he returns to his main theme and takes up the story of Caesar's conquest of Gaul, based on Caesar's *Gallic Wars*—although he fails to recognize the work as Caesar's own and attributes it instead to "Celsus."

In this first section, once the anonymous compiler begins his translation of the *Gallic Wars,* he remains for the most part faithful to the original text in its narrative development. Although there are numerous additions, moral comments, fictive elaborations of battles, glosses on place-names, and changes in the names of the Gallic peoples against whom Caesar wages war, only one major interpolation interrupts Caesar's account. A long and curious episode is intercalated between chapters 29 and 30 of Book 8, in which the author narrates a presumed combat between Caesar and the Gallic leader Drappés

Brenno, during which Caesar was captured but subsequently escaped with the aid of another Gallic chieftain. The singularity of this episode in light of the relative rarity of changes to the Latin account in this part of the *Faits des Romains* gives it an importance out of proportion to its relatively short length.

Once Gaul is subdued, Caesar returns to Rome to claim a triumph, but this is denied him because of Pompey's jealous machinations. For the author of the *Faits des Romains*, the Senate's refusal to grant Caesar the right to celebrate a triumph for his conquest of Gaul provides the *casus belli*—the "achoisons de la bataille"—between Caesar and Pompey. The political struggle over Caesar's triumph, the account of which derives variously from Suetonius, Lucan, and some remarks of the author's own, concludes part one of the *Faits des Romains* and serves as a bridge to the next major section, which is the account of the civil war between Caesar and Pompey.

Part two, which the majority of manuscripts entitle "Le livre de Lucan," inaugurates the author's use of the *Pharsalia*, although the initial chapters describing Caesar's crossing of the Rubicon come from Suetonius, mixed with passages from Lucan. The account of the civil war begins with Lucan's Book 3, where Lucan enumerates the peoples who sided with Pompey. At this point the translator introduces an account of the voyage to Paradise made by two lieutenants of Alexander, the *Alexandri Magni iter ad Paradisium*. The *Iter* was a narrative of Hebrew origin, known in the West by a Latin work that seems to have been redacted in the first half of the twelfth century and that appears in certain versions of the *Roman d'Alexandre*.[62] This anonymous translator's treatment of the material, however, differs from any of the standard sources.

After this, Lucan's account is followed through to its end with the deaths of Pompey and Cato and the war of Alexandria. Since Lucan's poem remained unfinished, however, the concluding sections of the translator's account of the civil war are based, though loosely, on the continuations of Caesar's *Commentaries*, the *Bellum Alexandrinum*, *Bellum Africae*, and *Bellum Hispaniense*. Into the account of Caesar's expedition to Alexandria the author interpolates a veritable romance between Caesar and Cleopatra and rewrites the history of Cleopatra, who is besieged by Achilles in the tower of the Phare. The eunuch Ganymede is metamorphosed into an Egyptian knight, who rescues from prison Arsinoé, the sister of Cleopatra and Ptolemy, and then seizes the throne by marrying her. Finally, the battles of Thapsus and Munda, against Juba and the sons of Pompey, respectively, are pure inventions in the style of *chansons de geste*, in which the author's poetic and fantastical elaborations overwhelm the little that derives from Latin authors. The end of the *Faits des Romains* returns to Suetonius, chapters 37–89, and offers an assessment of Caesar's achievements and character, moral and personal, terminating with an account of Caesar's death.[63]

To these principal texts the author added episodes, etymologies, and descriptions taken from Isidore of Seville's *Etymologies*, Josephus's *War of the Jews*, Eusebius's *Ecclesiastical History* and *Epistolae*, and Peter Comester's *History of the Maccabees*, as well as a brief segment concerning Cato from St. Augustine's *City of God*, which he mentions by name. Perhaps the most important of the secondary texts that he employed were learned *scholies* (glosses and commentary) on Lucan's *Pharsalia*, which Berthe Marti has identified as written by Master Arnulfus of Orléans.[64] He also cites briefly from the Bible, Cicero, Virgil, and Ovid and interpolates the episode from the *Alexandri Magni iter ad Paradisium* mentioned above. He occasionally takes the opportunity to christianize the sites to which his story carries him, commenting on biblical events and personages whose histories overlie the classical past.[65] His borrowing from medieval sources includes Geoffrey of Monmouth, either directly or through the vernacular adaptations of Geoffrey by Wace; the *Roman de Thèbes;* and the *Roman d'Alexandre*, the latter in particular for the description of Caesar's horse, which is modeled on Bucephalus. Although their origins are impossible to identify, there are also long explanatory digressions[66] and extensive interpolated scenes of battle executed in an epic style, all of which combine to make the translator the third most important "author" represented in the compilation.[67]

The author/translator's approach to his sources varies widely throughout the course of the *Faits*. The additions to and subtractions from the Latin sources do not operate evenly across the body of works presented. Although the translation of Caesar's *Gallic Wars*, with the noted exceptions, is a relatively straightforward affair, where the most consistent distortion of the original text takes the form of epic toning and the substitution of medieval for Roman names, the translation of Lucan is handled differently. In part, this difference is due to the quite distinct character of the two works. Caesar's account of the conquest of Gaul fit easily into the framework of medieval narratives of exemplary battles and heroic encounters between enemies. But Lucan's long and difficult verse epic, laden with mythological allusions, poetic figures, philosophical reflections, and obscure references to Roman political factions, posed quite a different problem, both in terms of the linguistic resources required for translation and in the Latin author's narrative procedures, which included frequent astrological and mythological digressions, moral apostrophes, and political laments. Although Lucan enjoyed considerable popularity in the Middle Ages as a historian and a source of aphorisms,[68] a direct rendering of Lucan lay just barely within the realm of a thirteenth-century vernacular writer's literary competence to translate and a medieval audience's capacity to comprehend. Not surprisingly, then, this part of the *Faits des Romains* exhibits much greater independence from its source than do, for example, the translations of Caesar and Suetonius, possessing the highest degree of both deletion and interpolation of episodes.

The author justifies his rewriting of his received material and the use of additional material, whether from other sources or from his own imagination, on the grounds of the inadequacy of his Latin models. When translating Lucan, for example, he is tempted to elaborate, since "Lucans s'em passe ci elecques si briemert, que nus ne puet savoir certain ordre de l'estoire par chose que il en die" (Lucan passes over this so briefly, that one is unable to know for certain the order of events by the things he says of it). Unfortunately, Sallust provided little help at this point in the narrative, which dealt with the war of Alexandria, for he "meïsmes n'en redist qui a conter face" (similarly fails to say anything that might furnish subject matter to recount). Although the author seeks to augment the deficiencies of Lucan and Sallust here by referring to the works of "Herodotus et Berosus, dui hystoriographe qui touchierent en lor estoires cest passage, en dient plus et auques s'acordent" (two historiographers who in their histories touch upon this passage, say more, and agree somewhat), it is impossible to identify any part of Herodotus or Berosius (a contemporary of Alexander the Great, fragments of whose *Chaldaica* had passed into Josephus) relevant to his discussion.[69] It seems likely, then, that the citation of "authors" is a false invocation of "authority" to conceal the author's own inventions.

The translator's departure from the sources for the sake of epic interpolation is similarly justified, for example in his account of the battle of Pharsalia, with the remark that "il i ot meinte bele joste et meint beau cop feru, dont Lucans ne parole pas; mes nos les escriverons einsi con nos les avons trovez es autres tretiez, en un livre meïsmes que Cesar fist de ses fez, et en Suetoine et aillors" (there were many fine jousts and many a fine blow delivered, of which Lucan does not speak; but we shall write about them as we have found them in other treatises, in a book that Caesar himself wrote of his deeds, and in Suetonius and elsewhere).[70] Despite the careful enumeration of alternative authorities, the ensuing narrative is a fictive elaboration in epic style based solely on the author's knowledge and deployment of the epic modes of Old French *chansons de geste*. For the most part, however, such epic additions are inserted without comment and so thoroughly woven into the fabric of the text as to fuse seamlessly with the Latin account. This is an ancient world in which antagonists in battle routinely engage in single combat with one another; where famous Roman fighters, such as Scipio at the battle of Thapsus, appear as a "biaus chevaliers, adroiz et boens" (handsome knight, agile and good);[71] in which Gneus, the son of Pompey, does battle with Caesar to avenge the death of his father, who was, he proclaims, "pleins de totes bontez, loiax chevaliers adurez et vassaux feelz vers sa cité et vers son païs" (full of all goodness, a loyal, experienced knight and a vassal faithful to his city and to his country);[72] where, at the naval battle before Marseille, the father of Argus is extolled in feudal terms as a man "qui avoit esté si preuz en sa jovente que il ne trovoit son paraill en vaselage n'a pié n'a cheval. Il estoit mes afebloiez de viellece, mes essamples de chevalerie estoit a cels qui le veoient et connoissoient" (who had been so *preu* in his youth that he did not find his equal in vassalage, neither on foot nor mounted. He was then enfeebled by old age, but he offered an example of chivalry to those who saw and knew him);[73] and where Caesar and Cleopatra fall into each other's arms with all the conventional passion of medieval romance lovers. To the uninitiated reader or hearer, ignorant of the original Latin source, ancient history as construed by the *Faits des Romains* must have seemed of a piece with the whole corpus of medieval literature traditionally sung and recounted in aristocratic circles, but now graced with the superior authority of prestigious ancient *auctores* and a classical literary pedigree. It therefore lent to chivalric culture the inherent legitimacy of antiquity without disturbing its essential ideological contours or ethical apparatus.

Viewed as a whole, the *Faits des Romains* reads less as a "life" of Caesar than as an inquiry into the roots and consequences of military and political ambition. Although he uses the frame provided by Suetonius, the author concentrates his attention on the military exploits generated by the Roman conquest of Gaul and the ensuing civil war. In his treatment, these events are causally related, since he believes that the Senate's denial of a triumph to Caesar for his successes in Gaul propelled the Roman general into open conflict with the state. Despite the employment of a wide variety of sources, both ancient and medieval, the two main sections formed by the translation of Caesar's

Bellum Gallicum and Lucan's *Bellum civile* take up fully 84 percent of the translated work. In both sections, the principal issue over which war is waged is liberty: the liberty of the Gauls in the face of Roman subjugation; the liberty of Romans in the face of Caesar's overweening political ambitions. As we shall see, the "wisdom" that the *Faits des Romains* seeks to promote turns, at its core, on the question of the untrammeled exercise of military and political power on the part of greedy and ruthless rulers. Insofar as Caesar emerges triumphant from both series of engagements, his success spells the death of liberty, a death mirrored in Caesar's own moral decline, which in turn, as handled by the anonymous translator, signifies the disruption of the values of the Roman world.

THE TRANSLATION OF CAESAR

Caesar's *Gallic Wars* was a work of self-promotion in which the Roman general advertised the greatness and utility of his war against the Gauls both as a personal triumph due to his exceptional military talents and as a potential benefit for the Roman world. To this end, Caesar sought to present the populations he subjected as worthy adversaries whose integration into the Roman world could be effected without undue strain. A notable feature of the *Gallic Wars*, indeed, is the fact that for Caesar, the "French" (that is, the Gauls) are barbarian allies, whereas the Britons and Germans (Saxons) are the "real" barbarians, whose absorption by Roman civilization appears scarcely possible.[74] Unlike the other "barbarian" peoples confronted by the Roman legions, the Gauls were civilizable.[75] In Caesar's *Gallic Wars*, they are depicted, if not on a par with the Romans, at least as worthy of forcible inclusion within the Roman political and military orbit. Since the anonymous translator worked on his text in the years 1213–1214, the distinction that Caesar had drawn in the *Gallic Wars* between the "French" and the "Saxons" and "Britons"—whose thirteenth-century descendants were at that moment in deadly alliance against Philip Augustus—conformed to the structure of political alignments in western Europe and may explain why Caesar's tale of conquest over the Gauls was less unpalatable to a prospective French audience than might otherwise be thought.

However, Caesar also was compelled to account for the difficulties that he encountered in subduing various Gallic peoples and for the persistence of revolts against Roman domination, even after the defeat and return of Vercingetorix. To do so, he resorted to an unflattering picture of the inherent instability, inconstancy, and impulsiveness of the Gauls, as well as their ferocity and credulity, apparent in their tendency to credit unfounded rumors, which continually led them into perfidious and faithless acts ranging from the breaking of treaties to outright rebellion. In translating the *Gallic Wars*, the thirteenth-century author systematically reworked the Caesarian image of the Gauls in ways favorable to the "French," who were their nominal equivalents. But this reinterpretation of Franco-Gallic "national" character did not extend to all the peoples that Caesar had termed "Gauls," nor was it applicable to the other barbarian tribes that had fallen victim to his sword and to his pen. The exclusionary tactics of rewriting that guided the author of the *Faits des Romains* is compelling testimony to the cultural and political agendas that he harbored and cannot be attributed simply to the desire to "modernize" his source in order to elucidate the text and enhance its didactic efficacy.

The "Gaul" that the thirteenth-century translator constructs is neither Roman Gaul as presented by Caesar nor precisely contemporary France under Philip Augustus. It is a Gaul seen from the perspective of Paris, not Rome; "beyond the Alps," in the *Faits des Romains*, designates Italy, not France.[76] The primary characteristic of this "new" Gaul is its size, for the author prefaces Caesar's famous statement concerning the tripartite division of Gaul by stressing that France in the days of Julius Caesar "estoit molt granz" (was very large).[77] It is a Gaul that includes Savoy—"toz cil dou païs de la estoient apeléz François et toz li païs estoit apelez France a cel tens" (all those from that country were called French and all the country was called France at that time)[78]—and Trier, which "a ce jor estoit la plus poissanz de France entre les autres citez en chevalerie, et gent de pié i avoit a foison" (in that day was the most powerful among the cities of France in chivalry, and it [also] had foot soldiers in abundance).[79] Yet it is also a Gaul thoroughly familiar to a thirteenth-century audience, in which the ancient cities and inhabitants of the north are metamorphosed into classical avatars of medieval French society. Caesar's Aquitani thus are identified as the Poitevins, the Morini as the Flemish, the Cantabri as the Gascons, and the Allobroges as the Burgundians. But they are all, as the translator notes at the beginning of his work, one people: "li messagier borguenon ou françois, tot est un" (Burgundian or French messengers, they are all one).[80]

More prevalent still is the identification of the French according to the cities they inhabit, a process that has the dual effect of reinscribing the ancient geography of Gaul as France and of reconstituting the adversaries against whom Caesar struggled as members of urban regions rather than tribal entities. No longer the tribal *barbari* of the *Gallic Wars*, the "François" are, like the Romans, a people who live in the city; hence they are "civilized" in the root sense of the word, all traces of "barbarism" effaced by the culturally neutral urban designations. Caesar's legions set forth to do battle against "cil de Rains," "cil de Biauves," and "cil de Soissons," all of whom are "François." Vercingetorix "de Clermont," seeking to raise an army to contend with the Romans, dispatches his messengers "partout as citez de France et manda que se tenissent en foi et en loiauté" (throughout the cities of France and commanded that they bind themselves in faith and loyalty). Responding to his call were "cil de Sens, de Paris, de Poitiers, de Caors, de Tors, d'Angiers, de Limoges et des autres citez."[81] Normans and Nivernais, Burgundians and Bretons, pass through these pages as emblematic representatives of the antiquity of France's geographic and social identity and the continuity of her political community.

Despite the overall tendency to homogenize past and present, pagan and Christian, *Galli* and *Franci*, the anonymous author nonetheless draws some fine distinctions in his treatment of the various populations he has assimilated to the "François." As a rule, "li François" seen as an ensemble are excused from the opprobrium that Caesar had heaped on them for their "légèreté." Although the translator acknowledges that Caesar placed little trust in the French—"por ce que il sot que François estoient appareillié a guerroier et a prendre noviax conselz tote jor, il se fioit petit en els" (because he knew that the French were always prepared to make war and to take new counsel, he had little faith in them)—their readiness to do battle and follow counsel hardly replicates Caesar's charge of pusillanimity, and Caesar's allegation of the notorious *infirmitatem Gallorum veritus* in the Latin text is simply suppressed. At worst, the French can be accused of overfrequent councils and of responding indiscriminately to interested rumor from passing merchants and travelers: "Lors prenoient conseill selonc ce que il ooient, a tel chief de foiz qui tornoit a lor nuisement, car li trespassant ne lor responnoient pas toz jors verité, mes selonc ce que il cuidoient que fust a lor plesir" (They took counsel according to what they heard, such that it often turned out to their harm, since passersby did not always answer [their inquiries] with the truth, but rather with what they thought would please them).[82]

Similarly, where Caesar claims that his Gallic auxiliaries inform upon their countrymen, the translator says in passing only that "espies i estoient" (there were spies), thus removing suspicions of treachery. Rather than fickle or treacherous, the inhabitants of France are portrayed as fierce warriors, committed to preserving their liberty. "Cil de Biauvés" are "de grant pooir et de tres grant fierté" (of great power and very fierce).[83] Those from Nevers are "home dur, cruel et de grant vertu, qui mout blasmoient toz cels de France qui rendu s'estoient en la main des Romains et avoient gitee arriere l'ancienne vertu de lor païs" (hard men, cruel and of great strength, who greatly blamed all those of France who had surrendered themselves to the hands of the Romans and had thrown away the ancient virtue of their country); the "Belges" are characterized as "soverain conbateor estoient en tote France" (sovereign fighters in all France), as are the Poitevins "qui bon conbateor furent et orent beles armes" (who were good fighters and bore excellent arms); the Champenois "sevent assez de fonde et de trere et de lancier" (were well acquainted with the use of a fronde and with the sword and lance).[84] Indeed, for the author of the *Faits des Romains*, "tote France estoient preste a bataille autresi con par nature" (all France was prepared to do battle, as if by nature),[85] exhibiting exceptional courage, the ability to withstand hardship, and a love of competition. Pride of place among them goes to the inhabitants of the Île-de-France and the "Parisis," "cil de la riviere de Sainne, ou li boen chevalier sont par nature et li hardi torneieor et meillor des autres" (those from the Seine river, where good knights are by nature, and bold tourneyers, better than the others).[86] It is in "cels de France," the author remarks in an addition to the Latin text, that Caesar places his greatest trust: "por lor hardement, car plus les avoit esprovez aspres et estables en totes batailles" (for their bravery, for he had found them courageous and steadfast in all battles).[87]

Yet, as Mireille Schmidt-Chazan has demonstrated, the translator's excision or mitigation of Caesar's criticisms is not total. He often lets stand isolated adverse judgments in the Latin text. But rather than apply them to the French as a whole, he reserves them for particular peoples from well-defined regions.[88] Thus, amid the general praise of the French for their warlike virtue, the Auvergnats are decried as "menteor . . . par nature et faignent que il sont frere as Romains et as Latins por ce que il vindrent de Troie" (liars . . . by nature, and they pretend that they are brothers to the Romans and Latins because they came from Troy).[89] In the same way, the scope of Caesar's remark on the return of the Aedui to Vercingetorix's rebellion—an act of betrayal that Caesar attributed to their having "treated frivolous hearsay as assured fact: some were influenced by avarice, others by anger and the recklessness which is specially characteristic of their race"[90]—is restricted by the translator to apply to "cil d'Ostum" who en furent si esmeü, c'onques n'i ot espace d'enquerre en nule verité, ainz alerent li un par avarice, li autres par ire, li autre[s] par folie, de croi[e]re tot quanque il ooient, car de nature avoient que il creïssent ce et coi de legier.[91]

were so [easily] moved, that they never had time [lit. space] to inquire into the truth; thus some proceeded from avarice, others from anger, others from folly, to believe everything they heard, for it was their nature to easily believe this and that.

And this despite the fact that Caesar had always held "cil d'Ostum" in the highest honor "por la foi qu'il avoient enciennement gardee vers Romains" (for the fealty that they had in ancient times maintained toward the Romans).[92]

Among the French, some come in for especially pointed criticism. For example, the Normans, alone among the "François," are said to lack courage in battle. The author transforms a rather bland comment of Caesar's on the Unelles—as being, like the Gauls, prompt in taking up arms, but lacking strength and resolve in sustaining reverses—into a direct attack on the Normans:

Si con dit Juliens, autresi come Normenz estoient prest a movoir barate et noise por petit, ensement il perdoient les cuers et les vertuz lues que il avoient une aversité d'aucun meschief.[93]

As Julius says, just as the Normans were ready to engage in treachery and tumults for very little cause, in the same way they lost heart and virtue as soon as they experienced a calamity of any misfortune.

The inability to persevere in enterprises rashly begun, a characteristic that Caesar attributes to the Gauls as a whole, is here shifted to the Normans, once again replicating in the ancient past the configurations and sentiments of thirteenth-century France at a moment of "national" struggle between the French and Normans, only recently conquered by Philip Augustus (in 1204–1205) and still suspect as potential allies for the Anglo-German coalition of 1213–1214.

Without doubt, however, the main target of the author's selective revisions of Caesar's account is the Germans, generally designated by the names of "Tyois" or "Sesnes." They alone merit the appellation of *barbari*, and they invariably appear in the text as a people "barbares et sauvages"—even when the Latin source refers only to "Germans."[94] The Germans who inhabit the territories beyond the Rhine appear in the *Faits des Romains* as cruel and ferocious beyond sense, a "gens forsené,"[95] habituated to thievery in their pursuit of plunder ("come genz qui estoient usé de larrecins et de roberies"),[96] who (rather surprisingly, given the general tenor of the Latin text on the warlike character of the Germans) are of less military value even than the "Hermines" ("mout meins a redoter que Hermines ne autres genz" [much less to be feared than the Hermines or other peoples])[97]—a disparaging phrase added to Caesar's account and referring to the Armenians defeated by Sulla. The Saxons are presented as "genz qui n'avoient loisir de conseill prendre ne de lor armes saisir" (a people who do not have the leisure to take counsel nor to bear arms). In place of the military valor that distinguishes the "François," Saxons resort to ruse (barate) and trickery (tricherie).[98] The Germans are a race of cowards ("ne sont pas de grant hardement"), and the Normans and English are unwise to ally themselves against the French with "such people," as the author interjects in an appreciation of the current political situation in France: "je tieng por fox et Anglois et Normanz, qui ont fole esperance et quident que Octes li escomeniez . . . doie France envaïr par itel genz" (I hold as foolish both the English and the Normans, who have vain hopes and think that Otto the excommunicated . . . could invade France with such people).[99] France, on the other hand, is a society where

> li chevalier . . . estoient toz jors en guerre et en bataille. Acostumé l'avoient avant la venue Cesar, car chascun an assilloient autrui, ou il se deffendoient de cels qui venoient sur els.
>
> the knights . . . were always engaged in war and in battle. They were accustomed to it before Caesar's advent, for each assailed the other, or defended themselves against those who attacked them.

In France, the exercise of war is not conducted merely for plunder, as among the Germans. Rather,

> qui plus estoit riches, plus avoit mesniee et serjanz environ soi. Qui plus pooit avoir grant conpaignie et de sa table et de sa meson, plus avoit, ce li sembloit, honor et cortoisie et grace.[100]
>
> he who was richer had more of an entourage and sergeants around him. He who was able to maintain a great company, both of his table and his household, had, so it seemed, greater honor and courtesy and grace.

As in the present, so in the past; as in the past, so in the present. The essential character of French society is chivalric, a world in which riches, honor, courtoisie, and favor are and always have been the determinants of social position and personal virtue. The transferral of the represented world of medieval chivalry to the ancient origins of the French people comes full circle and authorizes its continuance in the present. Because the French have always been a people distinguished by military prowess and valor, they will overcome the threatened coalition, just as surely as the Germans, the roots of whose cowardice burrow deep into the distant past, will suffer defeat. In the end, it is the maintenance of their *ancienne vertu* of military strength and moral honor that guarantees the liberty of "li François."

The crucial role of chivalric prowess in sustaining "French" liberty emerges most distinctively in the *Faits* in its treatment of the conflicts between Caesar and a series of Gallic leaders, whose meaning in the vernacular text takes on political and ethical dimensions absent from Caesar's narrative. The anonymous thirteenth-century translator consistently rewrites his Latin source to eliminate any suspicion of Gallic subordination toward Rome, both during the successive military confrontations and even, finally, in defeat.[101] Whether allies or enemies, the "François" are always treated as free peoples, routinely called for consultation to Caesar's numerous colloquies, and accorded the respect and fear due worthy adversaries. As handled in the *Faits des Romains*, the war between the Romans and the Gauls is a struggle between equal opponents, one fighting for domination and territorial expansion, the other striving to preserve its ancient liberty. Against Caesar's efforts to subjugate the Gauls, the "French" oppose a deep and perduring desire for autonomy that fuels their ferocity in the face of aggression. At times, the desire for liberty may even lead them to ally with the Romans. Thus the "François" applaud Caesar's conquest of the Helvetians, which they attribute not to Caesar's desire to avenge the shame that the Helvetians had visited upon the Romans in defeating Lucius Cassius, but to Caesar's recognition of the "conmun profit de tote France":

> car li Helveçois n'avoient guerpiz lor leus, qui plein estoit de tot bien, fors que por metre desoz lor piez tote France si grant come ele estoit en .iij. parties, et por estre seignor de tot et fere dou païs a lor volenté.[102]
>
> because the Helvetians left their spot, which was full of good things, only to subjugate [lit. place beneath their feet] all France, as great as she was in three parts, and in order to be lord of everything and to do what they wanted with the country.

Similarly, the French request Caesar's aid against the "Sesnes," who, under King Ariovistus, threaten to cross the Rhine in order that "il porront les François chacier de tote France" (they could chase the

French out of France), knowing full well that Ariovistus "veust avoir sor els cruel seignorie" (wished to exercise cruel lordship over them).[103]

But the most persistent threat to Gallic liberty comes from Caesar himself. When confronted with the specter of subjection to Rome, "François" of every sort and from every region relentlessly resist. Whereas Caesar found the continuous rebellion of the Gauls to be proof of their instability and inconstancy, the author of the *Faits* presents it as proof of their absolute commitment to preserving their autonomy. Thus the cities of Brittany, although subdued and in principle pacified, nonetheless rise up against the Roman victors, because "mielz se voloient abandoner a tote fortune que remanoir ou servage as Romains" (they preferred to abandon themselves to the whims of fortune rather than to remain in bondage to the Romans).[104] Indeed, Caesar was forced to conclude that "tote France pres s'apareilloit a movoir guerre, por ce meesmement que chascuns huem aime franchise par nature et het lien de servage" (almost all France was prepared to go to war, because each man loves liberty by nature and hates any tie of dependency).[105] *Franchise*, which in the *romans d'antiquité* tended to signify "nobility of character," "goodness," or "speech that bears witness to a noble heart"—all important qualities of the perfect courtly knight[106]—here takes on a decided inflection in the direction of "freedom." In the *Faits des Romains*, it is at one and the same time a condition strenuously defended by the French, a rallying cry for rebellion, and a structure of argumentation.

Thus Convictolitavis, on whom Caesar had conferred the leadership of "cil d'Ostum," determined to join the revolt against the Romans because, although "voirs est que je doi assez a Cesar por le bien que il m'a fet; mes je doi plus a comune franchise" (it is true that I owe Caesar much for the good that he has done me; but I owe more to the common liberty). And it is on this basis that he persuades the Aeduan messengers to join the ranks of the rebelling peoples of France in behalf of their "common liberty."[107] The guardians of the "common liberty" of the "François" are the Gallic tribal chieftains, here transformed into regional princes, against whom Caesar wages pitiless war but who emerge in their opposition to Roman aggression as national heroes fighting for the ancient liberties and customs of their followers. From first to last, they are treated as disinterested partisans of French freedom, who struggle against overwhelming odds to sustain traditional forms of Gallic self-government, waging war for causes both just and deeply embedded in the French past. To so present France's ancient rulers required the anonymous author of the *Faits des Romains* to revise considerably the picture that Caesar had painted of them. The underlying political preoccupations that guided his work emerge clearly in the ways that he redraws Caesar's image of Gallic tribal leaders as greedy, ambitious, and untrustworthy and refigures them as legitimate champions of "French" national honor and liberty.

THE GALLIC OPPOSITION

The first of the Gallic chieftains subjected to the author's legitimizing revisions is Dumnorix, of the "païs d'Ostum." In Caesar's account, Dumnorix was a notorious farmer of taxes who used the revenues from that enterprise to bribe his way to influence and a position of dominance among the Aedui, whom he was inciting to revolt against the Romans. According to Caesar:

> For several years, it was said, he had contracted at a low price for the customs and all the rest of the Aeduan taxes, for the simple reason that when he made a bid none durst bid against him. By this means he had at once increased his own prosperity and acquired ample resources for bribery; he maintained a considerable body of horses permanently at his own charges, and kept them about his own person; not only in his own but even in neighboring states his power was extensive.[108]

In place of this unflattering portrait, the author of the *Faits des Romains* depicts Dumnorix as a brave and powerful leader, who had won his followers' favor and cemented their loyalty by his capacity for "biau parler":

> Ce estoit Domnorix qui estoit si hardiz et de si grant pooir el pueple que nus n'osoit rien contre lui, car il avoit si la grace de toz par sa liberalité et par sa largece et par sa franchise et par son biau parler, que tuit le suivoient et voloient ce que il voloit.

> This was Dumnorix, who was extremely bold and possessed such great power over the people that no one dared to do anything against him, because he had so won the favor of all by his liberality and by his largesse and by his nobility of character [*franchise*] and fine speech, that everyone followed him and wished what he wished.

Although this Dumnorix also farms taxes, he does so not to bribe his way to influence, but to have

> de quoi il pooit granz largeces fere par la gent atrere a s'amor et por baer a noveles honors par assentement del pueple; et grant nombre de chevalerie avoit toz jors entor soi, que il meintenoit en totes choses de son avoir.[109]

the wherewithal to distribute great largesse in order to attract the love of the people and to aspire to new honors by the assent of the people; and he always had a great number of knights around him, whom he maintained in all things at his own expense.

He is an ideal medieval ruler, liberal with *largece*, eager for honors that are conferred upon him by the "assent of the people," whose favor and love he wins through that "fine speech" (*biau parler*) so essential, as Jean de Thuin noted, to the preservation of correct order in the chivalric world. He exhorts his followers to support the resistance, only to be cut down, dying with the cry upon his lips: "Je sui frans, et de franche cité" (I am free and from a free city).[110]

In this thirteenth-century vision of the ancient world of Gaul, the leader acts on the promptings of his followers, among whom he figures as a *primus inter pares* and whose wishes and counsels he is required to implement. Hence Ambiorix excuses himself from leading the Eburones in an attack against Caesar's troops sent to winter among his people on the grounds that he was bound by "French" custom to execute their demands, even against his better judgment, for in France ruler and subjects are contractually implicated in each other's "seignorie" and required to abide by the counsel of the majority:

> "et ce que je ai fet d'assaillir les tentes romaines n'a pas esté par ma volonté ne par mon jugement, ainz le m'a fet fere li pueples, qui a autretant de seignorie sor moi come je ai sor lui, car itex est nostre costume."

> "and what I did in attacking the tents of the Romans was not according to my own wishes nor my judgment, but I was made to do it by the people, who have as much lordship over me as I have over them, for such is our custom."

The fact that all the French together had decided to attack Caesar's legions wherever they were wintering only provided further incentive to join the rebellion, since

> ce estoit le comuns conselz de France d'assaillir totes les legions Cesar. . . . Ne li uns François ne puet escondire s'aide a l'autre a cest besoign, car cist conselz est de conmune franchise.[111]

> it was the common counsel of France to attack all Caesar's legions. . . . No Frenchman could refuse his aid to another in this need, for this counsel concerned the common liberty.

Counsel and consent are the twin pillars on which the *franchise* of the French stands or falls. They constitute the main vectors along which the lines of force in Gallic society run, its governing principles of cohesion and strength, and hence the essential elements that define its historical character. Consent to the common causes of liberty arrived at through deliberation in council cannot be refused, for the historical destiny of "li François" depends on adherence to the collective will of the princes.

The princes' title to leadership derives ultimately from their personal fortitude and valor, for it is, in this sense, their "chivalric" prowess that validates their ability to rule. The author of the *Faits des Romains* embellishes his history with innumerable micro-narratives of heroic valor among lesser figures, whose feats of bravery, recounted in heavily accented epic tones, contribute to the overall patterning of the narrative in epic style. Thus, in a small episode that recalls the actions of Roland at the battle of Roncevaux, Corbeus, the leader of the Beauvaisins (Bellovaci), although already defeated in battle, refuses to give up:

> Mes en nule maniere dou monde Corbeus ne vost le chanp guerpir, ne foïr n'ou bois n'aillors, ne partir soi de la bataille, n'estre menez a ce qu'il se vossist rendre par nul enortement de Romains; ainz le veïst l'en plus fier que lion plaier, abatre et ocirre plusors a tas devant soi. Tant que Romain nel porent plus sosfrir de mautalent,ançois li lancerent tant darz qu'il le ferirent parmi le cors et fu abatuz sanz relever. Mes bien si fu avant contenuz come vertueus dux.[112]

> In no way in the world did Corbeus wish to quit the field, or to flee into the woods or elsewhere, nor to remove himself from the battle, nor to be led to surrender by any urging of the Romans; rather one could see him, prouder than a lion, attack, strike, and kill several in a pile before him. To such an extent that the Romans in their anger could no longer endure it; therefore they threw so many javelins at him that they pierced him throughout his body and he was struck down without being able to get up again. But how well he had conducted himself before this as a virtuous leader.

Similarly, Vertiscus, "li princes de Rains," insisted on leading his host into battle despite his great age, which made it difficult for him to mount his horse:

> Il ne vost pas sosfrir que si chevalier alassent bataillier sanz lui, ne par viellece ne s'estoit escussez qu'il n'eüst receüe la provosté des chevaliers guier. [. . . He was considered] le prince prevost de tote la chevalerie de Renciens.[113]

> He could not stand to have his knights go into battle without him, nor did he excuse himself by reason of old age from receiving the

charge of commanding the knights. [. . . He was considered] the principal leader of all the chivalry of Reims.

The stories of even such minor princes as Corbeus and Vertiscus, taken from Caesar's account but consistently rewritten in language borrowed from the lexicon of medieval chivalry, build upon one another to heighten the sense of cyclical return and discursive recurrence that is an essential part of the narrative and historiographical strategies of the *Faits des Romains*. Narrative repetition creates a vast epic tableau out of alien classical *matière* that reinscribes its meaning for a medieval audience as a past that it makes its own. Ancient history becomes the ground of an ideology of chivalric identity whose distant origins tacitly argue the authentic status of the aristocracy's claim to a historical mission as warriors and leaders of France. The princes whose blood has been spilt since the beginning of time for the liberty of France are the true representatives of the ancient peoples of France. Their actions, guided by the common accord of leaders and followers in council, provide the paradigm of a French society governed according to ancient customs, offering a heritage of valor, honor, prowess, and virtue in the service of *franchise* that is the historical meaning and mandate of a specifically "French" antiquity.

Even more do the histories of ancient Gaul's emblematic chieftains such as Vercingetorix and—for the author of the *Faits des Romains*—Drappés Brenno disclose the contours of a French past potentially capable of reviving a lost world of aristocratic potency and chivalric virtue. In his account of the exploits of Vercingetorix and Drappés Brenno, the author of the *Faits des Romains* offers his thirteenth-century audience of readers and listeners a rectified history of ancient Gaul aimed at redeeming contemporary chivalric society.

Vercingetorix was not yet in the thirteenth century the national hero that nineteenth-century Frenchmen were to make of him, but he figured in the *Gallic Wars* as the principal Gallic chieftain fomenting revolt against Caesar. Caesar's depiction of Vercingetorix was a complicated admixture of admiration for his military skills, frustration with the continual rebellions that he excited and led, and scorn for the motley character of the followers that he admitted into his host, which Caesar disdains as "a levy of beggars and outcasts."[114] Curiously, the author of the *Faits des Romains* lets stand Caesar's adverse judgment on Vercingetorix's army and, if anything, darkens the picture, describing the warriors as a ragbag "de povres, d'eschis, d'endetez, de gent desperee, qui plus amoit guerre que pes" (of the poor, deprived, indebted, of desperate people, who loved war more than peace).[115]

Vercingetorix is moved to wage war, according to Caesar and our vernacular author, by a combination of personal ambition and "entencion de comune franchise recovrer" (intention to recover the common liberty). The narrative of his uprisings repeatedly raises questions about the nature of the Gallic leader's personal motives and goals, questions initiated by Caesar and allowed to linger in the vernacular text.[116] To the extent that the author of the *Faits* corrects the history of Gallic revolt against Caesar under Vercingetorix, his emendations of the past do not so much revise the image of the Gallic leader as reinterpret the global character of French rebellion and its meaning within the history of resistance to Roman domination.

In Caesar's view, Gallic princes had seized the opportunity created by his departure for Italy to sow discord among the people, already "chafing at their subjection to the sovereignty of Rome." In particular, he pointed to their alarm at the execution of Acco, chief of the Senones, and their concern that a similar fate might befall them.[117] In Caesar's eyes, then, Gallic motivation for the renewal of war derived from a combination of resentment over their defeat and subjugation to Roman rule and self-interested fear for their personal safety. The French author, in contrast, mitigates Caesar's judgment by adding that, although the French were afraid that Acco's cruel death at Caesar's hands "porroit avenir a chascun de nos" (could happen to each of us), more important was their belief that "tote France est en aventure . . . or si parra qui metra sa teste en aventure por conmune franchise recovrer" (the fate of France is in the balance . . . now it will be clear who is willing to place his head at risk in order to recover the common liberty). Indeed, so little did the French fear for their lives that they collectively determined that

> il voloient mielz estre tuit ocis em bataille, et a greignor honor lor torneroit, que il ne recovrassent la gloire de bataille que lor ancessor avoient eüe jadis.[118]
> they would prefer all to be killed in battle, and it would redound more greatly to their honor, rather than not recover the glory of battle that their ancestors formerly had.

Ancestral honor and glory require the prosecution of war in the name of liberty, not for the sake of personal security, but for "le conmun salu de France."[119] In answering Vercingetorix's call to arms, the "François" are responding to the imperatives of ancestry and the traditions of national honor by which liberty and glory have been sustained in the past. Vercingetorix is merely an instrument selected to lead the French to their historical destiny, an imperfect bearer of their aspirations for autonomy, perhaps, but in his military cunning a worthy opponent to Caesar's legions and, as the princes acclaim him, a "sovrains dux."[120]

Strikingly, Vercingetorix never acts alone. He is a chosen leader, "esleüz a prince et a comandeor par le conmun otroi des citez" (elected as prince and commander by the common consent of the cities) and bound by the common counsel of the other princes. His lordship (*seignorie*) and authority to command are established by election. The author of the *Faits des Romains* insists on the collective nature of decisions made in council in the conduct of war:

> Chascun matin fesoit [Vercingetorix] venir a soi princes et connoistables de tote s'ost por prendre conseill de tel atirement come au jor covenoit.[121]

> Each morning [Vercingetorix] had the princes and constables of all his host come to him in order to take counsel concerning the disposition of affairs that was necessary that day.

So compelling is the cause of national *franchise* that even those who allied with Caesar in the past join their compatriots against the Romans. Thus Commius, who loyally assisted Caesar in his wars in Britain and as a reward received Flanders and Thérouanne, nonetheless enters the fray on the side of French liberty:

> Neporquant tote France fu si a un acort de lor franchise venchier et ravoir et de recovrer lor premeraine gloire de bataille, qu'il ne menbra onques a nului d'amor ne de bienfet que Cesar lor eüst fet, ainz avoient tuit boene volenté de metre lor cors et lor avoirs en ceste guerre fornir.[122]

> Nevertheless, all France was of such an accord to avenge and repossess their freedom and recover their original glory of battle that no one remembered the love or benefits that Caesar had brought them; rather, they all wished to offer their bodies and goods for the prosecution of this war.

The war is fought in epic style, knight against knight, matching the *proece*, *vertu*, and *hardement* of each.[123] The French appetite for war is excited by "la memoire de l'encienne vertu des François" (the memory of the ancient virtue of the French). And it is precisely this memory that drives the Romans to conquer the French and deprive them of their laws, customs, and *franchise*. In the eyes of the French, the Romans seek nothing less than par envie de nostre boene renomee que nos avons toz jors eüe par noz victoires, demorer en noz heritages et acuivertir nos et tolir nostre franchise.[124]

out of envy of our good repute that we have always had by virtue of our victories, to dwell in our heritages and to enslave us and take away our liberty.

Although finally defeated in battle by Caesar, the French remain faithful to their ancestral traditions of liberty. Caesar recognizes only too well that if he left France to winter after subduing Vercingetorix, the French would rise up again, for

ne cuidoient François que ja i eüst cité qui volontiers ne s'entremeïst et preïst fes sor soi de sa franchise vanchier.[125]

the French did not believe that there was any city that would not willingly join in and take it upon itself to avenge its liberty.

Whatever the cost, freedom in France is to be defended, for in freedom lies the sole guarantee for the preservation of ancestral honor.

It is in the author's treatment of Vercingetorix's surrender to Caesar that his greatest changes to this section of the Latin source occur, changes consistent with the image of French history as the history of liberty that shapes his corrected vision of France's ancient past. Caesar's account emphasizes the final submission of the French in a ritual laying down of arms tantamount to an act of obeisance before a sovereign ruler. Caesar ordered the arms to be delivered up and the chiefs to be brought to him. Upon their arrival he was seated at the front of the camp, and the leaders approached him there: "Vercingetorix was surrendered, arms were thrown down."[126] The persistent use of the passive voice in the Caesarian text underscores the impotence of the "pacified" rebels, who no longer control their own deeds but are compelled to respond to the commands of others. The loss of *franchise* is a loss of agency, of the capacity to govern oneself.

In contrast, the author of the *Faits des Romains* converts Vercingetorix's final act of submission into a ritual of volition in which Vercingetorix *se rendit* (rendered himself) to Caesar, sovereign to sovereign, the agent of his self-surrender. It is, as Mireille Schmidt-Chazan remarks, a small detail, "mais combien révélateur de son souci de ne pas voir ternie si peu que ce soit l'image des Français."[127]In surrendering himself, Vercingetorix recovers the agency that Caesar had sought to take from him. The laying down of arms does not entail the loss of autonomy, only a momentary abandonment of the contest.

Caesar may set limits to French freedom of action, but he cannot destroy for all time their *franchise*.

To the degree that the story of Vercingetorix's resistance to Roman domination encodes the history of France as the history of French *franchise*, its meaning within the *Faits des Romains* lies within a semantic field of extraordinary breadth and complexity. *Franchise* is at once a status; a collection of personal attributes designating the inner qualities of nobility of character, virtue, and speech indicative of a noble heart; and an eponym for the French, who as *Franci* are *francs* (free, noble, etc.).[128] The social semantics of *franchise* move between these significations, drawing together into a single etymological and semantic lineage nobility of birth and status, nobility of moral being associated with high birth (i.e., courage, pride, prowess, liberality, etc.), propriety of speech, free status, and ethnic identity. To be French is to claim a legacy of personal characteristics and of ethical and linguistic propriety that replicates the semantic lineage of *franchise*. Given that the medieval inflections of *franchise* are socially coded to the highest degree, the history of France's ancient struggle for *franchise* (liberty) becomes, in the *Faits des Romains*, the history of the nobility, embodying in the ancient past a range of authoritative meanings associated with *franchise* as the social attribute and social prerogative of a class destined by ancestry, moral attainment, and exemplary *gestes* to be the guardians of the nation's honor. In light of the semantic fluidity within *franchise* between the senses of status, freedom, and autonomy, the effect of the author's insistent representation of the Gallic struggle against Caesar as the struggle for liberty is to recode the ancient past of the Gauls as the story of aristocratic autonomy. Resistance to Roman domination constitutes a legacy authorizing resistance to any attempt, past or present, to deprive the nobility of their rightful spheres of autonomous action, whether political, territorial, or sociomoral. The history of French liberty validates the aristocracy's struggle to preserve its autonomy in the face of any and all threats from above, including those of present-day rulers, that seek to deprive it of the *franchise* that is the defining mark of its status and character as a social class.

If Vercingetorix himself is a problematic figure, inappropriate in the eyes of the thirteenth-century translator as a representative of the full conspectus of chivalric values, the significance of his deeds nonetheless adequately articulates the necessary relations, semantically embedded in the term *franchise*, among status, rights, property, propriety, and autonomy that the genetic logic of lineage in the Middle Ages associated with a "free" (franc) nobility. In Drappés Brenno the author of the Faits des Romains was to find an opportunity to complete his vision of a "corrected past," and it is in this figure that the moral failings inherent in Vercingetorix are rectified.

The author interpolates the episode concerning Drappés Brenno between chapters 29 and 30 of Book 8, at the conclusion of the Gallic Wars, where it figures as the closing act of French resistance before the definitive submission of Gaul to Caesar. Placed after the defeat of Vercingetorix, as the climax of the Gallic struggle against the threat of subjugation to Rome, the interpolation revises and reverses the history of French defeat at the hands of the Romans, for it demonstrates the temporary character of that defeat and the undying fidelity to the pursuit of liberty that motivates French action.

The source of the episode is a passage in Hirtius's continuation of Caesar, in which he identifies Drappés as a Senonian who, at the first outbreak of the revolt in Gaul, "had collected desperadoes from anywhere and everywhere, calling slaves to liberty, summoning exiles from every state, and harboring brigands."[129] From the perspective of the Latin text, then, Drappés is no more appropriate a bearer of the traditions of French chivalry than Vercingetorix. If anything, his host transgresses more profoundly the principal boundaries of class and "national" identity in medieval society, for whom few social distinctions were greater than the barriers separating those who were slave and free, or those who possessed membership in a legal community and those who did not. The fact that the translator selects Drappés rather than Vercingetorix as the "national" hero of the ancient "François" would seem to be due to Drappés's position at the conclusion of the narrative, where he serves as both the finale and the final word on the character and meaning of France's ancestral past. Thus, whereas the pejorative implications of Vercingetorix's assembled host of "poor, dispossessed, and indebted" followers are allowed to stand, the author completely rewrites the account of Drappés from the inside out, effacing any trace of social or martial disabilities in him or in the French warriors who joined his army.

In Hirtius's version, Drappés sought to invade Provence but was routed and imprisoned under the walls of Uxellodunum, where he died of starvation. Using Drappés's campaign as a narrative frame, the author of the Faits des Romains reverses the sequence of events and their meaning. The "defection" of the Gauls is converted to a war:[130] the French campaign in Provence is answered by Caesar's in Sens, making French resistance to the Romans an act of defense. No longer composed of liberated slaves, exiles, and brigands, Drappés's army is a proper host of *soudoiers*, which he amasses "de partout . . . de privez et d'estranges."[131]

The battle between Drappés and Caesar is joined with all the traditional flourishes of epic encounters and, following the conventions of *chansons de geste*, takes the form of single combat. Caesar initiates the attack, hotly demanding engagement, while Drappés, equally avid for action, holds back in order to protect his host "come boens pastres qui se met entre les leus et ses oailles quant il les voit chacier" (like a good shepherd who places himself between the wolves and his sheep when he sees them being hunted). The pastoral metaphor places the leader of the Senonians within the traditions of Christian knighthood, whereas Caesar exhibits a rash and intemperate appetite for war, thereby, in Drappés's view, undermining the legitimacy of his lordship:

> Huem qui vehe le cors a un seul chevalier ne doit terre tenir n'avoir droit en ost mener n'en chevalerie governer.[132]

> A man who charges against a single knight should not hold land nor have the right to lead the host or to govern chivalry.

A long and vividly recounted series of thrusts and counter-thrusts ensues. At one point, when Drappés removes with a single blow a part of Caesar's scalp, he mocks the Roman's baldness, enraging Caesar, "qui mout estoit irez quant il ooit ramentevoir sa chauveté, si fu molt eschaufez quant il oï l'eschar Drappés" (who was very angry when he saw his baldness revealed; and he became very heated when he heard Drappés's jeer). From that moment, Caesar determines to kill Drappés, "qui tant de mal li avoit fet" (who had done him so much harm).[133] Whereas Drappés fights to protect his people and further the cause of French *franchise*, Caesar is driven by hatred of the enemy and a desire for revenge.

For once in this wholly fictitious account, the French remain undefeated. Instead, Caesar is captured and imprisoned in Sens. He is helped to escape by Cadorix, a knight of Melun who owed his life to Caesar, for Caesar had once protected him in the past when he led an embassy to Rome. In saving Caesar, Cadorix repays a debt of honor; his actions do not constitute a betrayal of the French, however unfortunate their consequences. And unfortunate they are, as Drappés recognizes:

> "Eschapez m'est," dist Drappés, "par mescheance. Se il fust pris, tote France eüst sa franchise recovree."[134]

"He escaped me," said Drappés, "by ill luck. If he had been taken, all France would have recovered her freedom."

Although Drappés endeavors to trick Caesar once more into capture, the effort fails. He and his companion Lucterius retreat from Sens, which is taken by Caesar and granted to Cadorix, whom Caesar designates as *prince et seignor*. Drappés is subsequently defeated at the siege of Alise (Uxellodunum) by Gaius Canines and taken prisoner. But even in defeat, he denies Caesar the final satisfaction of killing him. Rather than submit to Roman domination and vengeance, Drappés starves himself and, in a final act of self-mastery, "se lessa en ceste maniere de faim morir" (in this way let himself die of hunger).[135]

Throughout the account, the author of the *Faits des Romains* emphasizes the chivalric qualities that make Drappés a worthy leader of the French and a fearless antagonist to Caesar. His prowess, heroism, and concern for his followers contrast sharply with the cruelty and *démesure* with which Caesar pursues him. The preservation of Gallic liberty is opposed to Roman ruthlessness, the national hero to the "bald" conqueror. The narrative leaves little room for doubt concerning the inherent justice of the French cause, and Drappés's final act of suicide, which replicates and exaggerates Vercingetorix's assumption of agency in surrender, leaves unresolved the question of whether the French, under suitable leadership, might have escaped subjection to Rome. It thus interrogates the whole structure of Caesar's text, with its implicit assumption of the legitimacy of Roman conquest over Gaul as a civilizing mission.

Drappés himself is endowed with an entirely new status and lineage, one that connects him to a long tradition of ancient and medieval resistance to Rome. He is the "sire of Sens," *bons chevaliers et hardiz*, a descendant of "Brenne le premerain" (a name retrieved either from Geoffrey of Monmouth's *History of the Kings of Britain* or from Wace's *Roman de Brut*),[136]

> dont tot li prince de Sens retenoient les nons, que chascuns avoit non Brenno, ci com cist Drappés Brenno, et li autre qui furent jusqu'au tens Artur; car veritablement cil Brenno qui fu au tens Artu ne fu pas li premerains dont la citez de Sens fu renomee, mes uns autres qui assist Rome et la prist jusqu'au Capitoile au tens Camillus qui fut conciles de Rome ançois que Marius et Silla fussent.[137]
>
> of which all the princes of Sens kept the name, since each one had the name Brenno, like this Drappés Brenno, and the others who lived

up to the time of Arthur; for truly this Brenno who lived in
Arthur's time was not the first, on account of whom the city of Sens
was renowned, but the one who attacked Rome and took the city up
to the Capitol in the time of Camillus who was consul of Rome before Marius and Sulla.

In Drappés is revived the spirit of the first "Brenne." Like the
"Brenne" who preceded him and the "Brenne" who will come after
him in the time of Arthur, he opposes Roman domination. The sword
he wields is inherited from the first Brenne, founder of the line and
conqueror of Rome, and with it he, like Arthur, is empowered to perform feats of bravery and prowess that fulfill the imperatives of his
lineage. Even Caesar, engaged in mortal combat with the leader of the
Senonians, recognizes the revival of ancestral fortitude in him, proclaiming:

> En non Dieu, il samble que Brenno li premiers soit resucitez. Se cist
> vivoit longues, je cuit que il vodroit le Capitoile ancore asseoir une
> foiz.[138]

> In God's name, it seems as if Brenne the first were revived. If this
> one were to live a long life, I think that he would once again besiege
> the Capitol.

The associative logic of lineage here gathers into a single thread a
tightly braided structure of argument. Drappés, as the lineal descendant of "Brenne le premerain," not only bears within him the moral
and chivalric traditions of his own lineage, whose actions he replicates,
but looks forward to "li autre Brenne," historically associated with
Arthur, who similarly conducts a nearly successful campaign against
the Roman emperor Lucius. The allusion to Brenne and Arthur in
Drappés's fictionalized genealogy reinterprets Drappés's deeds in
terms of the later working out of the historical precedents they embody, and associates with him the legitimacy and ideal value ascribed
by medieval romance to Arthur's legendary realm. With the mention
of the Arthurian world, the legitimizing process comes full circle; ancient and medieval pasts fuse through the workings of descent as two
faces of a single history that constantly throw back their reflections to
one another, multiplying, as in facing mirrors, the repeated images of
the other. Because of this reciprocity of vision, the narrative of events
is submitted to a process of reinterpretation in which meaning inces-
santly circulates within the enclosed reflexivity of past and present.

The authorial act of interpolation in the *Faits des Romains* represents an intervention in history. The anonymous writer's revision of

Caesar's text is also a re-visioning of the past in light of the present and generates the same circularity of inscribed meaning. As authorial heir to the Latin source he translates, he repositions himself with respect to the textual legacy that he is endeavoring to pass down to contemporary society; he textually enacts the process of mastery over the past achieved in the refiguration of ancient history in the image of chivalric society. The story of Drappés's resistance to Caesar, thus, functions simultaneously on a variety of literary, interpretive, and historiographical levels. It rectifies the legacy of the past as handed down in the Caesarian text; it reinscribes the past within the legitimizing ideology of genealogy; it refigures the past in the image of the present.

The revision of the past that the translator effects in his reworking of Caesar's text does not only affect the interpretation of the interpolated episode concerning Drappés Brenno; it carries over as well to the meaning of the Gallic wars in their entirety. The definitive submission of the Gauls following Drappés's suicide is revised to emphasize the continued independence of the French and their social and political parity with the Romans. Hirtius had stressed the ease with which Caesar secured his conquest of Gaul: "by addressing the states in terms of honor, by bestowing ample presents upon the chiefs, by imposing no new burdens, he easily kept Gaul at peace after the exhaustion of so many defeats, under improved conditions of obedience."[139] The translator, in contrast, proclaims that Caesar's sole intent by these acts is to maintain the cities of France in peace and love.[140] Caesar does not compel the surrender of the French princes; rather, he calls them together in council, where he speaks to them *cortoisement* and gives them *riches dons* as befits an ally. He acts, that is, like the ideal courtly ruler toward his princes, respectful of their rights and liberal with largesse, by means of which he legitimizes his rule. Instead of submitting to Caesar, the French voluntarily accede to his rule,

> et por ce qu'il le troverent douz et debonaire et sanz grevement au derrien, il les tint assez plus legierement en pes.[141]
>
> and because they found him gentle and merciful and in the end without cause for blame, he maintained them all the more easily in peace.

French national honor and independence are preserved.

Ironically, the final narrative of the *Faits des Romains* calls into question the very basis of this historical scheme even as it unfolds. The textual revisions that the author imposes on the conclusion to the

Gallic wars profoundly contradict the overall thrust of the historiographical argument developed up to this point in the Old French
translation. To the extent that the author of the *Faits des Romains* had
"corrected" his Latin source in order to offer French history as the
history of liberty, he had opposed to the French desire to maintain
their *franchise* the ruthless ambition of the Romans and Caesar's insatiable appetite for territorial expansion. Although the narrative de-
nouement preserves the "liberty" of the French by construing their
surrender as an act of voluntary submission, it does so at the price of
reconfiguring the image of Caesar, who emerges in this final act as a
courtly ruler whom it is honorable to serve. The "voluntary" submission of Gaul becomes thereby an act of incorporation into the wider
orbit of Rome, a position that conceptually undermines the idea of
French freedom, unmasking it as the loss of autonomy.

By rewriting the final subjugation of the Gauls as an act of alliance,
the author of the *Faits des Romains* creates an interpretive impasse, in
which the contradictions generated by his narrative and ideological
goals subvert the historical framework that he had elaborated. And
this interpretive impasse discloses the discrepancies within aristocratic
ideology itself between the desire for autonomy and the realities of
monarchical government. As in the case of their ancient ancestors, the
fiction of the nobles' voluntary adherence to royal authority, consented to in open council, seeks to mantle the deeper historical reality
of decline and the necessity to submit to the centralizing policies of a
newly powerful king. The fantasy of French *franchise* as a legacy of
noble status, rights of lordship, and chivalric honor is fractured by the
inconsistency entailed in its articulation. Casting French submission
to Caesar as an act of voluntary self-surrender reveals the gap between ideological assertion and political reality.

The "corrected" past cannot, in the end, rectify the historical situation of the aristocracy, for it bears within it the same contradictions
in ideology and aspirations. The alternative vision to an unpalatable
present that the past re-visions merely reenacts the loss of autonomy
and sense of alienation that it attempts, in vain, to dissimulate. The
lack of coherence in the historical narrative discursively replicates the
contradictions of aristocratic life and underscores the inability of history to recuperate a pristine state of aristocratic freedom and authority. The failure of the ancient past to overcome the burdens of the
present betrays the limitations of history, just as the submission of the
"François" to Roman domination bespeaks the impossibility of sustaining liberty in the face of superior force. The past cannot redeem

the present, for it is too deeply marred by the contradictions of the contemporary world. The redemptive language of history is condemned to repeat again and again the terms of its own failure. The writing of history is compromised by the very conditions of the possibility of its production. The vernacular history of France's ancient past, in the end, discloses the very brokenness of contemporary experience that it disavows.

ᛋ⟋⚔⟍ᛏ

In recounting the earliest struggles of the "François" to secure their existence within a historical space understood as France, the *Faits des Romains* functions equally as a "livre des origines," as Mireille Schmidt-Chazan has called it,[142] and as the story of national resistance to illegitimate attempts by powerful rulers to restrict and undermine the natural, because ancient, freedom and autonomy of the "François." Understood as an allegory of contemporary society, the message of the *Faits des Romains* is that aristocratic resistance to royal centralization is historically authorized as the principal means to preserve the liberty of the French people.

That the author of the *Faits* meant his history of France's ancient past to be read in this way is confirmed by his treatment of Caesar in the translation of Lucan's *Pharsalia* that follows the *Gallic Wars*. At the same time, the translation of Lucan, found also in Jean de Thuin's *Hystore de Jules César*, which uses the *Faits des Romains* but offers a strikingly different image of the Roman emperor, addresses the question of the role of the hero in history, a question central to chivalric ideology. To the degree that the chivalric past is a heroic past, the paradigmatic value of heroic deeds and figures was critical to the attempt to ground aristocratic ideology in a legitimizing and usable past. The heroic character of medieval chivalry emerges in the vernacular histories of the *Faits des Romains* and the *Hystore de Jules César* as a problem around which the sociomoral character of aristocratic life is both organized and interrogated. Thus, it is to the issue of the heroic in ancient historiography that we must now turn.

4 The Question of the Heroic in Translations of Lucan's *Pharsalia*

Ancient History II

The development of chivalry in France by the thirteenth century had created a rich variety of cultic practices, a social lexicon, a body of sociomoral principles, and a prodigious literary corpus in the vernacular through which issues of knightly existence were explored and defined. Emblematic signs of knightly status in the form of titles, coats of arms, seals, and banners, accompanied by the emergence of ceremonial rituals of incorporation into the knightly class such as dubbing, all signaled the advent of the aristocracy's consciousness of itself as a social *ordo* governed by common juridical rules, accepted manners, and a shared knightly culture.[1]

In attaining the status of a caste, chivalry acquired an indelibly aristocratic character. Chivalric ideology took on the aspect of what Flori labels a *manifeste aristocratique*,[2] absorbing principles of Christian conduct and martial valor into the ideology of an ascendent class, for whom it served as social mythology.[3] As we saw in chapter 1, this developed social mythology was essentially defensive, shielding the aristocracy against successive attacks from the church for its failure to fulfill its secular mission; from the effects of economic competition due to the rising wealth of the bourgeoisie; from the threat to its monopoly on warfare posed by the emergence of professional mercenaries, Brabançons, and *cottereaux*; and from the consequences of monarchical consolidation. Beginning in the twelfth century, the *romans d'antiquité* inaugurated the process of historicizing chivalric ideology by tracing its origins to the distant worlds of Troy and Greece, creating a secular genealogy of morals and codes of behavior that also functioned, as Lee Patterson has demonstrated, as an "initiatory agent in the process by which medieval writing was gradually laicized."[4] By reestablishing the historical world as a locus of value in itself, the *romans d'antiquité* offered an alternative to the hitherto predominantly Christian cast of literate culture.

Yet almost immediately after its appearance in vernacular romance, the effort to create a secular lineage and history for chivalric culture appears to have been diverted. Already by the end of the twelfth century, chivalric ideology within the *romans* underwent a process of spiritualization by which the ethical codes and mores of the knightly classes were reinscribed according to the values of a pervasive Christian ethos. Increasingly spiritual in orientation and theme, the later *roman* in the thirteenth century abandoned the zone of the historical in favor of a transcendent vision of chivalry's mission within the context of an encompassing Christian eschatology. The literary task of explicating the historical roots and secular mission of chivalry was now assumed by the vernacular histories of antiquity, providing legitimacy in the form of historical precedent to the aims and aspirations of the lay aristocracy. Prose history displaced toward realism the formulaic structures of chivalric romance, adapting them to a roughly credible context that strengthened their representational character and, hence, their self-evident authenticity and authority as history.[5] Historiography, as the preeminent medieval literary genre devoted to realism, was perfectly suited to the historical expansion and objectification in the past of chivalric ideology.

To the extent that medieval chivalry organized itself around the imperatives of a martial existence and the attendant ethical prescriptions surrounding the exercise of arms and the conduct of war, chivalric ideology was fundamentally implicated in an attempt to moralize acts of violence by stipulating the conditions and causes under which and for which such violence served licit social purposes. For the vocation of warrior to become an ethical pursuit, legitimizing the social status of the aristocracy in the absence of its concrete performance of military functions (a situation increasingly true in the thirteenth century), it was necessary to present the profession of arms as possessing an inherent moral content.[6]

This moralization of violence found a natural ally in the heroic tradition, itself understood as a moral category of absolute value. The heroic past offered a vast and exploitable secular tradition, replete with relevant *exempla*; it is hardly surprising, therefore, that vernacular chroniclers sought to locate chivalric ideology within the traditions and economy of the heroic life of the ancient past. The historicization of chivalric life that had been initiated but aborted in Old French romance reappeared in the now thoroughly historical genre of the vernacular chronicle. But the vernacular chronicle's treatment of the heroic, precisely because staked on historical ground, necessarily involved an increasingly complex mediation of the ideals of chivalry with respect to the historical past that served as its locus. The goal of heroic idealization was ultimately subverted by the very historical— that is, realist—perspectives and procedures through which the past was seen and recreated. To understand why this occurred, it is useful to review briefly the principal characteristics of the heroic as they had been elaborated in earlier medieval literary forms.

"Heroic ages," Franz Bäuml has said, "appear to be born of a need for them by those conscious of their own present disadvantages."[7] In heroic literature, the values and qualities most prized by contemporary society take flight to the distanced plane of the absolute past, where they assume prescriptive status as social norms. Behind the idealizing impulse implicit in all heroic literature is the conviction that the past is the repository of all that is worthwhile, that the age of "fathers" and "forebears"—of, that is, "beginnings"—is the source of everything possessing social value. Contemporary society bows its head before the grandeur and majesty of this past, approaching it with an attitude, as Lee Patterson has pointed out, of "instinctive deference, even submissiveness."[8] The paradoxical effect of such submissiveness before the past is to purge it of its historical character, elevating it into a realm of transcendent being and value in which the figures and events located in a distanced past are separated from the corrosive effect of historical experience, hence robbed of their historicity. The idealizing procedures to which heroes and their deeds are subjected raise them above the flux of temporality into a timeless realm that is essentially ahistorical. The values that the past enshrines are canonized into immutable principles; the deeds enacted in the past become iconic images of success and failure, virtue and vice, which admit no internal complexity or development, since change transgresses the absolute boundary of ethical and historical authority that the heroic past seeks to erect between itself and the present.

The ideal hero is equally immutable. He is presented as a fully finished and completed being, appearing in heroic literature as "ready-made," entirely present in and of himself, incapable of either spiritual progress or regression. It is the fate of the hero to be what he is, a personality, Bakhtin noted, "absolutely equal to himself," without initiative or internal contradictions, who offers to others a view of himself that coincides completely with their view of him.[9] The hero is never trapped between the conflicting demands of inner and outer realities, for there is no gap between his inner self and the externalized self manifested to the world. He is a wholly "authentic" person, in the sense that his essential and externalized being are one. The hero in classic form can never be alienated, since he can never be other than what he appears to be. He lacks precisely that capacity for individuation or deviance from the norm that forms the modern understanding of what it means to be an individual. He is unique only insofar as he typifies in extravagant, even excessive, ways the values and attributes for which he stands. If there is a tragic undercurrent to all heroism, it resides in this obligatory character of the heroic, which commits the hero to acting out roles and scripts that have been written for him and that terminate, ultimately, in his death. The eulogy of power that constitutes heroic literature is governed by an inner dialectic whose inevitable outcome is defeat.[10]

The hero cannot learn from experience, since learning would carry him away from the path for which he has been destined. He labors under an absolute injunction to remain faithful to himself, whatever the personal, social, military, or political consequences, for himself or for the world that he fully represents in his person. And since "life" and "history" refuse to be governed by the same constraints that limit heroic action, the consequences of heroism are also often tragic for the world through which the hero moves and upon which he imposes his own limited understanding of choice and behavior.

The ineluctably tragic quality of the hero's action, which stems from this disjunction between the imperatives that shape his behavior and the needs of the world he serves so heroically, suggests a certain amount of bad faith on the part of the present that has constructed the heroic past in this way. If heroic ages are made by those in the present who are only too aware of their inferiority before the past, then the present exacts its revenge on the past by condemning the hero to the undoing of the world he both perfectly symbolizes and, ultimately, undermines through his undeviating, unthinking adherence to its precepts.

The utility of the heroic, from the point of view of the present, then, derives not so much from the model of historical success that it projects, since that success is rarely free of tragic consequences, but rather from its ability to furnish certain affirmations of secular values.

Especially in societies imbued with notions of the divine origin of all existence and value in the world, the heroic carves out a social space for what is human, secular, and temporal (however much, finally, it empties out the transitory and changeable from its concept of time). The heroic forms the basis of a "secular scripture,"[11] which competes with, although never entirely displaces, the divine scripture that stands at the center of such theologized societies. The creation of a new heroic past within the context of a culture saturated with theological concepts and moral ideas, therefore, favors the laicization of social values and functions as part of a broader movement involving the desacralization of the world. And since the ruling class in patriarchal societies like that of medieval Europe does belong, in a certain sense, to the world of "fathers," the heroic past both expresses its distance from other classes in society and argues for its independence from the clerical classes who are the guardians of the sacred scriptures. Because the prestige of the heroic lies in the past, an aristocratic class wishing to emphasize its social separation from all other classes looks to antiquity, using the temporal distance between the present and ancient past as a means of expressing the social distance that, it believes, rightfully obtains between it and its nearest social competitors. At the same time, it revives a tradition of secular values and scripts that it raises to the level of universality. As Maurice Keen has argued, the emphasis on classical exemplars of heroism in the High Middle Ages strengthened the conception of chivalry as an essentially secular institution. Unlike Roland, Charlemagne, and even Arthur, these antique examples were unabashedly pagan, thus less amenable to the ideological tampering—represented by clerical attempts such as the *Pseudo-Turpin Chronicle* or the later *romans*—to domesticate and turn them to theological purposes. The ancient past offered the Middle Ages a vast storehouse of exemplars for development as models of chivalry, and did so within a framework that was undeniably secular and pagan. Heroic classical texts such as the *Aeneid*, the *Thebaid*, even the *Pharsalia*, served as paradigms of secular value and chivalric prowess that the French aristocracy could make truly and *exclusively* its own.[12]

The values that medieval writers extracted from the ancient heroic past were the quintessential chivalric virtues of prowess, valor, fame, glory, loyalty, *franchise*, largesse, and courtesy, all of which, by the beginning of the thirteenth century, had become qualities specifically associated with chivalry understood as both a social order and an ideology of class. Heroic culture as constructed in vernacular writings of the twelfth and thirteenth centuries was in equal parts aristocratic and violent, celebrating and idealizing the military function that legitimized aristocratic dominance in medieval society, despite vastly diminished opportunities for its exercise in the conditions of thirteenth-century France. Indeed, the more restricted its field of action became, the more stridently did the aristocracy proclaim the ancient virtues of the battlefield. The almost incantatory affirmation of chivalric virtues found in Old French literature in this period assumes, Flori concluded, the "valeur d'exorcisme,"[13] addressing underlying fears concerning the historical obsolescence of the principles, beliefs, and prerogatives that had defined the social and political status of the warrior classes.

Yet this celebration of violence, even under the ritual guise of chivalric contests, carried its own burden of contradiction. The violent energy that is the *sine qua non* of heroic action also threatens to outrun society's capacity to contain it within socially acceptable bounds, to restrict it to the measured limits of the useful and praiseworthy. The heroic tendency is to struggle against such limits, to spill over into epic *démesure*, that violent rage and unreason which are the outer signs of a heroic energy that has loosed its bonds. The late medieval epic of revolt is marked by precisely this tendency for heroes to carry their violence beyond the legitimate spheres required by justice and to engulf the heroic world in its storm of rage and unthinking pursuit of vengeance.

Perhaps for this reason as well, the hero must die, for his very heroism has carried him beyond the society in whose name he acts but which his deeds now menace. The literary management of heroic violence always preserves the option of killing off the hero and thus putting a stop to the destruction that heroic *démesure* threatens. Short of this final solution, of course, lies the literary presentation of moral codes and hortatory or cautionary examples of heroic behavior, which profess to teach their audience how to live. The counterpoise to the violent energy that underlies all heroism and is to a certain extent the very condition of its being is the elaboration of an ethical code according to which men and events are characterized in terms of moral principles that establish typologies of good and evil.[14]

But the idealization of the hero and the past that had been conducted in vernacular literature of the twelfth century was not so easily accomplished in thirteenth-century vernacular translations of classical histories. The heroic, although grounded in history, is not ultimately hospitable to the relativizing consequences of historical perspectives. To the extent that the heroic past is an absolute past, it lacks any relativity (in the sense of change or temporal progression) and requires the preservation of an absolute boundary between it and the present. But a genuine historical consciousness makes it increasingly difficult to maintain this disjunction between past and present, if for no other reason than that the impulses that lead to the attempt to recover the past grow out of a desire for continuity and identification with it. History, by its very nature, threatens the structure of the heroic, because a historical treatment of the heroic past inevitably relativizes the values that the heroic past is meant to embody. Furthermore, if heroes make history, history can also "unmake" heroes,[15] and the literary management of heroic *démesure* through the death of the hero, by means of which imaginative literature escapes the full consequences of the violence unleashed in heroic action, is not an option necessarily available in historical accounts of the past.

One might ask, therefore, if in thus problematizing the heroic past that they were simultaneously engaged in creating, vernacular chroniclers were not expressing—consciously or unconsciously—the impossibility of sustaining the chivalric codes they sought to ground in antiquity. Could they remain faithful to the narrative plots of the classical histories they were translating while still advancing the heroic themes that prompted their forays into ancient history? In translating ancient histories, the chroniclers were bound to narratives not of their making, whose contents and ideological overtones were, therefore, less easily managed than might have been the case in forthrightly imaginative literature. Although, as we saw in the *Faits des Romains*, the translators who produced ancient histories in the early thirteenth century freely intervened in their sources, interpolating chivalric values and systematically rewriting them in epic and romance styles to suit the tastes and needs of aristocratic audiences for whom they labored, the use of historical texts, in and of itself, meant that chivalric models of conduct were imposed on, rather than produced by, the stories so retold.

The tragic undercurrents of ancient history are not redeemed by exemplary heroes in these vernacular texts, as they are in the *Pseudo-Turpin Chronicle*. Rather, the violence unleashed by the classical hero ends in the decline or destruction of the world he inhabits, signaling the dissolution of the ethical principles that had promoted its former glory and legitimized its exercise of power. If vernacular chroniclers wanted to reinforce the sense of historical mission and social prestige of a beleaguered elite, the message they actually conveyed was highly ambiguous, one more likely to induce fatalism than a sentiment of renewed vigor with which to address the social and political challenges to its authority in thirteenth-century France. The history that was called into being by the sponsorship of vernacular translations of ancient texts was at the same time called into question as the ground of chivalric ideology. Once again, it is the *Faits des Romains* that first addresses these issues and discloses the unintended consequences of the turn to the ancient past as warrant for the ideological needs of the present.

The *Faits des Romains* and the Translation of Lucan

In selecting Lucan's *Bellum civile*—or as it was popularly known, *Pharsalia*—as the base source for his treatment of Caesar's civil war against Pompey, the author of the *Faits des Romains* vastly enlarged the scope of his biography of Caesar beyond mere consideration of the Roman general's military achievements. But this expanded domain was purchased at the price of considerably complicating the task of writing a heroic life, a complication compounded by the nature of Lucan's text. Even to modern interpreters, Lucan's *Pharsalia* presents something of a puzzle, with respect both to the Roman author's literary design and to the attitudes that shaped his narrative.

Lucan's subject was the civil wars that began in 49 B.C., which he chose to treat in an immense epic poem of ten books. The poem was left unfinished, in its present state stopping with the events of the winter of 48–47, although it is logical to suppose, according to Ramsey MacMullen, that it might have been intended to continue to 46 or even 44.[16] The exact shape of the whole as originally conceived, in any case, cannot now be known. A much more serious problem for readers, however, lies in determining the exact nature of Lucan's message in the *Pharsalia*, which began as an attempt, in MacMullen's words, "to map out an epic in which the Emperor [Nero] and his ancestors received the most flattering tributes."[17] If that was Lucan's intent, it did not remain so for long. Although the first three books of the *Pharsalia* appeared without censure, presumably having won the approval of Nero, a breach between the emperor and Lucan at a special meeting of the Senate in A.D. 62 or 63, in which Nero was exhibiting his talents and Lucan walked out, radically reoriented the tone and polemic of the later books. After Book 3 of the *Pharsalia*, Lucan's bias against the Caesars took on a virulent, even violent, character. His venom against Nero, who banished him and his work, is acted out on the person of Caesar, who, in the later volumes, becomes the first in a line of "tyrants" responsible for the destruction of Roman liberty.[18] When Lucan was linked to the Pisonian conspiracy of 65, he was seized and tortured; he is said to have cut his veins, dying with lines from the unfinished *Pharsalia* on his lips.[19]

In the later books of the *Pharsalia*, the hatred of the Caesars that ultimately led Lucan to lay down his life in opposition to Nero works its way through the poem in long expostulations against tyranny and those who impose it, with gruesome details of severed limbs, hewn-off arms and legs, and gushing entrails distributed throughout the account of the civil war, replicating in its taste for blood and gore the bloodthirsty ambition of which Lucan accuses Caesar. Small wonder that Honorius Augustudonensis, in his *De artibus*, chose to exemplify tragedy with Lucan's work.[20] A dark and bitter tone pervades Lucan's depiction of civic virtue and *libertas* dethroned because of the ruthless pursuit of power by ambitious men willing to sacrifice family, state, tradition, and honor for the sake of personal gain.

The final struggle between Pompey and Caesar at the battle of Pharsalia betokens the twilight of the Roman world. The few remaining traces of Rome's past glory and virtue that appear in the figures of a Cato or Brutus, in the love between Pompey and his wife, in the willingness of some Romans to die for the cause of liberty, are destined to be extinguished in the general collapse of Roman traditions that resulted from the civil war and brought the once-great city low. Lucan's epic is a moral allegory, an investigation into the seductive effects of great power no longer bridled by virtue, when luxury, arrogance, self-indulgence, and greed combine to undermine the state that permits them to flourish.

It hardly needs saying that this was not an optimal framework on which to build an ideal image of Caesar. As Jeanette Beer forthrightly puts it: "Lucan's acrimony against the Caesars cannot fail to jar with the translator's presentations of Caesar as a heroic model for a thirteenth-century *imperator*."[21] The author of the *Faits des Romains* seems to have wavered constantly between a half-hearted attempt to vindicate the reputation of Caesar[22] and a desire to demonstrate, with Lucan, the socially pernicious consequences of intemperate ambition. The principal theme of this second part of the *Faits des Romains*, as of the first, is the struggle for liberty in the face of tyranny; the heroes of the civil war, if any exist, are those who prosecute the cause of freedom against the will of the few to dominate. Although there are consistent modifications to Lucan's text that involve the mitigation of es-

pecially harsh judgments and a tempering of Lucan's often violent tirades against Caesar, what is more striking is the degree to which the
anonymous translator lets stand the essentially pejorative picture of
the Roman ruler that Lucan had painted. Indeed, the *Faits* retains so
many of Lucan's acrimonious criticisms of Caesar and uses them so
pointedly that the choice of Lucan appears to have been made with the
full knowledge that Lucan presents a more complicated account of values than is normally supposed when talking about chivalric ideology.

This choice is all the more striking when the author of the *Faits des
Romains* is compared to Jean de Thuin, who, as we shall see, systematically removed all of Lucan's derogatory remarks concerning Caesar.
The differential pattern of translation is instructive, for it highlights
the options available to a thirteenth-century translator in his adaptation and revision of the Latin sources at his disposal. Whereas Jean de
Thuin recasts Lucan's poem as a heroic romance, creating an ideal portrait of Caesar as warrior and courtly lover, the *Faits des Romains* fails
to excise the damning portions of the *Pharsalia*, a failure especially
notable in light of its generically heroic matrix.

The heroic tradition to which Caesar was at once literary and literal
heir is invoked in the opening chapters of the *Faits des Romains*,
where the author appends to Suetonius's description of Caesar an account of his descent from Aeneas:

> Gaius fu ses principaus nons, car il fu apelez Juilles por ce que il fu
> deu lignage Iuli, qui fu filz Enee. De ce dist Virgiles: "Julius a
> magno demissum nomen Iulo"; ce est a dire que Juilles descendié
> deu lignage Enee, qui ot un fiuz qui ot non Iulus, dont li nons de
> Juilles fu estraiz.[23]

> Gaius was his principal name, since he was called Julius because he
> came from the line of Iülus [i.e., Ascanius], who was the son of Ae-
> neas. Of him Virgil says: "Julius a magno demissum nomen Iulo";
> that is to say, that Julius descends from the line of Aeneas, who had
> a son whose name was Iülus, from which the name Julius is derived.

Like his forefather Aeneas, Caesar claims a double lineage, both human and celestial, of which, we are informed, it was his wont to brag:
"Ilec loa Cesar oiant toz Juille sa tante . . . : 'La mere Juille ma tante
descendi de lignage a rois; ses peres fu deu lignage as diex. Or est
donques hautece et seinteez en mon lignage, car ge sui et de diex et de
rois' " (Then Caesar praised within everyone's hearing Julia his
aunt . . . : "The mother of my aunt Julia was descended from a line

of kings; her father came from a line of gods. Therefore, there is both nobility and sanctity in my lineage, for I am [descended] of both gods and kings").[24] The invocation of the Virgilian model and Trojan legend (in the person of Aeneas) at the outset of the *Faits* portends a mythic dimension to the heroic narrative that will ensue and seeks to place it firmly within the most prestigious epic traditions known to the Middle Ages. Caesar's ancestry is grounded in a past that is at once historical and divine and that situates his life within a commemorative ethic of the hero against which his own deeds will be measured and acquire meaning. Significantly, immediately after the battle of Pharsalia, Caesar travels to Troy, where he gazes upon the tombs of Achilles and Ajax and "meint autre noble Greu qui furent a la bataille de Troies" (many other noble Greeks who participated in the battle of Troy), burial sites now covered with grass and trees amid the ruined walls of the ancient city.[25] There, Caesar makes an offering at the tombs of his ancestors, "nies Enee et Aschanii et Iuli," imploring them to accept his gifts and prayers as those bestowed by a worthy successor.[26]

In the *Faits des Romains*, therefore, the history of Caesar's accomplishments, from the time of his birth until his climactic triumph at the battle of Pharsalia, unfolds within the framing context of a Virgilian paradigm of filial piety toward the legacy of the Trojan past. This past serves as warrant for the greatness that comes to Caesar as his natal patrimony and that it is his historical destiny to fulfill, a quasi-divine mandate passed down to him through the blood of his ancestors. The stones of the tombs and of the altar that the Trojans had erected to commemorate their dead now lie scattered on the ground, and "li leus n'estoit de nule biauté ne de nule conoissance" (the place was of no beauty and was scarcely known)—the text thus providing an elegiac setting for Caesar's orisons before the graves of his ancestors and reminding the reader/auditor of the mutability of human life and the evanescence of even the most heroic of peoples and deeds. Just as the fall of Troy, in Virgil's epic poem, effected the transferral of Trojan greatness to the shores of Rome in the person of Aeneas, so Caesar, heir to this imperial foundation, will complete the mission transmitted to him from the pious Aeneas and recuperate the past glory of Troy.

Yet the promise of the Virgilian model as an organizing framework for the account of Caesar's deeds is never realized; it is invoked, only to be ignored. Instead Caesar turns his back on his lineal mandate and chooses to measure himself against another, more powerful legend, which threatens to dwarf him in comparison with the majesty of the past. Sent as quaestor to "Gades" (Cadiz) in Spain, Caesar happens on a statue of Alexander the Great and

> l'esgarda et gemi et se tint por perecex. "Ha!," fist il a soi meïsmes, "con sui mauves, qui n'ai anquore rien fet dont ge doie lox avoir! et cil dont je voi ci l'ymage ot conquis pres que tot le monde quant il fu de mon aage."[27]
>
> looked upon it and sighed and considered himself lazy. "Ha!" he said to himself, "what a poor thing I am, I, who have not yet done anything for which I ought to have praise! while he whose image I see here had conquered almost the whole world when he was my age."

The spectacle of Alexander excites the Roman's ambition and determines him to undertake great things.[28] But Caesar's vow to persevere in greatness seems to be called into question the following night in a dream he has of raping his mother ("li fu vis en dormant que il gisoit charnelment o sa mere"), a dream that leaves him "mout confus" (greatly confused). Soothsayers hastily explain away the erotic content of the dream with the interpretation that "la terre est mere de toz, et einsi est ele ta mere" (the earth is the mother of everyone, and thus is she your mother). Caesar's dream, they assert, signifies that he, like Alexander, will possess "toute terre en ta subjection et seras sire deu monde" (the whole earth in your subjection and you will be lord of the world).[29] The rape of his mother oneirically figures Caesar's conquest of the world.

This eroticizing of heroic conquest as incestuous rape has a curious echo in the anonymous translator's final commentary on Caesar's conquest of Gaul. Translating the concluding chapters of Suetonius's *Vita* (I, 49) on Caesar's character, the author preserves the account of the "unnatural practices" in which Caesar is said to have engaged, whereby Caesar is accused of having been King Nicomedes' catamite. According to Suetonius, rumors persistently circulated that Caesar was the homosexual lover of Nicomedes of Bithynia; verses were composed to mock him, and Bibulus, Caesar's colleague as consul, described him in an edict as "the Queen of Bithynia."[30] The author of the *Faits des Romains* explains the prevalence of such remarks by the fact that Caesar "n'estoit pas lors dou pooir dont il fu puis, car encor n'avoit il pas France conquise ne Pompee sormonté" (Caesar was not at that time the powerful man that he later became, because he had not yet conquered France nor overcome Pompey).[31] The point to this linking of Caesar's homosexuality to the conquest of France soon becomes clear: at the time of Caesar's celebration of his triumph over France, the anonymous translator writes,

> li chevalier qui sivoient le curre qui Cesar portoit au Capitoile, entre les chançons que l'en soloit porter et chanter a lor triumphes, si chantoient et disoient: "Cesar a mise France soz soi; Nichomedes Cesar soz lui. Cesar a ore triumphe qui a France sozmise; Nichomedes n'en a point, qui a Cesar sozmis."[32]

> the knights who followed the chariot that bore Caesar to the Capitol, among the songs that one was accustomed to carry and sing at their triumphs, sang and said: "Caesar has placed France under him; Nicomedes [has placed] Caesar under him. Caesar, who made France submit, now has a triumph; Nicomedes, who made Caesar submit, does not."

Just as incestuous rape is the dream-image of Caesar's conquest of the world, so homosexual subjugation is the metaphorical equivalent of his conquest of France. What Caesar does to France, Nicomedes does to him. Caesar's military subjugation of France is the political equivalent, within the workings of this metaphor, of homosexual domination. The perverse erotic encounter between Nicomedes and Caesar ironically glosses the conquest of France and devalues its status as heroic deed. The subjugator of France is himself subjugated; his triumph is unmasked as a false celebration of virile prowess, a tribute not to a chivalric hero, but to a supine sexual object.

The triumphal context in which this erotic gloss on the conquest of France occurs is particularly important for the narrative and historiographical structure of the *Faits des Romains*, given that its explanation for the outbreak of civil war in Rome stresses Pompey's attempt to deny Caesar a triumph for his victory in Gaul as the primary *casus belli*. The issue of triumph is, in that sense, the narrative bridge between the first and second halves of the *Faits*, tying together the history of France and the history of Rome as twin threads of a single historical process. This narrative interlacing is reinforced by the author's revision of Lucan's text to highlight the importance and preponderance of French troops among Caesar's cohorts in the struggle against Pompey. Whereas in Lucan's version Caesar merely assembles the Roman troops dispersed among the garrisons of Gaul, in the *Faits des Romains* it is the subdued French who are called upon to compose Caesar's army.[33] Moreover, the translator specifies that "tote la fiance Cesar fu en cels de France por lor hardement, car plus les avoit esprovez aspres et estables en totes batailles" (Caesar placed all his faith in those of France on account of their bravery, for he had found them fierce and stable in all battles).[34]

The defeated French rise up to destroy the Roman world. If Caesar uses the Romans to conquer France, he uses the French to conquer Rome. The history of rectilinear progress that the Virgilian paradigm proffered turns back against itself in the symmetrical revenge that the French wreak upon the Roman world. It is a history not of fulfillment, but of doing and undoing, an endlessly repeating cycle of violence and destruction that pits brother against brother, father against son, ruler against ruled. The civil war that follows the conquest of France yields little ground for the display of those heroic virtues of bravery, loyalty, honor, and self-sacrifice that chivalric ideology sought to inculcate. Instead, the unleashing of heroic violence is consummated in the dissolution of the Roman world and the disruption of all value. And to the degree that the civil war is presented in the *Faits des Romains* as the inevitable consequence of Caesar's conquest of France, it redefines the significance of that conquest within the heroic economy of the past. Rather than a source of redemptive value, Caesar's heroism begets ambition, greed, lust, and disloyalty, whose full fury is set loose upon the Roman world.

In the end, the forces of violence within the Roman world that are unleashed in the civil war defeat the very possibility of heroic action. What remains are only small gestures, shards of decency in a world overrun by vengeance and destruction; and it is, finally, on the basis of these fragmentary, discontinuous, and incomplete gestures that the heroic character of the participants and the historical events they enact are judged. What emerges as historically telling for the moral adjudication of the hero in this narrative is not the grandeur and majesty of martial activities—those arabesques of bravery and military prowess that distinguish the medieval epic hero—but the capacity for small, intimate, and caring gestures that preserve a humane identity in the face of historical forces out of control, which threaten to devour all humanity. On this human scale, the deeds and character of Caesar are found wanting and those of his enemies affirmed.

The *Faits des Romains*, following Lucan, sets forth a series of counterportraits to Caesar in the persons of Pompey, Cato, and lesser figures, against which the Roman leader's character and deeds are measured. This series of juxtaposed portraits weaves an intricate argument about the fate of heroism and its consequences in the historical world that serves to interrogate notions of the heroic in the historical past and, by implication, in the chivalric present of thirteenth-century France.

CAESAR AND HIS RIVALS

Although Lucan in the *Pharsalia* consistently favors Pompey and his cause over Caesar, there remains a slight reticence in his treatment of Caesar's antagonist. If Caesar is the *tyrannus* who menaces Roman *libertas*, Pompey is yet a *dominus*, and there is, as Ramsey Mac-Mullen points out, "something fatal in wars fought only to choose a master."[35] Moreover, while sympathetic to Pompey, Lucan had already shown him to be a leader in decline, "a shadow of the mighty name" (*magni nominis umbra*) that he had once been.[36] Insofar as Lucan's principal theme is the abstract struggle for liberty against the forces of tyranny, neither protagonist in this struggle is free of blame for the war that leads to the destruction of the wider liberties of the Roman *populus*. No less than Caesar, Pompey strives for mastery, and although it is clear that, for Lucan, Pompey seeks power in the name of preserving the traditions of Rome, there is a feeling in Lucan's poem that the necessity for such a contest was already symptomatic of larger forces of historical decline in the Roman Republic. Alongside the specific causes of human greed, lust, arrogance, and desire for dominion that for Lucan were responsible for the outbreak of civil war lies a much broader view of the moral decline of the Republic, which inevitably produced men adapted to its conditions.[37]

In relegating to a secondary level the abstract theme that governs the development of Lucan's poem, the *Faits* personalizes the forces at work in the Roman world. Where Lucan saw Roman corruption as a general state to which the great wealth and power of Rome had given free rein, the medieval translator looks to individual moral traits and failings to explain the historical decadence that civil war generates. This narrowing of focus from the general to the specific and from the historical to the personal meant that the evaluation of the specific character of the participants in the civil war carried a much larger share of the historical argument than in Lucan. The significance of the Roman past to be conveyed to a medieval audience is articulated far more clearly in these portraits than in the abstract design of the *Faits des Romains* as a whole.

The picture that emerges of Caesar in the *Faits* complicates any attempt to create a heroic image of the noble warrior whose feats of arms and chivalric virtue vouchsafe the maintenance of social order and justice and, thus, serve to legitimize the prerogatives of a warrior class. In the *Faits des Romains*, Caesar simultaneously embodies and perverts the basic values of medieval chivalry. Among honor, largesse, liberty, lineage, and loyalty, only his prowess remains unaffected by the historical deeds whose consequences subvert the ideology of chivalry which the vernacular translator sought to extract from his ancient *matière*.

Caesar, to be sure, is cast by the thirteenth-century translator in a distinctively epic mold, a warrior without peer ("nus ne savoit de cheval ne d'armes plus de lui" [no one knew more than he about horses and arms])[38] who joins to his military prowess an unrivaled eloquence in speech and writing ("Amparlez estoit come nuls chevaliers mielz")[39] and who is, in keeping with the twin poles of medieval chivalry, equally committed to the pursuit of *chevalerie* and *clergie*.[40] But despite Caesar's personal prowess, his military campaigns, far from providing the stimulus to chivalric glory that the heroic leader should offer his followers, lead instead to the decline of chivalric virtues. The vast arena of warfare that is opened up by the prosecution of civil war solicits the emergence of honor, loyalty, and rectitude and offers a capacious stage on which to enact the theatrics of chivalric combat. The outcomes of these encounters, however, belie the virtue with which they are entered into.

Take, for example, the figure of Curio, Caesar's lieutenant, who leads his legions in Africa against Pompey's allies, Varus and Juba. Curio's battles against both opponents are rewritten with long epic amplifications that render them fully in the context of chivalric warfare as heroic examples of bravery and prowess. Yet in the end, despite the distinction that he has earned on the battlefield, Curio is denied the honor and acclaim that his chivalric skill should have brought him, for he fights, as it turns out, not for honor and glory, but for the booty with which tyrants like Caesar entice the loyalty of followers. What is tragic in the figure of Curio is not his early death in battle, for that is often the fate of even lesser heroes, but the corruption of his honor by the seductive specter of Caesar's gold. The *Faits* retains Lucan's ironic apostrophe to Curio's martial virtue, comparing him to Sulla and Marius and others who had purchased honor, while Curio sold his: "Tu sols vendis en ton tens ce que li autres orent acheté avant toi" (you alone sell in your time what others before you had bought).[41]

Just as Caesar's use of the enticements of wealth corrupts the meaning of honor and loyalty by devaluing the social currency of these chivalric virtues, so also does it pervert the significance of his largesse, itself already implicated in the transactional modalities of exchange.

Largesse, in twelfth-century Arthurian romance, had come to occupy a central place in the scheme of chivalric and courtly values, in which it figured as an absolute moral injunction on the ruler to reward his followers, a sign of the reciprocal social relations binding king and knight in a single system of social exchange and honor. So powerfully did it figure within the moral conspectus of the perfect courtly ruler that the legend of Alexander was largely rewritten in order to make him an exemplary model of royal largesse,[42] largesse being understood as a voluntary act of royal generosity by which the ruler dispensed goods and benefits to his followers in return for their equally voluntary allegiance to him and his causes. Although clearly motivated by economic considerations, largesse in Arthurian romance, as Erich Köhler noted, "was transformed into a condition necessary for the attainment of personal prestige and chivalric honor."[43] Largesse, in this sense, betokened the mutuality governing relations between king and knight, their equality of status within the network of complementary social relations and roles that constituted the unitary world of Arthurian chivalry. As an outer sign of the ties that bound the ruler to his knightly followers, the dispensation of largesse circulated exclusively within the social confines of medieval chivalry, as one more token of the class barriers separating aristocratic knights from all others.

Although Caesar was to achieve within courtly literature a reputation for largesse that rivaled Alexander's, the role that largesse plays in the *Faits des Romains* transgresses the social and moral boundaries within which it had functioned in earlier romance literature. Rather than a sign of social parity and mutuality, largesse in Caesar's hands is an instrument of political ambition, indiscriminately distributed as a means of purchasing political support:

> il donoit largement ou a riches ou a povres; ne frans ne sers ne s'en partoit escondiz. Neïs auquant des senators avoient de ses dons. Il toz seuls estoit refuiz et conforz et solaz des endetez et des colpables, et des joenes homes qui tot avoient despendu.[44]
>
> he gave profusely to rich and poor; neither freeman nor slave left [his presence] denied. Not a few of the senators received his gifts. He alone was the refuge and comfort and solace of the debt-ridden and culpable, and of the young men who had expended their all.

In his drive to power, Caesar proclaims himself a fountain of gifts to all who wish to benefit from his generosity, including *li ovrier*, who are paid out of the spoils of battle ("paié des despueilles et de la proie de ses batailles"). Publicly announcing his desire to disburse largesse, Caesar

> fist crier au pueple que tuit cil qui voudroient dons avoir et boivre et mengier venist a sa cort et uns et autres: il avroient tuit viande et dons a plenté.[45]
>
> proclaimed to the people that all those who wished to have gifts and drink and food should come to his court, one and all: they will have food and gifts in abundance.

Rather than enhancing class solidarity, Caesar's largesse excites the envy of the Roman nobility: "Tant en fist et tant dona dons, que mout des plus nobles Romains en orent envie, et se merveilloient li plusor et estoient esbahi a quoi ce devoit tendre" (He did so much and distributed so many gifts that the most noble Romans were envious of him, and many wondered and were frightened about where [such behavior] might lead).[46] Indeed, Caesar's intemperate ambition leads to the total disruption of social order, raising to power social inferiors and "basses genz":

> Et quant il conmença a monter en pooir, il mist avant en granz honors tex qui de bas lignage estoient, por ce que si ami orent esté en son mendre pooir. Quant l'en le blasmoit des basses genz si alever, il respondoit que, se larron robeor ou homicide li eüssent s'onor aidiee a deffendre si come cist, s'en feïst il autretant.[47]
>
> And when he began to rise in power, he placed at the fore in great honors those who were of low lineage, because they had been his friends when he was less powerful. When he was blamed for having elevated low-class men, he answered that, if thieves or murderers had helped to defend his honor as these had, he would do as much for them.

Not only does Caesar elevate his friends of low extraction to positions of honor in the state but—worse still—"dou fill a un soen serf fist il prevost et conestable de .iiij. legions de chevaliers" (he made the son of one of his slaves provost and constable of three legions of knights).[48] The actions of the unscrupulous ruler intrude those of servile status into the very heart of the aristocracy's martial function, making chivalric leaders out of domestic servants and menacing the elite with a perverse, because inverted, image of social order.

If, then, the thirteenth-century French aristocracy sought in the *Faits des Romains* (as so many scholars have argued) a ground for the exaltation of chivalric codes of behavior by the recovery of ideal models of prowess, virtue, largesse, and nobility, that history proved to be disappointingly deficient in furnishing such models. The comparisons between Caesar and his principal antagonists in the civil war disclose the complexities and uncertainties of the historical past. This is a world in which human pettiness, envy, lust for distinction, greed, political rivalry, and overweening ambition confound any attempt to align good and evil, justice and iniquity, hero and villain. The very complexity of the historical situation works against an "idealized" Caesarian narrative. Only the ruthless expurgation of these political complexities could produce a narrative that accorded with the restricted moral imperatives of medieval poetic heroism. It is noteworthy that the translator of the *Faits* did not elect to pursue such a cleansing policy. Instead he followed Lucan's lead in depicting Caesar as goaded by ambition to conquer Rome and the world, a process that, for Caesar, comes to entail the total elimination of his enemies and their heirs.

The author establishes from the outset the perspectives that will shape the *Faits's* presentation of Pompey and Caesar in relation to each other. The attitudes with which they approach the civil war disclose in telling ways the differences that so profoundly mark each antagonist. As Caesar takes the final step toward crossing the Rubicon, he sees before him an image of a large female figure "completely disheveled, with hair askew, arms uncovered and naked," who sighs, revealing herself as a personification of the city:

> "Ha! seignor home, ou volez vos aler outre ceste iaue? Ou volez vos porter mes banieres et mes ensaignes? Se vos estes mi citeain et vos venez por pes ne vos ne volez rien entreprendre vers moi, ci devez vos metre jus les armes et venir desarmé dusqu'an Rome, car pieça que jugemenz est donez que quiconques passera ceste iaue armez il sera tenuz por anemis mortex dou conmun de Rome."[49]

> "Ha! lord man, where do you wish to go beyond this river? Where do you wish to carry my banners and my flags? If you are my citizen and you come for peace and do not wish to undertake anything against me, you should lay down your arms here and come unarmed into Rome, because since long ago the judgment was made that whoever passes this river armed, he will be taken for a mortal enemy of the commune of Rome."

To Rome's evident distress at the prospect of civil war and clear articulation of the legal transgression that Caesar's crossing of the Rubicon will entail, placing him within the ranks of the city's "mortal enemies," Caesar responds with a rehearsal of the personal grievances he has suffered from the failure to acknowledge the honor he had accrued through his military victories on her behalf:

> "Ha! Rome, Rome, ja m'est il vis que ge voie Dieu quant je te voi. Ne va pas contre ce que je voill conmencier. Je n'ai pas pris armes contre toi, ainz revieng come cil que tu doiz reçoivre a honor por les batailles que je ai veincues, et me doiz rendre mon triumphe, car je ai esté il toens Cesar partot, et en terre et en mer, et me sui conbatuz por ta seignorie et por ta digneté acroistre. . . . Ge ne te quier pas nuire; cil te nuira, et celui doiz tu tenir por anemi, si come je meïsmes faz, qui metra descorde entre moi et toi."[50]

> "Ha! Rome, Rome, it seems to me that I see God when I see you. Do not oppose what I wish to begin. I have not taken up arms against you, but return as someone whom you should receive with honor on account of the battles that I have won, and you should render me my triumph, because I have been your Caesar everywhere, both on land and sea, and I have fought to augment your lordship and your dignity. . . . I do not seek to harm you; the one who will harm you, and whom you should consider an enemy, as I myself do, is he who shall sow discord between me and you."

The exercise of arms, in Caesar's partisan brief, suffices to earn him the distinctions that the Senate has wrongfully denied him. That he now, out of disappointment and a desire to avenge his honor, turns his arms against Rome herself, whose pitiful destiny is figured in her bare and unkempt state, is justified as a licit response to thwarted desires. The claims of personal honor override for Caesar the traditions of the state and permit him willfully to violate the laws that guarantee social order.

Significantly, whereas the image of Caesar progressively worsens over the course of the *Faits des Romains*, that of Pompey improves, until Pompey, in his devotion to the cause of Rome, in his love for his wife, and in his fidelity to the traditions of Roman *libertas*, becomes a heroic foil to Caesar. Pompey is consistently depicted as acting for the common good of the city. Where Caesar acts from motives of personal dissatisfaction, Pompey is moved to defend the common liberty, a theme insistently sounded in his exhortation to his followers to carry on the struggle against Caesar:

> "O seignor chevalier, prodonme loial, droit citeain de Rome, qui n'avez pas armes prises por voz privees besoignes, mes por le conmun profit, alez de boen cuer en ceste bataille. . . . Se Deu plest, ore est venue l'ore que Rome en sera vengie par mon conseill et par ma

main. Ne ce n'est pas bataille simplement ou vos devez aler, ainz est vengemenz de vostre païs."[51]

"O my lordly knights, loyal gentlemen, upright citizens of Rome, who have never taken up arms for the sake of private matters, but only for the common good, go with stout heart into this battle [Brindisium]. . . . If it please God, the hour has come when Rome will be avenged by my counsel and by my hand. It is not merely a battle into which you must enter, but also a vindication of your country."

Pompey's army is made up of loyal citizens who, like him, sacrifice themselves not for the sake of private gain, but for the common advantage (*profit*) of the state. Pompey's leadership takes the form of counsel and diligence, in which physical strength (*ma main*) is tempered by reason (*mon conseill*). Caesar, in contrast, is described as "enragiez et sanz mesure" (enraged and without measure). The phrase, which translates Lucan's "O rabies miseranda ducis" (What pitiable madness is Caesar's), places Caesar's actions within the lexical and discursive register of epic *démesure*. Its semantic range and literary resonances differ from Lucan's and, thus, locate the figure of Caesar in a new corpus of implicit intertextual references and allusions. No longer is Caesar a piteous figure, deranged by his pride and desire for honor; he is now the wrathful *bellator* of heroic epic, whose violent rage knows no bounds and, in that sense, is "without measure," a force unto itself that cannot be regulated.

As the narrative progresses, Caesar increasingly comes to represent an insatiable appetite for power that threatens, as Pompey warns his followers, to convert Roman citizens into slaves ("se vos ne deviez devenir tuit si serf").[52] The prowess and military cunning that had made Caesar the conqueror of France are now directed against his fellow countrymen, and with equal brutality. The lust for honor and dominion that drives Caesar spells the end of Roman traditions of liberty.

In contrast to Caesar, Pompey is invariably cast as the defender of liberty and the Roman traditions of honor and restraint that had allowed the city to flourish. As he pointedly declares on the eve of the battle of Pharsalia:

"Li roi, li duc, li conte, li senator, li prodome sont od nos por nostre droit et por nostre franchise desresnier. Se Catons li oncles et Camillus et Decius et li autre predome qui jadis furent estoient vif, nos avons si grant droit que il se metroient en ce perill avec nos come il firent jadis por la franchise de Rome garantir."[53]

"Kings, dukes, counts, senators, honorable men are with us in order
to defend our right and our liberty. If Cato the uncle and Camillus
and Decius and the other upright men who formerly lived were
alive, we have so much justice [on our side] that they would place
themselves in this peril with us, as they previously did to secure the
liberty of Rome."

We fight, proclaims Pompey, in order that "cil qui or sunt puissent
morir franc, et cil qui sunt a venir puissent nestre franc" (those who
are now [alive] might die free, and those who are to come might be
born free).[54] In Pompey, asserts the *Faits*, Rome had found a leader
worthy to champion the cause of liberty, who fought not for the renown or riches or honor that he might attain, but for the common
good of the people. "Bien," declares our author, "i paroit de quele
vertu il estoit" (It appears clearly what virtue he possessed).[55]

Perhaps the most touching evidence of Pompey's virtue emerges
from his relationship to his wife, Cornelia, which both Lucan and the
Faits starkly contrast with Caesar's wooing of Cleopatra. Pompey exhibits unfailing tenderness toward Cornelia and constant concern for
her well-being. When forced, finally, to send her to the island of Les-
bos before the battle of Pharsalia in order to ensure her safety, the
parting is a tearful wrenching for both, "car mout s'entramoient du
grant amor" (because they loved one another with great affection).
Cornelia's lament upon hearing of her husband's death is one of the
rhetorical jewels of the *Faits des Romains*. She matches in full those
exemplars of wifely virtue and conjugal fidelity that filled the pages of
Roman history and constituted a major aspect of its moral didacticism.

The story of Caesar and Cleopatra, to the contrary, remains within
the rhetorical frame of a cautionary tale of "luxure" utilized in Lucan's brief version, and this despite the fact that the translator seized
the opportunity to build a romance tale out of Lucan's passing remarks. It forms, in fact, one of the longest interpolated episodes in
this part of the *Faits des Romains*, and its negative character suggests,
once again, that the author was not primarily interested in the ideological fashioning of an ideal image from his Caesarean material. Caesar's self-abandonment to Cleopatra, his misguided and politically
dysfunctional alliance with her, prompted purely by erotic desire,
demonstrate a regressive surrender to instinctual forces that can only
be construed as morally reprehensible.

As developed in the *Faits des Romains*, Cleopatra, brilliantly clad in
dazzling gold, appears before Caesar to plead her cause against her
brother, Ptolemy, who, acting on the evil counsel of Photin, has

deprived her of the throne. But despite her tears, sighs, and "guise de fame qui devoit merci crier et requerre" (guise of a woman who must cry and beg for mercy), Caesar remains unmoved by her words. Instead, while his ears are closed to her pleas, his desire is excited by her appearance; indeed, he was "si corrompuz que il la vosist ja tenir une nuit entre ses braz et fust fet quanque ele demandoit" (so corrupted that he already wanted to hold her one night between his arms and let be done whatever she asked). And so it was ("Einsi fu il").[56] Although his reason remains obdurate, Caesar's lust takes hold of him, compelling him to surrender to Cleopatra's erotic enticements. That for Cleopatra such enticements were merely a means to political ends is made abundantly clear. She cloaks herself in splendor "por plere a Cesar et por enlacier le et atrere a sa volenté" (to please Caesar and to ensnare him and draw him to [do] her bidding).[57] The underlying immorality of her design is carefully registered by the translator, who notes that "tant s'estoit Cleopatra beau paree, que bel avival de puterie et de luxure avoit en li" (Cleopatra was so beautifully adorned, that there was in him a strong stirring of debauchery and lust).[58] Cleopatra's beauty, rather than being an aesthetic mantle to her sex, takes the form, in Jeanette Beer's phrase, of "degenerate display."[59] This is not a tale of amorous adventure, but a saga of lust and sexual manipulation for political gain.

The *Faits* repeats and embellishes Lucan's already harsh judgment on the affair between Caesar and Cleopatra as inherently shameful and disastrous in its consequences for Rome, delaying Caesar more than two years in Egypt while he languished in the delights of Cleopatra's bed.[60] Moreover, it adds, those in Caesar's camp are humiliated by the affair, since it was the lovers' practice to sail down the Nile, compelling Caesar's "knights" (*li chevalier Caesar*) to ride after them on the bank. They themselves reproach Caesar for the public shame that he visits upon Rome by his alliance with the Egyptian Queen:

> "Cesar, tu abesses l'onor de Rome, quant tu nos fez aler apres toi et apres une fame qui n'est mie t'espose. En ceste maniere tu ne te deduiz pas come dux de Rome, qui tant as encore a fere. Ce est vie de houlier. Tote chevalerie aville de ce que nos te suivons einsi."[61]

> "Caesar, you abase the honor of Rome when you make us follow after you and after a woman who is not your spouse. In this manner you do not conduct yourself like a leader of Rome, you who still have much to accomplish. This is the life of a libertine. All chivalry is dishonored by the fact that we thus follow you."

Rather than the heroic leader of military forces, Caesar acts the part of a libertine (*houlier*), whose sexual delinquencies are not confined to the privacy of the adulterous bed he shares with the queen, but used to coerce and humiliate his followers, sowing discontent and social shame among the knightly classes, whose loyalty he once had courted as arduously as he now courts Cleopatra. The interpolated love affair between Caesar and Cleopatra thus functions in the narrative as a foil to the fidelity of Pompey and Cornelia, and hence as a demonstration of the moral degeneracy to which unbridled power has brought the Roman general. It is Pompey in his tender care for his wife, not Caesar, who emerges from this comparison as the model worthy of emulation.

If the Pompey of the *Faits* displays a fatal weakness that makes him, too, something less than an ideal hero, it lies precisely in his tenderness, in a certain hesitancy to sacrifice others for the advancement of his own goals. Thus, although he had essentially defeated Caesar at the battle of Dyrrachium, Pompey—"qui mout estoit piteus"—fails to seal the victory by pursuing Caesar as he flees the field, for fear that to do so would lead to further deaths among his troops. Instead he sounds the retreat, enabling Caesar and the remainder of his army to escape.

Lucan in the *Pharsalia* had delivered an anti-imperial diatribe against this failure to destroy Caesar, which resulted in Rome's final loss of *sa franchise*. Had Pompey only overcome his distaste for further battle, the *Faits* translates, "Rome poïst avoir terminee sa dolor, ne ne covenist pas que tant roi et tant duc fussent mort en Thesaile come il furent puis" (Rome could have ended her sorrow, and it would not have been necessary for so many kings and dukes to have died in Thessaly as they did later).[62] From Pompey's failure to pursue victory to its bitter end arises the necessity for the battle of Pharsalia, the ultimate triumph of Caesar, and the destruction of Roman traditions of liberty. For Lucan, Pompey is, in the words of W. R. Johnson, "part scapegoat (victim of destiny, of Caesar, and of his own false friends) and part guilty leader (by virtue of his own defects and of the wider corruption and bad faith whose figurehead he was made to seem)." He thus serves the *Pharsalia* as "the ideal symbol both of the false promises of history and of the sickening dread that attends the recognition of the illusion of history."[63] In retaining Lucan's ambiguous portrait of Caesar's principal rival, the *Faits* incorporates the Roman author's sense of the radical inadequacies of those who champion freedom and of their ideals, offering to its audience a vision of the past already scented with the aroma of defeat.

Yet in the end, for both Lucan and the *Faits*, Pompey must be adjudged virtuous:

> Ce fu Pompee, qui toz les jors de sa vie avoit esté en honor sanz entremeslement de nule mesestance; . . . [he was one] qui onques n'ot cure d'orgueill ne n'ama mauvese conpaignie ne mauvese covoitise, mes franchise amoit sor tote rien, et por la franchise de Rome garder s'abandonoit a toz perilz.[64]

> Thus was Pompey, who all the days of his life remained steadfast in honor without the admixture of any affliction; . . . [he was one] who took no care for pride, nor did he love bad company or base concupiscence, but prized liberty above all other things, and in order to safeguard the liberty of Rome abandoned himself to all dangers.

His mutilated body, head severed from the torso, was recovered from the Nile, into which it had been thrown, and hastily buried in a pauper's grave by a loyal follower. Caesar, upon discovering the shameful site, allowed the corpse to rest there, so that all might know "que Pompee gisoit en si vil leu, et ce tornoit a sa honte" (that Pompey lay in such a vile spot, and that this redounded to his shame).[65] Not even to a dead enemy could Caesar accord the dignity of a proper burial place appropriate to a Roman citizen of Pompey's stature.[66] Pompey's mercy in sparing Caesar's life is answered by the degradation of his earthly remains in the inhospitable soil of Egypt.

If Pompey is a flawed heroic foil to Caesar, suspect in part as the representative of a tendency to domination in the Roman Republic, however much his personal virtue and commitment to liberty mitigate the historical implications of his status as *dominus,* the same cannot be said of Cato. The figure of Cato was so sanctified in Roman literature that his name had become a stereotype of virtue. Although the specifically Republican overtones in the classical veneration of the virtuous Roman meant little in the Middle Ages, he had continued to function as an exemplar of uncompromising virtue, free of any taint of corruption.

Cato first appears in the *Faits des Romains* when he delivers his speech before the Senate condemning the Catiline conspiracy. The question had been put by Cicero of whether the conspirators should be condemned to death. Caesar had counseled mercy in the name of senatorial traditions of clemency and compassion toward enemies.[67] Cato, conversely, recommended full punishment, stressing the seri-

ousness of the offense against the state and the threat that it posed to
the maintenance of liberty:

> "Ceste besoigne n'est pas de tonleu ne de paage ne de querele de
> conpaignons, ançois est de vostre franchise desfendre et de vos cors
> qui sont en peril."[68]

> "This affair is not a matter of taxes or tolls, nor a quarrel between
> companions, but involves the defense of your liberty and of your
> bodies, which are in danger."

Catiline had claimed that the roots of the conspiracy lay in the debt-
ridden poverty in which the conspirators were forced to live, while the
senatorial classes daily reveled in the honors, luxuries, and immense
wealth that Roman conquest had created and that the Senate had succeeded in monopolizing.[69] For Cato, however, the cause lay rather in
the "avarice," "luxure," and "covoitise" that had infected the citizens
of Rome as a consequence of the city's growing power. Forbearance toward conspirators, in these circumstances, was mere foolishness, an
inappropriate display of leniency toward those who merited the harsh-
est treatment that the state could mete out. Romans unwisely confided their destiny to the gods, proclaimed Cato, but "l'aide de Dieu ne
vient pas a la volenté de cels qui volent vivre come fames" (God's aid
does not come at the will of those who desire to live like women).[70]
Caesar's position, then, promotes a fatal feminization of once-sturdy,
masculine modes of behavior, whereas Cato promulgates a sterner
code.

Cato is a man who never bends before wrongdoing, whether for
praise, love, or hate; who declines to compete against the rich with
riches or against the trickster with treachery; who, instead,

> metoit vertu contre vertu, vergoingne avec mesure, abstinence avec
> innocence; mielz voloit estre preudom que senbler le; et por ce que
> meins covoitoit pris, loenge et gloire, plus en avoit.[71]

> matches virtue with virtue, modesty with reasonableness, abstinence
> with innocence; he preferred to *be* an honorable man than seem one;
> and because he little desired reward, praise, or glory, he had the
> more of them.

More pointed still is the contrast between Caesar's libertinism and
Cato's chastity. Cato had married Marcia while she was young. When
he became too old to sire offspring, although she was still capable of
bearing them, he urged her to marry again so as to continue to produce children, which she did. Christians should feel great shame,

interjects the *Faits*, at the example of such pagans who take women not "por lor luxure acomplir," but only in order to have children.[72] Moreover, although Cato received Marcia back, he never again touched her, and they lived out the remainder of their lives in perfect chastity. In public and private realms alike, Cato is the wholly moral being, unswayed by the fortunes of men or politics and undeviating from the path of virtue in the conduct of his life.

The virtues of Cato sketched in the Catiline conspiracy reappear in the context of the civil war, in which Cato places his moral authority on the side of Pompey and emerges as the principal defender of liberty after Pompey's demise. The *Faits* adds considerably to Lucan's account of the struggle between Caesar and Cato in order to enhance the heroic stature of Cato as warrior and thereby enable him to rival Caesar in this regard as well.[73] Unlike Caesar, however, Cato enters the struggle only with reluctance—primarily at the urging of Brutus, who persuades him to join Pompey's coalition and, after Pompey's death, to assume leadership of the forces against Caesar—because he recognizes that war between citizens is "folie et desverie" (madness).[74] Throughout the course of the struggle, he does what he does solely for the sake of defending Roman liberty:

> N'onques Catons ne s'entremist de meintenir guerre entre citeains
> por seignorie ou il tendist ne por crieme de servir, mes seulement
> por conmune franchise defendre et garantir; car il ne queroit estre ne
> sers ne sire, mes solement vivre en franchise avec son conmun. En
> chose que il feïst il ne querroit rien de son propre preu, ainz porcha-
> çoit toz jors le preu de toz en conmun.[75]

> Cato did not occupy himself with maintaining war between citizens
> out of a wish for lordship or out of fear of being enslaved, but only
> in order to defend and protect the common freedom; for he did not
> seek to be either slave or sire, but only to live in liberty with his
> community. In whatever he did, he never sought his own advantage,
> but always pursued the benefit of all in common.

Ever moved by the desire to safeguard the "conmun profit dou païs,"[76] Cato understands fully the threat to Roman freedom posed by Caesar's ambition. He deems Pompey lucky to have died so quickly after his defeat at Pharsalia, because otherwise he might have had to live on under Caesar, and "qui vit soz seignor, il n'a pas veraie franchise" (he who lives under a lord does not possess true freedom).[77]

Cato's speech to his followers as they prepare to join forces with Juba in the desert of Libya, a territory famous for its venomous snakes and brutal sun, acknowledges the uncertainty of their fates, but at the same time justifies the hardships they will endure by the inherent righteousness of their cause and the necessity to preserve their freedom, even in the face of death:

> "O li mien chevalier et li mien conpaignon, qui avez esleüe avec moi une seule voie de salu, ce est a morir en droite franchise plus qu'a vivre en servage . . . Mes ce vos doit conforter que l'en ne puet pas avoir auques de bien en cest siecle ne conquerre droite franchise a soi et a son païs sanz grant paine et sanz durs sentiers."[78]

> "Oh, my knights and my companions, who have elected with me the only worthy path, which is to die in just liberty rather than to live in servitude . . . But this should comfort you, that one cannot have any good in this life nor win true liberty for oneself and one's country without great difficulty and without taking the hard road."

By this speech Cato "grant essample donoit a toz de vertuz" (provided a great example of virtue for everyone).[79]

If Cato exhibits any failing in the eyes of the medieval translator, it derives from the fact that he took his own life by poison once it had become clear that the cause of Rome's *franchise* was lost. Yet even Cato's suicide is presented as the ultimate act in a life committed to the preservation of liberty, an act consonant with Roman, if not Christian, traditions: "grant essample dona d'amer vraie franchise, quant il s'ocist por itel franchise deffendre come Romein avoient a son tens" (he provided a great example of the love of real liberty when he killed himself in order to defend such liberty as the Romans possessed in his time).[80] As in the case of Drappés Brenno in the Gallic wars, suicide is the final rebuttal to Caesar's power, a denial of the Roman's drive to mastery in the name of a higher human struggle against the tyranny of the ambitious.

Given the traditional importance of Cato as a perfect exemplar of virtue, Cato's judgment of Pompey assumes a more than ordinary importance as a gloss on the relative justice and morality of Caesar and Pompey in the civil war. This judgment, moreover, leaves little doubt concerning the superior moral force of Caesar's antagonist. Pompey is characterized by Cato as a man of measure, reason, and virtuous behavior, devoted to principles of justice, and holding in reverence all that pertains to righteousness. His household is chaste and without luxury; nor is he corrupted by evil habits or the desire for riches. Never did he claim privilege or rulership over Rome by virtue of the battles he had waged or the lands he had conquered, nor gift nor triumph "se l'en ne li dona de boen gré" (unless it were given to him willingly). He knows both when to take up arms and when to lay them down and never wages war *against* but only *for* his country. Although he possessed great power and lordship (*seignorie*), he exercised them without diminishing the freedom of others. Indeed, proclaims Cato, "a peine seroit ore trovez ses parelz entre les meillors qui or sunt" (it would be difficult to find his equal today among the best who now live).[81]

Ultimately, however, even the deeds of the virtuous are doomed to historical defeat as the dream of freedom is transformed into the "nightmare of ruined Rome."[82] The violence that is unleashed in the civil war between Caesar and Pompey not only dissolves the values that had once guided the conduct of the Roman world, but, in pitting brother against brother, father against son, cousin against cousin, also signifies the disruption of lineage and, hence, of the very social principles in the name of which glory and military prowess had been so vigorously pursued. As Caesar's soldiers pointedly query:

> "Que nos profite ce que nos avons tant sanc espandu par toi es batailles de France, de Espaigne, de Tieche terre? Li guerredons que tu nos en renz, si est ce que tu nos fez conbatre au derien a noz parenz, a nos cosins, a nos freres."[83]

> "What does it profit us that we have spilled so much blood for you in the battles of France, of Spain, and the lands of Germany? The reward that you bestow upon us is that you require us in the end to fight against our parents, cousins, and brothers."

The heroic violence directed against the French returns to plague those who engaged in it. Loyalty to Caesar on the fields of France now entails loyalty in the slaughter of one's own lineage. The logic of Caesar's drive to mastery carries him from the far shores of Britain and France to the heart of Rome. Caesar's violence is displaced not outward but to the core of the civilization under whose banner he had taken up arms. It entails a betrayal not merely of the laws of the Roman Republic, of which his acts spell the end, but of the principles on which Roman society was founded. With brutal callousness, Caesar urges his troops to despoil whatever was left behind in Pompey's camp after the battle of Pharsalia, promising them tents filled with gold and silver, riches amassed from throughout the world. Yet the booty acquired in civil war is wrung from the broken bodies of fathers and brothers:

> Quant il furent si avugle et desvé de covoitise, quant il conmancerent a poindre et a aler par dessor armes, par dessor cors et menbres de lor peres et de lor freres, de lor parenz, de lor amis et de lor autres

voisins qui gisoient detrenchié par les chans a tas li uns sor les autres, droit as loges Pompee, ce fu merveille conment terre sostenoit itel gent.

When they were so blinded and maddened by greed, they began to charge and to go among the weapons and bodies and limbs of their fathers and brothers, of their relatives, of their friends and their neighbors, who lay hacked into pieces, piled up on the fields one upon the other, straight up to Pompey's tents; it was a wonder how the earth sustained such people.

Only too late do Caesar's followers recognize the fatal costs of war enacted against one's own society, a price not redeemed by the spoils taken from the dead bodies of relatives:

> Mout troverent es tentes grant tresor; mes poi lors sembla a ce que il cuidoient avoir fet et deservi. Se il eüssent tot l'or des minieres d'Espaigne et les haraines d'or que len seust trover em plusors fleuves, si lor semblast il poi a ce que il avoient de mal fet por Cesar et que il lor avoit promis.[84]

> Many found great treasure in the tents; but it seemed little to them in comparison to what they thought they had done and deserved. If they were to have all the gold from Spanish mines and the pebbles of gold that one might find in several rivers, it seemed to them little in light of the evil they had done for Caesar and what he had promised them.

Caesar's war promised glory and riches; instead it produced the destruction of Roman traditions, threatening Rome's very potential for survival: "Ce qui chaï en cele bataille ne fu recovré en meint aage por nule procreacion de lignee" (What [i.e., the generation that] fell in this battle was not recuperated for many ages through the procreation of lineages).[85] In a final act of outrage against his enemies, Caesar forbade his soldiers to bury Pompey's dead, thus depriving them of the right to honor their slain relatives.

If the French aristocracy sought in the past a redeemed vision of chivalric society, in which nobles occupied their rightful place as governors and defenders of the social order, what it found in turning to ancient history was the specter of a world turned upside down. The threat of social disorder haunts the pages of the classical past as persistently as it does the chivalric present. The lesson that ancient history teaches subverts the desire to use the past to reopen the contest for authority between aristocracy and monarchy, for the narration of Caesar's exploits underscores Cato's earlier warning that he who lives under a lord does not possess true freedom. Powerful rulers, by relying on the socially inferior to do their bidding, threaten the autonomy and prestige of noble classes, a fact as palpable in ancient as in contemporary history. Caesar offers no more hope for the revival of aristocratic social prestige and military function than does Philip Augustus, for both pursue the logic of rulership to its inevitable end in the elimination of rival sources of power.

Similarly, whatever heroicizing impulses may have been at work in the medieval translator's exploration of the ancient past as a source of heroic exemplars are frustrated by the hopelessly complex and contradictory conclusions to which his investigation of that past leads him. History itself, as both record and narrative source, subverts the historiographical project of grounding aristocratic ideology in an unproblematic past. The presentation of Caesar as chivalric hero is persistently shadowed by the violence and venom that marks Lucan's text. The distance inscribed between Latin source and medieval translation thus measures the rupture between historical reality and ideological assertion that the writing of vernacular history in the thirteenth century sought to dissemble. The inability of the *Faits des Romains* to sustain a heroic model of Caesar offers compelling testimony to the inherent contradictions in aristocratic life and ideology in thirteenth-century France. Rather than validate chivalric ideals, the history of Caesar, in the end, discloses the incapacity of the past to offer emotional sustenance and political legitimacy to a class in the process of losing its functional authority and political autonomy.

Jean de Thuin

The failure of the *Faits des Romains* to generate and sustain a heroic narrative of ancient history staked on historical grounds stems, in part, from the inherent contradictions implicit in such a historiographical project and, in part, from the incompatibility of its epic mode with the historical material itself. Insofar as a genuinely epic treatment of the heroic events and personages of the past required a timeless, unchanging, and deproblematized view of human motives and actions, the endeavor to inscribe ancient history within the literary and ideological framework of chivalric epic was bound to miscarry. In that sense, it might be said that the failure of the *Faits des Romains* is also a failure of mimesis, of the representational modes employed for forging a classical past governed by the ideological needs and literary tactics of contemporary society.

In Jean de Thuin's *Hystore de Jules César* we find a similar attempt to create an exemplary life of Caesar out of Lucan's complex and difficult poem, but one that pursues an entirely different set of literary strategies, both in its relation to its source and in the modes adopted for the re-creation of ancient history in accordance with medieval principles and values. Instead of the epic treatment of Lucan's Caesarean material that the *Faits* undertakes, Jean de Thuin consciously recasts his *Hystore* in a romance mode, using ancient history as a moral allegory of courtly ethics and behavior.

Of Jean de Thuin himself we know little beyond his name. The city of Thuin is in Hainaut, and the language of the earliest manuscripts (Vatican, Arsenal, and Saint-Omer) confirms this provenance.[86] H. Suchier noted two charters from Hainaut, dated to May and June of 1277, in which the name of a certain Jean de Thuin appears; in both he is identified as a knight, "avoué de Thuin." A third charter, from 1258, names the "advocate of Thuin" but fails to give Jean's name.[87] Yet although Suchier willingly identified the author of the *Hystore* with the *avoué* Jean, it seems highly unlikely that they were the same person. Both the ability to translate Lucan and obvious familiarity with school texts (such as those of the "Maistres d'Orléans"), which he frequently cited (albeit in a hostile vein), identify Jean as an educated cleric who had spent some time in university circles, probably in Paris. His translation of Lucan's difficult poem contains few errors, and he was clearly acquainted with a broad range of classical works and medieval commentaries on them. When translating, he often moved from one Latin source to another, completing deficiencies in Lucan with the aid of other ancient works.[88] In addition to Lucan, Jean was familiar with Caesar and his continuators, Suetonius, Ovid, Plutarch, Cassius Dio, Appian, and Isidore of Seville, as well as vernacular works such as the *Roman d'Enéas* and the first part of the *Roman de la Rose*.

Although the *Hystore* identifies itself simply as a translation of Lucan's *Pharsalia*, in fact, like the *Faits des Romains*, it employs Caesar's *Bellum civile* and its continuations, the *Bellum Alexandrinum*, *Africae*, and *Hispaniense*, to complete the narrative of the civil war after Lucan's *Pharsalia* gives out. In addition, Jean de Thuin often alludes to "li maistre d'Orliens," primarily in order to discredit the "fables" that he attributes to this source. In all likelihood, he used a set of glosses on ancient history, though not necessarily the same gloss by Master Arnulfus employed by the anonymous author of the *Faits des Romains*, since the *Hystore* never refers to the Maistre d'Orléans when dealing with passages derived from Lucan, but only in those portions of the text where the sources being translated are either the *Bellum Africae* or the *Bellum Hispaniense*.[89] His account of the death of Crassus, for example, derives from Cassius Dio, and less direct borrowings from Suetonius, Ovid, Isidore, and other classical and medieval authors are apparent. The portrait of Cleopatra, similarly, seems to be an imitation of the famous portrait of Iseult in *Tristan*. Salverda de Grave argues that the *Roman d'Enéas* was an important source for Jean, who used it not only for direct textual borrowings but also as a model for the interpolated love affair between Caesar and Cleopatra.[90] Similarly, the inserted love casuistry, or "traité d'amour," that follows the romance of Caesar and Cleopatra indicates Jean's knowledge of Ovid, Andreas Capellanus, and part one of the *Roman de la Rose*, although his own treatise differs considerably from any of these possible sources.

In the broadest sense, Jean's vocabulary, style, and troping of his historical material in romance modes demonstrate his wide acquaintance with the conventions and procedures of the earlier Old French *roman*. However, his use of these conventions for a specifically historical narrative effects a reduction in the range and richness of romance vocabulary and style. His own style tends, rather, to simplicity, fluidity, even a certain sobriety.[91] He is equally reductive in his handling of Lucan, removing the extravagant images, apostrophes, and extended similes with which Lucan liberally sprinkled his poem. At the same time, he adds to Lucan and his other sources the long epic amplifications of battle scenes that characterize vernacular histories of antiquity in this period. The interpolated scenes of battle appear to derive from his own imagination and familiarity with the epic conventions of the *chansons de geste*.

So closely modeled on romance conventions is the *Hystore de Jules César* that the principal scholarly investigations of the work have concentrated almost exclusively on the question of its textual relationship to the *Roumanz de Jules César*, a *roman* in Alexandrine laisses conventionally dated to the middle of the thirteenth century and attributed to Jacos de Forest.[92] Yet it is unclear, to date, whether Jacos de Forest in fact figures at all in the history of either text, and the question of who composed the *Roumanz* remains unresolved. Paul Hess entertained the possibility that Jean de Thuin was responsible both for the initial verse *Roumanz* and for its subsequent *dérimage*, in which he can be seen as responding to the growing demand in the thirteenth century for works in prose and to the period's tendency to identify historical truth with non-rhymed narrative.[93] Almost all scholars who have addressed the question of authorship acknowledge the superiority of the prose *Hystore* to the labored verse style of the *Roumanz*. If Jean recast the work in prose, he eliminated not only the mediocre versifying of the romance, but its superfluous descriptions and unwieldy turns of phrase as well, achieving in the process a fluidity and clarity of expression that make the *Hystore* a far more satisfying literary achievement.[94]

For our purposes, the priority of the *Roumanz* to the *Hystore*, particularly if Jean de Thuin is responsible for both versions, makes little difference. If anything, it testifies to the growing demand for historical works in vernacular prose in the thirteenth century, for if Jean did perform the *dérimage* of his earlier romance, one is justified in supposing that he did so because he believed a prose version of the life of Caesar would be more popular than, presumably, the *Roumanz* had been. The movement from verse to prose history is, in any case, a significant feature of Old French vernacular writing in this period, one paralleled by the *mise en prose* of vernacular romance as well, as represented in the prosing of Arthurian romance in the so-called Vulgate Cycle or prose Lancelot.

As has been noted, Jean de Thuin's effort in the *Hystore* to create an ideal portrait of Caesar as courtly warrior and lover entailed the systematic excision of Lucan's hostile attitudes and diatribes against the Roman ruler. The erasure involved precisely those aspects of the Latin source that had complicated beyond retrieval the image of Caesar in the *Faits des Romains*. This process of deletion is put into effect in the interest of maintaining ideological coherence, but ideological coherence is purchased at the cost of vastly constricting the scope and meaning of the narrative that results. Compared to the *Faits des Romains*, Jean's *Hystore* offers a greatly impoverished view of Caesar, of ancient history, and of the moral conspectus that defines the utility of the past for its medieval audience. Although Caesar is still seen against the background of the historical world of Rome, that world does not so much act on him as offer a stage for the enactment of his martial and amorous exploits. The intricate negotiations among ideological pressures, historical realities, moral desiderata, Latin source, and vernacular translation that govern the *Faits des Romains* and endow it with great interest and power are completely lacking in the *Hystore de Jules César*. Instead Jean de Thuin presents a reduced version of a Caesarean narrative, revised in order to preserve the coherence of the courtly ideology that simultaneously shaped and subtended the procedures he used in his reworking of Lucan's *Pharsalia*.

In moving from an epic to a romance mode in the patterning of his historical narrative, Jean not only constrained the scope of his account, but also redirected it to novel themes and concerns. The extent of this shift from an epic to romance mode in the literary refiguration of his received material should not, however, be overemphasized, since both types of amplification and rewriting are present in his text. Still, there is a significantly new tone and orientation to the *Hystore de Jules César* that sets it apart from the *Faits des Romains*—with which, it is clear, Jean de Thuin was familiar.[95] To the predominantly epic view of the heroic past that emerged from the *Faits des Romains*, Jean added—as the *roman* had added to the *chanson de geste*—the moral values and amorous ethics of *courtoisie*. The values expressed in courtly ideology were inserted into the historical narrative as evaluative norms that constructed a new version of the heroic past of classical antiquity.

To the medieval epic's emphasis on prowess, courage in the face of death, physical fortitude, fidelity to one's lord, loyalty, and *franchise*, courtly romance appended the specific notion of *courtoisie*—like chivalry, an ideal concept of class and man. By the thirteenth century, the idea of *courtoisie* had come to include a wide array of both intellectual and moral attributes that revolved around the cultivation of learning (*clergie*) and refinement in personal conduct and in the conduct of war, in the latter case entailing notions of mercy, largesse, honor, and comportment based on an exemplary morality.[96] The values expressed in *courtoisie* are directed to enhancing the personal fulfillment of the individual as an absolute moral ideal, rather than to facilitating the performance of political functions or historical tasks.[97] Heroic action or prowess, therefore, functions not so much in service to the society of which the hero is the emblematic representative, but in service to the hero's inner imperative for self-realization, even when that process of self-realization is achieved through service to women as love objects.

The shift from a predominantly epic to a predominantly romance mode, then, implicitly effects an interiorization of the historical forces that constitute the stage on which the hero acts.[98] This privatization and interiorization of historical forces is marked in Jean de Thuin, as we shall see, by the virtual disappearance of both Lucan's and the *Faits des Romains*'s obsession with *franchise* as a political concept of freedom appropriate for a free and noble class. In place of *franchise*, Jean substitutes *gentilleche* as the governing moral value of social life, whose attainment motivates historical actors and consumers of classical history alike. Refinement rather than freedom is the goal of the courtly hero, who strives to conquer love as arduously as he strives to overcome his enemies. The exemplary deeds of prowess that the courtly hero enacts become tokens of his fidelity to the objects of his desire, rather than to the political world within which they take place. Beauty and the desire to possess it, not military glory won on the battlefield, provide the wellspring of courtly conduct. The result is not only a moralizing of violence by *courtoisie*, but its aestheticizing as well.[99] Jean's long interpolated love affair between Caesar and Cleopatra, accompanied in his text by an extended love casuistry, relocates the history of Caesar within the moralized and aestheticized context of medieval courtly ideology. The *Hystore de Jules César* constructs a moral allegory from the amatory and martial exploits that it offers to its intended audience of *haut homes* as a means to excite and maintain in them that *gentilleche* which is at once a mark of noble status, a code of aristocratic behavior, and a collection of moral attributes appropriate for those destined by class and character to rule medieval society. The resulting work is an amalgam of classical, romance, and epic elements in somewhat unstable combination, the whole overlaid with moralizing lessons and religious prescriptions concerning the proper conduct of Christian knights and peoples, producing a sometimes strained blend of ancient history and medieval didacticism.

Hystore de Jules César

The didactic goals that guided Jean de Thuin in composing the *Hystore de Jules César* are clearly stated in the prologue to this translation of Lucan's *Pharsalia*. The story of Caesar's conquest of the world, Jean affirms, should prove profitable, for

> bien est drois ke si fait soient racontet en tel maniere que tout li haut home ki tiere ont a garder et a gouvrener, pour cou que il miex se maintiegnent en gentilleche et en toutes bontes, i prendent examples et enseignemens.[100]
>
> it is proper that his deeds be recounted in such a way that all the high men who have lands to protect and to govern, because they are accustomed to maintain themselves in gentility and in all good things, can find in it examples and lessons.

Like the author of the *Roman de Thèbes*, who writes "pour les clercs ou les chevaliers" and refuses to admit that any other auditors can understand the lessons of the past,[101] Jean's *Hystore* is class coded to the highest degree. It offers itself as sociomoral instruction for those who hold and govern lands, initiating them by historical example and precept into the cultural and social codes that constitute *gentilleche*, which would here seem to refer to that congeries of ideals of refinement and moral attributes normally associated with *courtoisie*. Yet this undertaking, apparently so innocuous on the surface, appears to the author to be fraught with dangers, for Jean fears that his worthy enterprise will generate the *mesdis*, the evil whispers, of the envious, who will turn to folly what he has written for the edification of *preudomes*.[102]

Jean de Thuin's conviction concerning the importance of history in supplying moral lessons to the present recurs in a long authorial interpolation that he inserts into the *Hystore de Jules César* upon the death of Scaeva, one of Caesar's faithful lieutenants, who was mortally wounded after an exceptional display of bravery at the battle of Dyrrachium. Lucan, although he acknowledged Scaeva's fortitude, had qualified his appreciation with the observation that Scaeva, "ready for any wickedness, knew not that valor in civil war is a heinous crime."[103] Jean, in contrast, seizes the opportunity of Scaeva's demise to meditate on the meaning of prowess, loyalty, honor, and rectitude, which represent, for him, the meaning of Roman history. The passage clearly captures the essential character of the moral conspectus that Jean and his contemporaries deemed essential for those *ki tiere doit gouvrener* and for which, they believed, ancient history could provide instruction. As in the preface, Jean speaks to a class holding and governing lands and identifiably aristocratic in both capacities:

> Haus hom ki tiere doit maintenir se doit tout adies tenir a prouece et
> a bonte por retenir s'ounour et pour garder ses homes; et s'il veut
> monter em pris et lui faire aloser, si doinst largement et merisse a
> ciaus ki siervice li font; si doit amer ses chevaliers et hounerer et
> aquellir entour lui et douner les biaus dons a cascun, si comme il a
> lui afiert; car il ne puet fere nul tresor ki tant li puist valoir a retenir
> tiere comme li tresors des chevaliers et des preudomes ki en tous be-
> soins se meteront pour lui aidier et pour autrui assalir. Et si doit
> haus hom maintenir droiture et loiaute et faire droite justice ne ne
> doit couvoitier don ne loier, car loiers fait maintes fois fallir droiture
> et metre le tort avant en maintes cours.[104]

> The lofty man who must maintain lands should always pursue prow-
> ess and goodness in order to preserve his honor and to retain his
> men; and if he wishes to rise in value and garner esteem, he should
> give generously and according to merit to those who provide him
> service; he should love and honor and gather around him his
> knights, and give fine gifts to each, as is his duty; for he can create
> no treasure which is as valuable in preserving [his] lands as the trea-

sure of knights and honorable men, who in all his needs are ready to aid him and to assail others [i.e., his enemies]. And the great man must maintain righteousness and loyalty and execute proper justice, and he must not demand gifts or recompense, because recompense often causes righteousness to fail and promotes wrongdoing in many courts.

In a broad sense, this is a highly conventional articulation of the principal moral qualities required of those possessing political authority in the Middle Ages, with the orthodox emphases on largesse, justice, and loyalty that romance writers since the twelfth century had stressed in their attempts to construct a unitary model of courtly virtue.[105] Like the writers of *romans*, Jeans exhorts *hauts homes* to adopt the culture of chivalry and *courtoisie* as a means of encouraging the loyalty of lesser vassals on whom their military strength depends. To maintain that loyalty, rulers and princes must demonstrate justice and rectitude in their dealings, mercy in their judgments, fairness in their deliberations, generosity in their rewards, and strength in combatting common enemies. Only in the acceptance and maintenance of a shared culture of chivalry is the prince vouchsafed success in his undertakings and the continued service of his followers. Although addressed to rulers, this passage takes as its point of view that of the chivalric knight.

Yet Jean's advocacy of courtly values reveals, even as it seeks to counteract, lines of fracture appearing within this putatively unitary world of shared values and mores. Those fractures appear first and most tellingly in the realm of speech. The spoilers in this fantasy of a shared courtly culture of virtue and authority are those who abuse the power of the word—the whisperers, evil speakers, calumniators, and lowborn (*vilain*) counselors, whose tongues poison the atmosphere of reason that should guide the exercise of power:

Nul haus hom ne doit amer losengier mesdisant, felon, mauparlier ne encusseour, car il blasment adies les boins par envie pour eus empirier . . . et si metent es tieres les mauveses coustumes et les vilaines et font rober le menue gent et destruire par lor acussasions.

Et pour cou proie jou coumunement a tous les haus homes k'il ne croient conseil de teus gens, mais tiegnent soi tous tans a conseil de francisse et de jentillece et de raison. Car mauves consaus fet souvent maint home blasmer et mesprendre encontre raison, et meismement il n'est mie avenant a haut hom k'il croie consel de vilain, ki fait vilounie apiertement et ki sans mesfet pourchace autrui mal.[106]

> No high man should favor evil-speaking flatterers, felons, false
> speakers, or slanderers, for they blame the good out of envy in order
> to cause them harm . . . and they introduce evil and bad customs in
> the lands and cause the lower orders to be robbed and destroyed by
> their accusations.
>
>   And for this reason I beg equally all the high men that they do
> not believe the counsel of such men, but hold themselves always to
> the counsels of nobility [*franchise*] and gentility and reason. For evil
> counsel often causes many men to place blame and err against rea-
> son, and similarly it is not proper for a high man to take counsel
> from villains, who openly perform villainies, and who without blame
> pursue the ill fortune of others.

The envious and ill-considered language of such men dislodges the
worthy and the good from their rightful places at the side of the ruler.
In abasing and vilifying the honorable, the counsel of the *vilain* produces *vilounie*, through which the base-born works his evil. The villain in this courtly world is not the enemy who must be faced on the
battlefield, but the liar and evil-speaker who threatens to stab one in
the back, and who "tampers with and diminishes conventional courtly
language."[107]
Nor is the effect of such speech confined to the realm of the court
or the reputation of the worthy, for once in place, evil counselors poison the rest of society by imposing "bad customs" that harm the poor.
A class that justifies its dominion on the basis of its capacity to protect
the *menue gent* (lower orders) inevitably destroys those whom it is
designated to safeguard when it degrades the worthy. The consequences of evil counsel and evil speech, in short, cannot be confined to
the court, but are let loose upon the whole world that labors under the
tutelage of the nobility.
If the abuse of speech promotes such disastrous developments in
the world of chivalry, then it is the word that must restore this fallen
universe. Culture must redeem politics; language must return virtue
and power to its proper path and rulers learn, as Jean proclaims, "biel
parler sans fol gas et sans mesdire d'autrui" (fine speech without foolish prattle and without speaking ill of others).[108] Redemptive language becomes the ethical counterpart of a corrected social order. Correct speech enacts a social morality, for language both mirrors and
constitutes social reality. Whereas evil speech destroys, *biel parler*
rescues and sustains society. Culture does not merely redeem politics;
it is its essential medium, for without proper speech (*bon conseil*)
there can be no proper action, hence no legitimate possession of

power. Linguistic propriety and political property are at root one; when language fails, the social order falls.

Jean's sensitivity to the moral efficacy of language underwrites his desire to offer Roman history to a medieval audience in a version that is both accessible and purged of its morally dubious components. This entailed, as V. L. Dedecek has indicated, a double movement in the task of translation: first, destruction, in which the patina of antiquity and the moral complexity of Lucan's poem are removed from the Old French account; second, construction, in which Lucan's work is appropriated for the thirteenth century by inserting within it, in Dedecek's words, "l'idéal chevaleresque avec sa bravoure et son amour courtois."[109] Both operate equally to reframe Lucan's account in what can only be called a "feudalizing" of Roman history, a rewriting of the Latin source so entirely in the political and cultural lexicon of the Middle Ages that its meaning threatens to disappear altogether. With Jean de Thuin, this procedure goes far beyond anything effected by the anonymous author of the *Faits des Romains* in his translation of the *Pharsalia*. As Dedecek observed, in reading the *Hystore de Jules César* "on n'a pas l'impression de lire une traduction d'une oeuvre antique. On dirait presque qu'on a sous les yeux un roman historique plutôt qu'un chapitre d'histoire."[110]

In the *Hystore de Jules César*, Rome is represented as a vast *seigneurie* in the hands of "trois des plus haus barons de Roume et des plus puissans" (three of the highest and most powerful barons of Rome).[111] They are surrounded by a crowd of "preudomes," bound to their "droit seigneur" by homage and an oath of fidelity. When Caesar determines to attack Rome, he calls upon the French to respond to the "ban":

> Cil firent le commandement de lor seignour, tant ke les os s'esmurent de France pour lui secourre encontre les Roumains, et bien sachies ke entre le Rosne et le Rin et Gironde ne demora hom ki peust armes porter, ke par ban ne l'i couvenist venir.

> They obeyed the command of their lord, so that the host moved from France to aid him against the Romans; and you should know that between the Rhône, the Rhine, and the Gironde there did not remain a single man capable of bearing arms who did not agree to come to him in accordance with the ban.

Indeed, Caesar's crossing of the Alps with his amassed host is explicitly compared to Charlemagne's expedition across the Pyrenees to Roncevaux:

> . . . et bien sachies c'onkes Karlemaines n'assambla tant de preu-
> doumes en .I. besoing, ne en Espagne ne en autre liu, que Cesar
> n'en eust adonques plus a son besoing.[112]

> . . . and you should know that Charlemagne never assembled so
> many honorable men for a single struggle, not in Spain or any other
> place, as Caesar had [gathered] now for his battle.

Caesar addresses his soldiers as "vassals" or "seigneurs compagnons"; they are led by a "maistres mareschaus."[113] Before the engagement at Pharsalia, Caesar urges his troops to battle by promising
them lands and fiefs as well as the honor to be won in warfare:

> et lor amonneste et prie que cascuns pense dou bien fere, car ceste
> bataille lor fera recouvrer lor tieres et lor fies et monter en hounour
> et en pris, et bien sacent tout cil ki preudoume i seront k'il lor
> reguerredounera au double lor travail.[114]

> and he admonished them and pleaded that each one think of doing
> well, for this battle will enable them to recover their lands and their
> fiefs and to rise in honor and value, and they should know truly that
> all those who will perform there as valiant knights will be rewarded
> doubly for their effort.

In contrast to the *Faits des Romains*, where the author retains the
names for Roman institutions yet endeavors to explain them to a medieval French audience unfamiliar with the offices and practices of Roman government, the *Hystore de Jules César* presents Roman functionaries as amalgamated with feudal administrators. Thus consuls
becomes "justicieres" and tribunes "connestables," and Codrus the
quaestor is identified as he who "rechevoit de par Rome les rentes
d'une citet" (receives on behalf of Rome the rents of a city).[115] Castles
are in the possession of the "hauts barons," who hold their courts
there. Towns are transformed into "bors," or "chastiaus," and are
variously inhabited by "paysans et ceux du bourg." Interestingly, one
of the more curious uses of the word *paysans* occurs in Jean's remark
that when Julius Caesar arrived in France he found "les paisans aspres
et combatans"[116]—a social devaluation of the Gallic tribes that the author of the *Faits des Romains* had been careful to avoid when confronted with translating Caesar's terminology for the *barbari*.

Like the anonymous translator of the *Faits*, though, Jean substitutes French designations for Roman geographical nomenclature. And
battles routinely take the form of epic combat, in which knights spur
their horses to meet one another "au jouster."[117] At the siege of
Marseille, "dames et damoiselles" watch from on high over the gate

of the city, like participants in a romance tournament.[118] In the account of the battle of Thapsus, Jean inserts an episode involving the sounding of the horn that is directly modeled on the *Chanson de Roland*. Pacidius, more wisely than Roland, determines to sound the horn, because he understands that "c'est plus grans honnors de demander le secours en combatant et d'atendre le que de fuir arriere et dont retorner apries . . . car li corners ne li coustera mie tant comme li jousters" (it entails greater honor to request help in fighting and to wait for it than to retreat and return later . . . because blowing the horn will not be as costly as fighting).[119] Labiiens, hearing the horn, returns to ambush Caesar's forces under Antony in a rout comparable to that at Roncevaux.

Far more significant than the feudal veneer and epic amplification to which Jean de Thuin submits Lucan's text, however, are the deletions he performs on it, deletions so extensive as to deform the underlying sense of the Latin poem. The most serious is the erasure of the principal themes that had governed Lucan's narrative and moral design, in which the civil war represented a struggle for liberty against tyranny in the defense of the *patria*.[120] The anonymous author of the *Faits des Romains*, to be sure, had tended to personalize this struggle, embodying it in the figures of Caesar and his antagonists. Nonetheless, he had retained the essential outline of Lucan's moral plot. In Jean's hands, though, Caesar emerges as an exemplary medieval ruler, motivated not by ambition, covetousness, or the wish for revenge, but by the promptings of glory, righteousness, and the desire to reap just rewards for heroic valor displayed on the battlefield.

To so present Caesar required a complete revision of the explanatory categories of Lucan's work. As in the *Faits des Romains*, the principal explanation for the outbreak of the civil war in the *Hystore de Jules César* stems from the Senate's refusal to grant Caesar a triumph for his conquest of Gaul, on the grounds that he had stayed too long in France. This denial of due recognition pushes Caesar to threaten that "puis ke on de droit li defaut, il le recouverra par force, s'il onques puet" (since they deprive him of his right, he will recover it by force, if ever he can).[121] But unlike the author of the *Faits*, Jean does not even hint that Caesar might be acting out of ambition or greed. Caesar's attack on Rome, as a consequence, is hedged with a legitimacy that would have been instinctively granted by a medieval audience as an attempt to redress a "defaut de droit." Insofar as Jean admits that other factors contributed to the outbreak of the civil war, they arise not from Caesar or his deeds, but rather from Pompey.

Pompey's covetousness and pride cause the Senate to refuse Caesar that which was rightfully his, and hence provides the *casus belli:*

> [Pompey] estoit si couvoiteus d'ounour tenir k'il ne voloit ke nus fust a lui pers de seignourie et voloit ke si commandement fuissent gardet sour tous autres et tenut. . . . [Il] doutoit que ses lox ne declinast et sa seignourie pour le los de Julle Cesaire, pour cou k'il savoit bien que Jules Cesar estoit plus conquerans de lui et miex vaillans. [122]

> [Pompey] was so desirous of possessing honor that he did not want anyone to be his equal in lordship and he wished that his commands would be maintained and held over all others. . . . [He] feared that his reputation and lordship would decline on account of the reputation of Caesar, because he knew that Julius Caesar was a greater conqueror than he and more valiant.

Thus, from the outset, Jean de Thuin reverses the moral valuation of Caesar and Pompey that in both Lucan and the *Faits des Romains* had endowed the *Pharsalia* with tragic overtones. Rather than as a flawed hero, Pompey is presented in the *Hystore* as moved solely by pride and cupidity, a man even tainted by cowardliness ("Pompeius n'avoit mie cuer de guerre mener" [Pompey had no heart for waging war]).[123] On these points Jean de Thuin leaves little room for doubt: "Ceste discorde . . . fu premierement esmeue par Pompee et par le grant orgueil des Roumains et par lor envie" (This discord was originally started by Pompey and by the great pride of the Romans and by their envy).[124] Even Cato is implicated in Pompey's conspiracy of envy to deny Caesar the recognition owed him: "Pompeus, Marchiaus et Catons, par la grant envie k'il avoient sour lui [Caesar], se sont traveilliet a lor pooir a ce k'il peussent arriere metre le partie de Cesar" (Pompey, Marcus, and Cato, on account of the great envy that they had of Caesar, worked with all their power so that they might set back Caesar's party).[125] Caesar's cause, by contrast, is entirely just; he fights, as he explains to his army, for his and their honor, since they, too, have been deprived of their rightful reward for the valor they exhibited in France. Those who fight in a just cause cannot fail to garner praise and honor:

> "Et ce est ce pour quoi je voel plus le guerre commenchier. Si vous proi a tous communement, premierement pour vos honnors et pour conkuerre los et pris et m'amour, ke vous aidant m'en soies; car tout cil qui aidant m'en seront, il conquerront hounour et m'amour, et li faillant honte et reprouvier et mon malgret."[126]

"And it is for this reason that I wish to open the war. I ask of you all together, that you come to my aid first to win your honors and praise and value and my love; because all who will aid me in this matter shall win honor and my favor, and those who fail [to do so shall have] shame, and reproof, and my ill will."

Indeed, Jean de Thuin goes so far in the disparagement of Pompey that Caesar's ultimate triumph in the civil war functions as a divine punishment imposed on Pompey for his desecration of the Temple in Jerusalem, where, after the conquest of the city, he had elected to stable his horses. [127] Thus did God, says Jean, avenge himself upon Pompey: "Et Diex li guerredouna si bien cest fait k'il souffri ke Jules Cesar le mata et desconfist" (and God so repaid him for this deed that he allowed Julius Caesar to strike him down and put him to flight). [128] God's unseen participation in the unfolding of the civil war is reiterated at the crucial moment of preparation for the battle of Pharsalia, when Pompey fatally hesitates to engage in combat:

Ensi blasmoient tuit Pompee de cou k'il tant detrioit la bataille encontre Cesar. Et ensi vait cascuns pourcachant se grevance et son encombrier, et voirs est k'il ensi plest a *nostre seignor* que, quant il veut destruire gens, k'i les destruit par lor coupes, si qu'il n'en puent blasmer ne encouper se eus meissmes non. [129]

Thus everyone blamed Pompey for having put off the battle against Caesar. And thus everyone went around acting on his grievance and his anger; and the truth is that it thus pleases Our Lord that, when He wishes to destroy men, He destroys them by their own flaws, in such a way that they can not place blame or fault for it on anyone except themselves.

Where Lucan and the author of the *Faits des Romains* provide intricate portraits of imperfect leaders caught up in historical processes beyond their control, to which they respond with moral and personal traits that govern their behavior and shape their fates, Jean de Thuin locates the forces that decide the final outcome of the clash between men outside of human events altogether. The conclusion is predetermined by God rather than determined by human character, motive, or deed. In this sense, Jean's translation of the *Pharsalia* not only diminishes the historical scope and significance of the civil war as the product of human behavior enmeshed within a complex skein of political and psychological factors, but also effaces its properly historical meaning by adducing a theological interpretation of both its cause and its consequences. The lesson that Roman history presents for the instruction of later generations is a thoroughly moralized one, testimony to a theological concept of God's operation and intervention in the affairs of men:

> Ensi se venga nostre sires de Pompee; et pour cou se doit cascuns garder a son pooir de mesprendre enviers nostre seignour et de meserrer. Car ja soit il ensi k'il detrit a aucune fois de vengier soi des meserrans viers lui, si·le set il bien guerredouner en point et en liu.[130]

> Thus Our Lord avenged himself on Pompey; and therefore let everyone beware with all his might not to do wrong against Our Lord or to follow an evil path. For, even though He might thus delay some time in taking vengeance against him who sins against Him, He knows very well how and where to repay him.

Within the essentially secular project of ancient historiography, therefore, Jean de Thuin reintroduces theological perspectives that threaten to undermine the significance of history itself as a repository of cultural codes and exemplary secular deeds. So powerful is his moralizing drive that the historical nature of his material is submerged beneath the didactic platitudes and explanatory arguments that he advances, robbing the classical past of its secular autonomy and utility.

In place of Lucan's view of Pompey as a flawed but essentially righteous leader of the Republican cause, Jean de Thuin consistently depicts him as a man who rashly promotes war but lacks the courage to prosecute it. He omits Pompey's sad speech to his troops before Pharsalia, as well as his reflections on the dire consequences of battle. When Pompey succeeds in escaping from the port of Brandiz, Jean demurs:

> Mais ceste fuite ne li doune preu d'ounour; car il s'en vait en estranges tieres, u il maura honteusement et a viute sans retorner arriere a Roume.[131]

> But this flight did not offer him the advantage of honor; he departed for foreign lands, where he died shamefully and in scorn without ever having returned to Rome.

Gone also is Cornelia's touching lament upon hearing of the death of her husband, together with Cato's apotheosis of Pompey with which Lucan opens Book 9 of the *Pharsalia*. Although Jean restores a long lamentation to Cornelia following Pompey's death, it does not correspond to Lucan's text,[132] and it addresses the evils of the times more powerfully than it does the passing of Pompey. Then too, as we saw above, Jean fails to include Lucan's anti-imperial diatribe occasioned by Pompey's failure to pursue the fleeing Caesar after the defeat administered at the battle of Dyrrachium.

Taken together, these changes essentially make of Pompey a secondary character in the life of Caesar, one among a host of enemies whom Caesar successfully overwhelms by his chivalric prowess and cunning as he sweeps before him the obstacles to his conquest of the world. This diminution of Pompey's role and significance in the history of the civil war, needless to say, completely deforms the structure of Lucan's narrative, and subtracts from it the complicated valences that Lucan saw as counterpoised in the war, themselves emblematic of the larger forces whose fates hung in the balance in the final resolution of Republican Rome's disastrous civil contest. Jean's *Hystore* is no longer a history of the struggle for liberty against tyranny, for it lacks a political context able to endow those terms with historical meaning. It is, rather, a celebration of Caesar's chivalric and courtly virtue, untroubled by countervailing forces or historical judgments.

The Caesar who emerges from the pages of Jean de Thuin's idealizing biography is no longer the ambitious, violent man of blood or the heroic *démesuré* depicted by Lucan and his thirteenth-century translator in the *Faits des Romains*. He has become, instead, the embodiment of those qualities associated with Jean de Thuin's notion of *gentilleche*: a noble, generous, and merciful conqueror, who combines prowess in battle with eloquence in speech and who exhibits in full that moral conspectus central to the ethical principles of courtly ideology.[133] Jean's handling of the Caesarean narrative converts it into a series of exemplary *gestes*, which then become available as illustrative matter for the long didactic passages that weigh down his account, themselves liberally sprinkled with hundreds of proverbs, *sententia*, and adages—adornments for his sermonizing discourse. One senses, Dedecek remarks, "la sincérité dans cette passion pour la perfection morale et dans ce zèle pour la formation du chevalier idéal."[134]

Jean's most profound revision to Lucan's negative image of Caesar's ethics involves the question of mercy, an attribute critical, Flori has demonstrated, to the evolving code of chivalric warfare in the High Middle Ages. Where Lucan saw Caesar as a harsh, often cruel leader, who indulged in mercy only to further his political goals, Jean de Thuin makes mercy Caesar's cardinal virtue, exploiting in his text the semantic resonance of *gentilleche* as both courtly refinement and merciful behavior. Once more, a comparison with the *Faits des Romains* discloses the lengths to which Jean went to expurgate any dubious implications in Caesar's conduct. Such implications had been present, for example, in the treatment in the *Faits* of Caesar's putative mercy toward Domitius, consul and praetor of Rome, who, failing to defend the city against attack by Caesar, was taken prisoner. Rather than beg for mercy, Domitius clearly preferred to die, "car desdaign sambloit a Luce Domice se il vivoit par la merci Cesar" (for it seemed contemptible to Lucius Domitius that he should live by Caesar's mercy).[135] However, to frustrate Domitius's laudable wish to die for the sake of his country, and to make an example of him before the remainder of Pompey's host, Caesar grants him his life.[136]

Whereas the *Faits* preserves Lucan's astute observation that, in pardoning Domitius, Caesar acted not out of mercy but to undermine Domitius's honor, Jean removes from his translation any trace of doubt concerning Caesar's motives. The *Hystore* completely revises the narrative import of Lucan's account by interpolating a plea for pardon on the part of those captured together with Domitius, while excising Domitius's request to die at the hand of a tyrant in the cause of preserving liberty. In place of Lucan's judgment that it was shameful for Domitius to have allowed himself to be pardoned for having honorably served the Republic, Jean admiringly reports Caesar's generosity toward his defeated enemy, whom he returns not only to life but also to the fight:

> "Pour cou ke je voeil ke vous soies tiesmougnages et examples de me bonte, premierement je vous otroi le vie; et se vous apries voles entour moi demorer, si i demores; u se ce non, reprendes vos armes et vous en rales a Pompee; et se vous puis me poes grever en estour et en bataille, onques pour cest pardon ke je chi vous fac ne m'espargnies."[137]

> "Because I wish that you stand as a witness and example of my goodness, in the first place I grant you your life; and if, afterwards, you wish to remain with me, then you shall do so; or if not, take up your arms again and return to Pompey, and if at some later time you are able to wound me in battle, do not spare me on account of this pardon that I here grant you."

In the same way, Afranius, driven back to waterless hills during the Spanish campaign, recognized the impossibility of his situation and the necessity to surrender to and request mercy from Caesar. Like Domitius, Afranius declares that " 'je vausisse mius ke jou meismes m'ochesisse a m'espee ke je ja vos criasse mierci' " ("I would prefer to kill myself with my own sword than ever to beg mercy from you"). But he is persuaded by Caesar's extraordinary reputation for the merciful treatment of defeated enemies to set aside his sense of shame at being captured and plead for his own life and the lives of his men:

"Mais la grans gentillece et li grans misericorde ke je sai ki est en vous me doune hardement ke je vous proie mierci, pour moi premierement et apries pour tous ces autres ki ci sont o moi. . . . Sire, tout avant je mec en vostre mierchit moi, et puis mes homes."[138]

"But the great gentility and mercy that I know you to possess emboldens me to request your mercy, for myself in the first place, and then for all the others who are with me. . . . Lord, first of all I place myself in your mercy, and then my men."

Jean leaves out from his account the entire political context of the civil war invoked by Afranius, which, owing to the winds of political fortune, had placed him in opposition to Caesar, toward whom he bore no personal animosity.[139] His decision to accept mercy for himself and his followers is blameless in this light, since it was by a fate not of his own choosing that he faced Caesar as a foe. Indeed, Jean stresses Caesar's merciful conduct by expanding Lucan's somewhat laconic statement that "Caesar facilis voltuque serenus / flectitur atque usus belli poenamque remittit" (Caesar readily gave way with unclouded brow; he excused them from service in his army and from all punishment)[140] into a full-blown paean to Caesar's joyful grant of pardon:

Quant Cesar a oie ceste requeste, sachies ke mout en fu lies, et nomeement pour cou k'il voit que la gens ki si estoit enorgeillie viers lui est ore humeliie et venue a se mierchit; et gentillece, ki en son cor estoit, francisse et pities et misericorde l'ont a cou amenet k'il pardoinst son maltalent a cascun, ensi comme Affranius li avoit requis.[141]

When Caesar heard this request, know that he was very happy about it, namely because he saw that the people who had been so prideful toward him now were humiliated and brought to his mercy; and gentility, which was in his heart, nobility and pity and mercifulness led him to forgive his anger at everyone, as Afranius had asked.

Yet even Caesar's mercy has its limits. Before the battle of Pharsalia, Caesar urges his men to spare neither cousin nor parent, "car ki espargne en bataille son anemi, il amenuise s'ounour et son pris" (for he who spares his enemy in battle diminishes his honor and praise).[142] Fortified by their leader's words, Caesar's troops force themselves to put aside all pity and go amid the opposing Romans, "ferant et navrant, abatant et ociant en tele maniere que mout i peust on veoir grant dolour; car li peres se combatoit au fil, li uns freres a l'autre, li parent ensamble et li .I. voisins a l'autre et s'entrevont ociant" (attacking and wounding, striking down and killing in such manner that one could see there great sorrow; for fathers fought against sons, brothers against one another, relatives together and neighbors went against one another killing).[143] What is missing from this description of the battle of Pharsalia is the horror evoked by Lucan—and reiterated in the *Faits des Romains*—at the spectacle of brothers smiting brothers, fathers killing sons, and neighbors clashing in deadly combat. Unlike the author of the *Faits*, Jean sees no logic connecting violence unleashed against foreign enemies and violence brought home. In his narrative, the imperatives of chivalric honor and prowess demand the same ruthless audacity against blood relatives as against any other enemy. The unique terror and tragedy of civil war and the social carnage that it produces, so powerfully articulated by Lucan, are wholly absent from his account.

The mitigation of Caesar's image as a harsh, even brutal, warrior, possessed with a taste for blood and relentless toward enemies, posed the greatest challenge to Jean de Thuin's efforts to idealize the Roman emperor, for it placed him in direct contradiction to his own Latin source. Other courtly virtues could be extracted much more easily from Lucan's narrative, and Jean was not reticent in exploiting the opportunities that the *Pharsalia* offered to extol Caesar's attributes and attainments. In his hands, Caesar epitomizes that combination of learning, refinement, honor, and prowess that is the mark of the ideal courtly hero.

Particularly interesting from this point of view is Jean de Thuin's use of the episode involving the poor boatman Amyclas, to whom Caesar offered a huge reward if he would take him to Antony at Brundisium. To disguise himself for the sea voyage, Caesar had donned the garb of a humble man. Lucan comments that "though the garb he wore was humble, he knew not how to speak the language of a private man."[144] Jean seizes the occasion to specify the courtly character of Caesar's language, which betrays his inherent nobility and refinement despite his attempt to mask them beneath a cloak of poverty. In response to Caesar's request to undertake the dangerous voyage, Amyclas answers:

> "Sire, je vous oi parler si courtoisement ke jou a vostre commandement me vauroie dou tout abandouner sour le francisse de vostre gentillece."[145]

> "My lord, I hear you speak so courteously that I would like at your command to abandon everything to the nobility of your gentility."

The speech of a ruler discloses the character of the man; eloquence in language and refinement of comportment are the ethical correlates of noble status. Central to the courtly ideal that Jean offers to his prospective audience is this presentation of a unitary model of refined language, moral being, and "francisse de gentillece." The semantic divergence of *franchise* as it appears in this passage from its political significance in the *Faits des Romains* is noteworthy. In Jean's lexicon, *franchise* has lost its connotation of political freedom and autonomy; its meanings circulate only within a more restricted courtly semantics of nobility and, in its coupling with *gentilleche*, refinement. Caesar here exemplifies the programmatic goal of the *Hystore de Jules César* as specified in the prologue, which is to teach rulers that *biel parler* and comportment appropriate for those of high social status.

The episode also affords Jean an opportunity to interpolate a review of Caesar's accomplishments, hence of his historical significance as ancient actor and of his moral utility as medieval exemplar. As a violent storm rocks the small craft in which Amyclas is transporting the Roman emperor, Caesar, afraid that he is about to die, laments that death will prevent all that he has desired to accomplish. Caesar's monologue, invented by Jean de Thuin, summarizes the attributes and achievements that make him an emblematic hero in the eyes of a thirteenth-century translator and authorize his moral utility for the medieval French aristocracy:

> "Ki donra mais les grans dons, si com je dounes les ai? Ki avera mes le non de prouece et ki maintera mais hounour ne hardement, issi com jou maintenut l'ai. Ciertes, se je muir ici, toute honnors morra o moi. Et nanpourquant je sai bien que j'ai tant fet de moi ke tous li mons en parlera apries me mort; et dira on ke je sousmis a moi Francois, Normans, Englois et Bretons et ke jou Pompee jetai de Roume et en oi toutes les hounours; et sans faille, de tant me reconforte jou que, de quele eure ke de moi defaille, mes bons los et mes bons nons duera a tous jours sans defallir."[146]

> "Who will distribute great gifts as I have? Who will ever have the renown for prowess and who will maintain honor and bravery, just as I have maintained it? Certainly, if I die here, all honors will die with me. And nonetheless, I know that I have accomplished so many deeds that the whole world shall speak of them after my death; and it will say that I subdued the French, Normans, English, and Britons, and that I threw Pompey out of Rome and possessed all its honors; and without fail, it greatly comforts me [to know] that, from the very hour that I pass away, my good praises and good name will last forever without decline."

Largesse, prowess, honor, glorious conquest in war, and everlasting fame, coupled with elegance in speech and deed: these are the qualities that Jean de Thuin solicits from the ancient past and proposes as an ethical paradigm for the French aristocracy. Their possession defines the sociomoral hierarchy of values and virtues that guarantee the social dominance of the aristocracy, whose hegemonic position in medieval society no longer rests exclusively on its capacity to deploy the instruments of military violence. The virtues of a warrior caste are amalgamated with the cultural leadership cultivated by aristocratic elites in classical civilization. Ancient history, precisely because it was a repository of learning, refinement, and cultural attainment, functioned as a privileged locus for the articulation of such values, construed as central to courtly ideology.[147] The vocation of warrior here becomes an ethically valorized pursuit, possessing an inherent moral content and cultural legitimacy.

THE "TREATISE ON LOVE"

Only one element of courtly ideology was lacking in the ancient past, and it is precisely in supplementing his classical source by its provision that Jean de Thuin most thoroughly refigures ancient history in the image of medieval society. That element is, of course, the belief in the transforming power of love, and it is in the creation of the love affair between Caesar and Cleopatra and in the "treatise on love" which he adds to his historical narrative that Jean de Thuin makes his most original contribution to the scope and significance of the Old French history of ancient Rome.[148]

The relative autonomy of the amorous episode and its accompanying "treatise on love" within the narrative structure of the *Hystore de Jules César* is confirmed by the fact that it was later copied independently by an anonymous compiler, a copy now preserved in MS. 2200 at the Bibliothèque de Sainte-Geneviève.[149] Whether Jean got the idea to interpolate an extended love affair between Caesar and Cleopatra from the *Faits des Romains* or elsewhere is unclear. His version is sufficiently different from that found in the *Faits des Romains*, most especially in its high-minded tone and idealizing thrust, to allow us to consider them as independent variations on the theme suggested by Lucan's brief, although vituperative, discussion of Cleopatra. It was probably Jean's desire to recast the affair in moral terms that accounts for his insertion of the "treatise on love," through which he attempts to control the meaning of the love between Caesar and Cleopatra.

N.H.J. van den Boogaard has identified and dated a similar Old French prose treatise on the art of love, comprising a very free translation of Ovid's *Ars amatoria*, which van den Boogaard believes was composed at approximately the same time as Jean's *Hystore* or slightly before.[150] It is unlikely, however, that Jean de Thuin either knew or used that work. As indicated above, Jean's sources for this interpolation are for the most part indirect, and they reveal his relatively wide acquaintance with courtly literature, including Ovid (whom he cites), Andreas Capellanus, the *Roman de la Rose* and earlier vernacular romances such as the *Roman d'Enéas*, from which he borrows turns of phrase and the highly conventional ideas that inform his work.

It seems clear that Jean's motives for including the episode and love casuistry stem from his desire to correct the nefarious image painted by Lucan of Caesar as a man who "even in the midst of his rage and fury, in that palace haunted by Pompey's ghost, while yet drenched with the blood of Pharsalia, . . . suffered adulterous love to mingle with his anxieties, and combined with war unlawful wedlock and spurious offspring."[151] Lucan's tirades against the Egyptian queen for the evils that she caused Rome and his scorn at Caesar's inability to withstand her amorous wiles would have seriously undermined the courtly portrait of the Roman leader that Jean was endeavoring to create. Significantly, he diverges as well from the moral opprobrium that the author of the *Faits des Romains* casts on the affair as an example of Caesar's uncontrolled *luxure* and lack of self-possession. In Jean's hands, Caesar's love of Cleopatra completes—indeed, epitomizes—the courtly character of the ancient ruler, demonstrating that he possessed a mastery of the codes of courtly behavior in love equal to his exemplary performance on the field of battle.

Since Lucan's animosity in reporting Caesar's relationship to the Egyptian queen centered on Cleopatra, the first task facing the thirteenth-century translator was to correct the degraded view of her that he found in his Latin source—a view, moreover, not previously dislodged in the *Faits des Romains*, despite the latter's more benign description of her physical attributes. The *Faits des Romains* had reserved the description of Cleopatra's beauty for *after* the onset of Caesar's love of her, deferring it to the feast that celebrates her reconciliation with her brother, Ptolemy. In Jean de Thuin, the portrait of the queen is placed at the opening of the romance, when Cleopatra appears for the first time before Caesar's eyes.[152] The sight of her beauty moves the emperor to love, a love unshaken in its strength by subsequent developments, either amatory or political. The result is an aestheticizing of the entire affair by means of which Cleopatra's

enticement of Caesar is displaced from the context of political mach-
ination, as it was presented in both Lucan and the *Faits des Romains*,
and reinterpreted according to the highest ideals of *courtoisie* and the
code of amatory etiquette that it sought to promulgate.

Jean's portrait of Cleopatra is copious, running to almost three
pages, methodical in its enumeration of her features and attire, and
highly stylized. Not only does Jean bring to bear the full panoply of
courtly aesthetic conventions in his description of her, but he explicitly places the Egyptian queen among the ranks of the great beauties
of courtly romance, comparing her to Helen of Troy and Iseult:

> com cele ki tant estoit biele c'onques autre dame ne fu plus, se ne fu
> Helaine ou Yseus de Cornuaille; et nanpourquant elle peut bien
> iestre ajoustee avoec ces deus de grant biaute.[153]

> as she who was so beautiful that never was there another woman
> more so, if not Helen or Iseult of Cornwall; and, nonetheless, she
> might well be added to [the list of] these two great beauties.

Cleopatra's tale of her political dilemma and appeal for Caesar's aid
against her brother, Ptolemy, and his evil counselor, Photin, follows
Lucan's text, but Jean adds to the conclusion a specifically courtly appeal to Caesar's sense of honor and *courtoisie*, which cannot fail to respond to her plea of distress:

> "Et d'autre part, sire, vous saves bien ke hom ki de haute lignie est
> estres, pour c'avillies n'en soit ne ses los n'en abaist ne s'ounour, ne
> doit refuser proiere ke dame li face."[154]

> "And on the other hand, my lord, you know well that a man who is
> born of high lineage, in order that neither his reputation nor his
> honor be injured or abased, must not refuse a plea that a woman
> puts to him."

True to form, Caesar is moved by her beauty and the imperatives of
the courtly code to look favorably upon her request. His reply rehearses the principal components of *courtoisie* that require him to enlist in her service and aid her in any way that he can:

> "Ciertes, dame, a dame ki rekiert aide si doucement com vous le re-
> queres mout doit on aidier de grant volente, et mout est grans hon-
> nors et grans courtoisie et grans francise d'aidier dame ki est
> desconseillie; et meismement vos dous samblans et vostre douce pa-
> role desiervent bien c'om vous doive aidier esforciement, pour quoi
> je vous dic loiaument ke jou me travaillerai de tout mon pooir de
> vous adrechier et de vous remetre en seignourie; et ke encontre vous
> vaura guerroier, ja, tant com je vive, guere ne li faudra."[155]

"Certainly, my lady, greatly should one give assistance, with all willingness, to a woman who requests aid as sweetly as you do, and it is a great honor and great courtesy and great nobility to help a woman who is deprived of protection; and especially your sweet appearance and gentle speech clearly earn you the right to be aided strenuously, for which reason I say to you loyally that I will work with all my power to ensure your right and to restore you in lordship; and whoever seeks to make war against you, so long as I live, will not fail to have war."

In keeping with the dialectic of what Robert Hanning has called the "chivalry topos" in romance, Caesar's love of Cleopatra spurs him to place at her command those martial powers that he possesses in full.[156]

Lucan's fierce hatred of the queen for the political turmoil and tragedy that her seduction of Caesar brought upon Rome has disappeared. In its place is an idealized version of Caesar's response as an act of courtesy owed to women by noble heroes. At no point does Caesar inquire into the justice of Cleopatra's cause or the military or political wisdom of committing himself and his forces to a struggle on her behalf. Unlike Lucan and the *Faits des Romains,* Jean de Thuin draws no distinction between the words that Cleopatra employs to persuade the Roman ruler to promote her political ambitions (against which, we recall, Caesar had closed his ears) and the beauty that entices him to accede to her demands. Her exemplary beauty casts an aesthetic mantle over war and wooing alike. Chivalric prowess is integrated into an aestheticized vision of courtly conduct that operates equally in love and war. And, following the conventions of this all-too-conventional narrative, Cleopatra rewards Caesar's profession of loyalty and service with a kiss.

In contrast to the troubadours' concept of courtly love, however, in which the adulterous relationship between lover and beloved is supposed to stop short of consummation and remain satisfied with a kiss, Caesar's affair with Cleopatra will proceed to its fulfillment in a fully eroticized encounter. Jean de Thuin faces here the impossibility of wholly managing a historical narrative not of his own devising. The love affair between Caesar and Cleopatra was far too well known for him to contain it within the bounds of lyric conventions, even if he had so desired. Perhaps for this reason, he interrupts the narrative of the affair to insert a small "treatise" on love, which enables him to reinterpret Caesar's behavior according to the rules governing "ce doit on apieler fine amour."[157] The love casuistry that Jean invents defines a code of love that allows him to control the interpretation of his historical narrative in ways favorable to Caesar. At the same time, the narrative is itself subsequently shaped to adhere to the rules of conduct and emotion required of a true courtly love. Narrative and treatise respond to each other in a circular fashion to gloss and decontaminate the potentially shameful consequences of the affair.

Jean de Thuin precedes his treatise on love with a report that Caesar was so taken and troubled with the great love that Cleopatra had aroused in him that he returned to his chambers, unable to sleep and moved to melancholy by desire for the queen.[158] His love for her drives all other thoughts from his mind, and he is totally captured by her image. "En tel maniere," says Jean, "le vait amors demenant, dont il m'est avis ke li diex d'amours a si bien esploitie ke mout s'en puet prisier, car il a navret le plus poissant home et souspris que on puist au monde trouver" (In this manner love went on agitating him, which I believe the God of Love so thoroughly achieved that he can take great pride in it, for he struck and caught unawares the most powerful man one could find in the world).[159] But it is, in a sense, exactly the greatness of Caesar that accounts for the strength of his passion, a courteous love commensurate with the magnitude of his chivalric prowess, as Jean is careful to note:

> Quant Amours a si poissant home com Julius Cesar estoit dou tout atrait a son commandement, mout me samble k'ele ait bien esploitie. Ele a vencut l'orgueil de celui ki onques ne fu esmaies pour guerre; dont je di c'Amours s'en doit mout esjoir et esbaudir et prisier, en tant k'ele est ore abandounee en si haut liu. S'ele par tout se gardoit ausi bien comme ele s'est ici gardee, en tant kele se tenist a ceus ki courtoisement le voelent siervir et de cuer sans vilains gas et sans losenge celeement.[160]

> When Love has brought under his command as powerful a man as Julius Caesar was, it seems to me that it has done well. It has conquered the pride of someone who was never frightened of war; therefore I say that Love ought to rejoice and take pleasure and pride in it, insofar as love today is abandoned in such high places. If only Love might maintain itself so well everywhere as it was here maintained, to the extent that it remained among those who wish to serve it *courtoisement* and with all their hearts, without base talk and without secret deceit.

Caesar becomes the paradigmatic courtly lover, the exemplification of the principles governing *courtoisie* that Jean will endeavor to set forth in the treatise on love that ensues.

This treatise is a highly conventional amalgam of the standard topoi on the "art of loving" as they had been set forth in a variety of medieval texts that Jean indirectly exploits for his own work. Beginning with a definition of love as a "legierete de cuer" (lightness of heart) and proceeding through its causes, mechanisms, character, and the distinction between "true" and "false" love, Jean lays out the conditions and codes according to which "wise men should love."

Perhaps most important for the narrative themes of his *Hystore* is his insistence that reason and measure are compatible with, even necessary for, the existence and maintenance of love, for "ki veut amer, k'il doit ouvrer par mesure et par sens" (he who wishes to love, he must proceed with measure and reason).[161] Indeed, the discourse terminates with a panegyric on "mesure," which for Jean de Thuin constitutes the essential quality of the "fin amant."[162] The effect of Jean's emphasis on reason and "mesure" is to guarantee that Caesar's conduct is seen to conform to a sanctioned ideal of moderation and courtliness that at the same time confronts and responds to the Lucanian subtext of Caesar as *démesuré*. The "treatise on love," in this sense, not only glosses the adulterous affair between Caesar and Cleopatra as an ideal form of *courtoisie*, but also addresses more profound issues concerning Caesar's chivalric character.

To the extent that his ability to win Cleopatra's love is a consequence of the greatness he has achieved on the field of battle, as she herself will proclaim, Cleopatra's love comes to Caesar as a reward for his feats of arms in war.[163] Chivalric prowess and courtly love are the twin faces of the exemplary hero, as Cleopatra emphasizes in her responses to the knight whom Caesar sends as *porte-parole* to plead his love for her. A man of such nobility, wealth, and accomplishment cannot, she confesses, be refused:

> "Ciertes, sire," ce dist la dame, "puis k'il est ensi ke je sui amee de si tres haut baron et d'oume ki tele seignorie a, mout m'en voeil d'ore en avant tenir plus chiere et doi; et meismement vous parles si tres biel et si courtoisement ke mout seroit la dame vilaine et sans science ki refuseroit vostre proiere pour iestre drue de si puissant prince k'en plus haut liu jou ne poroie m'amour asseoir."[164]

> "Certainly, my lord," said the lady, "since it appears that I am loved by so very high a baron and by a man who possesses such lordship, I wish henceforth to remain more welcoming, as I must; and especially [since] you speak so well and so courteously that a woman would have to be very base and without knowledge to refuse your request to be the beloved [*drue*] of so powerful a prince that there is no higher place in which I could lodge my love."

That Cleopatra judges correctly according to her "science" is confirmed by the knight, who enumerates Caesar's qualities to her:

> "il est biaus, preus et courtois, si ke on ne poroit ou monde trouver son parreill, et se haus princes doit iestre ames pour droite science, je vous di c'on ne poroit amer plus letre ne plus sage."[165]

> "he is handsome, valiant, and courteous, such that one cannot find his equal in the whole world, and if a high prince should be loved according to correct knowledge, I tell you that one could not love a more lettered or wiser [man]."

Reason and knowledge compel the acceptance of Caesar as suitor and lover, for he possesses in abundance those attributes of beauty, prowess, courtesy, and learning that epitomize the romance hero. Before the force of his achievements, Cleopatra can only acquiesce in his demands:

> "Je ne quier ja refuser m'amour a si haut prince comme il est, mais tant voil jou bien ke vous sachies de par moi ke plus me plest en lui cou que il est renoumes de prouece, de sens, de courtoisie et de bontet que quanques il me poroit douner."[166]

> "I do not wish to refuse my love to so high a prince as he is, but I want you to know that, for my part, I am pleased more by his renown for prowess, sense, courtesy, and goodness than by whatever he could give me."

Caesar's joy at hearing Cleopatra's reply, his impatience to be with her, his preparations for the visit, and his timidity in her presence— all are stock elements in a conventional romance plot. Finally, he declares his love for her and avows his perduring fidelity and service on her behalf:

> "Ciertes, madame," fet Caesar, "oil, et bien sachies ke je plus vous desir et aim que dame ne puciele ki soit orendroit en cest mont; si vous prie, dame, pour pitie ke par droit doit iestre trouvee en vous ke vous m'otroiies le don de vostre amour, et je vous proumec loiaument ke je serai en vostre siervice a tous besoins et ke ja mes ne vous faurai et tant ferai ke vous rares toute vostre honnour."

> "Certainly, madame," Caesar said, "hear and know that I desire and love you more than any woman or maiden who is now alive in this world; I beseech you, my lady, by whatever pity that naturally may be found in you, that you grant me the gift of your love, and I promise you faithfully that I will be in your service for all needs and that I will never fail you and will do such that you will have back all your honor."

Confronted with Caesar's nobility and *courtoisie*, and recognizing the wisdom of the choice offered her, Cleopatra yields:

> "jou ne seroie mie sage, se jou refusoie pour amic si vaillant prince comme vous iestes et si puissant."[167]

> "I would be very unwise if I refused as my lover such a valiant prince as you are and one so powerful."

In thus accepting Caesar as her lover, Cleopatra acts in accordance with the principles guiding *fine amour*, emerging in Jean's narrative as a perfect embodiment of the courtly lady. Lucan's notion that the Egyptian queen prostituted herself in order to win Caesar's aid in the political struggle against her brother has been effaced. And to underscore the queen's virtue, Jean de Thuin represents her as hesitant to agree to lie with Caesar, despite the strength of his demand. *She* is an honest woman, a passive recipient of Caesar's love and desire, who remains dignified and courteous in her every action to the end.[168] Indeed, Caesar's entry into her bedchamber is effected only by the bribing of her chamberlain, who arranges to lead him to the queen's bed after supper. Only then does Caesar consummate his love, a love now revealed as erotic desire, which refuses to be satisfied with a courtly exchange of a kiss:

> et Cesar a tant esploitie ke la dame li otroie toute se volente. Dont se sont ensemble couchie en .I. lit et gisent bras a bras, baisant et acolant et faisant tel deduit comme li amant doivent faire, quant il sont ensemble conjoint par amours et par le desir de l'un et de l'autre. Ensi se gist Cesar entre les bras s'amie, deduisant a se volente, ne il ne li souvient a celui point de guerre ne de mellee.[169]

> and Caesar acted with such ardor that the lady granted all his wishes. Thus they went to sleep together in one bed, lying arm in arm, kissing and embracing and experiencing such delight as lovers do, when they are joined together by love and the desire for one another. Thus did Caesar lie between the arms of his love, taking pleasure according to his will, and he did not think often at this time of war or conflict.

Despite Jean de Thuin's efforts to moralize the affair between Caesar and Cleopatra by cloaking it with a mantle of courtly convention, Caesar's regressive eroticism cannot be entirely suppressed. Nor, ultimately, does the erotic transaction obscure the history of war and violence that first brought Caesar to the realm of Egypt and that will lead him to complete the conquest of Rome and the destruction of the Republic. The courtly romance between Caesar and Cleopatra offers only an interlude, a moment of forgetfulness, as Jean indicates, in the martial violence that fundamentally governs the hero's life. Indeed, the affair is itself merely a prelude to the continuation of that violence in the war of Alexandria, undertaken for the sake of love. Erotic desire and military violence are the twin fonts of the primitive energy that constitutes the condition of the heroic life. Jean de Thuin's attempt to locate both within the moral framework of courtly conventions succeeds only to the extent that it removes from his narrative the tension between idealizing impulse and historical realities that had so powerfully shaped the historical vision of the *Faits des Romains*.

Just as Jean legitimizes the romance between Caesar and Cleopatra in terms of courtly convention, so also does he seek to validate the bloody history of Caesar's conquest of the world. He leaves no doubt as to the justice of Caesar's victory over Pompey or his right to rule Rome, for the mastery he attains over the empire betokens the restoration of justice and the revival of law. When Caesar the conqueror appeared in Rome,

> il fu recheus a grant honnor . . . i l'ont esleut a signour, et Cesar a tout saissi et tournet a lui cou ke li autre avoient eu, puis i a assis ses lois et ses commandemens.[170]

> he was received with great honor . . . they elected him as lord, and Caesar seized everything and turned to his own use what others had had; then he declared his laws and commandments.

In Jean de Thuin's idealizing narrative, Caesar's triumph redeems the violence of Rome's bloody civil war, restoring the empire to its former glory and reinstating its legitimacy through the declaration of "lois." That this process entails, as Jean notes in passing, the expropriation of others is the price society pays the hero who succeeds beyond all others:

> Ensi fu Cesar empereres de Rome et li plus poissans princes dou monde, car il en ot bien desous lui les trois parties, k'il ot toutes conquisses; ne onques rois ne empereres n'en conquist tant a son vivant con fist Cesar.[171]

> Thus Caesar was emperor of Rome and the most powerful prince in the world, for he had subjected to himself its three parts, all of which he had conquered; never was there king nor emperor who conquered as much in his lifetime as Caesar did.

The ambiguities concerning the events and personages of the past that so troubled the vision of ancient history translated into the terms of thirteenth-century France in the *Faits des Romains* do not impinge on Jean de Thuin's consciousness. He seeks to offer a wholly deproblematized view of ancient hero and history and holds out the promise that such a past can serve as social and moral guide for a present that aspires to similar levels of achievement.

Yet in the end, what lingers on in Jean's *Hystore* is a sense of resignation in the presence of the past, of the futility of human endeavor and ethical aspiration in a world that has lost its moral bearings. Beneath the veneer of idealism with which Jean de Thuin depicts the classical past runs a thread of surrender to forces beyond human control. Jean rewrites Cornelia's lament upon hearing of the death of Pompey, converting it from a *planctus* delivered on the loss of her husband to a lamentation on the decline of the times, which has produced a world in which Pompey's life and death no longer have meaning, for she asserts:

> "jou voi cascun jour alever les maves et amonter en hounour et en seignourie et eus douter et siervir, et se revoi viex tenir les preudoumes et les bons, qui voellent vivre simplement et ovrer loiaument; de ceus ne voi c'om apiaut nul en nule honnor, ains voi k'il sont tout adies a meschief et povre et besougnous et ensegnouriet par les malves."[172]

> "Every day I see evil persons rise in honor and lordship, while fear of them and service [paid] to them increases; and I see honorable men and the good set aside as antiquated, [although they] wish to live simply and behave faithfully; of these, I do not see any held in honor; rather I see that they are all now in misfortune, and poor and needy and dominated by the evil persons."

This is a world that elevates evil men (the "maves") and abases the honorable, in which it is impossible to lead a simple life and behave with loyalty and honor, for those who aspire to such a life find themselves poor and needy and in thrall to evildoers, a lesson that emerges as clearly from the field of war as from the mouths of bereft widows. Thus Scipio, whose outstanding courage in battle is amply narrated in the *Hystore de Jules César*, warns his companions:

> "Ciertes, mout est faus li hom ki trop se fie en l'eur de cest siecle; car quant il quide mius iestre asseur de bien avoir, dont li meschiet il plus, et li dechiet s'onnors."[173]

> "To be sure, that man is crazy who places too much confidence in the good fortune of this world, for when he thinks to be better assured of having goods, then misfortune strikes him hardest, and his honor declines."

History does not vouchsafe that the honorable will persevere or gain their just rewards. Human society is as likely to deprive *preudomes* of honor as elevate them in the eyes of their contemporaries, a moral that Jean de Thuin drives home in commenting on the death of Cato:

> Et pour sa mort que assavie soloit alever tous biens et oster et abaissier tous maus nous verrons encore si le siecle bestourner par tant ke prodons n'i avera son liu; et pour ce se puet on desconforter et trop durement espoenter.[174]

> He who in life was accustomed to elevate all good and remove and abase all evil, we shall see if, in his death, the times have so turned for the worse that the honorable man will not have his place; and for this reason one might grieve and painfully fear.

The spectacle of the past germinates discouragement and fear more often than encouragement and solace. And Jean de Thuin makes it all too clear that the inadequacy of the past is matched in the present, for it, no less than classical Rome, discloses the frailty of human society when confronted with the power of dishonorable men. To Cornelia's lament on the decline of the Roman world, Jean adds his own on the failings of contemporary society, which is no more protected from the ravages of the unworthy than the past:

> com cis siecles est frailles et niens, et com hom ki sens a en lui le doit tenir vill! On voit en cest siecle les mauves, les felons et les trahitours en grant dignite et en grant hounour, et cil ki sont preudoume et loial si n'ont fors povrete et meschief.[175]

> how this world is frail and nothing, and how a man who has good sense in him must hold it in contempt! One sees in this time the evil persons, the thieves and the traitors in great dignity and great honor, while those who are honorable men and loyal have nothing but poverty and misfortune.

The voice of the moralist ends in melancholic resignation before the enormity of the world's evil. For all Jean de Thuin's drive for idealism and consistency in the moral refiguration of his Caesarean narrative, his own moral posture and didactic goals betoken a sensibility better attuned to evil than heroism. The tale of courtly heroism and moral valor that he conveys to his medieval French audience ironically is undermined by the very moralism that informs his historiographical undertaking. It is no accident that Jean de Thuin concludes his romance with Caesar's triumphal entry into Rome as "li plus poissans princes dou monde." The narrative economy of his work conforms, as he declares, to the economy of Caesar's drive for mastery: "Et ore, puis ke nous avons tant menet nostre conte que Cesar a menet a fin son desirier, nous le vous laisserons a tant et nous en tairons" (And now, since we have brought our tale to the point at which Caesar accomplished his wish, we shall leave it to you and no longer speak of it).[176] The coherence of his moral vision of Caesar's history can be sustained only by a closure that forecloses access to the doomed future of the triumphant ruler.

In rewriting Lucan's *Pharsalia* as a romance narrative, enhanced by the long, interpolated love story of Caesar and Cleopatra, Jean de Thuin sought to erase the figure of Caesar the *démesuré* so pronounced in Lucan and in the *Faits des Romains*, while validating Caesar's endeavor to conquer the world. Jean moralizes the erotic, but fails to suppress it, just as he fails to obscure the violent origins of Caesar's seizure of power. The result is that, in his treatment, erotic desire and the desire to dominate are identical, and identically violent. Courtly ideology cannot, finally, disguise the violent impulses that prompt the actions of men like Caesar, for it is itself only a linguistic guise. Significantly, Jean's emphasis on language fails to produce a distinction between true and false, precisely because he resorts to a linguistic mode—that of romance—which by definition falsifies truth. In the end, his "romancing" of the past unwittingly reveals the "unromantic" meaning of both past romance and present history.

5 Contemporary Chronicles
The Contest over the Past

For French vernacular chroniclers, the question of how to construct what today we might call a "literature of fact"[1] entailed a novel set of literary problems relating to the content and representational strategies suitable for a historical discourse having as its subject the real events and actors of contemporary life. Insofar as the earliest works of Old French prose historiography, such as the translations of the *Pseudo-Turpin Chronicle* and classical histories, relied on both antecedent texts and the traditional literary techniques of epic and romance, they remained indebted to, and thus to some extent embedded within, romance conventions of poetic writing and oral performance, even as they sought to found a new genre of written prose history. From a formal perspective, then, it seems fair to conclude that only with the emergence of contemporary chronicles did vernacular prose historiography achieve a genuine autonomy, consolidating a generically specialized methodology and style along with a specialized subject matter understood as properly "historical."[2] To be sure, epic toning of battle accounts and romance techniques of narration continued to be employed to enliven accounts of the past and present. But in the main, contemporary chroniclers found the methods of earlier vernacular literary forms ill suited to the needs and goals of their own narratives. As Wlad Godzich and Jeffrey Kittay have indicated, "Traditional modes of transmission are put under strain, since their kinds of distance, dominance, transcendence and form now appear inappropriate" to the representation of contemporary historical events and topics.[3] In shifting the foci of their concern to contemporary events, whose claim to worthiness as objects of the historian's concern lay not in their ideal character but in their significance for the ongoing life of the communities for which historical texts were destined, chroniclers confronted novel problems in devising a discourse adequate to their task. That task, at its most basic, was to endow the discrete, concrete, and particular elements of contemporary reality with the same sense of moment and significance that medieval society normally accorded to an already valorized, traditional past. If vernacular historiography was to achieve generic autonomy as a "discourse of the real" and free itself from the ties that still bound it to the "discourse of the imaginary"—or, in Lacan's terminology, the "discourse of desire"—the problem confronting chroniclers, Suzanne Fleischman argues, was to make the real desirable.[4]

With respect to questions of content, the contemporary chronicler recast not only the temporal framework of his narrative, but the very nature of his investigation as well. The writing of contemporary history posed new difficulties in determining the criteria by which events were to be judged worthy of preservation. No longer a "given" established by the authority of prior texts, the importance of contemporary events now fell to the vernacular chronicler to determine, imposing on him an evaluative function that the translators of inherited Latin sources had mainly escaped. Although a long-standing rhetorical tradition declared that the historian's task was to preserve in memory deeds worthy of note—*notabilia facta*[5]—the exact characteristics and qualities that rendered events memorable or noteworthy remained subject to debate. The chronicler's ability to calculate the historical significance of the events he wished to recount was further complicated by a pervasive medieval bias in favor of considering as historically telling not "what really happened" but what was done—*res gestae*—and thus, perforce, by whom. The importance of events in the chronicle is gauged by the status of those who participate in them, in this way strengthening, if possible, the aristocratic character of vernacular historiography. Not surprisingly, therefore, the shift in subject matter from ancient to recent history is marked by an increase in the concern with and influence of the nobility on the form of the chronicle.[6]

From this perspective, aristocratic patronage of contemporary chronicles can be seen as a form of political action, an attempt to control the subject matter of history and the voices on the past as a means of dominating the collective memory of feudal society. To the extent that the patronage of contemporary history in the thirteenth century is prompted by political goals, it signals the beginning of an overt contest over the past that would scarcely have been conceivable in an earlier period when history represented primarily the trace of God's operation in human affairs. As long as meaning in history was generated and guaranteed by divine intervention and transcendent significance, the medieval nobility could scarcely have hoped to take control of the past, to make *its* history *the* history. The secularization and laicization of historical writing in the thirteenth century, by removing from view God's active participation in human affairs, brought history squarely into the realm of human contest and historiographical contestation.

Noble patronage of contemporary history similarly effected a change in the unit of historical investigation. In contrast to epic and romance, which treated the theme of individual heroic action in past times, the vernacular chronicle tended, instead, to provide a history of larger social collectivities. For the narration of the deeds of individual heroes the Old French chronicle substituted an account of aristocratic lineages, which were usually inserted within the narrative frame of royal dynastic history. The use of royal dynasties as an organizational device for aristocratic history in some cases paradoxically contradicted the ideological import of the chronicles themselves, at least to the degree that such chronicles sought to validate principles of aristocratic autonomy. But the absence in medieval Europe of a clear governmental entity like the Roman Republic meant that there was no natural political unit on which to focus historical narration. Old French romance had solved this problem by treating the individual adventures of chivalric knights as exemplary tales selected from a potentially much larger corpus of possible narratives that, had they ever been collected together, would recount the story of the noble class itself, understood as the plurality of knights. As a matter of practice, however, romance narration remained wedded to the account of single adventures of individual knights whose paths, and hence stories, intersected to produce an interlaced narrative that in sum represented the collective history of the Arthurian realm. Arthur, as head of the realm and arbiter of the Round Table, figuratively guaranteed the putative coherence of the tales both enacted and brought back and "deposited" at his court.[7] Early contemporary chroniclers such as the Anonymous of Béthune constructed their narratives along parallel lines, but their histories were constrained to a much higher degree by the need to establish a connection between the deeds and accomplishments of noble lineages and the larger political realities of the age. Inevitably, this meant viewing aristocratic activities within the "national" framework of royal history.

It is interesting to speculate whether the failure to conceive of a collective history of the nobility apart from the monarchy is itself emblematic of the relative weakness of the aristocracy in the face of the king's growing power. The apparent impossibility of grounding aristocratic history in a context independent of royal history might suggest that the outcome of the contest over the past was a foregone conclusion, since it was conducted within the terms already shaped, if not altogether determined by, the historical existence of monarchy. Was the conceptual dependence of aristocratic history on royal paradigms symptomatic of the historical necessity for aristocratic subordination to royal power, irrespective of any motives that might have animated the writing of contemporary history as a source of resistance to royal power? Or was the use of royal lineage as an organizing grid for the narration of contemporary history merely a traditional and convenient practice, facilitating the chronicler's narrative deployment of the diverse elements of his story? Alternatively, did the use of royal history as a model for aristocratic historiography implicitly argue for a parity of status between king and nobility? That is, did the representation of royal *gestes* as simply one thread among many interwoven into the fabric of the text constitute a narrative index of an underlying commonality of status, power, and historical significance that the chronicler believed obtained among king and nobles, both as real persons in the historical world and as subjects of the chronicler's discourse?

The answers to these questions will determine to a large degree our understanding of the nature and meaning of contemporary historiography in thirteenth-century France. Unfortunately, these answers are neither easy nor obvious. The titles employed by a contemporary chronicler such as the Anonymous of Béthune, who seemingly highlights the kings of France and England as the interpretive foci of his accounts, have traditionally led historians and literary scholars to classify them as works of royal history.[8] Because he wrote histories called the *Chronique des rois de France* and the *Histoire des ducs de Normandie et des rois d'Angleterre*, the Anonymous of Béthune is thought to represent a proto-nationalist tendency in Old French historiography, a tendency only fully realized fifty years later with the production of the *Grandes chroniques de France* at the Abbey of Saint-Denis. But does the use of royal history as title and narrative frame necessarily betoken ideological assent to monarchical hegemony? Conversely, if such assent is absent, why privilege the king by writing under the titular aegis of the royal name?

An approach, if not a definitive answer, to these questions lies in seeing the thirteenth-century contemporary chronicle as a site for the negotiation of competing interests. Because it treated the events and dilemmas of the present or the recent past, the contemporary chronicle was forced to abandon the supposed certainties and unified values embodied in a distanced, absolute past. Contemporary history no longer presented a valorized image of an idealized and stable world, but rather an image of an inconclusive present, whose full meaning could not be disengaged from a mere account of events in their unfolding, since those events were incomplete and harbored as yet unknown consequences. Furthermore, not only were events themselves incomplete, but the political environment in which the vernacular chronicle was generated—*by* which it was generated—enforced a sense of relative values and competing loyalties. Especially in the case of the Anonymous of Béthune, the rivalry between the Capetian and Plantagenet monarchies and their contest for the loyalties of and control over the lords of northern France required the recognition that it was impossible for one man to serve two masters. In a curious way, the conflict of loyalties generated by royal competition, which formed the political experience of the Anonymous of Béthune and his contemporaries, repeated the experience of the Romans during the civil war, as the *Faits des Romains* recounted that story. As we shall see, whether by conscious design or not, the Anonymous of Béthune replicates in his chronicles some of the narrative strategies employed in the *Faits des Romains* for representing a society riven by internal schisms and contested allegiances, in which the progress of war eventually pits blood relations against one another and spells the destruction of those principles of lineage and solidarity that had once formed the basis of the nobility's social cohesion and strength.

Unlike the earlier translators of the *Turpin* chronicle or ancient history, the chronicler of recent history felt no need to justify his activity as arising from a duty to transmit knowledge about the past or to provide ethical exempla for the edification of his audience. Characteristic of the recent chronicle was a belief that contemporary events possessed sufficient interest in and of themselves to warrant setting down by any chronicler fortunate enough to have witnessed them.[9] Instead, contemporary historiography tended to rely on a new system of authentication and authority in establishing its credibility. No longer able to draw on the prestige guaranteed by the use of prior Latin sources, the contemporary chronicler based the authority and truth of his history on the reliability of eyewitnesses, including, ideally, himself.[10] Historical writing, in this way, was transformed into a "witness discourse,"[11] the product of direct knowledge ascertained through visual and auditory experience, those things "seen" and "heard" in the course of the chronicler's own life. Truth in the chronicle was seen to result from "physical and temporal proximity" to the events recounted;[12] the immediacy of events guaranteed the referential validity of the chronicler's account. But since the chronicler was rarely the sole source of information for his history, the construction of a "witness discourse" inevitably entailed the multiplication of sources of authority—or voices—on the past. Competing with the knowledge and perspective on events that stemmed from the chronicler's own experience were views and information derived from other witnesses and other sites of knowledge to which he had access, whether directly or indirectly. In its very reliance on eyewitness testimony, the contemporary chronicle came to incorporate a plurality of perspectives, thereby enhancing its dialogic character. In the case of the Anonymous of Béthune, this dialogic character was actually represented by *two* versions of the same historical series of events, each embracing the perspective of one of the parties vying for political hegemony.

The contemporary chronicler's avoidance of overt moralization or polemical argumentation in favor of an apparently neutral and "factual" account of his subject matter has led some scholars to argue that behind the adoption of a posture of neutrality lay a demand for greater factual accuracy and realism on the part of an increasingly sophisticated and literate public. The overall movement in the development of vernacular historiography, William Sayers argues, is "from a theologically-oriented set of principles in the direction of a purely intellectual discipline whose goal is disinterested factual accuracy."[13] Naturally allied with the desire for such facticity was the employment of prose, since prose was the medium best suited to convey historical facts accurately. Hence Omer Jodogne, for example, sees the adoption of prose as a reflection of advances in the aristocracy's historical sensibility, now disencumbered of the need for imaginative amplification and able to focus on the concrete and realistic.[14] Similarly, Jean Frappier attributes the success of prose as a literary language to a growing taste for exactitude in narration and a desire to appear to be recounting an authentic story.[15] Prose was peculiarly adapted to meet the needs of such pretensions, since one of prose's subterfuges, as Godzich and Kittay have demonstrated, was to present itself as matter, not form.[16] It was, therefore, the style of choice for a historical discourse that claimed to be a faithful reproduction of the past, free of literary or "artistic" deformation.

Yet given the personal investment of the chronicler in the narration of a history in which he was also a participant, it is hardly surprising that the structure of his narrative rarely promoted a detached attitude toward events. Authorial investment in the political or moral significance of history to be conveyed to audiences simply assumes a new strategy of articulation in the contemporary chronicle. In place of the idealizing moralizations with which an author like Jean de Thuin interpellated his audience, there occurs in the course of the vernacular chronicle's development a gradual withdrawal of the author's voice, a diminution in the frequency of those narrative interjections by which earlier translators had established their presence in the text and impressed their personalities on it. Once embarked on his account of events, the vernacular chronicler leaves to the reader the task of extracting the lessons to be drawn from the historical narrative. Instead of making explicit the didactic import of his history, the vernacular chronicler retreats behind an increasingly reflective discourse, in the dual sense that he assumes that his narrative will transparently reflect an objective "reality" and that he strives to produce a more systematic, reflective treatment of his subject matter.[17] To be sure, individual points of view and ideological biases remain, but they are integrated into the narration of fact, behind which the historian hides his moral personality. The burden of interpreting the moral lessons implicit in the historian's account falls to the reader/auditor, while the chronicler takes refuge in that posture of impartiality that has become the hallmark of "objective" historiography.

It would be a mistake to believe that the façade of objectivity erected by vernacular chroniclers represented a genuine impartiality before the "facts" of history. If anything, the assumption of "neutrality" was a more powerful tool of partisanship, masking the play of interests that shaped the chronicler's perspective on present realities. In most cases, in fact, his coloration of his tale, structured to convey implicit if not overt messages, was sufficiently deft to leave little opportunity for ambiguity. As even Sayers notes:

> Few of the conditions of medieval life fostered an unprejudiced view
> of history and fewer still encouraged the expression of such a view
> in historical literature. The personality of the author, the circum-
> stances of patronage, the conception of the chronicle as a literary
> work designed for a specific public rather than as an independent and
> self-contained historical inquiry are of paramount interest in this
> respect.[18]

It is clear from the circumstances of patronage for vernacular historiography that few works of history were directed at audiences not already gained to the causes they upheld. In that sense, the chronicle functioned more as codification and ratification of the values, principles, and social aspirations of those it served than as the instigator of an innovative polemic.

The pluralism of perspectives that the chronicler included in his narrative, therefore, served not the goal of neutrality, but a higher partiality, one capable of generating an illusion of objectivity or "truth," a "truth" negotiated by the chronicler among the competing views that his chronicle set forth. Looked at in this way, the vernacular chronicler operated very much in the manner of the fictive "narrator" of a nineteenth-century realist novel, who controls the multiple, seemingly fragmented, viewpoints that make up the total discourse of the novel in order to produce a realist consensus that establishes narrative intelligibility and meaning.[19] Just as readers of realist fiction are led by the narrator to discover for themselves the connections between and significance of unfolding events and characters in the novel, so the vernacular chronicler (albeit with considerably less skill) politically managed his narration of events to confirm his own ideological viewpoint. As in the nineteenth-century novel, "realism" in the vernacular chronicle is nothing more than the visible symptom of this ideological turn.

Still, the realism of the thirteenth-century chronicle differs from that of the later European novel, though in both cases that realism, it is important to stress, is equally an effect of style. In thirteenth-century historiography, narrative realism derives from the chronicle's aim to function as a conveyor of information rather than to communicate social values to the community at large or to entertain. In lieu of its once frankly acknowledged desire to teach and to divert, the Old French chronicle increasingly claims to be a written monument to the actions, beliefs, and ideals of the past and present, which, in theory, it transparently reflects in a "true" narrative.

Realism's "truth," of course, is not the philosopher's *veritas*, but that humbler sort of truth that is the product of literary style: the truth found in verisimilitude. The goal of realist discourse is to render an image of the world "as it seems to be," and the measure of its success is not its ability to produce an exact replica of the world, impossible in any case, but to offer a simulacrum of how the world appears—an image of an image, as it were—whose persuasiveness lies in its strength of correspondence rather than in its identity to the object that it seeks to reproduce. For the realist historiographical text, correspondence is the crucial calculus, since it professes to represent a reality situated outside language itself. The closer to "reality," the less mediated its relation to the referent, the greater the apparent transparency of the historical text, the more credible it becomes. At the heart of all realist historical discourse, and no less so in the Middle Ages, lies a pervasive commitment to what Derrida has called the Western tradition of "logocentrism"—that is, the belief that words transparently represent things.

Obviously, few events in medieval society were as transparent as the chroniclers' narratives suggested.[20] Indeed, the very simplicity of the chronicle's representation of contemporary reality alerts us to its ideological function. Unlike the medieval epic, which had posited an ethical and sociopolitical ideal of chivalry as the central factor motivating behavior within feudal society and then endeavored to demonstrate the maintenance or disintegration of that ideal, and unlike the courtly romance, which had set forth a similar ideal in a more problematical and interrogative fashion, the contemporary chronicle "appears to provide an unreflective and unquestioning record of the resolution of fundamentally simple political problems through military and occasionally diplomatic means in an organically unified feudal world, one with few inner inconsistencies."[21] To achieve this "effect" of realism, however, the chronicler had to create a fictional "pseudo-reality" that could be recognized by both writers and their publics as a literary analogue of the "real" world.[22] The chronicler had to construct within the heart of his narrative a sense of space and time that conveyed the impression of a transparent extratextual reality replicated within the body of the text itself. In other words, the task of the chronicler shifted from that of "commenting on reality to constituting a reality."[23]

To some extent, prose was a natural instrument for the construction of such a "pseudo-reality," since prose proffers, Eugene Vance has argued, "a world where temporal and spatial perspectives prevail, one in which movement and action are in order."[24] But prose alone, especially in its early stages, could scarcely bear the full burden of creating a "realistic" stage for the literary representation of reality. One means of doing this was to embed within the historical account itself syntactical and narrative structures that formulated the sense of a coherent, causally motivated sequence of events capable of conveying the logic of historical development in time and space. For the vernacular chronicler to achieve this sense of historical coherence involved the creation of a new form of narration that departed sharply from the traditional procedures originally developed for vernacular oral composition and performance, procedures that had been carried over into the construction of both written romance narrative in the twelfth century and early-thirteenth-century histories.

Initially, the vernacular chronicler's method of narration appears to have been based on the uncodified but consciously practiced techniques of epic composition.[25] Epic narrative, generally, consisted of a series of episodes or tableaux serially ordered in paratactic juxtaposition along a temporal axis not of fixed dates (i.e., chronology) but of sequences. Because the connection between these juxtaposed scenes is serial rather than causal, the overall effect of such narrative organization is to produce a nondevelopmental, episodic narrative informed by a theme that is continually reexpressed in separate events, lending to epic its aura of existing in an eternal present, of constituting a series of "nows" placed side by side, which move forward in discrete, seemingly unrelated steps. In pure epic, the interrupted quality of the narrative line—a consequence of its unremitting parataxis—is reinforced by the inclusion of *laisses similaires*, subepisodic fragments in which the just-completed narrative element is repeated, thus further suspending the forward movement of the story. The structural pattern of epic literature is, therefore, basically repetitive and sequential, and it seems logical to conclude that it was a form of narration well suited to the ritual aims of the performed text and expressing, on the level of narrativity, epic's desire to revive the past and make it live in the present.

The purely serial arrangement of episodes characteristic of epic had its counterpart in the chronicle in the chronologically strung out but causally unrelated sequence of events that, as in epic, develop along a more or less clearly defined temporal axis. At first, vernacular history differed from Latin historiography (hence from its own Latin sources) in dividing the narrative into a series of episodic units, aimed at presenting sharply defined, visualized scenes in an action-oriented account. Nor was the Old French chronicle immune to the interruptions of plot line commonly found in contemporary fictional literature. While such interruptions obviously did not take the form of *laisses similaires*, the frequent discursive and episodic digressions to which the earliest Old French chronicles were prone produced comparable results in terms of the disruption of narrative continuity and movement.

As it developed, however, the vernacular chronicle progressively abandoned parataxis in favor of a hypotactic narrative construction, in

which individual scenes—the old building blocks of episodic narration—were gradually subordinated to a theme whose component
elements were united by logical, causal relations.[26] As Northrop Frye
has shown, causality in narrative develops with second-phase, or
metonymic, writing, which replaces the metaphoric language of myth
and presents itself as a verbal imitation of a reality outside itself,
thus strengthening the referential, "objective" status of historical
discourse.[27] The appearance of a synthetic, causal narrative in the vernacular chronicle represents, therefore, a literary preference for metonymic as against metaphoric discourse, for an ideological as against
an imaginative performance of history.

Another means of creating "pseudo-reality" was to organize the
chronicle in terms of the structure of an extratextual referent, one that
the chronicler's text claimed mimetically to represent. For thirteenth-
century vernacular chroniclers that referent was genealogy. By patterning his narrative along genealogical lines, the vernacular chronicler was able to create a seemingly coherent and realistic image of time
and social affiliation that could give structure and meaning to an account of contemporary history.

Thus the Anonymous of Béthune, in his *Histoire des ducs de Normandie et des rois d'Angleterre*, traces the history of the duchy of
Normandy and the kingdom of England, from the time of the Norman arrival in France to 1220, by interlacing the family histories of
the various ruling houses on both sides of the Channel, among which
his own patron's house of Béthune figures prominently. Each ruler in
the ducal and royal succession is given as full a *vita* as information
permits, and throughout the Anonymous shows extreme sensitivity
to questions of legitimate birth, hereditary rights, and the actions of
what he explicitly calls the *lignages*, producing a braided narrative
formed from the independent histories of each lineal grouping. In his
histories, the principle of narrative order derives from genealogical
succession, in which the most significant structural divisions of history are supplied by generational change.

Genealogy structured history by providing a metaphor of procre-
ative time and social affiliation that brought together into a connected
historical matrix the essential core of the chronicler's material. In this
way, it enabled chroniclers to organize their narratives as a sequence
of *gestes* performed by the successive representatives of one or more
lignages, whose personal characteristics and deeds, extensively chronicled in essentially biographical modes, bespoke the enduring meaning
of history as the collective action of noble lineages in relation to one

another and to those values to which their *gestes* gave life. Using genealogy as a myth of origin and an argument for continuity, the writer of a genealogically patterned history attempted to nullify aristocratic decline by reexpressing, with the greatest possible force and vividness, a cultural paradigm of origin, understood as the source of value in medieval society.[28]

Chroniclers such as the Anonymous of Béthune who discuss contemporary events integrate the contemporary history of Capetian France into its ancient (Trojan), Merovingian, and Carolingian past. But unlike the royal histories in Latin on which they draw for their material, these authors do not offer an exclusively monarchical past. Contemporary chroniclers turned to the dynastic past of France's or England's ruling houses not in an effort to validate the monarchy's right to govern, but as an essential political framework for considering the relations between a crisis-beset aristocracy and the increasingly powerful monarchies on both sides of the Channel. In so doing, they converted the historiographical text into a site for a contest over the past that is the textual analogue of the political contest for power and authority in contemporary society. At the same time, the writing of history served an expressive function, giving voice to aristocratic ambivalence about and resentment toward newly dominant kings. If, as I argued in chapter 2, vernacular historiography initially represented an attempt to deproblematize aristocratic culture in an age of anxiety whose social ground was the challenge to aristocratic autonomy posed by a resurgent monarchy, what the contemporary chronicle indicates is the impossibility of sustaining this deproblematized posture toward a past seen as a unitary source of authority, for that past spoke with more than one voice. The very complexity of contemporary history served to redefine and reinterpret both past and present as inherently complex structures of meaning over which it was difficult to establish control. The dual histories of the Anonymous of Béthune offer a rare opportunity to investigate this process, for in creating two parallel accounts of the same events, he exteriorized—and inscribed in separate texts—the inner tensions and ambiguities that underlay the impulse to historiographical production in thirteenth-century France.

The Anonymous of Béthune

As far as can be discerned from the language and content of his histories, it would appear that the Anonymous of Béthune was of Artesian extraction and had entered the service of Robert VII of Béthune sometime in the 1180s, in all likelihood in the capacity of *ménestrel*.

Even these bare facts are subject to dispute. Victor LeClerc, for example, conjectured that he was originally Flemish.[29] But Artois seems a more precise indication of his place of birth, as suggested not only by the language of his histories, but also by his solicitude for the fate of the region, his care in relating the events that occurred there as a result of Louis VIII's acquisition of the county, and, in particular, his emotional lament concerning the devastation wreaked by royal officials such as the *bailli* Nevelon, who administered Artois in Louis's name after its annexation to the royal domain.

Léopold Delisle proposed that the Anonymous be identified with a *maître* Matthieu, a cleric whose service in the household of Guillaume II of Béthune is recorded in a charter of April 1214, by which the grateful Guillaume bestowed upon him the sum of twelve livres, derived from an annual tax levied on the stalls of Béthune (*ad scopas Bethunie*).[30] But it is much more likely, as O. Holder-Egger originally proposed, that he was in the employ not of Guillaume, but of Robert VII of Béthune.[31] The evidence for this assertion rests on the Anonymous's treatment of his patron within the two histories that he composed and on the degree to which his narrative indicates that he was an eyewitness to events in which Robert VII participated.

To begin with, the detail with which he recounts the smallest matters relating to the house of Béthune—and among its members, to Robert VII especially—is out of proportion to the rather general character of the remainder of his chronicle. Moreover, not only is the Anonymous extraordinarily well informed about events in Flanders during the turbulent era of struggle against Philip Augustus that reached its climax in the battle of Bouvines; he also presents extremely accurate information on the departure of the Flemish barons to England and their service with John's army at the time of Prince Louis's invasion of England in 1216—information that can only stem from direct knowledge. It is logical to conclude, therefore, that he accompanied Robert of Béthune during the period when he served among the mercenary forces of John of England, a crossing of the Channel not made by Guillaume.

It is not certain, either, that the Anonymous was a cleric. As Charles Petit-Dutaillis already pointed out, his chronicles, although employing Latin historical works as sources, reveal no evidence of a clerical or classical education, and his writing is devoid of the sort of learned, classical allusions that mark even so secular a cleric as Guillaume le Breton.[32] More likely, he was a literate "siergans et menestreus," as Holder-Egger supposed, who had succeeded in attaching himself to the household of Robert of Béthune.[33]

The Anonymous's patron, Robert VII of Béthune, was the second son of Guillaume II. Shortly after 1194, Guillaume II had become lord of Béthune and advocate of Arras and, through his marriage in 1190 to Matilda, heiress to the seigneurie of Dendermonde in Flanders, lord of Dendermonde. The house of Béthune traced its ancestry back to Robert I Fasciculus, advocate of Arras around the year 1000 and possibly a descendant of the counts of Arras, given that he and his progeny continued to hold the office of advocate.[34] It is likely, in any case, that Robert I Fasciculus descended from Carolingian nobility, since the sources consider him a *princeps*, and his son and successor, Robert II, is called *nobilis* in 1066.[35] Galbert of Bruges specifically names Robert IV of Béthune (1090–1128) as belonging to the *primi terrae Flandriarum* and counts him among the peers (*pares*) of Flanders.[36] Although Robert IV was not expressly designated *nobilis*, all his descendants were considered to be noble in the twelfth and thirteenth centuries.

During the lifetime of his parents and elder brother, Daniel, Robert VII was a relatively poor knight without lands of his own, which perhaps explains his readiness to enlist on the side of King John, whose largesse to potential vassals in his bid for Flemish support against Philip Augustus was renowned.[37] Indeed, among the Flemish barons singled out for favors from King John, Robert VII figures most frequently in the rolls as the recipient of royal attention and gifts. Relations between the house of Béthune and the kings of England went back at least to the time of Henry II. The name of Béthune figures as one of the three peers to appear on the list of Flemish nobles confirming the *Recognitio Servitii*, acknowledging the service "that the barons and castellans and other men of the county of Flanders owe to Henry the king of England as [their] lord for the fiefs which they hold from him." The *Recognitio* is dated 1163, indicating that members of the family were already receiving money-fiefs, if not actual land, from the English king by the middle of the twelfth century.[38] Territorial grants to the Béthunes may have begun as early as 1175, when Count Philippe of Alsace had occasion to send Robert VII's grandfather, Robert V "Le Roux," on a mission to England, where, perhaps in return for services rendered, he obtained important holdings in fief. Robert's father, Guillaume II, also received lands in England from Henry II, grants rapidly augmented under Richard I and John. Privileges were added to possessions when Guillaume's brother, Jean of Béthune, *prévôt* of Douai and future bishop of Cambrai, was granted formal support by the king of England to obtain the deanship of York.[39] By the turn of the twelfth century, then, the whole Béthune family was to some extent already under English influence.

This pattern of service and reward continued well into the next generation. Both Robert and his brother Daniel are found on the receiving end of royal favors in the Close and Patent Rolls for John's reign. When Guillaume II died in 1214, John confirmed to Robert the full seisin of all the lands and revenues that his father had enjoyed in England, which now devolved to Robert by hereditary right.[40] On 11 April of the same year, the king offered Robert an additional one hundred pounds,[41] followed shortly thereafter by a gift of two hundred pounds.[42] Given this extraordinary pattern of royal generosity to Robert VII of Béthune, it is not surprising that when Count Ferrand of Flanders sent Baldwin of Nieuwpoort to England to request John's aid against Philip Augustus, the count's messenger immediately identified Robert as a particular royal favorite among the group of Flemish nobles gathered at the English court. According to the Anonymous, who had accompanied his master across the Channel, Baldwin met with "vi haus homes de Flanders . . . et plusiors autres bacelors" (six high men of Flanders . . . and several other bachelors), who elected Robert VII to plead the Flemish cause before the English king.[43] Robert did so successfully, helped to lead the expedition that surprised the French fleet at Damme, and continued to play an important role in the war against Philip Augustus throughout 1213 and 1214, eventually, after Bouvines, enlisting as a constable in the English army.

The Anonymous of Béthune's reporting of numerous incidents fully supports the notion that he was an eyewitness to the events he chronicled. Thus, for example, Holder-Egger believes that it was the Anonymous himself who read aloud to Robert of Béthune and the assembled Flemish barons the letters in 1216 from King John requesting Flemish aid against his rebellious barons, which he introduces into his narrative with the phrase "Or oiies que les lettres disoient" (Now hear what the letters said).[44] His account of the dismay felt by the Flemish barons in England when John signed Magna Carta without consulting them, and their ensuing confrontation with the king over the matter, constitutes one of the most vividly recounted moments in his history and has the feel of a report from a participant-observer. He is so well informed about the doings of the house of Béthune that in naming one of the prisoners taken by Philip Augustus's army under the walls of Damme on 1 June 1213, he adds that this prisoner had earlier been dubbed as a knight by his cousin, Robert of Béthune.[45] But it is especially in his account of the deliverance, in 1214, of the countess of Guines by Robert of Béthune and of the death of Robert's father, Guillaume II of Béthune, and the reaction of Guillaume's widow, Matilda, that he appears, as Delisle remarked, "se révéler un témoin oculaire des faits dont Béthune fut alors le théâtre."[46]

The Anonymous often includes summaries of conversations that took place among the principal actors in the events he chronicled as well as personal details about the participants, such as his description of Baldwin, count of Aumale, as a "preudom et loiaus et boins chevaliers; mais si estoit mehaigniés de la goute artetyque que il ne pooit aler .i. pas, ains le couvenoit porter" (honorable man and loyal and good knight; but he was so stricken with arthritic gout that he could not take a single step, but it was necessary to carry him).[47] His knowledge of the count's crippling gout betokens firsthand acquaintance. The Anonymous similarly relates Isabelle of Angoulême's scornful retort to her husband, King John, after he complained that he had lost all for her sake—a reference to the fact that Philip Augustus had used the occasion of John's marriage to Isabelle, then engaged to Hugh le Brun of Lusignan, to cite the English king to his court and to declare him forfeit of his continental possessions when John refused to appear. According to the Anonymous of Béthune, the haughty queen, cause of so much of the military conflict of the first decades of the thirteenth century, replied: " 'Sire, aussi ai-jou le melleur chevalier dou monde perdu por vous' "[48] ("My lord, I too have lost the best knight in the world for you"), a story that smacks of court gossip to which the Anonymous was privy. His understanding and description of the workings not only of the English court, but of the entourage of Philip Augustus as well, places him at the center of the major political events of his era, on which he provides precious and often unique information in vivid and amusing detail.

Scholars initially questioned whether the Anonymous was the author of both the *Histoire des ducs de Normandie et des rois d'Angleterre* and the *Chronique des rois de France*. In part, this doubt arose from the seeming illogic of a single chronicler producing two versions of virtually identical material, apparently written in quick succession one after the other. The two histories differ considerably in their opening sections, locating the events of contemporary history in distinct national histories and traditions that draw on quite divergent bodies of source materials. But with the narration of recent history, the texts cover essentially the same material in similar arrangement and include a large number of identical anecdotes, descriptions of historical actors, and reports of speeches and events. Although the chronicles do not precisely duplicate each other, their respective treatments of the same period of French and English history exhibit a striking degree of complementarity.

At present, though, based on the fundamental convergence of the material treated in the contemporary sections of the *Histoire* and the *Chronique,* most scholars have concluded that the Anonymous of Béthune was, indeed, the compiler of both works. In a large number of manuscripts the French and English histories are copied one after the other, suggesting that they were seen as deriving from a single author.[49] The most powerful argument for the Anonymous's authorship of both works, however, stems from his style of writing and methods of narration. In each text he employs a vigorous language aimed at pleasing a lay audience in a graceful and lively manner, creating a narrative through which he scatters amusing anecdotes, proverbial sayings, and memorable dialogues. Similarly, the narrative sequence of dynastic history is constantly interrupted in both works by the insertion of material relating to Flanders and the Béthunes, justified by remarks such as that found in the *Histoire des ducs de Normandie:* "Por chou que il m'estuet conter de .ij. estores, de celi d'Engletierre et de celi de Flandres, ne vous puis-jou pas toutes les choses conter en ordre" (Because I am endeavoring to recount two stories, that of England and that of Flanders, I cannot relate everything to you in order).[50] It is, in fact, the almost excessive preoccupation (excessive, that is, in terms of the overall economy of the works) with Flemish affairs that decisively marks them as the product of a single pen. One peculiarity to be noted is the virtual absence in the *Histoire* of any account of the battle of Bouvines, which is merely alluded to in a few lines, in contrast to the ten columns of manuscript text that it occupies in the *Chronique des rois de France,*[51] a distinction that surely must be attributed to the fact that the combined German, Flemish, and English forces were unsuccessful at Bouvines, concerning which the Anonymous, in his capacity as chronicler of the coalition in the *Histoire,* exercises a diplomatic reticence.

Despite the extensive community of subject matter shared by the *Histoire* and *Chronique,* contemporary history is not reproduced in identical terms in the two texts. Accounts of some events are more highly developed in the *Histoire,* and this work is characterized by a livelier sense of narrative development, providing more often than is found in the *Chronique* reported conversations, psychological portraits of the participants, most notably of King John, and a more precise presentation of events. This differential treatment of English and French history doubtless results from the fact that Robert of Béthune was allied for much of the period covered by the histories with John of England, and as Robert's companion the Anonymous had far greater knowledge of the events surrounding the war in England and Flanders than in France. Yet the *Chronique* is also notable for its exactitude, as its editor Delisle has signaled, requiring little correction other than for matters that came to the Anonymous via hearsay.[52]

It seems that the first of the histories written by the Anonymous was the *Histoire des ducs de Normandie et des rois d'Angleterre*, which Holder-Egger dates to 1220 or shortly after.[53] The *Histoire* opens with the passage "par la devision que li anciien home fisent dou monde, savons-nous que toute la tierre est enclose de la grant mer, ke on apiele *Occean*" (by the division that the ancients made of the world, we know that all the land is enclosed by a great sea, which is called *Ocean*), a translation into lucid thirteenth-century French prose of the beginning of Dudo of Saint-Quentin's *De moribus et actis primorum Normanniae ducum*.[54] Dudo's largely legendary account had been incorporated in an abridged form into Guillaume de Jumièges's *Historia Normannorum*, and Francisque Michel asserts that the opening section of the *Histoire* "n'est autre chose qu'une analyse de l'histoire des Normands de Guillaume de Jumièges, augmentée d'une suite peu considérable."[55]

This assertion is not entirely accurate, since the French text is at places closer to Dudo than to Guillaume de Jumièges and includes the translation of material found in Dudo but left out in Guillaume. Paul Meyer doubted, however, that the Anonymous was working from Dudo's text itself, which was rarely read in the thirteenth century and in which, in any case, he could not have found all the material included in his history. It is more likely, in Meyer's opinion, that the Anonymous used a compilation of Norman history in which most of Dudo's text figured. The work that best fits this description is the *Chronique de Normandie*, in a version such as that found in Cambridge II.6.24 and B.N. fr. 24431, to which, in its opening sections, the *Histoire* of the Anonymous is virtually identical.[56]

Beginning with the reign of William Rufus, the Anonymous increasingly develops the material found in the *Chronique de Normandie*, while continuing to exploit it through the reign of Henry I. He provides an extended discussion of the struggle between Stephen and Matilda over the disputed succession to the English throne, but merely scant notes relating to the reign of Henry II and an only slightly fuller treatment of the reign of Richard I. Beginning in 1199, after the death of Richard Lion-Heart, the text becomes a completely original account of events during the reign of King John and the beginning of the reign of Henry III, concluding in 1220. Given the Anonymous's heavy reliance on the *Chronique de Normandie* for his historical narrative prior to 1199, it is only the final section of the *Histoire* that has attracted the interest of editors and historians.

The *Chronique des rois de France* was written shortly after the *Histoire des ducs de Normandie et des rois d'Angleterre*, sometime between 1220 and 1223—that is, before the accession of Louis VIII (1223–1226)—though the actual narrative breaks off earlier, in 1217, in the middle of an account of the French expedition to England. The only complete text of the *Chronique* is found in B.N. nouv. acq. fr. 6295; however, it is marred by a scribal *bourdon* that occurs at the bottom of column A on folio 4v, resulting in the omission of the reigns of the Merovingian kings after Theodebert, son of Theoderic.[57]

The *Chronique des rois de France* is divided into four distinct sections, each of which draws on a different Latin source and all of which, for the sections prior to 1185, differ from the sources used in the *Histoire*. Part one traces the early history of French kingship from the time of the destruction of Troy and is based on a Latin chronicle from Saint-Denis known as the *Abbreviatio Regum Francorum*, in a version close to that published by George Waitz in the *Neues Archiv*.[58] Although the *Abbreviatio* carried its history to 1108 (with an early continuation to 1137), the Anonymous does not translate the entire text. Instead, arriving at the reign of Charlemagne, he inaugurates part two of the *Chronique* by inserting the vernacular version of the *Pseudo-Turpin Chronicle* (named by Walpole *Turpin I*), which is essentially the same as that found in B.N. fr. 1850.[59] It is preceded by an abridged version of the *Descriptio*, that is, of Charlemagne's journey to Jerusalem.[60] The only other manuscript of the *Chronique des rois de France* to incorporate the *Descriptio-Turpin* as an integral part of the history of the kings of France is Vat. Reg. Lat. 610, which also contains a continuation of the narrative up to the denunciation of the "False Baldwin" at Péronne in the presence of Louis VIII in 1225.[61]

Part three of the *Chronique* starts after the death of Charlemagne in 814 and is based on the Latin *Historia Regum Francorum usque ad annum 1214*, written by a monk of Saint-Germain-des-Prés,[62] although here again, the Anonymous does not translate the full text in his history, but only those portions up to 1185. The Anonymous's translation of the Latin *Historia* is completely independent of the translation of the same work made in the middle of the thirteenth century by the Ménestrel d'Alphonse de Poitiers.[63] It also possesses several interpolations, notably the *Visio Karoli Calvi* and the legend of Isembard and Gormond,[64] as well as a prose paraphrase of the verses engraved on the tomb of Louis VII at Barbeaux. The account for the years 1180–1184, in addition, contains two interpolations important for the political events of that period. The first concerns the marriage of Philip Augustus to Isabelle, daughter of the count of Hainaut, whom the Anonymous describes as "une sainte damoisele," doubtless to counteract the rather low esteem in which she was later held by the king, who sought to abandon her and their marriage in 1187.[65] The second involves his report on the "young Henry," eldest son of Henry II of England, as present in Philip Augustus's host in 1183.[66]

With the account of the Vermandois succession toward 1185 the Anonymous's chronicle becomes original, continuing to the beginning of 1217, at which point his history breaks off abruptly. Although Delisle believed that the last event reported by the Anonymous was the siege of Dover in 1216, Petit-Dutaillis demonstrates that it concerns, rather, the affair of Rye, which immediately preceded Prince Louis's return to France in February 1217. The port of Rye had been occupied by Henry III's troops, and Louis sought to retake it but was blocked at Winchelsea and might have lost everything if the prior of Waast had not sent aid. The Anonymous's chronicle concludes before the reader learns that Louis has been saved.[67] For events occurring after 1199, part four of the *Chronique* and the *Histoire des ducs de Normandie* display a striking degree of common material, though treated from subtly differing vantage points.

What is puzzling, however, is why the Anonymous should have written dual versions of contemporary history and which aristocratic audiences he had in mind in so doing. This is especially perplexing in the case of the *Chronique des rois de France*, written after the *Histoire des ducs de Normandie et des rois d'Angleterre*, since the Capetian focus of the work seems so at odds with the political sympathies and— by the time the work was initiated—history of defeated hostilities of the house of Béthune. The fact that both works are so often bound together in a single codex, sometimes directly following one another, at other times separated by intervening texts, suggests that scribes and copyists viewed them as complementary. In Walpole's opinion, "it is quite understandable that patrons wanted to have both works and that scribes copied them together, [since they were] addressed to feudal families whose interests were not restricted to one side of the channel."[68] According to Walpole, what appears in the manuscript tradition are

> the scattered copies of what was once a simple and organic work, written by one author for a particular public and adapted by him in language and content to its interests, a French prose history reaching from its traditional starting place in Troy down to contemporary thirteenth-century events . . . and the history of the Normans as part of the history of France.[69]

But this judgment accords badly with the fact that the *Histoire des ducs de Normandie et des rois d'Angleterre* was written first, suggesting that the original conception behind the work was to view it not in relation to the history of France, but in light of an autonomous Anglo-Norman tradition, embedded in a specifically Norman past that continued on to the present-day Angevins. For both chronicles, the parts anterior to the reigns of John Lackland and Philip Augustus employ compilations in Latin and French appropriate for their respective histories but, as we have seen, completely distinct from one another. Insofar as Anglo-Norman history is set against the background of the arrival of the Normans and their subsequent career of conquest in England, it is difficult to see it as an integral part of the history of France. Similarly, the Capetian past is traced back in an altogether traditional fashion to the Trojan origins of the Franks, the settlement of the Trojan remnant in France, and the foundation of French kingship with Pharamond, succeeded by the reigns of the Merovingian, Carolingian, and, ultimately, Capetian kings. From the perspective of French history, the Normans represent an intrusion into an otherwise continuous history, the essential linearity of which is not disrupted, since the royal future of the Normans lay not in France but in England. The recital of contemporary history thus does little to disturb the distinctive orientations of the two works, despite the fact that the events recounted overlap considerably.

What ties the two chronicles together most powerfully, in fact, is the intermediary and mediating role played in each by the Flemish, whose incessant crossings of the Channel bind together the histories of the royal powers contending for their allegiance. Any explanation of the motives that might have prompted the Anonymous to compose two distinct works of history that share a common present must, therefore, take into account the centrality, both literally and figuratively, of Flanders in their narrative structures.

One possible interpretation, advanced by Sayers, that incorporates the preoccupation with Flemish affairs as a principle of explanation is that the alternative versions represent an awkward but nonetheless significant attempt on the Anonymous's part to establish his historical impartiality, an impartiality "necessitated by the fact (never explicitly stated) that the house of his patron was divided in its support of the English and French monarchs."[70] But the effect of this dual inscription of a single history, if truly read as an organic whole as Walpole and, by implication, Sayers suggest, is not impartiality, but incoherence, for it creates a schism within the presumptive integrity of the past. Rather than impartiality, I would suggest, the Anonymous's doubling of the past contests the notion that there is a single, uniquely possible narrative of history grounded in a universal truth for which God, ultimately, serves as guarantee. In writing two completely distinct versions of the same story—a rare phenomenon at best among medieval chroniclers—the Anonymous of Béthune does not so much demonstrate his impartiality as exteriorize and set forth the political forces and choices that weighed on the house of Béthune during the turbulent era at the turn of the thirteenth century.

The challenge facing the Béthunes in this period was not merely military; first and foremost, it was a challenge that involved determining what posture the house of Béthune should assume toward the superior powers that vied for its support. Which side to choose? Which world to belong to? How to carve out a social and political space from which to negotiate with these powers from a position of strength and independence? These were choices that *had* to be made, questions that *had* to be answered, and there existed no clear-cut guidelines for reaching a solution—as witness the division in the decisions ultimately arrived at by individual members of the family, whose loyalties were divided between allegiance to the Capetians and allegiance to the Plantagenets. And it is important to emphasize that the struggle between French and English kings not only rent the loyalties of family members with respect to others, but divided the house itself, creating novel social and political cleavages within it and within the Flemish aristocracy as a whole.

In that sense the Anonymous, by rewriting the same segment of contemporary history alternatively from the point of view of the two main forces vying for political influence over contemporary Franco-Flemish society, created works embodying the new conditions under which his own patron's house of Béthune was compelled to operate, in a world in which competition for loyalty, authority, and political power had radically changed the social and political rules of the game. Just as Flanders was trapped politically between the rivalries of England and France, so the Anonymous's vision of history is fractured into competing versions, disclosing the incoherence of the nobility's position and the impossibility of negotiating a secure ground for the conduct of aristocratic life.

The French and English Histories

The most obvious sense in which the *Histoire des ducs de Normandie et des rois d'Angleterre* and the *Chronique des rois de France* embody distinct historical traditions with different meanings for their respective communities derives from the way the Anonymous of Béthune situates contemporary events with respect to the past in each work— that is to say, from the very structure of the histories that he elaborates. French history is located in a continuous tradition of royal descent from the Trojan Antenor; thus its meaning derives from a sequence of lineage, since the origin of the French peoples is already described in terms of a prestigious lineal ascent:

> Antenor estoit li plus sages chevaliers des Troiens et li plus raisnables. Il s'en vint a Pannone od grant gent que de son lignage, que del lignage Priamus qui avoit esté rois des Troiens aincois que la cites fu destruite.[71]

> Antenor was the wisest knight of the Trojans and the most reasonable. He went to Pannonia with many people both of his own lineage and of the lineage of Priam, who had been king of the Trojans before the city was destroyed.

Indeed, so powerful is the genealogical patterning of French history in the *Chronique* that Ms. B.N. fr. 17177 rubricates the entire work as "li livres de geanologie [sic] et coronikes [sic] des Roys de France."[72] At the same time, French history is unmistakenly chivalric, since Antenor is figured as the premiere *chevalier* of Troy, who saves not only his own lineage from total destruction but that of King Priam as well.

Led by an eponymous hero, Francio—from whom the "Franci" received their name—the Trojans eventually migrated to safety in the Danube Valley, where they built a city at Sicambria. There they remained, according to the traditional account incorporated by the Anonymous, until the Roman emperor Valentinian sought their aid against the Alani, aid granted by the Franks in return for a release from tribute for a period of ten years. But when Valentinian sought once again to exact tribute from them, they rebelled, proclaiming that "par lor sanc et par lor travail, ne jamais sous treu ne seroient" (by reason of the blood [they had spilled] and their work, never would they again submit to tribute).[73] Resisting the emperor's attack, they traveled to the Rhine and entered Gaul under the leadership of Marcomir, whose son Pharamond they elected as the first king, thus inaugurating the succession of kings who ruled France down to the present day. Although many versions of the legend of the Trojan origins of the French, no doubt prompted by the Valentinian episode, add to this account etymological explanations for the name *Franci* as derived from "free" (*franci*) or "fierce" (*ferox*—i.e., *ferancos* from *feroces*), the Anonymous is content to trace the name to its lineal progenitor, thereby fusing etymological and genealogical explanations, a point stressed by his rubric:

> Ci commence la geste de franche por coi il orent a non françois et dont il sont estrait et venu.[74]

> Here begin the deeds of France, and why [its people] have the name of French and whence they are descended and come.

In the *Histoire des ducs de Normandie*, English ascent is similarly traced to Trojan origins via a mythical, eponymous son of Antenor, from whom

> il estoient apielé Danois por chou que Danaus, qui [fu] fill Anthenor, quant il fu eschapés de la destruction de Troie, s'en ala là endroit et si fu sires de cel païs.

> They were called Danes on account of Danaus, who was the son of Antenor; when he escaped the destruction of Troy, he went to that place and was lord of this country.

But the Anonymous almost immediately abandons this account of Trojan descent in favor of an etymological explanation of the name *Norman*, rather than *Danish:*

> Encore estoient-il apielé Normant por une autre chose, por chou que [en] lor langages *nor* chou est byse en françois et *man* chou est hom; et quant ces deus sillebes sont ajoustées, si sonne li mos autant en lor langage comme en françois *hom de byse*.[75]

> They were also called Normans for another reason, because in their language *nor* means north [literally, "north wind"] in French and *man* is man; and when these two syllables are put together, the word sounds in their language such that [it would be] in French "man of the north."

Moreover, the Anonymous at once begins the tale of Norman conquest: impelled, he explains, by overpopulation in the north, the Normans came to the shores of France. Their Trojan descent, therefore, has no narrative weight in his account, except as a brief and essentially etymological reference. Despite a common legendary foundation, the histories of France and England remain distinct in their earliest origins.

The first problem facing the Anonymous in the construction of his histories, then, was to establish the relationship between the two dominant forces in the chronicles, that is, between England and France, even before they are brought into direct confrontation in the contemporary sections of the texts. It is fair to say, I think, that the Anonymous handles this task poorly, at least as far as the respective histories of the two monarchies are concerned. In the early parts of the chronicles, snippets of the other's history are interpolated, clearly because they are chronologically contemporaneous, even if thematically unrelated to the subject under discussion. Thus, for example, the Normans literally thrust themselves into the French realm after the death of Louis the Pious: "Ne demorra mie an un an apres sa mort que li Normant asaillierent France et gasterent Dorescatum .i. chastel" (There had scarcely passed a year after his death when the Normans assailed France and wasted Dorescatum, a castle). Only then does the Anonymous backtrack to explain that

> Normant sont danois de naissance et si les apela on primes normans en barbarine langue qui autre tant vaut que septentrionale por ce qu'il vindrent primes de cele partie.[76]

> Normans are Danes by birth, and one called them originally Normans in the barbarian tongue, which means essentially northern, since they first came from that region.

Notably absent, here, is any mention of the Trojan origins of the Normans that had figured at the beginning of the *Histoire des ducs de Normandie*.

Similarly, the Capetians first appear in Norman history in connection with the story of Hugh the Great's betrayal of his oath of loyalty to the young duke, Richard of Normandy, to whom King Louis had promised lands across the Seine that he now granted, instead, to Hugh:

> Hues li Grans fu decheus par la covoitise qui li entra ou cuer, si oublia ie sairement que il avoit fait à l'enfant, et fist au roi sairement contre l'enfant et contre Normendie.[77]

Hugh the Great was betrayed by the desire that entered his heart and thus forgot the oath that he had taken to the child, and swore an oath to the king against the child and against Normandy.

Normans and French enter each other's pasts as antagonists, stripped of the presumptive legitimacy that surrounds their deeds in their own narratives. Indeed, the communal nature of a shared past is represented in the Anonymous's narratives largely in the form of contestation between the principal actors. As we shall see, this problematizing of legitimacy in each chronicle vis-à-vis the other was bound to affect the Anonymous's general understanding of the character of French and English kings, leading him to produce histories in which monarchy on both sides of the Channel is seen constantly through the eyes of the "other." This pluralism of vision, effected through narrative interlacing, is a hallmark of the Anonymous of Béthune's historiography, endowing his histories with an oddly modern quality.

French and English kings are seen, moreover, not only in the light of their mutual and respective pasts, but also from the perspective of those whom they embroil in their antagonisms, whose actions take place within the tensions generated by royal competition. For example, when Duke Robert "the Magnificent" died in 1035, leaving behind his bastard son William to rule Normandy, the Anonymous reports that

> dès primes [William] ot grant travail et grant paine: ses lignages
> le guerroia, qui grant desdaing avoit de chou que il estoit dus et
> bastars. Li baron s'entre-guerroierent, et fremerent castiaus li .i. encontre les autres: dont il avint que Hues de Mont-Fort et Jakelins de
> Ferrieres s'entre'ocisent de guerre. Puis refu ocis li cuens de Deu qui
> Gillebers avoit non, et puis Teroldes qui maistres estoit de l'enfant.
> Puis refu ocis Obiers ki plus grans maistres estoit à l'enfant; et fu
> ocis el val de Rueil en dormant, de Guillaume le fill Rogier de Montegny. Chil Obiers estoit fils del frere la contesse Gomor. Puis crut
> moult durement et la guerre et li maus; tant monteplia la guerre que
> li rois Henris de France manda au duc Guillaume que jà à lui n'aroit
> amour ne pais tant comme Tiulieres tenist en estant.[78]

> From the beginning [William] had great travails and great difficulties: his lineage warred with him; [it] had great scorn for him because he was a duke and a bastard. The barons made war against
> each other, and fortified their castles one against the other; whence it
> happened that Hugh de Montfort and Jacques de Ferrieres killed each
> other in war. Then the count of Deu, whose name was Gillebers, was
> killed, and then Terold, who was master of the child. Then Obiers

was killed, who was even greater master to the child; and he was killed in the valley of Rueil while sleeping, by Guillaume, the son of Roger of Montegny. This Obiers was the son of the brother of the countess Gomor. Then both the war and evildoing grew especially harsh; the war so multiplied that the king, Henry of France, sent word to Duke William that he would never grant him peace or favor as long as Tuiliers remained standing.

This passage, which barely attains narrative intelligibility, is nonetheless a typical sample of the Anonymous's procedures. The misdeeds of kings, either alone or in competition with one another, generate war and wrongdoing, into the midst of which French and/or English nobles, named and identified in terms of their networks of affiliation, are thrust. Even before reaching contemporary events, the Anonymous's history offers a kaleidoscope of martial activities on both sides of the Channel, into which he inserts a discussion of the genealogical bonds of the noble lineages sucked into the whirl of royal warfare. As this sample demonstrates, the focus of attention is not the king himself, but the intricate play of interests and power among and within the nobility. Many pages of both chronicles are devoted to the genealogical identification of the nobles who participate in the events occasioned by royal activities, overwhelming by its sheer weight of words the thread of the narrative.

The most compelling evidence of a shared, perforce competitive, past comes precisely from this genealogical patterning of the histories. In his interweaving of the stories of the lineages that appear as actors the Anonymous most clearly articulates the communal and interdependent character of time, event, and history. Take, for example, two wholly characteristic interpolations, both representative of the Anonymous's concern with the affairs and personages of Flanders and Béthune. The first occurs in the *Histoire des ducs de Normandie*, where the Anonymous is discussing the money raised to ransom Richard Lion-Heart. He notes that, when Richard was liberated, the king left behind as hostages his nephew Otto of Germany and Baldwin of Béthune. Although the lineage of Otto, future emperor of Germany, goes unremarked, the Anonymous adds to the mention of Baldwin's name the following passage:

. . . Bauduin de Biethune, cui il fist puis conte d'Aubemalle par Havi le contesse, que il li donna à feme. Cele Havis avoit esté feme le conte de Mandeville, qui Guillaumes estoit apelés et n'en ot nul enfant. Quant li cuens fu mors si le donna li rois à Guillaume de Fors, qui en ot .i. fill, qui ot à non Guillaumes; et apriès Guil-

laume de Fors, la donna li rois à Bauduin de Biethune. Celui Bauduin
lassa-il en ostages por lui, avoec Othon son neveu.[79]

. . . Baldwin of Béthune, whom he later made count of Aubemarle,
by virtue of Havi the countess, whom he gave him in marriage. This
Havi had been the wife of the count of Mandeville, who was named
Guillaume, and he had no children by her. When the count died the
king gave her to Guillaume de Fors, who had a son by her, whose
name was Guillaume; and after Guillaume de Fors, the king gave her
to Baldwin of Béthune. This Baldwin he left as a hostage for him
with Otto his nephew.

It is noteworthy that this method of interlacing noble genealogies into
the body of the text functions, additionally, to introduce as significant
figures in the historical narrative the female branches of the family
trees discussed. Women appear as essential links in the chains of genealogies with which the Anonymous overlays his text, important
both for the land and wealth they bring to the noble family and in
their own right.

The density of the information adduced concerning the Anonymous's Béthune patrons is not restricted, moreover, to the immediate
generation of Robert VII, but reaches back at least two generations, as
demonstrated by the following passage on the death of Robert V at
Sutri on 18 January 1191 while accompanying Philippe of Alsace on
the Third Crusade:

morut à Sutre uns haus hom de sa terre, qui od lui s'en aloit, qui
ert apelés Robers; avoés ert de la cité d'Arras et sire del chastel de
Betune.

Grans damages fu de la mort à cel preudome; car ce ot esté uns
des meillors vavasors del monde. Mais sa terre ne remest pas sans
oir; car il ot v molt bons fils: Robert l'aisné, un saint home et bon
chevalier, qui après lui fu avoés, mais poi dura; Guillaume, qui refu
puis avoés et sire del chastel de Tenremonde par mariage, molt preudom et molt loials, mais molt ot d'aversités; Baudewin, uns très bons
chevaliers, qui puis fu cuens d'Aubemarle; Johan, un clerc, qui puis
fu evesques de Camberai; Cuenon, le puis né, qui puis fu maistre
chamberlens de l'empiere de Constantinople et uns des plus preudomes et des plus sages del monde; et ce parut bien en la terre tant
com il vesqui.[80]

there died at Sutri a high man of his [i.e., the count of Flanders's]
land, who had accompanied him, who was called Robert; he had been
avoué of the city of Arras and lord of the castle of Béthune.

The death of this honorable man was a great shame; for he had
been one of the best vavasors in the world. But his land did not

remain without heirs; for he had five very good sons: Robert the eldest, a holy man and a good knight, who after him was *avoué*, but he lived only a short while [d. 1193 or 1194]; Guillaume, who then was *avoué* and lord of the castle of Dendermonde through marriage, a very fine man and very loyal, but he experienced many adversities; Baldwin, a very good knight, who later was count of Aubemarle; Jean, a cleric, who later was bishop of Cambrai; Conon, the youngest, who later was master chamberlain of the empire of Constantinople and one of the best men and the most wise in the world; and this was clearly seen in the land while he lived.

Once again, what is notable is not only the length of the insertion or the extremely detailed knowledge of familial relations that the Anonymous of Béthune displays, but the laudatory tone he assumes in discussing members of the house of Béthune and their progenitors. The praise and concern lavished on the Flemish nobility, moreover, is not matched in his discussion of English and French kings and their ancestors, as the remarks about William the Conqueror and Hugh the Great cited above testify. Indeed, a great deal of the interest of the Anonymous's histories lies in this differential treatment of kings and nobles, for it confirms beyond doubt that his principal motive was not to celebrate the emerging authority of centralized monarchy, but rather to explore and interrogate the nature of aristocratic existence within the changed conditions of life and loyalty that royal competition and power were creating.

PORTRAITS OF RULERS AND RULED

As long as the Anonymous of Béthune is engaged essentially in translating prior sources, his depiction of rulers and their cohorts on both sides of the Channel remains relatively balanced. Following the lead of his base texts, he distributes praise and blame in an apparently impartial manner, and his narrative seems free of the ideological pressures that come into play when he reaches recent history. Thus, he presents past Norman rulers according to the merits of the case at hand, commending those whose honorable behavior and traits of personality earn his (or his source's) approval, while censuring those who violate the values and conduct appropriate for rulers entrusted by God with the governance of society. For example, he bestows upon Duke Richard of Normandy an encomium whose list of virtues is clearly derived from royal models:

> Li dus Richars fu moult preudom; il fu force des foibles, desfende-
> mens des veves et des orphenins, confors as caitis, apaisieres des

maus, bastons as avugles, releveres de Sainte Eglyse, lumiere as non veans, hautece des clers, aidieres as soufraiteus, honnours as evesques, ameres de pais, cultiveres de viertus, esperance as desconfortés, pitiés as dolours, aliance d'amour, sieges de lois, pastours des povres, examples des princes, droituriers en justice, veritables en parler, en consel porveans, en jugement loiaus, en toute honnesté, de boines meurs reluisans, et toutes les autres boines teches avoit herbregies en soi.[81]

The duke Richard was a very valiant man; he was the strength of the weak, defender of widows and orphans, comfort to the wretched, pacifier of wrongdoing, cane to the blind, rescuer of the Holy Church, light to those who did not see, grandeur of the clergy, aid to the suffering, honor to bishops, lover of peace, cultivator of virtue, hope to the disconsolate, pity to the sorrowing, bond of love, seat of laws, shepherd of the poor, example of princes, righteous in justice, truthful in speaking, in counsel farseeing, in judgment loyal, in everything honest, shining with good morals, and all the other good traits were lodged in him.

William Rufus, in contrast, although acknowledged as a "rois larges et vaillans," is nonetheless castigated because he

trop deshiretoit volentiers la gent; de chou ert-il trop mal entechiés. Il fist maint mal à Sainte Eglyse et as clers, et meismement as abbeyes, que il apetisoit de lor tierres et de lor rentes.[82]

very willfully disinherited the people; this was a considerable shortcoming of his. He did many wrongs to the Holy Church and to the clergy and especially to the abbeys, whose lands and rents he diminished.

One hears here, beneath the Anonymous's text, the voice of his clerical sources, reproduced with little change and with little apparent concern for making an independent judgment.

It is primarily when his chronicles become recent and original that the Anonymous of Béthune achieves real value, both as a narrator of history and as an index of the attitudes and concerns of the aristocratic audience for whom his histories were destined. Interestingly, his portraits of the French and English kings supply the same kind of gloss on the history he is narrating that the portraits offered in the *Faits des Romains* did, implicitly commenting on and evaluating the sources of both power and conflict with which those subject to royal authority must come to terms. The Anonymous's portraits of John and Philip Augustus disclose the complexity of the choices facing the French, and above all Flemish, aristocracy, caught between the contending ambitions of newly powerful and rich rulers, who did not hesitate to use their accumulated rights, skill, and wealth to impose their wishes on the realms over which they sought to achieve new levels of authority.

In his minute examination of the play of forces and personalities that shaped the destinies of France and England in the crucial first decades of the thirteenth century, the Anonymous of Béthune provides a unique view of how the aristocracy might have understood the processes by which an ascendant monarchy had transformed its conditions of existence. To the degree that he speaks for his patron, Robert of Béthune, he offers us a rare glimpse of how royal centralization in this period appeared to those most immediately affected by it. To be sure, his discussion of the impact of royal policies is refracted through the lens of royal personality; but his appreciation of the decisive role of kingship in determining the boundaries of aristocratic behavior indicates that he was keenly aware of the emerging shift in the balance of power between monarchy and aristocracy, an awareness that informed his depiction of the rulers around whom the political life of the thirteenth-century aristocracy gravitated. Through his portraits of John and Philip Augustus we can see an age in crisis, an age in which the conditions of political action and the meaning of loyalty had been radically transformed, leaving behind unresolved tensions that produced both open political strife and a less overt, but equally significant, sense of malaise.

THE KINGS OF ENGLAND AND FRANCE

The Anonymous of Béthune's view of the two monarchs whose actions and ambitions so powerfully shaped the histories of France and England in the early thirteenth century is informed by an acute sense of the personalities of these rulers. His treatment of both John and Philip Augustus is marked by an ironic distance that accentuates the realistic effect of his narrative. The ironic tone that characterizes his appraisal is perhaps best conveyed in the proverb he cites when discussing the dissension that arose between Richard Lion-Heart and Philip Augustus on the Third Crusade—the origins of which he attributes to an underlying current of competition between two proud and unyielding men:

> Voirs est que on dist que ja dui orgueilleus ne chevauceront bien un asne.[83]

Two proud men cannot ride the same ass.

At the root of the limited success of the Third Crusade lay, in the Anonymous's opinion, the inability of its leaders to cooperate, for their rivalry overrode any commitment to a larger cause. Thus, he argues:

> Li rois d'Engleterre ert orgueilleus sor tous homes; si ne daignoit estre obediens al roi de France son seignor, et li rois de Franche ne pooit souffrir son orgoeil, ne ne voloit. Por ce et por molt d'autres baras recommença la guerre entre'els molt grans et molt cruels.[84]

> The king of England was proud beyond all men; he did not deign to be obedient to the king of France his lord, and the king of France could not suffer his pride, nor did he wish to. For this and for many other pieces of roguery there recommenced the war between them, a great and very cruel one.

Although his explanation is couched in the language of personality, it is clear that the Anonymous understands the structural anomaly that fed the reluctance of English kings, vassals of the French king for their continental possessions, to be obedient to their nominal overlords. Indeed, it was this anomaly that underlay the struggle between Philip Augustus and John, for the former was determined to impose his authority and, if possible, reconquer for the French realm the continental holdings of his most powerful rival. As the Anonymous himself makes abundantly clear, Philip had repeatedly failed in the attempt to subdue Angevin rulers. The results of the renewed war that Philip initiated against Richard upon returning to France from the Third Crusade were, as the Anonymous indicates, hardly favorable to the French king:

> Si convint le roi de France soufrir molt d'aversités de cele guerre: car li rois Richars estoit trop riches et de terre et d'avoir, asés plus que li rois de France n'estoit.[85]

> The king of France had to suffer many adversities due to this war, because King Richard was extremely rich, both in land and in goods, much more than was the king of France.

Despite his persistent efforts to assert his authority and to regain territory, the resources of the French king proved hopelessly inadequate in the face of superior English wealth, martial force, and, in the case of Richard Lion-Heart, military cunning. Only against John was the French king finally successful, and the Anonymous argues persuasively that the cause of the English ruler's ultimate failure stemmed as much from the oddities and inconsistencies of his personality as from the improvement in French resources due to the king's acquisition of Vermandois and, in 1204, Normandy. In his handling of the struggle between John and Philip Augustus, the Anonymous provides a compelling picture of the complicated relationship and reciprocal influence of wealth, military power, behavior, and personality in shaping the events that culminated in the defeat of the English alliance at Bouvines and the final triumph of the king of France. His portrait of John skillfully articulates the precarious balance between power and legitimacy that, in a period when the bureaucratic structure of government was still relatively undeveloped by modern standards, depended finally on the personality of the king. The personal failings of rulers, therefore, assume a political significance for the governance of the realm and for the viability of those bound to them that is imbricated in the more fundamental issue of monarchical efficacy and legitimacy. The repercussions of royal success or failure were felt far beyond the court, and it is the Anonymous's clear understanding of the new precariousness of aristocratic life stemming from its dependency on monarchy that makes him such a valuable witness to noble consciousness in this period.

John Lackland.   Robert of Béthune's extensive involvement with John of England as a member of the English party in Flanders and recipient of English fiefs and rents in exchange for military service in John's host meant that the Anonymous of Béthune was advantageously placed to observe this complex and curious king. His view of John is hardheaded and not a little tinged with scorn; the resulting image is of a cruel and inconstant man, driven by greed, lust, and envy and afflicted with a strange lassitude at critical moments in the struggle that he engaged in so ferociously, yet fecklessly, against his French adversary. In the Anonymous's eyes, John appears to be a king who relied on money instead of leadership to garner the support necessary to prosecute his wars and who, when finally engaged in battle, exhibited that most despicable of characteristics in a chivalric world that prized bravery above all: cowardice. Reporting how, in 1206, John fled the castle of Thouars in Poitou when French troops commanded by the king surrounded it, the Anonymous sternly notes:

> Là parut bien la coardise le roi d'Engleterre: car od ce qu'il ne s'osa combatre, autre si tost que li rois de France se fu trahis arière, s'en rala il vers la mer et repassa en Engleterre.[86]

> There appeared clearly the cowardice of the king of England; for along with the fact that he did not dare to fight, as soon as the king

of France had withdrawn, he turned back to the sea and recrossed [the Channel] to England.

John's vicious tendencies, moreover, were not restricted to his enemies, but were directed equally at the *preudomes* upon whom, ultimately, the success of his reign relied. It would be difficult to find in contemporary vernacular historiography a portrait of a king as repugnant as the one the Anonymous here draws of John:

> Molt mal homme ot el roi Jehan: crueus estoit sor toz homes; de bieles femes estoit trop couvoiteus; mainte honte en fist as haus homes de la tierre: par coi il fu moult haïs. . . . Ses barons melloit ensamble quanques il pooit; moult estoit liés quant il veoit haine entre els. Toz les preudomes haoit par envie; moult li desplaisoit quant il veoit nullui bien faire. Trop estoit plains de males teces; mais de grant despens estoit: moult donnoit à mangier et larghement et volentiers; jà sa porte ne li huis de sa sale ne fussent gardé au mangier: tout chil mangoient à sa court qui mangier i voloient. As .iii. nataus donnoit volentiers grant plenté de reubes as chevaliers: de chou fu-il bien entechiés.[87]

> King John was a very evil man; he was cruel beyond all men; he was very covetous of beautiful women; because of this he shamed the high men of the land, for which reason he was greatly hated. . . . He set his barons against one another whenever he could; he was very happy when he saw hate between them. He hated all honorable men out of envy; it greatly displeased him when he saw anyone do good. He was full of bad traits; but he was free in spending: he gave away much to eat, both liberally and voluntarily; neither his gate nor the entrance to his hall was ever closed for eating: all those who wished to could eat at his court. On the three nativities [principal feast days] he willingly gave a large amount of robes to the knights: this was one of his good qualities.

Only in his apparent largesse does John demonstrate the moral qualities appropriate for a king. In all else his behavior shames not only the office he holds but also the subjects he rules, whose wives he coveted and sometimes took for his own use, earning the hatred of the nobility. Envious of the success of others, he set noble against noble and took pleasure in the hatreds between them that he had engendered. He made himself so despised and feared throughout the land, the Anonymous of Béthune proclaims, that

> toutes les gens tiesmoignoient que puis le tans le roi Artu n'avoit eu roi en Engletierre qui tant fust doutés en Engletierre, en Gales, en Eschoce ne en Yrlande, comme il estoit.[88]

all the people bore witness that since the time of King Arthur there had not been in England a king who was so feared throughout England, Wales, Scotland, and Ireland as he was.

At times, however, the king withdrew from the pressing concerns of the realm, retreating to a fantasy world in which he appeared to lose himself, concerned only with the care of his animals and pleasures of his marriage bed. For example, the Anonymous reports that when the news came to John that his castle at Chinon had fallen and one of his closest advisors, Hugh de Burgh, been taken prisoner, the king showed signs neither of regret nor outrage. In a rare use of the personal voice, the Anonymous displays his surprise at John's response:

> je ne sai quel duel il en ot au cuer; mais moult en fist poi de samblant. Toute tourna s'entente en deduit de chiens et d'oisiaus et à conjoïr la roine sa feme, que il moult amoit.[89]

> I do not know what sorrow he had in his heart; but he made little pretense about it. He turned all his attention to the pleasure of his dogs and birds and to the enjoyment of the queen his wife, whom he loved very much.

Nor was this an isolated response. Upon returning to England in 1214 after fleeing in panic the defense of his garrison at La Roche-au-Moine at the approach of French forces under Prince Louis, John "torna à deduire son cors: bois et rivieres antoit, et moult l'en plaisoit li deduis" (turned to the enjoyment of his body; he frequented woods and rivers and took great pleasure in this distraction).[90]

The Anonymous of Béthune's portrait of John could scarcely be darker. Lascivious and uxorious, indolent and self-indulgent, riven with envy, fear, and hatred, yet passionately in love with his wife and capable at rare moments of great energy, only to fall then into inexplicable periods of lassitude—these are the features of John's personality that the Anonymous sketches with compelling detail. If they had been merely personal idiosyncrasies, disagreeable and disappointing for the theatrics of kingship, which required a certain level of ceremonial dignity and charismatic force to be effective, the Anonymous's careful exposition of royal deficiencies would remain interesting but ultimately insignificant. Yet it is clear from his account of John's dealings with his vassals and followers—and with the Flemish most particularly—that the effects of royal incompetence and instability cast a widening shadow of political failure on the events of John's reign, drawing into the circle of his defeat all those associated with him.

A good example of the inconstancy with which John approached the problem of consolidating support among the Flemish—a critical task if he was to be successful against his Capetian rival—is to be found in a pair of reports on the king's treatment of Robert of Béthune, which veered wildly between attitudes of scorn and derision for his Flemish allies and indecorous importuning of their military aid. In the first instance, the Anonymous tells us that Count Ferrand of Flanders arrived in England after the burning of the French fleet at Damme and sent Robert of Béthune to Windsor where John was residing. Upon gaining access to the king, Robert conveyed the news of the count's arrival, whereupon the following conversation ensued:

> "Vostre sires, li cuens de Flandres, est arrivés en cest tierre."
> "Et k'atendés-vous dont," dist Robers, "que tantost n'alés à lui?"
> "Oés," dist li rois, "del Flamenc! Il cuide bien que che soit une grans chose de son segnour le conte de Flandres."
> "Par saint Jake!" dist Robiers, "je ai droit, ke si est chou."
> Li rois commencha lors à rire, si lor dist: "Mandés tost vos chevaus, car je m'en vois maintenant vers lui."[91]

> "Your lord, the count of Flanders, has arrived in this land."
> "And what are you waiting for then," said Robert, "that you do not go to him immediately?"
> "Listen," said the king, "to the Fleming! He thinks that he's a big deal, his lord the count of Flanders."
> "By Saint Jacques!" said Robert, "I am right, he is."
> The king began then to laugh and said to them: "Order up your horses, for I shall go to him straightaway."

The king's contempt for the count, upon whom his own military fortunes depended, and his open ridicule of Robert's claim for the dignity owed Ferrand as count of Flanders, which borders on the abusive, illustrate the political dangers posed for an aristocracy newly reliant on monarchy for its fate and the difficulties of sustaining loyalty to rulers who openly paraded their lack of respect for their vassals. In the cultic world of the feudal aristocracy, where questions of deference and precedence were as likely to instigate conflict as was competition for material gain, John's disdain for the protocols of honor governing relations between allies courted disaster. In this exchange, it is not the king but the poor knight who upholds the rules of social etiquette regulating feudal relations: Robert, not John, understands the implications of proper behavior for the conduct of political affairs, and he, ultimately, remains faithful to the ideals of kingship, even when monarchy itself derogates from them.

This last point is amply demonstrated by the second account, which involves the series of negotiations between John and his barons that led to the signing of Magna Carta, a story that the Anonymous labels as "l'ocoison de la guerre dont li rois Jehans moru deshiretés de la plus grant partie d'Engletierre" (the cause of the war by which John died disinherited of the greater part of England).[92] John, incapable of overcoming the baronial rebellion that had risen up against him, was compelled to sign a peace "comme li baron vaurrent" (as the barons wished), which he did without consultation: "onques n'i atendi le consel de son frere ne des Flamens" (he did not wait for the counsel of his brother nor of the Flemings). Only after signing did John communicate the terms of the peace laid out in Magna Carta, *sa chartre*, to his Flemish allies, who were outraged at the capitulation of their leader:

> Grant ire orent li Flamenc quant il oïrent les nouvieles de la vilaine pais que li rois avoit faite. Il vinrent à lui; mais il ne li fisent pas si boin samblant comme il avoient fait devant; nonpourquant il s'en alerent o lui jusques à Mierlebierge. Là fist-il une grant vilonnie; car il fist une grant masse de son tresor oster fors de la tour, si le fist porter en ses chambres, voiant les ielx as chevaliers de Flandres, ne onques riens ne lor en donna.
>
> Apriès cele vilenie que li rois fist, prisent li Flamenc congié à lui, si s'en repairierent en Flandres.[93]

> The Flemish were very angry when they heard the news of the base peace that the king had concluded. They came to him; but they did not present themselves in a manner as favorable to him as previously; nevertheless, they went with him to Merleberghe. There he did a terrible thing; for he had a great mass of his treasure taken from the tower and brought to his chambers, in the sight of all the knights of Flanders, but he did not give them anything from it.
>
> After this base deed of the king, the Flemings left him and returned to Flanders.

Furious that the king had negotiated peace without informing them, aware of John's dissembling nature, of which they were justly suspicious, and, finally, insulted and injured by his hoarding of money before their very eyes while they remained unpaid for their efforts on his behalf, the Flemish nobility appear, finally, to break their ties with a king so careless of their feelings, so unjust in his dealings with them, and so ineffectual in his government of the realm. Yet this is not the end of the story. For John, avid to reverse his situation by dethroning the committee of twenty-five barons that Magna Carta had created to regulate and constrain his actions, schemed how "il se porroit vengier d'els" (he might take vengeance on them).[94] To raise the necessary troops, the king sent letters to Robert of Béthune, imploring his aid:

> Li Rois d'Engletierre saluoit Robiert de Biethune comme son très chier ami et son home, si li mandoit que il connoissoit que il s'estoit mesfait enviers lui; mais pour Diu ne presist garde à son mesfait, ains euust pité et merchi de lui et de la couronne; car il vaurroit d'ore en avant del tout ouvrer par son consel.

> The king of England greeted Robert of Béthune as his most dear friend and his man, he sent word to him that he recognized that he had treated him badly; but for God's sake let him not heed his wrongdoing, but instead have pity and mercy on him and on the crown, for he wished from now on to do everything according to his counsel.

Before this spectacle of a king cravenly admitting his past error and begging for mercy and support, Robert of Béthune's sense of decency and fidelity carries the day:

> Quant Robiers ot les lettres oïes, mlt [*sic*] en eut grant pitié; il ne prist pas garde au mesfait le roi, ains se pena quanques il pot de querre gent et d'avancier le besoigne le roi à son pooir.[95]

> When Robert heard the letters, he was moved to great pity; he did not retain [his anger at] the king's misdeed, but strove with all his might to seek out men and to advance the king's cause.

Despite John's past history of royal abuse, betrayal, deception, and injustice, Robert of Béthune proves himself a staunch and steadfast supporter of the English crown, ready to forgive the king's misdeeds (*mesfait*) for the sake of loyalty to the needs of the throne. It is the ruled, not the ruler, who demonstrates a perduring commitment to the principles and bonds that provide the social cement of the medieval world. And, as the Anonymous discloses, it is this very commitment that will undermine those who faithfully, if foolishly, adhere to their demands.

That Robert's response stems from his character, not from the dire straits in which the English king found himself, is demonstrated by Robert's equal magnanimity with respect to his immediate overlord, the count of Flanders. Although, the Anonymous reports, Robert was at odds with Ferrand ("estoit mauvaisement dou conte de Flandres") on account of "la roine de Portygal s'antain, cui il avoit guerroié por chou qu'ele faisoit tort à son pere" (the queen of Portugal his aunt, with whom he had made war because she had wronged his father), nonetheless, when Ferrand requested the allegiance of his vassals in the break with Philip Augustus over the projected French expedition to England, Robert

> comme vaillans chevaliers, ne vaut onques por chou laissier que il estoit mauvaisement dou conte que il ne se penast de tout son pooir de se besoigne avancier.[96]
>
> like a valiant knight, did not wish that, just because he was at odds with the count, he not strive with all his might to advance his affairs.

In all his dealings, Robert of Béthune holds himself to the highest standards of behavior, despite repeated demonstrations that those to whom he offers his fealty and service do not maintain the same criteria in the conduct of their affairs, whether personal or political. Surrounded by rulers who repeatedly break oaths, violate rights, scheme to take revenge, and allow themselves extraordinary liberties in their drive to mastery, the nobility is hard put to find a path through which successfully to traverse the intricacies of contemporary political life. Whether the historical Robert of Béthune acted with the same degree of propriety and lofty idealism as the Anonymous's legitimizing portrait of him suggests is unknown. But the fact that the Anonymous locates the center of principled action and fidelity to the norms of medieval society in the nobility is significant.

From the perspective of the lesser nobility caught up in the wars and rivalries of overlords, political life had become a hazardous game whose rules were constantly shifting, threatening to submerge them in the vortex of violence that competition for power and territorial gain created. The contested and conflictual character of the Anonymous's history provides a narrative analogue of the contending forces that were so profoundly transforming the terms of aristocratic life in the early thirteenth century. And if the center of this vortex is the calm loyalty of the nobility, then the implication of the Anonymous's work is that this center will not hold, but will be drawn into the general crisis of conduct and values that monarchical conflict engenders. If John offers a particularly egregious example of royal misdeeds and deficient rulership, he represents but the outer limit of a more general tendency observable throughout the world inhabited by the Anonymous and his patron. When the Anonymous turns from England to France in the *Chronique des rois de France,* he finds no greater assurances for the long-term prosperity and viability of the nobility. No less than John, Philip Augustus is a king whose modes of operation and relations to the nobility over whom he is attempting to assert his authority threaten to undermine the principles that, in the past, had guided noble conduct and maintained them in relative independence and affluence.

Philip Augustus. Philip Augustus in no sense exhibited the extremes of cruelty, instability, or feckless leadership that marked the reign of John Lackland in England. Yet precisely because he was an effective and cunning ruler, he posed a greater threat to the autonomy of the French nobility. The Anonymous of Béthune's consideration of Philip Augustus is more nuanced than his opinion of John, but not, for all that, less critically aware of the impact that this tenacious and often unscrupulous king had on the lives of those he ruled.

The Anonymous begins his account of the reign of Philip Augustus with a translation of the summary judgment offered by his source for this part of the *Chronique des rois de France,* the *Historia Regum Francorum jusque ad annum 1214,* a passage that emphasized Philip's success in expanding the royal domain, fortifying its defenses, and ameliorating its cities—achievements, he repeats, that make the reign of Philip Augustus worthy of remembrance:

> Et sachiés que il ne soit mie à dire legiere chose de com grans sens cil rois Phelippes fu, et combien il acrut le règne de France, et coment il fist renoveler les fermetés des chastels ki deceues estoient, et com forment il fist fermer les cités et les bors et les chastels de France qui sans fermeté estoient, et coment il fist paver ses cités et ses bones viles.

> And know that it is not an easy thing to say what great sense this King Philip possessed, and how much he augmented the realm of France, and how he renovated the fortifications of the castles which had fallen down, and how forcefully he enclosed the cities and bourgs and castles of France, which were without fortification, and how he had his cities and his good villages paved.

In addition to these tasks of building and fortification, the Anonymous notes (and here he departs from the language of the *Historia*), Philip Augustus is also distinguished because

> il mist le règne de France fors de la signorie et de la poesté des rois d'Engleterre, qui tozjors ont esté rebelle as rois de France.[97]

> he placed the realm of France beyond the lordship and power of the kings of England, who always were rebellious toward the kings of France.

The Anonymous thus discloses from the outset a keen appreciation of Philip's determination to assert royal authority and impose his will on his independent and recalcitrant vassals.

The Anonymous attributes to Philip Augustus an early and unwavering commitment to defeat his enemies and extend his power. Thus, repeating a story found in his source, the Anonymous recounts how in 1181, when the most powerful barons had risen up against him, Philip found himself isolated at Compiègne as the counts of Flanders and Hainaut ravaged the nearby lands of Crépy-en-Valois, the count of Sancerre attacked Bourges and Lorris, and the duke of Burgundy destroyed the lands around Sens. Brought the news that the barons were devastating his realm, the young king—"qui enfès estoit," the Anonymous emphasizes—vowed:

> "se Dieu plaist, je croistrai en aage et en force et en sens, et il descroisteront de force et d'aage et de sens."[98]
>
> "if it pleases God, I shall grow in age and strength and sense, and they will diminish in strength and age and sense."

The tenacity of purpose and political skill with which Philip Augustus pursued the goal of securing royal suzerainty over the realm and eliminating rival sources of authority impressed the Anonymous of Béthune as forcefully as it did other contemporary observers.[99] The story of Philip at Senlis in 1181 serves as a narrative prelude to the Anonymous's account of the war between the count of Flanders, Philippe of Alsace, and the king, a war that demonstrated the truth of the young monarch's prediction, since "tot ce avint, si que on le vit" (all this came to pass, as we saw). By the conclusion of the truce of Boves in 1185, the Anonymous proclaims, "cil qui le conte de Flandres avoient aidié refistrent pais al rois; ne ainç puis ne s'osèrent vers lui mouvoir" (those who had aided the count of Flanders renewed peace with the king; after that they did not dare to move against him).[100]

Moreover, the Anonymous makes abundantly clear the ways in which the Flemish became embroiled in the wars that Philip Augustus prosecuted against his Angevin vassals, wars in which the Flemish nobility became pawns played by one king against the other. Thus, for example, he demonstrates how the Flemish under Baldwin IX were cleverly manipulated to enlist as Richard Lion-Heart's allies during the campaigns that Philip waged against the English king upon his return from the Third Crusade:

> Ensi adamagoit sovent par engien et par souprisure li rois d'Engleterre son liege seigneur le roi de France. Il li toli *par son engien* le

service del conte Bauduin de Flandres et de Hainau, qui jouenes hom estoit, à qui le conté de Flandres ert escheue de par sa mère, la contesse Margerite, qui fu suer al conte Phelippe de Flandres, et le conté de Heinau, qui ert escheue de par son père le conte Baudewin de Haynau.[101]

Thus did the king of England by cunning and by surprise often do damage to his liege lord the king of France. He took away from him *by his cunning* the service of count Baldwin of Flanders and Hainaut, who was a young man, to whom the county of Flanders had passed from his mother, the Countess Margaret, who was the sister of Count Philippe of Flanders, and the county of Hainaut, which had come to him from his father, Count Baldwin of Hainaut.

If brought into the war by the strategic manipulation of Richard, Baldwin IX did not lack reasons of his own to combat the French king. At issue was the persistent problem of Artois and the count of Flanders's unwillingness to acquiesce in the French possession of the county. As we saw in chapter 1, Artois represented that borderland of uncertainty about whether the king of France would succeed in subduing a powerful and independent barony and make it obedient to his will. At the time of his accession in 1195, Baldwin IX had done homage to Philip Augustus and recognized the concession of Artois, together with the overlordship of the counties of Guines and Boulogne. Nonetheless, he remained unreconciled to its loss. So disturbed over the alienation of Artois was Baldwin, the Anonymous of Béthune reports, that

> il fist tant à celui conte Baudewin qu'il demanda al roi de France Arras et Lens et Bapaumes et Saint Homer et Aire et Hesdin, qui li estoient doné en mariage avoec Ysabel la roine, la soror à celui conte Balduin, de qui il ot Loys, son fil. Et por ce que li rois ne li vout rendre, le guerroia il molt outrageusement, et il arst sa terre, et prist sor lui Saint Thomer et Aire et pluisors autres chasteaus, et assist la cité d'Arras.[102]

it meant so much to the count of Flanders that he demanded from the king of France Arras and Lens and Baupaume and Saint-Omer and Aire and Hesdin, which had been given to him [Philip Augustus] in marriage with Isabelle the queen, Count Baldwin's sister, by whom he had Louis, his son. And because the king did not wish to return it, he waged war on him furiously, and he burned his land, and took from him Saint-Omer and Aire and several other castles, and attacked the city of Arras.

Such war, once initiated, spread to engulf virtually the entire county of Flanders. As the Anonymous tells us, Philip Augustus's insistence on controlling Artois provided a convenient pretext for Flemish barons to go to war against their French overlord. Already in June 1197, Renaud of Boulogne and the counts of Guines and Saint-Pol allied themselves with Baldwin IX, openly withdrawing their homage from Philip Augustus and transferring it to the count of Flanders:

> Reinaus de Dantmartin, qui il ot fait conte de Boloigne, li failli, et devint homs le conte de Flandres, et Hue, li cuens de Saint Pol, autresi, et Baudewins, li cuens de Ghisnes.[103]

> Renaud of Dammartin, whom he [Philip Augustus] had made count of Boulogne, forsook him and became the man [vassal] of the count of Flanders; and Hugh, the count of Saint-Pol, did the same; and Baldwin, the count of Guines.

By September, Baldwin IX signed a solemn treaty with Richard I by which he reaffirmed the convention of mutual allegiance between Flanders and England. Before the treaty was even sealed, practically the entire Flemish nobility, led by Baldwin, was in open rebellion against Philip Augustus over the Artois succession, with the exception of Guillaume, the advocate of Béthune, and Guillaume, the castellan of Saint-Omer.[104] The Anonymous's own patron, Robert of Béthune, in contrast, did not share his father's loyalty to Philip but joined the Flemish coalition against the king.

So poorly did Philip Augustus fare in this campaign that he was compelled to sue for peace. But as had happened before in the king's dealings with the counts of Flanders, Philip was to repudiate this peace on the pretext that a rebellious vassal could not legitimately impose conditions on his lord. Instead the king set out to punish the counts of Boulogne and Saint-Pol for their defection, ravaging the lands of both:

> li rois, qui sa guerre avoit et à qui si baron faillirent, si com voz avés oï, fu sovent à grant meschief. Une fois mena il s'ost dusques à Hesdin por aler destruire la terre del conte de Boloigne et la terre [del] conte de Saint Pol.[105]

> the king, who was waging war and whom his barons had abandoned, as you have heard, often perpetrated great misfortune. One time he led his host to Hesdin in order to destroy the land of the count of Boulogne and the land of the count of Saint-Pol.

Compressed in the stark and straightforward narrative of events that the Anonymous of Béthune here offers are the most crucial issues confronting the Flemish aristocracy: royal competition that engenders an ever-widening circle of hostilities; monarchical ambition, which does not hesitate to employ treachery and broken vows in the further-ance of its goals; revenge taken against recalcitrant vassals; and, most destructive of all, the intense political conflict between Plantagenet and Capetian that divided the loyalties of families and set father against son and brother against brother. Indeed, so powerfully does the Anonymous of Béthune depict the forces dividing the Flemish ar-istocracy that we are justified in believing it was this intense conflict that stimulated the development of contemporary historiography by forcing chroniclers, and the society for which they spoke, to come to terms with their attitudes toward these competing authorities. At stake was not merely the question of which side to support according to a hypothetical calculus of the likely winner, but the very safety of Flemish lands and peoples. Trapped both politically and geographi-cally between royal belligerents, Flanders became the principal theater of warfare, the stage on which vying kings played out their drama of domination and exacted their revenge.

When Ferrand of Flanders refused, for example, to accompany Philip Augustus on his planned expedition to conquer England on the grounds that the king unjustly retained possession of Aire and Saint-Omer,[106] Philip assembled his host at Gravelines to make the Channel crossing. Prohibited by the papal legate from continuing with his in-vasion plans, Philip turned against Ferrand and went to Ypres to await the count and demand his compliance, "où li cuens vint à lui por merci crier" (where the count came to him to beg for mercy). But to no avail. Furious at the frustration of his designs, the king turned to wreak revenge on the obdurate count:

> Ains li commanda li rois qu'il feist cele nuit meisme son gré, ou, se ce non, vuidast la terre. Et li cuens s'en ala, ne revint pas al roi; et li roi prist la vile d'Ypre, et puis prist Bruges et Gant, dont il ot boens ostages.[107]
>
> Thus the king commanded that he do his bidding this very night, or, if not, he would waste his land. And the count departed, and did not return to the king; and the king took the town of Ypres, and then he took Bruges and Ghent, from which he had good hostages.

The beleaguered Ferrand was forced to flee to the island of Walcheren, while Philip occupied large areas of Flanders. According to the Anon-ymous's account in the *Histoire des ducs de Normandie*, it was this refusal to comply with Philip's wishes that led to the ultimate destruction of the count of Flanders: "par cel escondit fu puis li cuens toz destruis, et jetés en prison à Paris en la tour dou Louvre" (on account of this refusal the count was later completely destroyed, and thrown into prison in Paris in the tower of the Louvre).[108]

Indeed, between the firing of the French fleet at Damme in June 1213 and the battle of Bouvines on 27 July 1214, Flanders was the arena of innumerable skirmishes, pillaging, and arson, forced to bear the brunt of French hostilities while King John prepared his invasion force in relative leisure. Throughout this period, the county was subjected to extensive devastation. Prince Louis, in particular, brutally laid waste to the countryside, burning cities as he went. After taking and setting fire to Bailleul and Cassel, he turned on the neighboring town of Steenvoorde. So spectacular was the blaze that lit the city skies that Brother Guerin, Philip Augustus's chief counselor, who was present at Prince Louis's side, was moved to exclaim: "Seignor, or oés! Gardès si voz onques veistes nul estanfort miels taint en graine [i.e., scarlet] de cestui," a pun on the city's French name of Estanfort, which also designated a type of cloth fabricated there, dyed "scarlet" by the flames rising above the burning city. These words, asserts the Anonymous of Béthune, shocked the knights who were assembled within hearing of the king's counselor, who found them unseemly in a "home de religion."[109] The devastation brought upon the county touched every level of Flemish society, both urban and rural, whose losses were poignantly reflected, as we saw, in the *enquêtes* of 1247 by which Louis IX attempted to compensate the inhabitants of Flanders for damages done at this time.[110]

Capetian ruthlessness in the prosecution of war against Flanders, the Anonymous demonstrates, in the end left the Flemish little choice but to side with John against their French overlord. As he reports:

> Li cuens de Flandres, quant il vit que il ne poroit trover merchi au roi, il parla à ses homes et lor demanda consel. Si home li loerent que il envoiast en Engletierre au roi Jehan et s'en plainsist à lui, et si manda as chevaliers de sa tierre que il por Diu mesissent consel en son afaire et li aidassent à lor pooirs enviers le roi.[111]

> The count of Flanders, when he saw that he could not find mercy with the king, spoke to his men and requested counsel. His men counseled that he send [messengers] to England to King John and complain to him, and thus he ordered the knights of his land, for the sake of God, to take counsel in his affair and aid him with all their powers against the king.

Baldwin of Nieuwpoort, sent to England to meet with the Flemish barons gathered at the court of King John, reported to them how Philip Augustus had seized the land of Flanders, chased out the count, and "ne li voloit faire droit ne loi, ne merchi n'en voloit avoir" (did not wish to do right or justice to him, nor did he wish to be merciful).[112]

In a world where monarchs refused to act with justice and mercy and scorned the law in the pursuit of their own interests, loyalty to the principles of feudal service became not only precarious but infeasible. It is the Anonymous himself who draws this inference from the situation, exposing in dialogic form the forces and arguments that were fracturing the theoretical unity of reciprocal rights and obligations that supposedly bound the French realm together. When the Flemish barons approach the count to demand that he align himself with John of England, Ferrand at first counters with an articulation of the ethical barriers that render this shift in allegiance illegitimate:

> et il lor respondi qu'il estoit hom liges le roi de France, si n'oseroit chou faire se si home ne li looient.

> and he answered them that he was the liege man of the king of France, and thus that he would not dare to do this thing unless his men counseled it.

Against this scruple, however, the Flemish barons exert the full weight of their counsel to persuade Ferrand that in doing so he would remain blameless, for his withdrawal of loyalty resulted from royal wrongdoing and from this perspective was, in effect, a licit act of feudal *diffidatio*:

> Si home li disent que il bien le pooit faire. Encore dont ne la volt-il faire, se il ne li looient par conjurement. Lors les conjura que il li donnassent consel par la foi que il li devoient, se il sans blasmer le pooit faire; et il disent que il le pooit bien faire sans blasme, sour chou que li rois avoit esploitié viers lui.[113]

> His men said that he could very well do it. Yet he still did not wish to do it, unless they counseled him with an oath. Then he made them swear to counsel him, according to the fealty that they owed him, [as to] whether he could do it without blame; and they said that he could very well do it without blame, because the king had acted against him.

Yet again, the desire to remain faithful to law and right, to fulfill the feudal obligations of service and loyalty imposed on vassals high and low, is thwarted by the realities of contemporary political life, which subvert adherence to the rules governing feudal society. When rulers so freely violate the rights of those over whom they rule, for the ruled to persist in obedience to the legal terms of service and loyalty is mere folly.

Absent from the Anonymous's account, yet powerfully present in the silences that this absence generates, is the king himself. He does not debate the principles of justice with his barons; does not question the basis of his actions; does not negotiate to redress wrongs or recompense losses. Philip acts solely on the promptings of his own aims and angers, unmindful of the damage that he wreaks or the rights that he transgresses. His behavior is not bounded by the counsel of his vassals, as is Ferrand's. He acts virtually alone, with a sovereign (and sovereign's) insouciance for the norms laid down for the conduct of political life.

When the Anonymous inquires into the causes of this dangerous state of affairs, he brings before the reader the critical shifts in the conduct of royal government and sources of royal military strength that had contributed to rendering the nobility vulnerable to newly organized monarchies. Although he fails to report on the changed economic conditions that were operating to shift the balance of power and authority between kings and nobles in this period, his understanding of the structural transformations in royal modes of governing and fighting in the thirteenth century discloses a profound sensitivity to the underlying forces that were marginalizing the nobility's traditional role in the political and military governance of medieval society.

In the Anonymous's eyes, perhaps the most striking transformation in the form of royal government during the reign of Philip Augustus was the narrowing base of the royal *conseil*. In contrast to earlier Capetian kings, and to the king of England as well, by the opening of the thirteenth century the French monarch had excluded from his council the great barons who once had appeared there by virtue of their feudal tenure. In place of the barons, Philip Augustus increasingly relied on a restricted number of trusted counselors who formed part of an incipient service aristocracy and who owed their influence and whatever wealth they accumulated along the way to royal favor. These men were creatures of the king, recruited by him from among the lesser knights and clerks of the king—the *milites et clerici regis*—to fill the council and to execute royal orders, forming a corps of paid royal servitors responsive to the royal will and personally beholden to the king for advancement. With their rise to dominance in the *conseil*, royal government ceased to be the product of a collaborative effort between the king and the *proceres* of the realm, as earlier Capetians had envisaged it.

In the Anonymous's account we have a glimpse of the distaste with which the nobility looked on these men who had supplanted them in the royal council. The chronicler's principal characterization of Philip's counselors occurs in his record of the French king's sudden decision to undertake the invasion of England. According to the Anonymous, the king awoke one morning and, while lying abed, was seized by the plan to attack his rival across the Channel. Hastily he roused his chamberlain and demanded that he send for his *conseilliers*, namely:

> . . . frère Garin, un hospitelir, qui trop ert sire de lui. Car trop ert sages et bien en parles, et se ert il de basses gens; cil frère Garins fu puis evesques de Senlis. Ensement manda li rois Henris le Mareschal, un petit chevalier qui molt ert bien de lui: car molt l'avoit bien servi en ses guerres; si li ot doné li rois Argentuen en Normendie. Bertelmeu de Roie manda ensement li rois, un gras chevalier, qui molt ert bien de son conseil, et pluisors autres de ses conseillieres, et lor monstra que il voloit aler Engleterre conquerre.[114]

> . . . brother Guerin, a hospitaler, who was very much lord over him. For he was very wise and excellent in speech, and he came from the lower classes; this brother Guerin later was bishop of Senlis. The king also called for Henri the Maréchal, a small knight who was very much in his favor, because he had served him well in his wars; the king had given him Argentan in Normandy. Barthélemy of Roye he called for as well, a great knight who was very important in his council, and several others of his counselors, and he revealed to them that he wished to go and conquer England.

Concentrated in this brief report is an accurate assessment of the narrowing base and decline in social status of royal consultation during the reign of Philip Augustus. Key men of the royal *conseil* such as Guerin, acknowledged in the Latin histories of the period as *secundus a rege*,[115] and depicted even more forcefully by the Anonymous as "lord" (*sire*) of the king, had risen from virtual obscurity and low birth to positions of extraordinary influence, not only in the royal council but throughout the range of royal government, in the royal chancery as well as in affairs of justice, finance, and war.[116] A member of the crusading order of the Knights Hospitalers, Guerin in all likelihood had been discovered by Philip Augustus during the Third Crusade of 1190. Brought back to France by the king, he rapidly amassed prestige and property, no doubt by virtue of the cleverness and eloquence that the Anonymous attributes to him. Already by

1202–1203 he possessed houses at Saint-Léger-en-Yvelines, Orléans, and Lorris, and was later given another at Montreuil-Bellay.[117] As the Anonymous indicates, he was eventually elected bishop of Senlis, after which both he and his church continued to enjoy royal favors.

Also of humble origin was the second of Philip Augustus's principal counselors named in this account, Henri the Maréchal, a *petit chevalier* esteemed by the king for his military prowess and duly rewarded for his services with the great fief of Argentan in Normandy.[118] Henri already bears witness to the emergence of a service aristocracy composed of families of lesser knights who made their fortunes in royal service, since his father, Robert Clément, had served as a royal marshal and even guardian of the young Philip before 1181.[119]

Perhaps the most successful of these counselors was Barthélemy of Roye, who ultimately attained the position of grand chamberlain (in 1208) but whose sphere of duties, like Guerin's, encompassed a broad spectrum of administrative matters. Like Henri the Maréchal, Barthélemy was the son of minor lords, in his case a family of lesser knights of Roye in Vermandois, but he succeeded in accumulating even greater wealth than his colleague in the royal *conseil*. At the height of his career toward 1214 he had acquired extensive holdings in land, primarily as a result of royal gifts. After Philip's conquest of Normandy he was granted fiefs at Mantes, Montchauvet, and Acquiny, which he held together with houses in and around Paris and other gifts from the king, including money and jewels. As John Baldwin has indicated, "except for bestowing on him a great barony, the king could not have rewarded his faithful knight and grand chamberlain more handsomely."[120]

By the middle years of Philip Augustus's reign, these "new men" had wholly displaced the nobility in the royal council and, hence, in the system of rewards and benefits that service in the king's court implied. That the nobility resented the influence exercised over the king by this incipient service aristocracy and disdained the low social status of its members is clear from the muted scorn with which the Anonymous of Béthune labels them as "basse" and "petit." Already in the Old French *Couronnement de Loois*, a *chanson de geste* composed between 1131 and 1137 as part of the cycle of Guillaume d'Orange, the ancient emperor had counseled his son Louis to avoid accepting nonnobles into the royal council:

> "Et altre chose te vueil, filz, acointier,
> Que, se tu vis, il t'avra grant mestier:
> Que de vilain ne faces conseillier."[121]

"And one other thing I wish to teach you, son, which, if you live, will be very useful to you: that you do not make a counselor out of a villein."

Although Barthélemy of Roye and Henri the Maréchal might not constitute actual villeins (the case of Guerin is less clear), they clearly owed their social as well as political fortunes to the king. The intrusion of these lesser men into the royal court and their progressive monopolization of its primary offices, therefore, represented for the traditional nobility not merely a loss of influence and authority, but their exclusion from the benefits of royal largesse, which, as we know from contemporary romances, possessed a profound symbolic as well as economic significance for the nobility. The removal of the nobility from the king's court, in that sense, signaled a rupture in the symbolic conception of reciprocal services and benefits between nobility and monarch that had been a central component in traditional modes of feudal government. The Anonymous of Béthune's thinly veiled hostility toward the three principal counselors of the French king expresses in the language of personal scorn a more profound understanding of the structural transformations in royal administration that were marginalizing the nobility by distancing them from the sources of social and political power.[122]

Another major threat to the status and symbolic prestige of the nobility in this period, as we saw in chapter 1, was the gradual loosening of its monopoly over the use of arms and its right to fight in a distinctively noble style. Here, too, the Anonymous of Béthune indicates his awareness of how the spread of mercenary soldiers was changing the practice of warfare for kings and nobility alike. A condensed but powerful picture of this development emerges in his account of the wars between Richard Lion-Heart and Philip Augustus, in which the French king was condemned to suffer many adversities, the Anonymous explains,

> car li rois Richars estoit trop riches et de terre et d'avoir, asés plus que li rois de France n'estoit. S'avoit adès trop grant ost, que de ses homes que de ses souders. Les Flamens avoit, qui od lui estoient en soudées, et les Brabençons. S'avoit par somonce les Englois et les Normans et les Bretons et les Manseaus et les Angevins et les Poitevins. Adès avoit pluisors routes, par qoi il damagoit molt la terre al roi de France; car li routier estoient trop mal destruiseor de terres.
>
> Un routier i ot que on apeloit Markadé, qui molt fu de grant renon en cele guerre; non porquant si le desconfi sovent uns sergans le roi de France, que on apeloit Cadoc, qui autresi menoit route.

Celui Cadoc fist puis li rois de France chastellain de Gaillon par son service et por sa grant proece, dont plains estoit, et si estoit il petis.[123]

for king Richard was extremely rich in land and possessions, much more so than the king of France was. At that time he had a very large host, both of his vassals and of soldiers. He had the Flemings, who were in his pay, and the Brabançons. And he had, by virtue of [feudal] summons, the English and the Normans and the Bretons and those of Maine, and the Angevins and the Poitevins. At the same time he had several commoners, with whom he very much damaged the land of the French king; because commoners were terrible destroyers of lands.

There was a commoner named Mercadier, who was greatly renowned in this war; nonetheless, a sergeant of the king of France often defeated him, a man called Cadoc, who also led commoners. This Cadoc the king of France later made castellan of Gaillon [as a reward] for his service and for his great prowess, of which he was full, even though he was small.

Embedded in this passage are the marks of fundamental changes in the methods of military recruitment and the social quality of those who composed medieval armies, changes that were completely transforming the practice of warfare in the High Middle Ages. Formerly feudal armies are now fully penetrated by mercenary soldiers, the most famous of whom the Anonymous identifies by name, such as Mercadier and Cadoc.[124] Even feudal knights, as in the case of the Flemish serving in Richard's host, participate as paid members of the army, rather than fighting as a result of feudal service. Most striking, of course, is the presence of *routier* soldiers, whose damaging social presence in the host is disparaged by the charge that they are terribly destructive to the lands they attack. One hears through this charge a much broader complaint about their failure to observe those codes of comportment and military ethics that had served to define a distinctively noble style of fighting.

The Anonymous's remark about the destructive force of commoner soldiers can also be read as an index of the emotional response of the French aristocracy to the intrusion of non-noble contingents into the noble theater of war, a phenomenon that the French experienced as, in Duby's words, "un traumatisme profond."[125] To the extent that medieval French aristocrats defined themselves in functional terms as *bellatores*—"those who fought"—the performance of this social task had justified their rights to the labor and services of "those who worked" and "those who prayed."[126] To attack the aristocracy's prerogative to defend society through the exercise of military valor was, thus, to undermine the sources of its legitimacy by calling into question its exclusive military vocation, and with it the whole cultural edifice of chivalry that had endowed that military vocation with an almost sacred aura.

Curiously, despite his evident awareness of the pervasive presence of non-noble contingents among the armies of his day, when the Anonymous comes to record the battle of Bouvines he excludes any mention of them, even though they participated by the thousands in this major *bellum* of 1214. He does acknowledge that the communes of Flanders sent contingents to join the allied forces together with the Flemish nobility, who "ièrent venu molt efforciement" (who came there in great strength);[127] but in describing the actual battle he reconverts Bouvines into a purely aristocratic affair, orchestrated according to the rules of chivalric combat in which one champion opposes another in essentially single combat, backed up by the fighting of nameless, anonymous followers. Facing the French army across the fields of Bouvines is a great host of "bele gent et plenté de riches armes et de belles banières, et d'autre part autresi" (beautiful men and a host of rich arms and beautiful banners, on both sides). The battle itself is recounted in a series of paragraphs, each exalting the individual role of a single warrior: so, for example,

> Lors corrut li cuens de Flandres as Champenois, et li Champenois à lui, et ot trop bone meslée entre aus. Mais li Champenois furent mis arière.
> Lors corrut li viscuens de Meleun, en qui bataille se tenoient li quens de Pontieu et li cuens de Ghisnes et tot cil del fief Looys, le fil le roi, qui manoient entre Somme et la Lis. . . .
> Gauchiers de Chasteillon, li cuens de Saint Pol, corrut tot outre la bataille et la desrompi molt malement. Et quant ce vit Henris, li dus de Louvaign, qui encor n'ert asamblés, il se mist à la fuie et commencha la desconfiture.[128]

> The count of Flanders attacked the Champenois, and the Champenois him, and there was a great melée between them. But the Champenois were pushed back.
> Then the viscount of Meleun charged, in which battle line were the count of Ponthieu and the count of Guines and all those of the fief of Louis, the son of the king, who lived between the Somme and the Lys. . . .
> Gauchiers of Châtillon, the count of Saint-Pol, charged all over the battle line and disrupted it greatly. When Henri, the duke of Louvain, saw this, [although he] still had not entered the fray, he took flight and began the rout.

Although the language of battle here retains the simple, realistic style that the Anonymous employs throughout his chronicles, the form of presentation is reminiscent of the strophic rhythm of traditional epic song. In its concentration on noble combatants and their heroic encounters, the Anonymous attempts to reinscribe the battle of Bouvines as, in effect, Roncevaux. In this last arena of aristocratic glory—the increasingly rare pitched battle—the cultic world of the feudal aristocracy reasserts itself. As depicted by the Anonymous, Bouvines offers a final opportunity for the display of chivalric theatrics in a ritualized conduct of war that seeks to assert the centrality and crucial importance of the aristocracy to the military defense of medieval society. But the outcome of Bouvines will provide the final sign that this attempt is a vain gesture. The triumph of the French forces at Bouvines is a triumph for the king, marking his decisive victory over the barons of the realm and vindicating his pretensions to stand over and above the aristocracy.

Just as the Anonymous omits any discussion of the fighting except for that engaged in by the aristocracy, so also does he render the activity of the king as purely managerial in function. In contrast to the royal chronicler Guillaume le Breton, whose *Philippide* was written to celebrate the royal victory at Bouvines, the Anonymous of Béthune is curiously silent on the role of the king. In his account, Philip appears only before the battle, seated on his horse. The king did not appear to be afraid, the Anonymous claims, because he

> devisa et ordena molt sagement et molt seurement son afaire et non esbaiement, et fist crier que tuit, et chevalier et autre, ralaissent à lor batailles. [129]

> planned and ordered his affair very wisely and safely, and not in fright, and he had the order given that everyone, knights and the others, should return to their battle lines.

Royal action orders and initiates, but does not partake of, the fighting. In so situating the king outside the actual arena of battle, the Anonymous gives spatial expression to his understanding of the ways in which the French monarch had succeeded in disengaging himself from his membership in the world of the feudal aristocracy and surmounted the realm, over which he ruled as incontestable lord and governor. The victory at Bouvines marks the moment when the balance of power between monarch and aristocracy shifted decisively in favor of the Capetian king. In the wake of Bouvines, the Anonymous laments, "puis ne fu qui guerre li osast movoir" (there was no one who dared to make war against the king); his *bailli* en tel servage mist tote la terre de Flandres . . . que tot cil ki en ooient parler s'en esmerveilloient coment il le pooient souffrir ne endurer.[130]

placed all the land of Flanders in such servitude . . . that all who heard about it marveled how they could suffer and endure it.

Eight hundred years later, Henri Pirenne concurred in the Anonymous's judgment: "After Bouvines," he asserted, "the power of the French king became preponderant, so much so that at the end of the thirteenth century, the Low Countries seemed no more than an annex of the Capetian monarchy."[131]

𝄢𝅘𝅥𝅮𝄡

The two chronicles of the Anonymous of Béthune constitute the first step in the development of contemporary vernacular historiography, inaugurating a tradition of historical writing devoted to the narration of real events and actors that would achieve its mature expression in the Late Middle Ages in the work of chroniclers like Jean Froissart. Created in the turbulent decades surrounding the battle of Bouvines and shaped by the contest for loyalties and authority between vying monarchies on both sides of the Channel, the *Histoire des ducs de Normandie* and the *Chronique des rois de France* testify to the fracturing of a once-cohesive view of the past and of contemporary society's relation to it. The work of the Anonymous of Béthune sheds novel light on the essentially contested character of historical production in the Middle Ages, a process often masked beneath the valorized images of past and present that typify the tendentious and legitimizing narratives of much medieval historiography. In composing dual and alternative versions of the same sequence of events, his *Histoire* and *Chronique* are the first works of vernacular historiography to confront the ways in which the rise of a centralized monarchy had fundamentally changed the political situation in medieval France and to incorporate this changed situation as the very structure of a new kind of history capable of addressing the inherent instability and contested nature of the past.

With the triumph of monarchy at the battle of Bouvines, an era of aristocratic domination over medieval French society came to a close. Thereafter an ascendant monarchy progressively stamped its own style of rulership and dictated its own conception of social value on the realm, a process entailing a reevaluation of the ethical and moral precepts that had once served as the framework of royal behavior. The task of constructing a new image of the king now fell to royal chroniclers. Just as the locus of power and authority in medieval society moved inexorably toward the central monarchy, so also is the central concern of vernacular historiography displaced to the creation of royal history. With the rise of royal historiography in the middle decades of the thirteenth century, the question of the values and principles governing kingly comportment came to the fore. It is to the growth of royal historiography that we must turn now, to trace royal responses to the emerging world that royal power itself had done so much to create.

6 Royal History
Disengagement and Reconciliation

Until the mid–thirteenth century, vernacular historiography flourished far from the orbit of the royal court, emerging under the patronage of the aristocracy, who employed it as a vehicle for the investigation of the historical ground and ideological significance of aristocratic experience. Unlike the Plantagenets in England, Capetian monarchs in the early thirteenth century did little to foster narratives of royal history; royal encouragement of vernacular historiography does not emerge as a major preoccupation of French kings until the time of Louis IX, with the sponsorship of the *Chronique des rois de France* by the Ménestrel d'Alphonse de Poitiers, a writer resident in the household of King Louis's brother,[1] and, toward 1274, of the *Grandes chroniques de France* at the Abbey of Saint-Denis.

The relative disinterest of Capetian kings in promoting vernacular historiography is evident from the fragmentary nature of the first extant texts, which clearly failed to win the audiences necessary to preserve their existence in a manuscript culture. Although Latin chronicles treating the reign of Philip Augustus fared better, protected by the inherent authority and institutional support granted works in that discursive register, our knowledge of vernacular royal history in this period has been limited, until very recently, primarily to allusions to works subsequently lost or to fragments preserved from a larger corpus of texts.

Typical of the fate of royal historiography in Old French during this initial phase of production are the two folios discovered by C. R. Borland in the binding of a seventeenth-century law book housed at the Library of Edinburgh, which preserve by chance a translation into French verse of Guillaume le Breton's *Gesta Philippi Augusti*.

269

Borland and R.G.L. Ritchie identify the fragments with the lost work of Jean de Prunai, whose translation of Guillaume le Breton is mentioned by Guillaume Guiart in his *Branches des royaux lignages* at the beginning of the fourteenth century.[2] Guillaume Guiart declares that Jean de Prunai used both the *Philippide* and the *Gesta* for his verse history, and Borland and Ritchie have found sufficient resonances in the surviving folios to suggest that this is true.[3] Composed in all likelihood toward 1227, the fragments that survive treat the aftermath of Bouvines and include an account of events that led Prince Louis to renounce his attempt to win the crown of England.

Equally fragmentary is the surviving portion of a *Histoire de Philippe-Auguste* that Petit-Dutaillis ascribes to Michel of Harnes,[4] whose interest in history had earlier been expressed in his patronage of a vernacular *Pseudo-Turpin Chronicle* in 1206–1207. Michel of Harnes, as we have seen, was a staunch supporter of Philip Augustus at the battle of Bouvines, where he fought against his Flemish compatriots. The extant portion of Michel's *Histoire* was transcribed by André Duchesne from a parchment quire found in the library of the collegial church of Saint-Quentin, now available in volume 49 of the Collection Duchesne (fols. 163–168) at the Bibliothèque Nationale. It covers the years 1214–1216, thus, as in the case of Jean de Prunai, dealing essentially with the aftermath of Bouvines and the beginning of Prince Louis's expedition to England. What remains of this history suffices to indicate that it was the work of a contemporary well versed in events occurring in the north of France at the beginning of the thirteenth century. Pro-royalist and evincing strong regional affiliations, the author seeks to celebrate Philip's victory at Bouvines and the bravery of his son.[5] He terms Louis "mi sire," acknowledging his lordship of Artois, in which Harnes was situated.[6] For this and related reasons, Michel has been proposed as the author.

Michel of Harnes also demonstrates a concern to record the major events of his time, and his *Histoire* includes brief accounts of the triumph of the Ghibelline party and coronation of Frederick II in Germany; the Albigensian Crusade; the Fourth Lateran Council; and, especially, the conflict between King John and the English barons who had called Prince Louis to their aid. Since only the first folio is missing from the manuscript that Duchesne found at Saint-Quentin, it is unlikely that the original work covered events prior to the formation of the English-Flemish-German coalition in 1213. Although written at approximately the same time and covering the same events as the *Chronique des rois de France* of the Anonymous of Béthune, Michel's history differs considerably from that of the Anonymous, notably in his depiction of the dangers experienced by Otto on the field of Bouvines.[7] Unfortunately, apart from its generally laudatory tone on behalf of the Capetian monarch, which tells us something about the motives that prompted Michel's foray into historical composition, the chronicle in its present state is too truncated to analyze as a textual unit.

Still more shadowy is the work commissioned by a Burgundian lord, Giles of Flagi, who charged an anonymous author to write in French a history of Philip Augustus, of which only a 118-line fragment of the verse prologue remains, it too composed around the year 1227.[8] The "history of Saint-Denis" that the author professes to have translated must have been the *Gesta Philippi Augusti* of Rigord or Guillaume le Breton, and Meyer identifies the Burgundian chronicle with a "roman de Philippe le Conquérant," now lost, several copies of which were known to have been present in the library of Charles V.[9]

Despite the highly fragmentary nature of the extant vernacular corpus devoted to royal historiography in this period, it is hardly coincidental that the first stirring of royalist history, as yet developing independently of royal patronage, appears in the reign of Philip Augustus, at a moment when French kings were successfully consolidating their authority over the nobility and embarking on a career of military conquest and administrative centralization that would make them masters of the French realm. The clustering of texts around the year 1227, shortly after the king's death but while memories of the great events of his reign were still fresh, suggests the impulse to commemoration that his signal achievements helped to elicit.

But commemoration was scarcely the principal task confronting the development of royal historiography. If the rise of a newly powerful monarchy placed in question the ethical underpinning of the feudal world of the aristocracy, what has been too little appreciated is the extent to which the ethical crisis of the aristocracy touched the king as well. In part, this is because the sources that would allow us to follow royal reactions to the changing political climate have been lacking. Yet it is certain that the ideological consequences of the social and political transformations that the monarchy itself was implementing in thirteenth-century France were not confined to the nobility, but affected the moral predicates of royal ideology as well. Since the chivalric values that made up noble culture had been shared by—indeed, according to Flori, derived from—French kings, it could be expected that the monarchy would participate, whether directly or indirectly, in the refiguration of those aspects of chivalric and historical thought that had provided a common basis of action for royalty and nobility alike. Insofar as new conditions of social action demanded new forms of ethical and historical imagination in the thirteenth century, this demand weighed equally on the king, for the terms of his modes of operation had changed no less significantly than those of the aristocracy.

At the same time, royal historiographers needed to respond to the challenge posed by the contested past that vernacular writers such as the Anonymous of Béthune had created, for history, as the repository of tradition in medieval society, was the bearer of that society's sense of legitimacy. Just as custom—that is, precedent—reigned supreme in social life, so history, the record of political tradition, determined the parameters of political activity. Along with divine right, medieval governments justified their dominion on the grounds of what Max Weber called the "authority of the eternal yesterday."[10] At issue was not the mindless repetition of tradition, or an inability to innovate or create, but a compelling necessity to find in the past the means to explain and legitimize every deviation from tradition. In such a society, Joseph Strayer remarked, "every deliberate modification of an existing type of activity must be based on a study of individual precedents. Every plan for the future is dependent on a pattern which has been found in the past."[11] The eternal relevance of the past for the present made it a mode of experiencing the reality of contemporary life, and the examples the past offered had explanatory force in articulating the true and correct nature of present forms of political action. To have allowed the contested image of the past set forth by a chronicler like the Anonymous of Béthune to go unanswered risked jeopardizing the ultimate sources of historical—and hence political—legitimacy in medieval France.

The emergence of Old French royal history at the end of the reign of Philip Augustus, thus, must be seen in dialectical relation to the prior development of vernacular historiography and the contest over the past for which it served as a vehicle. Precisely because the king had triumphed over his feudal adversaries and was now powerful, he needed to validate his exercise of authority over those whom he had succeeded in submitting to his rule, to articulate a legitimizing vision of the monarch as the lawful and beneficent leader of society, whose actions and commands served the interests of the entire realm. But to do so meant distancing the king from the nobility, above whom he now claimed a preeminent position. The first task of royal historiography, therefore, was to disengage the king from the structures of thought and ethical values that had bound him to the nobility. Only then could royal propagandists begin to elaborate a new and encompassing structure of history that spoke in the name of the realm as a whole, hoping thereby to provide a mechanism for the aristocracy's integration into and reconciliation with royal authority.

Fortunately, it is now possible to begin to trace the impact of social and political change on royal ideology, for we have in hand a new text, only recently discovered at the Musée Condé in Chantilly, that represents the earliest known example of royal historiography in Old French. Significantly, it was composed sometime between 1210 and 1230—that is, at precisely that moment when the long thrust toward the recovery of royal power was brought to brilliant fruition by Philip Augustus.

The Chronique des rois de France *of the* Anonymous of Chantilly/Vatican

The existence of an Old French *Chronique des rois de France* at the Musée Condé in Chantilly was first reported by Ronald N. Walpole in 1978.[12] While engaged in a search for manuscripts of the vernacular *Pseudo-Turpin* in 1976, Walpole noticed that the version of *Pseudo-Turpin* contained in Chantilly MS. 869—a manuscript dating from the fifteenth century—strongly resembled one published by Claude Buridant from a thirteenth-century *Histoire des rois de France*, preserved at the Vatican in the collection of the queen of Sweden, Reg. Lat. 624. Although Elie Berger had noted the presence of this work at the Vatican in 1879 and had signaled its affinities with the *Grandes chroniques de France*,[13] no scholarly work was devoted to it for nearly a century, until Pierre Botineau undertook a thorough examination and was equally struck by the manuscript's resemblances to the vastly better known Dionysian compilation. Botineau would later argue, in fact, that it served as both source and model for the *Grandes chroniques*, thereby significantly transforming our understanding of the processes that contributed to the creation of that famous collection.[14] Shortly after this date Buridant published his edition of the *Pseudo-Turpin* found in the *Histoire*.[15] Although both Botineau and Buridant believed that Vatican 624 contained a unique version of the vernacular *Pseudo-Turpin*, Walpole was able to demonstrate that the text of Chantilly 869 provided a second exemplar. On this basis he suggested in passing that MS. 869 might, therefore, be a second copy of the whole *Chronique*.[16] In fact, not only has Walpole's hypothesis been fully confirmed by an examination of the text as a whole, but it is clear that MS. 869, although dating from the fifteenth century, possesses a much more complete version of the *Chronique des rois de France* than does Vatican 624. Whereas the Vatican version begins only with a life of Charlemagne, as translated from the *Vita Karoli* of Einhard, the text of Chantilly 869 includes a history of France from the Trojan origins of the Franks to Philip Augustus inclusively. For this reason, the ensuing discussion will be based for the most part on the manuscript of Chantilly, despite the chronological priority of the version found in Vatican 624.[17] Both manuscripts have now been submitted to a detailed analysis by Gillette Labory of the Institut de Recherche d'Histoire et des Textes, especially with respect to their common reliance on a group of Latin sources that also served Primat in the compilation of the *Grandes chroniques* at Saint-Denis.[18]

As Gillette Labory's investigation of the two manuscripts makes clear, Chantilly 869 is not a copy of Vatican 624, although the two versions are closely related. The older is Vatican 624, a manuscript dating from the end of the thirteenth or beginning of the fourteenth century, written in a rather negligent *littera textualis*, with relatively restricted decoration of mediocre execution, evidence of a copy of non-deluxe status in all likelihood commissioned for personal use.[19] The language of the scribe, according to both Buridant and Walpole, indicates a Burgundian copyist, possibly from the western part of that county.[20] Although the text at present begins only with the *Life of Charlemagne*, the original version almost certainly went back to the Trojan origins of the Franks, as several authorial interventions indicate.[21] The two manuscripts are for the most part made up of the same texts; however, there are sufficient divergences between them (especially, as we shall see, in their use of Latin sources) to warrant the conclusion that they represent two different redactions of the same work rather than faulty copies of a common exemplar.[22] In a general sense, the redaction represented by the manuscript of Chantilly offers a much more elaborated and complete stage of composition, containing a higher incidence of narrative embellishments, authorial interpolations, and the admixture of additional sources, which are translated with a greater freedom than is the case in Vatican 624.

The text of Chantilly 869 is a late copy, dating from the last quarter of the fifteenth century. It is a much more luxurious exemplar than that of Vatican 624, written in a careful *bâtarde* of the late fifteenth century in the language of the Île de France (Francien). It is highly decorated, possessing 12 large miniatures and 102 smaller ones.[23] The manuscript is incomplete at the end, owing to mutilation, which interrupts the Anonymous's translation of Guillaume le Breton's *Philippide* at verse 445 of Book 11 of that work.[24]

The anonymous author of the *Chronique des rois de France* evidently began his translation during the reign of Philip Augustus. This fact emerges from a long interpolation that the Anonymous inserts at folios 216r–v into his translation of the *Vita Ludovici Pii* by the Astronome. Because the facts that he is about to report concerning the deposition of the emperor by his sons are scandalous and scarcely credible, the Anonymous feels compelled to confirm the veracity of his account by noting his sources:

> Et des cy en avant orrez merveilles conter de cestui Loys, comme son filz et ses barons le menerent a ce qu'ilz lui osterent la couronne du chief et en firent moyne et de sa femme Judith l'emperiere nonnain a force. Tout en la maniere comment il fut si comme ie le treuve en l'ystoire de Saint Denys et Saint Germain des Pres dont ie extrait mot a mot ce conte, si comme il gisoit en Latin, de tous les faiz des roys de France et qui ont receu le royaume de France et tenu iusques au temps du gentilz roy Phelippe, auquel Dieu dont bonne vie et longue, si comme il nous est mestier, que les ennemis du royaume sont, la Dieu merciz, forment plaiez et mis soubz ses piez et tout par l'aide de Dieu et pour la priere de saincte eglise laquelle il a tousiours maintenue et deffendue, et saincte eglise lui comme son bon filz et son fort escu contre ses ennemys.

> From here on you will hear recounted the marvels of this Louis, how his son and his barons led him to the point that they deprived him of the crown and made him a monk, and [made] his wife Judith, the empress, a nun by force; all in the manner in which it occurred as I find it in the history of Saint-Denis and Saint-Germain-des-Prés, from which I extract word by word this story, as it appears in Latin, of all the deeds of the kings of France and who received the realm of France and held [it] up to the time of the noble King Philip, to whom may God grant a good and long life, as is our need, for the enemies of the realm are, by God's mercy, severely afflicted and put under his feet and all with the aid of God and for the prayer of Holy Church, which he has always maintained and defended, and Holy Church [has maintained and defended] him as its good son and its strong shield against its enemies.

Having prayed that the king be maintained in a long life to keep the enemies of the realm "mis soubz ses piez," the Anonymous continues by recalling Philip Augustus's conquest of Normandy, followed by a Norman genealogy pursued to John Lackland:

Ce fut cestui Phelipes qui adiousta au corps du royaume de France
toute Normandie avec ces sept eveschiez CCC et sept ans empres ce
que Charles le Simple dont vous orrez cy apres parler en ceste hystoire et la donna en mariage a sa fille Gillete, laquelle il donna a
femme a Rollon le Normant, lequel fut appellé Robert par un autre
non, qui depuis cellui Rollon qui Robert fut appellé si comme ie vous
ay dit engendra en celle fille de Charles le simple ung filz qui eut
nom Guillaume longue espee, Guillaume Richart et Robert son fre-
re.Et celui Robert engendra ung filz qui eut nom Guillaume le Bastard qui conquist Engleterre. Et cellui Guillaume eut ung filz qui fut
appellé Guillaume le Roy et Henry le Rous son frere. Empres ce
Leufroy le conte d'Angiers engendra Henry de la fille du vieil Henri
qui Mehaut l'emperiere eut non. Et cestui Hanri et Richart et Iehan
sans terre.[25]

It was this Philip who added all of Normandy to the body of the
realm of France, with its seven bishoprics, three hundred and seven
years after Charles the Simple, of whom you will hear spoken in this
history, gave it [Normandy] in marriage to his daughter Gillete,
whom he gave as a wife to Rollo the Norman, who was called Robert by another name; and afterwards this Rollo who was called Robert, as I have told you, engendered in this daughter of Charles the
Simple a son whose name was William Longsword, William, Richard, and Robert his brother. And this Robert begat a son whose
name was William the Bastard, who conquered England. And this
William had a son who was called William Rufus, and Henry the
Red his brother. After this Geoffrey the count of Anjou begat Henry
by the daughter of the old Henry, whose name was Matilda the em-
press. And this Henry [begat] Richard and John Lackland.

Despite the Anonymous's recognition of the importance of Philip
Augustus, he confesses that he has not yet discovered a Latin history
to translate that will allow him to report on the deeds of this worthy
king. Nonetheless, he vows that should he discover one, he will pursue his own history through the reign of Philip Augustus:

En cellui temps le vaillant roy Phelipes conquist Normandie par force
de guerre et se la vie de ce roy Phelipes nous venoit entre mains et
si fera elle se Dieu plaist quant ceste hystoire aura fait son cours
iusques a lui nous la traicterons si dignement comme nous porrons si
comme il est raison. Car il y a assez pour quoy si comme il est assez
apparaissant que bien vous sera conté en droit point et lieu.[26]

In this time the valiant King Philip conquered Normandy by force of
war, and if a life of this King Philip came into our hands (and so it
will if it pleasès God), when this history will have finished its course

up to him, we will treat him as worthily as we can, as is right.
For there is sufficient reason, as is quite apparent, which will be recounted to you at the right point and place.

The manner in which the Anonymous speaks of the king supports
the notion that Philip was still alive when he wrote these lines. Moreover, as Botineau has pointed out, it would seem that the king was already well advanced in his reign at the moment that the Anonymous
was translating the Astronome, because he mentions Prince Louis as
associated in the actions of his father and sharing with him the benefits of the church's prayers. Since Louis was not personally active in
the affairs of the realm until about 1210, the Anonymous probably did
not reach this part of his work before that date, perhaps not even until
Louis's important victory over King John of England at La Roche-au-
Moine in 1214.[27] The description of Philip Augustus as a "good son"
and defender of the church points to a date after 1213, for it was then
that the French king was formally reconciled with Queen Ingebourg,
whose previous repudiation and exile from the royal court had caused
the realm to be placed under interdict.[28]

Gillette Labory has attempted to provide a more specific date for the
inauguration of the *Chronique des rois de France* in referring to another interpolation that occurs in the account of a speech addressed by
King Chilperic (561–584) to the bishop of Rouen, whom the king
sought to condemn on the basis of false arguments fabricated by
Queen Fredegonde. The French, aroused by his words, the Anonymous writes, wished "le prandre et octire villainement" (to take and
kill him basely). This episode brings to mind similar occurrences that
continue to plague France, because there are still many in France, the
Anonymous maintains, "qui trop voluntiers feroient hontes et ville-
nies au clergie" (who all too willingly would enact shames and evil
deeds against the clergy). Nevertheless, such attacks are presently
avoided owing to royal protection: "se le roy, qui Dieu guerisse et doint
Dieu bonne vie et longue, ne nous deffendoit" (if the king, whom God
cure and grant a good and long life, did not defend us).[29] It appears
likely that Philip Augustus had fallen sick toward 1217, since after this
date he rarely appears in the registers of the Royal Chancery and
power seems to have passed into the hands of royal counselors like
Guerin and Barthélemy of Roye.[30] The Anonymous's prayer for the
king's recovery, thus, occurring as it does toward the beginning of his
work, would seem to indicate a period close to 1217 as the *terminus a
quo* for the inception of the *Chronique*. It is certain, in any case, that
the work was begun after 1210, possibly as late as 1213–1217, placing

its inspiration squarely in the years surrounding the momentous events that culminated in the battle of Bouvines.

The *terminus ad quem* is more easily established from comments concerning Jean of Brienne that the Anonymous added to his translation of verse 543 of Book 12 of Guillaume le Breton's *Philippide*. Jean of Brienne was elected emperor of Constantinople between 1229 and 1231. The Anonymous is aware of Jean's accession but fails to mention his death in 1237; it would appear, therefore, that he had concluded his long and arduous task of translation before the latter date.

SOURCES

The most complex aspect of the *Chronique des rois de France* involves the range of sources that the Anonymous utilized in the construction of his vernacular compilation, as those sources often were themselves compound texts compiled from a variety of Latin works. He explicitly mentions a large number of Latin and vernacular texts, both ecclesiastical and secular, that he claims either to have consulted or to which he refers the reader/auditor of his *Chronique*. Among the ecclesiastical sources he cites a "livre qui parle des fais aux apostoles" (a book which speaks of the deeds of the Apostles)[31]—a reference to the *Historia pontificalis;* Jerome's *Life of Saint Hylarion;*[32] several works of Gregory the Great, including the *Moralia in Iob*[33] and the *Dialogues;*[34] the *Life of Saint Sylvester,* which he professes to have used for the story of how the saint cured Constantine's leprosy;[35] as well as various Lives of the Saints, including the *Vie de Saint Fursin,*[36] the *Vie de Saint Germain des Prés,*[37] the *Vie de Saint Columban,*[38] Gregory the Great's *Life of Saint Benedict* (included in his *Dialogues IV*),[39] the *Vie de Saint Loup,* and the *Vie de Monsieur Saint Martin.*[40] In addition to these explicitly named texts we find generalized references to the Bible; to an "ancien livre" written by Saint Oain, archbishop of Rouen, recounting the death of King Dagobert;[41] to "livres de l'auctorité de l'eglise de monseigneur Saint Iaques de Galice" (books on the authority of the church of my lord Saint Jacques of Galicia), by which he means the *Codex Calixtinus,* used in connection with Charlemagne's expedition to Spain;[42] as well as praise for a "livre des faitz des arcevesques de Reins, qui est moult bonne et profitable a oyr" (a book on the deeds of the archbishops of Reims, which is very good and profitable to hear), a clear reference to the *Gesta episcoporum* of Reims.[43] He also cites an "escript" giving the ages of the world according to the Bible, which he asserts was "fait ou temps du preuz Charles Marteau" (made in the time of the brave Charles Martel).[44]

Included in the citations to secular sources explicit mention is made of "l'ystoire de Thebes,"[45] the "chanson de Girard de Rous-sillon,"[46] the "ystoire [i.e., chanson] d'Antioche,"[47] as well as more general references to "autres maistres qui ont traicté des hystoires" (other masters who have treated histories).[48] There are, as well, un-specified allusions to material found "en croniques et en ystoire," and other "maistres qui ont traicté des roys de France,"[49] in addition to the "chronique" of Gregory of Tours (i.e., the *Historia Francorum*), whose text the Anonymous complains has been corrupted by scribes.[50] Other information comes to him "en genelogie,"[51] and in certain "anciennes hystoyres,"[52] which mention "Aurelians, qui fut empereyr de Rome" (Aurelius, who was emperor of Rome). The Anonymous several times refers to "archaeological" evidence, such as the epitaphs found on the tombs of Clovis and Saint Germain, although in both cases he refers the inquiring reader not to the actual tombs, but to "histories" of Saint-Denis or Saint-Germain-des-Prés.[53] He often refers to letters and charters pertaining to the Abbey of Saint-Germain-des-Prés, and sprinkles his text with "proverbes de villain"[54] as well as sayings of classical authors such as Cicero and Cato.[55]

The ubiquity of these citations adds luster to the Anonymous's claim to learning and authority, although in truth he makes scant use of them and for the most part gleans his knowledge of their contents indirectly. In the composition of his work, instead, he largely relied on what he repeatedly refers to as the "hystoires" of Saint-Germain-des-Prés and Saint-Denis. At least for the initial portion of his work, preserved only in Chantilly 869, of which it constitutes the first 165 folios, what the Anonymous of Chantilly means by this dual reference is the *Continuation of Aimoin*, which would later also serve Primat as the base source for the initial portions of the *Grandes chroniques de France*.

Aimoin was a monk of Fleury who composed a *Historia Francorum* at the beginning of the eleventh century, during the abbacy of Abbot Abbon, to whom he addressed the dedicatory epistle.[56] For reasons that are not clear, Aimoin's text stopped in 634 and only later was completed with a number of continuations. Lemarignier has demon-strated that a copy of Aimoin was carried to Saint-Germain-des-Prés sometime between 1015 and 1025, where it was continually interpo-lated over the course of the next 150 years, with an initial continua-tion carrying the narration to 1031 and a second to 1165. Sometime toward 1175, the lives of Kings Louis VI and Louis VII by Suger were added to the manuscript. The Saint-Germainian provenance of the *Continuatio* is apparent from the fact that numerous interpolations concern the history of the abbey and all of its abbots are named.[57] The prototype of this redaction is found in B.N. Lat. 12711, from which all the manuscripts possessing interpolations and continuations derive.[58]

In her 1976 thesis for the Ecole des Chartes, Christine le Stum was able to identify Vatican Reg. Lat. 550 as the oldest of the copies and to demonstrate that it was written at Saint-Denis at the beginning of the thirteenth century, where it served as the basis for the famous collection of Latin histories compiled there in midcentury that appears in B.N. Lat. 5925.[59] When the Anonymous of Chantilly/Vatican speaks, therefore, of the "hystoires" of Saint-Germain and Saint-Denis, either of these versions of the *Continuation of Aimoin*—B.N. Lat. 12711 or Vat. Reg. Lat. 550—may figure as the source that he consulted (see Appendix).

Unfortunately, as Gillette Labory has demonstrated, the Anonymous's use of the *Continuation of Aimoin* cannot be perfectly matched to readings found exclusively in either B.N. Lat. 12711 or Vatican 550. Thus, while the *Continuation* is certainly his principal source, it is impossible to demonstrate that he directly translated either of these manuscripts. Moreover, the Anonymous consistently supplements the Latin sources found in this compilation with additional material. For example, in treating the reign of Charlemagne, he includes a translation of Einhard's *Vita Karoli* (also present in Vatican 550) and adds a version of the *Pseudo-Turpin Chronicle* (absent in both Latin versions of the *Continuation*). Walpole has identified the version of *Pseudo-Turpin* present in the *Chronique des rois de France* as belonging to the family of texts he terms *Turpin I* and not—as Buridant had believed—an independent redaction.[60]

The Anonymous follows his translations of the *Vita Karoli* and *Pseudo-Turpin* with a translation of the Astronome's *Life of Louis the Pious*, an arrangement similarly found in Vatican 550. Nevertheless, neither Vatican 624 nor Chantilly 869 wholly conforms to the text found there.[61] For the period succeeding Louis the Pious the Anonymous consistently attempted to fill in the gaps present in his Latin source by amalgamating additional texts. This part of his work can be divided into three sections, covering inclusively the time period from Charles the Bald to Philip I. In part one, the Anonymous added to the Latin compilation's reliance on the *Historia Francorum Senonensis* and the *Annales Bertiniani* of Hincmar (with, in Vatican 550, pieces from other chronicles such as the *Abbreviatio Regum Francorum* and the chronicle of Adon inserted) supplementary material taken from the *Miracula Sancti Benedicti* as well as interpolations drawn from the *Historia Regum Francorum usque ad annum 1214,* written by a monk of Saint-Germain-des-Prés during the reign of Philip Augustus and initially composed in 1205 but almost immediately continued to 1214.[62] Also included in this portion of the *Chronique* in Vatican 624, but absent from Chantilly 869, is an abridged version of the *Visio Karoli,* which, although it lacks the references to Saint-Denis, does evoke Charles's gift to Saint-Denis of the relics putatively brought back by Charlemagne from the Holy Land. After reporting on the Norman incursions that led to the Treaty of Sainte-Claire-sur-Epte in 911, Rollo's baptism in 912, and his marriage with the daughter of Charles the Simple, the Anonymous concludes with an allusion to the Norman genealogy that he had already recounted in the interpolation into the Astronome's *Vita Ludovici Pii* cited above, which offers a basis for a proximate dating of his work.

In section two, covering the period subsequent to Charles the Bald, Vatican 624 offers a different text from that found in Chantilly 869, one made up of extracts from an abridged French chronicle of the kings of France up to Louis VII, followed by a version of the *Chronique de Normandie* close to that published by Francisque Michel in 1839 and characterized by Paul Meyer as a "free translation of Guillaume de Jumièges."[63] This narrative is abruptly interrupted after the account of the taking of the castle of Tillières by Henry I. At folio 73 of Vatican 624, then, the text returns without explanation to the reign of Louis IV d'Outremer, as recounted in the *Continuation of Aimoin*—the same text found in Chantilly 869—and reiterates all the reigns whose history had already been traced until the reign of Philip I inclusively.

For the third section, which deals with the events surrounding the *mutatio regni* or Capetian accession, the Anonymous uses the *Historia Francorum Senonensis* via the *Continuation of Aimoin,* as did Primat later in the *Grandes chroniques,* despite the highly prejudicial character of this account to Capetian legitimist sentiments.[64] One notable addition here is a long passage borrowed from Odorannus concerning the conjugal problems of Robert the Pious and the intervention of Saint Savinian in a vision to Queen Constance.[65] For the years 1096 to 1099 up to the First Crusade the Anonymous faithfully reproduces the *Continuation of Aimoin,* but with the commencement of the Crusade he once again interpolates his text with the addition of a long passage taken from the *Historia Regum Francorum* that reports on the genesis of the Crusade, followed by a list of those who took the cross. On folio 259v of Chantilly 869 and folio 78r of Vatican 624 there occurs a reference to "l'ystoire d'Antioche," in all likelihood an allusion to the original version of the *Chanson d'Antioch* by Richard the Pilgrim, now known only in its revised form.[66] The Anonymous then returns to his Latin compilation for the account of the Crusade, continuing to follow it for the succession of events through the reign of Philip I, to which he adds only a notice on the foundation of the Abbey of Cîteaux taken from the *Historia*.[67]

After the death of Philip I, the Anonymous of Chantilly/Vatican translates the *Vita Ludovici Grossi* of Suger, which he introduces with a long preamble:

> De ce roy Loys dont nous avons ores commencé à conter nous avons ia parlé en l'ystoire devant du roy, jasoit ce que ce fust tant seulement en brief de ce qu'il fut couronné roy empres la mort du roy Phelipes son pere en la cite d'Orlyans. Mais l'abbé Sugges de Saint Denys qui fut norry son clerc et qui moult l'ayma rescript ses faitz et sa vie ou il moustra bien quelle amour il avoit vers lui. Ceste vie et les faitz de ce noble roy Loys le gros avons commencé à compter en Françoys ainsi comme l'abbé Sugges le conte en Latin, si comme nous avons peu. Mais trop nous griefve durement ceste chose a faire. Car a telle chose entreprandre ne se doit nul tirer avant s'il n'est parfait en escriptures car ne scayt qu'il est forte chose de translater de Latin en Françoys senon celui qui a ce fait et qui a essayé le cas; comment qu'il nous griefve le nous convient faire, car nous en sommes contraints et n'en oserions rien contredire ne reffuser. Mais je prie moult à ceulx qui ce livre liront qu'ilz ne me blasment ne repreignent de ceste chose entreprandre, car bien sachent que je le fays comme par force comme celui qui n'est pas suffisant à faire tel euvre. Ce vous avons dit pour nous excuser, mais poursuivons l'ystoire si comme le vaillant abbé Sugges le conte. . . . [68]

> Of this King Louis, about whom we have now begun to narrate, we have already spoken in the preceding history of the king, even though this was only in brief, concerning how he was crowned king after the death of King Philip his father in the city of Orléans. But the Abbot Suger of Saint-Denis who was raised his cleric and who greatly loved him wrote up his deeds and his life where he shows very clearly what love he possessed for him. This life and deeds of the noble King Louis the Fat we have begun to relate in French just as the Abbot Suger recounts it in Latin, to the extent that we have been able. But it chafes us sorely to do this task. For no one should attempt to undertake such a thing unless he is perfect in writing, for no one can know how difficult a thing it is to translate from Latin

into French unless he has done it himself and attempted it. However much it grieves us, we have to do it because we are constrained to do so and would not dare to contradict or refuse. But I heartily pray those who read this book that they not blame or reproach me for having undertaken this thing, for they should know that I do it as if forced, as someone who is inadequate to perform such a work. We have said this to excuse ourselves, but let us continue the history as the valiant Abbot Suger relates it. . . .

The Anonymous's complaints about the difficulty of translating Suger's convoluted Latin are well founded, and he was not alone in finding the task daunting. Botineau has proved that, beginning with the *Vita Ludovici Grossi*, Primat made extensive use of the Anonymous's own translation when similarly confronted with the intricacies of Suger's Latin, although prior to the life of Louis VI the resemblances between the *Grandes chroniques* and the Anonymous are exceptional and largely insignificant.[69] For the reigns of Louis VI and Louis VII, however, the *Grandes chroniques* constitute, in Botineau's words, "rien d'autre qu'une adaptation d'une traduction vieille d'une cinquantaine d'années, et si le ms. 5925 a été utilisé pour cette période, ç'a été seulement . . . pour quelques vérifications."[70] There could scarcely be stronger confirmation of the extent to which the elaboration of the *Grandes chroniques* must be situated within the context of the prior development of vernacular historiography, from which it draws and to which it responds.[71] The French translation of Suger's *Vita Ludovici* differs, though, in Vatican 624 and Chantilly 869: whereas the text of Chantilly is complete, that of Vatican 624 lacks a section corresponding to approximately thirty folios in Chantilly.[72]

The Anonymous precedes his translation of the life of Louis VII, known as the *Historia gloriosi regis Ludovici*, with another protracted preamble that recalls his account of the life of Louis VI just completed, announces the life of his son to come, and indulges in a personal complaint about the length and arduous character of his enterprise, which he undertakes not in order to garner praise among men but to win God's favor and to support the efforts of those who work to promote the growth and peace of the French realm.[73] In addition to this prologue, the Anonymous also interpolates at folio 303v a passage in praise of the king that he takes from the *Historia Regum Francorum*—the origin of many of his interpolations in this portion of the *Chronique*, doubtless because he found his source insufficiently laudatory concerning the king's achievements.

Despite the Anonymous's statement that with the *Life of Louis VII* he had at last come to the end of his extensive effort of translation, in the Chantilly manuscript the text of the *Historia gloriosi* is followed by a translation of Odo of Deuil's *De profectione Ludovici Septimi ad Orientem*, the account by the monk of Saint-Denis of the first two years of Louis's disastrous crusading venture. This text does not appear in Vatican 624, which instead proceeds immediately to a translation of Guillaume le Breton's *Philippide*, a Latin verse panegyric of over nine thousand lines, written by the king's chaplain to commemorate Philip's victory at Bouvines.

The *Philippide* of Guillaume le Breton constitutes the final work translated in the *Chronique des rois de France*. The Anonymous here makes good his promise on folio 216v to include an account of the reign of Philip Augustus should one come to his attention. Evidently the Anonymous was unaware of Rigord's *Gesta Philippi Augusti*, which existed at this time in a single manuscript copy at the Abbey of Saint-Denis and which, at the moment that the Anonymous was complaining about the absence of a Latin source for the life of Philip Augustus, was already being summarized by Guillaume le Breton as the prefatory section to his own Latin prose chronicle of Philip's deeds, also titled *Gesta Philippi Augusti*.[74] Guillaume indirectly confirms the Anonymous's difficulty in finding a source for Philip's reign, for he explains in the preface to his own *Gesta* that he has written a history of Philip's reign that includes an abridged version of Rigord's work, since that work was "a paucis habetur et adhuc multitudini non communicatur."[75] The translation of Guillaume's *Philippide* in the vernacular compilation is significant, for it represents the only French version of Guillaume's poem known to exist in the Middle Ages.

The version of Guillaume's text that the Anonymous employs has been identified by Botineau and Buridant as the second redaction, completed sometime between 1224 and 1226, in all likelihood in the exemplar designated "L" by Delaborde, now at the British Library, Additional 21212. This identification is made possible because the Anonymous incorporates into the body of his translated text notes found on the margins of the British manuscript.[76] There is no introduction in the *Chronique* to the translation of the *Philippide*, in contrast to the extensive prologues produced for the reigns of Louis VI and Louis VII. It is possible to determine that the Anonymous worked on the translation of the *Philippide* after the death of Louis VIII in 1226, because he interpolates into his account of Louis's consecration in 1223 the comment that the unfortunate king's reign was all too brief ("mais ce fu trop poi as François et à Seinte Yglise et au monde").[77] The full text of the *Chronique* was not completed, as we saw, until some point between the accession of Jean of Brienne as emperor of Jerusalem in 1229–1231 and prior to his death in 1237.

Botineau conjectured that this translation of the *Philippide* might represent a version of the lost prose work commissioned by Giles of Flagi, only the verse prologue of which has survived. But the fact that the Anonymous fails to introduce this section of his compilation with a prologue comparable to those found at the head of the *Lives* of Louis VI and Louis VII, though a deviation in practice, cannot be made to authorize the supposition that the translation of the *Philippide* originally formed an independent vernacular text simply appropriated for use by the Anonymous.[78] Botineau himself was quick to indicate the weak nature of his hypothesis, concluding that the Anonymous's work, "malgré nos efforts, garde son anonymat."[79]

The Author

No less so does the author preserve his anonymity. Despite his frequent interventions in the text in the form of interpolations, opinions, and expressions of personal fatigue, the Anonymous nowhere names himself. That he was a cleric is almost certain, given the pious sermonizing with which he adorns his narrative and his frequent comments on the clerical mores of his day, both negative and positive. His extensive employment of the "croniques" of Saint-Germain-des-Prés and Saint-Denis might seem to connect him in some fashion to those Parisian abbeys, especially the former, since he retains a large number of the interpolations concerning the affairs of Saint-Germain that are present in the *Continuation of Aimoin* but later suppressed by Primat in the *Grandes chroniques*. At the same time, he evidently knew about or had visited the Abbey of Saint-Denis. He reports from Aimoin that at the time of Dagobert, the king ordered two bronze doors to be taken from the church of Saint-Hilaire of Poitiers and placed in the church of Saint-Denis; however, during their transport one of the doors fell into the Seine. To this account the Anonymous adds a personal note that "l'autre fut amenee iusques à Saint Denys et on la y peut encores veoir qui vieult" (the other was brought to Saint-Denis, and whoever wishes to can still see it there).[80] Still, his lack of knowledge of Rigord argues strongly that he did not reside or work at Saint-Denis, since he surely would have discovered Rigord's history and its continuation by Guillaume le Breton had he consulted the monastic library. In light of his ignorance of Rigord, and in the absence of any indication tying him more closely to the Abbey of Saint-Germain-des-Prés, it is impossible to specify a clerical institution to which he might have belonged or to localize his working milieu more precisely than Paris.

Gillette Labory suggests that an indication of his possible birthplace is furnished by a comment inserted into his account of the battle of Dormelles. According to the Latin text, the battle raged "super fluvium Arvenna nec procul a Doromelle vico." To this vague description the Anonymous adduces precise topographical details, explaining that the battle took place "en la province de Sens, pres d'une ville qui a nom Dormelles, qui est a troys petite[s] lieues de Moret le Chastel et se logierent sur la riviere d'Arvenne qui court par celle ville" (in the province of Sens, near a village called Dormelles, which is three short leagues from Moret le Chastel, there [the knights] lodged themselves by the river of Arvenne, which runs by this village).[81] Beyond his evident familiarity with the environs of Dormelles, however, the Anonymous offers no further clues concerning his place of origin.

Throughout the course of his work, the Anonymous frequently intervenes to complain about the length of the enterprise he has undertaken[82] and to express his discontent that its enormous size is preventing him from other pressing tasks. Thus he asserts:

> Nous avons autre chose a faire que moult voluntiers metrions a fin ceste present euvre se nous povions.[83]

> We have other things to do so that we would willingly put an end to this present work if we could.

Yet despite his haste to conclude his work, he defends his digressions on the grounds, for example, that

> Pour ce si ne se doivent pas courroucer ceulx qui ceste hystoire oient qui moult y peuvent aprandre et y aprandront, s'ilz veullent escouter ce qu'elle dira ça en avant, en ce qu'elle ajoindra a soy de ce qu'elle prandra es choses et es avantures qui sont avenues aux autres royaumes et que qu'elle die si revient-elle tousiours a sa droicte matiere des roys de France de quoy elle traicte a la maniere que l'eaue fait qui decourt par son eschenau droit aux fousses qui sont entour l'eschenau se tourne et les emplist. Et quant elle les a emplies si revient a son droit eschenau et fait son droit cours.[84]

> Those who hear this history should not be angered for there is much they can and will learn, if they wish to listen to what it will say from this point forward, insofar as it will add material concerning things and events which have occurred in other kingdoms; and no

matter what is said, the history always comes back to its proper matter of the kings of France, in the manner of water which overflows its channels, twisting through the ditches that surround it and filling them. And when it has filled them, it returns to its channel and resumes its original course.

Still, he looks forward to the day when he will receive due recompense for the enormous labor he has expended:

> Je vous lairay tout ce à dire pour plus haster s'il se povoit faire de venir a la fin de ceste euvre qui si longuement m'aura tenu et tant travaillie; ne je ne tiendroie point mon travail pour perdu si je povoie venir a fin de ceste euvre et si j'en avoie le *guerdon* que j'en ay desservy. Car le bon homme qui travaille à labourer sa terre, si elle ne lui rent son fruit à sa droicte heure, il se peut bien tenir pour destruit.[85]

> I will leave aside saying all this in order to hasten more quickly, if it can be done, to come to the end of this work which will have held me for so long and so greatly vexed [me]; I would not consider my work as lost if I could come to the end of this work and if I had from it the *reward* that I have deserved. For the good man who works to labor in his fields, if they do not return to him their fruit at the appointed hour, he considers himself destroyed.

Unfortunately, the Anonymous does not specify for us the person from whom he expects to receive his reward. Of the patron for his work, he says only that it was commissioned by someone

> a qui nous ne pourrions riens esconduire ne reffuser que nous peussions faire, qui nous a fait entreprandre ceste pesant euvre dont ne vendrons ia au bout si non par l'aide de Dieu.[86]

> to whom we can deny or refuse nothing that we are capable of doing, who has made us undertake this present work, at whose end we will never arrive, except with the help of God.

Although the terms of this remark would appear to point to a personage of high, even royal, status, it seems unlikely that the patron was Philip Augustus, whose monumental disinterest in historical and literary patronage is universally acknowledged. Gillette Labory suggests a patron such as Michel of Harnes, whose interest in historical writing is well known, but the text does not provide evidence for this attribution.[87] What is clear is that the work is royalist in inspiration, suggesting that the Anonymous was a Parisian cleric who worked in the orbit of—though probably not directly at—the royal court. My reason for this conclusion stems from his long ignorance of the work of Guillaume le Breton, of whose *Gesta Philippi Augustus* he is unaware and whose *Philippide* he uses only in the second redaction, and this despite his avowed search for a Latin source for Philip Augustus's reign. Rather, like the monk of Saint-Germain-des-Prés who composed the *Historia Regum Francorum jusque ad annum 1214*, he likely formed part of a circle of historical writers who were impressed by the extraordinary achievements of the monarchy under Philip Augustus and who sought to convey to their contemporaries a sense of the importance and significance of the events of their own day. The Anonymous of Chantilly/Vatican claims a special place within that circle as the first royalist historian of the kings of France to write in Old French, producing, fifty years before the composition of the *Grandes chroniques,* a narrative of French history that in its influence on the Dionysian compilation would powerfully condition all subsequent versions of royal historiography in France.

If we cannot identify the patron for whom the Anonymous wrote his *Chronique des rois de France,* we can at least garner a relatively clear picture of the motives that inspired him and the historiographical goals that he set himself. With most medieval chroniclers, the Anonymous of Chantilly/Vatican shares a belief in the moral utility of history as, he claims, a "mirouer de vie," the knowledge of which can benefit all:

> Pour ce si dirons a ceulx qui l'escoutent qu'il ne leur tourne pas a ennuy ne a charge mais a plaisance de raconter maintes chouses qui sont moult prouffitables et ou l'on peut maintes bons exemples prandre et se mirer et garder des avantures qui sont avenues car, si comme dit le bon clerc, hystoire et [*sic*] le mirouer de vie que par l'ystoyre on aprant ce qui est bon et on eschive ce qui est mauvais et perilleux.[88]

> For this reason we say to those who are listening [to our history] that it will not become boring or a burden to them, but a pleasure in the recounting of many things which are very advantageous and from which one can derive many good examples, and reflect upon them and take heed of the adventures which have taken place because, as the good clerk says, history is the mirror of life, in that through history one learns what is good and avoids what is bad and dangerous.

To this wholly conventional view of the utility of history the Anonymous adds a more particular concern with demonstrating the "richness" of history's political matter, "riche" precisely, as he says, "car elle traicte des plus nobles gens et des plus riches de cuer et des plus entreprenans" (because it narrates the deeds of the most noble people and those richest in heart and most enterprising); it is, therefore, a fit subject for the rich and noble men of his own age, for whom his history is intended.[89] His audience he clearly identifies, as do most vernacular chroniclers, as those untutored in Latin, for whose sake he undertakes to present history. In pursuit of his goal of transmitting the knowledge stored up in Latin works to a lay audience, the Anonymous is careful to insist on his scrupulosity in translation, assuring his readers that he translates literally—*mot à mot*—taking nothing away and adding no lies, but recounting all "comme je le treuve en escript" (as I find it written).[90]

Sprinkled throughout the text are also numerous aids to the reader—explanations, for example, of the ancient geography of France, the changing names of cities, of certain customs either still in force or long since abandoned by the French. So we find on folio 106 the following explanation of the name of King Clotaire, a characteristic sample of the Anonymous's efforts to clarify his material for the reader:

> Icellui Clotaire est appellé le jeune Clotaire pour son aiol qui eut nom Clotaire qui est appellé le vieulx Clotaire et par raison puet estre appellé le premier Clotaire celui qui est son ayol pour l'amor de lui qui est le second and pour ung autre qui cy empres vendra qui le tiers Clotaire porra estre appellé par ces deux de quoy nous avons parlé si comme nous l'avons trouvé en l'ystoire; de celui qui le tiers Clotaire est appellé veult l'ystoire parler si comme vous orrez si vous voulez escouter. Mais or retournons arriere et parachevons de dire de cestui Clotaire, le pere de Dagobert, qui nous avons entre mains.[91]

> This Clotaire is called the young Clotaire after his ancestor who had the name Clotaire, who is called the old Clotaire; and for this reason he who is his ancestor might be called the first Clotaire for the love of him who is the second and for another who will come after and who could be called the third Clotaire for those two of whom we have spoken, as we have found it in *l'ystoire*; of him who is called the third Clotaire *l'ystoire* will speak, as you will hear if you wish to listen. But now let us turn back and finish speaking of this Clotaire, the father of Dagobert, whom we have between our hands.

One can be grateful that he did not attempt to straighten out the various Theoderics of the Merovingian line.

The Anonymous is, moreover, keenly aware of the insufficiency of his sources, repeatedly complaining that he is unable to complete his discussion of a particular topic because "l'ystoire n'en dit rien"; the lacunae in the texts range from the length of a reign, the genealogy of a high baron, and the deployment of battle lines to a general absence of causal explanation and even, in the case of Einhard's attempt to mask the licentious behavior of Charlemagne's daughters, to the cover-up of royal scandal, of which he writes:

> Il fist moult semblant qu'il n'en sceust riens. Aussi come si nulle suspecon mauvaise de nulle folie ne fust iamais yssue ne espandue d'elles . . . ains en parle si couvertement que a poines peuz entendre qu'il en vouloit dire, mais nous povons forment entendre par ces paroles que ce puet estre.[92]

> [Einhard] makes it appear as if he knew nothing of it, and as if no suspicion of wrongdoing or folly ever attached to them . . . rather, he speaks of them in such a hidden manner that we can scarcely understand what he wishes to say; but nonetheless, we are able to understand by his words what might have happened.

Here again he underlines the difference between history, which is true, and the *chansons de geste*, which retail lies; he declines to complete his narration by purveying false or invented information. When "l'ystoire" says nothing about some matter, he does "not wish to add anything, unless it is the truth of history which declares it," for he says

> je ne vueil pas ressembler les baveurs qui en noz chancons mancongeresses nous decouppent parmy un chevalier tout a tour de son cheval a ung seul coup. Mais l'ystoire qui est vraye et qui n'entend que à retraire la verite dit bien et afferme pour vray que . . . [93]

> I do not wish to resemble the singers who in our lying songs cut through a knight together with his horse completely with a single blow. But the history which is true and intends only to treat the truth says and affirms as true that . . .

In an obvious attempt to reinforce the demand for historical narratives sharply differentiated from epic, the Anonymous insists on the historian's exclusive purchase on truth and his own claim to respect as a practitioner of history. Concluding the long interpolation into the Astronome's *Vita Ludovici Pii*, he concedes that "while in many ways and from many people you have heard spoken and recounted the deeds of this pious emperor, Louis," nonetheless, he alone is worthy of belief, for, he avers, "les menteurs qui vous en chantent ne scevent pas la ou j'en suis et la ou je vous en diray. Et telle chose vous en vueil dire que onques nul n'oy ne ne sceut si non cellui qui a oye l'ystoire comme j'ay" (the liars who sing of Louis to you do not know what I know and what I will tell you. For I wish to say to you such things as no one ever hears or knows, except he who has heard history as I have).[94]

Still, there are limits to the Anonymous's own capacity to resist the insidious attractions of the *chansons de geste*. Having arrived at the end of his translation of two different accounts of the deeds of Charles Martel, both of which he has faithfully transmitted "without the addition of lies," he professes himself amazed that

> je n'y ay trouve la grant guerre qui fut entre cestui Charles et Girard de Roussillon, dont les vielleurs chantent et dont il est si grant renommee; et si la guerre fut si fiere d'eulx .ii. et telle comme on dit, trop fut grant merveilles quant elle ne fut mise en ceste hystoyre, mesmement pour ce que l'on dit que celui Girard fonda une abbaie a chacune foys qu'il desconfit Charles Marteau. Et celui Charles aussi fonda une abaye a chacuneffoys qu'il desconfist cellui Girard. Et dient que Charles en fonda .xiii. et Girard .xii. qui tant de foys se desconfirent chacun son compaignon, Charles Girart .xiii. foys et Girart Charles .xii. foys. Et doit l'une des abbayes que Girart fonda estre en Vizelais et l'autre en Poictiers, si comme le commun des gens le dit. Pour ce, je suis tout esbahy et esmerveillé comme si tres riche guerre et si haulte euvre comme de fonder abbayes fut laissee a mectre en cest hystoire des rois de France, s'il fut vray. Je ne dit pas qu'il soit mençonge ne ne veulx pas tesmoigner qu'il soit vray pour les chançons des vielleurs qui trop mectent en doubtance et en souspeçon.[95]

I have not found any mention of the great war that took place between this Charles and Girard of Roussillon, of which the jongleurs sing, and which is so famous; and if, indeed, the war was as fierce between them as is said, it is astonishing that it was not included in this history, especially since they say that Girard founded an abbey each time that he routed Charles Martel. And Charles also founded an abbey each time that he routed Girard. And they say that Charles founded thirteen of them, and Girard twelve, for just so many times did each defeat his companion; Charles, Girard, thirteen times, and Girard, Charles, twelve times. And one of the abbeys that Girard founded was supposed to be in Vézelay, and another in Poitiers, as the common opinion of the people has it. For this reason, I am astonished and amazed that such an important [*riche*] war and such high works as the founding of abbeys were left out of this history of the kings of France, if they were true. I'm not saying that it is a lie,

> but neither do I wish to testify that it is true, on account of the *chansons* of the *vielleurs,* which place everything in doubt and suspicion.

In the presence of this "doubt and suspicion," the Anonymous takes refuge in a counsel of interpretive anarchy. "For the time being," he advises,

> or en die chacun ce qu'il vouldra selon son avis car je en dy tant comme je en puis dire. Elle n'est pas en l'ystoire de monseigneur Saint Denis ne en celle de monseigneur Saint Germain des Prez, et maintes autres guerres qui ou temps de cestui Charles avindrent et les maistres qui les hystoires des roys de France compillerent et firent qui mieulx en doyvent estre creuz. Atant me tais ores a parler de ce et m'en retourne au cours de l'ystoire.[96]

> let everyone say of it what he will according to his own opinion, for I have said all that I can. It is not in the history of Saint-Denis nor in that of Saint-Germain-des-Prés, and many other wars occurred in the time of this Charles, and we ought perhaps to believe in the masters who composed and compiled the histories of the kings of France. Henceforth I shall cease to speak of this and return to the course of the history.

The influence of the *chansons de geste* on the Anonymous is not confined to the inclusion of stories borrowed from that medieval genre, but permeates his style throughout the *Chronique des rois de France.* Beginning with the opening account of the fall of Troy, he rewrites virtually all battle accounts in an epic style, amplifying his Latin sources with vivid narrative details of "beaulx chevaulx, bel escu d'or et d'azur et de sinope et de diverse couleurs,"[97] and extended scenes of single combat, horses hewn in half with a single blow, and the remaining panoply of epic clichés. This use of the rhetorical devices furnished by the *chansons de geste* goes hand in hand with the Anonymous's harsh criticism of the mendacious tendencies of epic narrative noted above.

In general, the Anonymous's style is marked by a certain syntactic looseness, with negatives often left unexpressed, nominal subjects omitted, and even verbs dropped.[98] He often indulges in exceptionally long sentences, over which he fails to retain his grasp of syntax and meaning. In its imprecision, his style seems closer to oral than to written composition, despite his insistence on the literalness and exacting standards that guided his labor of translation. His grammatical solecisms are so pervasive that they cannot be ascribed to scribal error, however marred the manuscripts might be in that quarter as well.

In the first half of the *Chronique* especially, the Anonymous frequently interpolates comments of a moralizing turn, directed at the contemporary mores of rulers, knights, clerics, and so forth. He is particularly concerned with the lack of charity and mercy among his clerical contemporaries, whom he excoriates for their grasping avarice. Thus, for example, having recounted the story of Pasquaises, who was noted for his alms to the poor, the Anonymous turns his scorn on his confreres, whose behavior he compares invidiously with the practices of the past:

> Mais les clercs et les prevostz qui ores sont ne le semblent de rien. . . . Jamais d'eulx n'ystra nul bien pour les pauvres si non bien pou ains les despendent et sont si deurs vers les pouvres comme gens qu'ilz ne cognoissent. Et quant il leur vient force d'argent de leur patrimoine, ilz le mectent en leurs bourses.[99]

> But the clerics and provosts who now live do not resemble him at all. . . . There never issues from them any good for the poor except a little; instead they spend and are very harsh toward the poor, whose existence they barely acknowledge. And when they get any amount of money from their patrimony, they put it in their purses.

Nor is covetousness and its constant companion, envy, restricted to the clergy. These two vices, in the Anonymous's opinion, permeate all of medieval society from top to bottom:

> Plusieurs examples de plusieurs hystoires l'on peust traire avant que eust loisir de monstrer comment ces deux vices mortelz confundent tous ceulx du monde, les roys, les contes, les barons, les evesques, les arcevesques, et evesques et tous les autres prelatz de saincte eglise et tout l'autre peuple empres.[100]

> One could treat several examples from several histories before having leisure to demonstrate how these two mortal vices confound all those in the world: kings, counts, barons, bishops, archbishops, and bishops [sic] and all the other prelates of the Holy Church and all other peoples as well.

The Anonymous complains of the decline in bravery since the time of Clotaire II's defeat of the Saxons and condemns the cowardice of the French nobility who, although highly praised by the people for their practice of arms, in fact expose themselves to danger only with great hesitation.[101] Numerous kings are criticized for their *puteries:* for example, Gontron, whom the Anonymous asserts lost all his nobility and goodness "car il fut trop lechierre et putier et trop s'i habandonna qui refusa loyal mariage" (for he was very lecherous and debauched and gave himself over to it too much, refusing loyal marriage);[102] and the brothers of Sigebert, king of Metz, on account of "leurs puteries qu'ilz maintenoient de leurs meschines qu'ilz tenoient comme telle vie ne appartiegne a roys" (their debaucheries that they maintained with young girls, leading a life that did not belong to kings);[103] and even Dagobert who, after the birth of his son Sigibert, changed his good ways and

> a luxure s'abandonna il si tres durement que avec troys femmes haultes dames qu'il tenoit come ioynes il avoit avec elles et tenoit ung grant troupeau et ung grant nombre d'autres femmes agaiges.[104]
>
> abandoned himself to lust so ardently that, together with three women [who were] high-born ladies whom he maintained as play-things, he had and kept a great herd and a large number of other paid women.

The textual universe of the Anonymous of Chantilly/Vatican is inhabited by forces that constantly threaten to undermine the workings of medieval society and to contravene the ethical principles that guide it. Prime among them is the turbulent rebellion of the nobility who, out of pride and greed, thwart the king's rightful exercise of authority in order to pursue political and territorial ambitions. Although this theme permeates the *Chronique des rois de France*, nowhere is it so pointedly treated as in the final section devoted to the translation of Guillaume le Breton's *Philippide*, for it was a central concern of Guillaume's work as well. Writing to celebrate the king's victory at Bouvines, Guillaume took the opportunity to rehearse the major accomplishments of the reign of Philip Augustus. One informing theme of the *Philippide* is Guillaume's demonstration that Bouvines decisively condemns the rebellion of the great barons and expresses the feudal supremacy of the king of France.[105] In contrast to Rigord and to Guillaume's own earlier *Gesta Philippi Augusti*, the *Philippide* makes the defeat of the feudal nobility a principal part of the basic transformations that the French monarchy had effected during the reign of Philip Augustus, allowing the king to emerge at the end of his life as the undisputed and sole governor of the realm. The seven thousand verses that precede the account of Bouvines in the *Philippide* present the preliminaries of the victory and lay the basis for an understanding of the slow process by which, over thirty-five years, the king had prepared his triumph.[106] In Guillaume's verse panegyric, Bouvines marks that moment when the Capetian king succeeded in disengaging himself from the feudal principles and structures that had inhibited the growth of royal power. His triumph is at the same time a triumph for a new conception of the realm and of the king's place in it.[107] The Anonymous of Chantilly/Vatican's keen awareness of the significance of these developments governs his translation of the *Philippide* and converts it into a polemic against the chivalric code that hitherto had ensnared both king and nobility. In his hands, the *Philippide* comes to function as a poignant warning to those on both sides of the struggle between monarchy and aristocracy that adherence to the principles and conduct mandated by chivalric ideology betokens disaster.

The Translation of the Philippide

The Anonymous of Chantilly/Vatican attempts to provide a faithful, though not wholly literal, translation of Guillaume le Breton's verse text. The task he faced was formidable on several levels. Not only did he have to de-rhyme and cast into the newly emerging language of vernacular prose Guillaume's often complex and obscure Latin verses, but the very act of translation into Old French indicates that he was aiming at a public very different from the clerical and court circles to which Guillaume's learned and classicizing work was addressed. Whereas Guillaume elaborated his narrative on the model of Walter of Châtillon's *Alexandreis*[108] and ornamented his text with classical allusions and Virgilian topoi,[109] the Anonymous of Chantilly reshaped his source to suit the tastes and expectations of a lay audience accustomed to conventions of Old French epic and romance. The translation of Guillaume le Breton's Latin into Old French placed the text within a lexical and discursive register that connected it to the body of romance literature and transformed it into something resembling a prose romance work.

To be sure, the Anonymous takes directly from Guillaume the themes and accounts that organize this section of the *Chronique*, translating often in literal fashion the verses of his Latin source, a source inaccessible to those for whom his work was intended. But in moving from Latin verse to Old French prose he locates his account in an entirely new corpus of implicit intertextual references and allusions. While on the level of content there is little substantive difference between the *Philippide* and the *Chronique*, the linguistic transformation of Guillaume's classically inspired Latin into the lexicon and semantic resonances of Old French literature effects not merely a change in the tone of the work, but also an ideological displacement that, in the employment of the language of chivalric romance, generates a novel set of textual problematics. Although many of the issues discussed below appear first in Guillaume's *Philippide*, I do not attempt systematically to distinguish the differences between Latin source and vernacular translation. From the point of view of its intended audience, the message of the *Chronique des rois de France*, although powerfully indebted to the *Philippide*, is for all intents first transmitted to the French aristocracy in the *Chronique* itself. As with all other examples of vernacular historiography in this book, the distinction between Latin source and vernacular chronicle is marked only when there are significant deviations that disclose a particular authorial intention.

The opening sections of Guillaume's *Philippide* are concerned with the king's struggles against the great barons of France, fomented by "plusieurs barons, plusieurs contes et plusieurs ducs qui regardoient son jeune aage" (several barons, several counts, and several dukes who were mindful of his [the king's] young age). Combining to attack the monarchy, the great barons failed to respect the love and honor that they were bound to pay him "comme hommes liges a son seigneur ou chevaliers a leur roy" (as liege men to their lord or knights to their king).[110] In particular, Philippe of Alsace, count of Flanders, acknowledged by all as a man of "sens," "conseil," "hault lignage," and "grant renomee,"[111] although nominally tutor to the king, schemed how he might take advantage of the relative youth of Philip Augustus to wage war against the monarch. For his part, the young king endeavored to defend the realm, proud, as the *Chronique* proclaims, of "la noblesce de sa nouvelle chevalerie" (the nobility of his new knighthood).[112]

As we saw in chapter 1, the dispute between the two Philips concerned the complex negotiations over the Vermandois succession. Between 1181 and 1185, the count of Flanders persistently pursued his wife's claims to the territories of Vermandois, Valois, and Amiens in a series of wars against the French monarch, advancing his frontiers to within sixty kilometers of Paris. In 1184 he even planned an invasion of the French capital, threatening to implant his dragon standard on the Petit Pont.[113] Only when the two armies faced each other across the Somme did the count yield to a peace treaty, concluded at Boves in 1185.[114]

In this part of the *Philippide*, the burden of the arguments advanced concerning the Vermandois succession is carried by a series of alternating speeches between Philippe of Flanders and Philip Augustus. For both king and count, the issues in conflict are couched in the language of feudal laws of inheritance and tenure, laws presumably acknowledged by both parties to govern the respective rights of the king and his vassal, but which Philip Augustus consciously violates in the interests of enhancing royal power.

The basis of Philippe of Flanders's tenure of Vermandois and its allied counties had been a grant by Louis VII in 1179, confirmed by Philip Augustus himself upon his formal accession to the throne in 1180, but which the king now sought to revoke, demanding that the counties be returned "sans force et sans debat."[115] Against this assertion of royal will, Philippe of Flanders takes his stand on the grounds of fidelity to feudal law and the maintenance of the traditional legal order:

> "Ce que vous me demandez me donna voustre pere et vous mesmes m'avez ja confermé le don par voz lettres royaulx. Pour cette raison ay je desclairé mon droit en ce que vous requerez.
>
> "Ne troublez pas la paix du royaume, et que ceulx qui vous doivent obeïr ne vous soient ennemys. Il ne appartient pas que don de roy soit ainsi quassé. Ne n'est pas chose honneste que le roy se desdie. . . . Je suis saisi de par vostre pere et de par vous, et ma tenue me deffand ma droicture et semble estre grant honte de faire dire a force a nullui par quelle raison il tient en possession ce qu'il tient. Ne ce n'est point a alleguer comme ce me aye esté donné loyaument de mes seigneurs liges, et ainsi excuse droicte loyaulté et droit tiltre la letre que j'ay du fons de ceste querelle que je tiens sans faire tort a nully. Et bien sachez droictement que nulle chose qui aye esté donnee loyaument a ung homme ne la doit perdre sans forfait."[116]

> "What you demand from me your father gave me and you yourself confirmed the gift by your royal letters. For this reason have I declared my right in what you request.
>
> "Do not trouble the peace of the realm lest those who should obey you become your enemies. It is not proper that the gift of a king be thus broken. Nor is it honest for a king to repudiate his own actions. . . . I was seized by your father and by you, and my tenure defends my right and it seems a great shame to compel someone to declare the basis by which he has in his possession that which he holds. Nor is it at all necessary to assert, since this has been loyally given to me by my liege lords, and thus proper loyalty and proper title justifies the understanding that I have of the basis of this quarrel: that I hold without doing wrong to anyone. And know beyond doubt that nothing which has been loyally given to a vassal should be lost without forfeit."

To this appeal to the traditional customs and usages of the kingdom, Philip Augustus answers with an argument whose shallowness
only underscores the arbitrary nature of his demands, responding first
that brief tenure is no guarantee of possession and that, in any case,
the gift of a child is not tenable before law.[117] The king's position con-
veniently overlooks Louis VII's perfectly legitimate grant of 1179, not
to mention the fact that Philippe of Flanders's ultimate title to the
counties derived from his wife's inheritance, which was ceded to him
in 1164. More important, Philip Augustus's willful transgression of
the principles of feudal law involved in his breaking the implicit feudal
contract between king and count—*sans forfeit*, the text stresses—represents the disturbance, indeed breakdown, of traditional relationships
of power in French medieval society and points up the king's newly
arbitrary exercise of authority.[118] The growth of royal power and
Philip's clear intention to use it to enhance the position of the king relative to his vassals signified for the aristocracy both a hated innovation and a gross violation of the legal basis of royal authority, which
hitherto had restrained the king's actions within the limits imposed by
legal order.

In the account of the war that ensues, the contrast between the
count's adherence to the governing principles and values of the feudal
world of the aristocracy, on the one hand, and the goals that shape
the royal exercise of power, on the other, is sharpened. When at last
Ralph, castellan of Boves and ally of the Flemish count, closes the
castle doors against Philip Augustus, the king rejoices, "car or avoit
il trouve voye par laquelle il monstreroit sa force et ce qu'il avoit
pieca en pensee, il demoustreroit vertu et prouesce" (for now he
had found a way to show his force, and he would demonstrate his
strength [*vertu*] and prowess, as he had had it in mind for a long
time).[119] Alongside the more obvious explanation of Philip Augustus's
political motives for wishing to engage the enemy is found the
argument (already present in the *Philippide*) that prowess, if unexer-
cised, will "dry up" and wither away, while contrarily, when practiced, it grows in force and multiplies its fruits.[120] The passage
demonstrates the extent to which the young king had imbibed the
chivalric values of his age and desired to present himself to the
world, as the earlier passage had asserted, in the full "noblesce de sa
nouvelle chevalerie."[121]

At the siege of Boves, Philippe of Flanders challenges his royal antagonist to open combat, denigrating the practice of siege warfare
while invoking the virtues of prowess, bravery, and the pursuit of
glory to be won on the battlefield. "Departe," the count exclaims,

"huy, l'espee tranchant ce debat et de fers de lances et avec coups de fortune soit hui departie ceste guerre et affinee" (Depart, and now let the cutting sword determine this quarrel, and with iron lances and blows of fortune let this war proceed and be concluded).[122] Philip Augustus is prepared to accept the challenge to do battle, despite the fact that evening is coming on, when at the last moment the king's advisors—Guillaume, archbishop of Reims, and Thibaut of Blois—rush up. Scorning the risk involved in open battle, they advance the values of calculation, restraint, and planning in a language that emphasizes a lexicon of order and reason. Proclaims the archbishop:

> "Gentilz Roy, tel temps ne telle heure ne requiert pas bataille. Ne si puissant roy ne se doit point combatre de nuyt, aincoys convient avant ordonner et deviser ses batailles et bailler a chacune son connestable et que chacun sache quel lieu il doit tenir et qui il doit suivre. . . . Bon roy, ne te mesprise mie tant que toy qui es sire de si grant empire de gens, que tu te vueilles et ton peuple mectre en tel peril."[123]

> "Gentle King, such a time and hour is not fit for battle. A powerful king must not fight at night; rather it is appropriate for him first to order and plan his battle lines, to delegate to each its constable, so that everyone might know what place he should hold and whom he should follow. . . . Do not, you who are lord of such a great empire of men, make the mistake of placing yourself and your people in such peril."

They excoriate the young king, calling him a *vil chevalier*, ready to place his troops in danger for the sake of a misguided notion of honor, and they counsel him against *avanture*—a word redolent of chivalric pursuits—in favor of management, preservation of resources, and strategy. *Proesce*, in their mouths, loses its chivalric significance of individual prowess and acquires the connotation of calculation of advantage, consideration of the needs of state against those of personal honor. Thus, the archbishop concludes:

> "N'aviengne ore ia que France commence ores a donner cause de joye a ses ennemys. Ne se mectre a l'avanture des destinees doubteuses, comme celle qui iusques a heure a esté bien euree d'avoir victoire de ses ennemys et de mectre soubz soy le coul des orguilleux."[124]

> "Let it not happen that France now begin to give cause for joy to her enemies, nor that she place herself at the *avanture* [fortune] of dubious destinies. For France until now has been fortunate enough to have victory over her enemies and to place beneath her the necks of the proud."

Avoid, Guillaume insists, the example of Alexander, "qui tous ses chevaliers blasmoient pour ce qu'il se abatit sur ses ennemys et fut secoura de pou de ses gens" (whom all his knights blamed for the rash abandon with which he entered into war with the aid of so few men). [125]

The rejection of the example of Alexander is a rejection of that ideal, heroic world of epic and romance that Philippe of Flanders had called upon in demanding battle, made all the more pointed when we remember that in the prologue to *Perceval* Chrétien de Troyes had explicitly compared the count of Flanders with Alexander and seen in Philippe of Alsace the finest flower of contemporary chivalry. [126] It is telling that it is precisely Alexander's chivalric excess that is here castigated as unbefitting a king. The *Chronique* thus anticipates the particular inflection placed in the late Middle Ages on Alexander's *magnanimitas*, which had originally signified the Macedonian's indomitable spirit, greatness of mind, and ambitious bravery. By the end of the Middle Ages, as George Cary has demonstrated, the term, when applied to Alexander, had taken on the connotation of excess, a valor in which all thought of restraint was suppressed, hence a trait dangerous for the conduct of war and government alike. [127] The pejorative cast given to the chivalric concept of *magnanimitas* offers an indication of the relatively subtle processes by which courtly ideology was slowly undergoing revision in the light of monarchical needs and interests. The *Chronique des rois de France* represents an early instance of this transformation within the domain of historiography.

In the end, the royal victory at Boves was a bloodless one, disappointing as chivalric theater, perhaps, but politically profitable: "Qui tous rendoient a Dieu graces, qui si legierement avoit donné victoire au roy sans le blecier ne octire, et sans batailles" (All gave thanks to God that he had so easily given victory to the king, without wounding or killing him and without battle). [128] The victory at Boves is sealed with a miracle, [129] and is thus presented by both Guillaume le Breton and the Anonymous of Chantilly/Vatican as divinely mandated.

The antinomies expressed in this opening section of the *Philippide*—between feudal tradition, prowess, boldness, and chivalry, on the one hand, and royal power, calculation, and the management of resources, on the other—are repeated throughout the remainder of the narrative in a series of escalating confrontations between the king and his barons that lead to the final conflict at Bouvines. Yet with each reprise, the consequences of allegiance to the values that constitute chivalric ideology become more severe, so that the progress of the chronicle entails a deepening critique of the ethical underpinnings of courtly society.

Perhaps the clearest illustration of the affect of obedience to the imperatives of courtly conduct is provided by the struggle between Philip Augustus and Richard Lion-Heart, the outcome of which, as presented in the *Chronique*, unleashes the forces of epic *démesure*. Here, too, the precipitating issue is a question of feudal custom, in this case the king's right to receive homage and service from Richard for his continental holdings, "tel comme droicture de fie requiert" (as the law of fiefs demands),[130] homage that Richard neglects to perform. Philip was enraged by Richard's failure to fulfill his feudal obligations and

> moult lui vint a grant despit ce qu'on lui efforcoit son droit et son fief. Comme il soit grant desplaisir a si hault homme comme lui qui estoit roy de France pour requerre son droit souffrir et endurer tant d'esconduitz. Pour son fie requerre s'appareilla. Car il lui estoit chose layde des lors en avant de plus le requerre par parolles sans plus fere.[131]
>
> there arose in him a [sense] of great outrage that one went against his right and his fief. For it was a great displeasure to so lofty a man as he, who was king of France, to have to ask that his law be obeyed and to endure so much disobedience. He was prepared to demand his fief. For it appeared unseemly to him that from this time forth he should request it in words without doing anything more.

Gone are the days when French kings demanded the performance of feudal service but accepted their inability to secure it. Philip declares himself prepared to make good on all rights and dues owed the monarchy, by force if necessary.

Throughout the various stages of this struggle, the *Chronique* plays on the contradictions in courtly ideology that increasingly entrap both kings in courses of action from whose disastrous consequences there is no escape, until loyalty to chivalric notions of honor becomes a form of false consciousness. When, for example, at one point in the war between the two kings, Richard arrives at Beauvais with a small troop of soldiers to find arrayed there a large host of French forces, he is caught between his rational recognition of the danger entailed in engaging battle and his shame of flight, an inner conflict that the *Chronique* explicitly designates as one between honor and calculation:

> En ceste maniere s'esbahit le noble roy Richart de ses ennemys qu'il vit si pres qu'il n'osa assaillir. Nonobstant que la noblesse de son

cueur ne l'en laissoit pas reculer arriere. Mais il eust eu honte de
fouyr, ja soit ce qu'il y eust preu et de les assaillir ne lui estoit
prouffit. Car il n'y eust point eu de honneur. Mais au derrenier
le vaillant roy mist arrieres son prou pour foyr honte et pour
conquerir honneur que il a son povoir vouloit aquerre.[132]

In this way the noble king Richard was afraid of his enemies, whom
he saw so close by that he dared not attack. Notwithstanding, the
nobility of his heart did not permit him to withdraw. But he was
ashamed to flee, although it would have been more advantageous,
and there was no profit in attacking them. Because there would have
been no honor in it [i.e., flight]. But in the end the valiant king put
aside his advantage to flee shame and to conquer honor, which he
wished to acquire with his power.

Contrasted here is Richard's pursuit of *preu* (advantage) and *prouffit*
(profit) with *prouesce*, through the suggestion that Richard will abandon his *preu* for the sake of prowess and honor. Thus inflamed by *hardiesce* and *prouesce*, Richard commits his knights to a doomed fight,
only to watch them be cut down and lost.[133]

Yet this is not the end of it, for in seeking to avenge his defeat, the
English king is led to greater and greater excesses, which in turn call
forth a reciprocal chain of cruel and unjust acts on the part of the
French king. When Philip Augustus defeats the Welsh mercenary
forces whom Richard had called to his aid, Richard strikes back in a
frenzy by throwing from a high rock overlooking the Seine three
French prisoners whom he happened to have in his guard.[134] As if this
were not enough to sate his anger, he had the eyes of fifteen prisoners
gouged out and sardonically returned the blinded men to Philip under
the guidance of a one-eyed knight, whose partial sight had been preserved for just this purpose. So provoked, Philip retaliated in kind,
drowning three and blinding fifteen English prisoners, who were
similarly led back to Richard by the wife of one of them. And the king
did this "affin que aucun ne cuidast qu'il fust de mendre courage ne
mendre force ne moins hardy que le roy Richart" (so that no one
would think that he had less courage or was less bold [*hardy*] than
Richard).[135]

On this spurious battlefield of matched cruelties and injustices,
the meaning of honor and courage is deformed and the pursuit of
proesce and *hardiesce* leads to epic *démesure*. The world of chivalric
actors turns against itself in a demonic rage that will ultimately
consume it, "car leur fait les ayde mieulx a les deffouler et abatre"
(for their deeds cause them to stumble and be brought down).[136] Even

the king is not free of the seduction of the chivalric code, but the clear message of the *Philippide* is that to rule successfully he must become so.

Repeatedly, assent to the dictates of *proesce* proves to be the way of disaster, for it blinds men just as surely as Richard had blinded his prisoners to the true needs of society and diverts them from the recognition of their proper interests. The moral vision of the battle-field as an arena of personal honor and glory, so crucial to the ethical imagination of the aristocracy, has become a darkened realm of self-deceit and blind failure, incapable of sustaining the meaningful pursuit of chivalric action within the terms set forth by traditional chivalric morality.

A final, and tragic, instance of the way in which codes of chivalry have become emptied of meaning and serve only to beguile and mislead those who honor them is furnished by the case of the young Arthur of Brittany. Before the siege of Mirabeau, Arthur begs his Poitevin knights to forbear attacking the castle in which Eleanor of Aquitaine awaits the arrival of her son, King John, until Philip Augustus can send reinforcements to aid them. His speech rehearses the arguments advanced by Guillaume of Reims to the young Philip Augustus before the battle of Boves, for he counsels restraint, discretion, and the consideration of advantage in a discourse of reason:

> "O nobles barons de quelle prouesce et de quelle valeur Poictou est renommé par tout le monde et de qui la puissance et la vertu est souvent esprouvee en maintes grans cops.
>
> "Vous cognoissez bien et savez quant qu'il convient a guerre et bien appercoit voustre discrection les avantures qui peuvent avenir. . . . Parquoy je dy en conseil et le loe pour nostre prou, que . . . nous les actandons troys jours. Pour voir trop petit d'actancte est demeure de temps et si fait mainteffoys grant bien et pour mieulx saillir les sailleurs s'esloignent mainteffoys et le sage enseigne à eschiver les dommages qui pevent avenir."[137]

> "Oh noble barons of such prowess and valor [for which] Poitou is renowned throughout the world and whose power and strength is often tested in many huge blows.
>
> "You know only too well what is needed to make war and your discretion clearly perceives the outcomes that can arrive. . . . Therefore I say in council and advise it for the sake of our advantage, that . . . we wait three days. In truth, this is a very little delay and length of time, and it can achieve many times its worth; to better attack besiegers often withdraw, and the wise man teaches [us] to avoid harm that can arrive."

But the Poitevin lords, "les meilleurs chevaliers du monde," belittling his caution and mocking the cowardly King John, urge instead immediate attack. "By such words they enflamed the heart of the young *chevalier* [Arthur] and made him bolder and more greedy for victory, *comme jouvencel eschauffé de la première vertu.*"[138] Predictably, the attack on Mirabeau results in Arthur's capture and eventual murder at the hands of the despised John, disclosing the fatal logic of a chivalric *vertu défrenée*, which cannot be avoided even by the circumspect Arthur.

Taken together, these episodes give voice to a profound critique of the ethical structure of chivalric ideology, which, by the reign of Philip Augustus, had come to prize above all else courage and what Duby has called the "arabesques of boldness."[139] As such, they are also a powerful criticism of the cultic world of the feudal aristocracy based on chivalric morality and on a courtly model of socially derived value. In this world, as Simon de Montfort makes clear in his speech to the host assembled for the Albigensian Crusade (recounted somewhat later in the *Chronique des rois de France*), the greatest moral failure is occasioned through derogation from ancestral honor. Simon begins his exhortation to his companions in arms by recalling their descent from the noble lineage of Troy and their chivalric legacy as the heirs of Charlemagne, Roland, and Oliver, thus summoning up the primary historical myths of descent—the Trojan and Carolingian—in medieval France:

> "O mes barons chevaliers extraitz de la noble lignee de Troye, heritiers de Charles le puissant et de Rolant et du fort Ogier qui pour la foy de Jhesucrist deffendre et exaulcer avez laissez femmes et enfans et voustre doulce contree, voz villes, voz terres et voz amys. . . ."

> "Oh my barons, knights descended from the noble line of Troy, heirs of Charles the powerful and of Roland and of the strong Ogier, who in order to defend and exalt the faith of Jesus Christ have left behind wives and children and your sweet country, your towns, your lands, and your friends. . . ."

To this is added an invocation of the great tradition of biblical warriors—the "saints hommes de jadis des chevaliers de Dieu" (holy men of yesteryear, the knights of God) such as Judas Maccabee, Jonathan, and Simon—thus underscoring the sacred character of chivalric pursuits undertaken in defense of the church and its teachings.

But more important for Simon de Montfort than the aura of sanctity that crusading ventures cast upon the exercise of arms are the imperatives of lineage, in which personal honor and family pride demand the performance of consummate acts of valor, however dangerous the undertaking or tragic the consequences. Thus, he continues by warning the "barons" and "chevaliers" who follow him:

> "Ayez memoire de vos peres et de voz successeurs dont vous estes yssuz et extraitz. Or vous gardez de forligner, et ceulx de nostre contree dont tant de bons chevaliers sont yssuz et extraitz, que par avanture, dont Dieu vous gard et deffende, mauvais reproche ne viengne de vous à voz amys ne à nostre contree."[140]

> "Remember your fathers and your successors, from whom you are issued and descended. Now take care not to fail [them], and those of our country, whence so many good knights have come forth and descended, that by chance, from which may God guard and defend you, no ill reproach may stem from you to your friends nor to your country."

Where Guillaume le Breton's Latin poem says only *ne patres sibi dissimiles*,[141] Simon's speech yields the verb *forlignier*: to degenerate from the virtues of one's ancestors, to fail the traditions of the lineage. His exhortation is based on the assumption of an inherited virtue, existing in all heirs and needing only to be called forth to be mobilized.

Yet, the *Philippide* seems to argue, this has become a world in which fidelity to ancestral traditions of honor and obedience to feudal custom and usage no longer guarantee protection against the forfeiture of rights and possessions or success in the prosecution of one's causes. Blinded to its true purposes, the feudal aristocracy has dethroned prudence, wisdom, and justice in a specious glorification of honor and has become, therefore, the agent of its own imminent defeat at Bouvines.

One of the clearest demonstrations of this development in the *Philippide* is provided by the case of Renaud of Boulogne. Renaud, whose constant defections between the parties of the king and his antagonists gave new meaning to the medieval definition of treachery, was nonetheless acknowledged by all (including Guillaume le Breton) for his exemplary military performance on the field of Bouvines. Unrivaled in the courage and prowess with which he wielded arms in battle, Renaud is, however, in Guillaume's view, fatally marred by pride and recklessness, which lead him to betray his lord and join the losing side.

The issue that opened the final breach between the count and monarch was Philip Augustus's confiscation in 1211 of Renaud's castle of Mortain in Normandy, on suspicion of Renaud's intended betrayal. When Renaud declined to render the castle to the king, Philip had him declared forfeit of both the castle of Mortain and the county of Boulogne, taking Mortain into his own hands and assigning Boulogne to Prince Louis, who, as lord of Artois, was the count of Boulogne's immediate overlord. Renaud, in response, rejoined the English coalition, remaining henceforth an implacable enemy of the Capetian king.

In a long apostrophe addressed to the count, in which Guillaume le Breton assumes authorial omniscience and foretells Renaud's defeat at the battle of Bouvines, the royal chaplain excoriates Renaud for his treachery in abandoning the royal cause, and for his pride and rashness, which lead him to misperceive the correct course of action and hence cause his downfall. In a faithful translation of Guillaume's text, the *Chronique* continues with the assertion that, blinded by pride, Renaud has failed to understand that

> se tu venisses humblement et doulcement mis au bas ton orgueil a tousiours, te laissast [the king] sa paix et te rendroit et plus te donneroit encores.

> if you would come humbly and gently lay down your pride forever, the king would grant you his peace and would render to you [your possessions] and would even give you more.

But the count turned an obdurate ear on those who counseled him to repair his break with the king: "Et des ce que tu ne veulx croyre bon conseil, aincoys de ton cueur endurcy, tu cours a ton esciant a ton dommage" (And since you do not wish to believe good counsel, but rather harden your heart, you run to your ruin knowingly). From Renaud's stubborn pride and rejection of reason flow the consequences that await him at Bouvines:

> Va donc et cueilla [*sic*] verge dont tu soies batu et tire avec toy et ducs et contes et barons a la mort. Et par le venim de ta langue met en liens avec toy les cueurs de plusieurs, lesquelz comme avuglez ne voient mie le peril ou tu les moynes ne n'appercoivent pas la meschance que Fortune leur a apparaillé.[142]

> Go then and gather rods by which you shall be beaten and drag along with you dukes and counts and barons to their death. And by the poison of your tongue bind to you the hearts of many, who, like the blind, fail to see the peril into which you lead them and do not perceive the unhappiness that Fortune has prepared for them.

The repercussions of Renaud's rash actions are not confined to him alone, but embroil all those similarly motivated by false pride and arrogant disregard of rational counsel. However high their lineage, great their prowess, firm their convictions in the putative justice of their cause, their resolute rebellion against their proper overlord will cause them "to stumble and be brought down." The *orgueil* that so misleads Renaud and his allies to their ultimate demise is no longer the sinful pride of rebellion against God, but a secularized desire for independence, an unwillingness to submit to the will of the king. In the eyes of Guillaume le Breton and his vernacular translator, aristocratic aspirations for autonomy constitute a rejection of those tenets of loyalty, obedience, and, above all, subordination on which the Capetian monarch newly insisted and whose infraction he was prepared to punish with all the force at his disposal.

Against this image of an aristocratic world ensnared within a web of false consciousness and internal contradictions, the *Philippide* poses that of the king and his court, a world of rising monarchical power in constant strife with the feudal aristocracy. Only by learning to disengage and distance himself from the values of aristocratic society can the king triumph over his adversaries. Thus, the progress of the historical narration entails not just a devaluation of chivalric morality, but a complementary valorization of a new set of royal virtues, one that places the claims of state above those of personal honor, that demands loyalty, obedience, and subordination, and that seeks to "mectre soubz soy le coul des orgueilleux."[143] Here, action is guided not by the promptings of inherited status or the demands of honor, but by counsel. Not the old Frankish and feudal *concilium*, given and received according to custom, with its legal and potentially constitutional edge, its ritual function in open, public assemblies, but the counsel of creatures of the king, of a private, domestic, even familial order, furnished by an incipient service aristocracy that, already by the time of Philip Augustus, had succeeded in supplanting the barons and prelates in the royal court and in the court of the king's mind. That this represents a departure from the practices of former Capetian kings is made abundantly clear in the *Chronique*, which earlier had praised Philip's father, Louis VII, for his habit of always taking counsel from the prelates and barons of the realm:

> De ce se conseilla le roy a ses evesques et a ses barons. Et jasoit ce que nul ne doubtast qu'il ne fust plain de moult grant sens, nonobstant si ordonnoit il tousiours les plusieurs choses par le conseil de plusieurs de ses gens.[144]

> About this the king took counsel with his bishops and his barons. And, although no one doubted that he was full of very great sense, notwithstanding he always ordered various things according to the counsel of several of his men.

Moreover, the *Chronique* points out, Louis's adherence to taking counsel stemmed both from his personal humility and from a deep commitment to the *usage* and *coustume* of the realm, for he knew perfectly well that "de ce qu'il eust peu faire à son voloir comme sire" (although he could have done as he wished as lord), he preferred "se conseilloit à ses subgetz" (to take counsel with his subjects).[145]

Not so Philip Augustus. The architects of royal victory at Bouvines are precisely those base-born men and administrative *arrivistes* whom the Anonymous of Béthune, in his *Chronique des rois de France*, had characterized as *un gras chevalier, un petit chevalier*, and one *de basse gens*. In the *Philippide* they are named—Walter the Chamberlain, Barthélemy of Roye, and Guerin of Senlis—and the *Chronique* describes them as:

> Ceulx qui tousiours est [*sic*] avec le roy en guerres, et en batailles, et en ostelz et en palais, et ne souloit guieres aler nulle part sans eulx. Car ceulx pour voir souloient estre et aler avec lui plus continuellement que nul autre et lui aidoient et de conseil et de chevalerie et de quant que chacun d'eulx povoit. . . . Car à ces troys en qui il croyoit moult il souloit prendre son conseil et descouvrir son cueur de ce qu'il vouloit faire.[146]

> Those who are always with the king in wars, in battles, and in his hostels and his palaces, for he was scarcely accustomed to go anywhere without them. For these in truth were accustomed to be and to go with him more continually than any other and aided him with both *conseil* and *chevalerie* and in any way that each of them could. . . . Because in these three in whom he believed the most, the king was accustomed to take his counsel and to open his heart concerning what he wanted to do.

It is they, and especially Guerin, who at the battle of Bouvines see to it that the royal forces before the opening of combat are "arrayed and ordered each one in his battle line, knights of great prowess and inspired by boldness [but now disciplined by royal supervision], who maintained their lines closely pressed together [i.e., collectively] and held themselves at the ready to fight and run against the enemy whenever the trumpets would sound the call to battle."[147] As at Boves, so at Bouvines, royal victory is sealed with miracles, compelling testimony to the divine will that guides the king's cause.

By Bouvines, Philip Augustus had learned his lesson well. His triumph is the triumph of management and planning over *proesce* and *hardiesce*; of the collectivity over the individual; of, in effect, the bureaucratic state over the feudal aristocracy. Philip's lesson is also the lesson of the *Philippide* and the intended lesson of the *Chronique des rois de France*. Even before he had discovered a text of the *Philippide*, the Anonymous of Chantilly/Vatican had expressed his desire to write a life of Philip Augustus, which he believed merited treatment because "the king strove to augment and pacify the realm."[148] He prays that God might "give to Philip a good and long life, so that the enemies of the crown might, with God's grace, be severely afflicted and *mis soubz ses piez*."[149] What is involved here, both in the translation of the *Philippide* and in the *Chronique des rois de France* as a whole, is an extended metaphor for the shift from feudal to administrative kingship that characterized the governmental innovations of the reign of Philip Augustus.[150]

The defeat of the aristocracy at Bouvines is a defeat for those codes of conduct and ethical aspirations that had for so long served to define the aristocracy's sense of itself and its role in feudal society, but which now stand revealed as dysfunctional in a new era of monarchical consolidation and authority. The contradiction between the high ideals of courtly ideology and the realities of royal power can no longer be masked, and the futility of persevering in the defense of chivalric values is all too patent. Even the king must abandon his allegiance to chivalric notions of honor and glory. Neither he nor his barons can maintain the pretense that he is a *primus inter pares*, a *chevalier* among *chevaliers*, for he now has his foot too firmly set upon the neck of the proud.

ᚱ᚜᚛

The critical task facing the king after defeating his enemies on the field of battle was to overcome any bitterness that the aftermath of war might leave and to reconcile the rebellious barons to the exercise of royal authority. Conquered enemies had to be converted to loyal supporters and persuaded of the legitimacy and justice of Capetian rule, to which, henceforth, they were compelled to submit. Guillaume le Breton and his Old French translator were keenly aware of this need, and it forms a counterpoint in the *Philippide* to the saga of the king's victory.

The account of Philip's conquest and assumption of royal authority over Normandy at Rouen in 1205 offers a good example of the care the royal chroniclers took to underline the king's efforts to reconcile his opponents by convincing them of the beneficence of Capetian government. The *Philippide* painstakingly rehearses the city's hostility to the prospect of incorporation into the Capetian realm, reporting the hatred its proud inhabitants felt toward the French king:

> Surquetout, l'orguilleuse commune de celle cite qui avoit hayne mortelle a nostre roy vouloit mieulx estre vaincue a force que soy soubz mectre de son gre a sa seigneurie, ne le recevoir a amour.

> Above all, the proud commune of this city, which mortally hated our king, preferred to be vanquished by force than to submit itself willingly to his lordship, or to receive him in love.

Inevitably, the city fell to the king's superior strength and was compelled to witness the demolition of its walls, ordered by Philip Augustus so that it would not be tempted to rebel against him, "ne oster le jou de la seigneurie de soubz eulx" (nor to remove the yoke of lordship from them). Unable to escape the imposition of royal authority, Rouen and all Normandy "furent contraints a le servir et lui obeyr comme a leur propre roy qu'il estoit" (were constrained to serve and obey him as their proper king, which he was).[151]

After recounting the submission of Normandy, the *Philippide* goes back to the time of Charles the Simple and repeats the earliest history of the county, narrating the story of how Rollo received Normandy from Charles and subsequently married his daughter, whose heirs held Normandy thereafter, until God "la rendit au bon et sage roy Phelipe par maintes guerres et par grans poines qu'il y souffrit" (gave it to the good and wise King Philip through many wars and by the great difficulties that he suffered there). The purpose of this journey into the past is to confirm the legitimacy of the king's claim to the duchy and to demonstrate that the institution of French rule over Normandy represents not a new conquest, but its reintegration into the "corps du royaume."[152]

Yet Philip Augustus does not rest with this display of his historical rights to Normandy, however valuable they are in establishing the legitimacy of his conquest. Instead, he actively seeks to win over the Rouennais:

> Mais le bon roy Phelipe leur voulut mieulx estre debonnaire que moustrer cruaulte et pour les acoustumer de l'amer petit a petit les traicta doulcement qu'ilz ne se plaingnissent d'estre grevez ne adestroit de nouvelles coustumes. Car comme sage il leur octroya de tenir telles loys et telz coustumes et leur conferma generallement comme ilz avoient tenues devant.[153]

> But the good king Philip preferred to be merciful to them [rather] than to show cruelty, and in order to accustom them to love him

little by little he treated them gently so that they would not complain of having new customs imposed on them. For, like a wise man, he granted them [the right] to maintain such law and such customs and generally confirmed them as they had been held before.

Philip's preservation of Norman custom, with a few exceptions duly noted in the *Philippide*, and his "doux" treatment of his new subjects lest he give them cause for complaint point to a king not so much mindful of the legal rights of those entrusted to his care as conscious of the need to reconcile the vanquished to his rule in order that they might, as the *Philippide* asserts, "serve and obey him as their proper king."

Philip Augustus was willing to show royal mercy even to his most bitter enemies, such as Renaud of Boulogne. Renaud, the *Philippide* reminds the reader, deserved to be killed and have his land taken away from his heirs for his *mesprison* toward the king. Indeed, Guillaume le Breton had reported some refinements in the tradition of disposing of traitors available to Philip, such as placing the offender in a sack with a monkey and a serpent and then throwing them bound together into the sea, whereupon the serpent entered the body of the condemned man "o par la boiche ou par lou darrier" (through the mouth or the rear).[154]

But the "bons roy" wished to show himself "feiaus" toward his "home non feoill." Philip therefore promised to pardon Renaud of Boulogne if the count would swear to be faithful in the future, since, the king professed to his quondam vassal, "no one had been as great a friend to us than you."[155] Renaud, therefore, was placed in a "legiere prison," on the expectation that his fidelity to the king was finally assured. Within three days, however, Renaud, traitorous to the end, sent secret letters to the Emperor Otto "contre le roi et contre le regne." Only at this point was the king's patience with his treacherous ally finally exhausted, and Renaud was condemned to languish in prison at Péronne until his death.

Having thus disposed of his enemies, mercifully and with justice, the king at last commemorated his hard-earned victory, parading through the streets of Paris in a triumph reminiscent of Roman generals returning from war. As Duby has argued, Philip Augustus's celebration of a triumph after the battle of Bouvines offered up a new image of the French monarchy, in which the Capetian king had at last succeeded in disengaging himself from membership in any of the three orders—"those who pray, those who fight, and those who work"—by which medieval society conventionally designated its social structure.[156] After Bouvines, the king stood outside and above the realm, its undisputed head and lawful sovereign. The royal triumph at Bouvines marks that moment when political power and authority passed decisively and irretrievably into the hands of the French monarchy. For the defeated northern French aristocracy, it similarly marked a turning point, demonstrating unmistakably that the era of uncontested aristocratic domination over medieval society had come to a close.

Confronted by the king's superior power, French nobles had little alternative but to reconcile themselves to the political realities of their age. For monarchy and aristocracy alike, vernacular historiography functioned as a central arena for negotiating such a reconciliation. The *Chronique des rois de France* of the Anonymous of Chantilly/Vatican represents the first effort of royalist historians to present to an aristocratic audience in the language of their class a new image of Capetian government in order to reconcile those most affected by royal centralization to the "new order of things," to proclaim not only the power of monarchy but its inhering righteousness as well.

Fifty years later, the *Grandes chroniques de France* would complete this process. But if we ask ourselves why the monks of Saint-Denis, after compiling an extensive series of Latin chronicles, should have undertaken to translate its Latin corpus into the vernacular, that decision must now be seen in dialectical relation to the prior development of vernacular historiography. As Sayers remarked, the *Grandes chroniques* signal "the recognition by the French monarchy and its ecclesiastical affiliate of the role of vernacular historical literature in the life of the newly constructed state and represent the initial step in the decisive orientation of the historical interests of the lettered public toward the France of the Capetian monarchy."[157] Like the work of the Anonymous of Béthune and the *Chronique des rois de France,* the *Grandes chroniques* spoke to the aristocracy in the language of its class and on the subject from which it drew its own sense of identity. Building on the themes and historical material of its vernacular predecessors, the *Grandes chroniques* sought to forge a new vision of the French past.

This vision, as it as elaborated by the monks of Saint-Denis, was unmistakenly royal in character, casting back upon the contested past of French history the long shadow of the king, who emerges from its pages as the principle of the unity of the realm. As a Venetian ambassador remarked at the beginning of the sixteenth century, "There are states more fertile and richer than France, such as Hungary and

Italy. There are greater and more powerful states, such as Germany and Spain; but none is so thoroughly unified."[158] In France, the king dominates the crown as the principle of French community, emerging "as the sole symbol of unity in the kingdom, far above the many communities it ruled."[159] There was no tension in France between dynastic patriotism and popular nationalism, and the cult of kingship, of the king as *pater patriae*, evolved naturally and without strain into a patriotic cult of the kingdom of France.[160]

In this evolution, vernacular historiography played a part. The language of the chronicles is filled with references to "France" and "li Franceis" that reveal a new consciousness of the nation as a historical entity. Vernacular chronicles bestowed upon the maturing state a sense of historical identity. Thirteenth-century Capetian monarchs, Strayer once remarked, "had to invent the France which they claimed to rule . . . they had to expand the idea of France to make it match the expansion of their own power."[161] France in the thirteenth century was no longer the feudal monarchy of Louis VI, nor yet the absolute monarchy of the Ancien Régime, but something in between, "still medieval but already modern."[162] It was, essentially, a developed monarchical state with claims to national loyalty. Beginning with the *Chronique des rois de France* of the Anonymous of Chantilly/Vatican and continued more fully in the *Grandes chroniques*, royal historiography in the vernacular helped to construct a new vision of history more appropriate to the operation of the emerging national monarchy in the thirteenth century. In that sense, thirteenth-century vernacular historiography provides us with an important point of access to the medieval shaping of literary frames—figurations of collective life—for the perception, recording, and revision of social experience.

Epilogue

In a given country's history of historical writing, relatively few periods witness the foundation of a new structure of historical memory, a vision of the past sufficiently strong and durable that it establishes a veritable canon of historical thought and writing, shaping for centuries to come a nation's consciousness of its course of development and essential character. France, in the opinion of Pierre Nora, has witnessed only three such historiographical transformations during the entire span of her history. The first of these occurred with the redaction of the *Grandes chroniques de France* at the Abbey of Saint-Denis in the thirteenth century.[1] The *Grandes chroniques* condensed the genealogical and dynastic memory of France into a simple edifice that inaugurated a new understanding of French history as the history of the *trois races* of kings: Merovingians, Carolingians, and Capetians. The appearance of the initial installment of the *Grandes chroniques de France* in 1274, therefore, represents a significant moment not merely in the history of medieval France, but in the unfolding of French historical consciousness.

The *Grandes chroniques de France* provided both a fundamental record of French royal history in the Middle Ages and an implicit body of doctrine concerning the function of monarchy in the life of the nation. In recounting the history of French kings, the monks of Saint-Denis framed a context in which the changing nature of the French monarchy could be related to the past, a past that conferred retrospective legitimacy on the monarchy and thus aided in the expansion and definition of the state that constitutes an essential aspect of the political history of France in the Middle Ages. The ideological elements that formed a permanent part of the chroniclers' view of

French kingship helped to clarify for the nation the inner meaning of French history, which was a shared legacy of the past to all who acknowledged their membership in a "French" realm ruled over the centuries with apparent justice and wisdom by the kings of France.[2]

Already present in the Grandes chroniques is the basic articulation of French medieval history as a dynastic chronicle narrating the succession of kings from Pharamond forward, with critical nodal points of meaning clustered around a few hallmark figures, principally Clovis, Charlemagne, Philip Augustus, St. Louis, and Philip the Fair. As Michel Tyvaert has demonstrated, both the structure and sense of critical conjuncture around these select figures continued unchanged until the seventeenth century.[3] In many ways, a comparable structure and rhythm of French history can still be found in Robert Fawtier's Les rois Capétiens, first published in 1960 and reissued in both French and English several times since. A durable canon, indeed. It is, thus, of more than passing interest to inquire, if only fleetingly, into the forces that helped to shape the Grandes chroniques and the tradition of French royal historiography for which it stands.

All scholars agree that Primat's history, although structured around the genealogy of the three "races" of French kingship, is as much a saga of the French nation as it is a chronicle of the kings of France.[4] To the extent that French history was understood to begin with the Trojans, the origins of France went back to a period that antedated the institution of kingship. In the beginning was the nation, not the monarchy. Only later did the princes and people determine to set a king over them as lord and ruler "like other nations."[5] The legendary origin of the French monarchy with the election of Pharamond postdates the legendary origin of the French people with the exile of the Trojans after the fall of Troy, their wanderings in Sicambria, and eventual migration to the Seine Valley.

To be sure, Primat's historiographical goals in compiling the Grandes chroniques were thoroughly royalist in inspiration, and his roman des roys, as the medieval manuscripts most often termed it,[6] was precisely that: a vernacular history of the kings of France, whose rulership over the French realm owed more to the grace of God than to the election of the people. Hedged round with the aura of sacred kingship and exercising a dynastic right to the throne of France, the French monarchy quickly liberated itself from its dependency on popular election, which disappears from the Grandes chroniques almost as soon as it is mentioned.[7] If the participation of the "people" in the election or, more aptly, acclamation of French kings is occasionally still mentioned, the "people" so designated represent a small elite of princes and barons, who alone play a role alongside the king as actors in the medieval drama of French history recorded in the *Grandes chroniques*. Nonetheless, as Bernard Guenée has recently stressed, "ce rôle, à côté du roi et parfois même avant le roi, est primordial. . . . Tout au long de l'histoire de France, les 'barons' pèsent d'un poids décisif. L'oeuvre de Primat c'est le roman des rois, l'histoire du royaume, mais aussi l'épopée des barons du royaume."[8]

It is difficult not to see in Primat's intense concern to integrate the French nobility into the chronicle of royal history a reflection of that impulse toward reconciliation which, I am arguing, figures as a primary factor in the rise of royally sponsored vernacular historiography in thirteenth-century France. In recounting the history of the kings of France in Old French prose, the *Grandes chroniques* and its literary heirs adopted a language and literary form first devised for the elaboration of a historiography of resistance to royal authority. Historical writing in Old French prose had begun as the historiography of a lost cause, offering a threatened elite a vehicle through which to recuperate a sense of social worth and political legitimacy. The French aristocracy's romancing of the past, in that sense, entailed both the *mise en roman*—the recasting of historical writing into Old French—and the quest for a lost world of chivalric power, ethical value, and aristocratic autonomy, all of which had been severely undermined by the growth of royal government in the thirteenth century.

It is significant that the vast bulk of the texts treated in this study originated in an area of intense political conflict during the latter half of Philip Augustus's reign, and it is doubly significant that the majority of the *known* patrons of the earliest histories can be shown to have belonged to the English—that is, anti-Capetian—party in Flanders. The highly restricted geographical scope of the patronage phenomenon, in my opinion, provides the key to what is fundamentally at issue in this body of texts. For these patrons, sponsorship of vernacular histories written down in the "truthful" language of prose became a means of asserting the truthfulness of aristocratic ideology, which, precisely because it was "true" in the past, bore an inherent, and historically validated, legitimacy. In this way historical discourse inscribed both in its content and in its linguistic code an ideologically motivated argument about the historical necessity for the aristocracy to preserve its status and functional role in medieval society.

With the expansion of the aristocracy's interest in the past to include the history of classical antiquity, and principally that of Rome under Caesar, vernacular historiography found an analogue of the aristocracy's present crisis, and thus a means to address the most troubling issues confronting contemporary French society. The ancient past was transfigured into an image of medieval chivalry, making clear the political preoccupations that subtended such a rewriting of history. The conflation of classical past and contemporary chivalry argued for the historical antiquity of the aristocracy's social ethics and military roles and sought to legitimize its claim to an autonomy that was at once cultural and political. Yet in the end, ancient history proved unable to offer either emotional solace or historical precedent for a resurgent aristocracy, for the classical past of Rome disclosed the same complexities and contradictions that menaced aristocratic life in the thirteenth century.

With the emergence of the contemporary chronicle, vernacular historiography consolidated its generic identity, while at the same time bringing the contested nature of past and present to the fore as the focus of historical narration. This contested past, as set forth by a chronicler such as the Anonymous of Béthune, challenged royal legitimacy by offering an account of both past and present that was no longer exclusively monarchical. Royal historians answered this contested past by creating a historiographical corpus that not only responded to the rise of aristocratic vernacular historiography and the challenges implicit in it, but also allowed for a reconciliation of the now defeated aristocracy with an increasingly powerful monarchy by integrating aristocratic history into the framework of royal history.

Somewhat paradoxically, French kings and their propagandists, victors in the contest for power and authority that had set aristocracy and monarchy at odds for nearly a century, adopted the language and literary forms of the defeated aristocracy as the means both to conciliate the losers and to proclaim their own, newly won, hegemony over the French realm. With the creation of Old French royal historiography, the winners in this struggle for political authority absorb and revalorize the terms and language of the losers for their own purposes. The French aristocracy, no longer able to impose its needs and concerns in the governance of the realm, contributed to the dominant ideology its own defeated discourse, thus achieving on a literary level the success that eluded it on the political. From this perspective, it is hardly surprising that Primat accorded such a large place in his historical text to the nobility, for the French aristocracy constituted the first and most crucial audience for his *roman des roys*. Indeed, until well into the second half of the fourteenth century, copies of the *Grandes chro-*

niques were commissioned and circulated almost exclusively among the courts of northern France,[9] that is, among the same audiences originally responsible for the rise of vernacular prose historiography. It is, perhaps, one of the finer ironies in the history of medieval historiography that the original quest involved in the French aristocracy's romancing of the past should issue, ultimately, not in an idyll of a lost age, but in a new vision of the French nation.

The *Continuation of Aimoin* and the Sources of the Anonymous of Chantilly/Vatican

The two principal manuscripts of the *Continuation of Aimoin*—B.N. Lat 12711 and Vat. Reg. Lat. 550—differ in several ways. The Vatican manuscript omits some of the interpolations pertaining to Saint-Germain-des-Prés found in 12711, yet it also adds two texts absent in 12711: Einhard's *Vita Karoli* and the *Pseudo-Turpin Chronicle*. Although both manuscripts include material taken from Suger for the life of Louis VI, in 12711 the king's biography includes only a few chapters of Suger's *Vita*, which follow an interpolated segment due to an unknown continuator, whereas Vat. 550 possesses the whole of Suger's original work. The Vatican manuscript terminates at the conclusion of the life of Louis VI, while 12711 continues with the *Historia gloriosi Regis Francorum Ludovici Septimi*, a compound life of Louis VII comprising the fragment composed by Suger before 1151, together with an addendum written by a monk of Saint-Germain-des-Prés that carries the narrative to the birth of Philip Augustus in 1165.[1]

The Latin redactions are fundamentally similar up to the reign of Dagobert, but they diverge in their handling of Aimoin, who for his part had based his account on the chronicle of the Pseudo-Fredegarius, supplemented by additions taken from the *Liber historiae Francorum* and the *Gesta Dagoberti*. In 12711, the *Gesta Dagoberti* are introduced only after the death in 629 of Dagobert's father, Clothair—that is, at the beginning of Dagobert's reign. In Vat. 550, on the contrary, the *Gesta* begin much earlier, inserted after the chapter that treats the thirty-fourth year of Clothair's rule.[2] Notably, the Anonymous of Chantilly/Vatican follows neither 12711 nor Vat. 550 directly in this portion of his translation. Rather, he translates the text of Aimoin as found in 12711 through the forty-third year of Clothair's reign but

then, as Vat. 550 had done after the regnal year thirty-four, introduces the *Gesta Dagoberti* at folio 101v under a chapter entitled "Cy
comme le roy Dagobert fonda Saint-Denys en France." Thus, on the
basis of her detailed study of both manuscripts in relation to Chantilly
MS. 869, Gillette Labory concludes that, while it is true that the *Continuation of Aimoin* constitutes the principal source for the Anonymous, it is impossible to demonstrate that he directly translated 12711
or Vat. 550.[3] The divergence from both versions that characterizes his
handling of the *Gesta Dagoberti* appears elsewhere; indeed, beginning
with Dagobert, the Anonymous of Chantilly/Vatican increasingly departs from the chronological order given in the *Continuation of Aimoin* and enhances that source with additional material.

In the fashion of Vat. 550, the Anonymous includes a translation of
the texts of Einhard's *Vita Karoli* and the *Pseudo-Turpin Chronicle*.
This contrasts with 12711, which for the years 741–819 follows the
Annales of Einhard and then the so-called *Royal Annals*. Walpole has
identified the version of the *Pseudo-Turpin Chronicle* present in the
Chronique des rois de France as belonging to the family of texts that
he terms *Turpin I* and not—as Buridant had claimed—an independent
redaction.[4] In contrast to other portions of the *Chronique*, in this section Vatican 624 handles the Latin source in a much freer fashion than
Chantilly 869, not so much translating as combining several Latin
versions in places (e.g., in the section on the Seven Liberal Arts),
omitting certain phrases found in the Latin, and adding or embellish-
ing others.[5]

Having arrived at the year 819, B.N. Lat. 12711 returns chronologically to the beginning of the reign of Charlemagne's son, Louis the
Pious, inserting that king's biography by the Astronome. The Anonymous also follows his translations of the *Vita Karoli* and *Pseudo-
Turpin* with a translation of the Astronome, an arrangement similarly
found in Vat. 550. But, although the Anonymous follows the scheme
found in Vat. 550, neither Vatican 624 nor Chantilly 869 wholly conforms to the text found there.[6]

In addition, the Anonymous includes a work that does not figure in
either of the two Latin compilations, known as the *Conquestio Ludovici Imperatoris* or *Complainte de Louis le Pieux*, which purports to be
a complaint composed by the Emperor Louis when he was deposed and
imprisoned by his sons at Saint-Médard in Soissons.[7] This text, which
is not found in the *Vita Hludowici* or in the *De gestis Ludovici* of The-
gan, or in various contemporary *Annales*, derives from a translation
of the *Life* of Saint Sebastian, the work of Odilon, a monk of Saint-

Médard de Soissons, who lived at the end of the ninth and beginning of the tenth centuries.[8] The Anonymous introduces this text with the claim that he found it "at the end of the history of Saint-Germain-des-Prés":

> ie vous reciteré ung petit de sa [the Emperor's] prison qu'il eut la ou Lothier son filz le mist à Saint Medart de Soissons, si comme je l'ay trouvé en la fin de l'ystoire monseigneur Saint Germain des Prez si comme celuy ampereur Loys mesmes le recite et si comme il se plaint de ces filz qu'ilz contre luy se releverent.[9]

> I will recite for you a little concerning the Emperor's imprisonment, which he experienced there where his son Lothar placed him, at Saint-Médard of Soissons, as I found it at the end of the history of monseigneur Saint-Germain-des-Prés, as the Emperor Louis himself recounts it and as he complains that these sons rose up against him.

Interestingly, although the Anonymous continued to use the *Continuation of Aimoin*, after this point in his narrative he no longer cites an "ystoire Saint Germain," having here specified the precise termination of his copy of the "cronique" of Saint-Germain.[10]

Notes

INTRODUCTION

1. C. Vann Woodward, "The Lost Cause" (review of *Socialism and America*, by Irving Howe), *New York Review of Books*, 30 January 1986, p. 26.

2. Raymond Williams, *Culture* (Glasgow, 1981), p. 201; cited in Alan Sinfield, "Questions in Cultural Materialism and New Historicism: Sexualities, Imperialism, the Humanities" (typescript), p. 5.

3. Jacques Le Goff, "Social Realities and Ideological Codes in the Early Thirteenth Century: An *Exemplum* of James of Vitry," in *The Medieval Imagination*, trans. Arthur Goldhammer (Chicago, 1988), p. 181.

4. Eugene Vance, "Signs of the City: Medieval Poetry as Detour," *New Literary History* 4 (1973): 557.

5. "Literary language," Vance demonstrates, "has mechanisms of its own that allow it to register, codify, and absorb incongruities of an ethical system without ever articulating denotatively what forces are involved" (ibid., p. 559).

6. M. M. Bakhtin, *The Dialogic Imagination*, ed. Michael Holquist, trans. Caryll Emerson and Michael Holquist (Austin, 1981), p. 259.

7. Carroll Smith-Rosenberg, "The Body Politic," in *Coming to Terms: Feminism, Theory, Politics*, ed. Elizabeth Weed (New York, 1989), p. 101. I would like to thank Professor Smith-Rosenberg for letting me read her paper in draft.

CHAPTER ONE

1. On the condition of the French nobility at the beginning of the thirteenth century, see Georges Duby, "Situation de la noblesse de France au début du XIIIe siècle," in *Hommes et structures du moyen âge* (Paris,

1973), pp. 343–352; and the English translation, "The Transformation of the Aristocracy: France at the Beginning of the Thirteenth Century," in *The Chivalrous Society*, trans. Cynthia Poston (Berkeley and Los Angeles, 1977), pp. 178–185. Also useful for the social and political history of the period is the collection of articles based on a colloquium organized on the occasion of the eight hundredth anniversary of Philip Augustus's accession to the throne, *La France de Philippe Auguste: le temps des mutations*, ed. R.-H. Bautier (Paris, 1982).

2. Malcolm Parkes, "The Literacy of the Laity," in *The Medieval World*, ed. David Daiches and Anthony Thorlby (Literature and Western Civilization) (London, 1973), p. 555. See also my "Forging the Past: The Language of Historical Truth in the Middle Ages," *History Teacher* 17 (1984): 267–288.

3. This version has been edited by Ian Short, *The Anglo-Norman Pseudo-Turpin Chronicle of William of Briane*, Anglo-Norman Text Society, 25 (Oxford, 1973). See also his "A Note on the Pseudo-Turpin Translations of Nicolas of Senlis and William of Briane," *Zeitschrift für romanische Philologie* 86 (1970): 525–532. Short believes that Briane translated directly from a Latin source; André de Mandach, however, disagrees in "Réponse à M. Ian Short," *Zeitschrift für romanische Philologie* 86 (1970): 533–537.

4. Theodor Auracher published an edition of Nicolas's text based on the Paris MSS. in *Die sogenannte Poitevinische Übersetzung des Pseudo-Turpin* (Halle, 1877).

5. Ian Short found a reference to a Johannes, chaplain to Renaud of Boulogne, in the *Rotuli litterarum clausarum*, ed. Thomas Duffus Hardy (London, 1833), p. 153, for the year 1213; see Short, *Anglo-Norman Pseudo-Turpin Chronicle*, p. 7; and Ronald N. Walpole, *The Old French Johannes Translation of the Pseudo-Turpin Chronicle: A Critical Edition* (Berkeley and Los Angeles, 1976), 1:95.

6. An edition of Michel of Harnes's copy was edited by A. Demarquette in *Précis historique sur la maison de Harnes de 963 à 1230 suivi d'une version romane attribué à Michel de Harnes de la Chronique de Faux Turpin* (Douai, 1856).

7. B.N. fr. 2168, fol. 156v. This copy is written in Picard, doubtless William of Cayeux's own dialect (Cayeux is near Abbeville in Ponthieu). See Ronald N. Walpole, "Charlemagne's Journey to the East: The French Translation of the Legend by Pierre de Beauvais," *University of California Publications in Semitic Philology* 11 (1951): 440–443.

8. This version is characteristically represented by B.N. fr. 1850, first published by Frederick Wulff, *La chronique dite Turpin* (Lund, 1881); it was subsequently renamed "Turpin I" by Walpole, who has provided a critical edition based on all the extant manuscripts, together with a summary of the various recensions, in *Le Turpin français dit le Turpin I* (Tor-

onto, 1985). Additional versions of the *Pseudo-Turpin* in vernacular dialects were produced later in the thirteenth century. See chapter 2.

9. On the Anonymous of Béthune and the two histories he composed for Robert of Béthune, see below.

10. Ronald N. Walpole, ed., *An Anonymous Old French Translation of the Pseudo-Turpin Chronicle: A Critical Edition of the Text Contained in Bibliothèque Nationale MSS fr. 2137 and 17203 and Incorporated by Philippe Mouskés in His Chronique Rimée*, Medieval Academy of America, 89 (Cambridge, Mass., 1979).

11. This text remains unedited. The base manuscript of the first recension is B.N. fr. 20125. The *Histoire ancienne* was among the most popular medieval historical works and is preserved in some fifty-nine manuscripts, forty-seven of which belong to the first recension. On the manuscript tradition, see Brian Woledge, *Bibliographie des romans et nouvelles en prose française antérieur à 1500: supplément 1954–1973*, Publications Romanes et Françaises, 130 (Geneva, 1975). Although unpublished, the *Histoire ancienne* has been the object of considerable study, beginning with Paul Meyer, "Les premières compilations françaises d'histoire ancienne," *Romania* 14 (1885): 1–81. Especially useful are the studies by Guy Raynaud de Lage, "L' 'Histoire ancienne jusqu'à César' et les 'Faits des Romains,' " *Le moyen âge*, 4th ser., 4 (1949): 5–16; idem, "Les romans antiques dans 'L'histoire ancienne jusqu'à César,' " *Le moyen âge*, 4th ser., 12 (1957): 267–309; idem, "Les romans antiques et la représentation de l'antiquité," in *Les premiers romans français*, Publications Romanes et Françaises, 138 (Geneva, 1976), pp. 127–159; idem, "L'histoire ancienne," in *Dictionnaire des lettres françaises*, vol. 1: *Le moyen âge* (Paris, 1964), pp. 377–378. A detailed study of the Macedonian section and its sources is provided by D.J.A. Ross, "The History of Macedon in the 'Histoire ancienne jusqu'à César': Sources and Compositional Method," *Classica et mediaevalia* 24 (1963): 181–231. Meyer sought to identify the clerical author of the *Histoire ancienne* with Wauchier de Denain (see his "Wauchier de Denain," *Romania* 32 [1903]: 583–586), in which opinion he was joined by Ferdinand Lot ("Compte-rendu de J. Frappier: *Etude sur la 'Mort le Roi Artu*,' " *Romania* 64 [1938]: 111–122), but the reasoning behind this attribution remains unconvincing to most students of the text.

12. F. Settegast, ed., *Li hystore de Julius César: eine altfranzösische Erzählung in Prosa von Jehan de Tuim* (Halle, 1881). For an interesting discussion of Jean de Thuin, see J. Frappier, "La peinture de la vie et des héros antiques dans la littérature française du XIIe et du XIIIe siècle," in *Histoire, mythes et symboles: études de littérature française*, Publications Romanes et Françaises, 137 (Geneva, 1976), pp. 21–54.

13. L.-F. Flutre and K. Sneyders de Vogel, eds., *Li fet des Romains: compilé ensemble de Saluste et de Suetoine et de Lucan*, 2 vols. (Paris, 1937–1938). On the manuscript and textual tradition, see L.-F. Flutre, *Les*

manuscrits des Faits des Romains (Paris, 1932); and idem, *Li Faits des Romains dans les littératures française et italienne du XIIIe au XIVe siècle* (Paris, 1933). The dating of the work to 1211–1214 is discussed by K. Sneyders de Vogel, "La date de la composition des Faits des Romains," *Neophilologus* 17 (1932): 213–214, 271. Among the many studies of this history the most comprehensive is that of Jeanette M. A. Beer, *A Medieval Caesar*, Etudes de Philologie et d'Histoire, 30 (Geneva, 1976). See also Mireille Schmidt-Chazan, "Les traductions de la 'Guerre des Gaules' et le sentiment national au moyen âge," *Annales de Bretagne et des pays de l'ouest* 87 (1980): 387–407; and Paul Meyer, "Les premières compilations d'histoire ancienne," 1–32. On the public for ancient history and on the later use of the *Faits des Romains*, see Jacques Monfrin, "Les traducteurs et leur public en France au moyen âge," in *L'humanisme médiéval dans les littératures romanes du XIIe au XIVe siècle*, ed. A. Fourrier (Paris, 1964), pp. 247–262; Bernard Guenée, "La culture historique des nobles: le succès des *Faits des Romains* (XIIIe–XVe siècles)," in *La noblesse au moyen âge*, ed. Philippe Contamine (Paris, 1976), pp. 261–288; and Robert Bossuat, "Traductions françaises des *Commentaires* de César à la fin du XVe siècle," *Bibliothèque d'humanisme et Renaissance* 3 (1943): 253–411.

14. The first mention of the Chantilly manuscript appeared in a review article by Ronald N. Walpole, "La traduction du Pseudo-Turpin du Manuscrit Vatican Regina 624: à propos d'un livre récent," *Romania* 99 (1978): 484–514. While engaged in a search for manuscripts of the vernacular *Turpin*, Professor Walpole noticed that the version of Turpin contained in Chantilly MS. 869, closely resembled one published in 1976 by Claude Buridant (*La traduction du Pseudo-Turpin du Manuscrit Vatican Regina 624*, Publications Romanes et Françaises, 142 [Geneva, 1976]) from a thirteenth-century manuscript preserved at the Vatican. He suggested that perhaps the Chantilly exemplar was a second copy of the text as a whole, although his own observations were confined to the section on *Pseudo-Turpin*, a new edition of which he later published as *Turpin I*. The existence of the Vatican manuscript was first noted by Elie Berger in 1879 ("Notice sur divers manuscrits de la Bibliothèque Vaticane," *Bibliothèque des Ecoles Françaises d'Athènes et de Rome* 6 [1879]: 10), but it was not until Pierre Botineau undertook a complete study of it that its importance as one of the earliest histories of France in Old French was appreciated; see his "L'histoire de France en français de Charlemagne à Philippe-Auguste: la compilation du MS. 624 du fonds de la reine à la Bibliothèque Vaticane," *Romania* 90 (1969): 79–99. Unfortunately, both Buridant and Botineau were unaware of the existence of the second and more complete version of the text at Chantilly. Walpole's suggestion that MS. 869 might be a second copy of the chronicle is confirmed by an examination of the work as a whole. For a full description of both manuscripts, see Ronald N.

Walpole, "Prolégomènes à une édition du Turpin français dit le Turpin I," *Revue d'histoire des textes* 10 (1980): 199–230; 11 (1981): 325–370.

15. The only complete manuscript version of the *Chronique des rois de France* is B.N. nouv. acq. fr. 6295. On the Anonymous of Béthune, see Léopold Delisle, "Notice sur la chronique d'un anonyme de Béthune du temps de Philippe-Auguste," *Notices et extraits des manuscrits* 34, pt. 1 (1891): 365–380; Paul Meyer, "Notice sur le MS. II.6.24 de la Bibliothèque de Cambridge," *Notices et extraits des manuscrits* 32, pt. 2 (1888): 37–81; Charles Petit-Dutaillis, *Etude sur la vie et le règne de Louis VIII* (1894; reprint Paris, 1964), p. xx; idem, "Une nouvelle chronique du règne de Philippe-Auguste, l'Anonyme de Béthune," *Revue historique* 50 (1892): 63–71; Ronald N. Walpole, "L'Anonyme de Béthune," in *Dictionnaire des lettres françaises*, vol. 1: *Le moyen âge* (Paris, 1964), pp. 130–131; as well as his extremely thorough and useful discussion of the place of *Turpin* in the manuscript tradition of the Anonymous's work in "Philip Mouskés and the Pseudo-Turpin Chronicle." The final, contemporary section of the Anonymous's *Chronique* is published by Léopold Delisle, ed., *Chronique des rois de France de l'Anonyme de Béthune, Recueil des historiens des Gaules et de la France* 24:750–775.

16. Anonymous of Béthune, *Histoire des ducs de Normandie et des rois d'Angleterre*, ed. Francisque Michel (Société de l'Histoire de France) (Paris, 1840).

17. Charles Petit-Dutaillis, "Fragment de l'histoire de Philippe-Auguste, roy de France: chronique en français des années 1214–1216," *Bibliothèque de l'Ecole des Chartes* 87 (1926): 98–141; and Léopold Delisle, "Chronique française des rois de France par un anonyme de Béthune (Fragment de l'histoire de Philippe-Auguste)," *Histoire littéraire de France* 32 (1898): 219–234.

18. *Les Grandes chroniques de France*, ed. J. Viard, 10 vols. (Société de l'Histoire de France) (Paris, 1920–1953). On the *Grandes chroniques*, see Gabrielle M. Spiegel, *The Chronicle Tradition of Saint-Denis: A Survey*, Medieval Classics: Texts and Studies, 10 (Brookline, Mass., 1978), pp. 72–88.

19. Henry's return of Louis's horse and accoutrements is reported by Ordericus Vitalis, *Ecclesiastical History*, ed. and trans. Majorie Chibnall (Oxford, 1978), 6:240. Suger, who covers this event in his *Vita Ludovici Grossi*, ed. and trans. Henri Waquet (Les Classiques de l'Histoire de France au Moyen Age) (Paris, 1964), p. 198, acknowledges Louis's defeat but omits the humiliating details.

20. See John W. Baldwin, *The Government of Philip Augustus: Foundations of French Royal Power in the Middle Ages* (Berkeley and Los Angeles, 1986), pp. 8–9.

21. Thus the famous story, reported by Suger (*Vita Ludovici Grossi*, p. 38), of Philip I who, when finally taking the castle of Montlhéry under his

protection, warned his son Louis VI to keep it always in his possession, since the troubles it had fomented had made it impossible for the king to travel between Paris and Orléans without attack.

22. Baldwin, *Government of Philip Augustus*, p. 13.

23. " . . . Quanto melius pretiique majoris oppidum illud existeret, tanto carius idem, cum ad manus meas devolveretur, haberem" (Gerald of Wales, *Liber de principis instructione*, ed. George F. Warner, in *Rerum Britannicarum medii aevi scriptores* [Rolls Series], 21[8], distinctio 3, chap. 25, p. 289). See also R.-H. Bautier, "Philippe Auguste: la personnalité du roi," in *La France de Philippe Auguste*, p. 35.

24. " . . . De quo rex Ludovicus, antequam natus esset, talem in somnis vidit visionem; videbatur ei quod Philippus filius suus tenebat calicem aureum in manu sua, plenum humano sanguine, de quo propinabat omnibus principibus suis, et omnes in eo bibebant" (Rigord, *Gesta Philippi Augusti*, in *Oeuvres de Rigord et de Guillaume le Breton*, ed. Henri-François Delaborde, vol. 1 [Société de l'Histoire de France] [Paris, 1882], p. 8).

25. Cf. the judgment of R.-H. Bautier: "Jamais à aucune époque de l'histoire de France, sinon au temps de Louis XI, la duplicité royale et l'absence totale de scrupules n'auront été poussées aussi loin" ("Philippe Auguste," p. 45).

26. Gastinel's comments come in the midst of a portrait of Philip Augustus that he presents at the close of his account of the king's reign; *Chronicon Sancti Martini Turonensis*, ed. M. Brial, in *Recueil des historiens des Gaules et de la France* 18:304. Cf. R.-H. Bautier, " Philippe Auguste," p. 35.

27. *Chronicon Turonensis*, p. 304.

28. *Chronique des rois de France*, p. 764.

29. See Eric Bournazel, *Le gouvernement capétien au XIIe siècle, 1108–1180: structures sociales et mutations institutionnelles* (Paris, 1975), chaps. 3 and 4.

30. Ibid., pp. 151ff. Cf. Baldwin, *Government of Philip Augustus*, p. 124.

31. Baldwin, *Government of Philip Augustus*, p. 260.

32. "Car à ces troys en qui il croyoit moult il souloit prandre son conseil et descouvrir son cueur de ce qu'il vouloit faire" (Chantilly MS. 869, fol. 378v). "Ceulx qui tousiours est [sic] avec le roy en guerres, en batailles, et en ostelz et en palais, et ne souloit guieres aler nulle part sans eulx. Car ceulx pour voir souloient estre et aler avec lui plus continuellement que nul autre et lui aidoient et de conseil et de chevalerie et de quant que chacun d'eulx povoit" (ibid., fol. 385r).

33. Baldwin, *Government of Philip Augustus*, pp. 262–263.

34. E. Bournazel and J.-P. Poly, "Couronne et mouvance: institutions et représentations mentales," in *La France de Philippe Auguste*, p. 225.

35. Cited in Baldwin, *Government of Philip Augustus*, p. 261.

36. The first writer to articulate this principle was Suger, who, in the *De Rebus in Administratione sua Gestis*, claimed that King Philip I of France would have done homage to the Abbey of Saint-Denis for the lands of the Vexin, which he held in fief from the abbot *si non rex esset* (if he were not king); in *Oeuvres complètes de Suger*, ed. A. Lecoy de la Marche (Paris, 1867), p. 162. For an explanation of Suger's reasoning, see Gabrielle M. Spiegel, "History as Enlightenment: Suger and the *Mos Anagogicus*," in *Abbot Suger and Saint-Denis: A Symposium*, ed. Paula L. Gerson (New York, 1986), pp. 17–27. For the development of the idea of royal suzerainty between the time of Suger and that of Philip Augustus, see Jean-François Lemarignier, *La France médiévale: institutions et sociétés* (Paris, 1970), pp. 256ff.

37. *Scripta de Feodis ad Regem Spectantibus et de Militibus ad Exercitum Vocandis*, ed. L. Delisle, N. de Wailly, and Jourdain, in *Recueil des historiens des Gaules et de la France* 23:605–723. Cf. Gérard Sivéry, "La description du royaume de France par les conseillers de Philippe-Auguste et par leurs successeurs," *Le moyen âge*, 4th ser., 39 (1984): 81.

38. Charles Petit-Dutaillis, *Le déshéritement de Jean Sans Terre et le meurtre d'Arthur de Bretagne: étude critique sur la formation et la fortune d'une légende* (Paris, 1925).

39. Philippe Contamine, "L'armée de Philippe Auguste," in *La France de Philippe Auguste*, p. 586–587.

40. See Georges Duby, *Le dimanche de Bouvines* (Paris, 1973), p. 104.

41. Georges Duby, "Les transformations sociales dans le milieu aristocratique," in *La France de Philippe Auguste*, p. 712.

42. Thus the famous complaint by Suger that, whereas William Rufus was rich and prodigal, a "wonderful paymaster of soldiers and expert in hiring them" (*mirabilisque militum mercator et solidatur*), the young Louis VI was forced to rely on sheer prowess and personal energy in combatting his wealthy rival; see Suger, *Vita Ludovici Grossi*, p. 8.

43. Baldwin, *Government of Philip Augustus*, p. 168.

44. Contamine, "Armée de Philippe Auguste," p. 584.

45. Guillaume le Breton, *Philippide*, in *Oeuvres de Rigord et de Guillaume le Breton*, vol. 2, chant. XI, v. 85, p. 321. Cf. Contamine, "Armée de Philippe Auguste," p. 585.

46. For a general discussion of this topic, see Gérard Sivéry, *L'économie du royaume de France au siècle de Saint Louis (vers 1180–vers 1315)* (Lille, 1984); and Robert Fossier, *La terre et les hommes en Picardie jusqu'à la fin du XIIIe siècle*, 2 vols. (Louvain, 1968).

47. Sivéry, *Economie du royaume*, chap. 3: "L'économie rurale et les prix," passim.

48. Ibid., p. 109.

49. Ibid., p. 20.

50. Fossier, Terre et hommes, pp. 607–608.
51. Ibid., pp. 609–610.
52. Duby, "Transformation of the Aristocracy," p. 184.
53. Fossier, Terre et hommes, p. 610.
54. See Sivéry, Economie du royaume, p. 128.
55. Fossier, Terre et hommes, p. 620.
56. Duby, "Transformation of the Aristocracy," p. 183.
57. Sivéry, Economie du royaume, p. 265.
58. Ibid., pp. 55, 266.
59. Ibid., p. 59.
60. Ibid., p. 25.
61. Ibid., p. 266.
62. Ibid., p. 301.
63. Ibid., pp. 52–53.
64. Ibid., p. 299.
65. Ibid., pp. 96–97.
66. Fossier places particular emphasis on the rise in salaries, which he believes so added to the expenses of rural cultivation that, more than anything else, it compromised a seigneurial lord's efforts to reestablish the equilibrium of his enterprise on the basis of a continuation of ancient domainal practices; see Terre et hommes, p. 607.
67. Sivéry, Economie du royaume, p. 132.
68. Ibid., p. 129; Fossier, Terre et hommes, p. 580.
69. Attempts to compensate for falling returns from perpetual cens by the commutation of corvées or a rise in the rate of cens in cases where a change of tenants permitted reevaluation brought Flemish lords only meager cash supplements. Greater gains could be made from terrages, rents taken in kind instead of specie, since their ultimate value reflected market fluctuations; but terrages operated principally on newly cleared land rather than the old seigneurial estates. The most successful response to the progressive decline in the value of the cens and related seigneurial revenues was to introduce the new system of short-term leases, or fermages, which allowed proprietors to revalue rents every three, six, nine, twelve, or eighteen years (see Sivéry, Economie du royaume, p. 21). But here again, it was generally churches or parvenus, newly installed on landed estates, who benefited from this development, not the nobility, whose seigneuries were structured in accordance with traditional patterns and whose exactions were limited by custom.
70. H. E. Warlop, The Flemish Nobility Before 1300, 4 vols. (Kortrijk, 1975–1976), 1:281.
71. P. Feuchère, "La noblesse du nord de la France," Annales: économies, sociétés, civilisations 6 (1951): 312n.3.
72. August Potthast, Regesta Pontificum Romanorum, vol. 1 (Graz, 1957), no. 8160, p. 703.

73. Ibid., no. 8716, p. 748. The pope, acting on behalf of the house of Béthune, instructed the appropriate ecclesiastical dignitaries to take action against the usurers to compel them to return that which they held unlawfully and, if necessary, to threaten them with the full weight of the penalties imposed for usury by the Lateran council. Ibid., no. 8819, p. 757.

74. Warlop, *Flemish Nobility* 1:282.

75. Ibid.

76. Ibid.

77. Ibid., 2:529n.308.

78. Ibid., 1:292.

79. Henri Pirenne, *Histoire de Belgique,* vol. 1 (Brussels, 1921), p. 144.

80. Chrétien de Troyes, *Le roman de Perceval (ou le conte du Graal),* ed. William Roach (Geneva, 1956), p. 1 (prologue, lines 11–15). On patronage at the court of Flanders under Philippe of Alsace generally, see Mary D. Stanger, "Literary Patronage at the Medieval Court of Flanders," *French Studies* 11 (1957): 214–229.

81. *Genealogiae Comitum Flandriae continuatio Claromariscensis Flandriae generosa,* ed. L. C. Bethmann, in *Monumenta Germaniae historica, Scriptores* 9:327 [hereafter cited as *Flandria generosa*]. Like Pirenne, the author of the *Flandria generosa* considered the rule of Philippe of Alsace one of the most important in medieval Flemish history; this chronicler eulogized the count after his death as "nobilissimus omnium qui fuerant ante ipsum in Flandria, divitiis et honoribus affluens, prudentia et potentia magnus, fervens in iustitia, fortis et probus ad arma, unique Machabeorum non inmerito comparandus" (p. 329).

82. Léon Louis Borrelli de Serres, *La réunion des provinces septentrionales à la couronne par Philippe-Auguste Amiénois, Artois, Vermandois, Valois* (Paris, 1899), pp. ix–xii.

83. Elizabeth of Vermandois's infidelity is reported in the *Vita et gestis Henrici II et Ricardi, Angliae Regum* of the so-called "Benedict" of Peterborough (ed. T. Hearne, in *Recueil des historiens des Gaules et de la France* 13:163) and in Ralph of Diceto's *Ymagines Historiarum* (in *Recueil des historiens des Gaules et de la France* 13:198). Since the lovers were discovered the same year that Elizabeth made her grant to Count Philippe, Borrelli de Serres surmises that it was the price the count extracted for her transgression; see *Réunion,* p. xxvi, n. 2.

84. Louis's was clearly an act of confirmation, despite the tendency of some historians, following Guillaume le Breton, to treat the cession of Vermandois, Amiénois, and Valois as a direct grant from the king, as Borrelli de Serres makes abundantly clear (*Réunion,* p. xxvi, n. 3).

85. *Flandria generosa,* p. 327.

86. Baldwin, *Government of Philip Augustus,* p. 6.

87. Cited in Pirenne, *Histoire de Belgique,* p. 145.

88. Borrelli de Serres, *Réunion,* p. xxiii.

89. In the Anonymous of Chantilly/Vatican's *Chronique des rois de France*, Philip Augustus is reported as proclaiming to Philippe of Alsace: "Ce que mon pere vous octroya à Rains à avoir et tenir par aucun temps ne vous puet pas garantir si brief temps que l'avez tenue. Et de ce que vous vantez que je l'ay confermé, je dy au contraire que nulle vigueur n'a d'estre tenue possession nulle qui est donnée d'enfant qui est en tutelle" (Chantilly MS. 869, fol. 334v). Cf. Guillaume le Breton, who in the *Philippide* (chant. II, lines 21–30, p. 41) pretended that Philippe of Alsace had no right to Elizabeth's lands:

> Nullo jure, nisi quod rex ad tempus habenda
> Hec eadem senior dederat Ludovicus eidem,
> Et puer acta patris rex confirmaverat illi
> De facili. Quid enim non impetrasset ab illo,
> Cujus erat tutor, didascalus atque patrinus?
> Rex super hoc semel ac iterum convenit eundem
> Ut sibi restituat ea que spectare sciuntur
> Ad fiscum proprie, nec regni jura minoret
> Que debent magis augeri de jure per illum
> Qui datus est doctor illi, custosque fidelis.

The claim that Vermandois et al. belonged to the royal domain is, of course, false, as is the notion that Philip Augustus was incompetent by reason of youth to issue legal enactments, also reported by Rigord (*Gesta Philippi Augusti*, p. 41).

90. Rigord, *Gesta Philippi Augusti*, p. 40. Cf. Borrelli de Serres, *Réunion*, p. xxxii.

91. Rigord claims that the report concerning the harvest of Boves was told to him by canons of Amiens (*canonici Ambianenses*); see *Gesta Philippi Augusti*, p. 44.

92. Alexander Cartellieri, *Philipp II. August, König von Frankreich*, vol. 1: *1165–1189* (Leipzig, 1899), pp. 126–129.

93. Philippe assigned Matilda the towns of Aire and Saint-Omer. See Thérèse de Hemptinne, "Aspects des relations de Philippe Auguste avec la Flandre au temps de Philippe d'Alsace," in *La France de Philippe Auguste*, p. 259n.23.

94. Baldwin, *Government of Philip Augustus*, p. 18.

95. This is surmised by Hemptinne, "Aspects des relations de Philippe Auguste avec la Flandre," p. 259.

96. Baldwin, *Government of Philip Augustus*, p. 18.

97. Borrelli de Serres, *Réunion*, pp. xxxviii–lx.

98. Baldwin, *Government of Philip Augustus*, p. 26.

99. Borrelli de Serres, *Réunion*, p. xl.

100. Philip's actions at this time indicate that such plans were afoot. As soon as Philippe of Alsace was safely buried, the king announced that he would leave the Holy Land and return to France at the earliest possible

moment. Meanwhile, he wrote to the nobles and bourgeois of Péronne (and probably Saint-Quentin as well) to secure their oaths of fidelity in light of the count of Flanders's death and his own hereditary claim (Borelli de Serres, *Réunion*, p. lx.) He also instructed his mother, as regent, and his uncle, the archbishop of Reims, to occupy Artois in the name of his son, Prince Louis. And, in what is perhaps the most surprising move, best known to us from the account of Gislebert of Mons, chancellor to Baldwin V of Hainaut, Philip Augustus sent envoys to Paris with orders to invade Flanders. Gislebert, who heard the news of Philip's planned attack in Italy while traveling to Rome to enter into negotiations concerning a disputed election to the bishopric of Liège, quickly dispatched a messenger to Mons, who made such good speed that he overtook the royal envoys sent by Philip, affording Baldwin advance notice of the invasion. Gislebert reports that when his party had arrived at the town of Borgo-San-Donino: "rumores de morte comitis Flandrensis certos habuerunt. Dominus etenim rex Francorum a transmarinis partibus pro tota terra comitis Flandrie occupanda milites quosdam in detrimentum comitis Hanoniensis mittebat, scilicet Petrum de Maisnil et Robertum de Waurin, Hellini senescalci fratrem, et quosdam alios, quorum quidam in Ytalia mortui sunt; sed Petrus et Robertus in Franciam et Flandriam pervenerunt. Gislebertus autem clericus rumores illos comiti Hanoniensi domino suo per festinum cursorem significavit, ita quod comes Hanoniensis rumores illos octo diebus citius prescivit, quam Franci vel Flandrenses homines prescirent; quod quidem ei profuit. Comes enim sibi providit; ita quantotius rumores ad Francos et ad Flandrenses pervenerunt, ipse terram Flandrensem iure hereditario uxorem suam Margharetam comitissam contingentem occupavit" (in *Chronicon Hanoniense*, ed. Wilhelm Arndt, *Monumenta Germaniae historica, Scriptores* 11:574). On these events see also Pirenne, *Histoire de Belgique*, p. 147.

101. Baldwin, *Government of Philip Augustus*, p. 81.

102. See ibid., pp. 99–100, for the revenues from Vermandois et al.; pp. 247–248 for those of Normandy.

103. Borrelli de Serres, *Réunion*, p. xlvi.

104. Henri Malo, *Un grand feudataire: Renaud de Dammartin et la coalition de Bouvines* (Paris, 1898), p. 52.

105. Baldwin, *Government of Philip Augustus*, p. 91.

106. Ibid.

107. Rigord's account of this breach emphasizes the disloyalty of Philip Augustus's vassals, especially Renaud, whom Philip had graciously confirmed in his possession of Boulogne, despite his forcible marriage to the heiress Ida; see *Gesta Philippi Augusti*, pp. 137–138.

108. *Chronique des rois de France*, p. 759.

109. Malo, *Grand feudataire*, p. 57.

110. Bautier, "Philippe Auguste," p. 39.

111. " . . . Dusque à Hesdin por aler destruire la terre del conte de Boloigne et la terre [del] conte de Saint Pol" (*Chronique des rois de France*, p. 759).

112. Malo, *Grand feudataire*, p. 58.

113. Cartellieri, *Philipp II. August* 1:192.

114. Malo, *Grand feudataire*, pp. 61–62.

115. *Forma Pacis facte apud Goleton inter Philippum regem Francorum et Joannem Angliae regem*, ed. M. Brial, in *Recueil des historiens des Gaules et de la France* 17:53.

116. Baldwin, *Government of Philip Augustus*, p. 96.

117. Malo, *Grand feudataire*, p. 69.

118. Warlop, *Flemish Nobility* 1:264.

119. Gaston G. Dept, "Les influences anglaises et françaises dans le comté de Flandre au début du XIIIème siècle," in *Université de Gand, recueil de travaux publiés par la faculté de philosophie et lettres*, 59 (Gand/Ghent, 1928), p. 33.

120. Ibid., pp. 74–75.

121. Roger of Wendover, *Flores historiarum*, ed. F. Liebermann and R. Pauli, in *Monumenta Germaniae historica, Scriptores* 28:45.

122. Baldwin, *Government of Philip Augustus*, p. 276.

123. Ibid., p. 203.

124. In the opinion of Cartellieri; see *Philipp II. August*, vol. 4: *1199–1223* (Leipzig, 1922), p. 309.

125. T. Leuridan, *Les châtellains de Lille* (Lille, 1873), p. 124.

126. Malo, *Grand feudataire*, p. 145; Baldwin, *Government of Philip Augustus*, p. 208. In return for his adherence to the English cause, John lavished territories upon the count of Boulogne, granting him the manors of Dunham, Kirketon, and Bampton in the county of Essex; Kirketon and Ridal in Lincolnshire; Norton and Ixning in Suffolk; and Wrestlingworth in Bedfordshire, with their rights and dependencies (see *Rotuli litterarum clausarum*, p. 116). In addition, for the other fiefs that Renaud claimed in England and Normandy, John promised him an annual rent of one thousand pounds for three years (Malo, *Grand feudataire*, p. 146).

127. Dept, "Influences anglaises et françaises," pp. 110–111.

128. Baldwin, *Government of Philip Augustus*, p. 275.

129. "Philippus . . . quod nos dilecto et fideli hostro Michaeli de Harn . . . damus sexaginta libras et decem solidos parisiensium, percipiendos annuatim in festo sancti Remigii in guionagio Perone, tenendos tam ab ipso quam heredibus ejus de uxore sua desponsata, de nobis et heredibus nostris, in feodo et hominagio" (J. Monicat and J. Boussard, eds., *Recueil des actes de Philippe-Auguste*, vol. 3 [Paris, 1966], no. 1245, p. 368). Michel of Harnes was, in fact, one of the mainstays of the French party, together with Jean de Nesles and Siger de Gand. But even Siger de Gand

attempted at this time to cross over to the English party, although he withdrew his efforts soon afterward. Both he and Jean de Nesles, castellan of Bruges, were chased from their lands in August 1213, and with their departure the French party in Flanders momentarily collapsed. See Dept, "Influences anglaises et françaises," p. 119.

130. Baldwin, *Government of Philip Augustus*, p. 209.

131. Ibid., p. 211.

132. See the letter close to Robert of Béthune in *Rotuli litterarum clausarum*, p. 133.

133. Baldwin, *Government of Philip Augustus*, p. 210.

134. Pirenne, *Histoire de Belgique*, p. 152.

135. The counts of Boulogne and Flanders, for example, ravaged the lands of Guines, settling old scores under the pretext that the count of Guines was allied with the French king; see Baldwin, *Government of Philip Augustus*, p. 213.

136. Warlop, *Flemish Nobility* 1:265.

137. Malo, *Grand feudataire*, p. 211.

138. Dept, "Influences anglaises et françaises," p. 141.

139. Pirenne, *Histoire de Belgique*, p. 154.

140. Baldwin, *Government of Philip Augustus*, p. 268.

141. Pirenne, *Histoire de Belgique*, p. 154.

142. See William C. Jordan, *Louis IX and the Challenge of the Crusade* (Princeton, 1979), chap. 3.

143. Gérard Sivéry, "L'enquête de 1247 et les dommages de guerre en Tournaisis, en Flandre gallicante et en Artois," *Revue du nord* 59 (1977): 10.

144. Ibid., p. 8.

145. Ibid., p. 9.

146. Ibid., p. 12.

147. Ibid.

148. Ibid., p. 16.

149. Ibid., p. 17.

150. Ibid., p. 11.

151. Ibid., p. 14.

152. Ibid., p. 12.

153. Dept, "Influences anglaises et françaises," p. 150.

154. Ibid., p. 151.

155. " . . . Optamus rogantes quatenus, pro loco et tempore, nobis in auxilio et consilio velitis assistere contra ipsum, qui parati sumus manum auxiliarem vobis pro viribus extendere" (Thomas Rymer, ed., *Foedera*, vol. 1 [London, 1727], p. 277).

156. Dept, "Influences anglaises et françaises," p. 149.

157. Ibid., p. 154.

CHAPTER TWO

1. On the beginning of vernacular prose historiography, see Paul Meyer, "Discours de M. Paul Meyer, membre de l'Institut, président de la Société pendant l'exercice de 1889–1890 [quelques vues sur l'origine et les premiers développements de l'historiographie française]," *Annuaire-Bulletin de la Société de l'Histoire de France* 27 (1890): 82–106; William J. Sayers, "The Beginnings and Early Development of Old French Historiography, 1100–1274" (Ph.D. diss., University of California, Berkeley, 1966); Brian Woledge and H. P. Clive, *Répertoire des plus anciens textes en prose française depuis 842 jusqu'aux premières années du XIIIe siècle*, Publications Romanes et Françaises, 79 (Geneva, 1964); Omer Jodogne, "La naissance de la prose française," *Bulletin de la Classe des Lettres et des Sciences Morales et Politiques, Académie Royale de Belgique*, 5th ser., 49 (1963): 296–308; Henry J. Chaytor, *From Script to Print: An Introduction to Medieval Literature* (Cambridge, 1945); Diana B. Tyson, "Patronage of French Vernacular History Writers in the Twelfth and Thirteenth Centuries," *Romania* 100 (1979): 180–222; Walpole, "Philip Mouskés and the Pseudo-Turpin Chronicle"; Brian Woledge, "La légende de Troie et les débuts de la prose française," in *Mélanges de linguistique et de littérature romanes offerts à Mario Roques*, vol. 2 (Paris, 1953), pp. 313–324.

2. Jodogne, "Naissance de la prose française," p. 297.

3. Ibid., p. 299. See C. A. Robson, *Maurice de Sully and the Medieval Vernacular Homily* (Oxford, 1952).

4. Woledge and Clive, *Répertoire des plus anciens textes*, p. 21.

5. Mary B. Speer and Alfred Foulet, "Is *Marques de Rome* a De-rhymed Romance?" *Romania* 101 (1980): 361. See also Wlad Godzich and Jeffrey Kittay, *The Emergence of Prose: An Essay in Prosaics* (Minneapolis, 1987), p. 81.

6. See Godzich and Kittay, *Emergence of Prose*, p. xx.

7. Cited in Peter Dembowski, "Learned Latin Treatises in French: Inspiration, Plagiarism, and Translation," *Viator* 17 (1986): 258.

8. James J. Murphy, *Rhetoric in the Middle Ages* (Berkeley and Los Angeles, 1974), p. 49.

9. On this medieval view of human language, see R. Howard Bloch, "Medieval Misogyny," in *Continuity and Change: Political Institutions and Literary Monuments in the Middle Ages*, ed. Elisabeth Vastergaard (Odense, Den., 1986), p. 107.

10. Tertullian, *The Apparel of Women* (The Fathers of the Church) (New York, 1959), p. 126. For a penetrating discussion of Tertullian's treatment of feminine adornment and its relation to the medieval discourses on both sexuality and language, see Bloch, "Medieval Misogyny." Much of the ensuing discussion is based on Bloch's article.

11. *Apparel of Women*, pp. 135–136, 131.

12. See E. Jane Burns, *Arthurian Fictions: Rereading the Vulgate Cycle* (Columbus, Ohio, 1985), p. 23.

13. J. Murphy, *Rhetoric in the Middle Ages*, p. 49.

14. See R. Howard Bloch, *The Scandal of the Fabliaux* (Chicago, 1986), p. 41. On Alain de Lille, see Jan Ziolkowski, *Alan of Lille's Grammar of Sex: The Meaning of Grammar to a Twelfth-Century Intellectual*, The Medieval Academy of America, Speculum Anniversary Monographs, 10 (Cambridge, Mass., 1985).

15. Alain de Lille, *The Plaint of Nature*, trans. and with a commentary by James J. Sheridan (Toronto, 1980), p. 134.

16. *La mort Aymeri de Narbonne: chanson de geste*, ed. J. Couraye du Parc (Société des Anciens Textes Français) (Paris, 1884).

17. See Michel Zink, "Une mutation de la conscience littéraire: le langage romanesque à travers des exemples français du XIIe siècle," *Cahiers de civilisation médiévale* 24 (1981): 3–27, for much of what follows.

18. Benoît de Sainte-Maure, *Roman de Troie*, ed. L. Constans, 6 vols. (Société des Anciens Textes Français) (Paris, 1904–1912), line 37.

19. See, most recently, Roger Dragonetti, *Le mirage des sources: l'art du faux dans le roman médiéval* (Paris, 1987), esp. chap. 2: "Citation des sources."

20. Burns, *Arthurian Fictions*, p. 19.

21. As David Hult explains, the semantic range in the word *geste*, which encompasses family, orally recounted tale, prior written text, and historical deed, results in this case in a situation in which "the documentary nature of the events and heroes is already incorporated into the narrated action, effecting a subversion of the normally intuited relationship between action and narrated account: if the present poem is based on (a) previous *geste(s)*, guaranteeing the historicity of the events, the latter are in turn predicated upon earlier written accounts"; see his " 'Ci falt la geste': Scribal Closure in the Oxford *Roland*," *Modern Language Notes* 97 (1982): 897.

22. For the existential character of oral performance, see Eugene Vance, "Roland et la poétique de la mémoire," *Cahiers d'études médiévales* 1 (1975): 103–115; and the expanded English version of this article in idem, *Mervelous Signals: Poetics and Sign Theory in the Middle Ages* (Lincoln, Neb., 1986), 51–85. See also Paul Zumthor, "The Text and the Voice," *New Literary History* 16 (1984): 67–92.

23. Zink, "Mutation de la conscience littéraire," p. 11.

24. Benoît de Sainte-Maure, *Chronique des ducs de Normandie*, ed. Carin Fahlin, 3 vols., Bibliotheca Ekmaniana, 56 (Uppsala, 1951–1979), line 2139.

25. Zink, "Mutation de la conscience littéraire," p. 15.

26. See Dominique Boutet and Armand Strubel, *Littérature, politique et société dans la France au moyen âge* (Paris, 1979), p. 12; and P. Meyer, "Discours," p. 93.

27. Franz H. Bäuml, "Varieties and Consequences of Medieval Literacy and Illiteracy," *Speculum* 55 (1980): 256.

28. *Jean Bodels Saxonlied*, vol. 1, ed. F. Menzel and E. Stengel, Ausgaben und Abhandlungen aus dem Gebiete der romanischen Philologie, 99 (Marburg, 1906), p. 11.

29. Zink, "Mutation de la conscience littéraire," p. 19.

30. Ibid., p. 20.

31. Ibid., p. 26.

32. Chrétien de Troyes, *Erec et Enide*, ed. and trans. Carleton W. Carroll, with an introduction by William W. Kibler, Garland Library of Medieval Literature, ser. A, vol. 25 (New York, 1987), lines 23–26.

33. Sayers, "Beginnings and Early Development of Old French Historiography," p. 288.

34. Cited in Bernard Guenée, *Histoire et culture historique dans l'occident médiéval* (Paris, 1980), p. 19n.20. This was, of course, a standard medieval position, which had passed into rhetorical handbooks and chronicles via Isidore of Seville, who identified truth as the characteristic separating history (*res quae factae sunt*) from fable (*fabulae vero sunt quae nec factae sunt nec fieri possunt*; I, 44.5). Already in the *Gesta Guillelmi ducis Normannorum et regis Anglorum* of Guillaume de Poitiers, composed between 1071 and 1077, fiction is associated with poetry, and prose is extolled as a truthful medium; see Jeanette M. A. Beer, *Narrative Conventions of Truth in the Middle Ages* (Geneva, 1981), pp. 13–14. But it is not for another century that the debate over the relative truth of poetry and prose moves into vernacular literature.

35. Cited in David Hult, "Lancelot's Two Steps: A Problem in Textual Criticism," *Speculum* 61 (1986): 854n.58.

36. R. Howard Bloch, *Etymologies and Genealogies: A Literary Anthropology of the French Middle Ages* (Chicago, 1983), p. 15. On the rise of silent reading, see the important article by Paul Saenger, "Silent Reading: Its Impact on Late Medieval Script and Society," *Viator* 13 (1982): 367–414.

37. See Gail Berkeley Sherman, "Saints, Nuns, and Speech in the Canterbury Tales," in *Images of Sainthood in Medieval Europe*, ed. Renate Blumenfeld-Kosinski and Timea Szell (Ithaca, 1991), p. 144.

38. Robert Hanning, *The Individual in Twelfth-Century Romance* (New Haven, 1977), p. 143.

39. Walter J. Ong calls this patterning of social experience "the formulaic constitution of thought" in *Orality and Literacy: The Technologizing of the Word* (London, 1982), pp. 23–24. Cf. Bäuml, "Varieties and Consequences of Medieval Literacy and Illiteracy," p. 243.

40. Earlier anthropologists—like Jack Goody in *The Domestication of the Savage Mind* (Cambridge, 1977) and in his collaborative essay with Ian Watt, "The Consequences of Literacy," in *Literacy in Traditional Societies,* ed. J. R. Goody (Cambridge, 1968)—have stressed the ways in which, they believe, oral cultures tend to efface the pastness of the past in the interests of preserving a homeostatic view of culture in which variables, such as the distinction between past and present, are continually eliminated in the course of transmission from one generation to the next or from one group to another. They argue that this homeostatic management of the past means that the salient features of a society's history are constantly redefined in terms of the present, a process facilitated by the absence of institutional mechanisms for the archival preservation of statements that would reveal difference. Goody and Watt's view of primary oral cultures—and consequently of the enormous rupture introduced by writing—has achieved wide circulation and adherence outside of anthropology, especially among literary historians. But it has recently come under attack within anthropology itself, both for the overly sharp distinction that it draws between oral and literate modes of communication and for its tendency to homogenize an oral culture into a single entity, free of internal opposition and contradictions. See, for example, Brian V. Street, *Literacy in Theory and Practice* (Cambridge, 1984).

More recent field work in anthropology demonstrates that the public recitation of, for example, the lineage traditions of a tribal grouping are not necessarily agreed to in private by those whose ancestors were the subjects of the account. Although publicly the dissenting families will *seem* to defer to the consensual account offered by tribal spokesmen, in private the members of these families will offer their own versions as "true," if secretly held. William Murphy analyzes this difference between apparent public consensus and private, secret knowledge in terms of "frontstage"/"backstage" discourse; see his "Creating the Appearance of Consensus in Mende Political Discourse," *American Anthropologist* 92 (1990): 25–42. Similar findings have been made by Warren L. d'Azevedo among the Gola ("Uses of the Past in Gola Discourse," *Journal of African History* 3, no. 1 [1962]: 11–34) and Ben G. Blount ("Agreeing to Agree on Genealogy: A Luo Sociology of Knowledge," in *Sociocultural Dimensions of Language Use,* ed. Mary Sanches and Ben G. Blount [New York, 1975], pp. 117–135). This new work in anthropology should warn us against overhasty generalizations about the homogeneous character of oral cultures as lacking internal differentiation or dissidence. There are strong motives both for the tribe as a whole to accept the "public," agreed-upon version of its ancestral past and for individuals and families to preserve their own dissenting traditions in private. But the fact that such secret, publicly withheld traditions *are* articulated means that the consensual view is a communally constructed fiction that is consciously maintained, if not necessarily believed in by all those who participate in its fabrication. This fact emerges powerfully in Blount's account of an assembly of elders called for the purpose of recounting Luo genealogy to him (the investigator), in which the final product—the agreed-upon Luo genealogy—resulted only after often heated negotiations among participants and was privately disavowed by some of those who had helped to construct it. In effect, among the Luo anyway, no single reading of the historical picture gains universal adherence as accurate; rather, a particular account is accepted provisionally for the immediate future, with the frank recognition that it is the product of negotiated interests and authority. Obviously, given the impossibility of field work, we are not able to document the existence of a comparable gap between public and private history in medieval Europe, but since our view of the functioning of medieval oral culture is to a large degree derived, in the first place, from anthropological work such as Goody's, it behooves us to take seriously the evolving view of oral cultures among anthropologists themselves. For a recent overview of this question, see David William Cohen, "The Undefining of Oral Tradition," *Ethnohistory* 36 (1989): 9–18.

41. Cited in Evelyn Birge Vitz, "Orality, Literacy, and the Early Tristan Material: Béroul, Thomas, Marie de France," *Romanic Review* 78 (1987): 303.

42. For a discussion of diglossia, see Nancy S. Struever, "The Study of Language and the Study of History," *Journal of Interdisciplinary History* 4 (1974): 405.

43. Godzich and Kittay, *Emergence of Prose*, p. 195.

44. For the distinction between a written and a "textualized" language, see Walter J. Ong, "Orality, Literacy and Medieval Textualization," *New Literary History* 16 (1984): 5.

45. André Vauchez reports the existence of a well-documented piece of etymological whimsy in the thirteenth century, which proclaimed that the word *laicus* was derived from the Latin *lapis*, "stone," because the layman was hard and unacquainted with literature; see his "Lay People's Sanctity in Western Europe: Evolution of a Pattern (Twelfth and Thirteenth Centuries)," in *Images of Sainthood in Medieval Europe*, p. 24.

46. Bäuml, "Varieties and Consequences of Medieval Literacy and Illiteracy," p. 244.

47. "Multa, Magister Giralde, scripsitis, et multum adhuc scribitis; et nos multa diximus. Vos scripta dedistis, et nos verba. Et quanquam scripta vestra longe laudabiliora sint, et longaeviora, quam dicta nostra, quia tamen haec aperta, communi quippe idiomate prolata, illa verba, quia Latina, paucioribus evidentia, nos de dictis nostris fructum aliquem reportavimus" (Gerald of Wales, *Opera omnia*, vol. 5, ed. James F. Dimock, in *Rerum Britannicarum medii aevi scriptores* [Rolls Series], 21[5] [London, 1867], pp. 410–411).

48. This evolution has been traced by David Hult, "Vers la société de l'écriture: *Le roman de la rose*," *Poétique* 50 (1982): 155–172, on which the ensuing discussion is based.

49. Ibid., p. 163.

50. Brian Stock, *The Implications of Literacy: Written Language and Models of Interpretation in the Eleventh and Twelfth Centuries* (Princeton, 1983), chap. 2. For the theoretical concepts informing Stock's notion of "textual communities," see his collected essays in *Listening for the Text: On the Uses of the Past* (Baltimore, 1990).

51. On the signs of oral delivery, see Ruth Crosby, "Oral Delivery in the Middle Ages," *Speculum* 11 (1936): 88–110, as well as the more technical exposition of oral epic by Joseph J. Duggan, *The Song of Roland: Formulaic Style and Poetic Craft* (Berkeley and Los Angeles, 1973). For a list of the collection of literary attributes associated with orality see Ong, *Orality and Literacy*, pp. 37ff.

52. For an interesting discussion of this process as applied to the techniques of epic composition, see Franz H. Bäuml, "Transformations of the Heroine: From Epic Heard to Epic Read," in *The Role of Women in the Middle Ages*, ed. Rosemarie Morwedge (Albany, 1975), pp. 23–40.

53. Godzich and Kittay, *Emergence of Prose*, p. 195.

54. Brian Stock, "Medieval Literacy, Linguistic Theory, and Social Organization," *New Literary History* 16 (1984): 13–29.

55. On the technical ways in which prose does this, see Godzich and Kittay, *Emergence of Prose*, pp. 35ff.

56. Walpole, *Old French Johannes Translation of the Pseudo-Turpin Chronicle*, p. xi. André de Mandach, however, suggests that earlier versions went back as early as the end of the eleventh century; see his *Naissance et développement de la chanson de geste en Europe*, vol. 1: *La geste de Charlemagne et de Roland*, Publications Romanes et Françaises, 69 (Geneva, 1961). Mandach's extremely early dating suggests that the composition of the *Pseudo-Turpin Chronicle* preceded the oldest extant manuscript of the *Song of Roland* (the Oxford version, from ca. 1100), and Mandach seems to believe it possible that the *Turpin* antedated the writing down of the *Chanson de Roland*. But the *Turpin*'s obvious attempt to exploit the popularity of the *Chanson de Roland* for the purposes of ecclesiastical propaganda makes this implausible. The earliest firm evidence for the composition of the *Pseudo-Turpin* would place it somewhat later, between 1116 and 1145, but most likely about 1120–1130. In all probability, it was the work of a French cleric who lived and wrote in northern France, possibly at Aix-la-Chapelle. See C. Meredith-Jones, "Historia Karoli Magni et Rotholandi, ou Chronique de Pseudo-Turpin" (Doc. thesis, Université de Paris, 1936).

57. Vance, *Mervelous Signals*, p. 84.

58. This version has been edited by Short, *Anglo-Norman Pseudo-Turpin Chronicle of William of Briane*. See also his "Note on the Pseudo-Turpin Translations." Short believes that Briane translated directly from a Latin source; Mandach disagrees, in "Réponse à M. Ian Short."

59. Theodor Auracher published an edition of Nicolas's text based on the Paris MSS. in *Die sogenannte Poitevinische Übersetzung des Pseudo-Turpin*. For a general discussion of both the Latin and old French manuscript tradition of the *Pseudo-Turpin Chronicle*, see Mandach, *Naissance et développement de la chanson de geste*.

60. B.N. fr. 124, fol. 1r.

61. They are B.N. fr. 124, B.N. fr. 5714, and the so-called "Lee" manuscript, now published by André de Mandach, *Chronique dite Saintongeaise texte Franco-Occitan inédit "Lee": à la découverte d'une chronique gasconne du XIIIe siècle et de sa poitevinisation* (Tübingen, 1970). See also C. Meredith-Jones, "The Chronicle of Turpin in Saintonge," *Speculum* 13 (1938): 160–179.

62. Ian Short found a reference to a "Johannes," a chaplain of Renaud of Dammartin, in the *Rotuli litterarum clausarum*, I, 153, for the year 1213. See Ian Short, *Anglo-Norman Pseudo-Turpin Chronicle of William of Briane*, p. 7; and Walpole, *Old French Johannes Translation*, p. 95.

63. On Pierre de Beauvais's translation, see Max L. Berkey, Jr., "Pierre de Beauvais: An Introduction to His Works," *Romance Philology* 18 (1964–1965): 387–398; Gaston Paris, "La traduction de la légende latine du voyage de Charlemagne à Constantinople par Pierre de Beauvais," *Romania* 21 (1892): 263–264; Ronald N. Walpole, "Two Notes on Charlemagne's Journey to the East: The French Translation of the Latin Legend by Pierre de Beauvais," *Romance Philology* 7 (1953–1954): 130–142. Walpole provided an edition of the text in "Charlemagne's Journey to the East." It is possible that Pierre de Beauvais also prepared a French version of the *Translatio* and *Miracula* of the *Liber Sancti Jacobi*, dated 1212, for Yolande of Saint-Pol, although there is some question as to which Yolande was the intended recipient of this work. Gaston Paris originally suggested the countess of Saint-Pol, but Max L. Berkey believes that "la countesse Yollent" mentioned in the prologue refers to Yolande de Coucy, daughter of Raoul I de Coucy and Agnes of Hainaut, a niece of Baldwin VIII of Flanders ("Pierre de Beauvais," p. 395). Both Walpole ("Charlemagne's Journey to the East," p. 440) and Mandach, however, believe that it was addressed to Yolande of Saint-Pol (see Mandach, "Le livre de Saint-Jacques de Compostelle par Pierre de Beauvais [1212]: à propos d'une édition récente," *Vox Romanica* 30 (1971): 287–291). If this is so, it would have served as a natural complement to Yolande's earlier patronage of the *Pseudo-Turpin* translation executed by Nicolas of Senlis, since the *Pseudo-Turpin* also formed part of the *Liber Sancti Jacobi*.

64. Renaud's Johannes version was published by Walpole, *The Old French Johannes Translation of the Pseudo-Turpin Chronicle,* while that of Michel of Harnes was edited by A. Demarquette in *Précis historique sur la maison de Harnes 963 à 1230 suivi d'une version romane attribué à Michel de Harnes de la Chronique du Faux Turpin.* The manuscript stemma established by Walpole demonstrates that, contrary to earlier assertions that Michel copied Renaud's translation, Michel's version is an independent copy of the second redaction of the Johannes *Turpin* (*Old French Johannes Translation,* p. 58). On Michel himself, see Demarquette, *Précis historique sur la maison de Harnes.* For the political activities of both Renaud and Michel, see chapter 1.

65. B.N. fr. 2168, fol. 156v. This copy is written in Picard, doubtless William of Cayeux's own dialect. Cayeux is near Abbeville in Ponthieu. See Ronald N. Walpole, "Charlemagne's Journey to the East," pp. 440–443.

66. Walpole, *Old French Johannes Translation,* pp. 53ff.

67. This version is characteristically represented by B.N. fr. 1850, published by Wulff, *La chronique dite Turpin.*

68. The Anonymous's *Histoire des ducs de Normandie et des rois d'Angleterre* is published by Francisque Michel. Léopold Delisle has published the last, original portion of the *Chronique des rois de France,* beginning in 1185, in the *Recueil des historiens des Gaules et de la France* 24:750–775. The only complete manuscript of the Anonymous's *Chronique des rois de France* is that of B.N. nouv. acq. fr. 6295. On the Anonymous of Béthune, see Léopold Delisle, "Notice sur la chronique d'un anonyme de Béthune"; P. Meyer, "Notice sur le MS. II.6.24 de la Bibliothèque de Cambridge"; Petit-Dutaillis, *Etude sur la vie et le règne de Louis VIII,* p. xx; idem, "Une nouvelle chronique du règne de Philippe-Auguste"; Walpole, "L'Anonyme de Béthune"; and Walpole's extremely thorough and useful discussion of the place of *Turpin* in the manuscript tradition of the Anonymous's works in "Philip Mouskés and the Pseudo-Turpin Chronicle."

69. Published by Ronald N. Walpole, *An Anonymous Old French Translation of the Pseudo-Turpin Chronicle: A Critical Edition of the Text Contained in Bibliothèque Nationale MSS. fr. 2137 and 17203 and Incorporated by Philip Mouskés in His Chronique Rimée,* Medieval Academy of America, 89 (Cambridge, Mass., 1979). One final Francien version of the *Pseudo-Turpin Chronicle,* which dates from the decade 1220–1230 and which appears in the newly discovered *Chronique des rois de France* (see chapter 6), has been published by Walpole under the title of *Turpin I* (*Le Turpin français dit le Turpin I*) (Toronto, 1985). See also his "Prolégomènes à une édition du Turpin français dit le Turpin I," *Revue d'histoire des textes* 10 (1980): 199–230; 11 (1981): 325–370. Several manuscripts

of the Anonymous of Béthune use this version, in place of the Artesian version. Its place in the *Chronique des rois de France* will be discussed in chapter 5. Additional versions of the *Pseudo-Turpin* in vernacular dialects were produced later in the thirteenth century, notably a Burgundian translation, published by Walpole, "The Burgundian Translation of Pseudo-Turpin Chronicle in Bibliothèque Nationale (French MS. 25438)," *Romance Philology* 2 (1948–1949): 177–255; 3 (1949–1950): 83–116, as well as those cited in Ian Short, "The Pseudo-Turpin Chronicle: Some Unnoticed Versions and Their Sources," *Medium aevum* 38 (1969): 1–22.

70. Walpole, *Old French Johannes Translation*, p. 58.

71. See Galbert's *The Murder of Charles the Good, Count of Flanders*, ed. and trans. James Bruce Ross (New York, 1967), p. 91.

72. Warlop, *Flemish Nobility* 1:178.

73. Fossier, *Terre et hommes*, p. 659.

74. Galbert, *Murder of Charles the Good*, pp. 196, 230; see also the excellent discussion of the status of various members of the nobility by J. B. Ross in the introduction to that work, p. 29.

75. Fossier, *Terre et hommes*, p. 658.

76. F. Vercauteren, "Etude sur les châtelains comtaux en Flandre du XIe au début du XIIIe siècle," in *Etudes d'histoire dédiées à la mémoire de Henri Pirenne* (Brussels, 1937), p. 438.

77. William Stubbs, ed., *The Historical Works of Gervase of Canterbury*, in *Rerum Britannicarum medii aevi scriptores* (Rolls Series), 73 (London, 1879), 1:294.

78. Delisle, Wailly, and Jourdain, *Scripta de feodis*, pp. 682–685.

79. See Petit-Dutaillis, "Fragment de l'histoire de Philippe-Auguste," p. 103.

80. Monicat and Boussard, eds., *Recueil des actes de Philippe-Auguste*, vol. 3, no. 1245, p. 369.

81. Ferdinand Lot and Robert Fawtier, *Le premier budget de la monarchie française: le compte général de 1202–1203* (Paris, 1932), no. 152. I am indebted to Professor John Baldwin for drawing my attention to this entry.

82. Warlop believes that Michel II died about 1195, which would require Michel III to be the referent of the entry in the "budget" of 1202–1203. But since Warlop was unaware of this mention in the royal accounts, it is possible that the elder Michel was still alive at the turn of the century.

83. See chapter 1. Supporting evidence for this chronology comes from a list of *feoda* copied into register A, which includes Michel's fief-rent. Dept dates this list to approximately 1208 on historical grounds. However, according to John Baldwin, the entry concerning Michel must have been transcribed between August 1204 and February 1205 because it is written in the hand of the first scribe. Baldwin also dates between 1204 and 1207–1208 the list of knights-banneret in register A, in which Michel of Harnes

figures twice: under *milites Flandrie* (where his name is crossed out) and under *milites Attrebatensis*, the change explained by the royal acquisition of Artois, in which Harnes was located. I would like to thank Professor Baldwin for communicating this information to me.

84. Rita Lejeune staunchly defends the accuracy of Jean Renart's political alignments in "Le roman de Guillaume de Dole et la principauté de Liège," *Cahiers de civilisation médiévale Xe–XIIe siècles* 17 (1974): 20. Indeed, it is on the basis of his accurate depiction of contemporary political factions that Lejeune redates the *Roman de Guillaume de Dole* to 1208–1210.

85. See chapter 6.

86. Walpole, "Philip Mouskés and the Pseudo-Turpin Chronicle," p. 389. Diana Tyson follows Walpole in seeing the literary sponsorship of historical texts by the nobility as stemming from the patrons' desire to imitate the example of friends and neighbors ("Patronage of French Vernacular History Writers," p. 218).

87. "Et pour ce que rime se viveult [*sic*] a faitier a mos conquis hors d'istoire, viveult [*sic*] Michel que cest livre soit fait sans rime" (B.N. fr. 573, fol. 147r). Pierre de Beauvais, in his *Bestiaire*, expresses himself in identical terms: "Et pour ce que rime se vieut a faitier de moz concueilliz hors de verite, mist il sanz rime cest livre selonc le latin dou livre que Physiologes uns boens clers d'Athenes traita" (B.N. nouv. acq. fr. 13521, fol. 22r). On this manuscript see Paul Meyer, "Notices sur deux anciens manuscrits français ayant appartenu au marquis de la Clayette (Bibliothèque Nationale, Moreau 1715–1719)," *Notices et extraits des manuscrits de la Bibliothèque Nationale* 33, pt. 1 (1890): 1–90.

88. "L'estoire traitie par rime samble menchonge" (B.N. fr. 1621, fol. 208r).

89. "Mes que que li autre aient osté et mis, ci poez oïr la verité d'Espaigne selonc le latin de l'estoire que li cuens Renauz de Boloigne fist par grant estuide cerchier et querre es livres a monseignor Saint Denise" (Walpole, *Old French Johannes Translation*, p. 130).

90. "Por che que l'estoire traitie par rime samble menchonge est cheste sans rime mise en romans selonc le raison del latin que Torpins meisme fist et traita" (B.N. fr. 1621, fol. 208r).

91. Cf. Sayers, "Beginnings and Early Development of Old French Historiography," p. 110.

92. That some medieval writers were suspicious of the historical veracity of the *Pseudo-Turpin Chronicle* is evident from the fact that an author would sometimes add a personal note of warning to readers that Archbishop Turpin should not command their unquestioning belief. An example is furnished by Alberic of Trois-Fontaines's *Chronica* (ed. P. Scheffer-Boichorst, in *Monumenta Germaniae historica, Scriptores* 23:719). See

Walpole, "Philip Mouskés and the Pseudo-Turpin Chronicle," p. 368. It is also clear that the Abbey of Saint-Denis possessed a copy of the *Pseudo-Turpin Chronicle* from at least 1124, but did not incorporate it within its narrative accounts of the kings of France until 1274, with Primat's compilation of the *Grandes chroniques de France*. Notably, it appears first in the vernacular, rather than the Latin (i.e., quasi-official), corpus of chronicles, despite the fact that Vincent of Beauvais had already inserted it into his *Speculum historiale* around 1250.

93. According to Ronald N. Walpole, Renaud and Michel did no more than sponsor independent copies of the composite Old French *Descriptio-Turpin* made by an unknown author shortly before 1206 (*Old French Johannes Translation*, p. 58).

94. It had long been fashionable for jongleurs to appeal to the authority of Saint-Denis as a means of reassuring audiences of the authenticity of their narratives and as a mark of their special access to new and historically significant material, distinct from that purveyed by rival storytellers (Chaytor, *From Script to Print*, p. 123). Although it is probable that the version of the Latin *Turpin* copied by the clerks of Baldwin VIII and subsequently used by Nicolas of Senlis came from Saint-Denis (Mandach, *Naissance et développement de la chanson de geste* 1:93), this is clearly not the case for other versions. Jules Lair has argued that Saint-Denis owned a manuscript of the *Pseudo-Turpin* in the middle of the twelfth century, although it is also true that the *Turpin* was not incorporated into the compilations of French histories such as the *Gesta gentis Francorum*, the *Nova gesta Francorum*, or the *Abbreviatio* made at the abbey in the course of the century; see "Mémoire sur deux chroniques latines composées au XIIe siècle à l'abbaye de Saint-Denis," *Bibliothèque de l'Ecole des Chartes* 35 (1874): 543–580. Indeed, it was not until 1274, in the vernacular *Grandes chroniques*, that the *Turpin* was integrated into the Dionysian version of the French history, although the Anonymous of Béthune had earlier effected such an integration; see Spiegel, *Chronicle Tradition of Saint-Denis*.

95. See Eugene Vance, *Mervelous Signals*, p. 155; and Struever, "Study of Language."

96. R. Howard Bloch, *Medieval French Literature and Law* (Berkeley and Los Angeles, 1977), p. 10.

97. Godzich and Kittay, *Emergence of Prose*, p. 195.

98. Sayers, "Beginnings and Early Development of Old French Historiography," p. 445.

99. As Robert Hanning proposed; see "The Social Significance of Twelfth-Century Chivalric Romance," *Mediaevalia et humanistica*, n.s., 3 (1972): 24.

100. Jodogne, "Naissance de la prose," p. 302.

101. Tyson, "Patronage of French Vernacular History Writers," p. 222.

102. Sayers, "Beginnings and Early Development of Old French Historiography," pp. 132, 451. The close relation between patron and the form and subject matter of Old French literature is thematized by Chrétien de Troyes in the prologue to the *Roman de la Charette*. As Michelle Freeman has indicated, the *Charette* depicts Marie de Champagne, patroness of the poem, as Chrétien's "better half in this poetic collaboration." She is not just Chrétien's Muse, but is presented as exercising control over the work to the extent that she has designated the subject matter and specified its style of treatment. See Freeman, *The Poetics of Translatio Studii and Conjointure: Chrétien de Troyes's "Cligès,"* French Forum Monographs, 12 (Lexington, Ky., 1979), pp. 30–31. The patron here figures as a kind of unofficial co-author, who may, as in the case of Baldwin VIII's search for a copy of the *Pseudo-Turpin Chronicle*, provide an author's source material or, indirectly, influence the form and manner in which the work is cast. Cf. Burns, *Arthurian Fictions*, p. 30.

103. B.N. fr. 5713, fol. 1v.

104. B.N. fr. 1444, fol. 115r. Cf. B.N. fr. 5713, fol. 1v.

105. Bakhtin, *Dialogic Imagination*, p. 15. In Bakhtin's sense, the "absolute past" is a "specifically evaluating [hierarchical] category." In the epic world of the "absolute past," terms like "beginning," "first," "earlier," "founder," "ancestor," are not simple temporal markers but "valorized temporal categories, and valorized to an extreme degree." The effect of this totalizing valorization of the past is to cut it off absolutely from all subsequent times, especially that of the oral singer and his audience.

106. I am indebted to Phyllis Rackin for this notion of verbal substitutes for an absent social past. See her "Genealogical Anxiety and Female Authority: The Return of the Repressed in Shakespeare's Histories" (typescript); idem, *Stages of History: Shakespeare's English Chronicles* (Ithaca, 1990); and idem, "Anti-Historians: Women's Roles in Shakespeare's Histories," *Theatre Journal* 37 (1985): 329–344. I am grateful to Professor Rackin for making her unpublished work available to me.

107. To some extent this shift in literary function might be attributed to the new role of oral, or performed, epic for an illiterate subgroup within a literate society. Franz Bäuml believes that since illiterate subgroups in a literate society no longer depend on oral epic to preserve the data necessary for the guidance of society, epic literature functions in this situation rather as a "preserver of data useful for the conduct of daily life" ("Transformations of the Heroine," p. 30). This need not imply, however, that such a shift is due entirely to epic's adaptation to the newly textualized communicative situation.

108. See Guenée, *Histoire et culture historique*, p. 346, on the function of examples and precedents in historiographical writing in the Middle Ages.

109. B.N. fr. 1621, fol. 208r. Cf. Walpole, *Old French Johannes Translation*, p. 130.

110. Walpole, *Old French Johannes Translation*, p. 131.

111. Ibid., p. 160.

112. Claude Buridant, ed., *La traduction du Pseudo-Turpin du manuscrit Vatican Regina 624*, Publications Romanes et Françaises, 142 (Geneva, 1976), p. 95.

113. Walpole, "Charlemagne's Journey to the East," p. 446. Cf. B.N. fr. 834, fol. 15v.

114. Buridant, *Traduction du Pseudo-Turpin*, p.107.

115. Pierre de Beauvais, "Charlemagne's Journey to the East," p. 446.

116. Henri-François Delaborde, "Pourquoi Saint Louis faisait acte de servage à Saint Denis," *Bulletin de la Société Nationale des Antiquaires*, 1897, 256.

117. Walpole, *Old French Johannes Translation*, p. 132.

118. Ibid., p. 143.

119. "Toz cels qu'il trova en prison mist hors. Les povres et le nuz vesti. . . . Les debotez de lor heritages remist en lor honors" (ibid., p. 143).

120. Ibid.

121. Ibid., p. 162.

122. Ibid., p. 161.

123. As Eugene Vance (*Mervelous Signals*, p. 61) has insightfully argued, Ganelon's deceitful behavior destroys the stability of meaning in language, dislocating signs from their referents and, thus, "compromising language."

124. Walpole, *Anonymous Old French Translation*, p. 69. See also idem, *Le Turpin français dit le Turpin I*, pp. 32–33; and idem, *Old French Johannes Translation*, p. 162.

125. Walpole, *Le Turpin français dit le Turpin I*, p. 33.

126. Ibid.

127. Walpole, *Anonymous Old French Translation*, p. 78.

128. Ibid.

129. Walpole, *Old French Johannes Translation*, p. 169.

130. Walpole, *Anonymous Old French Translation*, p. 79.

131. See Guenée, *Histoire et culture historique*, p. 320.

132. Walpole, *Old French Johannes Translation*, p. 130.

133. Ibid.

134. See Ong, *Orality and Literacy*, p. 43.

135. Buridant, *Traduction du Pseudo-Turpin*, p. 85.

136. Walpole, *Old French Johannes Translation*, p. 134.

137. Walpole, *Anonymous Old French Translation*, p. 42.

138. B.N. fr. 834, fol. 15r.

139. See J. Longnon, *Les compagnons de Villehardouin: recherches sur les croisés de la quatrième croisade*, Hautes Etudes Médiévales et Modernes, 30 (Geneva, 1978).

140. See the discussion of the importance of Crusading themes in romance literature in Erich Köhler, *L'aventure chevaleresque: idéal et réalité dans le roman courtois*, with a preface by Jacques Le Goff (Paris, 1974), p. 110.

141. Georges Duby, "Remarques sur la littérature généalogique en France aux XIe et XIIe siècles," in *Hommes et structures du moyen âge* (Paris, 1973), pp. 287–298; and Léopold Genicot, *Les généalogies*, Typologie des Sources du Moyen Age Occidental, 15 (Turnhout, Bel., 1975).

142. See Gabrielle M. Spiegel, "Political Utility in Medieval Historiography: A Sketch," *History and Theory* 14 (1975): 314–325; and idem, "Genealogy: Form and Function in Medieval Historical Narrative," *History and Theory* 22 (1983): 43–53.

143. For this formulation, see Goody and Watt, "Consequences of Literacy," p. 33.

144. Cf. Michel Sot, "Historiographie épiscopale et modèle familial en Occident au IXe siècle," *Annales: économies, sociétés, civilisations* 33 (1978): 434.

145. In a genealogy included in a manuscript of Arras, Bibliothèque Municipale, MS. 163; see Mandach, *Naissance et développement de la chanson de geste* 1:139; and Walpole, *Anonymous Old French Translation*, p. 29.

146. Walpole, *Anonymous Old French Translation*, p. 7.

147. B.N. fr. 1621, fol. 208r.

148. Bakhtin, *Dialogic Imagination*, p. 13.

149. For an anthropological discussion of this use of the past, see Clifford Geertz, "Politics Past, Politics Present: Some Notes on the Uses of Anthropology in Understanding the New States," in *The Interpretation of Cultures* (New York, 1973), pp. 327–341.

150. See Köhler, *L'aventure chevaleresque*, p. 26; also Boutet and Strubel, *Littérature, politique et société*, p. 87.

151. See Gabrielle M. Spiegel, "The Reditus regni ad stirpem Karoli Magni: A New Look," *French Historical Studies* 7 (1971): 145–174; and K. F. Werner, "Die Legitimität der Kapetinger und die Entstehung des Reditus regni Francorum ad stirpem Karoli Magni," *Welt als Geschichte* 12 (1952): 203–225.

152. Cited in Jacques Le Goff, "Philippe Auguste dans les 'Exempla,' " in *La France de Philippe Auguste*, p. 151.

153. Yvon Lacaze has demonstrated that a comparable use of epic tradition and historical writing among Burgundian and Flemish nobles in opposition to the centralizing forces of the French monarchy continues well

into the fourteenth and fifteenth centuries. Like his forebears, Philippe le Bon used vernacular historiography, in particular the *Chronique de Baudouin d'Avesnes* (itself a reworking of the thirteenth-century vernacular histories of authors like the Anonymous of Béthune, including the *Pseudo-Turpin*) to justify his politics of independence vis-à-vis the French monarchy of Charles VII. See Lacaze, "Le rôle des traditions dans la genèse d'un sentiment national au XVe siècle: la Bourgogne de Philippe le Bon," *Bibliothèque de l'Ecole des Chartes* 129 (1971): 303–385.

154. Sayers, "Beginnings and Early Development of Old French Historiography," p. 439.

155. Guenée, *Histoire et culture historique*, p. 222.

156. The Anonymous inserts an episode from *Gormond and Isembard* and the vision of Charles the Bald (*Visio Karoli*). See Léopold Delisle, "Notice sur la chronique d'un anonyme de Béthune," p. 367; and Walpole, "Philip Mouskés and the Pseudo-Turpin Chronicle," p. 353.

157. Walpole, *Old French Johannes Translation*, p. 97.

158. Vitz ("Orality, Literacy, and the Early Tristan Material," p. 300) questions to what extent and until when the appearance of interpellations such as "oyez" in the text indicate the persisting vocal presence of a live narrator. She believes that at some point in the thirteenth century calls for the listeners' attention became merely nostalgic, evoking a rapidly disappearing if not extinguished world of oral performance.

CHAPTER THREE

1. Li livre est mout anciiens
    Qui tesmoingne l'estoire a voire;
    Por ce fet ele miauz a croire.

Chrétien de Troyes, *Cligès*, ed. W. Foerster (Halle, 1910), lines 24–26.

2. Des doint qu'ele i soit retenue
    Et que li leus li abelisse
    Tant que ja mes de France n'isse
    L'enors qui s'i est arestee.

Ibid., lines 35–38.

3. E por ço me vueil travaillier
    En une estoire comencier
    Que de latin, ou jo la truis,

    La voudrai si en romanz metre
    Que cil qui n'entendent la letre
    Se puissent deduire el romanz.

Benoît de Sainte-Maure, *Roman de Troie*, lines 33–39.

4. Cited in Dembowski, "Learned Latin Treatises in French," p. 257.

5. See Boutet and Strubel, *Littérature, politique et societé,* p. 15.

6. Maurice Keen, for example, appreciates the duality of the medieval approach to the past: "If the laymen of the twelfth century pictured the classical past in terms of contemporary conditions, that does not mean that they were unaware of the great space of time that divided them from it, or that it was essentially a part of history" (*Chivalry* [New Haven, 1984], p. 110).

7. Jacques Monfrin, "Humanisme et traductions au moyen âge," in *L'humanisme médiévale dans les littératures romanes du XIIe au XIVe siècle,* ed. A. Fourrier (Paris, 1964), p. 217.

8. See, for example, Zink, "Mutation de la conscience littéraire," p. 22.

9. Raymond J. Cormier, "The Problem of Anachronism: Recent Scholarship on the French Medieval Romances of Antiquity," *Philological Quarterly* 53 (1974): 157.

10. Frappier, "Peinture de la vie et des héros antiques," p. 52.

11. Ibid., p. 53.

12. Ibid., pp. 30–31; cf. Cormier, "Problem of Anachronism," p. 151.

13. Frappier, "Peinture de la vie et des héros antiques," p. 53.

14. Etienne Gilson, *Héloise et Abélard: études sur le moyen âge et l'humanisme* (Paris, 1938), p. 222.

15. Peter Dembowski, in contrast, maintains that adaptation was a necessary stage for the romance author/translator to go through before he was sufficiently confident of his abilities to undertake a literal translation of ancient writers, a psychological tendency that he believes explains why strict translations as we understand them did not become the norm until the late fourteenth and fifteenth centuries; see his "Learned Latin Treatises in French," pp. 255–269.

16. See Sayers, "Beginnings and Early Development of Old French Historiography," p. 34.

17. Bakhtin, *Dialogic Imagination,* pp. 13, 20.

18. See, for example, Frappier, "Peinture de la vie et des héros antiques," p. 24, who follows in this Woledge, "La légende de Troie et les débuts de la prose française," p. 314. See also Anthime Fourrier, *Le courant réaliste dans le roman courtois en France au moyen âge,* vol. 1: *Les débuts (XIIe siècle)* (Paris, 1960).

19. See the discussion of the *Roman d'Enéas* in Lee Patterson, "Virgil and the Historical Consciousness of the Twelfth Century: The *Roman d'Enéas* and *Erec et Enide*," in *Negotiating the Past: The Historical Understanding of Medieval Literature* (Madison, Wis., 1987), pp. 157–195.

20. This text remains unedited. The base manuscript of the first recension is B.N. fr. 20125. The *Histoire ancienne* was among the most popular medieval historical works and is preserved in some fifty-nine manuscripts, forty-seven of which belong to the first recension. On the manuscript tradition, see Woledge, *Bibliographie des romans et nouvelles antérieurs à*

1500. Although unpublished, the *Histoire* has been the object of considerable study, beginning with P. Meyer, "Les premières compilations françaises d'histoire ancienne," *Romania* 14 (1885): 1–18. See also Jacques Monfrin, "Les traducteurs et leur public en France au moyen âge," *Journal des savants*, 1964, 5–20; idem, "Les traducteurs et leur public," in *L'humanisme médiéval*; idem, "La connaissance de l'antiquité et le problème de l'humanisme en langue vulgaire dans la France du XVe siècle," in *The Late Middle Ages and the Dawn of Humanism Outside Italy*, ed. G. Verbeke and J. Ijsewijn (Louvain, 1972); and idem, "Humanisme et traductions." Especially useful are the studies of Guy Raynaud de Lage: "L' 'Histoire ancienne jusqu'à César' et les 'Faits des Romains' "; "Romans antiques dans l' 'Histoire ancienne jusqu'à César' "; "Romans antiques et la représentation de l'antiquité"; "L' 'Historia britonum': source de l' 'Histoire ancienne jusqu'à César,' " in *Les premiers romans français*, Publications Romanes et Françaises, 138 (Geneva, 1976), pp. 1–4; and "L'histoire ancienne." A detailed study of the Macedonian section and its sources is provided by Ross, "History of Macedon in the 'Histoire ancienne jusqu'à César.' " The second recension of the *Histoire ancienne* is characterized by the substitution of a prose version of Benoît de Sainte-Maure's *Roman de Troie* in place of the original Trojan narration. On this recension see, in addition to the works cited above, François Avril, "Trois manuscrits napolitains des collections de Charles V et de Jean de Berry," *Bibliothèque de l'Ecole des Chartes* 127 (1970): 291–328; G. Mazzoni and A. Jeanroy, "Un nouveau manuscrit du Roman de Troie et de l'Histoire ancienne avant César," *Romania* 27 (1898): 574–581; Clem C. Williams, Jr., "A Case of Mistaken Identity: Still Another Trojan Narrative in Old French Prose," *Medium aevum* 53 (1984): 59–72.

21. The work is clearly dedicated to Roger of Lille, who attained his majority and entered the office of castellan in 1211. He died in 1229, hence the broad dates. There is no general agreement among scholars as to a more specific determination for the period of the *Histoire ancienne*'s composition. The traditional dating is 1223–1230, but Ferdinand Lot has demonstrated on what thin grounds this is based; see his "Compte-Rendu de J. Frappier: *Etude sur la 'Mort le Roi Artu*,' " *Romania* 64 (1938): 120–122. Raynaud de Lage (see above, note 20) favors a comparatively earlier date than customarily assumed, before 1213 but after 1208, making the *Histoire ancienne* exactly contemporary to the *Faits des Romains*. On Roger of Lille, see Leuridan, *Châtellains de Lille*.

22. The sections are those designated by P. Meyer, "Premières compilations d'histoire ancienne," pp. 38–49.

23. B.N. fr. 20125, fol. 2v. On the complex relationship of the *Histoire ancienne* to its romance sources, see Raynaud de Lage, "Romans antiques dans l' 'Histoire ancienne,' " passim.

24. See Woledge, *Bibliographie des romans et nouvelles*, pp. 42ff.

25. B.N. fr. 20125, fols. 10v, 41v, 43r, 62r, 180v, 273v–274r. The moralizations are discussed by Guy Raynaud de Lage, "La morale de l'histoire," *Le moyen âge,* 4th ser., 18 (1963): 365–369, and Renate Blumenfeld-Kosinski, "Moralization and History: Verse and Prose in the 'Histoire ancienne jusquà César' (in B.N. fr. 20125)," *Zeitschrift für romanische Philologie* 97 (1982): 41–46.

26. Conversely, ten—or nearly half—of the moralizations fall within the first section devoted to biblical history, where no such contamination might be feared.

27. B.N. fr. 20125, fols. 10v, 14r.

28. See Blumenfeld-Kosinski, "Moralization and History," p. 44; and P. Meyer, "Premières compilations françaises de l'histoire ancienne," p. 58.

29. For Lambert's list of the works collected in the library of the count of Guines, see Lambert of Ardres, *Historia Comitum Ghisnensium,* ed. G. H. Pertz, in *Monumenta Germaniae historica, Scriptores* 24:598.

30. Jacques Le Goff, "Naissance du roman historique au XIIe siècle," *Nouvelle revue française* 238 (1972): 171.

31. See Spiegel, "Political Utility in Medieval Historiography."

32. Erich Köhler came to a similar conclusion in considering the universal import of the Arthurian world of romance, which he sees as a response to royal centralization: "Les efforts de centralisation nationale de la monarchie française . . . devaient inciter les puissances féodales à donner à leur existence des fondements universalistes" (*L'aventure chevaleresque,* p. 43). Thus, in the verse preface to the *Histoire ancienne,* commissioned toward 1213 by Roger of Lille, ancient history could be offered as a prologue to the history of Flanders and other French principalities. See B.N. fr. 20125, fols. 2r–2v.

33. John G. A. Pocock, "The Origins of the Study of the Past," *Comparative Studies in Society and History* 4 (1962): 217.

34. Keen, *Chivalry,* p. 102.

35. Le Goff, "Naissance du roman historique," p. 173.

36. Bakhtin, *Dialogic Imagination,* p. 31.

37. Northrop Frye, *The Great Code: The Bible and Literature* (New York, 1982), p. 43. For Frye, in fact, the narrative aspect of all literature "is a recurrent act of symbolic communication: in other words a ritual." What Frye means is that narrative functions ritually as an imitation of human action as a whole, rather than as mimesis, or the imitation of a particular practice. In that sense, ritual is something continuously latent in the order of words, that is, in narrative. See his *Anatomy of Criticism* (New York, 1969), pp. 105, 109.

38. See especially Mircea Eliade, *The Myth of the Eternal Return, or Cosmos and History,* trans. Willard Trask (Princeton, 1965), p. 5.

39. Burns, *Arthurian Fictions,* p. 148.

40. Vance, *Mervelous Signals*, p. 83.

41. B.N. fr. 20125, prologue, fol. 2v. Cf. Guenée, *Histoire et culture historique*, p. 276. That Roger was in control of the shape and content of the text we know from interpolated comments indicating a certain level of disagreement between author and patron. The clerical translator wished to emphasize biblical history, whereas Roger of Lille expressed a decided preference for pagan history. Thus, having arrived at a point in his recounting of biblical history where the exodus of the Jews from Egypt normally would have been narrated, the author excuses himself for disrupting the narrative thread on the grounds that Roger insisted that he treat pagan history before returning to the Hebrews: "Or seroit drois et mesure que ie avant des fiz Israel, c'est de la lignee les fiz Jacob, vos deisse et contasse avant et continuasse l'estoire comment et par quele ochoison il issirent d'Egypte et commant et par co grant paine il conquisterent la terre de Chananee, mes non ferai ore; ains dirai premereinement des paiens qui adonques regnerent et commencerai au meaus que ie porrai des rois et des regnes trosques a la destruction de Troies, quar si le veut ce me sambla et commande mes sires; et lores apres ce revendrai et repairerai as Ebruis" (B.N. fr. 20125, fols. 82v–83r). Similarly, Roger was not particularly interested in incorporating an account of Trojan history, which he believed to be widely known, preferring to enhance, instead, his knowledge of Roman history. Thus the author was once again compelled to cut short his narrative, although he clearly insisted that no "ancient history" would be complete without some discussion of the city's deeds and fate: "Or vos conterai de la destruction de Troies et l'ochoison mout brefment, quar ensi le me proie mes sires por ce que l'estorie est tant oïe, mais n'avenoit moi que de si grant fait con la ot ne feust on entre les autres ramenbrance la ou ele devroit estre" (ibid., fol. 123v). Twenty-five folios later he acknowledges the return to the "matter" that principally interests his patron: "De ce ne vos voil or plus dire, ains voill revenir a la matere por cui tote cheste choze et ceste hystorie fu comencee, c'est de Rome et des Romains et de lors ores et coment la cités fu primes comencee" (ibid., fol 148r). Cf. a similar remark at fol. 187r concerning the history of Cyrus, also abandoned in favor of Roman history.

42. Raynaud de Lage, "Les romans antiques dans l' 'Histoire ancienne,' " p. 274.

43. Many scholars have claimed that the patronage lavished at the court of Henry II in England on the historical *romans,* involving the successive production of the *Roman de Troie* by Benoît de Sainte-Maure, the *Roman d'Enéas,* and the *Roman de Brut* and *Roman de Rou* by Wace, functioned in the Angevin realm as the genealogical foundation for Plantagenet aspirations to political hegemony. Thus, Michel Zink points out that the *Enéas* begins with a summary of the *Roman de Troie* and the *Brut* begins with a summary of *Enéas,* while Wace writes the *Roman de Rou* as a con-

tinuation of the *Brut*. These authors appear to be writing the history of the origins of the English monarchy in the distant worlds of Troy and Rome, an argument strengthened by the retrospective genealogy that opens the *Roman de Rou,* which suggests that they were all writing the same history. See Zink, "Mutation de la conscience littéraire," pp. 12–13. Although a widely held view, not all historians of Old French literature agree. Frappier, in particular, finds the idea that the succession of the *Roman de Troie, Brut, Rou,* and *Chronique des ducs de Normandie* were intended to form part of a coherent ensemble devoted to the "prehistory" of the Anglo-Norman and Angevin dynasties "outrées pour le moins" ("Peinture de la vie et des héros antiques," p. 23n.4.)

44. Settegast, *Li hystore de Julius César,* p. 2 (hereafter cited as *Hystore de Jules César*). One is reminded of Wace's forthright admission that

> Jeo parouc a la riche gent
> Ki unt les rentes e le argent
> Kar pur eus sunt li livre fait
> E bon dit fait e bien retrait.

Roman de Rou, ed. A. J. Holden (Société des Anciens Textes Français) (Paris, 1970–1973), 1:167, lines 163–166.

45. B.N. fr. 20125, fol. 1v.

46. Flutre and Sneyders de Vogel, *Li fet des Romains* 1:2 (hereafter cited as *Faits des Romains*).

47. *Hystore de Jules César,* p. 105.

48. I am indebted for this idea to Vance, *Mervelous Signals,* p. 157.

49. L.-F. Flutre, "Li faits des Romains," *Annales de l'Université de Paris* 8 (1933): 276.

50. Beer, *Medieval Caesar,* pp. 72–74. In Beer's view, the large and heterogeneous region of "Gaul" that Caesar ruled foreshadowed the augmented realm over which Philip Augustus hoped to rule and from which he derived his very name of Augustus. However, although it is true that court propagandists frequently employed antique models as legitimizing fictions to enhance royal ideology in medieval France, that does not seem to be the case here. Royal ideology in this period tended to draw on Carolingian themes, thus only indirectly on the Roman models that influenced them. Even if Guenée had not demonstrated the *Faits*'s independence of royal patronage—and the total lack of interest in Roman history evinced by the monarchy under Philip Augustus—the treatment accorded Caesar in the *Faits* provides sufficient grounds to question the notion that it sought to capture the interest of the king or to promote royal causes. The ways in which the anonymous translator reworked Caesar's *Gallic Wars* bears witness to interpretive goals at variance with promoting royal ideology.

51. As in Vat. Reg. Lat. 893. See P. Meyer, "Premières compilations françaises d'histoire ancienne," p. 23.

52. Flutre, "Faits des Romains," p. 270; and idem, *Les manuscrits des Faits des Romains* (Paris, 1932), pp. 1–3.

53. *Faits des Romains* 2:48.

54. Guenée, "Culture historique des nobles," p. 267.

55. Ibid., p. 269.

56. *Faits des Romains* 1:274.

57. Guillaume le Breton, *Gesta Philippi Augusti,* in *Oeuvres de Rigord et de Guillaume le Breton* 1:240–241.

58. *Faits des Romains* 1:365.

59. See also Sneyders de Vogel, "Date de la composition des Faits," p. 271.

60. *Faits des Romains* 1:18–19.

61. See Flutre's discussion in ibid., 2:19–20.

62. Ibid., pp. 161–162. The interpolation occurs in the edited text on p. 397. The *Alexandri Magni iter ad Paradisium* was published in 1859 by J. Zacher. On its use in the *Roman d'Alexandre,* see Paul Meyer, *Alexandre le Grand dans la littérature française du moyen âge,* 2 vols. (Paris, 1886).

63. For a more detailed account of the structure and sources of the *Faits des Romains,* see Flutre, *Les manuscrits des Faits,* pp. 11–26.

64. Berthe Marti, "Arnulfus and the *Faits des Romains,*" *Modern Language Quarterly* 2 (1941): 3–23; see pp. 15ff. for a direct comparison of texts.

65. For example, he elaborates for his audience on the site of Bithynia, where Caesar undertook his first "chevalerie," explaining that it was also the place where "seinz Luch [St. Luke] li evangelistes i transi. La l'envoia Marcus Thermus, uns prevoz de Rome, por assenbler un estoire de nes a destruire Mitilene: ce est uns isles ou la nes seint Pol [St. Paul] brisa quant Festus, li procurerres de la terre d'outre mer, l'envoioit lïé a Rome a Noiron, a cui il avoit feit son apel contre les Juïs, qui por la foi Jhesu Crist le voloient ocirre" (*Faits des Romains* 1:10). See also, e.g., pp. 452, 554.

66. For example, on the meaning of the eagle, which the Romans carried as their insignia (p. 350), on the etymology of place-names (pp. 390, 372), on proverbial sayings that appear in Lucan (p. 394), or on the Roman practice of granting triumphs to victorious generals (pp. 56ff.).

67. Jeanette Beer (*Medieval Caesar,* p. 29) has quantified the relative contributions of the major sources in the *Faits des Romains* and identified the importance of the compiler's additions.

68. See Eva M. Sanford, "The Study of Ancient History in the Middle Ages," *Journal of the History of Ideas* 5 (1944): 39.

69. *Faits des Romains* 1:645; and commentary by Flutre, 2:207–208.

70. Ibid., 1:522.

71. Ibid., p. 675.

72. Ibid., p. 695.

73. Ibid., pp. 417–418. Lucan says merely that "infelix Argi genitor, non ille iuventae / Tempore Phocaicis ulli cessurus in armis; / Victum aevo robur cecidit, fessusque senecta / Exemplum, non miles erat" (in his prime he would have matched any man of the Phocaean army, but conquering age had brought low his strength, and the feeble old man could not fight but could show the way to others; *Bellum civile*, III, 727–730).

74. I am indebted for this view of the *Gallic Wars* to my colleague Arthur Eckstein of the University of Maryland.

75. The importance of this point to the translator's modes of rewriting his Latin source has been stressed by Schmidt-Chazan, "Traductions de la 'Guerre des Gaules,' " p. 389. My own view of the meaning and goals of the *Faits des Romains*, arrived at before the publication of Schmidt-Chazan's superb article, is substantially at one with hers, and I owe a great deal to her careful presentation of the evidence supporting it. Her article confirmed my belief that the appeal of the *Faits des Romains* for a thirteenth-century audience lay in the fact that it furnished an essential, and hitherto lacking, account of the early history of France, and not in its presentation of an imperial model for French kings. I have been guided throughout by her attentive and sensitive reading of the medieval translation in relation to the Latin source, a debt I happily acknowledge here.

76. See Beer, *Medieval Caesar*, p. 75.

77. *Faits des Romains* 1:79.

78. Ibid., p. 137.

79. Ibid., p. 178.

80. Ibid., p. 32.

81. Ibid., p. 241.

82. Ibid., p. 157.

83. Ibid., p. 118.

84. Ibid., p. 124, 335, 356.

85. Ibid., p. 334.

86. Ibid., p. 356.

87. Ibid., p. 357.

88. Schmidt-Chazan, "Traductions de la 'Guerre des Gaules,' " p. 391.

89. *Faits des Romains* 1:356.

90. "Impellit alios avaritia, alios iracundia et temeritas, quae maxime illi hominum generi est innata" (*The Gallic Wars*, ed. and trans. H. J. Edwards [Cambridge, Mass., 1963], VII, 42).

91. *Faits des Romains* 1:264.

92. Ibid., p. 209.

93. Ibid., p. 148.

94. Again, see the fine discussion in Schmidt-Chazan, "Traductions de la 'Guerre des Gaules,' " p. 394.

95. *Faits des Romains*, e.g. 1:117, 364.

96. Ibid., p. 233.
97. Ibid., p. 105.
98. Ibid., p. 161.
99. Ibid., p. 365.
100. Ibid., p. 223.
101. See Beer, *Medieval Caesar*, p. 82.
102. *Faits des Romains* 1:98.
103. Ibid., p. 100.
104. Ibid., p. 141.
105. Ibid., p. 142.
106. See Glyn Sheridan Burgess, *Contribution à l'étude du vocabulaire pré-courtois* (Geneva, 1970), pp. 57–67.
107. *Faits des Romains* 1:261.
108. *Gallic Wars*, I, 18.
109. *Faits des Romains* 1:90–91.
110. Ibid., p. 181.
111. Ibid., p. 193.
112. Ibid., pp. 308–309.
113. Ibid., p. 304.
114. In agris habet dilectum egentium ac perditorum; *Gallic Wars*, VII, 4.
115. *Faits des Romains* 1:241.
116. For example, one question that arises concerns whether Vercingetorix betrayed the French when he disappeared to forage for food. The French accused him of secretly treating with the Romans for reasons of personal ambition, because "il voloit mielz estre rois par l'otroi Cesar que par le conmun benefice as François." To this charge Vercingetorix successfully responded that he had gone only to forage and that, in any case, "il ne tendoit . . . a avoir de Cesar roiaume ne seignorie par nule traïson, car il l'avroit bien par victoire que il veoit tote apareilliee, et François meïsmes le veoient auques" (ibid., p. 250). It is not immaterial to these charges that Vercingetorix's father, Celtillus, had held the chieftainship of all Gaul and had been put to death ("by the state," says Caesar) because he had desired to be king.
117. *Gallic Wars*, VII, 1.
118. *Faits des Romains* 1:239.
119. Ibid., p. 240.
120. Ibid., p. 251.
121. Ibid., p. 260.
122. Ibid., p. 287.
123. See the interpolated account of battle in ibid., pp. 283ff.
124. Ibid., pp. 288–289.
125. Ibid., p. 298.
126. *Gallic Wars*, VII, 89.

127. Schmidt-Chazan, "Traductions de la 'Guerre des Gaules,' " p. 393.

128. See the chapter on *franc* and *franchise* in Burgess, *Contribution à l'étude du vocabulaire pré-courtois.*

129. *Gallic Wars,* VIII, 30.

130. A point well made by Beer, *Medieval Caesar,* p. 89.

131. *Faits des Romains* 1:315.

132. Ibid., p. 316.

133. Ibid., pp. 316–319.

134. Ibid., p. 321.

135. Ibid., p. 331.

136. Geoffrey, in chapter 43 of his history, identifies a Brenne of Sens: "Itali arbitrati sunt brennium Senonesque Gallos adesse." In Wace (*Roman de Brut,* lines 2904ff.), Brenne is mentioned, but not the Senonais. Brenne, chief of the Senonais who captured Rome, derives from the *scholies* on Lucan, I, 179. See Flutre's commentary in *Faits des Romains* 2:140.

137. *Faits des Romains* 1:317.

138. Ibid.

139. *Gallic Wars,* VIII, 49.

140. "Ses seuls proposemenz fu de tenir totes les citez de France en ferme pes et amor" (*Faits des Romains* 1:334).

141. Ibid., p. 335.

142. Schmidt-Chazan, "Traductions des 'Guerres des Gaules,' " p. 407.

CHAPTER FOUR

1. On the origins of chivalry, its organizing principles and rituals, see especially Jean Flori, *L'idéologie du glaive: préhistoire de la chevalerie,* Travaux d'Histoire Ethico-Politique, 43 (Geneva, 1983), and its sequel, *L'essor de la chevalerie, XIe–XIIe Siècles,* Travaux d'Histoire Ethico-Politique, 46 (Geneva, 1986). A good overview of the phenomenon also is found in Keen, *Chivalry.* For the development of armorial insignia and of seals, see Michel Pastoureau, "La diffusion des armoiries et les débuts de l'héraldique," in *La France de Philippe Auguste,* pp. 737–759; and Brigitte Bedos Rezak, "Les sceaux aux temps de Philippe Auguste," in ibid., pp. 33–57.

2. Flori, *L'essor de la chevalerie,* p. 342.

3. This process of rendering values class-specific is very close to what Northrop Frye has called "kidnapping" romance, in which general values are integrated into the ideology of a ruling class, where they express that class's dreams of its own social functions and the idealized acts of protection and responsibility that it invokes to justify those functions. It is this process of "kidnapping" romance that Frye attributes to the medieval

chivalric romance. See Frye, *The Secular Scripture: A Study of the Structure of Romance* (Cambridge, Mass., 1976), p. 57.

4. Patterson, "Virgil and the Historical Consciousness of the Twelfth Century," in *Negotiating the Past*, p. 158.

5. For a general view of this process within romance genres, see Frye, *Secular Scripture*, pp. 36ff. For the theoretical basis of the displacement of concepts from one discursive code to another within the social group, see Vance, *Mervelous Signals*, p. 119.

6. See Köhler, *L'aventure chevaleresque*, p. 79.

7. Bäuml, "Transformations of the Heroine," p. 27.

8. Patterson, "The Romance of History and the Alliterative *Morte Arthure*," in *Negotiating the Past*, p. 198.

9. Bakhtin, *Dialogic Imagination*, p. 34.

10. Thus, as Frye (*Secular Scripture*, p. 67) points out, heroic literature tends to make all heroes of action ultimately tragic heroes.

11. The phrase was coined by Northrop Frye, referring to romance.

12. Thus Lee Patterson argues that "from the twelfth century onward, the *Aeneid* served as a central paradigm for all who would protect secular history from apocalyptic judgment" ("Virgil and the Historical Consciousness of the Twelfth Century," in *Negotiating the Past*, p. 170).

13. Flori, *L'essor de la chevalerie*, p. 341.

14. Cf. Sayers, "Beginnings and Early Development of Old French Historiography," p. 44.

15. As Hanning cogently argues in "The Social Significance of Twelfth-Century Chivalric Romance," p. 8.

16. Ramsey MacMullen, *Enemies of the Roman Order: Treason, Unrest, and Alienation in the Empire* (Cambridge, Mass., 1966), p. 24.

17. Ibid.

18. According to W. R. Johnson, Lucan was led by his disaster to shape a poem that he did not want and had not intended to write: "Lucan wants to defend the greatness of Rome. He wants somehow to save it from the ruin that has overtaken it and continues, in his lifetime, to engulf it. But even as he attempts this rescue, he knows that his effort is doomed. He knows that ruin is inevitable" (in *Momentary Monsters: Lucan and His Heroes* [Ithaca, 1987], pp. 14–15; see also p. 85).

19. MacMullen, *Enemies of the Roman Order*, p. 24.

20. "Tragoediae sunt que bella tractant, ut Lucanus" (cited in Marilyn Bendena, "The Translations of Lucan and Their Influence on French Medieval Literature, Together with an Edition of the *Roumans de Jules César* by Jacos de Forest" [Ph.D. diss., Wayne State University, 1976], p. 17). See also Jesse Crosland, "Lucan in the Middle Ages, with Special Reference to the Old French Epic," *Modern Language Review* 25 (1930): 42.

21. Beer, *Medieval Caesar*, p. 138.

22. As Crosland has proposed, "Lucan in the Middle Ages," p. 34.

23. *Faits des Romains* 1:8.

24. Ibid., p. 15.

25. Ibid., p. 614.

26. Ibid., p. 616.

27. Ibid., pp. 15–16.

28. "Lors li crut ses hardemenz, et se pensa que il emprendroit greignors choses que il n'avoit fet ançois et voudroit monter en greignor pris" (ibid., p. 16).

29. Ibid.

30. See Suetonius, *The Twelve Caesars*, trans. Robert Graves (Baltimore, 1957), p. 30.

31. *Faits des Romains* 1:720.

32. Ibid., p. 721.

33. Ibid., p. 356 and note at 2:150.

34. Ibid., p. 357.

35. MacMullen, *Enemies of the Roman Order*, p. 25.

36. *Bellum civile*, I, 135.

37. On this theme in Lucan, see MacMullen, *Enemies of the Roman Order*, p. 34.

38. *Faits des Romains* 1:724.

39. Ibid., p. 723.

40. "Tot son tens voloit gaster ou en chevalerie ou en clergie, sanz les hores de boivre et de mengier" (ibid., p. 724).

41. Ibid., p. 448.

42. See George Cary, *The Medieval Alexander*, ed. D.J.A. Ross (Cambridge, 1956); see also Keen, *Chivalry*, p. 99.

43. Köhler, *L'aventure chevaleresque*, p. 28.

44. *Faits des Romains* 1:341.

45. Ibid., p. 340.

46. Ibid., p. 341.

47. Ibid., p. 731.

48. Ibid., pp. 734–735.

49. "Une grant ymage tote eschevelee, qui avoit ses chevex derroz, et avoit ses braz descoverz et nuz" (ibid., p. 348).

50. Ibid.

51. Ibid., p. 377.

52. Ibid., p. 378.

53. Ibid., p. 516.

54. Ibid., p. 517.

55. Ibid., p. 539.

56. Ibid., pp. 625, 626.

57. Ibid., p. 623.

58. Ibid., p. 627.

59. Jeanette M. A. Beer, "Stylistic Heterogeneity in the Middle Ages: An Examination of the Evidence of *Li Fet des Romains*," in *Jean Misrahi Memorial Volume: Studies in Medieval Literature*, ed. Hans R. Runte, H. Niedzielski, and W. L. Hendrickson (Columbia, S.C., 1977), p. 108.

60. "Maufé, ce dist Lucans, l'i aporterent, car il n'en vint onques se mal non et hontes as Romains. Car onques la biautez Helaine ne fist tant de mal a cels de Troies conme la biauté de ceste fist a cels de Rome, ne mes de ce que Troies fu abatue, Rome remest en estant" (*Faits des Romains* 1:623).

61. Ibid., p. 657.

62. Ibid., p. 493.

63. Johnson, *Momentary Monsters*, p. 69. In Johnson's powerful analysis of the *Pharsalia*, it is "this bitter recognition, not only of freedom's defeat but also of the deceptive hope that freedom's defeat was not inevitable, that accounts for the dark, angry laughter which overwhelms Lucan's Pompey."

64. *Faits des Romains* 1:567, 571.

65. Ibid., p. 570.

66. Johnson argues that in the *Pharsalia*, Caesar's refusal to grant proper burial for his enemies—not only for Pompey, but especially for those slain at Pharsalia—constitutes Lucan's way of representing Caesar as an "artist in death, loath to have his masterpiece [the battle of Pharsalia] ruined by funerals, since it is the number of corpses and the sheer quantity of gore which betoken not only his triumph, but also his unique luck, his right to be *the* survivor" (*Momentary Monsters*, p. 102).

67. *Faits des Romains* 1:37–39.

68. Ibid., p. 40.

69. As Catiline proclaimed to his followers: "Vos veez que un po de senators ont toute la seignorie et la richesce de la cité de Rome. . . . Mes nos, qui deüssienmes estre avant, soumes tenu vil; ne nus ne nos apele a nule hautece, qui deüssiemes estre cremu et redouté. Il ont la grace, le pooir, l'onor, la richece; nos somes deguerpi en perilz, nos somes debouté et jugié, nos somes en poverte" (ibid., p. 23).

70. Ibid., p. 43.

71. Ibid., p. 45.

72. Ibid., p. 369. See also p. 371: "Et merveille estoit il ne touchast ja a fame charnaument nule foiz, se ne fust por enfant engendrer, ainz contrestoit verteusement as aguillons de luxure."

73. See Jeanette M. A. Beer, "A Medieval Cato—Virtus or Virtue?" *Speculum* 47 (1972): 56.

74. *Faits des Romains* 1:368.

75. Ibid., pp. 574–575.

76. Ibid., p. 371.

77. Ibid., p. 586.

78. Ibid., p. 593.

79. Ibid., p. 611.

80. Ibid., p. 689.

81. This judgment is rendered as "Li tesmoinz Caton des mors Pompee" and functions as a funeral eulogy, but delivered to Cornelia and Pompey's sons Gneus and Sextus upon their learning of Pompey's death. Ibid., p. 585.

82. The phrase is Johnson's, *Momentary Monsters,* p. 69.

83. *Faits des Romains* 1:457.

84. Ibid., p. 541.

85. Ibid., p. 517.

86. Settegast, ed., *Hystore de Julius César,* p. xxxii [hereafter cited as *Hystore de Jules César*].

87. H. Suchier, "Jehan von Thuim," *Zeitschrift für romanische Philologie* 6 (1882): 386.

88. On Jean's translation procedures and sources, see V. L. Dedecek, *Etude littéraire et linguistique de "Li Hystore de Julius César" de Jehan de Tuim,* Publications of the University of Pennsylvania Series in Romanic Languages and Literature, 13 (Philadelphia, 1925), p. 87.

89. Ibid., p. 82. See also G. de Poerck, "Les Faits des Romains: à propos de deux ouvrages récents," *Revue belge de philologie et d'histoire* 15 (1936): 639.

90. J. J. Salverda de Grave, "Un imitateur du 'Roman d'Enéas' au XIIIe siècle en France," *Studi medievali,* n.s., 5 (1932): 309–316.

91. Compare the analysis of Jean's style by Dedecek, *Etude littéraire et linguistique,* pp. 89ff.

92. The scholars who have considered the relationship between Jean de Thuin's *Hystore de Jules César* and Jacos de Forest's *Roumanz de Jules César* are F. Settegast, "Jacos de Forest e la sua fonte," *Giornale di filologia* 2 (1879): 172–178; idem in *Li hystore de Jules César;* G. Paris, "Compte-rendu de F. Settegast, *Li hystore de Julius César";* Suchier, "Jehan von Thuim," p. 386; G. Bertoni, "Un nuovo manoscritto del 'Roman de Julius César,' " *Archivum Romanicum* 15 (1931): 76–82; Paul Hess, *Li roumanz de Julius César: ein Beitrag zur Cäsargeschichte im Mittelalter* (Winterthur, 1956); R. Bossuat, "Compte-rendu de Paul Hess, *Li roumanz de Julius César,"* *Le moyen âge,* 4th ser., 12 (1957): 383–385; Jean-Charles Payen, "Compte-rendu de Paul Hess, *Li roumanz de Julius César: ein Beitrag zur Cäsargeschichte im Mittelalter,"* *Romance Philology* 11 (1957–1958): 173–176. Despite this reasonably full treatment, the question remains more or less open, as Frappier indicates; see his "Peinture de la vie et des héros antiques," p. 47n.61. Marilyn Bendena, who provides an edition of the *Roumanz de Jules César* in her 1976 Ph.D. dissertation, "The Translations of Lucan," simply follows Settegast in seeing the *Roumanz* as a versification of Jean's text and adds nothing to the debate.

In the opinion of Settegast, the editor of Jean's *Hystore*, the striking similarities between the texts of Jean and of Jacos de Forest—which cover the same material in the same order and often in the same words—indicated that "one of the two works was merely a version of the other" (*Hystore de Jules César*, p. vi), thereby raising the question of which came first. Put in slightly different terms: Was the *Hystore* a prosification or *dérimage* of the *Roumanz*, or the *Roumanz* a versification of the *Hystore*? The question, when posed this way, is not without interest for the development of Old French literature in the thirteenth century. Neither prologue to the texts offers any clue to the solution of this problem, but in support of his claim for the priority of the *Hystore* to the *Roumanz*, Settegast pointed to a passage found in B.N. fr. 1457, fol. 147v, in which Jacos alludes to a source: "Si com l'estoire dist et en apres Jehanz" (ibid., p. vi)—seemingly a clear reference to Jean de Thuin, on whom, therefore, his own verse romance would seem to depend. Settegast additionally presented five passages in which Jacos de Forest's reliance on Jean's *Hystore* appeared beyond issue.

But already in his review of Settegast's edition, Gaston Paris raised doubts concerning what he considered to be Settegast's somewhat hasty conclusion. To begin with, it appeared strange to Paris that none of the faults common to the four manuscripts in which Jean's *Hystore* is preserved—that is, Vat. Reg. 834; Bibliothèque de l'Arsenal, Paris, MS. 3344; Bibliothèque Royale, Brussels, MS. 15700; and Bibliothèque Municipale de Saint-Omer, MS. 722—reappears in Forest's verse text. Indeed, Settegast himself had pointed out several places where Jacos de Forest had ameliorated the readings found in the *Hystore*, presumably by consulting a manuscript of Lucan independent of the manuscripts on which the *Hystore* was based. More telling, Jacos de Forest's amplifications are in closer agreement with Lucan's *Pharsalia* or Caesar's *Bellum civile* (the Latin sources for the cited passages), thus suggesting a direct dependence on the Latin originals (G. Paris, "Compte-rendu de F. Settegast," pp. 380–381). Far from drawing the conclusion from these observations that the *Roumanz* antedated the *Hystore*, however, Paris suggested that both texts derived from a lost prose version that was more developed than Jean's, and thus closer to the *Roumanz*. The *Hystore* of Jean de Thuin, in Paris's view, represented an abbreviated redaction of this lost prose version.

This remained the received wisdom on the relationship between the two works until a new manuscript of the *Roumanz* was discovered in 1931 by G. Bertoni in the Bibliothèque Bodmeriana. The manuscript dates from the end of the thirteenth century and originated from the hand of a copyist belonging to eastern France, probably Lorraine ("Un nuovo manoscritto," p. 77). In this new manuscript, the poem is not attributed, as in B.N. fr. 1457, to Jacos de Forest; rather, in the passages corresponding to those in which the name "Jacos" normally figured, one finds "Jehan," that is, the same name found in manuscripts of the *Hystore*. This finding raised the possibility that Jean de Thuin was the author not only of the *Hystore*, but of the *Roumanz* as well, relegating Jacos de Forest to the status of "un plagiaro" (ibid., p. 78).

Bertoni's tantalizing suggestion that Jean de Thuin wrote both the verse *Roumanz* and the prose *Hystore* remained without further proof or investigation, and it was not until Paul Hess undertook a complete review of the problem in a new study of the manuscript tradition that an apparent solution to the question of the relationship between the two texts emerged. Comparing the two works, Hess demonstrated that the *roman* was not only more developed and more faithful to the Latin sources than the history, but that the prose *Hystore* preserved in an unexpected way a large number of words that figured in the rhyme of the verse text, a phenomenon often found in works created by the process of "dérimage" or prosification in the thirteenth century (*Li roumanz de Julius César*, pp. 25–27). See also R. Bossuat, "Compte-rendu de Paul Hess," p. 384. On the general question of the practice and procedures of *dérimage*, see Speer and Foulet, "Is *Marques de Rome* a Derhymed Romance?" From this, Hess not unreasonably concluded that the *Roumanz de Jules César* preceded the *Hystore*, and that the latter text was a prose revision of the earlier romance. If so, it is likely, according to Bossuat ("Compte-rendu de Paul Hess," p. 384), that neither work was written before the last third of the thirteenth century, meaning that the date traditionally given to the *Hystore*, 1242, should be revised accordingly. Payen ("Compte-rendu de Paul Hess," p. 175), in contrast, considers it likely that the *Roumanz* was written at the beginning of the thirteenth century, making the traditional date of 1242 perfectly possible.

93. Hess, *Roumanz de Julius César*, pp. 28–29.

94. This is the opinion of both Payen, "Compte-rendu de Paul Hess," p. 175; and Frappier, "Peinture de la vie et des héros antiques," p. 47.

95. See L.-F. Flutre, "Li faits des Romains," p. 272, who points to a number of passages that demonstrate that Jean not only knew the *Faits des Romains* but also had a copy of it before him while writing his book and from which he drew certain expressions, scenes, and interpretations. F. Settegast, the editor of the *Hystore*, stresses, however, the relative independence of Jean from the *Faits des Romains*: "*Li Faits* et il testo di Jehan de Tuim sono fra loro indipendenti; le somiglianze che reciprocamente presentano, provengono d'all avera ambedue in parte la medesima fonte, Lucano" ("Jacos de Forest e la sua fonte," p. 176)—although Settegast does agree that several passages indicate that Jean knew the *Faits*. In general, although Jean may have known the *Faits des Romains*, his direct borrowings from it remain scant and appear only incidentally in some surface features, when present at all.

96. See, among others, Köhler, *L'aventure chevaleresque*, p. 149; and, for the origins and development of courtly ideals, C. Stephen Jaeger, *The Origins of Courtliness: Civilizing Trends and the Formation of Courtly Ideals 939–1210* (Philadelphia, 1985).

97. Cf. Erich Auerbach, "The Knight Sets Forth," in *Mimesis: The Representation of Reality in Western Literature*, trans. Willard R. Trask (Princeton, 1953), p. 134.

98. See the discussion of this process in courtly romance in Lee Patterson's analysis of the *Roman d'Enéas* in "Virgil and the Historical Consciousness of the Twelfth Century," in *Negotiating the Past*, p. 177.

99. Stephen Jaeger has emphasized the centrality of beauty to courtly ideals, including beauty of conduct. He cites a long passage from Saxo Grammaticus's *Gesta Danorum*, book X, in which the ideal of beauty in conduct is employed for the subjection of the "chaotic impulses" of the warrior classes in service to the duties of social life. See Jaeger, *Origins of Courtliness*, pp. 137–188.

100. *Hystore de Jules César*, p. 2.

101. He writes:

> Or s'en tesent de cest mestier,
> Se ne sont clerc ou chevalier
> Car ausi pueent escouter
> Conme li asnes a harper.

Le roman de Thèbes, ed. Guy Renaud de Lage (Paris, 1969), vol. 1, lines 13–16.

102. "Mes tant i a k'il redoute sour toute riens les mesdis des envios, k'il ne li atournent a folie cou k'il fait pour sens et pour edefiier les cuers des preudoumes ki l'estore en ascoutereont" (*Hystore de Jules César*, p. 3).

103. "Pronus ad omne nefas et qui nesciret, in armis / Quam magnum virtus crimen civilibus esset" (*Bellum civile*, VI, 147–148, trans. J. D. Duff [Cambridge, Mass., 1927], p. 315).

104. For the full passage, see *Hystore de Jules César*, pp. 102–105.

105. As Köhler has so brilliantly demonstrated in *L'aventure chevaleresque*.

106. *Hystore de Jules César*, pp. 103–104.

107. See Vance, *Mervelous Signals*, p. 124.

108. *Hystore de Jules César*, p. 105.

109. Dedecek, *Etude littéraire et linguistique*, p. 49.

110. Ibid.. Jean himself, in the *explicit*, refers to his *Hystore* as *le roumant*: "Et Diex soit warde de tous ciaus ki le matere en recevront et ki le roumant oront" (*Hystore de Jules César*, p. 245). The reference here, of course, signifies a work in the vernacular, the same sense in which, as late as the end of the thirteenth century, a work of quasi-official history like

the *Grandes chroniques de France* is still called "Le Roman des Rois." See Guenée, *Histoire et culture historique*, p. 321.

111. *Hystore de Jules César*, p. 4.

112. Ibid., p. 25.

113. Ibid., p. 23.

114. Ibid., p. 113.

115. Ibid., p. 140.

116. Ibid., p. 6. Even stranger is Jean's assertion that Ptolemy had his "plus haus barons" dubbed in accordance with Egyptian custom (ibid., p. 202)!

117. Ibid., p. 220.

118. Ibid., p. 53.

119. Ibid., pp. 221–222.

120. It is true that traces of Lucan's themes remain in certain speeches, notably those of Cato (see, e.g., ibid., pp. 147ff.), whom it would have been impossible to represent as anything other than an upholder of Roman traditions of *franchise* and still make sense of his actions or their motivations. But the dominant tone of the *Hystore* differs strikingly both from Lucan and from the vernacular *Faits des Romains*.

121. *Hystore de Jules César*, p. 12.

122. Ibid., pp. 12–13.

123. Ibid., p. 40.

124. Ibid., p. 12.

125. Ibid., pp. 17–18.

126. Ibid., p. 22.

127. "D'autre part a .I. jor ki passes iert Pompeius avoit conduites les os de Roume outre mer, et tant fisent adont li Roumain par lor esfort k'il prisent Jerusalem et roberent et destruisent, et Pompeius si fist brisier le temple Domini et i fist ses chevaus establer" (ibid., p. 40).

128. "Ensi se venga nostre sires de Pompee" (ibid.). The *Faits des Romains* reports the same incident, but without the certainty that Pompey's defeat results from an act of divine retribution: "Une chose fist Pompee en Jerusalen, par que l'en quide que ceste dereenne mesestance li avenist, car il souffri que si home establerent lor chevax ou temple." This report is, furthermore, immediately followed by a passage praising Pompey's humility and moral character, which has the effect of mitigating the consequences of the reported sacrilege. See *Faits des Romains* 1:571–572. The source for the story of Pompey stabling horses in the Temple at Jerusalem is Peter Comester's *Historiae diversae*, chap. 9: "et irruentes Romani profanaverunt templum et, ut alibi legitur, equos in porticibus stabulaverunt. Ob quam rem traditur numquam de caetero pugnasse Pompeium quin vinceretur, qui hactenus fortunatissimus fuerat" (cited in *Faits des Romains* 2:194).

129. *Hystore de Jules César*, p. 111.

130. Ibid., p. 40.

131. Ibid., p. 39.

132. See the remarks on this point by Dedecek, *Etude littéraire et linguistique*, p. 36.

133. On Jean's view of Caesar, see, in addition to Dedecek, Frappier, "Peinture de la vie et des héros antiques," pp. 46ff.; and Crosland, "Lucan in the Middle Ages," p. 34.

134. Dedecek, *Etude littéraire et linguistique*, p. 80.

135. *Faits des Romains* 1:376.

136. "Ge voil que tu vives par ma merci et par mon don, tot soit ice que tu voilles morir. Que cil qui se tienent a Pompee i prengnent essample et soient en boene esperance de ma merci quant jes avrai conquis, car je les tieng ja por veincuz" (ibid.).

137. *Hystore de Jules César*, p. 33.

138. Ibid., p. 66.

139. Cf. Lucan, *Bellum civile*, IV, 344–363.

140. Ibid., IV, 363–364.

141. *Hystore de Jules César*, pp. 66–67.

142. Ibid., p. 124.

143. Ibid., p. 125.

144. "Quamquam plebeio tectus amictu, indocilis privata loqui" (*Bellum civile*, V, 537–538).

145. *Hystore de Jules César*, p. 83.

146. Ibid., p. 85.

147. On the ancient sources of courtly ideology, see especially Jaeger, *Origins of Courtliness*, who has traced the roots of courtly principles in Germanic literature to classical sources preserved and reactivated in the courtly world of the twelfth century.

148. Dedecek, in fact, calls the interpolated romance Jean's "chef d'oeuvre" (*Etude littéraire et linguistique*, p. 39).

149. The relevant portion of MS. 2200 (fols. 191v–197v) was published by Arthur Långfors in "Deux traités sur l'amour tirés du Manuscrit 2200 de la Bibliothèque Sainte-Geneviève," *Romania* 56 (1930): 362–373, who believed that he had discovered an original work. Flutre demonstrated, however, that the text found at Sainte-Geneviève was merely a copy of Jean de Thuin; see his "Sur un traité d'amour courtois du Ms. 2200 de la Bibliothèque de Sainte-Geneviève," *Romania* 59 (1933): 270–276.

150. See N.H.J. van den Boogaard, "L'art d'aimer en prose," in *Etudes de civilisation médiévale (IXe–XIIe siècles): mélanges offerts à E.-R. Labande* (Poitiers, 1974), pp. 687–698.

151.   . . . et in media rabie medioque furore
Et Pompeianis habitata manibus aula

Sanguine Thessalicae cladis perfusus adulter
Admisit Venerem curis, et miscuit armis
Inlicitosque toros et non ex coniuge partus.

Bellum civile, X, 72–76; translation by J. D. Duff, p. 594.

152. Cf. the discussion in Frappier, "Peinture de la vie et des héros antiques," p. 51n.71.

153. *Hystore de Jules César*, p. 160.

154. Ibid., pp. 163–164.

155. Ibid., p. 164.

156. Hanning, "Social Significance of Twelfth-Century Chivalric Romance," pp. 4ff. See also idem, *The Individual in Twelfth-Century Romance* (New Haven, 1977).

157. *Hystore de Jules César*, p. 169.

158. " . . . Est couchies pour soi reposer, mais il ne puet; car amours le met en tante pensee et en tant travaus que il n'i puet reposer ne dormir, ains vait tournant en son lit et retournant, et se delite toutes voies de ramenbrer le grant biaute de cele ki son cuer a entierement, si k'il ne puet penser a autre chose" (ibid., p. 167).

159. Ibid.

160. Ibid., pp. 167–168.

161. Ibid., p. 170.

162. Ibid., pp. 171ff. See also the comments on Jean de Thuin by Crosland, "Lucan in the Middle Ages," p. 34.

163. See Dedecek's remarks on the placement of the love affair at the end of the *Hystore* as, in effect, making an argument that Cleopatra's love figures as recompense for the "faits d'armes de ce chevalier parfait" (*Etude littéraire et linguistique*, p. 91).

164. *Hystore de Jules César*, p. 182.

165. Ibid., p. 183.

166. Ibid.

167. Ibid., p. 187.

168. See the discussion of this in Dedecek, *Etude littéraire et linguistique*, p. 62.

169. *Hystore de Jules César*, p. 190.

170. Ibid., pp. 79–80.

171. Ibid., p. 245.

172. Ibid., p. 143.

173. Ibid., p. 232.

174. Ibid., p. 241.

175. Ibid., p. 139.

176. Ibid., p. 245.

CHAPTER FIVE

1. Lorraine Daston compellingly argues that the idea of historical "fact" as we understand that term did not emerge until the seventeenth century; see her "The Prehistory of Objectivity," in *Rethinking the Physical World: Essays in Honor of Erwin N. Hiebert*, ed. Mary Jo Nye, Joan Richards, and Roger Stuewer (Cambridge, forthcoming). In the Middle Ages, what we call "facts" were a complex amalgam of *res gestae*, "things done" that could never have the hard-edged, stubborn status of "facts" (even when *res verae que factae sunt*, "true things that were done," as Isidore of Seville called history), since they could never be seen or understood apart from the ideological and interpretive systems of thought and theory *by which* they were apprehended. Even today, the question of history's status as a putatively objective, i.e. "factual," form of knowledge about the past, a knowledge communicated in narratives obviously mediated by literary techniques of representation, remains the subject of often violent disagreement, as the publication of Hayden White's *Metahistory* in 1973 disclosed. On the modern debate concerning the status of historical knowledge in relation to the literary modes employed for the communication of that knowledge, see Angus Fletcher, ed., *The Literature of Fact* (New York, 1976); the collection of essays in Dominick LaCapra and Steven L. Kaplan, eds., *Modern European Intellectual History: Reappraisals and New Perspectives* (Ithaca, 1982); Hayden White, "The Question of Narrative in Contemporary Historical Theory," *History and Theory* 23 (1984): 1–33; and Gabrielle M. Spiegel, "History, Historicism, and the Social Logic of the Text in the Middle Ages," *Speculum* 65 (1990): 59–86.

2. On these developments see also Sayers, "Beginnings and Early Development of Old French Historiography," pp. 338ff.

3. Godzich and Kittay, *Emergence of Prose*, p. 167.

4. Suzanne Fleischman, "On the Representation of History and Fiction in the Middle Ages," *History and Theory* 22 (1983): 280.

5. Cf. Guenée, *Histoire et culture historique*, p. 23.

6. On this see Sayers, "Beginnings and Early Development of Old French Historiography," p. 111.

7. On the knight's deposition of his tale of adventure at the Arthurian court, see Burns, *Arthurian Fictions*, pp. 7ff.

8. For example, Walpole, "Philip Mouskés and the Pseudo-Turpin Chronicle"; Sayers, "Beginnings and Early Development of Old French Historiography"; Petit-Dutaillis, "Une nouvelle chronique du règne de Philippe-Auguste"; and idem, *Etude sur la vie et le règne de Louis VIII*.

9. Cf. Sayers, "Beginnings and Early Development of Old French Historiography," p. 160.

10. Michael Clanchy has demonstrated the tenacity of the medieval preference for eyewitness testimony over the evidence of written documents and the pervasive medieval belief in the greater reliability of visual and aural over written communication, even in the realm of law courts. See his *From Memory to Written Record: England 1066–1307* (Cambridge, Mass., 1979).

11. The phrase is that of Godzich and Kittay, *Emergence of Prose,* p. 155.

12. Cf. the discussion of this phenomenon in ibid., p. 153.

13. Sayers, "Beginnings and Early Development of Old French Historiography," p. 167.

14. Jodogne, "Naissance de la prose française," p. 307.

15. Jean Frappier, "Le roman en prose en France au XIIIe siècle," in *Grundriss der romanischen Literaturen des Mittelalters,* vol. 4, pt. 1 (Heidelberg, 1978), p. 505. For a more general treatment of the desire for verisimilitude and "realism" in romance literature, see Fourrier, *Le courant réaliste dans le roman courtois,* vol. 1: *Les débuts.*

16. Godzich and Kittay, *Emergence of Prose,* p. 175.

17. Walter J. Ong has commented that in the passage from a primarily oral to a primarily written culture, the attempt to create a narrative form appropriate for writing, as distinct from the narrative structures employed in oral performance, necessitated the abandonment of the poet's voice, if for no other reason than to transform the episodic, paratactic structure characteristic of orally delivered stories, a transformation that was initiated but remained incomplete, Ong claims, until the rise of a print culture. As he indicates: "A narrator in an oral culture normally and naturally operated in episodic patterning, and the elimination of narrative voice appears to have been essential at first to rid the story line of patterning. The original voice of the oral narrator took on various new forms when it became the silent voice of the writer, as the distancing reflected by writing invited various fictionalizations of the decontextualized reader and writer. But until print, the voice's allegiance to episode always remained firm" (*Orality and Literacy,* p. 148).

18. Sayers, "Beginnings and Early Development of Old French Historiography," p. 284.

19. On this function of the narrator in realist fiction, see Elizabeth Deeds Ermarth, *Realism and Consensus in the English Novel* (Princeton, 1983), chaps. 1–3.

20. Sayers, "Beginnings and Early Development of Old French Historiography," p. 333.

21. Ibid., p. 450.

22. On the need for such a "pseudo-reality" and the techniques employed by vernacular writers in its creation, see Bäuml, "Varieties and Consequences of Medieval Literacy and Illiteracy," pp. 237–265, esp. 257ff.

23. Ibid., p. 265.

24. Eugene Vance, " 'Aucassin et Nicolette' as a Medieval Comedy of Signification and Exchange," in *The Nature of Medieval Narrative*, ed. Minnette Grunmann-Gaudet and Robin F. Jones, French Forum Monographs, 22 (Lexington, 1980), p. 62.

25. These techniques are discussed in Duggan, *Song of Roland*. For medieval narrative generally, see William R. Ryding, *Structure in Medieval Narrative* (The Hague, 1971).

26. Sayers points to the beginning use of constructions such as *"tant* (or *si)* . . . *que,"* which introduce a consecutive clause as an explicit stating of the causal relation between two events. Initially, words like *si* that serve as syntactic links between clauses endeavor to suggest close causal connections, although the actions so united are not really placed in the relation of cause and effect, but function merely in terms of a temporal succession. See his "Beginnings and Early Development of Old French Historiography," p. 410. As the vernacular chronicle matured, however, a growing concern with causality appears in the use of terms like *ochoison,* enabled, as the use of prose became more flexible and grammaticalized, by an increasing ability to master the intricacies of hypotactic construction. At some point, the logic of sequence becomes the logic of sequential causality. On the weak grammatical structure of early Old French textual discourse, see Suzanne Fleischman, "Philology, Linguistics, and the Discourse of the Medieval Text," *Speculum* 65 (1990): 19–37. Fleischman attributes the weak syntactical structure of written vernacular to its still strong ties to orality.

27. Frye, *The Great Code*, pp. 7–8.

28. For an anthropological discussion of this process of nullification by recourse to pristine origins, as in the Balinese state, see Geertz, "Politics Past, Politics Present," p. 334.

29. Victor LeClerc, "Notices supplémentaires chroniques [Anonyme de Béthune]," *Histoire littéraire de la France* 21 (1895): 670.

30. " . . . Dedi Magistro Matheo, clerico meo, qui michi diu et benigne servit, pro salute anime mee, duodecim libras monete currentis Bethunie annuatim accipiendas ad scopas Bethunie, ex una et altera parte, ad clausum Pasca, sicut eas capere consuevi. . . . " A copy of this charter was sent to Delisle by M. Guesnon according to a *vidimus* from the year 1302, in the Archives of the Pas-de-Calais (Trésor des Chartes Artois, A.5.23). The same charter is found on fol. 20v of the cartulary of Saint-Barthélmi de Béthune, also at the archives; it is cited in Delisle, "Notice sur la chronique d'un anonyme de Béthune," p. 369.

31. "Auctor, miles quidam, forte 'siergans et menestreus' Roberti de Bethunia fuisse, hunc in bello Flandrensi a. 1213. 1214 in itineribus et in bello Anglico a. 1215 et 1216 comitatus esse videtur" (O. Holder-Egger,

ed., "Ex historiis Ducum Normanniae et regum Angliae," in *Monumenta Germaniae historica, Scriptores* 26:700).

32. Petit-Dutaillis, "Une nouvelle chronique du règne de Philippe-Auguste," p. 69. On Guillaume, see Spiegel, *Chronicle Tradition of Saint-Denis*, pp. 63ff.; and Baldwin, *Government of Philip Augustus*, pp. 362ff.

33. See above, note 31.

34. See Warlop, *Flemish Nobility*, p. 45. There is, however, no evidence to support this hypothesis.

35. Ibid., p. 149.

36. Galbert of Bruges, *The Murder of Charles the Good*, pp. 29, 196.

37. See chapter 1.

38. Warlop, *Flemish Nobility* 1:261.

39. Dept, "Influences anglaises et françaises," p. 55.

40. "Preceptus est Vic. Notingham quod faciat habere Robertus de Beton. plenarium saisum de omnibus terris et redditibus, unde Willemus pater ipsius Roberti fuit saisitus in domino suo ut de suo die qua obiit et que ipsum Robertum hereditarie contingunt et valorem illarum terrarum par literas suas sigillatas scire aciat domino Just" (Hardy, ed., *Rotuli litterarum clausarum*, p. 208).

41. "Liberate de thesauro nostro Roberto de Bethun. centum librum de termino Pasch. futuri de feodo suo" (ibid., p. 184b).

42. "Rex omnibus &c Noveritis nos concessisse quod assedebimus dilecto et fideli nostro Robert. de Betun. ducento libratas terre in Angliam ad Pasch. anno regni nostro XVII de quibus se pacatum tenere debebit" (Thomas Duffus Hardy, *Rotuli litterarum patentium* [London, 1835], p. 138).

43. "Il meismes fu eslius à moustrer la parole devant le roi" (*Histoire des ducs de Normandie et des rois d'Angleterre*, p. 128).

44. Holder-Egger, ed., "Ex historiis Ducum Normanniae et regum Angliae," p. 700.

45. "Hues de la Bretaigne, que Robers de Betune, qui cousins il ert, avoit fait novel chevalier" (*Chronique des rois de France*, B.N. nouv. acq. fr. 6295, fol. 55r). Cf. *Histoire des ducs de Normandie et des rois d'Angleterre*, p. 133: "Hues de la Bretaigne, uns cousins Robert de Biethune, qui nouviaus chevaliers estoit." See also Delisle, "Notice sur la chronique d'un anonyme de Béthune," p. 374.

46. Delisle, "Notice sur la chronique d'un anonyme de Béthune," p. 374. These matters are reported in the *Chronique des rois de France* on fol. 56r and in the *Histoire des ducs de Normandie et des rois d'Angleterre* on pp. 141–142.

47. *Histoire des ducs de Normandie et des rois d'Angleterre*, p. 100.

48. Ibid., p. 104.

49. On the manuscript tradition of the Anonymous's histories, see Walpole, *Anonymous Old French Translation of the Pseudo-Turpin Chronicle;* idem, *Le Turpin français dit le Turpin I;* idem, "Philip Mouskés and the Pseudo-Turpin Chronicle"; idem, "Prolégomènes à une édition du Turpin français"; Delisle, "Chronique française des rois de France par un Anonyme de Béthune"; idem, "Chronique des ducs de Normandie," *Histoire littéraire de la France* 32 (1898): 182–194; idem, "Notice sur la chronique d'un anonyme de Béthune"; idem, "Annales [B.N. fr. 10130]," *Histoire littéraire de la France* 32 (1898): 207–208; Marc Du Pouget, "Recherches sur les chroniques latines de Saint-Denis: commentaire et édition critique de la *Descriptio Clavi et Corone Domini* et de deux autres textes relatifs à la légende Carolingienne" (Thesis, Ecole de Chartes, 1977); Philippe Lauer, "Louis IV d'Outremer et le fragment d'Isembart et Gormont," *Romania* 26 (1897): 161–174; LeClerc, "Notices supplémentaires chroniques"; Paul Meyer, "Notice du Manuscrit fr. 17177 de la Bibliothèque Nationale," *Bulletin de la Société des Anciens Textes Français,* 1895, pp. 80–118; idem, "Notice sur le MS. II.6.24 de la Bibliothèque de Cambridge"; idem, "Compte-Rendu de L. Delisle, 'Notice sur la chronique d'un anonyme de Béthune du temps de Philippe-Auguste,' " *Romania* 21 (1892): 302–303; Alain Marechaux, "Chronique d'un Anonyme de Béthune" (Thesis, Université de Lille, 1976); Petit-Dutaillis, "Une nouvelle chronique du règne de Philippe-Auguste"; idem, *Etude sur la vie et le règne de Louis VIII;* Woledge and Clive, *Répertoire des plus anciens textes en prose française.*

50. *Histoire des ducs de Normandie et des rois d'Angleterre,* p. 127.

51. B.N. nouv. acq. fr. 6295, fols. 55v–59r. Cf. Léopold Delisle, introduction to *Chronique des rois de France,* in *Recueil des historiens des Gaules et de la France* 24:752.

52. Delisle, "Chronique française des rois de France," p. 228.

53. Holder-Egger, ed., "Ex historiis Ducum Normanniae," p. 700. The *Histoire des ducs de Normandie et des rois d'Angleterre* is found in the following manuscripts: B.N. nouv. acq. fr. 6295; Cambridge II.6.24.; B.N. fr. 24431; B.N. fr. 2137; B.N. fr. 10130; Ashburnham 54; Arsenal 3516; Vat. Reg. Lat. 936; B.N. fr. 4946; B.N. fr. 4619; B.N. fr. 12203; B.N. fr. 24210; Berne 307; and Lille 536.

54. See P. Meyer, "Notice sur le MS. II.6.24 de la Bibliothèque de Cambridge," p. 42.

55. *Histoire des ducs de Normandie et des rois d'Angleterre,* p. i.

56. P. Meyer, "Notice sur le MS. II.6.24 de la Bibliothèque de Cambridge," pp. 43–44. Other manuscripts of the *Chronique de Normandie* are found in B.N. fr. 10130, B.N. fr. 2137, and Arsenal 3516; in more developed redactions in Berne 307 and B.N. fr. 4946; and, as incorporated by the Anonymous of Béthune, in B.N. fr. 17203 and B.N. fr. 12203. There is also a version posterior to the Anonymous in B.N. fr. 4619,

which dates from the fourteenth century. Francisque Michel published the text following 2137 and 24431 in *Les chroniques de Normandie* (Rouen, 1939), and O. Holder-Egger published fragments of what can be called the common version in the *Monumenta Germaniae historica, Scriptores* 26:702–703.

57. I discovered this by accident when comparing B.N. nouv. acq. fr. 6295 with B.N. fr. 10130, which covers the material omitted by the scribe of 6295, as do other manuscripts. The manuscripts containing the *Chronique des rois de France* in various forms of development are Cambridge II.6.24; Ashburnham 54; B.N. fr. 24431; B.N. fr. 17177; Arsenal 3516; Bibliothèque Ste-Geneviève 792; and an abridged copy found in the Vatican, Reg. Lat. 610. On them see preceding note.

58. On the *Abbreviatio*, see Spiegel, *Chronicle Tradition of Saint-Denis*, pp. 41ff.; Lair, "Mémoire sur deux chroniques Latines"; and George Waitz, "Über die sogenannte Abbreviatio gestorum regum," *Neues Archiv der Gesellschaft für ältere deutsche Geschichtskunde* 7 (1882): 385–390.

59. On this version of *Pseudo-Turpin*, see Walpole, "Prolégomènes à une édition du Turpin français."

60. Marc du Pouget has edited the French versions of the *Descriptio*. I would like to thank him for sending me a copy of the typescript of his edition.

61. For a description of Vat. Reg. Lat. 610, see Walpole, "Prolégomènes à une édition du Turpin français," pp. 214ff. Although 610 covers the same historical period as B.N. nouv. acq. fr. 6295, it does so in a much abridged version, leaving 6295 as the most complete text of the *Chronique*.

62. The full text of the *Historia* has never been edited, but fragments appear in the *Recueil des Historiens des Gaules et de la France* 7:259, 9:41, 10:277, 11:319, 12:217, 17:424; as well as in the *Monumenta Germaniae historica, Scriptores* 26:394–396.

63. On this text, see chapter 6.

64. On the Anonymous's use of the episode of Isembart and Gormond, see Lauer, "Louis IV d'Outremer et le fragment d'Isembart et Gormont."

65. See above, chapter 1.

66. "Li jouene rois Henris d'Engleterre . . . l'ert venus servir od grant ost" (*Chronique des rois de France*, p. 754).

67. See Petit-Dutaillis, "Une nouvelle chronique du règne de Philippe-Auguste," p. 68.

68. Walpole, "Philip Mouskés and the Pseudo-Turpin Chronicle," p. 350.

69. Ibid., p. 351.

70. Sayers, "Beginnings and Early Development of Old French Historiography," p. 191.

71. *Chronique des rois de France,* B.N. nouv. acq. fr. 6295, fol. 4r. The first three parts of the *Chronique* remain unedited. I will cite from the manuscript except in cases where the quotation comes from part 4, edited by Delisle in volume 24 of the *Recueil des historiens des Gaules et de la France.* All citations not followed by reference to a manuscript hereafter derive from the edited portion of the *Chronique.*

72. B.N. fr. 17177, fol. 252v.

73. B.N. nouv. acq. fr. 6295, fol. 4r.

74. Ibid.

75. *Histoire des ducs de Normandie et des rois d'Angleterre,* p. 2. "Byse" normally means "north wind" and is used here metaphorically for that which comes out of the north.

76. B.N. nouv. acq. fr. 6295, fols. 34v–35r.

77. *Histoire des ducs de Normandie et des rois d'Angleterre,* p. 29.

78. Ibid., pp. 58–59.

79. Ibid., p. 88.

80. *Chronique des rois de France,* pp. 756–757.

81. *Histoire des ducs de Normandie et des rois d'Angleterre,* pp. 38–39.

82. Ibid., p. 66.

83. *Chronique des rois de France,* p. 758.

84. Ibid.

85. Ibid.

86. Ibid., pp. 762–763.

87. *Histoire des ducs de Normandie et des rois d'Angleterre,* p. 105.

88. Ibid., p. 109.

89. Ibid., p. 104.

90. Ibid., p. 109.

91. Ibid., p. 140.

92. Ibid., p. 145.

93. Ibid., pp. 149–151.

94. Ibid., p. 151.

95. Ibid., p. 153.

96. Ibid., pp. 128–129.

97. *Chronique des rois de France,* p. 754.

98. Ibid.

99. See chapter 1.

100. *Chronique des rois de France,* p. 754.

101. Ibid., p. 758; emphasis added.

102. Ibid., pp. 758–759.

103. Ibid., p. 759.

104. "N'en ot gaires baron en cele marche de Flandres, fors Willaumes, l'avoé de Betune, et Guillaume le chastelain de Saint Homer, qui malvais samblant ne li feissent" (ibid.).

105. Ibid.

106. The fullest report of this development by the Anonymous of Béthune appears in the *Histoire des ducs de Normandie et des rois d'Angleterre* (p. 120), in which he explains that "li rois [Philip] manda toz les haus barons de sa tierre à parlement, si lor requist que il venissent o lui en Engletierre pour le regne conquerre. Tout li otriierent, fors li cuens de Flandres, qui ne li vaut otriier se il ne li rendoit Saint-Omer et Aire, que ses fils Looys li avoit tolu."

107. *Chronique des rois de France*, p. 765.

108. *Histoire des ducs de Normandie et des rois d'Angleterre*, p. 120.

109. *Chronique des rois de France*, p. 766.

110. See chapter 1.

111. *Histoire des ducs de Normandie et des rois d'Angleterre*, p. 126.

112. Ibid., p. 128.

113. Ibid., p. 131.

114. *Chroniques des rois de France*, p. 764. The wording of this account in the *Histoire des ducs de Normandie et des rois d'Angleterre* is slightly different, especially with respect to Guerin, whom the Anonymous there designates as *maistres* of the royal council (p. 120).

115. For example, by Guillaume le Breton, *Gesta Philippi Augusti*, p. 256.

116. On this development, as well as on the background and functions of Philip Augustus's other counselors and servitors, see Baldwin, "The King's New Men," in *Government of Philip Augustus*, pp. 101ff.

117. Ibid., pp. 115–116.

118. Ibid., p. 123.

119. On the familial background of Henri, see ibid., p. 113.

120. Ibid., p. 111.

121. E. Langlois, ed., *Le couronnement de Louis: chanson de geste du XIIe siècle* (Paris, 1925), p. 7, lines 204–206.

122. The case of England differs significantly from that of France, since the English king maintained a large and raucous court. This difference was noted still in 1227 by a citizen of Caen, who sent an intelligence report to Henry III in which he said that he had overheard the castellan of Caen and a certain Master Nicolas, a clerk of Guerin, contending that the English kings were foolish not to follow the practice of the French monarch in taking counsel. Whereas Philip Augustus had consulted only Guerin and Barthélemy de Roye, they declared, English kings took counsel from many. (Cited in Baldwin, *Government of Philip Augustus*, p. 125.) Although the size of the English court remained large, the issue of "new men" was no less important across the Channel. An echo of this appears in the Anonymous's discussion of William Marshall, who rose to the position of justiciar of England but who, the Anonymous affirms, "n'estoit mie de grant linage." Like his French counterparts, William, in addition to

380 / Notes to Pages 264-269

the riches that he had earned from tournaments, enormously benefited through his participation in government, a fact the Anonymous is quick to point out: "Et por chou k'il estoit justice d'Engletierre, s'estoit-il moult acreus de grans tierres et de haus mariages: par coi il avoit moult grant pooir." Indeed, so great was the influence and wealth amassed by William Marshall, according to the Anonymous of Béthune, that it excited King John's rage: "Li rois se courecha à la justice pour deus choses: l'une fu por chou que il le doutoit por sa poissance; l'autre si fu por chou que il avoit couvoitise d'avoir de ses deniers, dont il avoit assés: par coi il le raienst, et li fist puis assés de maus" (*Histoire des ducs de Normandie et des rois d'Angleterre*, pp. 115–116).

123. *Chronique des rois de France*, p. 758.

124. The Anonymous also discusses Eustache le Moine, perhaps the most famous mercenary of all, in his *Histoire des ducs de Normandie et des rois d'Angleterre*, pp. 167ff.

125. Duby, "Transformations sociales dans le milieu aristocratique," p. 717.

126. For a fuller discussion of this ideological justification and its connection to the theory of the three orders, see Georges Duby, *Les trois ordres, ou l'imaginaire du féodalisme* (Paris, 1978).

127. *Chronique des rois de France*, p. 768.

128. Ibid., pp. 768–769.

129. Ibid., p. 768.

130. Ibid., p. 770.

131. Pirenne, *Histoire de Belgique*, p. 154.

CHAPTER SIX

1. On the Ménestrel, see Ernst Langlois, "Notices et extraits des manuscrits français et provençaux de Rome antérieurs au XVIe siècle," *Notices et extraits des manuscrits de la Bibliothèque Nationale*, 33, pt. 2 (1889): 57; Paulin Paris, "Premières compilations de l'histoire générale des Français," *Histoire littéraire de la France* 21 (1895): 734–736; Natalis de Wailly, "Examen de quelques questions relatives à l'origine des chroniques de Saint-Denys," *Mémoires de l'Institut Royal de France, Académie des Inscriptions et Belles-Lettres* 17, pt. 1 (1847): 379–407; Mandach, *Chronique dite Santongeaise Texte Franco-Occitan inédit "Lee."* Kathleen James has produced a critical edition of the text in a doctoral thesis: "Critical Edition of *La Chronique d'un ménestrel d'Alphonse de Poitiers* as contained in B.N. fr. 5700" (Ph.D. diss., University of Maryland, College Park, 1984). The Ménestrel's text is a literal translation of the *Historia Regum Francorum jusque ad annum 1214*, with three final chapters drawing on the *Speculum historiale* of Vincent of Beauvais, and was written around 1260.

2. For C. R. Borland and R.G.L. Ritchie's argument and their edition of the folio leaves, see "Fragment d'une traduction française en vers de la chronique en prose de Guillaume le Breton," *Romania* 42 (1913): 1–22. According to Guillaume Guiart, Jean de Prunai had used both of Guillaume's accounts of the reign of Philip Augustus, that is, his *Philippide* as well as the *Gesta Philippi Augusti*, which he in turn consulted in the compilation of his own verse history of French kingship.

3. He says:

> Mis frere Jehan de Prunai
> Les ot *tous deuz* à exemplaire
> Ce dit il, por son roman faire,
> Qui gracious est à devise.
> Cil romans ensaingne et devise
> Comment cils roys, par ses merites,
> Conquist les terres de sus dites.

Cited in LeClerc, "Notices supplémentaires chroniques [Jean de Prunai]," p. 674.

4. Petit-Dutaillis, "Fragment de l'Histoire de Philippe-Auguste," which also provides an edition of the manuscript. On this text, see also Delisle, "Chronique française des rois de France par un Anonyme de Béthune."

5. Between 1212 and 1217 Philip Augustus frequently selected Michel of Harnes to act as pledge on behalf of Flemish barons such as Hellin de Warrin, Rabot de Rumes, Gautier de Ghistelle, Alard de Bourghelles, Gautier de Vormizeele, Rasse de Gavre, together with other lords of the region, whose names reappear in the *Histoire*. See Petit-Dutaillis, "Fragment de l'histoire de Philippe-Auguste," p. 104. On Michel's role as pledge, see also Baldwin, *Government of Philip Augustus*, p. 268.

6. Collection Duchesne, vol. 49, fol. 166r.

7. Michel reports that Girard la Truie struck the Emperor's horse with his sword through its left eye and skull, killing it: "Girars la Truie se departi de la bataille le roi et vint assembler à Othon l'Emperor moult hardiment et moult se combati à lui; et tant fist qu'il feri le cheval l'Emperor Othon d'un coté à pointe qu'il feroit parmi le senestre oel en la cervele" (ibid., fol. 163r). Girard was himself subsequently killed by "li bon sirgant de Braibant."

8. The prologue is published by A. Meyer, "Prologue en vers français d'une histoire perdue de Philippe-Auguste," *Romania* 6 (1877): 494–498.

9. The catalogue of Charles's library mentions two items: "997 bis. Le livre du roi Philippe le Conquerant rimé" and "997 ter. Le roman du roi Philippe le Conquerant, les Macabées, Pamphilet et les epistres Seneque, partie en rime et partie en prose, en lettre de note." The catalogue thus indicates rhymed works, at least for the "livre du roi Philippe," but Meyer queries whether it is certain that the works were rhymed throughout. No

rhymed "roman" of Philip Augustus is known to exist, a fact strengthening Meyer's conviction that the work commissioned by Giles of Flagi should be identified with the text housed in the royal library. See ibid., p. 496.

10. Hans H. Gerth and C. Wright Mills, eds., *From Max Weber* (New York, 1958), p. 78.

11. Joseph Strayer, "Introduction," in *The Interpretation of History*, ed. Jacques Barzun (Princeton, 1943), p. 10.

12. Walpole, "La traduction du Pseudo-Turpin."

13. Berger, "Notice sur divers manuscrits de la Bibliothèque Vaticane."

14. See Botineau, "L'histoire de France en français de Charlemagne à Philippe-Auguste" and his unpublished "Une source des *Grandes chroniques de France*: l'histoire de France en prose française de Charlemagne à Philippe-Auguste." I would like to thank Gillette Labory of the Institut de Recherche d'Histoire et des Textes for letting me read a copy of Botineau's article at the Institut.

15. Buridant, ed., *Traduction du Pseudo-Turpin.*

16. Walpole, "Traduction du Pseudo-Turpin," p. 513. Walpole proposed the hypothesis provisionally, acknowledging that it "devra être contrôlée sur place," but recognized that "si, en effet, cette opinion s'avère justifiée, nous aurons dans le ms. de Chantilly un texte plus complet de la chronique française, dont le commencement, M. Botineau nous l'a fait voir, manque dans le ms. du Vatican."

17. I acknowledge that, from a technical perspective, it would be preferable to begin all work with Vatican 624, but since my interest in the *Chronique* lies largely in its ideological stance and historiographical procedures, the advantages of using a complete rather than truncated exemplar of the text are obvious. From the point of view of ideology, the two versions diverge very little, except insofar as they occasionally employ different sources. Since I have studied both versions, such differences, if telling, will be noted. From the point of view of historiographical methods and concepts, Chantilly 869 is actually to be preferred, since it includes a far greater number of authorial interpolations in which the Anonymous of Chantilly/Vatican discourses on his practices, modes of working, moralizations, and sources, inter alia. Claude Buridant is currently engaged in preparing an edition of Vatican 624, which will be collated with Chantilly 869. It can be expected that this edition will bring into relief the precise and nuanced distinctions between the two versions, as only such a careful collation of the two manuscripts can illuminate.

18. Gillette Labory, "Essai d'une histoire nationale au XIII siècle: la Chronique de l'Anonyme de Chantilly-Vatican," *Bibliothèque de l'Ecole des Chartes* 148 (1990): 301–354. I would like to thank Madame Labory for making a typescript of her article available to me before its publication.

19. Walpole, "Prolégomènes à une édition du Turpin français," p. 203.

20. Ibid., pp. 205–206.

21. As Botineau indicates, the author several times refers his hearers/ readers to earlier material that has already been recounted—e.g., "ci comme l'estoire l'a ja dit ariers" (fol. 1r)—although the allusions are to matters not included in previous pages of the manuscript in its current, truncated state. See his "Histoire de France en français de Charlemagne à Philippe-Auguste," p. 83. Additional references of this sort are found on fols. 6v and 7r.

22. Labory, "Essai d'une histoire nationale," p. 302.

23. See the detailed description of the manuscript given in appendix 1 of ibid., pp. 347–348.

24. See Claude Buridant, "La traduction du *Philippide* de Guillaume le Breton dans la *Chronique des rois de France*" (Thèse de Doctorat, Lille, III), p. 11. What is missing from the text of Chantilly, therefore, represents the end of the *Philippide*, that is, lines 446–718 of Book 11 and all of Book 12, which can be read in the Vatican text.

25. Chantilly MS. 869, fols. 216r–216v.

26. Ibid., fol. 216v.

27. Botineau, "Histoire de France en français," p. 87.

28. Cf. Labory, "Essai d'une histoire nationale," p. 306. For these events, see Baldwin, *Government of Philip Augustus*, p. 210.

29. Chantilly MS. 869, fol. 57r.

30. Labory, "Essai d'une histoire nationale," p. 307 and note 23.

31. Chantilly MS. 869, fol. 11r.

32. "Monseigneur Saint Jheroisme fait mencion de ces gens c'est des francoys en ung livret qu'il fait de la vie monseigneur St. Hylarion" (ibid., fol. 29v).

33. "Son livre des moralitez qu'il fist soubz iob la ou il fait mencion de ceulx d'angleterre qui sont convertiz a la foy de ihesucrist" (ibid., fol. 81v).

34. " . . . Qu'il avoit faitz des vies des saints pour ce qu'il la savoit a bonne crestienne et a proudedame" (ibid., fol. 83r).

35. " . . . Et qui ce vouldroit savoir plus appartement lise la vie de monseigneur saint Sauvestre et illec le trouvera sans faillir" (ibid., fol. 110r).

36. "Mais de cestui roy Sigilbert ne puis trouver es anciennes hystoires si non tant qu'on en treuve en la vie Saint Fursin" (ibid., fol. 17r).

37. " . . . Si come dit la vie de monseigneur Saint Germain de Paris" (ibid., fol. 65r).

38. "Ceste convenance lui [Theoderic] octroya Clotaire si come l'ystoire le dit. Mais la vie de Saint Columbain dit que ces deux freres [Theoderic and Theodebert] requistrent Clotaire d'ayde" (ibid., fol. 91v).

39. " . . . Il n'est point a doubter se celui hault seigneur eut en sa fin grant gloyre et grant honneur, car il fist en terre tant de miracles tant

come il vesquit que si monseigneur Saint Gregoyre le Pape qui est renommé par tout le monde et en auctorité n'eust escripte sa vie et ne l'eust tesmoigne que sans doubtance on l'eust trop bien creu tant estoient grans les miracles" (ibid., fol. 38r).

40. "Comme celui Saint Loup fut de grant merite et de grant sainctete come l'on treuve en sa vie par les miracles que Dieu fist pour lui en terre. . . . Car l'en treuve en la vie monseigneur Saint Martin que le dyable vint devant lui" (ibid., fols. 106r, 230v).

41. Ibid., fol. 117v.

42. Ibid., fol. 177v.

43. Ibid., fol. 256v.

44. Ibid., fol. 127r.

45. " . . . Et maintes en a a ce menez par mainteffois qui desheritoient et s'entre'octioient si come vous avez oy de tous en l'ystoire de Thebes des deux freres germains qui s'entreguerroient pour ce que chacun vouloit avoir par soy tout le royaume" (ibid., fol. 86v).

46. Ibid., fol. 129v.

47. " . . . Ou il y eut donnez maintes riches cops si come l'ystoire d'Antioche qui en fut faicte le devise de la prise de celle terre qui lors fut conquise par ces barons qui vous avez oy nommez fut si comme je treuve en escript" (ibid., fol. 259v).

48. Ibid., fol. 93r.

49. Ibid., fol. 123v.

50. "Mais en une cronique que Saint Gregoyre fist qui fut arcevesque de Tours on trouve que ung roy Sigilbert envoya ung sien filz qui Cloderique ot non au roy de France pour le secourir contre les Gotiens, et dit encores celle cronique que ces deux, Sigilbert et Cloderique son filz, furent puis octis par la tricherie des francoys et que les francoys pristrent leur tresors et leur royaume. Mais pour ce que le livres ou nous trouvasmes ce escript estoit trop corrumpu par le vice aux escripvains ne peusmes pas clerement encerchier ne savoir de quelz gens celui Sigilbert fut roy ne pour quoy il fu octis, mais tant en dit que les francoys pristrent leurs tresors et le royaume" (ibid., fol. 17r).

51. Ibid., fol. 125v.

52. Ibid., fol. 39r.

53. In the case of Clovis, he assures the reader that he can find the king's epitaph "en l'ystoyre de Saint Denis ou a Saint Germain des Pres" (fol. 21v). For that of St. Germain, he sends him to the saint's life: "Et pour la joye du hault miracle fist ung moult riche epithafe sur sa tombe par vers que nous cy entrelairons. Car nous avons autre chose a faire que moult voluntiers metrions a fin ceste present euvre se nous povions. Et qui aura talant de savoir cest epitafe trouver le peut si en lui ne demeure en la vie de monseigneur St. Germain des Prez" (ibid., fol. 53v).

54. E.g., "selon le proverbe du villain qui dit: Comme plus on exaulte le felon et desloyal et tant plus il s'orguillist contre son bienffacteur" (ibid., fol. 300r).

55. In a clear allusion to Cicero's conception of history, the Anonymous proclaims the moral utility of history: "car si com dit le bon clerc hystoire et [sic] le mirouer de vie que par l'ystoyre on aprant ce qui est bon et on eschive ce qui est mauvais et perilleux." And, citing Cato on the dangers of laziness: "et s'en fouyt oysivete qui fait maintes maulx a ceulx qui l'ayment et la maintienent, si comme dit Chaton" (ibid., fols. 42r, 261v).

56. See Alexandre Vidier, *L'historiographie à Saint-Benoît-sur-Loire et les miracles de Saint Benoît* (Paris, 1965), p. 73.

57. On the Continuation of Aimoin at Saint-Germain-des-Prés, see Simon Luce, "La Continuation d'Aimoin et le manuscrit Latin 12711 de la Bibliothèque Nationale," in *Notices et documents publiés pour la Société de l'Histoire de France à l'occasion du cinquantième Anniversaire de sa fondation* (Paris, 1884), pp. 57–70; and Jean-François Lemarignier, "Autour de la royauté française du IXe au XIIIe siècle. Appendice: la Continuation d'Aimoin et le manuscrit Latin 12711 de la Bibliothèque Nationale," *Bibliothèque de l'Ecole des Chartes* 113 (1955): 25–36.

58. See Labory, "Essai d'une histoire nationale," p. 309.

59. On B.N. lat. 5925, see Spiegel, *Chronicle Tradition of Saint-Denis*, pp. 68–71.

60. See his "Traduction du Pseudo-Turpin," as well as the pair of articles entitled "Prolégomènes à une édition du Turpin français."

61. As discovered by Labory, "Essai d'une histoire nationale," p. 317.

62. Ibid., p. 321. On the *Historia Regum Francorum* text, see Paulin Paris, "Historium Regum Francorum," *Histoire littéraire de la France* 21 (1895): 731–734; Léopold Delisle, "Chroniques et annales diverses," *Histoire littéraire de la France* 32 (1898): 535–537; and Spiegel, *Chronicle Tradition of Saint-Denis*, p. 81.

63. See Botineau, "Histoire de France en français," p. 85.

64. On the anti-Capetian sentiments of the *Historia Francorum Senonensis*, see Werner, "Die Legitimität des Kapetinger"; and Spiegel, "The Reditus Regni ad stirpem Karoli Magni."

65. Odorannus's text is edited by L.-M. Duru in the *Bibliothèque de l'Yonne Auxerre-Paris* 2 (1852): 397–398. See Botineau, "Histoire de France en français," p. 85n.2.

66. Ibid., p. 86n.1.

67. Labory, "Essai d'une histoire nationale," p. 325.

68. Chantilly MS. 869, fol. 261r. Cf. Vatican 624, fol. 78r.

69. Botineau, "Une source des *Grandes chroniques de France*," p. 1.

70. Ibid., p. 15.

71. Following Botineau, Labory concurs that the evidence of Primat's systematic use of the Anonymous's *Chronique des rois de France*, beginning with the lives of Louis VI and Louis VII, is sufficiently dense to ascribe to the *Chronique* "le rôle d'ébauche ou premier état des *Grandes chroniques*" ("Essai d'une histoire nationale," p. 346).

72. Ibid., p. 326.

73. "Des ores en avant puis que nous sommes delivrez et aquictez, si comme nous avons peu, de conter et traicter en françoys la haulte vie et les nobles faitz du vaillant et du puissant roy Loys le gros qui tant de pesans faitz et tant de dures poines soustint et souffrit en son temps pour son royaume de France accroistre et deffendre des grans assaulx et des fieres incursions et des pesans guerres que ses ennemys qui la couronne de France vouloient abbaiser et desacroistre le esmurent, si nous convient a poursuivre et a raconter les erremens et le estre et la vie et les faitz de son bon filz le roy Loys. Celui qui par la divine inspiracion fonda l'abbaye de Saint Port que nous appelons Barbeel. . . . Ne ja ne nous soit travail ne poine ne charge de parachever ceste euvre. Car bien devrions estre louez de tel euvre comme nous avons entrepris et presque mise a fin, se nous querions ne covoitons le louer des hommes. Mais nous ne covoitons mie la louange des hommes que celle de Dieu le Seigneur de toute creature par lequel les roys regnent et par lequel toutes choses ont commencement et entendement et vie et duquel toute louange doit venir. Car pour neant se travaille qui d'aucun bien qu'il fait requiert le los des hommes. Et telz gens n'en recevront ja autre loyer si comme l'escripture tesmoigne que seulement la gloyre et le los du monde. Ce ne nous doit mie estre poine ne travail se nous travaillons a escripre et tractier la vie et les faitz de ceulx qui se travaillent à accroistre et appaisier le royaume et leur terre par la force desquelx et par la puissance d'eulx nous et noz biens sommes asseur et en paix. Atant commencons l'ystoire qui conte et dit que le jeune Loys le filz du gros roy Loys" (Chantilly MS. 869, fols. 297v–298r). Cf. Vat. Reg. Lat. 624, fol. 116r.

74. On Rigord and Guillaume le Breton's *Gesta Philippi Augusti*, see Spiegel, *Chronicle Tradition of Saint-Denis*, pp. 56–68.

75. Guillaume le Breton, *Gesta Philippi Augusti*, p. 169.

76. Botineau, "Histoire de France en français," p. 86; Buridant, "Traduction de la *Philippide*," pp. 2–3.

77. Vat. Reg. Lat. 624, fol. 155r. This section of the *Philippide* is missing in the manuscript of Chantilly.

78. Botineau tentatively puts forth the hypothesis that the *Chronique des rois de France* and the prose translation of Guillaume le Breton were originally independent works, only later united in a single manuscript, which he suggests would help to explain that character of hard juxtaposition offered on one side by Vatican 624's history of Charlemagne to the death of Louis VII—whose unity appears certain—and the translation of

the *Philippide*, added as a continuation without the slightest explanation ("Histoire de France en français," p. 94). Yet the discovery of Chantilly 869 makes this highly unlikely, since the same hard juxtaposition without explanation is found there, suggesting that it was part of the original work. Diana Tyson accepts Botineau's hypothesis and, on that basis, identifies Giles of Flagi as the patron of the *Chronique des rois de France;* there is, however, absolutely no evidence for this in the text itself. See Tyson, "Patronage of Vernacular History Writers," p. 214.

79. Botineau, "Histoire de France en français," p. 98.

80. Chantilly MS. 869, fol. 109r. Cf. Labory, "Essai d'une histoire nationale," p. 342.

81. Chantilly MS. 869, fol. 87r. Cf. Labory, "Essai d'une histoire nationale," p. 342.

82. For example, he compares himself to a ship at sea that still has a long way to sail before reaching port: "mais pour ce que nostre nef est encores en la haultemer et a encores trop a sigler avant qu'elle preigne port, n'en dirons rien que nous en ceste riche hystoyre ne voulons riens aiouster" (Chantilly MS. 869, fol. 29r).

83. Ibid., fol. 53v.

84. Ibid., fol. 12r.

85. Ibid., fol. 226v; emphasis added.

86. Ibid., fol. 32v. It is striking that Primat uses a similar formula in explicating the origins of the *Grandes chroniques,* proclaiming that he had taken up his pen "par le commandement de tel home que il ne pout ne ne dut refuser" (*Les grandes chroniques de France,* ed. J. Viard, 10 vols. [Paris, 1920–1953], 1:1).

87. Labory, "Essai d'une histoire nationale," p. 4.

88. Chantilly MS. 869, fol. 42r.

89. Ibid., fol. 29r.

90. E.g., "Or escoutez et je vous raconterai tout mot a mot la privee vie de ce gentil empereur . . . tout ainsi dy je comme je le treuve en escript" (ibid., fol. 171r).

91. Ibid., fol. 106r.

92. Ibid., fol. 172r.

93. Ibid., fol. 87r.

94. Ibid., fol. 216r.

95. Ibid., fol. 129v.

96. Ibid.

97. Ibid., fol. 3r. The full passage reads: "Ce jour peussiez veoir maints beaulx chevaulx de pris en celle place qui la terre faisoient crosser sur leurs piez et maint bel escu d'or et d'azur et de sinople et de diverse couleur qui contre la clarté dou soleil resplendissoient et maintes banieres et maintes penonceaulx venteller au vent."

98. On his style, see Buridant, "Traduction de la *Philippide*," pp. 6ff.

99. Chantilly MS. 869, fol. 11r.

100. Ibid., fol. 86v.

101. "Ceste haulte prouesce fist ce roy Clotaire le pere de Dagoubert. Mais maintenant en y a de telz en France qui sont moult aprisez et honnourez d'armes au ditz des gens qui a grant poines se mectroient ia en telle avanture comme il fist" (ibid., fol. 105v).

102. Ibid., fol. 45v.

103. Ibid., fol. 46r.

104. Ibid., fol. 109r.

105. As John Baldwin has argued in "Le sens de Bouvines," *Cahiers de civilisation médiévale* 39 (1987): 123.

106. For this analysis see Duby, *Dimanche de Bouvines*, p. 195.

107. Duby has forcefully argued this point in *Les trois ordres*.

108. On the importance of Walter's poem for Guillaume's conception of his task, see Baldwin, *Government of Philip Augustus*, p. 398.

109. For some examples, see Duby, *Dimanche de Bouvines*, pp. 194, 199.

110. Chantilly MS. 869, fol. 331r. The full passage reads: "ils ne pensoient pas a la vertu ne a vigour de son [Philip Augustus's] cueur ne a l'amour ne a l'onneur qu'ilz lui devoient porter comme hommes liges a son seigneur ou chevaliers a leur roy."

111. Ibid., fol. 334r.

112. Ibid., fol. 331r.

113. " 'Je n'ay riens fait,' dist lors le conte Phelipe, 'si je ne brise les portes de Paris et se je ne fiche mon estandart et mon enseigne sur petit pont' " (ibid., fol. 335v).

114. See chapter 1.

115. Chantilly MS. 869, fol. 334r.

116. Ibid., fols. 334r–334v.

117. "Ce que mon pere vous octroya a Rains a avoir et tenir par aucun temps ne vous puet pas garantir si brief temps que l'avez tenue. Et de ce que vous vous vantez que je l'ay confermé, je dy au contraire que nulle vigueur n'a d'estre tenue possession nulle qui est donnée d'enfant qui est en tutelle" (ibid., fol. 334v).

118. Thus, as Eric Köhler points out, "si le seul fondement légal de l'auctorité est le respect des lois et non le gouvernement lui-même, et si les lois subsistent dans le droit coutumier de la féodalité, la royauté nationale ne pourra se libérer des entraves de l'état féodal que sous le signe d'une théorie du 'rex legibus solutus,' même si la théorie est en retard sur la pratique" (*L'aventure chevaleresque*, p. 13).

119. Chantilly MS. 869, fol. 336r.

120. "Laquelle [prouesce], s'elle ne se travaille a vigueur maintenir, elle seche ne ne se fait pas cognoistre s'elle ne treuve ou a present est l'ennemy; et si elle se travaille en proesse elle croist en force et moultiplie son

fruit qu'elle donne a ceulx qui l'ayment" (ibid., fols. 336r–336v). Cf. Guillaume le Breton's *Philippide*, II, 300:

> Que nisi se factis exerceat, arida marcet,
> Nec se prodit, ubi presentem non habet hostem;
> Si vero fuerit exercita, crescit et auget
> Fructus ipsa suos, quos donat amantibus ipsam.

121. Chantilly MS. 869, fol. 331r.

122. Ibid., fol. 336v–337r.

123. Ibid., fol. 337r.

124. Ibid.

125. Ibid.

126. See Chrétien de Troyes, *Le roman de Perceval*, prologue, lines 11–15.

127. Cary, *Medieval Alexander*, pp. 198–203.

128. Chantilly MS. 869, fol. 337v.

129. Ibid. This miracle is first reported by Rigord, who claimed that the fields on which the French forces had been encamped and the harvests trampled revived and flourished after the departure of French troops, while those occupied by Flemish forces remained barren. See Rigord, *Gesta Philippi Augusti*, p. 44. The story is incorporated by Guillaume le Breton and thus enters the *Chronique des rois de France*.

130. Chantilly MS. 869, fol. 338r.

131. Ibid.

132. Ibid., fol. 352.

133. Guillaume le Breton's Latin text has Richard balance the claims of *utilitas* and *honor*, but lacks the specific linguistic play between *preu*, *prouffit*, and *prouesce*, a play already present in the vernacular word, since the Old French *preu* (from the Latin *prodis*, price) designates either (or both) a qualitative merit (prowess) or a quantitative one (advantage). I am indebted to Brigitte Cazelles for this etymology. In contrast, the Latin text uses the wholly distinct terms of utility and honor, between which there are no comparable etymological and semantic resonances: "Illud [i.e., retreat] honore caret, sed plus habet utilitatis; / Utilitate vacat istud, precellit honore. / Utile postposuit demum rex fortis honori, / Quem retinere studet quantum licet" (*Philipidde*, V, lines 204–207).

134. " . . . Les fist tresbucher comme cruel d'ung rochier hault en la riviere de Seyne de la ou il fist depuis faire les murs de Gaillait" (Chantilly MS. 869, fol. 353r).

135. Ibid. Cf. *Philippide* V, lines 323–24: "Ipsum Richardo ne quis putet esse minorem / Viribus aut animo, vel eundem forte timere."

136. Chantilly MS. 869, fol. 354v.

137. Ibid., fol. 358r.

138. Ibid., fol. 358v. The full wording is: "Par telz parolles aguisoient le cueur du jeune chevalier et le faisoient plus couvoiteux et plus hardy d'avoir victoire comme jouvencel eschauffé de la premiere vertu."

139. Duby, *Dimanche de Bouvines*, p. 127.

140. Chantilly MS. 869, fol. 372r.

141. *Philippide*, VIII, 688.

142. Chantilly MS. 869, fol. 375v.

143. Ibid., fol. 337r.

144. Ibid., fol. 321v.

145. The full passage reads: "Et avoit cy moult sage humilité, car lui seul se mectoit darriere, qui estoit lors ieune d'aage, plusieurs vieulx hommes et se gouvernoit par usage et la coustume de ceulx qui estoient esprouvez; et a merveilles estoit plain de grant franchise et de grant liberalité, qui de ce qu'il eust peu faire à son voloir comme sire et comme sage ouvrier il se conseilloit à ses subgetz" (ibid.).

146. Ibid. fols. 385r, 378v.

147. " . . . Rengez et ordonnez chacun en sa bataille, chevaliers de grant prouesce et inspirez de grant hardiesce qui tenoient leurs eschielles serrees et se tenoient prests tous de vistement combatre et courir sur eulx de quelque heure que les trompectes sonneroient l'assemblée de bataille" (ibid., fol. 387r).

148. "Nous travaillons à escriptre et traitier la vie et les faitz de ceulx qui se travaillent a accroistre et appaisier leur royaume" (ibid., fol. 298r).

149. Ibid., fol. 216r.

150. On this development, see C. Warren Hollister and John W. Baldwin, "The Rise of Administrative Kingship: Henry I and Philip Augustus," *American Historical Review* 83 (1978): 867–905.

151. Chantilly MS. 869, fol. 368r.

152. Ibid., fol. 368v.

153. Ibid.

154. Vat. Reg. Lat. 624, fol. 196r.

155. Ibid.

156. Duby, *Les trois ordres*, p. 178.

157. Sayers, "Beginnings and Early Development of Old French Historiography," pp. 448–449.

158. Cited in P. Viollet, *Droit public: histoire des institutions politiques et administratives de France*, 3 vols. (Paris, 1898–1903), 2:20.

159. Gavin Langmuir, "Community and Legal Change in Capetian France," *French Historical Studies* 6 (1970): 286.

160. Joseph Strayer speaks of the cult of the kingdom of France as early as 1300; see his *On the Medieval Origins of the Modern State* (Princeton, 1970), p. 54.

161. Joseph Strayer, "France, the Holy Land, the Chosen People, the Most Christian King," in *Action and Conviction in Early Modern France*, ed. T. E. Rabb and J. E. Siegel (Princeton, 1970), p. 5.

162. Bernard Guenée, "L'histoire de l'état en France à la fin du moyen âge vue par les historiens français depuis cent ans," *Revue historique* 232 (1964): 346.

EPILOGUE

1. See his "Between Memory and History: Les Lieux de Mémoire," *Representations* 26 (1989): 21. The other two, in Nora's view, occur, first, with the destruction of the legend of the French monarchy's Trojan origins and the restoration of France's Gallic heritage in Etienne Pasquier's *Recherches de la France* (1599), which also effected a significant shift away from the kind of dynastic history represented by the *Grandes chroniques* to a more "modern" understanding of the history of a people as a nation; and second, with the historiography of the late Restoration, which ushered in the modern conception of France as a nation-state.

2. See Spiegel, *Chronicle Tradition of Saint-Denis*, p. 130.

3. Michel Tyvaert, "L'image du roi: légitimité et moralité royales dans les histoires de France au XVIIe siècle," *Revue d'histoire moderne et contemporaine* 21 (1974): 521–546.

4. See Spiegel, *Chronicle Tradition of Saint-Denis*, pp. 72–89; and, for a more recent insistence on this point, Bernard Guenée, "Les grandes chroniques de France: le 'Roman aux roys' (1274–1518)," in *La nation*, ed. Pierre Nora, vol. 1 (Paris, 1986), pp. 189–213; and Raymonde Foreville, "L'image de Philippe Auguste dans les sources contemporaines," in *La France de Philippe Auguste*, pp. 122ff.

5. "Li François, qui vourent avoir roi aussi comme les autres nations" (*Grandes chroniques* 1:19).

6. Guenée, *Histoire et culture historique*, p. 340.

7. A point well made by Guenée, "Les grandes chroniques de France," p. 195.

8. Ibid.

9. For the manuscript diffusion of the *Grandes chroniques*, see ibid., pp. 203ff; and Guenée, *Histoire et culture historique*, p. 321.

APPENDIX

1. On this see Labory, "Essai d'une histoire nationale," p. 7.

2. Ibid., p. 8.

3. Ibid., p. 24.

4. See his "La traduction du Pseudo-Turpin," as well as the two articles entitled "Prolégomènes à une édition du Turpin français."

5. Walpole, "La Traduction du Pseudo-Turpin," p. 513.

6. As discovered by Labory, "Essai d'une histoire nationale," p. 12.

7. Ibid., p. 13.

8. Ibid. Odilon's Latin text is published in the *Acta Sanctorum*, Jan. 2:292–293. See also *Grandes chroniques* 4:112n.2. Primat appears to have followed the Anonymous's lead in including a translation of the *Conquestio Ludovici* in the *Grandes chroniques*, which he claims, like the Anonymous, to have taken from the "croniques Saint Germain des Prez." In fact, the translations by the Anonymous of Chantilly-Vatican and Primat differ considerably, so it cannot be supposed that Primat used the Anonymous, although he may have derived the idea of including the complaint from his vernacular predecessor's work. See Botineau, "Une source des *Grandes chroniques*," p. 2.

9. Chantilly MS. 869, fol. 220r.

10. Gillette Labory, "Le métier d'historien au XIIIe siècle: la 'Chronique des rois de France' de l'Anonyme de Chantilly-Vatican" (typescript, n.d.), p. 7.

Bibliography

PRIMARY SOURCES

Manuscripts

Anonymous of Béthune, *Chronique des rois de France*
    Bibliothèque Nationale, Paris: nouv. acq. fr. 6295; fr. 17177, fr. 10130; fr.
        17203; fr. 24331
    Bibliothèque de l'Arsenal, Paris: MS. 3516
    Bibliothèque Sainte-Geneviève, Paris: MS. 792
    Cambridge, University Library: II.6.24
Chronique d'un ménestrel d'Alphonse de Poitiers
    Bibliothèque Nationale, Paris: fr. 5700; fr. 13565; fr. 4961; fr. 2815
Pseudo-Turpin Chronicle
    Bibliothèque Nationale, Paris: fr. 124; fr. 5714; fr. 5713; fr. 2464; fr. 573; fr.
        10554; fr. 2168; fr. 1444; fr. 1621; fr. 1850; fr. 906; fr. 17203; fr. 2137;
        nouv. acq. fr. 10232
    Bibliothèque de l'Arsenal, Paris: MSS. 3516, 2995
    Bibliothèque Royale, Brussels: MSS. 12193–12194, 10437–10440, 10437
Pierre de Beauvais
    Bibliothèque Nationale, Paris: fr. 834 (Collected Works); nouv. acq. fr. 13521
        (*Bestiaire en prose*)
    Bibliothèque Royale, Brussels: MS. 10437
Descriptio-Turpin
    Bibliothèque Royale, Brussels: MSS. 12193–12194, 10437
Anonymous of Chantilly/Vatican, *Chronique des rois de France*
    Musée Condé, Chantilly: MS. 869
    Vatican: Regina Lat. 624
Histoire ancienne jusqu'à César
    Bibliothèque Nationale, Paris: fr. 20125; fr. 9682; fr. 20126; fr. 1386; fr. 686;
        fr. 12586; nouv. acq. fr. 3576; fr. 9685; fr. 251; fr. 182; fr. 168; fr. 821
Fragment de l'histoire de Philippe-Auguste
    Bibliothèque Nationale, Paris: Collection Duchesne, vol. 49, fols. 163–168.
Historia Regum Francorum jusque ad annum 1214
    Bibliothèque Nationale, Paris: Lat. 17008
Aimoinis Continuatio
    Bibliothèque Nationale, Paris: Lat. 12711

Printed Sources

Alan of Lille. *The Plaint of Nature*. Trans. and with a commentary by James J. Sheridan. Toronto, 1980.

Anonymous of Béthune. *Chronique des rois de France*. Ed. Léopold Delisle. In *Recueil des historiens des Gaules et de la France* 24:750–775.

——. *Histoire des ducs de Normandie et des rois d'Angleterre*. Ed. Francisque Michel. Société de l'Histoire de France. Paris, 1840.

Augustine. *Christian Instruction (De Doctrina Christiana)*. Trans. John J. Gavigan, O.S.A. The Fathers of the Church. New York, 1950.

Auracher, Theodor. *Die sogennante Poitevinische Übersetzung des Pseudo-Turpin*. Halle, 1877.

Benedict of Peterborough. *Vita et gestis Henrici II et Ricardi, Angliae Regum*. Ed. T. Hearne. In *Recueil des historiens des Gaules et de la France* 13:142–182.

Benoît de Sainte-Maure. *Chronique des ducs de Normandie*. Ed. Carin Fahlin. 3 vols. Bibliotheca Ekmaniana, 56. Uppsala, 1951–1979.

——. *Le roman de Troie*. Ed. L. Constans. 6 vols. Société des Anciens Textes Français. Paris, 1904–1912.

Buridant, Claude, ed. *La traduction du Pseudo-Turpin du manuscrit Vatican Regina 624*. Publications Romanes et Françaises, 142. Geneva, 1976.

Chrétien de Troyes. *Cligès*. Ed. W. Foerster. Halle, 1910.

——. *Erec and Enide*. Ed. and trans. Carleton W. Carroll, with an introduction by William W. Kibler. Garland Library of Medieval Literature, ser. A, vol. 25. New York, 1987.

——. *Le roman de Perceval (ou le conte du Graal)*. Ed. William Roach. Geneva, 1956.

Chronicon Sancti Martini Turonensis. Ed. Michel Brial. In *Recueil des historiens des Gaules et de la France* 18:290–320.

Le couronnement de Louis: chanson de geste du XIIe siècle. Ed. E. Langlois. Paris, 1920.

Enéas: roman du XIIe Siècle. Ed. J.-J. Salverda de Grave. 2 vols. Les Classiques Français du Moyen Age. Paris, 1973.

Li Fet des Romains: compilé ensemble de Saluste et de Suetoine et de Lucan. Ed. L.-F. Flutre and K. Sneyders de Vogel. 2 vols. Paris, 1937–1938.

Forma Pacis facte apud Goleton inter Philippum regem Francorum et Joannem Angliae regem. Ed. M. Brial. In *Recueil des historiens des Gaules et de la France* 17:51–54.

Galbert of Bruges. *The Murder of Charles the Good, Count of Flanders*. Ed. and trans. James Bruce Ross. New York, 1967.

Genealogiae Comitum Flandriae continuatio Claromariscensis: Flandriae Generosa. Ed. L. Bethmann. In *Monumenta Germaniae historica, Scriptores* 9:326–334.

Gerald of Wales. *Liber de principis instructione*. Ed. George F. Warner. In *Rerum Britannicarum medii aevi scriptores* (Rolls Series), 21[8].

Gervase of Canterbury. *The Historical Works of Gervase of Canterbury*. Ed. William Stubbs. In *Rerum Britannicarum medii aevi scriptores* (Rolls Series), 73. London, 1879.

Girart de Rousillon: chanson de geste. Ed. W. Mary Hacket. 3 vols. Société des Anciens Textes Français. Paris, 1953–1955.

Gislebert of Mons. *Chronicon Hanoniense.* Ed. Wilhelm Arndt. In *Monumenta Germaniae historica, Scriptores* 21:481–601.

Grandes chroniques de France. Ed. J. Viard. 10 vols. Société de l'Histoire de France. Paris, 1920–1953.

Guillaume le Breton. *Gesta Philippi Augusti.* In *Oeuvres de Rigord et de Guillaume le Breton,* ed. Henri-François Delaborde, vol. 1. Société de l'Histoire de France. Paris, 1882.

———. *Philippide.* In *Oeuvres de Rigord et de Guillaume le Breton,* ed. Henri-François Delaborde, vol. 2. Société de l'Histoire de France. Paris, 1885.

Hardy, Thomas Duffus, ed. *Rotuli litterarum clausarum.* London, 1833.

———. *Rotuli litterarum patentium.* London, 1835.

Historia Regum Francorum usque ad annum 1214. Ed. Michel Brial. In *Recueil des historiens des Gaules et de la France* 17:423–428.

Holder-Egger, O. "Ex historiis Ducum Normanniae et regum Angliae." In *Monumenta Germaniae historica, Scriptores* 26:699–717.

Hugh of Saint-Victor. *The Disdascalion.* Trans. Jerome Taylor. New York, 1961.

Jean de Thuin. *Li hystore de Julius César: eine altfranzösische Erzählung in Prosa von Jehan de Tuim.* Ed. F. Settegast. Halle, 1881.

Jean Bodels Saxonlied. Vol. 1. Ed. F. Menzel and E. Stengel. Ausgaben und Abhandlung aus dem Gebiete der Romanischen Philologie, 99. Marburg, 1906.

John of Garland. *The Parisiana Poetria of John of Garland.* Ed. Traugott Lawler. New Haven, 1974.

Lambert of Ardres. *Historia Comitum Ghisnensium.* Ed. G. H. Pertz. In *Monumenta Germaniae historica, Scriptores* 24:550–642.

Lecoy de la Marche, A., ed. *Oeuvres complètes de Suger.* Paris, 1867.

Lot, Ferdinand, and Robert Fawtier. *Le premier budget de la monarchie française: le compte général de 1202–1203.* Bibliothèque de l'Ecole des Hautes Etudes. Paris, 1932.

Mandach, André de. *Naissance et développement de la chanson de geste en Europe.* Vol. 2: *Chronique de Turpin Texte Anglo-Normand inédit de Willem de Briane (Arundel 220).* Publications Romanes et Françaises, 77. Geneva, 1963.

Matthew of Vendôme. *Ars versificatoria (The Art of the Versemaker).* Trans. Roger P. Parr. Milwaukee, 1981.

Ménestrel d'Alphonse de Poitiers. *Abrégé de l'histoire de France.* In *Recueil des historiens des Gaules et de la France* 10:278–280, 11:319, 12:22–27, 17:429–432.

La mort Aymeri de Narbonne: chanson de geste. Ed. J. Couraye du Parc. Société des Anciens Textes Français. Paris, 1884; reprint 1966.

La mort le roi Artu: roman du XIIIe Siècle. Ed. Jean Frappier. Textes Littéraires Français. Geneva, 1954.

Ordericus Vitalis. *Ecclesiastical History.* Ed. and trans. Majorie Chibnall. 6 vols. Oxford, 1969–1980.

Pierre de Beauvais. "Charlemagne's Journey to the East: The French Translation of the Legend by Pierre de Beauvais." Ed. Ronald N. Walpole. *University of California Publications in Semitic Philology* 11 (1951): 445–452.

Potthast, August. *Regesta Pontificum Romanorum.* Vol. 1. Graz, 1957.

Ralph of Diceto. *Ymagines historiarum.* In *Recueil des historiens des Gaules et de la France* 13:183–205.
Recueil des actes de Philippe-Auguste. Ed. Henri-François Delaborde, Charles Petit-Dutaillis, J. Boussard, and Michel Nortier. 4 vols. Paris, 1916–1979.
Rigord. *Gesta Philippi Augusti.* In *Oeuvres de Rigord et de Guillaume le Breton,* ed. Henri-François Delaborde, vol. 1. Société de l'Histoire de France. Paris, 1882.
Roger of Wendover. *Flores historiarum.* Ed. F. Liebermann and R. Pauli. In *Monumenta Germaniae historica, Scriptores* 28:3–73.
Roman de Thèbes. Ed. Guy Raynaud de Lage. 2 vols. Les Classiques Français du Moyen Age. Paris, 1969–1971.
Rymer, Thomas, ed. *Foedera.* Vol. 1. London, 1727.
Scripta de Feodis ad Regem Spectantibus et de Militibus ad Exercitum Vocandis. Ed. L. Delisle, N. de Wailly, and Jourdain. In *Recueil des historiens des Gaules et de la France* 23:605–723.
Short, Ian, ed. *The Anglo-Norman Pseudo-Turpin Chronicle of William of Briane.* Anglo-Norman Text Society, 25. Oxford, 1973.
Suger. *Vita Ludovici Grossi.* Ed. and trans. Henri Waquet. Les Classiques de l'Histoire de France au Moyen Age. Paris, 1964.
Tertullian. *The Apparel of Women.* The Fathers of the Church. New York, 1959.
Thomae de Chobham summa confessorum. Ed. F. Broomfield. Analecta Mediaevalia Namurcensia, 25. Louvain, 1968.
Tote l'istoire de France (Chronique Saintongeaise). Ed. F. Bourdillon. London, 1897.
Wace. *Le roman de Rou.* Ed. A. J. Holden. 3 vols. Société des Anciens Textes Français. Paris, 1970–1973.
Walpole, Ronald N. *An Anonymous Old French Translation of the Pseudo-Turpin Chronicle: A Critical Edition of the Text Contained in Bibliothèque Nationale MSS. fr. 2137 and 17203 and Incorporated by Philippe Mouskés in His Chronique Rimée.* Medieval Academy of America, 89. Cambridge, Mass., 1979.
———."The Burgundian Translation of Pseudo-Turpin Chronicle in Bibliothèque Nationale (French MS. 25438)." *Romance Philology* 2 (1948–1949): 177–215.
———.*The Old French Johannes Translation of the Pseudo-Turpin Chronicle: A Critical Edition.* 2 vols. Berkeley and Los Angeles, 1976.
———. *Le Turpin français dit le Turpin I.* Toronto, 1985.
Wulff, Frederick. *La chronique dite Turpin.* Lund, 1881.

SECONDARY SOURCES

Auerbach, Erich. *Mimesis: The Representation of Reality in Western Literature.* Trans. Willard R.Trask. Princeton, 1953.
Avril, François. "Trois manuscrits napolitains des collections de Charles V et de Jean de Berry." *Bibliothèque de l'Ecole des Chartes* 127 (1970): 291–328.
Azevedo, Warren L. d'. "Uses of the Past in Gola Discourse." *Journal of African History* 3, no. 1 (1962): 11–43.
Bakhtin, M. M. *The Dialogic Imagination.* Ed. Michael Holquist, trans. Caryll Emerson and Michael Holquist. Austin, 1981.

Baldwin, John W. *The Government of Philip Augustus: Foundations of French Royal Power in the Middle Ages.* Berkeley and Los Angeles, 1986.
———. "Le sens de Bouvines." *Cahiers de civilisation médiévale* 30 (1987): 119–130.
Barbero, Alessandro. *L'aristocrazia nella società francese dei medioevo.* Bologna, 1987.
Baron, D. "Note sur les manuscrits du voyage de Wilbrand d'Oldenbourg." *Le moyen âge,* 4th ser., 30 (1975): 499–506.
Barthes, Roland. "Historical Discourse." In *Introduction to Structuralism,* ed. Michael Lane, pp. 145–155. New York, 1970.
Barzun, Jacques, ed. *The Interpretation of History.* Princeton, 1943.
Bäuml, Franz. "Medieval Texts and the Two Theories of Oral-Formulaic Composition: A Proposal for a Third Theory." *New Literary History* 16 (1984): 31–49.
———. "Transformations of the Heroine: From Epic Heard to Epic Read." In *The Role of Women in the Middle Ages,* ed. Rosemarie Morwedge, pp. 23–40. Albany, 1975.
———. "Varieties and Consequences of Medieval Literacy and Illiteracy." *Speculum* 55 (1980): 237–265.
Bautier, Robert-Henri. "L'historiographie en France au Xe et XIe siècles." In *La storiografia altomedievale,* Settimane di Studio del Centro Italiano di studi sull'alto medioevo, 17, pp. 793–850. Spoleto, 1970.
———. "Philippe Auguste: la personnalité du roi." In *La France de Philippe Auguste: le temps des mutations,* ed. R.-H. Bautier, Actes du colloque international organisé par le C.N.R.S., Paris, 29 septembre–4 octobre 1980, pp. 33–57. Paris, 1982.
———, ed. *La France de Philippe Auguste: le temps des mutations.* Actes du colloque international organisé par le C.N.R.S., Paris, 29 septembre–4 octobre 1980. Paris, 1982.
Bedos Rezak, Brigitte. "Les sceaux aux temps de Philippe Auguste." In *La France de Philippe Auguste: le temps des mutations,* ed. R.-H. Bautier, Actes du colloque international organisé par le C.N.R.S., Paris, 29 septembre–4 octobre 1980, pp. 721–735. Paris, 1982.
Beer, Jeanette M. A. "Epic Imitation: Its Serious and Comic Potential in Two Medieval Histories." In *Charlemagne et l'épopée romane,* Actes du VIIe Congrès International de la Société Rencesvals, Liège, 28 août–4 septembre, *Les congrès et colloques de l'Université de Liège* 76 (1978): 415–421.
———. *A Medieval Caesar.* Etudes de Philologie et d'Histoire, 30. Geneva, 1976.
———. "A Medieval Cato—Virtus or Virtue?" *Speculum* 47 (1972): 52–59.
———. *Narrative Conventions of Truth in the Middle Ages.* Geneva, 1981.
———. "Stylistic Heterogeneity in the Middle Ages: An Examination of the Evidence of *Li Fet des Romains.*" In *Jean Misrahi Memorial Volume: Studies in Medieval Literature,* ed. Hans R. Runte, H. Niedzielski, and W. L. Hendrickson, pp. 100–114. Columbia, S.C., 1977.
Bendena, Marilyn. "The Translations of Lucan and Their Influence on French Medieval Literature, Together with an Edition of the *Roumans de Jules César* by Jacos de Forest." Ph.D. diss., Wayne State University, 1976.

Berger, Elie. "Notice sur divers manuscrits de la Bibliothèque Vaticane." Bibliothèque des Ecoles Françaises d'Athènes et de Rome 6 (1879): 10.

Berkey, Max L. "The Liber Sancti Jacobi: The French Adaptation by Pierre de Beauvais." Romania 86 (1965): 77–103.

———. "Pierre de Beauvais: An Introduction to His Works." Romance Philology 18 (1964–1965): 387–398.

Bertoni, G. "Un nuovo manoscritto del 'Roman de Julius Cesar.' " Archivum Romanicum 15 (1931): 76–82.

Bloch, R. Howard. Etymologies and Genealogies: A Literary Anthropology of the French Middle Ages. Chicago, 1983.

———. "Etymologies et généalogies: théories de la langue, liens de parenté et genre littéraire au XIIIe siècle." Annales: économies, sociétés, civilisations 36 (1981): 946–962.

———. Medieval French Literature and Law. Berkeley and Los Angeles, 1977.

———. "Medieval Misogyny." In Continuity and Change: Political Institutions and Literary Monuments in the Middle Ages, ed. Elisabeth Vastergaard, pp. 87–117. Odense, Den., 1986.

———. The Scandal of the Fabliaux. Chicago, 1986.

Blount, Ben G. "Agreeing to Agree on Genealogy: A Luo Sociology of Knowledge." In Sociocultural Dimensions of Language Use, ed. Mary Sanches and Ben G. Blount, pp. 117–135. New York, 1975.

Blumenfeld-Kosinski, Renate. "Moralization and History: Verse and Prose in the 'Histoire ancienne jusqu'à César' (in B.N. fr. 20125)." Zeitschrift für romanische Philologie 97 (1981): 41–46.

Borland, C. R. and R.G.L. Ritchie. "Fragment d'une traduction française en vers de la chronique en prose de Guillaume le Breton." Romania 42 (1913): 1–22.

Borrelli de Serres, Léon Louis. La réunion des provinces septentrionales à la couronne par Philippe-Auguste Amiénois, Artois, Vermandois, Valois. Paris, 1899.

Bossuat, Robert. "Compte-rendu de Paul Hess, Li roumanz de Julius César: ein Beitrag zur Cäsargeschichte im Mittelalter." Le moyen âge, 4th ser., 12 (1957): 383–385.

———. "Traductions françaises des Commentaires de César à la fin du XVe siècle." Bibliothèque d'humanisme et Renaissance 3 (1943): 253–411.

Botineau, Pierre. "L'histoire de France en français de Charlemagne à Philippe-Auguste: la compilation du MS. 624 du Fonds de la Reine à la Bibliothèque Vaticane." Romania 90 (1969): 79–99.

———. "Une source des Grandes chroniques de France: l'histoire de France en prose française de Charlemagne à Philippe Auguste." Typescript, n.d..

Bourgain, Pascale. "L'emploi de la langue vulgaire dans la littérature au temps de Philippe Auguste." In La France de Philippe Auguste: le temps des mutations, ed. R.-H. Bautier, Actes du colloque international organisé par le C.N.R.S., Paris, 29 septembre–4 octobre 1980, pp. 765–784. Paris, 1982.

Bournazel, Eric. Le gouvernement capétien au XIIe siècle, 1108–1180: structures sociales et mutations institutionelles. Paris, 1975.

Bournazel, E., and J.-P. Poly. "Couronne et mouvance: institutions et représentations mentales." In La France de Philippe Auguste: le temps des mutations, ed. R.-H. Bautier, Actes du colloque international organisé par le C.N.R.S., Paris, 29 septembre–4 octobre 1980, pp. 217–234. Paris, 1982.

Boutet, Dominique. "Les chansons de geste et l'affermissement du pouvoir royal (1100–1250)." *Annales: économies, sociétés, civilisations* 37, (1982): 3–14.

Boutet, Dominique, and Armand Strubel. *Littérature, politique et société dans la France au moyen âge.* Paris, 1979.

Burgess, Glyn Sheridan. *Contribution à l'étude du vocabulaire pré-courtois.* Geneva, 1970.

Buridant, Claude. "La traduction du *Philippide* de Guillaume le Breton dans la *Chronique des rois de France.*" Thèse de doctorat, Lille, III.

Burns, E. Jane. *Arthurian Fictions: Rereading the Vulgate Cycle.* Columbus, Ohio, 1985.

Calin, William. *The Old French Epic of Revolt: Raoul de Cambrai, Renaud de Montauban, Gormond et Isembard.* Geneva, 1962.

Cartellieri, Alexander. *Philipp II. August, König von Frankreich.* 4 vols. Leipzig, 1899–1922.

Cary, George. *The Medieval Alexander.* Ed. D.J.A. Ross. Cambridge, 1956.

Chaytor, Henry J. *From Script to Print: An Introduction to Medieval Literature.* Cambridge, 1945.

Clanchy, M. T. *From Memory to Written Record: England 1066–1307.* Cambridge, Mass., 1979.

Cohen, David William. "The Undefining of Oral Tradition." *Ethnohistory* 36 (1989): 9–18.

Colker, M. L. "The 'Karolinus' of Egidius Parisiensis." *Traditio* 29 (1973): 199–325.

Contamine, P. "L'armée de Philippe Auguste." In *La France de Philippe Auguste: le temps des mutations,* ed. R.-H. Bautier, Actes du colloque international organisé par le C.N.R.S., Paris, 29 septembre–4 octobre 1980, pp. 577–593. Paris, 1982.

Cormier, Raymond J. "The Problem of Anachronism: Recent Scholarship on the French Medieval Romances of Antiquity." *Philological Quarterly* 53 (1974): 145–157.

Crosby, Ruth. "Oral Delivery in the Middle Ages." *Speculum* 11 (1936): 88–110.

Crosland, Jessie. "Lucan in the Middle Ages, with Special Reference to the Old French Epic." *Modern Language Review* 25 (1930): 32–51.

Daston, Lorraine. "The Prehistory of Objectivity." In *Rethinking the Physical World: Essays in Honor of Erwin N. Hiebert,* ed. Mary Jo Nye, Joan Richards, and Roger Stuewer. Cambridge, forthcoming.

Dedecek, V. L. *Etude littéraire et linguistique de "Li Hystore de Julius César" de Jehan de Tuim.* Publications of the University of Pennsylvania Series in Romanic Languages and Literature, 13. Philadelphia, 1925.

Delaborde, Henri-François. "Pourquoi Saint Louis faisait acte de servage à Saint Denis." *Bulletin de la Société Nationale des Antiquaires,* 1897, 254–257.

Delisle, Léopold. "Annales [B.N. fr. 10130]." *Histoire littéraire de la France* 32 (1898): 207–208.

———. "Chronique des ducs de Normandie." *Histoire littéraire de la France* 32 (1898): 182–194.

———. "Chronique française des rois de France par un anonyme de Béthune (fragment de l'histoire de Philippe-Auguste)." *Histoire littéraire de la France* 32 (1898): 219–234.

———. "Chroniques et annales diverses." *Histoire littéraire de la France* 32 (1898): 535–537.

———. "Notice sur la chronique d'un anonyme de Béthune du temps de Philippe-Auguste." *Notices et extraits des manuscrits* 34, pt. 1 (1891): 365–380.

———. *Nouvelles acquisitions latines et françaises, 1875–1891.* Paris, n.d..

Demarquette, A. *Précis historique sur la maison de Harnes de 963 à 1230 suivi d'une version romane attribué à Michel de Harnes de la Chronique du Faux Turpin.* Douai, 1856.

Dembowski, Peter. "Learned Latin Treatises in French: Inspiration, Plagiarism, and Translation." *Viator* 17 (1986): 255–269.

———. "Recent Studies in Old French Literature." *Medievalia et humanistica* 15 (1987): 193–205.

Dept, Gaston G. "Les influences anglaises et françaises dans le comté de Flandre au début du XIIIe siècle." In *Université de Gand, recueil de travaux publiés par la faculté de philosophie et lettres,* p. 59. Gand/Ghent, 1928.

Dragonetti, Roger. *Le mirage des sources: l'art du faux dans le roman médiéval.* Paris, 1987.

———. *La vie et la lettre au moyen âge.* Paris, 1980.

Du Pouget, Marc. "Recherches sur les chroniques latines de Saint-Denis: commentaire et édition critique de la *Descriptio Clavi et Corone Domini* et de deux autres textes relatifs à la légende carolingienne." Thesis, Ecole des Chartes, 1977.

Duby, Georges. "The Diffusion of Cultural Patterns in Feudal Society." In *The Chivalrous Society,* trans. Cynthia Poston, pp. 171–177. Berkeley and Los Angeles, 1977.

———. *Le dimanche de Bouvines.* Paris, 1973.

———. "Remarques sur la littérature généalogique en France aux XIe et XIIe siècles." In *Hommes et structures du moyen âge,* pp. 287–298. Paris, 1973.

———. "Situation de la noblesse de France au début du XIII siècle." In *Hommes et structures du moyen âge,* pp. 343–352. Paris, 1973.

———. "The Structure of Kinship and Nobility." In *The Chivalrous Society,* trans. Cynthia Poston, pp. 134–148. Berkeley and Los Angeles, 1977.

———. "Structures de parenté et noblesse dans la France du nord aux XIe et XIIe siècles." In *Hommes et structures du moyen âge,* pp. 267–285. Paris, 1973.

———. "The Transformation of the Aristocracy: France at the Beginning of the Thirteenth Century." In *The Chivalrous Society,* trans. Cynthia Poston, pp. 178–185. Berkeley and Los Angeles, 1977.

———. "Les transformations sociales dans le milieu aristocratique." In *La France de Philippe Auguste: le temps des mutations,* ed. R.-H. Bautier, Actes du colloque international organisé par le C.N.R.S., Paris, 29 septembre–4 octobre 1980, pp. 711–719. Paris, 1982.

———. *Les trois ordres, ou l'imaginaire du féodalisme.* Paris, 1978.

Duggan, Joseph J. *The Song of Roland: Formulaic Style and Poetic Craft.* Berkeley and Los Angeles, 1973.

Eliade, Mircea. *The Myth of the Eternal Return, or Cosmos and History.* Trans. Willard R. Trask. Princeton, 1965.

Ermarth, Elizabeth Deeds. *Realism and Consensus in the English Novel.* Princeton, 1983.

Feuchère, P. "La noblesse du nord de la France." *Annales: économies, sociétés, civilisations* 6 (1951): 306–318.

Flach, Jacques. "Le comté de Flandre et ses rapports avec la couronne de France du IXe au XIIe siècle." *Revue historique* 115 (1914): 1–33, 241–271.

Fleischman, Suzanne. "On the Representation of History and Fiction in the Middle Ages." *History and Theory* 22 (1983): 278–310.

————. "Philology, Linguistics, and the Discourse of the Medieval Text." *Speculum* 65 (1990): 19–37.

Fletcher, Angus, ed. *The Literature of Fact.* New York, 1976.

Flori, Jean. *L'essor de la chevalerie, XIe–XIIe siècles.* Travaux d'Histoire Ethico-Politique, 46. Geneva, 1986.

————. *L'idéologie du glaive: préhistoire de la chevalerie.* Travaux d'Histoire Ethico-Politique, 43. Geneva, 1983.

Flutre, L.-F. "Encore un manuscrit des Faits des Romains." *Neophilologus* 21 (1936): 19–21.

————. "Li Faits des Romains." *Annales de l'Université de Paris* 8 (1933): 269–276.

————. *Li Faits des Romains dans les littératures française et italienne du XIIIe au XIVe siècle.* Paris, 1933.

————. *Les manuscrits des Faits des Romains.* Paris, 1932.

————. "Un nouvel emprunt aux Faits des Romains." *Neophilologus* 21 (1936): 16–19.

————. "Sur un traité d'amours courtois du Ms. 2200 de la Bibliothèque Sainte-Geneviève." *Romania* 59 (1933): 270–276.

Foreville, Raymonde. "L'image de Philippe Auguste dans les sources contemporaines." In *La France de Philippe Auguste: le temps des mutations,* ed. R.-H. Bautier, Actes du colloque international organisé par le C.N.R.S., Paris, 29 septembre–4 octobre 1980, pp. 115–130. Paris, 1982.

Fossier, Robert. *La terre et les hommes en Picardie jusqu'à la fin du XIIIe siècle.* 2 vols. Louvain, 1968.

Fourrier, Anthime. *Le courant réaliste dans le roman courtois en France au moyen âge.* Vol. 1: *Les débuts (XIIe siècle).* Paris, 1960.

Frappier, Jean. "La peinture de la vie et des héros antiques dans la littérature française du XIIe et du XIIIe siècle." In *Histoire, mythes et symboles: études de littérature française,* Publications Romanes et Françaises, 137, pp. 21–54. Geneva, 1976.

————. "Le roman en prose en France au XIIIe siècle." In *Grundriss der romanischen Literaturen des Mittelalters,* vol. 4, pt. 1, pp. 503–512. Heidelberg, 1978.

Freeman, Michelle A. *The Poetics of Translatio Studii and Conjointure: Chrétien de Troyes's "Cligès."* French Forum Monographs, 12. Lexington, Ky., 1979.

————. "Transpositions structurelles et intertextualité: le 'Cligès' de Chrétien." *Littérature* 41 (1981): 50–61.

Frye, Northrop. *Anatomy of Criticism.* New York, 1969.

————. *The Great Code: The Bible and Literature.* New York, 1982.

————. *The Secular Scripture: A Study of the Structure of Romance.* Cambridge, Mass., 1976.

Geertz, Clifford. "Politics Past, Politics Present: Some Notes on the Uses of Anthropology in Understanding the New States." In *The Interpretation of Cultures,* pp. 327–341. New York, 1973.

Genicot, Léopold. *Les généalogies.* Typologie des Sources du Moyen Age Occidental, 15. Turnhout, Bel., 1975.

Gerth, Hans H., and C. Wright Mills, eds. *From Max Weber.* New York, 1958.

Gillingham, John. "The Unromantic Death of Richard I." *Speculum* 54 (1979): 18–41.

Gilson, Etienne. *Héloise et Abélard: études sur le moyen âge et l'humanisme.* Paris, 1938.

Godzich, Wlad, and Jeffrey Kittay. *The Emergence of Prose: An Essay in Prosaics.* Minneapolis, 1987.

Goody, Jack. *The Domestication of the Savage Mind.* Cambridge, 1977.

Goody, Jack, and Ian Watt. "The Consequences of Literacy." In *Literacy in Traditional Societies,* ed. J. R. Goody, pp. 27–68. Cambridge, 1968.

Guenée, Bernard. "La culture historique des nobles: le succès des *Faits des Romains* (XIIIe–XVe siècles)." In *La noblesse au moyen âge,* ed. Philippe Contamine, pp. 261–288. Paris, 1976.

————. "Les Grandes chroniques de France: le 'Roman aux roys' (1274–1518)." In *La nation,* ed. Pierre Nora, 1:189–213. Paris, 1986.

————. "Histoire, annales, chroniques: essai sur les genres historiques du moyen âge." *Annales: économies, sociétés, civilisations* 28 (1973): 997–1016.

————. "L'histoire de l'état en France à la fin du moyen âge vue par les historiens français depuis cent ans." *Revue historique* 232 (1964): 331–360.

————. *Histoire et culture historique dans l'occident médiéval.* Paris, 1980.

————. "L'historien par les mots." In *Le métier d'historien au moyen âge: études sur l'historiographie médiévale,* ed. B. Guenée, pp. 1–17. Paris, 1977.

Hanning, Robert. *The Individual in Twelfth-Century Romance.* New Haven, 1977.

————. "The Social Significance of Twelfth-Century Chivalric Romance." *Mediaevalia et humanistica,* n.s., 3 (1972): 3–29.

Hemptinne, Thérèse de. "Aspects des relations de Philippe Auguste avec la Flandre au temps de Philippe d'Alsace." In *La France de Philippe Auguste: le temps des mutations,* ed. R.-H. Bautier, Actes du colloque international organisé par le C.N.R.S., Paris, 29 septembre–4 octobre 1980, pp. 255–261. Paris, 1982.

Hess, Paul, *Li roumanz de Julius César: ein Beitrag zur Cäsargeschichte im Mittelalter.* Winterthur, 1956.

Hollister, C. Warren, and John W. Baldwin. "The Rise of Administrative Kingship: Henry I and Philip Augustus." *American Historical Review* 83 (1978): 867–905.

Hult, David. " 'Ci falt la geste': Scribal Closure in the Oxford *Roland.*" *Modern Language Notes* 97 (1982): 890–905.

————. "Lancelot's Two Steps: A Problem in Textual Criticism." *Speculum* 61 (1986): 836–858.

————. "Vers la société de l'écriture: *Le roman de la rose.*" *Poétique* 50 (1982): 155–172.

Hunt, Tony. "The Structure of Medieval Narrative." *Journal of European Studies* 3 (1973): 295–328.

Jaeger, C. Stephen. *The Origins of Courtliness: Civilizing Trends and the Formation of Courtly Ideals 939–1210*. Philadelphia, 1985.

James, Kathleen. "Critical Edition of *La chronique d'un ménestrel d'Alphonse de Poitiers* as contained in B.N. fr. 5700." Ph.D. diss., University of Maryland, College Park, 1984.

Jodogne, Omer. "Le caractère des oeuvres 'antiques' dans la littérature française du XIIe au XIIIe siècle." In *L'humanisme médiéval dans les littératures romanes du XIIe au XIVe siècle*, ed. A. Fourrier, pp. 55–83. Paris, 1964.

———. "La naissance de la prose française." *Bulletin de la Classe des Lettres et des Sciences Morales et Politiques, Académie Royale de Belgique*, 5th ser., 49 (1963): 296–308.

Johnson, W. R. *Momentary Monsters: Lucan and His Heroes*. Ithaca, 1987.

Jordan, William C. *Louis IX and the Challenge of the Crusade*. Princeton, 1979.

Keen, Maurice. *Chivalry*. New Haven, 1984.

———. "Chivalry, Heralds, History." In *The Writing of History in the Middle Ages*, ed. R.H.C. Davis and J. M. Wallace-Hadrill, pp. 393–414. Oxford, 1981.

Kittay, Jeffrey. "On Octo (Response to 'Rethinking Old French Literature: The Orality of the Octosyllabic Couplet' by Evelyn Birge Vitz)." *Romanic Review* 78 (1987): 291–298.

Köhler, Erich. *L'aventure chevaleresque: idéal et réalité dans le roman courtois*. Preface by Jacques Le Goff. Paris, 1974.

———. "Observations historiques et sociologiques sur la poésie des troubadours." *Cahiers de civilisation médiévale* 7 (1964): 27–51.

———. "Zur Entstehung des altfranzösischen Prosaromans." In *Troubador Lyrik und höfischer Roman*, Neue Beiträge zur Literaturwissenschaft, 15, pp. 213–223. Berlin, 1962.

Labory, Gillette. "Essai d'une histoire nationale au XIIIe siècle: la Chronique de l'Anonyme de Chantilly-Vatican." *Bibliothèque de l'Ecole des Chartes* 148 (1990): 301–354.

———. "Le métier d'historien au XIIIe siècle: la 'Chronique des rois de France' de l'Anonyme de Chantilly-Vatican." Typescript, n.d.

LaCapra, Dominick, and Steven L. Kaplan, eds. *Modern European Intellectual History: Reappraisals and New Persepctives*. Ithaca, 1982.

Lacaze, Yvon. "Le rôle des traditions dans la genèse d'un sentiment national au XVe siècle: la Bourgogne de Philippe le Bon." *Bibliothèque de l'Ecole des Chartes* 129 (1971): 303–385.

Lair, Jules. "Mémoire sur deux chroniques latines composées au XIIe siècle à l'Abbaye de Saint-Denis." *Bibliothèque de l'Ecole des Chartes* 35 (1874): 543–580.

Långfors, Arthur. "Deux traités sur l'amour tirés du Manuscrit 2200 de la Bibliothèque Sainte-Geneviève." *Romania* 56 (1930): 361–388.

Langlois, E. "Notices et extraits des manuscrits français et provencaux de Rome antérieurs au XVIe siècle." *Notices et extraits des manuscrits de la Bibliothèque Nationale* 33, pt. 2 (1890): 18 (Reg. 610, Anonyme de Béthune); 60–61 (Reg. 824, Hystore de Julius César).

Langmuir, Gavin. "Community and Legal Change in Capetian France." *French Historical Studies* 6 (1970): 275–286.

Lauer, Philippe. "Louis IV d'Outremer et le fragment d'Isembart et Gormont." *Romania* 26 (1897): 161–174.

LeClerc, Victor. "Notices supplémentaires chroniques." *Histoire littéraire de la France* 21 (1895): 669–671 (Anonyme de Béthune); 674 (Jean de Prunai).

Le Goff, Jacques. "Naissance du roman historique au XIIe siècle." *Nouvelle revue française* 238 (1972): 163–173.

———. "Philippe Auguste dans les 'Exempla.' " In *La France de Philippe Auguste: le temps des mutations*, ed. R.-H. Bautier, Actes du colloque international organisé par le C.N.R.S., Paris, 29 septembre–4 octobre 1980, 145–154. Paris, 1982.

———. "Social Realities and Ideological Codes in the Early Thirteenth Century: An *Exemplum* by James of Vitry." In *The Medieval Imagination*, trans. Arthur Goldhammer. Chicago, 1988.

Lejeune, Rita. "Le roman de Guillaume de Dole et la principauté de Liège." *Cahiers de civilisation médiévale Xe–XIIe siècles* 17 (1974): 1–24.

Lemarignier, Jean-François. "Autour de la royauté française du IXe au XIIIe siècle. Appendice: la Continuation d'Aimoin et le manuscrit Latin 12711 de la Bibliothèque Nationale." *Bibliothèque de l'Ecole des Chartes* 113 (1955): 25–36.

———. *La France médiévale: institutions et sociétés*. Paris, 1970.

Leuridan, T. *Les châtellains de Lille*. Lille, 1873.

Lévi-Strauss, Claude. *Myth and Meaning*. New York, 1979.

Longnon, Jean. *Les compagnons de Villehardouin: recherches sur les croisés de la quatrième croisade*. Hautes Etudes Médiévales et Modernes, 30. Geneva, 1978.

Lord, Albert B. *The Singer of Tales*. Harvard Studies in Comparative Literature, 24. Cambridge, Mass., 1960.

Lot, Ferdinand. "Compte-rendu de J. Frappier: étude sur la 'Mort le Roi Artu.' " *Romania* 64 (1938): 111–122.

Luce, Simon. "La Continuation d'Aimoin et le manuscrit Latin 12711 de la Bibliothèque Nationale." In *Notices et documents publiés pour la Société de l'Histoire de France à l'occasion du cinquantième anniversaire de sa fondation*, pp. 57–70. Paris, 1884.

MacMullen, Ramsey. *Enemies of the Roman Order: Treason, Unrest, and Alienation in the Empire*. Cambridge, Mass., 1966.

Malo, Henri. *Un grand feudataire: Renaud de Dammartin et la coalition de Bouvines*. Paris, 1898.

Mandach, André de. *Chronique dite Santongeaise texte Franco-Occitan inédit "Lee": à la découverte d'une chronique gasconne du XIIIe siècle et de sa poitevinisation*. Tübingen, 1970.

———. "Le livre de Saint-Jacques de Compostelle par Pierre de Beauvais (1212): à propos d'une édition récente." *Vox Romanica* 30 (1971): 287–300.

———. *Naissance et développement de la chanson de geste en Europe*. Vol. 1: *La geste de Charlemagne et de Roland*. Publications Romanes et Françaises, 69. Geneva, 1961.

———. "Réponse à M. Ian Short." *Zeitschrift für romanische Philologie* 86 (1970): 533–537.

Marechaux, Alain. "Chronique d'un anonyme de Béthune." Thesis, Université de Lille, 1976.

Marti, Berthe. "Arnulfus and the *Faits des Romains*." *Modern Language Quarterly* 2 (1941): 3–23.

Mazzoni, G., and A. Jeanroy. "Un nouveau manuscrit du Roman de Troie et de l'Histoire ancienne avant César." *Romania* 27 (1898): 574–581.

Meredith-Jones, C. "The Chronicle of Turpin in Saintonge." *Speculum* 13 (1938): 160–179.

———. "Historia Karoli Magni et Rotholandi, ou Chronique du Pseudo-Turpin." Doc. thesis, Université de Paris, 1936.

———. Review of *Naissance et développement*, by André Mandach. *Speculum* 37 (1962): 634–637.

Meyer, A. "Prologue en vers français d'une histoire perdue de Philippe-Auguste." *Romania* 6 (1877): 494–498.

Meyer, Paul. *Alexandre le Grand dans la littérature française du moyen âge*. 2 vols. Paris, 1886.

———. "Compte-rendu de Léopold Delisle, 'Notice sur la chronique d'un anonyme de Béthune du temps de Philippe-Auguste.' " *Romania* 21 (1892): 302–303.

———. "Discours de M. Paul Meyer, membre de l'Institut, président de la Société pendant l'exercice de 1889–1890 [quelques vues sur l'origine et les premiers développements de l'historiographie française]." *Annuaire-Bulletin de la Société de l'Histoire de France* 27 (1890): 82–106.

———. "Fragments des manuscrits français. V. Fragment d'un ms. du Roman de Jules César par Jacot de Forest." *Romania* 35 (1906): 58–63.

———. "Notice du Manuscrit fr. 17177 de la Bibliothèque Nationale." *Bulletin de la Société des Anciens Textes Français*, 1895, 80–118.

———. "Notice sur le MS. II.6.24 de la Bibliothèque de Cambridge." *Notices et extraits des manuscrits de la Bibliothèque Impériale* 32, pt. 2 (1888): 37–81.

———. "Notices sur deux anciens manuscrits français ayant appartenu au marquis de la Clayette (Bibliothèque Nationale, Moreau 1715–1719)." *Notices et extraits des manuscrits de la Bibliothèque Nationale* 33, pt. 1 (1890): 1–90.

———. "Les premières compilations françaises d'histoire ancienne." *Romania* 14 (1885): 1–81.

———. "Wauchier de Denain." *Romania* 32 (1903): 583–586.

Moland, Louis. "Charlemagne à Constantinople et à Jerusalem." *Revue archéologique*, n.s., 2, no. 3 (1861): 36–50.

Monfrin, Jacques. "La connaissance de l'antiquité et le problème de l'humanisme en langue vulgaire dans la France du XVe siècle." In *The Late Middle Ages and the Dawn of Humanism Outside Italy*, ed. G. Verbeke and J. Ijsewijn, pp. 131–170. Louvain, 1972.

———. "Humanisme et traductions au moyen âge." In *L'humanisme médiéval dans les littératures romanes du XIIe au XIVe siècle*, ed. A. Fourrier, pp. 217–246. Paris, 1964.

———. "Les traducteurs et leur public en France au moyen âge." *Journal des savants*, 1964, 5–20.

———. "Les traducteurs et leur public en France au moyen âge." In *L'humanisme médiéval dans les littératures romanes du XIIe au XIVe siècle*, ed. A. Fourrier, pp. 247–262. Paris, 1964.

Morf, H. "Notes pour servir à l'histoire de la légende de Troie en Italie et en Espagne." *Romania* 21 (1892): 18–38.

Murphy, James J. *Rhetoric in the Middle Ages*. Berkeley and Los Angeles, 1974.

Murphy, William P. "Creating the Appearance of Consensus in Mende Political Discourse." *American Anthropologist* 92 (1990): 25–42.

Nora, Pierre. "Between Memory and History: Les Lieux de Mémoire." *Representations* 26 (1989): 7–25.

Ong, Walter, J. *Orality and Literacy: The Technologizing of the Word*. London, 1982.

———. "Orality, Literacy, and Medieval Textualization." *New Literary History* 16 (1984): 1–12.

Paris, Gaston. "Chronique des séances de l'Académie des Inscriptions et Belles-Lettres [on B.N. nouv. acq. fr. 6295]." *Romania* 20 (1891): 371–373.

———. "Compte-rendu de F. Settegast, *Li hystore de Julius César*." *Romania* 12 (1883): 380–383.

———. "La traduction de la légende latine du voyage de Charlemagne à Constantinople par Pierre de Beauvais." *Romania* 21 (1892): 263–264.

Paris, Paulin. "Historia Regum Francorum." *Histoire littéraire de la France* 21 (1895): 731–734.

———. "Premières compilations de l'histoire générale des Français [on the Ménestrel d'Alphonse de Poitiers]." *Histoire littéraire de la France* 21 (1895): 734–736.

Parkes, Malcolm. "The Literacy of the Laity." In *The Medieval World*, ed. David Daiches and Anthony Thorlby, pp. 555–577. Literature and Western Civilization. London, 1973.

Pastoureau, Michel. "La diffusion des armoiries et les débuts de l'héraldique." In *La France de Philippe Auguste: le temps des mutations*, ed. R.-H. Bautier, Actes du colloque international organisé par le C.N.R.S., Paris, 29 septembre–4 octobre 1980, pp. 737–759. Paris, 1982.

Patterson, Lee. "The Historiography of Romance and the Alliterative *Morte Arthure*." *Journal of Medieval and Renaissance Studies* 13 (1983): 1–32.

———. *Negotiating the Past: The Historical Understanding of Medieval Literature*. Madison, Wis., 1987.

Payen, Jean-Charles. "Compte-rendu de Paul Hess, *Li roumanz de Julius César: ein Beitrag zur Cäsargeschichte im Mittelalter*." *Romance Philology* 11 (1957–1958): 173–176.

———. "L'humanisme médiéval dans les littératures romanes du XIIe au XIVe siècle." *Le moyen âge*, ser. 4, 21 (1966): 129–137.

Petit-Dutaillis, Charles. *Le déshéritement de Jean Sans Terre et le meurtre d'Arthur de Bretagne: étude critique sur la formation et la fortune d'une légende*. Paris, 1925.

———. *Etude sur la vie et le règne de Louis VIII*. 1894; reprint Paris, 1964.

———. "Fragment de l'histoire de Philippe-Auguste, roy de France: chronique en français des années 1214–1216." *Bibliothèque de l'Ecole des Chartes* 87 (1926): 98–141.

————. "Une nouvelle chronique du règne de Philippe-Auguste, l'Anonyme de Béthune." *Revue historique* 50 (1892): 63–71.

Pirenne, Henri. *Histoire de Belgique.* Vol. 1. Brussels, 1921.

Pocock, John G. A. "The Origins of the Study of the Past." *Comparative Studies in Society and History* 4 (1962): 209–246.

Poerck, G. de. "Les Faits des Romains: à propos de deux ouvrages récents." *Revue belge de philologie et d'histoire* 15 (1936): 621–652.

Poirion, Daniel. "Histoire de la littérature médiévale et histoire sociale: perspective de recherche." In *Grundriss der romanischen Literaturen des Mittelalters* 1:13–16. Heidelberg, 1980.

————. "Literary Meaning in the Middle Ages: From a Sociology of Genres to an Anthropology of Works." *New Literary History* 10 (1979): 401–408.

Rackin, Phyllis, "Anti-Historians: Women's Roles in Shakespeare's Histories." *Theatre Journal* 37 (1985): 329–344.

————. "Genealogical Anxiety and Female Authority: The Return of the Repressed in Shakespeare's Histories." Typescript. N.d.

————. *Stages of History: Shakespeare's English Chronicles.* Ithaca, 1990.

Ranum, Orest. *Artisans of Glory: Writers and Historical Thought in Seventeenth-Century France.* Chapel Hill, 1980.

Raynaud de Lage, G. "L'histoire ancienne." In *Dictionnaire des lettres françaises,* vol. 1: *Le moyen âge,* pp. 377–378. Paris, 1964.

————. "L' 'Histoire ancienne jusqu'à César' et les 'Faits des Romains.' " *Le moyen âge,* 4th ser., 4 (1949): 5–16.

————. "L' 'Historia britonum': source de l' 'Histoire ancienne jusqu'à César.' " In *Les premiers romans français,* Publications Romanes et Françaises, 138, 1–4. Geneva, 1976.

————. "La morale de l'histoire." *Le moyen âge,* 4th ser., 18 (1963): 365–369.

————. "Les romans antiques dans 'l' 'Histoire ancienne jusqu'à César.' " *Le moyen âge,* 4th ser., 12 (1957): 267–309.

————. "Les romans antiques et la représentation de l'antiquité." In *Les premiers romans français,* Publications Romanes et Françaises, 138, pp. 127–159. Geneva, 1976.

Riffaterre, Michael. "L'intertexte inconnu." *Littérature* 41 (1981): 4–7.

Robson, C. A. *Maurice de Sully and the Medieval Vernacular Homily.* Oxford, 1952.

Ross, D.J.A. "The History of Macedon in the 'Histoire ancienne jusqu'à César': Sources and Compositional Method." *Classica et mediaevalia* 24 (1963): 181–231.

Rouse, Richard H. "Florilegia and Latin Classical Authors in Twelfth- and Thirteenth-Century Orléans." *Viator* 10 (1979): 131–160.

Ryding, William W. *Structure in Medieval Narrative.* The Hague, 1971.

Saenger, Paul. "Silent Reading: Its Impact on Late Medieval Script and Society." *Viator* 13 (1982): 367–414.

Said, Edward. "On Repetition." In *The Literature of Fact,* ed. A. Fletcher, pp. 135–158. New York, 1976.

Salverda de Grave, J. J. "Un imitateur du 'Roman d'Enéas' au XIIIe siècle en France." *Studi medievali,* n.s., 5 (1932): 309–316.

Sanford, Eva M. "The Study of Ancient History in the Middle Ages." *Journal of the History of Ideas* 5 (1944): 21–43.

———. "The Use of Classical Authors in the Libri Manuales." *Transactions and Proceedings of the American Philological Association* 55 (1924): 190–248.

Sayers, William. "The Beginnings and Early Development of Old French Historiography, 1100–1274." Ph.D. diss., University of California, Berkeley, 1966.

Schmidt-Chazan, Mireille. "Les traductions de la 'Guerre des Gaules' et le sentiment national au moyen âge." *Annales de Bretagne et des pays de l'ouest* 87 (1980): 387–407.

Settegast, F. "Jacos de Forest e la sua fonte." *Giornale di filologia* 2 (1879): 172–178.

Sherman, Gail Berkeley. "Saints, Nuns, and Speech in the Canterbury Tales." In *Images of Sainthood in Medieval Europe*, ed. Renate Blumenfeld-Kosinski and Timea Szell, pp. 136–160. Ithaca, 1991.

Short, Ian. "A Note on the Pseudo-Turpin Translations of Nicolas of Senlis and William of Briane." *Zeitschrift für romanische Philologie* 86 (1970): 525–532.

———. "The Pseudo-Turpin Chronicle: Some Unnoticed Versions and Their Sources." *Medium aevum* 38 (1969): 1–22.

Sivéry, Gérard. "La description du royaume de France par les conseillers de Philippe-Auguste et par leurs successeurs." *Le moyen âge*, ser. 4, 39 (1984): 65–85.

———. *L'économie du royaume de France au siècle de Saint Louis (vers 1180–vers 1315)*. Lille, 1984.

———. "L'enquête de 1247 et les dommages de guerre en Tournaisis, en Flandre gallicante et en Artois." *Revue du nord* 59 (1977): 7–18.

Smalley, B. "Sallust in the Middle Ages." In *Classical Influences on European Culture*, ed. R. R. Bolgar, 1st International Conference on Classical Influences, King's College, Cambridge, 1969, pp. 165–175. Cambridge, 1971.

Sneyders de Vogel, K. "La date de la composition des Faits des Romains." *Neophilologus* 17 (1932): 213–214, 271.

———. "Recherches sur les Faits des Romains." *Romania* 59 (1933): 41–72.

Sot, Michel. "Historiographie épiscopale et modèle familial en Occident au IXe siècle." *Annales: économies, sociétés, civilisations* 33 (1978): 433–449.

Speer, Mary B. "Beyond the Frame: Verisimilitude, *Clergie*, and Class in the *Roman de Marques de Rome*." *Romance Philology* 35 (1981): 305–334.

Speer, Mary B., and Alfred Foulet. "Is *Marques de Rome* a Derhymed Romance?" *Romania* 101 (1980): 336–365.

Spiegel, Gabrielle M. *The Chronicle Tradition of Saint-Denis: A Survey*. Medieval Classics: Texts and Studies, 10. Brookline, Mass., 1978.

———. "Forging the Past: The Language of Historical Truth in the Middle Ages." *History Teacher* 17 (1984): 267–288.

———. "Genealogy: Form and Function in Medieval Historical Narrative." *History and Theory* 22 (1983): 43–53.

———. "History as Enlightenment: Suger and the *Mos Anagogicus*." In *Abbot Suger and Saint-Denis: A Symposium*, ed. Paula L. Gerson, pp. 17–27. New York, 1986.

———. "History, Historicism, and the Social Logic of the Text in the Middle Ages." *Speculum* 65 (1990): 59–86.

―――. "Moral Imagination and the Rise of the Bureaucratic State: Images of Government in the *Chroniques des rois de France*, Chantilly, Ms. 869." *Journal of Medieval and Renaissance Studies* 18 (1988): 157–173.

―――. "Political Utility in Medieval Historiography: A Sketch." *History and Theory* 14 (1975): 314–325.

―――. "*Pseudo-Turpin*, the Crisis of the Aristocracy, and the Beginnings of Vernacular Historiography in Thirteeth-Century France." *Journal of Medieval History* 12 (1986): 207–223.

―――. "The Reditus regni ad stirpem Karoli Magni: A New Look." *French Historical Studies* 7 (1971): 145–174.

―――. "Social Change and Literary Language: The Textualization of the Past in Thirteenth-Century French Historiography." *Journal of Medieval and Renaissance Studies* 17 (1987): 129–148.

Stanger, Mary D. "Literary Patronage at the Medieval Court of Flanders." *French Studies* 11 (1957): 214–229.

Stock, Brian. *The Implications of Literacy: Written Language and Models of Interpretation in the Eleventh and Twelfth Centuries*. Princeton, 1983.

―――. *Listening for the Text: On the Uses of the Past*. Baltimore, 1990.

―――. "Medieval Literacy, Linguistic Theory, and Social Organization." *New Literary History* 16 (1984): 13–29.

Strayer, Joseph. "France, the Holy Land, the Chosen People, the Most Christian King." In *Action and Conviction in Early Modern France*, ed. T. E. Rabb and J. E. Siegel, pp. 3–16. Princeton, 1969.

―――. *On the Medieval Origins of the Modern State*. Princeton, 1970.

Street, Brian V. *Literacy in Theory and Practice*. Cambridge, 1984.

Struever, Nancy S. "The Study of Language and the Study of History." *Journal of Interdisciplinary History* 4 (1974): 401–415.

Suchier, H. "Jehan von Thuim." *Zeitschrift für romanische Philologie* 6 (1882): 386.

Tyson, Diana B. "Patronage of French Vernacular History Writers in the Twelfth and Thirteenth Centuries." *Romania* 100 (1979): 180–222.

Tyvaert, Michel. "L'image du roi: légitimité et moralité royales dans les histoires de France au XVIIe siècle." *Revue d'histoire moderne et contemporaine* 21 (1974): 521–546.

Vance, Eugene. " 'Aucassin et Nicolette' as a Medieval Comedy of Signification and Exchange." In *The Nature of Medieval Narrative*, ed. Minnette Grunmann-Gaudet and Robin F. Jones, French Forum Monographs, 22, pp. 57–77. Lexington, Ky., 1980.

―――. *Mervelous Signals: Poetics and Sign Theory in the Middle Ages*. Lincoln, Neb., 1986.

―――. "Roland et la poétique de la mémoire." *Cahiers d'études médiévales* 1 (1975): 103–115.

―――. "Signs of the City: Medieval Poetry as Detour." *New Literary History* 4 (1973): 557–574.

van den Boogaard, N.H.J. "L'art d'aimer en prose." In *Etudes de civilisation médiévale (IX–XII siècles): mélanges offerts à E.-R. Labande*, pp. 687–698. Poitiers, 1974.

Vauchez, André. "Lay People's Sanctity in Western Europe: Evolution of a Pattern (Twelfth and Thirteenth Centuries)." In *Images of Sainthood in Medieval Europe*, ed. Renate Blumenfeld-Kosinski and Timea Szell, pp. 21–32. Ithaca, 1991.

Vercauteren, F. "Etude sur les châtelains comtaux en Flandre du XIe au début du XIIIe siècle." In *Etudes d'histoire dédiées à la mémoire de Henri Pirenne*, pp. 425–449. Brussels, 1937.

Vidier, Alexandre. *L'historiographie à Saint-Benoît-sur-Loire et les miracles de Saint Benoît*. Paris, 1965.

Viollet, P. *Droit public: histoire des institutions politiques et administratives de la France*. 3 vols. Paris, 1898–1903.

Vitz, Evelyn Birge. "Orality, Literacy, and the Early Tristan Material: Béroul, Thomas, Marie de France." *Romanic Review* 78 (1987): 299–310.

Wailly, Natalis de. "Examen de quelques questions relatives à l'origine des chroniques de Saint-Denys." *Mémoires de l'Institut Royal de France, Académie des Inscriptions et Belles-Lettres* 17, pt. 1 (1847): 379–407.

Waitz, George. "Über die sogennante Abbreviatio gestorum regum." *Neues Archiv für ältere deutsche Geschichtskunde* 7 (1882): 385–390.

Walpole, Ronald N. "L'Anonyme de Béthune." In *Dictionnaire des lettres françaises*, vol. 1: *Le moyen âge*, pp. 130–131. Paris, 1964.

———. "The Burgundian Translation of Pseudo-Turpin Chronicle in Bibliothèque Nationale (French MS. 25438)." *Romance Philology* 2 (1948–49): 177–255; 3 (1949–1950): 83–116.

———. "Note to the Meredith-Jones Edition of the 'Historia Karoli Magni et Rotholandi, ou Chronique du Pseudo-Turpin.'" *Speculum* 22 (1947): 260–262.

———. "Philip Mouskés and the Pseudo-Turpin Chronicle." *University of California Publications in Modern Philology* 26 (1947): 327–440.

———. "Prolégomènes à une édition du Turpin français dit le Turpin I." *Revue d'histoire des textes* 10 (1980): 199–230; 11 (1981): 325–370.

———. "La traduction du Pseudo-Turpin du Manuscrit Vatican Regina 624: à propos d'un livre récent." *Romania* 99 (1978): 484–514.

———. "Two Notes on Charlemagne's Journey to the East: The French Translation of the Latin Legend by Pierre de Beauvais." *Romance Philology* 7 (1953–1954): 130–142.

Warlop, H. E. *The Flemish Nobility Before 1300*. 4 vols. Kortrijk, 1975–1976.

Werner, K. F. "Die Legitimität der Kapetinger und die Entstehung des Reditus regni francorum ad stirpem Karoli Magni." *Welt als Geschichte* 12 (1952): 203–225.

White, Hayden. *The Content of the Form: Narrative Discourse and Historical Representation*. Baltimore, 1987.

———. "Historicism, History, and the Figurative Imagination." *History and Theory* 14, supp. 14 (1975): 48–67.

———. *Metahistory: The Historical Imagination in Nineteenth-Century Europe*. Baltimore, 1973.

———. "The Question of Narrative in Contemporary Historical Theory." *History and Theory* 23 (1984): 1–33.

Williams, Clem C., Jr. "A Case of Mistaken Identity: Still Another Trojan Narrative in Old French Prose." *Medium aevum* 53 (1984): 59–72.

Woledge, Brian. *Bibliographie des romans et nouvelles en prose française antérieur à 1500: supplément 1954–1973*. Publications Romanes et Françaises, 130. Geneva, 1975.

———. "Encore des manuscrits des Faits des Romains." *Neophilologus* 24 (1939): 39–42.

———. "La légende de Troie et les débuts de la prose française." In *Mélanges de linguistique et de littérature romanes offerts à Mario Roques* 2:313–324. Paris, 1953.

———. "Un manuscrit des Faits des Romains." *Romania* 59 (1933): 564–566.

Woledge, Brian, and H. P. Clive. *Répertoire des plus anciens textes en prose française depuis 842 jusqu'aux premières années du XIIIe siècle*. Publications Romanes et Françaises, 79. Geneva, 1964.

Woodward, C. Vann. "The Lost Cause" (review of *Socialism and America*, by Irving Howe). *New York Review of Books*, 30 January 1986, 26–29.

Zink, Michel. "Une mutation de la conscience littéraire: le langage romanesque à travers des exemples français du XIIe siècle." *Cahiers de civilisation médiévale* 24 (1981): 3–27.

Ziolkowski, Jan. *Alan of Lille's Grammar of Sex: The Meaning of Grammar to a Twelfth-Century Intellectual*. Medieval Academy of America, Speculum Anniversary Monographs, 10. Cambridge, Mass., 1985.

Zumthor, Paul. *Histoire littéraire de la France médiévale (VIe–XIVe siècles)*. Paris, 1954.

———. "Intertextualité et mouvance." *Littérature* 41 (1981): 8–16.

———. "The Text and the Voice." *New Literary History* 16 (1984): 67–92.

Index

Compositor: BookMasters, Inc.
       Text: 11/13 Aldus
   Display: Aldus
   Printer: Braun-Brumfield, Inc.
    Binder: Braun-Brumfield, Inc.